DIMENSIONS
OF
DRAMA

LAURENCE PERRINE
Southern Methodist University

HARCOURT BRACE JOVANOVICH, INC.
New York   Chicago   San Francisco   Atlanta

ISBN: 0-15-517655-2

Library of Congress Catalog Card
Number: 72-85636

Printed in the United States of America

Cover photograph by Susan Faludi of *Galaxy*, a dance-theatre piece by Alwin Nikolais.

Preface

Dimensions of Drama has been prepared for the student who is beginning a serious study of imaginative literature; its objective is to help him understand, enjoy, and prefer good plays.

The chapter discussions and the plays illustrating the elements of drama appeared originally in *Literature: Structure, Sound, and Sense,* an anthology that included the poetry and short story texts, *Sound and Sense* and *Story and Structure.* (In this separate publication on the drama, *Everyman* has been substituted for Edward Albee's *The Sandbox,* since the latter play was not available for reprinting in this edition.)

The chapter discussions in *Dimensions of Drama* concentrate on problems unique to drama rather than on the aspects of language or narration that drama has in common with poetry or fiction. The discussion follows the plan used in the poetry and short story volumes—a presentation of the elements of drama, illustrated by nine plays. Two additional plays are included for further reading.

L. P.

Contents

Plays for Further Reading

The
Elements
of Drama

CHAPTER ONE

The Nature
of Drama

Drama, like prose fiction, utilizes plot and characters, develops a theme, arouses emotion or appeals to humor, and may be either escapist or interpretive in its dealings with life. Like poetry, it may draw upon all the resources of language, including verse. Much drama *is* poetry. But drama has one characteristic peculiar to itself. It is written primarily to be *performed*, not read. It normally presents its action (1) *through* actors, (2) *on* a stage, and (3) *before* an audience. Each of these circumstances has important consequences for the nature of drama. Each presents the playwright with a potentially enormous source of power, and each imposes limitations on the directions his work may take.

Because a play presents its action *through* actors, its impact is direct, immediate, and heightened by the actor's skills. Instead of responding to words on a printed page, the spectator sees what is done and hears what is said. The experience of the play is registered directly upon his senses. It may therefore be fuller and more compact. Where the work of prose fiction may tell us what a character looks like in one paragraph, how he moves or speaks in a second, what he says in a third, and how his auditors respond in a fourth, the acted play presents this material all at once. Simultaneous impressions are not temporally separated. Moreover, this experience is interpreted by actors who may be highly skilled in rendering nuances of meaning and strong emotion. Through facial expression, gesture, speech rhythm, and intonation, they may be able to make a speaker's words more expressive than can the reader's unaided imagination. Thus, the performance of a play by skilled actors expertly directed gives the playwright[1] a tremendous source of power.

But the playwright pays a price for this increased power. Of the four major points of view open to the fiction writer, the dramatist is practically limited to one—the *objective,* or *dramatic.* He cannot directly comment on the action or the characters. He cannot enter the minds of his characters and tell us what is going on there. Although there are ways around these limitations, each has its own limitations. Authorial commentary may be placed in the mouth of a character, but only at the risk of distorting characterization and of leaving the character's reliability uncertain. (Does the character speak for the author or only for himself?) Entry can be made into a character's mind through the conventions of the soliloquy and the aside. In the *soliloquy,* a character is presented as speaking to himself—that is, he is made to think out loud. In the *aside,* a character turns from the person with whom he is conversing to speak directly to the audience, thus letting the audience know what he is really thinking or feeling as opposed to what he pretends to be thinking or feeling. Both of these devices can be used very effectively in the theater, but they interrupt the action and must therefore be used sparingly. Also, they are inappropriate if the playwright is working in a strictly realistic mode.

Because a play presents its action *on* a stage, it is able powerfully to focus the spectator's attention. The stage is lighted; the theater is dark; extraneous noises are shut out; the spectator is almost literally pinned to his seat; there is nowhere he can go; there is nothing else to look at; there is nothing to distract. The playwright has extraordinary means by which to command the undivided attention of his audience. He is not, like the fiction writer or the poet, dependent on the power of his words alone.

But the necessity to confine his action to a stage, rather than to the imagination's vast arena, limits the playwright in the kind of materials he can easily and effectively present. For the most part, he must present human beings in spoken interaction with each other. He cannot easily use materials in which the main interest is in unspoken thoughts and reflections. He cannot present complex actions that involve nonhuman creatures such as dogs or charging bulls. He finds it more difficult to shift scenes rapidly than the writer of prose fiction does. The latter may whisk his reader from heaven to earth and back again in the twinkling of an eye, but the playwright must usually stick to one setting for an

---

[1] The word *wright*—as in *playwright, shipwright, wheelwright, cartwright,* and the common surname *Wright*—comes from an Anglo-Saxon word meaning a workman or craftsman. It is related to the verb *wrought* (a past-tense form of *work*) and has nothing whatever to do with the verb *write.*

extended period of time, and may feel constrained to do so for the whole play.[2] Moreover, the events he depicts must be of a magnitude appropriate to the stage. He cannot present the movements of armies and warfare on the vast scale that Tolstoi uses in *War and Peace*. He cannot easily present adventures at sea or action on a ski slope. Conversely, he cannot depict a fly crawling around the rim of a saucer or falling into a cup of milk. At best he can present a general on a hilltop reporting the movements of a battle or two persons bending over a cup of milk reacting to a fly that the members of the audience cannot see.

Because a play presents its action *before* an audience, the experience it creates is a communal experience, and its impact is intensified. Reading a short story or a novel is a private transaction between the reader and a book, but the performance of a play is public. The spectator's response is affected by the presence of other spectators. A comedy becomes funnier when one hears others laughing, a tragedy more moving when others are present to carry the current of feeling. A dramatic experience, in fact, becomes more intense almost exactly to the extent that it is shared and the individual spectator becomes aware that others are having the same experience. This intensification is partly dependent on the size of the audience, but more on their sense of community with each other. A play will be more successful performed before a small audience in a packed auditorium than before a larger audience in a half-filled one.

But, again, the advantage given the playwright by the fact of theatrical performance is paid for by limitations on the material he can present. His play must be able to hold the attention of a group audience. A higher premium than in prose fiction is placed on a well-defined plot,

[2] The ease, and therefore the rapidity, with which a playwright can change from one scene to another depends, first, on the elaborateness of the stage setting and, second, on the means by which one scene is separated from another. In ancient plays and in many modern ones, stage settings have been extremely simple, depending only on a few easily moved properties or even entirely on the actors' words and the spectators' imaginations. In such cases, change of scenes is made fairly easily, especially if the actors themselves are allowed to carry on and off any properties that may be needed. Various means have been used to separate scenes from each other. In Greek plays, dancing and chanting by a chorus served as a scene-divider. More recently, the closing and opening or dropping and raising of a curtain has been the means used. In contemporary theater, with its command of electrical technology, increased reliance has been placed on darkening and illuminating the stage or on darkening one part of it while lighting up another. But even where there is no stage scenery and where the shift of scene is made only by a change in lighting, the playwright can hardly change his setting as rapidly as the writer of prose fiction. On the stage, too frequent shifts of scene make a play seem jerky. A reader's imagination, on the other hand, can change from one setting to another without even shifting gears.

swift exposition, strong conflict, dramatic confrontations. Unless the play is very brief, it must usually be divided into parts separated by an intermission or intermissions, and each part must work up to its own climax or point of suspense. It must be written so that its central meanings may be grasped in a single hearing. The spectator at a play cannot back up and rerun a passage whose import he has missed; he cannot, in one night, sit through the whole performance a second time. In addition, the playwright must avoid extensive use of materials that are purely narrative or lyrical. Long narrative passages must be interrupted. Descriptive passages must be short, or eliminated altogether. Primarily, human beings must be presented in spoken interaction with each other. Clearly, many of the world's literary masterpieces—stories and poems that enthrall the reader of a book—would not hold the attention of a group audience in a theater.

Drama, then, imposes sharp limitations on its writer but holds out the opportunity for extraordinary power. The successful playwright combines the power of words, the power of fiction, and the power of dramatic technique to make possible the achievement of that extraordinary power.

DISCUSSION TOPICS

1. Movie production is in many ways more flexible than stage production, and movies are more easily brought to a mass audience. What limitations of stage performance discussed in this chapter can be minimized or circumvented in a movie production? In view of the greater flexibility of moving pictures as a medium, why is there still an eager audience for plays? What advantages do stage performances have over moving pictures?
2. If plays are written to be *performed*, what justification is there for reading them?

August Strindberg

THE STRONGER

CHARACTERS

MRS. X., *an actress, married*
MISS Y., *an actress, unmarried*
A WAITRESS

SCENE. *The corner of a ladies' cafe. Two little iron tables, a red velvet sofa, several chairs. Enter* MRS. X., *dressed in winter clothes, carrying a Japanese basket on her arm.*

MISS Y. *sits with a half-empty beer bottle before her, reading an illustrated paper, which she changes later for another.*

MRS. X. Good afternoon, Amelia. You're sitting here alone on Christmas eve like a poor bachelor!

MISS Y. *(Looks up, nods, and resumes her reading.)*

MRS. X. Do you know it really hurts me to see you like this, alone, in a café, and on Christmas eve, too. It makes me feel as I did one time when I saw a bridal party in a Paris restaurant, and the bride sat reading a comic paper, while the groom played billiards with the witnesses. Huh, thought I, with such a beginning, what will follow, and what will be the end? He played billiards on his wedding eve! (MISS Y. *starts to speak*) And she read a comic paper, you mean? Well, they are not altogether the same thing.

(A WAITRESS *enters, places a cup of chocolate before* MRS. X. *and goes out.)*

MRS. X. You know what, Amelia! I believe you would have done better to have kept him! Do you remember, I was the first to say "Forgive him?" Do you remember that? You would be married now and have a home. Remember that Christmas when you went out to visit your fiancé's parents in the country? How you gloried in the happiness of home life and really longed to quit the theatre forever? Yes, Amelia dear, home is the best of all—next to the theatre—and as for children—well, you don't understand that.

MISS Y. *(Looks up scornfully.)*

(MRS. X. sips a few spoonfuls out of the cup, then opens her basket and shows Christmas presents.)

MRS. X. Now you shall see what I bought for my piggywigs. [*Takes*

THE STRONGER: First performed in 1889.

up a doll] Look at this! This is for Lisa, ha! Do you see how she can roll her eyes and turn her head, eh? And here is Maja's popgun.

(*Loads it and shoots at* Miss Y.)

Miss Y. (*Makes a startled gesture.*)

Mrs. X.   Did I frighten you? Do you think I would like to shoot you, eh? On my soul, if I don't think you did! If you wanted to shoot *me* it wouldn't be so surprising, because I stood in your way—and I know you can never forget that—although I was absolutely innocent. You still believe I intrigued and got you out of the Stora theatre, but I didn't. I didn't do that, although you think so. Well, it doesn't make any difference what I say to you. You still believe I did it. (*Takes up a pair of embroidered slippers*) And these are for my better half. I embroidered them myself—I can't bear tulips, but he wants tulips on everything.

Miss Y. (*Looks up ironically and curiously.*)

Mrs. X. (*putting a hand in each slipper*)   See what little feet Bob has! What? And you should see what a splendid stride he has! You've never seen him in slippers! (Miss Y. *laughs aloud.*) Look! (*She makes the slippers walk on the table.* Miss Y. *laughs loudly.*) And when he is grumpy he stamps like this with his foot. "What! damn those servants who can never learn to make coffee. Oh, now those creatures haven't trimmed the lamp wick properly!" And then there are draughts on the floor and his feet are cold. "Ugh, how cold it is; the stupid idiots can never keep the fire going." (*She rubs the slippers together, one sole over the other.*)

Miss Y. (*Shrieks with laughter.*)

Mrs. X.   And then he comes home and has to hunt for his slippers which Marie has stuck under the chiffonier—oh, but it's sinful to sit here and make fun of one's husband this way when he is kind and a good little man. You ought to have had such a husband, Amelia. What are you laughing at? What? What? And you see he's true to me. Yes, I'm sure of that, because he told me himself—what are you laughing at?—that when I was touring in Norway that brazen Frederika came and wanted to seduce him! Can you fancy anything so infamous? (*pause*) I'd have torn her eyes out if she had come to see him when I was at home. (*pause*) It was lucky that Bob told me about it himself and that it didn't reach me through gossip. (*pause*) But would you believe it, Frederika wasn't the only one! I don't know why, but the women are crazy about my husband. They must think he has influence about getting them theatrical engagements, because he is connected with the government. Perhaps you were after him yourself. I didn't use to trust you any too much. But now I know he never bothered his head about you, and you always seemed to have a grudge against him someway.

(*Pause. They look at each other in a puzzled way.*)

Mrs. X.   Come and see us this evening, Amelia, and show us that you're not put out with us—not put out with me at any rate. I don't know, but I think it would be uncomfortable to have you for an enemy. Perhaps it's because I stood in your way (*more slowly*) or—I really—don't know why—in particular.

(*Pause.* MISS Y. *stares at* MRS. X *curiously.*)

MRS. X (*thoughtfully*) Our acquaintance has been so queer. When I saw you for the first time I was afraid of you, so afraid that I didn't dare let you out of my sight; no matter when or where, I always found myself near you—I didn't dare have you for an enemy, so I became your friend. But there was always discord when you came to our house, because I saw that my husband couldn't endure you, and the whole thing seemed as awry to me as an ill-fitting gown—and I did all I could to make him friendly toward you, but with no success until you became engaged. Then came a violent friendship between you, so that it looked all at once as though you both dared show your real feelings only when you were secure—and then—how was it later? I didn't get jealous—strange to say! And I remember at the christening, when you acted as godmother, I made him kiss you—he did so, and you became so confused—as it were; I didn't notice it then—didn't think about it later, either—have never thought about it until—now! (*Rises suddenly.*) Why are you silent? You haven't said a word this whole time, but you have let me go on talking! You have sat there, and your eyes have reeled out of me all these thoughts which lay like raw silk in its cocoon—thoughts—suspicious thoughts, perhaps. Let me see—why did you break your engagement? Why do you never come to our house any more? Why won't you come to see us tonight?

(MISS Y. *appears as if about to speak.*)

MRS. X. Hush, you needn't speak—I understand it all! It was because —and because— and because! Yes, yes! Now all the accounts balance. That's it. Fie, I won't sit at the same table with you. (*Moves her things to another table.*) That's the reason I had to embroider tulips—which I hate—on his slippers, because you are fond of tulips; that's why (*throws slippers on the floor*) we go to Lake Mälarn in the summer, because you don't like salt water; that's why my boy is named Eskil—because it's your father's name; that's why I wear your colors, read your authors, eat your favorite dishes, drink your drinks—chocolate, for instance; that's why—oh—my God—it's terrible, when I think about it; it's terrible. Everything, everything came from you to me, even your passions. Your soul crept into mine, like a worm into an apple, ate and ate, bored and bored, until nothing was left but the rind and a little black dust within. I wanted to get away from you, but I couldn't; you lay like a snake and charmed me with your black eyes; I felt that when I lifted my wings they only dragged me down; I lay in the water with bound feet, and the stronger I strove to keep up the deeper I worked myself down, down, until I sank to the bottom, where you lay like a giant crab to clutch me in your claws—and there I am lying now.

I hate you, hate you, hate you! And you only sit there silent—silent and indifferent; indifferent whether it's new moon or waning moon, Christmas or New Year's, whether others are happy or unhappy; without power to hate or to love; as quiet as a stork by a rat hole—you couldn't scent your prey and capture it, but you could lie in wait for it! You sit here in your corner of the café—did you know it's called "The Rat Trap" for you?—and read the papers to see if misfortune hasn't befallen someone, to see if someone hasn't been given notice at the theatre, perhaps; you sit here and calculate about your next victim and reckon on your chances of recompense like a pilot in a shipwreck. Poor Amelia, I pity you, nevertheless, because I know you are unhappy, unhappy like one who has been wounded, and angry because you are wounded. I can't be angry with you, no matter how much I want to be— because you come out the weaker one. Yes, all that with Bob doesn't trouble me. What is that to me, after all? And what difference does it make whether I learned to drink chocolate from you or some one else. (*Sips a spoonful from her cup*) Besides, chocolate is very healthful. And if you taught me how to dress—tant mieux!—that has only made me more attractive to my husband; so you lost and I won there. Well, judging by certain signs, I believe you have already lost him; and you certainly intended that I should leave him— do as you did with your fiancé and regret as you now regret; but, you see, I don't do that—we mustn't be too exacting. And why should I take only what no one else wants?

Perhaps, take it all in all, I am at this moment the stronger one. You received nothing from me, but you gave me much. And now I seem like a thief since you have awakened and find I possess what is your loss. How could it be otherwise when everything is worthless and sterile in your hands? You can never keep a man's love with your tulips and your passions—but I can keep it. You can't learn how to live from your authors, as I have learned. You have no little Eskil to cherish, even if your father's name was Eskil. And why are you always silent, silent, silent? I thought that was strength, but perhaps it is because you have nothing to say! Because you never think about anything! (*Rises and picks up slippers.*) Now I'm going home—and take the tulips with me—*your* tulips! You are unable to learn from another; you can't bend—therefore, you broke like a dry stalk. But I won't break! Thank you, Amelia, for all your good lessons. Thanks for teaching my husband how to love. Now I'm going home to love him. (*Goes.*)

QUESTIONS

1. Much of the action of this play lies in the past, but to reconstruct that action we must separate what is true from what is untrue and from what may

or may not be true in Mrs. X's account of it. Point out places where Mrs. X (a) is probably lying, (b) is clearly rationalizing, (c) has very likely or has certainly been deceived, (d) is clearly giving an accurate account. In each case, explain your reason for your opinion. To what extent can we be certain of what has happened in the past?

2. Now put together as reliable an account as possible of the past relationships of Mrs. X, her husband, and Miss Y. How did the friendship between the two women start? How did it proceed? How and why did it terminate? In what two ways have the two women consciously or unconsciously been rivals? In what ways and by what means has Miss Y influenced Mrs. X's behavior and her life?

3. In a sense the play has two plots, one in the past and one in the present, though the plot in the present is really only the culminating phase of that in the past. At what point does Mrs. X discover something about the past that she had not known before? What is it she discovers? How does she react to the discovery? Why can this discovery be called the turning point of the play?

4. Trace the successive attitudes expressed by Mrs. X toward Miss Y, together with the real attitudes underlying the expressed attitudes. At what points do the expressed attitudes and the real attitudes coincide? At what points do they clearly differ?

5. What kind of person is Mrs. X? Characterize her.

6. Although Miss Y says nothing during the course of the play, we can infer a good deal about her from her reactions to Mrs. X, from her past actions, and from what Mrs. X says about her (cautiously interpreted). What kind of person is she? How, especially, does she differ from Mrs. X? What is the nature of her present life? Would this role be easy or difficult to act?

7. Although Mr. X never appears, he also is an important character in the play. What kind of man is he?

8. To which character does the title refer? Consider carefully before answering, and support your answer with a reasoned argument, including a definition of what is meant by "stronger."

Anton Chekhov

THE BRUTE

A Joke in One Act

English Version *by* ERIC BENTLEY

CHARACTERS

MRS. POPOV, *widow and landowner, small, with dimpled cheeks.*
MR. GRIGORY S. SMIRNOV, *gentleman farmer, middle-aged.*
LUKA, *Mrs. Popov's footman, an old man.*
GARDENER
COACHMAN
HIRED MEN

The drawing room of a country house. MRS. POPOV, *in deep mourning, it staring hard at a photograph.* LUKA *is with her.*

LUKA. It's not right, ma'am, you're killing yourself. The cook has gone off with the maid to pick berries. The cat's having a high old time in the yard catching birds. Every living thing is happy. But you stay moping here in the house like it was a convent, taking no pleasure in nothing. I mean it, ma'am! It must be a full year since you set foot out of doors.

MRS. POPOV. I must never set foot out of doors again, Luka. Never! I have nothing to set foot out of doors *for.* My life is done. *He* is in his grave. I have buried myself alive in this house. We are *both* in our graves.

LUKA. You're off again, ma'am. I just won't listen to you no more. Mr. Popov is dead, but what can we do about that? It's God's doing. God's will be done. You've cried over him, you've done your share of mourning, haven't you? There's a limit to everything. You can't go on weeping and wailing forever. My old lady died, for that matter, and I wept and wailed over her a whole month long. Well, that was it. I couldn't weep and wail all my life, she just wasn't worth it. (*He sighs.*)As for the neighbours, you've forgotten all about them, ma'am. You don't visit them and you don't let them visit you. You and I are like a pair of spiders—excuse the expression, ma'am— here we are in this house like a pair of spiders, we never see the light of day. And it isn't like there was no nice people around either. The whole county's swarming with 'em. There's a regiment quartered at Riblov, and the officers are so good-looking! The girls can't take their eyes off them—There's a ball at the camp every Friday—The military band plays most every day of the week —What do you say, ma'am? You're young, you're pretty, you could enjoy yourself! Ten years from now you may want to strut and show your feathers to the officers, and it'll be too late.

Mrs. Popov (*firmly*).   You must never bring this subject up again, Luka. Since Popov died, life has been an empty dream to me, you know that. *You* may think I am alive. Poor ignorant Luka! You are wrong. I am dead. I'm in my grave. Never more shall I see the light of day, never strip from my body this . . . raiment of death! Are you listening, Luka? Let his ghost learn how I love him! Yes, *I* know, and *you* know, he was often unfair to me, he was cruel to me, and he was unfaithful to me. What of it? *I* shall be faithful to *him*, that's all. I will show him how *I* can love. Hereafter, in a better world than this, he will welcome me back, the same loyal girl I always was—

Luka.   Instead of carrying on this way, ma'am, you should go out in the garden and take a bit of a walk, ma'am. Or why not harness Toby and take a drive? Call on a couple of the neighbours, ma'am?

Mrs. Popov (*breaking down*).   Oh, Luka!

Luka.   Yes, ma'am? What have I said, ma'am? Oh dear!

Mrs. Popov.   Toby! You said Toby! He adored that horse. When he drove me out to the Korchagins and the Vlasovs, it was always with Toby! He was a wonderful driver, do you remember, Luka? So graceful! So strong! I can see him now, pulling at those reins with all his might and main! Toby! Luka, tell them to give Toby an extra portion of oats today.

Luka.   Yes, ma'am.

(*A bell rings.*)

Mrs. Popov.   Who is that? Tell them I'm not at home.

Luka.   Very good, ma'am. (*Exit.*)

Mrs. Popov (*gazing again at the photograph*).   You shall see, my Popov, how a wife can love and forgive. Till death do us part. Longer than that. Till death re-unite us forever! (*Suddenly a titter breaks through her tears.*) Aren't you ashamed of yourself, Popov? Here's your little wife, being good, being faithful, so faithful she's locked up here waiting for her own funeral, while you—doesn't it make you ashamed, you naughty boy? You were terrible, you know. You were unfaithful, and you made those awful scenes about it, you stormed out and left me alone for weeks—

(*Enter* Luka.)

Luka (*upset*).   There's someone asking for you, ma'am. Says he must—

Mrs. Popov. I suppose you told him that since my husband's death I see no one?

Luka. Yes, ma'am. I did, ma'am. But he wouldn't listen, ma'am. He says it's urgent.

Mrs. Popov (*shrilly*). I see no one!!

Luka. He won't take no for an answer, ma'am. He just curses and swears and comes in anyway. He's a perfect monster, ma'am. He's in the dining room right now.

Mrs. Popov. In the dining room, is he? I'll give him his come uppance. Bring him in here this minute.

(*Exit* Luka.)

(*Suddenly sad again.*) Why do they do this to me? Why? Insulting my grief, intruding on my solitude? (*She sighs.*) I'm afraid I'll have to enter a convent. I will, I *must* enter a convent!

(*Enter* Mr. Smirnov *and* Luka.)

Smirnov (*to* Luka). Dolt! Idiot! You talk too much! (*Seeing* Mrs. Popov. *With dignity.*) May I have the honour of introducing myself, madam? Gregory S. Smirnov, landowner and lieutenant of artillery, retired. Forgive me, madam, if I disturb your peace and quiet, but my business is both urgent and weighty.

Mrs. Popov (*declining to offer him her hand*). What is it you wish, sir?

Smirnov. At the time of his death, your late husband—with whom I had the honour to be acquainted, ma'am—was in my debt to the tune of twelve hundred rubles. I have two notes to prove it. Tomorrow, ma'am, I must pay the interest on a bank loan. I have therefore no alternative, ma'am, but to ask you to pay me the money today.

Mrs. Popov. Twelve hundred rubles? But what did my husband owe it to you for?

Smirnov. He used to buy his oats from me, madam.

Mrs. Popov (*to* Luka, *with a sigh*). Remember what I said, Luka: tell them to give Toby an extra portion of oats today!

(*Exit* Luka.)

My dear Mr.—what was the name again?

Smirnov. Smirnov, ma'am.

Mrs. Popov. My dear Mr. Smirnov, if Mr. Popov owed you money, you shall be paid—to the last ruble, to the last kopeck. But today—you must excuse me, Mr.—what was it?

Smirnov. Smirnov, ma'am.

Mrs. Popov. Today, Mr. Smirnov, I have no ready cash in the house.

(Smirnov *starts to speak.*)

Tomorrow, Mr. Smirnov, no, the day after tomorrow, all will be well. My steward will be back from town. I shall see that he pays what is owing. Today, no. In any case, today is exactly seven months from Mr. Popov's death. On such a day you will understand that I am in no mood to think of money.

SMIRNOV. Madam, if you don't pay up now, you can carry me out feet foremost. They'll seize my estate.

MRS. POPOV. You can have your money.

(*He starts to thank her.*)

Tomorrow.

(*He again starts to speak.*)

That is: the day after tomorrow.

SMIRNOV. I don't need the money the day after tomorrow. I need it today.

MRS. POPOV. I'm sorry, Mr.—

SMIRNOV (*shouting*). Smirnov!

MRS. POPOV (*sweetly*). Yes, of course. But you can't have it today.

SMIRNOV. But I can't wait for it any longer!

MRS. POPOV. Be sensible, Mr. Smirnov. How can I pay you if I don't have it?

SMIRNOV. You don't have it?

MRS. POPOV. I don't have it.

SMIRNOV. Sure?

MRS. POPOV. Positive.

SMIRNOV. Very well. I'll make a note to that effect. (*Shrugging.*) And then they want me to keep cool. I meet the tax commissioner on the street, and he says, 'Why are you always in such a bad humour, Smirnov?' Bad humour! How can I help it, in God's name? I need money, I need it desperately. Take yesterday: I leave home at the crack of dawn, I call on all my debtors. Not a one of them pays up. Footsore and weary, I creep at midnight into some little dive, and try to snatch a few winks of sleep on the floor by the vodka barrel. Then today, I come here, fifty miles from home, saying to myself, 'At last, at last, I can be sure of something,' and you're not in the mood! You give me a mood! Christ, how can I help getting all worked up?

MRS. POPOV. I thought I'd made it clear, Mr. Smirnov, that you'll get your money the minute my steward is back from town?

SMIRNOV. What the hell do I care about your steward? Pardon the expression, ma'am. But it was you I came to see.

MRS. POPOV. What language! What a tone to take to a lady! I refuse to hear another word. (*Quickly, exit.*)

SMIRNOV. Not in the mood, huh? 'Exactly seven month since Popov's death,' huh? How about me? (*Shouting after her.*) Is there this interest to pay, or isn't there? I'm asking you a question: is there this interest to pay, or isn't there? So your husband died, and you're not in the mood, and your steward's gone off some place, and so forth and so on, but what *I* can do about all that, huh? What do *you* think I should do? Take a running jump and shove my head through the wall? Take off in a balloon? You don't know my *other* debtors. I call on Gruzdeff. Not at home. I look for Yaroshevitch. He's hiding out. I find Kooritsin. He kicks up a row, and I have to throw him through the window. I work my way right down the list. Not a kopeck. Then I come to you, and God damn it to hell, if you'll pardon the expression, you're not in the mood! (*Quietly, as he realizes he's talking to air.*) I've spoiled them all, that's what, I've let them play me for a sucker. Well, I'll show them. I'll show this one. I'll stay right here till she pays up. Ugh! (*He shudders with rage.*) I'm in a rage! I'm in a positively towering rage! Every nerve in my body is trembling at forty to the dozen! I can't breathe, I feel ill, I think I'm going to faint, hey, you there!

(*Enter* LUKA.)

LUKA. Yes, sir? Is there anything you wish, sir?

SMIRNOV. Water! Water!! No, make it vodka.

(*Exit* LUKA.)

Consider the logic of it. A fellow creature is desperately in need of cash, so desperately in need that he has to seriously contemplate hanging himself, and this woman, this mere chit of a girl, won't pay up, and why not? Because, forsooth, she isn't in the mood! Oh, the logic of women! Come to that, I never have liked them, I could do without the whole sex. Talk to a woman? I'd rather sit on a barrel of dynamite, the very thought gives me gooseflesh. Women! Creatures of poetry and romance! Just to see one in the distance gets me mad. My legs start twitching with rage. I feel like yelling for help.

(*Enter* LUKA, *handing* SMIRNOV *a glass of water.*)

LUKA. Mrs. Popov is indisposed, sir. She is seeing no one.

SMIRNOV. Get out.

(*Exit* LUKA.)

Indisposed, is she? Seeing no one, huh? Well, she can see me or not, but I'll be here, I'll be right here till she pays up. If you're sick for a week, I'll be here for a week. If you're sick for a year, I'll be here for a year. You won't get around *me* with your widow's weeds and your schoolgirl dimples. I know all about dimples. (*Shouting through the window.*) Semyon, let the horses out of those shafts, we're not leaving, we're staying, and tell them to give the horses some oats, yes, oats, you fool, what do you think? (*Walking away from the window.*) What a mess, what an unholy mess! I didn't sleep last night, the heat is terrific today, not a damn one of 'em has paid up, and here's this—this skirt in mourning that's not in the mood! My head aches, where's that— (*He drinks from the glass.*) Water, ugh! You there!

(*Enter* LUKA.)

LUKA. Yes, sir. You wish for something, sir?

SMIRNOV. Where's that confounded vodka I asked for?

(*Exit* LUKA.)

(SMIRNOV *sits and looks himself over.*) Oof! A fine figure of a man *I* am! Unwashed, uncombed, unshaven, straw on my vest, dust all over me. The little woman must've taken me for a highwayman. (*Yawns.*) I suppose it wouldn't be considered polite to barge into a drawing room in this state, but who cares? I'm not a visitor, I'm a creditor—most unwelcome of guests, second only to Death.

(*Enter* Luka.)

Luka (*handing him the vodka*). If I may say so, sir, you take too many liberties, sir.

Smirnov. What?!

Luka. Oh, nothing, sir, nothing.

Smirnov. Who in hell do you think you're talking to? Shut your mouth!

Luka (*aside*). There's an evil spirit abroad. The Devil must have sent him. Oh! (*Exit* Luka.)

Smirnov. What a rage I'm in! I'll grind the whole world to powder. Oh, I feel ill again. You there!

(*Enter* Mrs. Popov.)

Mrs. Popov (*looking at the floor*). In the solitude of my rural retreat, Mr. Smirnov, I've long since grown unaccustomed to the sound of the human voice. Above all, I cannot bear shouting. I must beg you not to break the silence.

Smirnov. Very well. Pay me my money and I'll go.

Mrs. Popov. I told you before, and I tell you again, Mr. Smirnov. I have no cash, you'll have to wait till the day after tomorrow. Can I express myself more plainly?

Smirnov. And *I* told *you* before, and *I* tell *you* again, that I need the money today, that the day after tomorrow is too late, and that if you don't pay, and pay now, I'll have to hang myself in the morning!

Mrs. Popov. But I have no cash. This is quite a puzzle.

Smirnov. You won't pay, huh?

Mrs. Popov. I *can't* pay, Mr. Smirnov.

Smirnov. In that case, I'm going to sit here and wait. (*Sits down.*) You'll pay up the day after tomorrow? Very good. Till the day after tomorrow, here I sit. (*Pause. He jumps up.*) Now look, do I have to pay that interest tomorrow, or don't I? Or do you think I'm joking?

Mrs. Popov. I must ask you not to raise your voice, Mr. Smirnov. This is not a stable.

Smirnov. Who said it was? Do I have to pay the interest tomorrow or not?

Mrs. Popov. Mr. Smirnov, do you know how to behave in he presence of a lady?

Smirnov. No, madam, I do not know how to behave in the presence of a lady.

Mrs. Popov. Just what I thought. I look at you, and I say: ugh! I hear you talk, and I say to myself: 'That man doesn't know how to talk to a lady.'

Smirnov. You'd like me to come simpering to you in French, I suppose.

'*Enchanté, madame! Merci beaucoup* for not paying zee money, *madame! Pardonnez-moi* if I 'ave disturbed you, *madame!* How *charmante* you look in mourning, *madame!'*

Mrs. Popov.   Now you're being silly, Mr. Smirnov.

Smirnov (*mimicking*). 'Now you're being silly, Mr. Smirnov.' 'You don't know how to talk to a lady, Mr. Smirnov.' Look here, Mrs. Popov, I've known more women than you've known pussy cats. I've fought three duels on their account. I've jilted twelve, and been jilted by nine others. Oh, yes, Mrs. Popov, I've played the fool in my time, whispered sweet nothings, bowed and scraped and endeavoured to please. Don't tell me I don't know what it is to love, to pine away with longing, to have the blues, to melt like butter, to be weak as water. I was full of tender emotion. I was carried away with passion. I squandered half my fortune on the sex. I chattered about women's emancipation. But there's an end to everything, dear madam. Burning eyes, dark eyelashes, ripe, red lips, dimpled cheeks, heaving bosoms, soft whisperings, the moon above, the lake below—I don't give a rap for that sort of nonsense any more, Mrs. Popov. I've found out about women. Present company excepted, they're liars. Their behaviour is mere play acting; their conversation is sheer gossip. Yes, dear lady, women, young or old, are false, petty, vain, cruel, malicious, unreasonable. As for intelligence, any sparrow could give them points. Appearances, I admit, can be deceptive. In appearance, a woman may be all poetry and romance, goddess and angel, muslin and fluff. To look at her exterior is to be transported to heaven. But I have looked at her interior, Mrs. Popov, and what did I find there—in her very soul? A crocodile. (*He has gripped the back of the chair so firmly that it snaps.*) And, what is more revolting, a crocodile with an illusion, a crocodile that imagines tender sentiments are its own special province, a crocodile that thinks itself queen of the realm of love! Whereas, in sober fact, dear madam, if a woman can love anything except a lapdog you can hang me by the feet on that nail. For a man, love is suffering, love is sacrifice. A woman just swishes her train around and tightens her grip on your nose. Now, you're a woman, aren't you, Mrs. Popov? You must be an expert on some of this. Tell me, quite frankly, did you ever know a woman to be—faithful, for instance? Or even sincere? Only old hags, huh? Though some women are old hags from birth. But as for the others? You're right: a faithful woman is a freak of nature—like a cat with horns.

Mrs. Popov.   Who *is* faithful, then? Who *have* you cast for the faithful lover? Not man?

Smirnov.   Right first time, Mrs. Popov: man.

Mrs. Popov (*going off into a peal of bitter laughter*).   Man! Man is faithful! that's a new one! (*Fiercely.*) What right do you have to say this, Mrs. Smirnov? Men faithful? Let me tell you something. Of all the men I have ever known my late husband Popov was the best. I loved him, and there are women who know how to love, Mr. Smirnov. I gave him my youth, my happiness, my life, my fortune. I worshipped the ground he trod on—and what happened? The best of men was unfaithful to me, Mr. Smirnov. Not once in a while. All the time. After he died, I found his desk drawer full of love letters. While he was alive, he was always going away for the week-end. He squandered my money. He made love to other women before my very eyes. But, in spite of all, Mr. Smirnov, I was faithful. Unto death. And beyond. I am *still* faithful, Mr. Smirnov! Buried alive in this house, I shall wear mourning till the day I, too, am called to my eternal rest.

SMIRNOV (*laughing scornfully*). Expect me to believe that? As if I couldn't see through all this hocus-pocus. Buried alive! Till you're called to your eternal rest! Till when? Till some little poet—or some little subaltern with his first moustache—comes riding by and asks: 'Can that be the house of the mysterious Tamara who for love of her late husband has buried herself alive, vowing to see no man?' Ha!

MRS. POPOV (*flaring up*). How dare you? How dare you insinuate—-?

SMIRNOV. You may have buried yourself alive, Mrs. Popov, but you haven't forgotten to powder your nose.

MRS. POPOV (*incoherent*). How dare you? How—?

SMIRNOV. Who's raising his voice now? Just because I call a spade a spade. Because I shoot straight from the shoulder. Well, don't shout at me, I'm not your steward.

MRS. POPOV. I'm not shouting, you're shouting! Oh, leave me alone!

SMIRNOV. Pay me the money, and I will.

MRS. POPOV. You'll get no money out of me!

SMIRNOV. Oh, so that's it!

MRS. POPOV. Not a ruble, not a kopeck. Get out! Leave me alone!

SMIRNOV. Not being your husband, I must ask you not to make scenes with me. (*He sits.*) I don't like scenes.

MRS. POPOV (*choking with rage*). You're sitting down?

SMIRNOV. Correct, I'm sitting down.

MRS. POPOV. I asked you to leave!

SMIRNOV. Then give me the money. (*Aside.*) Oh, what a rage I'm in, what a rage!

MRS. POPOV. The impudence of the man! I won't talk to you a moment longer. Get out. (*Pause.*) Are you going?

SMIRNOV. No.

MRS. POPOV. No?!

SMIRNOV. No.

MRS. POPOV. On your head be it. Luka!

(*Enter* LUKA.)

Show the gentleman out, Luka.

LUKA (*approaching*). I'm afraid, sir, I'll have to ask you, um, to leave, sir, now, um—

SMIRNOV (*jumping up*). Shut your mouth, you old idiot! Who do you think you're talking to? I'll make mincemeat of you.

LUKA (*clutching his heart*). Mercy on us! Holy saints above! (*He falls into an armchair.*) I'm taken sick! I can't breathe!!

MRS. POPOV. Then where's Dasha? Dasha! Dasha! Come here at once! (*She rings.*)

LUKA. They gone picking berries, ma'am, I'm alone here—Water, water, I'm taken sick!

MRS. POPOV (*to* SMIRNOV). Get out, you!

SMIRNOV. Can't you even be polite with me, Mrs. Popov?

MRS. POPOV (*clenching her fists and stamping her feet*). With you? You're a wild animal, you were never house-broken!

SMIRNOV. What? What did you say?

MRS. POPOV. I said you were a wild animal, you were never house-broken.

SMIRNOV (*advancing upon her*). And what right do you have to talk to me like that?

MRS. POPOV. Like what?

SMIRNOV. You have insulted me, madam.

MRS. POPOV. What of it? Do you think I'm scared of you?

SMIRNOV. So you think you can get away with it because you're a woman. A creature of poetry and romance, huh? Well, it doesn't go down with me. I hereby challenge you to a duel.

LUKA. Mercy on us! Holy saints alive! Water!

SMIRNOV. I propose we shoot it out.

MRS. POPOV. Trying to scare me again? Just because you have big fists and a voice like a bull? You're a brute.

SMIRNOV. No one insults Grigory S. Smirnov with impunity! And I don't care if you *are* a female.

MRS. POPOV (*trying to outshout him*). Brute, brute, brute!

SMIRNOV. The sexes are equal, are they? Fine: then it's just prejudice to expect men alone to pay for insults. I hereby challenge—

MRS. POPOV (*screaming*). All right! You want to shoot it out? All right! Let's shoot it out!

SMIRNOV. And let it be here and now!

MRS. POPOV. Here and now! All right! I'll have Popov's pistols here in one minute! (*Walks away, then turns.*) Putting one of Popov's bullets through your silly head will be a pleasure! Au revoir. (*Exit.*)

SMIRNOV. I'll bring her down like a duck, a sitting duck. I'm not one of your little poets, I'm no little subaltern with his first moustache. No, sir, there's no weaker sex where I'm concerned!

LUKA. Sir! Master! (*He goes down on his knees.*) Take pity on a poor old man, and do me a favour: go away. It was bad enough before, you nearly scared me to death. But a duel—!

SMIRNOV (*ignoring him*). A duel! That's equality of the sexes for you!

That's women's emancipation! Just as a matter of principle I'll bring her down like a duck. But what a woman! 'Putting one of Popov's bullets through your silly head . . .' Her cheeks were flushed, her eyes were gleaming! And, by God, she's accepted the challenge! I never knew a woman like this before!

LUKA. Sir! Master! Please go away! I'll always pray for you!

SMIRNOV (*again ignoring him*). What a woman! Phew!! *She's* no sour puss, *she's* no cry baby. She's fire and brimstone. She's a human cannon ball. What a shame I have to kill her!

LUKA (*weeping*). Please, kind sir, please, go away!

SMIRNOV (*as before*). I like her, isn't that funny? With those dimples and all? I like her. I'm even prepared to consider letting her off that debt. And where's my rage? It's gone. I never knew a woman like this before.

(*Enter* MRS. POPOV *with pistols.*)

MRS. POPOV (*boldly*). Pistols, Mr. Smirnov! (*Matter of fact.*) But before we start, you'd better show me how it's done, I'm not too familiar with these things. In fact I never gave a pistol a second look.

LUKA. Lord, have mercy on us, I must go hunt up the gardener and the coachman. Why has this catastrophe fallen upon us, O Lord? (*Exit.*)

SMIRNOV (*examining the pistols*). Well, it's like this. There are several makes: one is the Mortimer, with capsules, especially constructed for duelling. What you have here are Smith and Wesson triple-action revolvers, with extractor, first-rate job, worth ninety rubles at the very least. You hold it this way. (*Aside.*) My God, what eyes she has! They're setting me on fire.

MRS. POPOV. This way?

SMIRNOV. Yes, that's right. You cock the trigger, take aim like this, head up, arm out like this. Then you just press with this finger here, and it's all over. The main thing is, keep cool, take slow aim, and don't let your arm jump.

MRS. POPOV. I see. And if it's inconvenient to do the job here, we can go out in the garden.

SMIRNOV. Very good. Of course, I should warn you: I'll be firing in the air.

MRS. POPOV. What? This is the end. Why?

SMIRNOV. Oh, well—because—for private reasons.

MRS. POPOV. Scared, huh? (*She laughs heartily.*) Now don't you try to get out of it, Mr. Smirnov. My blood is up. I won't be happy till I've drilled a hole through that skull of yours. Follow me. What's the matter? Scared?

SMIRNOV. That's right. I'm scared.

MRS. POPOV. Oh, come on, what's the matter with you?

SMIRNOV. Well, um, Mrs. Popov, I, um, I like you.

MRS. POPOV (*laughing bitterly*). Good God! He likes me, does he? The gall of the man. (*Showing him the door.*) You may leave, Mr. Smirnov.

SMIRNOV (*quietly puts the gun down, takes his hat, and walks to the* door. *Then he stops and the pair look at each other without a word. Then, approaching gingerly*). Listen, Mrs. Popov. Are you still mad at me? I'm in the devil of a temper myself, of course. But then, you see—what I mean is—it's this way—the fact is— (*Roaring.*) Well, is it my fault, damn it, if I like you? (*Clutches the back of a chair. It breaks.*) Christ, what fragile furniture you have here. I like you. Know what I mean? I could fall in love with you.

Mrs. Popov. I hate you. Get out!

Smirnov. What a woman! I never saw anything like it. Oh, I'm lost, I'm done for, I'm a mouse in a trap.

Mrs. Popov. Leave this house, or I shoot!

Smirnov. Shoot away! What bliss to die of a shot that was fired by that little velvet hand! To die gazing into those enchanting eyes. I'm out of my mind. I know: you must decide at once. Think for one second, then decide. Because if I leave now, I'll never be back. Decide! I'm a pretty decent chap. Landed gentleman, I should say. Ten thousand a year. Good stable. Throw a kopeck up in the air, and I'll put a bullet through it. Will you marry me?

Mrs. Popov (*indignant, brandishing the gun*). We'll shoot it out! Get going! Take your pistol!

Smirnov. I'm out of my mind. I don't understand anything any more. (*Shouting.*) You there! That vodka!

Mrs. Popov. No excuses! No delays! We'll shoot it out!

Smirnov. I'm out of my mind. I'm falling in love. I *have* fallen in love. (*He takes her hand vigorously; she squeals.*) I love you. (*He goes down on his knees.*) I love you as I've never loved before. I jilted twelve, and was jilted by nine others. But I didn't love a one of them as I love you. I'm full of tender emotion. I'm melting like butter. I'm weak as water. I'm on my knees like a fool, and I offer you my hand. It's a shame, it's a disgrace. I haven't been in love in five years. I took a vow against it. And now, all of a sudden, to be swept off my feet, it's a scandal. I offer you my hand, dear lady. Will you or won't you? You won't? Then don't! (*He rises and walks toward the door.*)

Mrs. Popov. I didn't say anything.

Smirnov (*stopping*). What?

Mrs. Popov. Oh, nothing, you can go. Well, no, just a minute. No, you can go. Go! I detest you! But, just a moment. Oh, if you knew how furious I feel! (*Throws the gun on the table.*) My fingers have gone to sleep holding that horrid thing. (*She is tearing her handkerchief to shreds.*) And what are you standing around for? Get out of here!

Smirnov. Goodbye.

Mrs. Popov. Go, go, go! (*Shouting.*) Where are you going? Wait a minute! No, no, it's all right, just go. I'm fighting mad. Don't come near me, don't come near me!

SMIRNOV (*who is coming near her*).   I'm pretty disgusted with myself—falling in love like a kid, going down on my knees like some moongazing whippersnapper, the very thought gives me gooseflesh. (*Rudely.*) I love you. But it doesn't make sense. Tomorrow, I have to pay that interest, and we've already started mowing. (*He puts his arm about her waist.*) I shall never forgive myself for this.

MRS. POPOV.   Take your hands off me, I hate you! Let's shoot it out!

(*A long kiss. Enter* LUKA *with an axe, the* GARDENER *with a rake, the* COACHMAN *with a pitchfork,* HIRED MEN *with sticks.*)

LUKA (*seeing the kiss*).   Mercy on us! Holy saints above!

MRS. POPOV (*dropping her eyes*).   Luka, tell them in the stable that Toby is *not* to have any oats today.

QUESTIONS

1. In what way are Mrs. Popov and Smirnov alike? In what ways, respectively, do both transgress the norms of reason? Who in the play serves as the voice of reason?

2. What are the sources of Mrs. Popov's fidelity to the memory of her late husband? Is there a name for her attitude?

3. In what respect do Mrs. Popov and Smirnov undergo a reversal of roles—that is, how is Mrs. Popov in the latter part of the play like Smirnov in the earlier part, and Smirnov in the latter part like Mrs. Popov in the earlier part?

4. At what point does the turning point in the play come? What causes it?

5. Is the sudden change in Mrs. Popov's feelings believable? What explanations can be given for it?

6. Does either character undergo a change in character?

7. What is the significance of Mrs. Popov's final speech?

8. Unlike "The Stronger," this play has a number of soliloquies and three asides. What is their effect? Why do they "work" here when they would be out of place in "The Stronger"?

9. How do you visualize the stage action when Smirnov shows Mrs. Popov how to hold the revolver?

Anonymous

EVERYMAN

CHARACTERS

MESSENGER	GOOD DEEDS
GOD	KNOWLEDGE
DEATH	CONFESSION
EVERYMAN	BEAUTY
FELLOWSHIP	STRENGTH
COUSIN	DISCRETION
KINDRED	FIVE WITS
GOODS	ANGEL

DOCTOR

Here beginneth a treatise how the High Father of Heaven sendeth Death to summon every creature to come and give account of their lives in this world, and is in manner of a moral play.

Enter MESSENGER *as Prologue.*

MESSENGER. I pray you all give your audience,
And hear this matter with reverence,
By figure a moral play—
The *Summoning of Everyman* called it is,
That of our lives and ending shows   5
How transitory we be all day.
This matter is wondrous precious,
But the intent of it is more gracious,
And sweet to bear away.
The story saith: Man, in the beginning,   10
Look well, and take good heed to the ending,
Be you never so gay!
Ye think sin in the beginning full sweet,
Which in the end causeth the soul to weep,
When the body lieth in clay.   15
Here shall you see how Fellowship and Jollity,
Both Strength, Pleasure, and Beauty,
Will fade from thee as flower in May.
For ye shall hear how our Heaven King
Calleth Everyman to a general reckoning.   20

EVERYMAN: The author and date of this play are unknown. The earliest existing printed versions date from the early 1500s.

Give audience, and hear what he doth say. (*Exit.*)

(GOD *speaks from above.*)

GOD. I perceive, here in my majesty,
How that all creatures be to me unkind,
Living without dread in worldly prosperity.
Of ghostly° sight the people be so blind,   25
Drowned in sin, they know me not for their God.
In worldly riches is all their mind,
They fear not my rightwiseness, the sharp rod;
My love that I showed when I for them died
They forget clean, and shedding of my blood red;   30
I hanged between two, it cannot be denied;
To get them life I suffered to be dead;
I healed their feet, with thorns hurt was my head.
I could do no more than I did, truly;
And now I see the people do clean forsake me.   35
They use the seven deadly sins damnable,
As pride, covetise,° wrath, and lechery,
Now in the world be made commendable;
And thus they leave of angels the heavenly company.
Every man liveth so after his own pleasure,   40
And yet of their life they be nothing sure.
I see the more that I them forbear
The worse they be from year to year;
All that liveth appaireth° fast.
Therefore I will, in all the haste,   45
Have a reckoning of every man's person;
For, and° I leave the people thus alone
In their life and wicked tempests,
Verily they will become much worse than beasts;
For now one would by envy another up eat;   50
Charity they all do clean forget.
I hoped well that every man
In my glory should make his mansion,
And thereto I had them all elect,°
But now I see, like traitors deject,°   55
They thank me not for the pleasure that I to them meant,
Nor yet for their being that I them have lent.

---

25. ghostly: spiritual.   **37. covetise:** covetousness.   **44. appaireth:** becomes
worse.   **47. and:** if; so used frequently throughout the play.   **54. elect:** numbered among the redeemed.   **55. deject:** abject.

I proffered the people great multitude of mercy,
And few there be that asketh it heartily;
They be so cumbered with worldly riches,   60
That needs on them I must do justice,
On every man living without fear.
Where art thou, Death, thou mighty messenger?

(*Enter* DEATH.)

DEATH. Almighty God, I am here at your will,
Your commandment to fulfil.   65
    GOD. Go thou to Everyman,
And show him, in my name,
A pilgrimage he must on him take,
Which he in no wise may escape;
And that he bring with him a sure reckoning   70
Without delay or any tarrying. (*Exit* GOD.)
    DEATH. Lord, I will in the world go run over all,
And cruelly out search both great and small.
Every man will I beset that liveth beastly
Out of God's laws, and dreadeth not folly.   75
He that loveth riches I will strike with my dart,
His sight to blind, and from heaven to depart,
Except that alms be his good friend,
In hell for to dwell, world without end.

(EVERYMAN *enters, at a distance.*)

Lo, yonder I see Everyman walking;   80
Full little he thinketh on my coming.
His mind is on fleshly lusts and his treasure,
And great pain it shall cause him to endure
Before the Lord, Heaven King.
Everyman, stand still! Whither art thou going   85
Thus gaily? Hast thou thy Maker forgot?
    EVERYMAN. Why askest thou?
Wouldst thou wete?°
    DEATH. Yea, sir, I will show you:
In great haste I am sent to thee   90
From God out of his Majesty.
    EVERYMAN. What, sent to me?
    DEATH. Yea, certainly.
Though thou have forgot him here,

88. wete: know.

He thinketh on thee in the heavenly sphere,   95
As, ere we depart, thou shalt know.
    EVERYMAN. What desireth God of me?
    DEATH. That shall I show thee:
A reckoning he will needs have
Without any longer respite.   100
    EVERYMAN. To give a reckoning, longer leisure I crave.
This blind matter troubleth my wit.
    DEATH. On thee thou must take a long journey;
Therefore thy book of count° with thee thou bring;
For turn again thou can not by no way.   105
And look thou be sure of thy reckoning,
For before God thou shalt answer and show
Thy many bad deeds, and good but a few,
How thou hast spent thy life, and in what wise,
Before the Chief Lord of paradise.   110
Have ado that we were in that way,°
For, wete thou well, thou shalt make none attourney.°
    EVERYMAN. Full unready I am such reckoning to give.
I know thee not. What messenger art thou?
    DEATH. I am Death, that no man dreadeth.°   115
For every man I 'rest,° and no man spareth;
For it is God's commandment
That all to me should be obedient.
    EVERYMAN. O Death! thou comest when I had thee least in mind!
In thy power it lieth me to save.   120
Yet of my goods will I give thee, if thou will be kind;
Yea, a thousand pound shalt thou have,
If thou defer this matter till another day.
    DEATH. Everyman, it may not be, by no way!
I set not by° gold, silver, nor riches,   125
Nor by pope, emperor, king, duke, nor princes.
For, and I would receive gifts great,
All the world I might get;
But my custom is clean contrary.
I give thee no respite. Come hence, and not tarry.   130
    EVERYMAN. Alas! shall I have no longer respite?
I may say Death giveth no warning.
To think on thee, it maketh my heart sick,

---

104. **count**: accounts. 111. **Have ado . . . way**: get busy so that we may be on
the way. 112. **thou shalt . . . attourney**: you shall have no attorney to plead
for you. 115. **no man dreadeth**: fears no man. 116. **'rest**: arrest. 125. **set not
by**: care nothing for.

For all unready is my book of reckoning.
But twelve year and I might have abiding,   135
My counting-book I would make so clear,
That my reckoning I should not need to fear.
Wherefore, Death, I pray thee, for God's mercy,
Spare me till I be provided of remedy.

    DEATH. Thee availeth not to cry, weep, and pray;   140
But haste thee lightly that thou were gone that journey,
And prove thy friends if thou can.
For wete thou well the tide abideth no man;
And in the world each living creature
For Adam's sin must die of nature.   145

    EVERYMAN. Death, if I should this pilgrimage take,
And my reckoning surely make,
Show me, for saint charity,
Should I not come again shortly?

    DEATH. No, Everyman; and thou be once there,   150
Thou mayest never more come here,
Trust me verily.

    EVERYMAN. O gracious God, in the high seat celestial,
Have mercy on me in this most need!
Shall I have no company from this vale terrestrial   155
Of mine acquaintance that way me to lead?

    DEATH. Yea, if any be so hardy,
That would go with thee and bear thee company.
Hie thee that thou were gone to God's magnificence,
Thy reckoning to give before his presence.   160
What! weenest° thou thy life is given thee,
And thy worldly goods also?

    EVERYMAN. I had weened so, verily.

    DEATH. Nay, nay; it was but lent thee;
For, as soon as thou art gone,   165
Another a while shall have it, and then go therefrom
Even as thou hast done.
Everyman, thou art mad! Thou hast thy wits five,
And here on earth will not amend thy life;
For suddenly I do come.   170

    EVERYMAN. O wretched caitiff! whither shall I flee,
That I might 'scape endless sorrow?
Now, gentle Death, spare me till tomorrow,
That I may amend me

161. **weenest:** think.

With good advisement.° 175
DEATH. Nay, thereto I will not consent,
Nor no man will I respite,
But to the heart suddenly I shall smite
Without any advisement.
And now out of thy sight I will me hie; 180
See thou make thee ready shortly,
For thou mayst say this is the day
That no man living may 'scape away. (Exit DEATH.)
EVERYMAN. Alas! I may well weep with sighs deep.
Now have I no manner of company 185
To help me in my journey and me to keep;
And also my writing is full unready.
How shall I do now for to excuse me?
I would to God I had never been get!
To my soul a full great profit it had be, 190
For now I fear pains huge and great.
The time passeth; Lord, help, that all wrought.
For though I mourn it availeth naught.
The day passeth, and is almost a-go;
I wot° not well what for to do. 195
To whom were I best my complaint to make?
What if I to Fellowship thereof spake,
And showed him of this sudden chance?
For in him is all mine affiance,°
We have in the world so many a day 200
Been good friends in sport and play.
I see him yonder, certainly;
I trust that he will bear me company;
Therefore to him will I speak to ease my sorrow.

(Enter FELLOWSHIP.)

Well met, good Fellowship, and good morrow! 205
FELLOWSHIP. Everyman, good morrow, by this day!
Sir, why lookest thou so piteously?
If any thing be amiss, I pray thee me say,
That I may help to remedy.
EVERYMAN. Yea, good Fellowship, yea, 210
I am in great jeopardy.
FELLOWSHIP. My true friend, show to me your mind.
I will not forsake thee to my life's end

175. advisement: warning. 195. wot: know. 199. affiance: trust.

In the way of good company.

EVERYMAN. That was well spoken, and lovingly. 215

FELLOWSHIP. Sir, I must needs know your heaviness;
I have pity to see you in any distress;
If any have you wronged, ye shall revenged be,
Though I on the ground be slain for thee,
Though that I know before that I should die. 220

EVERYMAN. Verily, Fellowship, gramercy.°

FELLOWSHIP. Tush! by thy thanks I set not a straw!
Show me your grief, and say no more.

EVERYMAN. If I my heart should to you break,°
And then you to turn your mind from me, 225
And would not me comfort when you hear me speak.
Then should I ten times sorrier be.

FELLOWSHIP. Sir, I say as I will do, indeed.

EVERYMAN. Then be you a good friend at need;
I have found you true here before. 230

FELLOWSHIP. And so ye shall evermore;
For, in faith, and thou go to hell,
I will not forsake thee by the way!

EVERYMAN. Ye speak like a good friend. I believe you well;
I shall deserve it, and I may. 235

FELLOWSHIP. I speak of no deserving, by this day!
For he that will say and nothing do
Is not worthy with good company to go;
Therefore show me the grief of your mind,
As to your friend most loving and kind. 240

EVERYMAN. I shall show you how it is:
Commanded I am to go a journey,
A long way, hard and dangerous,
And give a strait° count without delay
Before the high judge, Adonai.° 245
Wherefore, I pray you, bear me company,
As ye have promised, in this journey.

FELLOWSHIP. That is matter indeed! Promise is duty;
But, and I should take such a voyage on me,
I know it well, it should be to my pain. 250
Also it maketh me afeared, certain.
But let us take counsel here as well as we can,
For your words would fear° a strong man.

---

221. **gramercy:** thanks. 224. **break:** reveal. 244. **strait:** strict. 245. **Adonai:** an Old Testament name for God. 253. **fear:** frighten.

EVERYMAN. Why, ye said if I had need,
Ye would me never forsake, quick° nor dead, 255
Though it were to hell, truly.
FELLOWSHIP. So I said, certainly,
But such pleasures be set aside, the sooth to say.
And also, if we took such a journey,
When should we come again? 260
EVERYMAN. Nay, never again till the day of doom.
FELLOWSHIP. In faith, then will not I come there!
Who hath you these tidings brought?
EVERYMAN. Indeed, Death was with me here.
FELLOWSHIP. Now, by God that all hath bought, 265
If Death were the messenger,
For no man that is living today
I will not go that loath° journey—
Not for the father that begat me!
EVERYMAN. Ye promised otherwise, pardie.° 270
FELLOWSHIP. I wot well I said so, truly;
And yet if thou wilt eat, and drink, and make good cheer,
Or haunt to women the lusty company,
I would not forsake you while the day is clear,
Trust me verily! 275
EVERYMAN. Yea, thereto you would be ready.
To go to mirth, solace, and play,
Your mind will sooner apply
Than to bear me company in my long journey.
FELLOWSHIP. Now, in good faith, I will not that way. 280
But and thou wilt murder, or any man kill,
In that I will help thee with a good will!
EVERYMAN. O, that is a simple advice indeed!
Gentle fellow, help me in my necessity;
We have loved long, and now I need, 285
And now, gentle Fellowship, remember me!
FELLOWSHIP. Whether ye have loved me or no,
By Saint John, I will not with thee go.
EVERYMAN. Yet, I pray thee, take the labor, and do so much for
me
To bring me forward, for saint charity, 290
And comfort me till I come without the town.
FELLOWSHIP. Nay, and thou would give me a new gown,
I will not a foot with thee go;

255. quick: living. 268. loath: loathsome. 270. pardie: by God.

But, and thou had tarried, I would not have left thee so.
And as now God speed thee in thy journey,   295
For from thee I will depart as fast as I may.
    EVERYMAN. Whither away, Fellowship? Will you forsake me?
    FELLOWSHIP. Yea, by my fay,° to God I betake° thee.
    EVERYMAN. Farewell, good Fellowship! For thee my heart is sore;
Adieu for ever! I shall see thee no more.   300
    FELLOWSHIP. In faith, Everyman, farewell now at the end!
For you I will remember that parting is mourning.

                                  (*Exit* FELLOWSHIP.)

    EVERYMAN. Alack! shall we thus depart indeed
(Ah, Lady, help), without any more comfort?
Lo, Fellowship forsaketh me in my most need.   305
For help in this world whither shall I resort?
Fellowship here before with me would merry make,
And now little sorrow for me doth he take.
It is said, "In prosperity men friends may find,
Which in adversity be full unkind."   310
Now whither for succor shall I flee,
Sith° that Fellowship hath forsaken me?
To my kinsmen I will, truly,
Praying them to help me in my necessity;
I believe that they will do so,   315
For "kind° will creep where it may not go.°"
I will go say,° for yonder I see them go.
Where be ye now, my friends and kinsmen?

    (*Enter* KINDRED *and* COUSIN.)

    KINDRED. Here be we now, at your commandment.
Cousin, I pray you show us your intent   320
In any wise, and do not spare.
    COUSIN. Yea, Everyman, and to us declare
If ye be disposed to go any whither,
For, wete you well, we will live and die together.
    KINDRED. In wealth° and woe we will with you hold,   325
For over his kin a man may be bold.
    EVERYMAN. Gramercy, my friends and kinsmen kind.
Now shall I show you the grief of my mind.
I was commanded by a messenger

---

298. fay: faith. betake: commend. 312. Sith: since. 316. kind: kinship. go:
walk. 317. say: assay, try. 325. wealth: weal, happiness.

That is a high king's chief officer;
He bade me go a pilgrimage, to my pain,
And I know well I shall never come again;
Also I must give a reckoning straight,
For I have a great enemy that hath me in wait,°
Which intended me for to hinder. 335
    KINDRED. What account is that which ye must render?
That would I know.
    EVERYMAN. Of all my works I must show
How I have lived, and my days spent;
Also of ill deeds that I have used 340
In my time, sith life was me lent;
And of all virtues that I have refused.
Therefore I pray you go thither with me,
To help to make mine account, for saint charity.
    COUSIN. What, to go thither? Is that the matter? 345
Nay, Everyman, I had liefer fast bread and water
All this five year and more.
    EVERYMAN. Alas, that ever I was bore!
For now shall I never be merry
If that you forsake me. 350
    KINDRED. Ah, sir, what! Ye be a merry man!
Take good heart to you, and make no moan.
But one thing I warn you, by Saint Anne,
As for me, ye shall go alone.
    EVERYMAN. My Cousin, will you not with me go? 355
    COUSIN. No, by our Lady! I have the cramp in my toe.
Trust not to me, for, so God me speed,°
I will deceive you in your most need.
    KINDRED. It availeth not us to tice.°
Ye shall have my maid with all my heart; 360
She loveth to go to feasts, there to be nice,°
And to dance, and abroad to start;
I will give her leave to help you in that journey,
If that you and she may agree.
    EVERYMAN. Now show me the very effect of your mind. 365
Will you go with me, or abide behind?
    KINDRED. Abide behind? Yea, that will I, and I may!
Therefore, farewell till another day. (*Exit* KINDRED.)
    EVERYMAN. How should I be merry or glad?

---

334. hath me in wait: lies in wait for me. **357. speed:** prosper. **359. tice:**
entice. **361. nice:** wanton, gay.

For fair promises men to me make,   370
But when I have most need, they me forsake.
I am deceived; that maketh me said.
    COUSIN. Cousin Everyman, farewell now,
For verily I will not go with you;
Also of mine own life an unready reckoning   375
I have to account; therefore I make tarrying.
Now, God keep thee, for now I go. (*Exit* COUSIN.)
    EVERYMAN. Ah, Jesus! is all come hereto?
Lo, fair words maketh fools fain;°
They promise and nothing will do, certain.   380
My kinsmen promised me faithfully
For to abide with me steadfastly,
And now fast away do they flee.
Even so Fellowship promised me.
What friend were best me of to provide?   385
I lose my time here longer to abide.
Yet in my mind a thing there is:
All my life I have loved riches;
If that my good now help me might,
He would make my heart full light.   390
I will speak to him in this distress.
Where art thou, my Goods and riches?

    (GOODS *speaks from within.*)

    GOODS. Who calleth me? Everyman? What, hast thou haste?
I lie here in corners, trussed and piled so high,
And in chests I am locked so fast,   395
Also sacked in bags—thou mayest see with thine eye—
I cannot stir; in packs low I lie.
What would ye have? Lightly me say.°
    EVERYMAN. Come hither, Goods, in all the haste thou may.
For of counsel I must desire thee.   400

    (*Enter* GOODS.)

    GOODS. Sir, and ye in the world have sorrow or adversity,
That can I help you to remedy shortly.
    EVERYMAN. It is another disease that grieveth me;
In this world it is not, I tell thee so.
I am sent for another way to go,   405
To give a strict count general
Before the highest Jupiter of all;

379. fain: joyful.   **398. Lightly me say:** tell me quickly.

And all my life I have had joy and pleasure in thee,
Therefore I pray thee go with me,
For, peradventure, thou mayst before God Almighty 410
My reckoning help to clean and purify;
For it is said ever among,
That "money maketh all right that is wrong."
    GOODS. Nay, Everyman; I sing another song,
I follow no man in such voyages; 415
For, and I went with thee,
Thou shouldst fare much the worse for me;
For because on me thou did set thy mind,
Thy reckoning I have made blotted and blind,
That thine account thou cannot make truly; 420
And that hast thou for the love of me.
    EVERYMAN. That would grieve me full sore,
When I should come to that fearful answer.
Up, let us go thither together.
    GOODS. Nay, not so! I am too brittle, I may not endure; 425
I will follow no man one foot, be ye sure.
    EVERYMAN. Alas! I have thee loved, and had great pleasure
All my life-days on goods and treasure.
    GOODS. That is to thy damnation, without lesing!°
For my love is contrary to the love everlasting. 430
But if thou had me loved moderately during,°
As to the poor to give part of me,
Then shouldst thou not in this dolor be,
Nor in this great sorrow and care.
    EVERYMAN. Lo, now was I deceived ere I was ware, 435
And all I may wyte° my spending of time.
    GOODS. What, weenest thou that I am thine?
    EVERYMAN. I had weened so.
    GOODS. Nay, Everyman, I say no;
As for a while I was lent thee, 440
A season thou hast had me in prosperity.
My condition is man's soul to kill;
If I save one, a thousand I do spill;°
Weenest thou that I will follow thee
From this world? Nay, verily. 445
    EVERYMAN. I had weened otherwise.
    GOODS. Therefore to thy soul Goods is a thief;

---

429. lesing: lying. **431. during:** while living. **436. wyte:** blame on. **443.
spill:** destroy.

For when thou art dead, this is my guise,°
Another to deceive in the same wise
As I have done thee, and all to his soul's reprief.°　　　　　450
　　EVERYMAN. O false Goods, curséd may thou be!
Thou traitor to God, that hast deceived me
And caught me in thy snare.
　　GOODS. Marry!° thou brought thyself in care,°
Whereof I am right glad.　　　　　455
I must needs laugh, I cannot be sad.
　　EVERYMAN. Ah, Goods, thou hast has long my heartly love;
I gave thee that which should be the Lord's above.
But wilt thou not go with me indeed?
I pray thee truth to say.　　　　　460
　　　GOODS. No, so God me speed!
Therefore farewell, and have good day. (*Exit* GOODS.)
　　EVERYMAN. O, to whom shall I make my moan
For to go with me in that heavy journey?
First Fellowship said he would with me gone;　　　　　465
His words were very pleasant and gay,
But afterward he left me alone.
Then spake I to my kinsmen, all in despair,
And also they gave me words fair,
They lacked no fair speaking,　　　　　470
But all forsook me in the ending.
Then want I to my Goods, that I loved best,
In hope to have comfort, but there had I least;
For my Goods sharply did me tell
That he bringeth many into hell.　　　　　475
Then of myself I was ashamed,
And so I am worthy to be blamed;
Thus may I well myself hate.
Of whom shall I now counsel take?
I think that I shall never speed　　　　　480
Till that I go to my Good Deeds.
But alas! she is so weak
That she can neither go nor speak.
Yet will I venture on her now.
My Good Deeds, where be you?　　　　　485

　　(GOOD DEEDS *speaks from the ground.*)

　　GOOD DEEDS. Here I lie, cold in the ground.

---

448. **guise:** custom.　450. **reprief:** reproach.　454. **Marry:** "by Mary," a mild oath.　**care:** trouble.

Thy sins hath me sore bound,
That I cannot stir.
    EVERYMAN. O Good Deeds, I stand in fear!
I must you pray of counsel,   490
For help now should come right well.
    GOOD DEEDS. Everyman, I have understanding
That ye be summoned account to make
Before Messias, of Jerusalem King;
And you do by me,° that journey with you will I take.   495
    EVERYMAN. Therefore I come to you my moan to make;
I pray you that ye will go with me.
    GOOD DEEDS. I would full fain, but I cannot stand, verily.
    EVERYMAN. Why, is there anything on you fall?
    GOOD DEEDS. Yea, sir, I may thank you of all;°   500
If ye had perfectly cheered° me,
Your book of count full ready had be.
Look, the books of your works and deeds eke.°
Behold how they lie under the feet,
To your soul's heaviness.   505
    EVERYMAN. Our Lord Jesus help me!
For one letter here I can not see.°
    GOOD DEEDS. There is a blind reckoning in time of distress!°
    EVERYMAN. Good Deeds, I pray you, help me in this need,
Or else I am for ever damned indeed.   510
Therefore help me to make my reckoning.
Before the Redeemer of all thing,
That King is, and was, and ever shall.
    GOOD DEEDS. Everyman, I am sorry of your fall,
And fain would I help you, and I were able.   515
    EVERYMAN. Good Deeds, your counsel I pray you give me.
    GOOD DEEDS. That shall I do verily;
Though that on my feet I may not go,
I have a sister that shall with you also,
Called Knowledge,° which shall with you abide,   520
To help you to make that dreadful reckoning.

    (*Enter* KNOWLEDGE.)

    KNOWLEDGE. Everyman, I will go with thee, and be thy guide,
In thy most need to go by thy side.

---

495. **do by me:** follow my advice. 500. **of all:** for everything. 501. **cheered:** cherished. 503. **eke:** also. 507. **one . . . see:** I cannot make out a single letter. 508. **There . . . distress:** the account is hard to read in time of trouble. 520. **Knowledge:** i.e., knowledge of sin.

EVERYMAN. In good condition I am now in every thing,
And am wholly content with this good thing;   525
Thanked be God my Creator.
    GOOD DEEDS. And when he hath brougth thee there,
Where thou shalt heal thee of thy smart,
Then go you with your reckoning and your Good Deeds together
For to make you joyful at heart   530
Before the blesséd Trinity.
    EVERYMAN. My Good Deeds, gramercy!
I am well content, certainly,
With your words sweet.
    KNOWLEDGE. Now go we together lovingly   535
To Confession, that cleansing river.
    EVERYMAN. For Joy I weep; I would we were there!
But, I pray you, give me cognition°
Where dwelleth that holy man, Confession.
    KNOWLEDGE. In the house of salvation,   540
We shall find him in that place,
That shall us comfort, by God's grace.

    (Enter CONFESSION.)

Lo, this is Confession. Kneel down and ask mercy,
For he is in good conceit° with God almighty.
    EVERYMAN. O glorious fountain, that all uncleanness doth clarify,   545
Wash from me the spots of vice unclean,
That on me no sin may be seen.
I come, with Knowledge, for my redemption,
Redempt with hearty and full contrition;
For I am commanded a pilgrimage to take,   550
And great accounts before God to make.
Now, I pray you, Shrift,° mother of salvation,
Help my Good Deeds for my piteous exclamation.
    CONFESSION. I know your sorrow well, Everyman.
Because with Knowledge ye come to me,   555
I will you comfort as well as I can,
And a precious jewel I will give thee,
Called penance, voider of adversity.
Therewith shall your body chastised be
With abstinence and perseverance in God's service.   560
Here shall you receive that scourge of me

    (Gives EVERYMAN a scourge.)

---

538. cognition: understanding.   **544. conceit:** favor.   **552. Shrift:** absolution.

Which is penance strong that ye must endure
To remember thy Savior was scourged for thee
With sharp scourges and suffered it patiently.
So must thou ere thou 'scape° that painful pilgrimage.   565
Knowledge, keep him in this voyage,
And by that time Good Deeds will be with thee.
But in any wise be sure of mercy,
For your time draweth fast, and ye will saved be;
Ask God mercy, and He will grant truly;   570
When with the scourge of penance man doth him bind,
The oil of forgiveness then shall he find. (*Exit* CONFESSION.)
EVERYMAN. Thanked be God for his gracious work!
For now I will my penance begin;
This hath rejoiced and lighted my heart,   575
Though the knots be painful and hard within.
KNOWLEDGE. Everyman, look your penance that ye fulfil,
What pain that ever it to you be,
And Knowledge shall give you counsel at will
How your account ye shall make clearly.   580

(EVERYMAN *kneels*.)

EVERYMAN. O eternal God! O heavenly figure!
O way of rightwiseness! O goodly vision!
Which descended down in a virgin pure
Because he would Everyman redeem,
Which Adam forfeited by his disobedience.   585
O blessèd Godhead! elect and high divine,
Forgive me my grievous offence;
Here I cry thee mercy in this presence.
O ghostly treasure! O ransomer and redeemer!
Of all the world hope and conductor,   590
Mirror of joy, and founder of mercy,
Which illumineth heaven and earth thereby,
Hear my clamorous complaint, though it late be.
Receive my prayers; unworthy in this heavy life.
Though I be a sinner most abominable,   595
Yet let my name be written in Moses' table.°
O Mary! pray to the Maker of all thing,
Me for to help at my ending,
And save me from the power of my enemy,

565. 'scape: finish. 596. table: tablets, i.e., among the saved.

For Death assaileth me strongly. 600
And, Lady, that I may by means of thy prayer
Of your Son's glory to be partner,
By the means of his passion I it crave.
I beseech you, help my soul to save. (*He rises.*)
Knowledge, give me the scourge of penance. 605
My flesh therewith shall give you a quittance.°
I will now begin, if God give me grace.
    KNOWLEDGE. Everyman, God give you time and space.
Thus I bequeath you in the hands of our Savior,
Now may you make your reckoning sure. 610
    EVERYMAN. In the name of the Holy Trinity,
My body sore punished shall be. (*Scourges himself.*)
Take this, body, for the sin of the flesh.
Also thou delightest to go gay and fresh,
And in the way of damnation thou did me bring; 615
Therefore suffer now strokes of punishing.
Now of penance I will wade the water clear,
To save me from purgatory, that sharp fire.

    (GOOD DEEDS *rises.*)

    GOOD DEEDS. I thank God, now I can walk and go,
And am delivered of my sickness and woe. 620
Therefore with Everyman I will go, and not spare;
His good works I will help him to declare.
    KNOWLEDGE. Now, Everyman, be merry and glad!
Your Good Deeds cometh now, ye may not be sad.
Now is your Good Deeds whole and sound, 625
Going upright upon the ground.
    EVERYMAN. My heart is light, and shall be evermore.
Now will I smite faster than I did before.
    GOOD DEEDS. Everyman, pilgrim, my special friend,
Blessèd be thou without end. 630
For thee is prepared the eternal glory.
Ye have me made whole and sound,
Therefore I will bide by thee in every stound.°
    EVERYMAN. Welcome, my Good Deeds; now I hear thy voice,
I weep for very sweetness of love. 635
    KNOWLEDGE. Be no more sad, but ever rejoice;
God seeth thy living in his throne above.

606. a quittance: full payment. 633. stound: trial.

Put on this garment to thy behoof,°
Which is wet with your tears,
Or else before God you may it miss,   640
When you to your journey's end come shall.
    EVERYMAN. Gentle Knowledge, what do ye it call?
    KNOWLEDGE. It is the garment of sorrow;
From pain it will you borrow,°
Contrition it is   645
That getteth forgiveness;
It pleaseth God passing well.
    GOOD DEEDS. Everyman, will you wear it for your heal?

    (EVERYMAN *puts on garment of contrition.*)

    EVERYMAN. Now blesséd be Jesu, Mary's Son,
For now have I on true contrition.   650
And let us go now without tarrying;
Good Deeds, have we clear our reckoning?
    GOOD DEEDS. Yea, indeed I have it here.
    EVERYMAN. Then I trust we need not fear.
Now, friends, let us not part in twain.   655
    KNOWLEDGE. Nay, Everyman, that will we not, certain.
    GOOD DEEDS. Yet must thou lead with thee
Three persons of great might.
    EVERYMAN. Who should they be?
    GOOD DEEDS. Discretion and Strength they hight,°   660
And thy Beauty may not abide behind.
    KNOWLEDGE. Also ye must call to mind
Your Five Wits° as for your counselors.
    GOOD DEEDS. You must have them ready at all hours.
    EVERYMAN. How shall I get them hither?   665
    KNOWLEDGE. You must call them all together,
And they will hear you incontinent.°
    EVERYMAN. My friends, come hither and be present,
Discretion, Strength, my Five Wits, and Beauty.

    (*Enter* DISCRETION, STRENGTH, FIVE WITS, *and* BEAUTY.)

    BEAUTY. Here at your will we be all ready.   670
What will ye that we should do?
    GOOD DEEDS. That ye would with Everyman go,
And help him in his pilgrimage.
Advise you, will ye with him or not in that voyage?

---

638. **behoof:** benefit.   644. **borrow:** redeem.   660. **hight:** are called.   663. **Five Wits:** five senses.   667. **incontinent:** at once.

STRENGTH. We will bring him all thither,   675
To his help and comfort, ye may believe me.
DISCRETION. So will we go with him all together.
EVERYMAN. Almighty God, lovéd may thou be!
I give thee laud° that I have hither brought
Strength, Discretion, Beauty, and Five Wits. Lack I naught.   680
And my Good Deeds, with Knowledge clear,
All be in company at my will here.
I desire no more to my business.
    STRENGTH. And I, Strength, will by you stand in distress,
Though thou would in battle fight on the ground.   685
    FIVE WITS. And though it were through the world round,
We will not depart for sweet nor sour.
    BEAUTY. No more will I, unto death's hour,
Whatsoever thereof befall.
    DISCRETION. Everyman, advise you first of all,   690
Go with a good advisement and deliberation.
We all give you virtuous monition
That all shall be well.
    EVERYMAN. My friends, hearken what I will tell:
I pray God reward you in his heavenly sphere.   695
Now hearken, all that be here,
For I will make my testament
Here before you all present:
In alms half my goods I will give my hands twain
In the way of charity, with good intent,   700
And the other half still shall remain,
I it bequeath to be returned there it ought to be.
This I do in despite of the fiend of hell,
To go quite out of his peril
Ever after and this day.   705
    KNOWLEDGE. Everyman, hearken what I say;
Go to Priesthood, I you advise,
And receive of him in any wise
The holy sacrament and ointment together,°
Then shortly see ye turn again hither;   710
We will all abide you here.
    FIVE WITS. Yea, Everyman, hie you that ye ready were.
There is no emperor, king, duke, nor baron,
That of God hath commission
As hath the least priest in the world being;   715
For of the blesséd sacraments pure and benign

679. laud: praise.   **709. The . . . together:** Communion and extreme unction.

He beareth the keys, and thereof hath the cure
For man's redemption—it is ever sure—
Which God for our soul's medicine
Gave us out of his heart with great pain,   720
Here in this transitory life, for thee and me.
The blessèd sacraments seven there be:
Baptism, confirmation, with priesthood good,
And the sacrament of God's precious flesh and blood,
Marriage, the holy extreme unction, and penance.   725
These seven be good to have in remembrance,
Gracious sacraments of high divinity.
    EVERYMAN. Fain would I receive that holy body
And meekly to my ghostly father I will go.
    FIVE WITS. Everyman, that is the best that ye can do.   730
God will you to salvation bring,
For priesthood exceedeth all other thing;
To us Holy Scripture they do teach,
And converteth man from sin, heaven to reach;
God hath to them more power given,   735
Than to any angel that is in heaven.
With five words he may consecrate
God's body in flesh and blood to make,
And handleth his Maker between his hands.
The priest bindeth and unbindeth all bands,   740
Both in earth and in heaven.
Thou, ministers all the sacraments seven,
Though we kissed thy feet, thou wert worthy;
Thou art the surgeon that cureth sin deadly:
No remedy we find under God   745
But all only priesthood.
Everyman, God gave priests that dignity,
And setteth them in his stead among us to be;
Thus be they above angels, in degree.

    (EVERYMAN *goes out to receive the last rites of the church.*)

    KNOWLEDGE. If priests be good, it is so, surely.   750
But when Jesus hanged on the cross with great smart,
There he gave out of his blessèd heart
The same sacrament in great torment.
He sold them not to us, that Lord omnipotent.
Therefore Saint Peter the Apostle doth say   755
That Jesus' curse hath all they
Which God their Savior do buy or sell,

Or they for any money do take or tell.°
Sinful priests giveth the sinners example bad;
Their children sitteth by other men's fires, I have heard;   760
And some haunteth women's company
With unclean life, as lusts of lechery.
These be with sin made blind.
    Five Wits. I trust to God no such way we find.
Therefore let us priesthood honor,   765
And follow their doctrine for our souls' succour.
We be their sheep, and they shepherds be
By whom we all be kept in surety.
Peace! for yonder I see Everyman come,
Which hath made true satisfaction.   770
    Good Deeds. Methinketh it is he indeed.

    (*Re-enter* Everyman.)

    Everyman. Now Jesu be your alder speed.°
I have received the sacrament for my redemption,
And then mine extreme unction.
Blesséd be all they that counseled me to take it!   775
And now, friends, let us go without longer respite.
I thank God that ye have tarried so long.
Now set each of you on this rood° your hand,
And shortly follow me.
I go before, there I would be. God be our guide.   780
    Strength. Everyman, we will not from you go,
Till ye have done this voyage long.
    Discretion. I, Discretion, will bide by you also.
    Knowledge. And though this pilgrimage be never so strong,°
I will never part you fro.°   785
Everyman, I will be as sure by thee
As ever I did by Judas Maccabee.

    (*They go to a grave.*)

    Everyman. Alas! I am so faint I may not stand,
My limbs under me do fold.
Friends, let us not turn again to this land,   790
Not for all the world's gold;
For into this cave must I creep
And turn to earth, and there to sleep.
    Beauty. What, into this grave? Alas!

---

758. tell: count.　**772. your alder speed:** the help of you all.　**778. rood:** cross.
784. strong: hard.　**785. fro:** from.

EVERYMAN. Yea, there shall you consume, more and less.   795
BEAUTY. And what, should I smother here?
EVERYMAN. Yea, by my faith, and never more appear.
In this world live no more we shall,
But in heaven before the highest Lord of all.
BEAUTY. I cross out all this; adieu; by Saint John!   800
I take my cap in my lap and am gone.
EVERYMAN. What, Beauty, whither will ye?
BEAUTY. Peace! I am deaf. I look not behind me,
Not and thou would give me all the gold in thy chest.

                                        (*Exit* BEAUTY.)

EVERYMAN. Alas, whereto may I trust?   805
Beauty goeth fast away from me;
She promised with me to live and die.
STRENGTH. Everyman, I will thee also forsake and deny.
Thy game liketh me not at all.
EVERYMAN. Why, then ye will forsake me all?   810
Sweet Strength, tarry a little space.
STRENGTH. Nay, sir, by the rood of grace,
I will hie me from thee fast,
Though thou weep till thy heart to-brast.°
EVERYMAN. Ye would ever bide by me, ye said.   815
STRENGTH. Yea, I have you far enough conveyed.
Ye be old enough, I understand,
Your pilgrimage to take on hand.
I repent me that I hither came.
EVERYMAN. Strength, you to displease I am to blame;   820
Yet promise is debt, this ye well wot.
STRENGTH. In faith, I care not!
Thou art but a fool to complain.
You spend your speech and waste your brain.
Go, thrust thee into the ground. (*Exit* STRENGTH.)   825
EVERYMAN. I had weened surer I should you have found.
He that trusteth in his Strength
She him deceiveth at the length.
Both Strength and Beauty forsaketh me,
Yet they promised me fair and lovingly.   830
DISCRETION. Everyman, I will after Strength be gone;
As for me I will leave you alone.
EVERYMAN. Why, Discretion, will ye forsake me?
DISCRETION. Yea, in faith, I will go from thee;

814. **to-brast:** burst.

For when Strength goeth before 835
I follow after evermore.
EVERYMAN. Yet, I pray thee, for the love of the Trinity,
Look in my grave once piteously.
DISCRETION. Nay, so nigh will I not come.
Farewell, every one! (*Exit* DISCRETION.) 840
EVERYMAN. O all thing faileth, save God alone,
Beauty, Strength, and Discretion;
For when Death bloweth his blast,
They all run from me full fast.
FIVE WITS. Everyman, my leave now of thee I take; 845
I will follow the other, for here I thee forsake.
EVERYMAN. Alas! then may I wail and weep,
For I took you for my best friend.
FIVE WITS. I will no longer thee keep;
Now farewell, and there an end. (*Exit* FIVE WITS.) 850
EVERYMAN. O Jesu, help! All hath forsaken me!
GOOD DEEDS. Nay, Everyman; I will bide with thee,
I will not forsake thee indeed;
Thou shalt find me a good friend at need.
EVERYMAN. Gramercy, Good Deeds! Now may I true friends see. 855
They have forsaken me, every one;
I loved them better than my Good Deeds alone.
Knowledge, will ye forsake me also?
KNOWLEDGE. Yea, Everyman, when ye to death shall go;
But not yet, for no manner of danger. 860
EVERYMAN. Gramercy, Knowledge, with all my heart.
KNOWLEDGE. Nay, yet I will not from hence depart
Till I see where ye shall be come.
EVERYMAN. Methink, alas, that I must be gone
To make my reckoning and my debts pay, 865
For I see my time is nigh spent away.
Take example, all ye that this do hear or see,
How they that I loved best do forsake me,
Except my Good Deeds that bideth truly.
GOOD DEEDS. All earthly things is but vanity. 870
Beauty, Strength, and Discretion do man forsake,
Foolish friends and kinsmen, that fair spake,
All fleeth save Good Deeds, and that am I.
EVERYMAN. Have mercy on me, God most mighty;
And stand by me, thou Mother and Maid, holy Mary! 875
GOOD DEEDS. Fear not, I will speak for thee.
EVERYMAN. Here I cry God mercy!

GOOD DEEDS. Short° our end, and 'minish° our pain.
Let us go and never come again.
　　EVERYMAN. Into thy hands, Lord, my soul I commend.　　　880
Receive it, Lord, that it be not lost.
As thou me boughtest, so me defend.
And save me from the fiend's boast,
That I may appear with that blessèd host.
That shall be saved at the day of doom.　　　　　　　　885
In manus tuas—of might's most
For ever—*commendo spiritum meum.*°

　　(EVERYMAN *and* GOOD DEEDS *go into the grave.*)

　　KNOWLEDGE. Now hath he suffered that we all shall endure;
The Good Deeds shall make all sure.
Now hath he made ending.　　　　　　　　　　　　　　890
Methinketh that I hear angels sing
And make great joy and melody
Where Everyman's soul received shall be.
　　ANGEL. Come, excellent elect spouse to Jesu!
Here above thou shalt go　　　　　　　　　　　　　　895
Because of thy singular virtue.
Now the soul is taken the body fro,
Thy reckoning is crystal clear.
Now shalt thou into the heavenly sphere,
Unto the which all ye shall come　　　　　　　　　　　900
That liveth well before the day of doom. (*Exit* KNOWLEDGE.)

　　(*Enter* DOCTOR *as Epilogue.*)

　　DOCTOR.° This moral men may have in mind;
Ye hearers, take it of worth, old and young,
And forsake Pride, for he deceiveth you in the end,
And remember Beauty, Five Wits, Strength, and Discretion,　　905
They all at the last do Everyman forsake,
Save his Good Deeds there doth he take.
But beware, and they be small
Before God he hath no help at all.
None excuse may be there for Everyman.　　　　　　　910
Alas, how shall he do then?
For, after death, amends may no man make,
For then mercy and pity doth him forsake.

878. **Short:** shorten.　**'minish:** diminish.　**886–87. In manus . . . meum:** "Into thy hands I commend my spirit."　**902. Doctor:** teacher.

If his reckoning be not clear when he doth come,
God will say, *"Ite, maledicti, in ignem aeternum."* °   915
And he that hath his account whole and sound,
High in heaven he shall be crowned.
Unto which place God bring us all thither,
That we may live body and soul together.
Thereto help the Trinity!   920
Amen, say ye, for saint charity.

Thus endeth this moral play of EVERYMAN.

QUESTIONS

1. Composed by an unknown author probably before 1500, *Everyman* is a characteristically medieval play, yet it has been produced in recent years on radio and stage with notable success. What qualities continue to make it effective and moving?

2. *Everyman* belongs to a class of medieval plays known as moralities. Briefly, a morality is a moral allegory in dramatic form. What characteristics of this play make it an allegory? On what central metaphor is the allegory based?

3. Unlike most plays, this play is frankly didactic (intended to teach). List its didactic devices. Does this didacticism weaken the force or appeal of the play? Why or why not? What are the central lessons of the play? Draw up a brief account of the religious doctrines it embodies.

4. Of what relative importance are plot, character, and theme in the play? Discuss the importance of each.

5. At what points in the play does Everyman undergo a change of mood or attitude? Chart the rising and falling of his morale. What causes each change?

6. Everyman has four soliloquies during the first half of the play, none during the second half. Can you relate this fact to the action and meaning of the play? What effect do the soliloquies have?

7. Discuss the characterization of (a) God, (b) Death, (c) Everyman. How is each conceived? How might they have been conceived differently?

8. What sort of stage setting would you design for this play? Would it be effective if performed on the steps of a cathedral? How would you present God? How old an actor would you choose for Everyman? What parts would you assign to female actors? How would you costume the various characters?

9. Contrast the play with *The Stronger* and *The Brute*. What qualities does it lack that they have? What qualities does it have that they lack?

915. Ite maledicti, in ignem aeternum: "Go, ye accursed, into everlasting fire."

CHAPTER TWO

Realistic and Nonrealistic Drama

As in fiction and poetry, so in drama, literary truth is not the same as fidelity to fact. Fantasy is as much the property of the theater as of poetry or the prose tale. Shakespeare in *A Midsummer Night's Dream* and *The Tempest* uses fairies and goblins and monsters as characters, and in *Hamlet* and *Macbeth* he introduces ghosts and witches. These supernatural characters, nevertheless, serve as a vehicle for truth. When Bottom, in *A Midsummer Night's Dream*, is given an ass's head, the enchantment is a visual metaphor. The witches in *Macbeth* truthfully prefigure a tragic destiny.

Because it is written to be performed, however, drama adds still another dimension of possible unreality. It may be realistic or unrealistic in mode of production as well as in content. Staging, make-up, costuming, and acting may all be handled in such a way as to emphasize the realistic or the fanciful.

It must be recognized, however, that all stage production, no matter how realistic, involves a certain necessary artificiality. If an indoor scene is presented on a picture-frame stage, the spectator is asked to imagine that a room with only three walls is actually a room with four walls. In an arena-type theater, he must imagine all four walls. Both types of presentation, moreover, require adjustments in the acting. In a traditional theater, the actors most of the time must be facing the missing fourth wall. In an arena-type theater, they must not turn their backs too long on any "wall." Both types of presentation, in the interests of effective presentation, require the actors to depart from an absolute realism.

From this point on, the departure from the appearance of reality may be little or great. In many late nineteenth- and early twentieth-century productions, an effort was made to make stage sets as realistic as possible. If the play called for a setting in a study, there had to be real book shelves on the wall and real books on the shelves. If the room contained a wash basin, real water had to flow from the taps. More recently, however, plays have been performed on a stage furnished only with drapes and platforms. In between these two extremes, all degrees of realism are possible. The scenery may consist of painted flats, with painted bookshelves and painted books and painted pictures on the wall. Or, instead of scenery, a play may use only a few movable properties to suggest the required setting. Thornton Wilder's famous play *Our Town* (1938) utilized a bare stage, without curtain, with exposed ropes and backstage equipment, and with a few chairs, two ladders, and a couple of trellises as the only properties. For a scene at a soda fountain, a plank was laid across the backs of two chairs. In fact, provision of elaborately realistic stage sets has been the exception rather than the rule in the long history of the theater. Neither in Greek nor in Shakespearean theater was setting much more than suggested.

But the choice of realistic or unrealistic stage sets, costuming, and make-up may lie with the producer rather than the playwright. When we move to the realm of language and the management of dialogue, the choice is entirely the playwright's. Here again all degrees of realism and nonrealism are possible. In the realistic theater of the early twentieth century, playwrights often made an elaborate effort to reproduce the flat quality of ordinary speech, with all its stumblings and inarticulateness. In real life, of course, few lovers speak with the eloquence of Romeo and Juliet, and many people, in daily conversation, have difficulty getting through a grammatically correct sentence of any length or complexity. They break off, they begin again, they end lamely with an apology, a grammatical blunder, a "you know." Such broken-backed and inadequate speech, skillfully used by the playwright, may faithfully render the quality of human life at some levels, yet its limitations for expressing the heights and depths of human experience are obvious. Most dramatic dialogue, even when most realistic, is more coherent and expressive speech in actual life. Art is always a heightening or an intensification of reality; else it would have no value. The heightening may be little or great. It is greatest in poetic drama. The love exchanges of Romeo and Juliet, spoken in rhymed iambic pentameter and at one point taking the form of a perfectly regular sonnet, are absurdly unrealistic if judged as an imitation of actual speech, but they vividly express the emotional truth of passionate, idealistic young love. It is no criticism of Shakespearean tragedy, therefore, to say that in real life people do not speak in blank verse. The deepest purpose of the playwright is not to imitate actual human speech but to give accurate and powerful expression to human thought and emotion.

All drama asks us to accept certain departures from reality—certain dramatic *conventions*. That a room with three walls or fewer may represent one with four walls, that the actors speak in the language of the audience whatever the nationality of the persons they play, that the actors stand or sit so as to face the audience most of the time—these are all necessary conventions. Other conventions are optional—for example, that the characters may reveal their inner thoughts through soliloquies and asides or may speak in the heightened language of poetry. The playwright working in a strictly realistic mode will avoid the optional conventions, for they conflict with the realistic method that he has chosen to achieve his purpose. The playwright working in a freer mode will feel free to use any or all of them, for they make possible the revelation of dimensions of reality unreachable by a strictly realistic method. Hamlet's famous soliloquy that begins "To be or not to be," in which he debates in blank verse the merits of continued life and suicide, is unrealistic on two counts, but it enables Shakespeare to present Hamlet's introspective mind more powerfully than he otherwise could have done. The characteristic device of Greek drama, a chorus—a group of actors speaking in unison, often in a chant, while going through the steps of an elaborate formalized dance—is another unrealistic device but a useful one for conveying communal or group emotion. It has been revived, in different forms, in many modern plays. The use of a narrator, as in *Our Town* and Tennessee Williams' *Glass Menagerie*, is a related unrealistic device that has served playwrights as a vehicle for dramatic truth.

In most plays, however unreal the world into which we are taken, this world is treated as self-contained, and we are asked to regard it temporarily as a real world. Thus Shakespeare's world of fairies in *A Midsummer Night's Dream* is real to us while we watch the play. Because of Shakespeare's magic, we quite willingly make that "temporary suspension of disbelief" that, according to Coleridge, "constitutes poetic faith." And the step from crediting Bottom as real, though we know in fact he is only a dressed-up actor, to regarding Bottom with an ass's head as real is relatively a small one. But some playwrights abandon even this much attempt to give their work an illusion of reality. They deliberately violate the self-containment of the fictional world and keep reminding us that we are only seeing a play. In *Everyman,* for instance, the opening speaker announces that we are about to see a play and tells us what its moral is; God begins the play itself by speaking, apparently, directly to the audience; at the conclusion a "doctor" (or teacher) reiterates the moral of the play. More important, however, the names of the characters and the nature of the dialogue throughout the play remind us that these characters are not really persons but only abstractions. Nevertheless, for most audiences Everyman quickly becomes an intensely real personage.

The adjective *realistic,* then, as applied to literature, must be regarded as a descriptive, not an evaluative, term. When we call a play realistic, we are saying something about its mode of presentation, not praising nor dispraising it. Realism indicates fidelity to the outer appearances of life. The serious dramatist is interested in life's inner meanings, which he may approach through ether realistic or unrealistic presentation. Great plays have been written in both the realistic and the nonrealistic modes. It is not without significance, however, that the three greatest plays in this book are probably *Oedipus Rex, Othello,* and *The Misanthrope*—one originally written in quantitative Greek verse, one in English blank verse, and one in French rimed couplets. Human truth, rather than fidelity to fact, is the highest achievement of literary art.

EXERCISE

1. Which of these three short plays did you find most entertaining? which most revealing? which most moving? Do you find any correlation between the achievement of these purposes and the degree of "realism" used?

Henrik Ibsen

AN ENEMY OF THE PEOPLE

CHARACTERS

DR. THOMAS STOCKMANN, *Medical Officer of the Municipal Baths*
MRS. STOCKMANN, *his wife*
PETRA, *their daughter, a teacher*
EJLIF ⎱
MORTEN ⎰ *their sons, aged 13 and 10 respectively*
PETER STOCKMANN, *the Doctor's elder brother; Mayor of the Town and Chief Constable, Chairman of the Baths' Committee, etc., etc.*
MORTEN KIIL, *a tanner* (MRS. STOCKMANN's *adoptive father*)
HOVSTAD, *editor of the* People's Messenger
BILLING, *subeditor*
CAPTAIN HORSTER
ASLAKSEN, *a printer*
MEN, *of various conditions and occupations, some few women, and a troop of schoolboys—the audience at a public meeting.*

The action takes place in a coast town in southern Norway.

ACT I

SCENE. DR. STOCKMANN's *sitting-room. It is evening. The room is plainly but neatly appointed and furnished. In the right-hand wall are two doors; the farther leads out to the hall, the nearer to the doctor's study. In the left-hand wall, opposite the door leading to the hall, is a door leading to the other rooms occupied by the family. In the middle of the same wall stands the stove, and, further forward, a couch with a looking-glass hanging over it and an oval table in front of it. On the table, a lighted lamp, with a lampshade. At the back of the room, an open door leads to the dining-room. BILLING is seen sitting at the dining table, on which a lamp is burning. He has a napkin tucked under his chin, and MRS. STOCKMANN is standing by the table handing him a large plate-full of roast beef. The other places at the table are empty, and the table somewhat in disorder, a meal having evidently recently been finished.*

MRS. STOCKMANN.   You see, if you come an hour late, Mr. Billing, you have to put up with cold meat.

AN ENEMY OF THE PEOPLE: First performed in 1882.

BILLING (*as he eats*). It is uncommonly good, thank you—remarkably good.

MRS. STOCKMANN. My husband makes such a point of having his meals punctually, you know—

BILLING. That doesn't affect me a bit. Indeed, I almost think I enjoy a meal all the better when I can sit down and eat all by myself and undisturbed.

MRS. STOCKMANN. Oh well, as long as you are enjoying it—. (*Turns to the hall door, listening*) I expect that is Mr. Hovstad coming too.

BILLING. Very likely.

(PETER STOCKMANN *comes in. He wears an overcoat and his official hat, and carries a stick.*)

PETER STOCKMANN. Good evening, Katherine.

MRS. STOCKMANN (*coming forward into the sitting-room*). Ah, good evening—is it you? How good of you to come up and see us!

PETER STOCKMANN. I happened to be passing, and so— (*Looks into the dining-room*) But you have company with you, I see.

MRS. STOCKMANN (*a little embarrassed*). Oh, no—it was quite by chance he came in. (*Hurriedly*) Won't you come in and have something, too?

PETER STOCKMANN. I! No, thank you. Good gracious—hot meat at night! Not with my digestion.

MRS. STOCKMANN. Oh, but just once in a way—

PETER STOCKMANN. No, no, my dear lady; I stick to my tea and bread and butter. It is much more wholesome in the long run—and a little more economical, too.

MRS. STOCKMANN (*smiling*). Now you mustn't think that Thomas and I are spendthrifts.

PETER STOCKMANN. Not you, my dear; I would never think that of you. (*Points to the Doctor's study*) Is he not at home?

MRS. STOCKMANN. No, he went out for a little turn after supper—he and the boys.

PETER STOCKMANN. I doubt if that is a wise thing to do. (*Listens.*) I fancy I hear him coming now.

MRS. STOCKMANN. No, I don't think it is he. (*A knock is heard at the door.*) Come in! (HOVSTAD *comes in from the hall.*) Oh, it is you, Mr. Hovstad!

HOVSTAD. Yes, I hope you will forgive me, but I was delayed at the printer's. Good evening, Mr. Mayor.

PETER STOCKMANN (*bowing a little distantly*). Good evening. You have come on business, no doubt.

HOVSTAD. Partly. It's about an article for the paper.

PETER STOCKMANN. So I imagined. I hear my brother has become a prolific contributor to the "People's Messenger."

HOVSTAD. Yes, he is good enough to write in the "People's Messenger" when he has any home truths to tell.

MRS. STOCKMANN (to HOVSTAD). But won't you—? (Points to the dining-room.)

PETER STOCKMANN. Quite so, quite so. I don't blame him in the least, as a writer, for addressing himself to the quarters where he will find the readiest sympathy. And, besides that, I personally have no reason to bear any ill will to your paper, Mr. Hovstad.

HOVSTAD. I quite agree with you.

PETER STOCKMANN. Taking one thing with another, there is an excellent spirit of toleration in the town—an admirable municipal spirit. And it all springs from the fact of our having a great common interest to unite us— an interest that is in an equally high degree the concern of every right-minded citizen—

HOVSTAD. The Baths, yes.

PETER STOCKMANN. Exactly—our fine, new, handsome Baths. Mark my words, Mr. Hovstad—the Baths will become the focus of our municipal life! Not a doubt of it!

MRS. STOCKMANN. That is just what Thomas says.

PETER STOCKMANN. Think how extraordinarily the place has developed within the last year or two! Money has been flowing in, and there is some life and some business doing in the town. Houses and landed property are rising in value every day.

HOVSTAD. And unemployment is diminishing.

PETER STOCKMANN. Yes, that is another thing. The burden of the poor rates has been lightened, to the great relief of the propertied classes; and that relief will be even greater if only we get a really good summer this year, and lots of visitors—plenty of invalids, who will make the Baths talked about.

HOVSTAD. And there is a good prospect of that, I hear.

PETER STOCKMANN. It looks very promising. Enquiries about apartments and that sort of thing are reaching us every day.

HOVSTAD. Well, the doctor's article will come in very suitably.

PETER STOCKMANN. Has he been writing something just lately?

HOVSTAD. This is something he wrote in the winter; a recommendation of the Baths—an account of the excellent sanitary conditions here. But I held the article over, temporarily.

PETER STOCKMANN. Ah,—some little difficulty about it, I suppose?

HOVSTAD. No, not at all; I thought it would be better to wait till the spring, because it is just at this time that people begin to think seriously about their summer quarters.

PETER STOCKMANN. Quite right; you were perfectly right, Mr. Hovstad.

HOVSTAD. Yes, Thomas is really indefatigable when it is a question of the Baths.

PETER STOCKMANN. Well—remember, he is the Medical Officer to the Baths.

HOVSTAD. Yes, and what is more, they owe their existence to him.

PETER STOCKMANN. To him? Indeed! It is true I have heard from time to time that some people are of that opinion. At the same time I must say I imagined that I look a modest part in the enterprise.

MRS. STOCKMANN. Yes, that is what Thomas is always saying.

HOVSTAD. But who denies it, Mr. Stockmann? You set the thing going and made a practical concern of it; we all know that. I only meant that the idea of it came first from the doctor.

PETER STOCKMANN. Oh, ideas—yes! My brother has had plenty of them in his time—unfortunately. But when it is a question of putting an idea into practical shape, you have to apply to a man of different mettle, Mr. Hovstad. And I certainly should have thought that in this house at least—

MRS. STOCKMANN. My dear Peter—

HOVSTAD. How can you think that—?

MRS. STOCKMANN. Won't you go in and have something, Mr. Hovstad? My husband is sure to be back directly.

HOVSTAD. Thank you, perhaps just a morsel. (*Goes into the dining-room.*)

PETER STOCKMANN (*lowering his voice a little*). It is a curious thing that these farmers' sons never seem to lose their want of tact.

MRS. STOCKMANN. Surely it is not worth bothering about! Cannot you and Thomas share the credit as brothers?

PETER STOCKMANN. I should have thought so; but apparently some people are not satisfied with a share.

MRS. STOCKMANN. What nonsense! You and Thomas get on so capitally together. (*Listens*) There he is at last, I think. (*Goes out and opens the door leading to the hall.*)

DR. STOCKMANN (*laughing and talking outside*). Look here—here is another guest for you, Katherine. Isn't that jolly! Come in, Captain Horster; hang your coat up on this peg. Ah, you don't wear an overcoat. Just think, Katherine; I met him in the street and could hardly persuade him to come up! (CAPTAIN HORSTER *comes into the room and greets* MRS. STOCKMANN. *He is followed by* DR. STOCKMANN.) Come along in, boys. They are ravenously hungry again, you know. Come along, Captain Horster; you must have a slice of beef. (*Pushes* HORSTER *into the dining-room.* EJLIF *and* MORTEN *go in after them.*)

MRS. STOCKMANN. But, Thomas, don't you see—?

DR. STOCKMANN (*turning in the doorway*). Oh, is it you, Peter? (*Shakes hands with him.*) Now that is very delightful.

PETER STOCKMANN. Unfortunately I must go in a moment—

DR. STOCKMANN. Rubbish! There is some toddy just coming in. You haven't forgotten the toddy, Katherine?

MRS. STOCKMANN. Of course not; the water is boiling now. (*Goes into the dining-room.*)

PETER STOCKMANN. Toddy too!

DR. STOCKMANN. Yes, sit down and we will have it comfortably.

PETER STOCKMANN. Thanks, I never care about an evening's drinking.

DR. STOCKMANN. But this isn't an evening's drinking.

PETER STOCKMANN. It seems to me—. (*Looks towards the dining-room*) It is extraordinary how they can put away all that food.

DR. STOCKMANN (*rubbing his hands*). Yes, isn't it splendid to see young people eat? They have always got an appetite, you know! That's as it should be. Lots of food—to build up their strength! They are the people who are going to stir up the fermenting forces of the future, Peter.

PETER STOCKMANN. May I ask what they will find here to "stir up," as you put it?

DR. STOCKMANN. Ah, you must ask the young people that—when the time comes. We shan't be able to see it, of course. That stands to reason—two old fogies, like us—

PETER STOCKMANN. Really, really! I must say that is an extremely odd expression to—

DR. STOCKMANN. Oh, you mustn't take me too literally, Peter. I am so heartily happy and contented, you know. I think it is such an extraordinary piece of good fortune to be in the middle of all this growing, germinating life. It is a splendid time to live in! It is as if a whole new world were being created around one.

PETER STOCKMANN. Do you really think so?

DR. STOCKMANN. Ah, naturally you can't appreciate it as keenly as I. You have lived all your life in these surroundings, and your impressions have got blunted. But I, who have been buried all these years in my little corner up north, almost without ever seeing a stranger who might bring new ideas with him—well, in my case it has just the same effect as if I had been transported into the middle of a crowded city.

PETER STOCKMANN. Oh, a city—!

DR. STOCKMANN. I know, I know; it is all cramped enough here, compared with many other places. But there is life here—there is promise—there are innumerable things to work for and fight for; and that is the main thing. (*Calls*) Katherine, hasn't the postman been here?

MRS. STOCKMANN (*from the dining-room*). No.

DR. STOCKMANN. And then to be comfortably off, Peter! That is something one learns to value, when one has been on the brink of starvation, as we have.

PETER STOCKMANN. Oh, surely—

DR. STOCKMANN. Indeed I can assure you we have often been very hard put to it, up there. And now to be able to live like a lord! To-day, for instance, we had roast beef for dinner—and, what is more, for supper too. Won't you come and have a little bit? Or let me show it you, at any rate? Come here—

PETER STOCKMANN. No, no—not for worlds!

DR. STOCKMANN. Well, but just come here then. Do you see, we have got a table-cover?

PETER STOCKMANN. Yes, I noticed it.

DR. STOCKMANN. And we have got a lamp-shade too. Do you see? All out of Katherine's savings! It makes the room so cosy. Don't you think so? Just stand here for a moment—no, no, not there—just here, that's it! Look now, when you get the light on it altogether—I really think it looks very nice, doesn't it?

PETER STOCKMANN. Oh, if you can afford luxuries of this kind—

DR. STOCKMANN. Yes, I can afford it now. Katherine tells me I earn almost as much as we spend.

PETER STOCKMANN. Almost—yes!

DR. STOCKMANN. But a scientific man must live in a little bit of style. I am quite sure an ordinary civil servant spends more in a year than I do.

PETER STOCKMANN. I daresay. A civil servant—a man in a well-paid position—

DR. STOCKMANN. Well, any ordinary merchant, then! A man in that position spends two or three times as much as—

PETER STOCKMANN. It just depends on circumstances.

DR. STOCKMANN. At all events I assure you I don't waste money unprofitably. But I can't find it in my heart to deny myself the pleasure of entertaining my friends. I need that sort of thing, you know. I have lived for so long shut out of it all, that it is a necessity of life to me to mix with young, eager, ambitious men, men of liberal and active minds; and that describes every one of those fellows who are enjoying their supper in there. I wish you knew more of Hovstad—

PETER STOCKMANN. By the way, Hovstad was telling me he was going to print another article of yours.

DR. STOCKMANN. An article of mine?

PETER STOCKMANN. Yes, about the Baths. An article you wrote in the winter.

DR. STOCKMANN. Oh, that one! No, I don't intend that to appear just for the present.

PETER STOCKMANN. Why not? It seems to me that this would be the most opportune moment.

DR. STOCKMANN. Yes, very likely—under normal conditions. (*Crosses the room.*)

PETER STOCKMANN (*following him with his eyes*). Is there anything abnormal about the present conditions?

Dr. Stockmann (*standing still*).   To tell you the truth, Peter, I can't say just at this moment—at all events not to-night. There may be much that is very abnormal about the present conditions—and it is possible there may be nothing abnormal about them at all. It is quite possible it may be merely my imagination.

Peter Stockmann.   I must say it all sounds most mysterious. Is there something going on that I am to be kept in ignorance of? I should have imagined that I, as Chairman of the governing body of the Baths—

Dr. Stockmann.   And I should have imagined that I—. Oh, come, don't let us fly out at one another, Peter.

Peter Stockmann.   Heaven forbid! I am not in the habit of flying out at people, as you call it. But I am entitled to request most emphatically that all arrangements shall be made in a business-like manner, through the proper channels, and shall be dealt with by the legally constituted authorities. I can allow no going behind our backs by any roundabout means.

Dr. Stockmann.   Have I ever at any time tried to go behind your backs!

Peter Stockmann.   You have an ingrained tendency to take your own way, at all events; and that is almost equally inadmissible in a well-ordered community. The individual ought undoubtedly to acquiesce in subordinating himself to the community—or, to speak more accurately, to the authorities who have the care of the community's welfare.

Dr. Stockmann.   Very likely. But what the deuce has all this got to do with me?

Peter Stockmann.   That is exactly what you never appear to be willing to learn, my dear Thomas. But, mark my words, some day you will have to suffer for it—sooner or later. Now I have told you. Good-bye.

Dr. Stockmann.   Have you taken leave of your senses? You are on the wrong scent altogether.

Peter Stockmann.   I am not usually that. You must excuse me now if I—(*calls into the dining-room*) Good night, Katherine. Good night, gentlemen. (*Goes out.*)

Mrs. Stockmann (*coming from the dining-room*).   Has he gone?

Dr. Stockmann.   Yes, and in such a bad temper.

Mrs. Stockmann.   But, dear Thomas, what have you been doing to him again?

Dr. Stockmann.   Nothing at all. And, anyhow, he can't oblige me to make my report before the proper time.

Mrs. Stockmann.   What have you got to make a report to him about?

Dr. Stockmann.   Hm! Leave that to me, Katherine.—It is an extraordinary thing that the postman doesn't come.

(Hovstad, Billings and Horster *have got up from the table and come into the sitting-room.* Ejlif *and* Morten *come in after them.*)

BILLING (*stretching himself*).   Ah—one feels a new man after a meal like that.

HOVSTAD.   The mayor wasn't in a very sweet temper tonight, then.

DR. STOCKMANN.   It is his stomach; he has a wretched digestion.

HOVSTAD.   I rather think it was us two of the "People's Messenger" that he couldn't digest.

MRS. STOCKMANN.   I thought you came out of it pretty well with him.

HOVSTAD.   Oh yes; but it isn't anything more than a sort of truce.

BILLING.   That is just what it is! That word sums up the situation.

DR. STOCKMANN.   We must remember that Peter is a lonely man, poor chap. He has no home comforts of any kind; nothing but everlasting business. And all that infernal weak tea wash that he pours into himself! Now then, my boys, bring chairs up to the table. Aren't we going to have that toddy, Katherine?

MRS. STOCKMANN (*going into the dining-room*).   I am just getting it.

DR. STOCKMANN.   Sit down here on the couch beside me, Captain Horster. We so seldom see you——. Please sit down, my friends.

(*They sit down at the table.* MRS. STOCKMANN *brings a tray, with a spirit-lamp, glasses, bottles, etc., upon it.*)

MRS. STOCKMANN.   There you are! This is arrack, and this is rum, and this one is the brandy. Now every one must help himself.

DR. STOCKMANN (*taking a glass*).   We will. (*They all mix themselves some toddy.*) And let us have the cigars. Ejlif, you know where the box is. And you, Morten, can fetch my pipe. (*The two boys go into the room on the right.*) I have a suspicion that Ejlif pockets a cigar now and then!—but I take no notice of it. (*Calls out*) And my smoking-cap too, Morten. Katherine, you can tell him where I left it. Ah, he has got it. (*The boys bring the various things.*) Now, my friends. I stick to my pipe, you know. This one has seen plenty of bad weather with me up north. (*Touches glasses with them*) Your good health! Ah! it is good to be sitting snug and warm here.

MRS. STOCKMANN (*who sits knitting*).   Do you sail soon, Captain Horster?

HORSTER.   I expect to be ready to sail next week.

MRS. STOCKMANN.   I suppose you are going to America?

HORSTER.   Yes, that is the plan.

MRS. STOCKMANN.   Then you won't be able to take part in the coming election.

HORSTER.   Is there going to be an election?

BILLING.   Didn't you know?

HORSTER.   No, I don't mix myself up with those things.

BILLING.   But do you not take an interest in public affairs?

HORSTER.   No, I don't know anything about politics.

BILLING.   All the same, one ought to vote, at any rate.

HORSTER. Even if one doesn't know anything about what is going on?

BILLING. Doesn't know! What do you mean by that? A community is like a ship; every one ought to be prepared to take the helm.

HORSTER. Maybe that is all very well on shore; but on board ship it wouldn't work.

HOVSTAD. It is astonishing how little most sailors care about what goes on on shore.

BILLING. Very extraordinary.

DR. STOCKMANN. Sailors are like birds of passage; they feel equally at home in any latitude. And that is only an additional reason for our being all the more keen, Hovstad. Is there to be anything of public interest in tomorrow's "Messenger"?

HOVSTAD. Nothing about municipal affairs. But the day after tomorrow I was thinking of printing your article—

DR. STOCKMANN. Ah, devil take it—my article! Look here, that must wait a bit.

HOVSTAD. Really? We had just got convenient space for it, and I thought it was just the opportune moment—

DR. STOCKMANN. Yes, yes, very likely you are right; but it must wait all the same. I will explain to you later.

(PETRA comes in from the hall, in hat and cloak and with a bundle of exercise books under her arm.)

PETRA. Good evening.

DR. STOCKMANN. Good evening, Petra; come along.

(Mutual greetings; PETRA takes off her things and puts them down on a chair by the door.)

PETRA. And you have all been sitting here enjoying yourselves, while I have been out slaving!

DR. STOCKMANN. Well, come and enjoy yourself too!

BILLING. May I mix a glass for you?

PETRA (coming to the table). Thanks, I would rather do it; you always mix it too strong. But I forgot, father—I have a letter for you. (Goes to the chair where she had laid her things.)

DR. STOCKMAN. A letter? From whom?

PETRA (looking in her coat pocket). The postman gave it to me just as I was going out—

DR. STOCKMANN (getting up and going to her). And you only give to me now!

PETRA. I really had not time to run up again. There it is!

DR. STOCKMANN (seizing the letter). Let's see, let's see, child! (Looks at the address) Yes, that's all right!

MRS. STOCKMANN. Is it the one you have been expecting so anxiously, Thomas?

DR. STOCKMANN. Yes, it is. I must go to my room now and——. Where shall I get a light, Katherine? Is there no lamp in my room again?

MRS. STOCKMANN. Yes, your lamp is all ready lit on your desk.

DR. STOCKMANN. Good, good. Excuse me for a moment——. (*Goes into his study.*)

PETRA. What do you suppose it is, mother?

MRS. STOCKMANN. I don't know; for the last day or two he has always been asking if the postman has not been.

BILLING. Probably some country patient.

PETRA. Poor old dad!—he will overwork himself soon. (*Mixes a glass for herself*) There, that will taste good!

HOVSTAD. Have you been teaching in the evening school again to-day?

PETRA (*sipping from her glass*). Two hours.

BILLING. And four hours of school in the morning—

PETRA. Five hours.

MRS. STOCKMANN. And you have still got exercises to correct, I see.

PETRA. A whole heap, yes.

HORSTER. You are pretty full up with work too, it seems to me.

PETRA. Yes—but that is good. One is so delightfully tired after it.

BILLING. Do you like that?

PETRA. Yes, because one sleeps so well then.

MORTEN. You must be dreadfully wicked, Petra.

PETRA. Wicked?

MORTEN. Yes, because you work so much. Mr. Rörlund says work is a punishment for our sins.

EJLIF. Pooh, what a duffer you are, to believe a thing like that!

MRS. STOCKMANN. Come, come, Ejlif!

BILLING (*laughing*). That's capital!

HOVSTAD. Don't you want to work as hard as that, Morten?

MORTEN. No, indeed I don't.

HOVSTAD. What do you want to be, then?

MORTEN. I should like best to be a Viking.

EJLIF. You would have to be a pagan then.

MORTEN. Well, I could become a pagan, couldn't I?

BILLING. I agree with you, Morten! My sentiments, exactly.

MRS. STOCKMANN (*signalling to him*). I am sure that is not true, Mr. Billing.

BILLING. Yes, I swear it is! I am a pagan, and I am proud of it. Believe me, before long we shall all be pagans.

MORTEN. And then we shall be allowed to do anything we like?

BILLING. Well, you see, Morten——.

Mrs. Stockmann. You must go to your room now, boys; I am sure you have some lessons to learn for to-morrow.

Ejlif. I should like so much to stay a little longer—

Mrs. Stockmann. No, no; away you go, both of you.

(*The boys say good-night and go into the room on the left.*)

Hovstad. Do you really think it can do the boys any harm to hear such things?

Mrs. Stockmann. I don't know; but I don't like it.

Petra. But you know, mother, I think you really are wrong about it.

Mrs. Stockmann. Maybe, but I don't like it—not in our own home.

Petra. There is so much falsehood both at home and at school. At home one must not speak, and at school we have to stand and tell lies to the children.

Horster. Tell lies?

Petra. Yes, don't you suppose we have to teach them all sorts of things that we don't believe?

Billing. That is perfectly true.

Petra. If only I had the means I would start a school of my own, and it would be conducted on very different lines.

Billing. Oh, bother the means—!

Horster. Well if you are thinking of that, Miss Stockmann, I shall be delighted to provide you with a schoolroom. The great big old house my father left me is standing almost empty; there is an immense dining-room downstairs—

Petra (*laughing*). Thank you very much; but I am afraid nothing will come of it.

Hovstad. No, Miss Petra is much more likely to take to journalism, I expect. By the way, have you had time to do anything with that English story you promised to translate for us?

Petra. No, not yet; but you shall have it in good time.

(Dr. Stockmann *comes in from his room with an open letter in his hand.*)

Dr. Stockmann (*waving the letter*). Well, now the town will have something new to talk about, I can tell you!

Billing. Something new?

Mrs. Stockmann. What is this?

Dr. Stockmann. A great discovery, Katherine.

Hovstad. Really?

Mrs. Stockmann. A discovery of yours?

Dr. Stockmann. A discovery of mine. (*Walks up and down.*) Just let them come saying, as usual, that it is all fancy and a crazy man's imagination! But they will be careful what they say this time, I can tell you!

PETRA. But, father, tell us what it is.

DR. STOCKMANN. Yes, yes—only give me time, and you shall know all about it. If only I had Peter here now! It just shows how we men can go about forming our judgments, when in reality we are as blind as any moles—

HOVSTAD. What are you driving at, Doctor?

DR. STOCKMANN (*standing still by the table*). Isn't it the universal opinion that our town is a healthy spot?

HOVSTAD. Certainly.

DR. STOCKMANN. Quite an unusually healthy spot, in fact—a place that deserves to be recommended in the warmest possible manner either for invalids or for people who are well—

MRS. STOCKMANN. Yes, but my dear Thomas—

DR. STOCKMANN. And we have been recommending it and praising it —I have written and written, both in the "Messenger" and in pamphlets—

HOVSTAD. Well, what then?

DR. STOCKMANN. And the Baths—we have called them the "main artery of the town's life-blood," the "nerve-centre of our town," and the devil knows what else—

BILLING. "The town's pulsating heart" was the expression I once used on an important occasion—

DR. STOCKMANN. Quite so. Well, do you know what they really are, these great, splendid, much praised Baths that have cost so much money— do you know what they are?

HOVSTAD. No, what are they?

MRS. STOCKMANN. Yes, what are they?

DR. STOCKMANN. The whole place is a pesthouse!

PETRA. The Baths, father?

MRS. STOCKMANN (*at the same time*). Our Baths!

HOVSTAD. But, Doctor—

BILLING. Absolutely incredible!

DR. STOCKMANN. The whole Bath establishment is a whited, poisoned sepulchre, I tell you—the gravest possible danger to the public health! All the nastiness up at Mölledal, all that stinking filth, is infecting the water in the conduit-pipes leading to the reservoir; and the same cursed, filthy poison oozes out on the shore too—

HORSTER. Where the bathing-place is?

DR. STOCKMANN. Just there.

HOVSTAD. How do you come to be so certain of all this, Doctor?

DR. STOCKMANN. I have investigated the matter most conscientiously. For a long time past I have suspected something of the kind. Last year we had some very strange cases of illness among the visitors—typhoid cases, and cases of gastric fever—

MRS. STOCKMANN. Yes, that is quite true.

DR. STOCKMANN. At the time, we supposed the visitors had been infected before they came; but later on, in the winter, I began to have a different opinion; and so I set myself to examine the water, as well as I could.

MRS. STOCKMANN. Then that is what you have been so busy with?

DR. STOCKMANN. Indeed I have been busy, Katherine. But here I had none of the necessary scientific apparatus; so I sent samples, both of the drinking-water and of the sea-water, up to the University, to have an accurate analysis made by a chemist.

HOVSTAD. And have you got that?

DR. STOCKMANN (showing him the letter). Here it is! It proves the presence of decomposing organic matter in the water—it is full of infusoria. The water is absolutely dangerous to use, either internally or externally.

MRS. STOCKMANN. What a mercy you discovered it in time.

DR. STOCKMANN. You may well say so.

HOVSTAD. And what do you propose to do now, Doctor?

DR. STOCKMANN. To see the matter put right—naturally.

HOVSTAD. Can that be done?

DR. STOCKMANN. It must be done. Otherwise the Baths will be absolutely useless and wasted. But we need not anticipate that; I have a very clear idea what we shall have to do.

MRS. STOCKMANN. But why have you kept this all so secret, dear?

DR. STOCKMANN. Do you suppose I was going to run about the town gossiping about it, before I had absolute proof? No, thank you. I am not such a fool.

PETRA. Still, you might have told us—

DR. STOCKMANN. Not a living soul. But to-morrow you may run round to the old Badger—

MRS. STOCKMANN. Oh, Thomas! Thomas!

DR. STOCKMANN. Well, to your grandfather, then. The old boy will have something to be astonished at! I know he thinks I am cracked—and there are lots of other people think so too, I have noticed. But now these good folks shall see—they shall just see—! (Walks about, rubbing his hands.) There will be a nice upset in the town, Katherine; you can't imagine what it will be. All the conduit-pipes will have to be relaid.

HOVSTAD (getting up). All the conduit-pipes—?

DR. STOCKMANN. Yes, of course. The intake is too low down; it will have to be lifted to a position much higher up.

PETRA. Then you were right after all.

DR. STOCKMANN. Ah, you remember, Petra—I wrote opposing the plans before the work was begun. But at that time no one would listen to me. Well, I am going to let them have it, now! Of course I have prepared a report for the Baths Committee; I have had it ready for a week, and was only waiting for this to come. (Shows the letter.) Now it shall go off at once. (Goes into his room and comes back with some papers.) Look at that! Four closely written sheets!—and the letter shall go with them. Give me a bit of paper, Katherine—something to wrap them up in. That will do! Now give it to—to—(*stamps his foot*)—what the deuce is her name?—give it to the maid, and tell her to take it at once to the Mayor.

(MRS. STOCKMANN *takes the packet and goes out through the dining-room.*)

PETRA. What do you think uncle Peter will say, father?

DR. STOCKMANN. What is there for him to say? I should think he would be very glad that such an important truth has been brought to light.

HOVSTAD. Will you let me print a short note about your discovery in the "Messenger"?

DR. STOCKMANN. I shall be very much obliged if you will.

HOVSTAD. It is very desirable that the public should be informed of it without delay.

DR. STOCKMANN. Certainly.

MRS. STOCKMANN (*coming back*). She has just gone with it.

BILLING. Upon my soul, Doctor, you are going to be the foremost man in the town!

DR. STOCKMANN (*walking about happily*). Nonsense! As a matter of fact I have done nothing more than my duty. I have only made a lucky find —that's all. Still, all the same—

BILLING. Hovstad, don't you think the town ought to give Dr. Stockmann some sort of testimonial?

HOVSTAD. I will suggest it, anyway.

BILLING. And I will speak to Aslaksen about it.

DR. STOCKMANN. No, my good friends, don't let us have any of that nonsense. I won't hear of anything of the kind. And if the Baths Committee should think of voting me an increase of salary, I will not accept it. Do you hear, Katherine—I won't accept it.

MRS. STOCKMANN. You are quite right, Thomas.

PETRA (*lifting her glass*). Your health, father!

HOVSTAD and BILLING. Your health, Doctor! Good health!

HORSTER (*touches glasses with* DR. STOCKMANN). I hope it will bring you nothing but good luck.

DR. STOCKMANN. Thank you, thank you, my dear fellows! I feel tremendously happy! It is a splendid thing for a man to be able to feel that he has done a service to his native town and to his fellow-citizens. Hurrah, Katherine!

(*He puts his arms round her and whirls her round and round, while she protests with laughing cries. They all laugh, clap their hands and cheer the* DOCTOR. *The boys put their heads in at the door to see what is going on.*)

ACT II

SCENE. *The same. The door into the dining-room is shut. It is morning.* MRS. STOCKMANN, *with a sealed letter in her hand, comes in from the dining-room, goes to the door of the* DOCTOR'S *study and peeps in.*

MRS. STOCKMANN. Are you in, Thomas?

DR. STOCKMANN (*from within his room*). Yes, I have just come in. (*Comes into the room*) What is it?

MRS. STOCKMANN. A letter from your brother.

DR. STOCKMANN. Aha, let us see! (*Opens the letter and reads*) "I return herewith the manuscript you sent me"—(*reads on in a low murmur*) Hm!—

MRS. STOCKMANN. What does he say?

DR. STOCKMANN (*putting the papers in his pocket*). Oh, he only writes that he will come up here himself about midday.

MRS. STOCKMANN. Well, try and remember to be at home this time.

DR. STOCKMANN. That will be all right; I have got through all my morning visits.

MRS. STOCKMANN. I am extremely curious to know how he takes it.

DR. STOCKMANN. You will see he won't like it's having been I, and not he, that made the discovery.

MRS. STOCKMANN. Aren't you a little nervous about that?

DR. STOCKMANN. Oh, he really will be pleased enough, you know. But, at the same time, Peter is so confoundedly afraid of anyone's doing any service to the town except himself.

MRS. STOCKMANN. I will tell you what, Thomas—you should be good-natured, and share the credit of this with him. Couldn't you make out that it was he who set you on the scent of this discovery?

DR. STOCKMANN. I am quite willing. If only I can get the thing set right. I—

(MORTEN KIIL *puts his head in through the door leading from the hall, looks around in an inquiring manner and chuckles.*)

MORTEN KIIL (*slyly*). Is it—is it true?

MRS. STOCKMANN (*going to the door*). Father!—is it you?

DR. STOCKMANN. Ah, Mr. Kiil—good morning, good morning!

MRS. STOCKMANN. But come along in.

MORTEN KIIL. If it is true, I will; if not, I am off.

DR. STOCKMANN. If what is true?

MORTEN KIIL. This tale about the water-supply. Is it true?

DR. STOCKMANN. Certainly it is true. But how did you come to hear it?

MORTEN KIIL (*coming in*). Petra ran in on her way to the school—

DR. STOCKMANN. Did she?

Morten Kiil. Yes; and she declares that—. I thought she was only making a fool of me, but it isn't like Petra to do that.

Dr. Stockmann. Of course not. How could you imagine such a thing!

Morten Kiil. Oh well, it is better never to trust anybody; you may find you have been made a fool of before you know where you are. But it is really true, all the same?

Dr. Stockmann. You can depend upon it that it is true. Won't you sit down? (*Settles him on the couch.*) Isn't it a real bit of luck for the town—

Morten Kiil (*suppressing his laughter*). A bit of luck for the town?

Dr. Stockmann. Yes, that I made the discovery in good time.

Morten Kiil (*as before*). Yes, yes, yes!—But I should never have thought you the sort of man to pull your own brother's leg like this!

Dr. Stockmann. Pull his leg!

Mrs. Stockmann. Really, father dear—

Morten Kiil (*resting his hands and his chin in the handle of his stick and winking slyly at the* Doctor). Let me see, what was the story? Some kind of beast that had got into the water-pipes, wasn't it?

Dr. Stockmann. Infusoria—yes.

Morten Kiil. And a lot of these beasts had got in, according to Petra —a tremendous lot.

Dr. Stockmann. Certainly; hundreds of thousands of them, probably.

Morten Kiil. But no one can see them—isn't that so?

Dr. Stockmann. Yes; you can't see them.

Morten Kiil (*with a quiet chuckle*). Damme—it's the finest story I have ever heard!

Dr. Stockmann. What do you mean?

Morten Kiil. But you will never get the Mayor to believe a thing like that.

Dr. Stockmann. We shall see.

Morten Kiil. Do you think he will be fool enough to—?

Dr. Stockmann. I hope the whole town will be fools enough.

Morten Kiil. The whole town! Well, it wouldn't be a bad thing. It would just serve them right and teach them a lesson. They think themselves so much cleverer than we old fellows. They hounded me out of the council; they did, I tell you—they hounded me out. Now they shall pay for it. You pull their legs too, Thomas!

Dr. Stockmann. Really, I—

Morten Kiil. You pull their legs! (*Gets up.*) If you can work it so that the Mayor and his friends all swallow the same bait, I will give ten pounds to a charity—like a shot!

Dr. Stockmann. That is very kind of you.

Morten Kiil. Yes, I haven't got much money to throw away, I can tell you; but if you can work this, I will give five pounds to a charity at Christmas.

(Hovstad *comes in by the hall door.*)

Hovstad. Good morning! (*Stops.*) Oh, I beg your pardon—

Dr. Stockmann. Not at all; come in.

Morten Kiil (*with another chuckle*). Oho!—is he in this too?

Hovstad. What do you mean?

Dr. Stockmann. Certainly he is.

Morten Kiil. I might have known it! It must get into the papers. You know how to do it, Thomas! Set your wits to work. Now I must go.

Dr. Stockmann. Won't you stay a little while?

Morten Kiil. No, I must be off now. You keep up this game for all it is worth; you won't repent it, I'm damned if you will!

(*He goes out;* Mrs. Stockmann *follows him into the hall.*)

Dr. Stockmann (*laughing*). Just imagine—the old chap doesn't believe a word of all this about the water-supply.

Hovstad. Oh that was it, then?

Dr. Stockmann. Yes, that was what we were talking about. Perhaps it is the same thing that brings you here?

Hovstad. Yes, it is. Can you spare me a few minutes, Doctor?

Dr. Stockmann. As long as you like, my dear fellow.

Hovstad. Have you heard from the Mayor yet?

Dr. Stockmann. Not yet. He is coming here later.

Hovstad. I have given the matter a great deal of thought since last night.

Dr. Stockmann. Well?

Hovstad. From your point of view, as a doctor and a man of science, this affair of the water-supply is an isolated matter. I mean, you do not realise that it involves a great many other things.

Dr. Stockmann. How, do you mean—let us sit down, my dear fellow. No, sit here on the couch. (Hovstad *sits down on the couch,* Dr. Stockmann *on a chair on the other side of the table.*) Now then. You mean that—?

Hovstad. You said yesterday that the pollution of the water was due to impurities in the soil.

Dr. Stockmann. Yes, unquestionably it is due to that poisonous morass up at Mölledal.

Hovstad. Begging your pardon, doctor, I fancy it is due to quite another morass altogether.

Dr. Stockmann. What morass?

Hovstad. The morass that the whole life of our town is built on and is rotting in.

Dr. Stockmann. What the deuce are you driving at, Hovstad?

HOVSTAD. The whole of the town's interests have, little by little, got into the hands of a pack of officials.

DR. STOCKMANN. Oh, come!—they are not all officials.

HOVSTAD. No, but those that are not officials are at any rate the officials' friends and adherents; it is the wealthy folk, the old families in the town, that have got us entirely in their hands.

DR. STOCKMANN. Yes, but after all they are men of ability and knowledge.

HOVSTAD. Did they show any ability or knowledge when they laid the conduit-pipes where they are now?

DR. STOCKMANN. No, of course that was a great piece of stupidity on their part. But that is going to be set right now.

HOVSTAD. Do you think that will be all such plain sailing?

DR. STOCKMANN. Plain sailing or no, it has got to be done, anyway.

HOVSTAD. Yes, provided the press takes up the question.

DR. STOCKMANN. I don't think that will be necessary, my dear fellow, I am certain my brother—

HOVSTAD. Excuse me, doctor; I feel bound to tell you I am inclined to take the matter up.

DR. STOCKMANN. In the paper?

HOVSTAD. Yes. When I took over the "People's Messenger" my idea was to break up this ring of self-opinionated old fossils who had got hold of all the influence.

DR. STOCKMANN. But you know you told me yourself what the result had been; you nearly ruined your paper.

HOVSTAD. Yes, at the time we were obliged to climb down a peg or two, it is quite true; because there was a danger of the whole project of the Baths coming to nothing if they failed us. But now the scheme has been carried through, and we can dispense with these grand gentlemen.

DR. STOCKMANN. Dispense with them, yes; but we owe them a great debt of gratitude.

HOVSTAD. That shall be recognised ungrudgingly. But a journalist of my democratic tendencies cannot let such an opportunity as this slip. The bubble of official infallibility must be pricked. This superstition must be destroyed, like any other.

DR. STOCKMANN. I am whole-heartedly with you in that, Mr. Hovstad; if it is a superstition, away with it!

HOVSTAD. I should be very reluctant to bring the Mayor into it, because he is your brother. But I am sure you will agree with me that truth should be the first consideration.

DR. STOCKMANN. That goes without saying. (*With sudden emphasis*) Yes, but—but—

HOVSTAD. You must not misjudge me. I am neither more self-interested nor more ambitious than most men.

DR. STOCKMANN.   My dear fellow—who suggests anything of the kind?

HOVSTAD.   I am of humble origin, as you know; and that has given me opportunities of knowing what is the most crying need in the humbler ranks of life. It is that they should be allowed some part in the direction of public affairs, Doctor. That is what will develop their faculties and intelligence and self-respect—

DR. STOCKMANN.   I quite appreciate that.

HOVSTAD.   Yes—and in my opinion a journalist incurs a heavy responsibility if he neglects a favourable opportunity of emancipating the masses—the humble and oppressed. I know well enough that in exalted circles I shall be called an agitator, and all that sort of thing; but they may call what they like. If only my conscience doesn't reproach me, then—

DR. STOCKMANN.   Quite right! Quite right, Mr. Hovstad. But all the same—devil take it! (*A knock is heard at the door.*) Come in!

(ASLAKSEN *appears at the door. He is poorly but decently dressed, in black, with a slightly crumpled white neckcloth; he wears gloves and has a felt hat in his hand.*)

ASLAKSEN (*bowing*).   Excuse my taking the liberty, Doctor—

DR. STOCKMANN (*getting up*).   Ah, it is you, Aslaksen!

ASLAKSEN.   Yes, Doctor.

HOVSTAD (*standing up*).   Is it me you want, Aslaksen?

ASLAKSEN.   No; I didn't know I should find you here. No, it was the Doctor I—

DR. STOCKMANN.   I am quite at your service. What is it?

ASLAKSEN.   Is what I heard from Mr. Billing true, sir—that you mean to improve our water-supply?

DR. STOCKMANN.   Yes, for the Baths.

ASLAKSEN.   Quite so, I understand. Well, I have come to say that I will back that up by every means in my power.

HOVSTAD (*to the Doctor*).   You see!

DR. STOCKMANN.   I shall be very grateful to you, but—

ASLAKSEN.   Because it may be no bad thing to have us small tradesmen at your back. We form, as it were, a compact majority in the town—if we choose. And it is always a good thing to have the majority with you, Doctor.

DR. STOCKMANN.   That is undeniably true; but I confess I don't see why such unusual precautions should be necessary in this case. It seems to me that such a plain, straight-forward thing—

ASLAKSEN.   Oh, it may be very desirable, all the same. I know our local authorities so well; officials are not generally very ready to act on proposals that come from other people. That is why I think it would not be at all amiss if we made a little demonstration.

HOVSTAD.   That's right.

DR. STOCKMANN. Demonstration, did you say? What on earth are you going to make a demonstration about?

ASLAKSEN. We shall proceed with the greatest moderation, Doctor. Moderation is always my aim; it is the greatest virtue in a citizen—at least, I think so.

DR. STOCKMANN. It is well known to be a characteristic of yours, Mr. Aslaksen.

ASLAKSEN. Yes, I think I may pride myself on that. And this matter of the water-supply is of the greatest importance to us small tradesmen. The Baths promise to be a regular gold-mine for the town. We shall all make our living out of them, especially those of us who are householders. That is why we will back up the project as strongly as possible. And as I am at present Chairman of the Householders' Association—

DR. STOCKMANN. Yes—?

ASLAKSEN. And, what is more, local secretary of the Temperance Society—you know sir, I suppose, that I am a worker in the temperance cause?

DR. STOCKMANN. Of course, of course.

ASLAKSEN. Well, you can understand that I come into contact with a great many people. And as I have the reputation of a temperate and law-abiding citizen—like yourself, Doctor—I have a certain influence in the town, a little bit of power, if I may be allowed to say so.

DR. STOCKMANN. I know that quite well, Mr. Aslaksen.

ASLAKSEN. So you see it would be an easy matter for me to set on foot some testimonial, if necessary.

DR. STOCKMANN. A testimonial?

ASLAKSEN. Yes, some kind of an address of thanks from the townsmen for your share in a matter of such importance to the community. I need scarcely say that it would have to be drawn up with the greatest regard to moderation, so as not to offend the authorities—who, after all, have the reins in their hands. If we pay strict attention to that, no one can take it amiss, I should think!

HOVSTAD. Well, and even supposing they didn't like it—

ASLAKSEN. No, no, no; there must be no discourtesy to the authorities, Mr. Hovstad. It is no use falling foul of those upon whom our welfare so closely depends. I have done that in my time, and no good ever comes of it. But no one can take exception to a reasonable and frank expression of a citizen's views.

DR. STOCKMANN (shaking him by the hand). I can't tell you, dear Mr. Aslaksen, how extremely pleased I am to find such hearty support among my fellow-citizens. I am delighted—delighted! Now, you will take a small glass of sherry, eh?

ASLAKSEN. No, thank you; I never drink alcohol of that kind.

DR. STOCKMANN. Well, what do you say to a glass of beer, then?

ASLAKSEN. Nor that either, thank you, Doctor. I never drink anything as early as this. I am going into town now to talk this over with one or two householders, and prepare the ground.

DR. STOCKMANN. It is tremendously kind of you, Mr. Aslaksen; but I really cannot understand the necessity for all these precautions. It seems to me that the thing should go of itself.

ASLAKSEN. The authorities are somewhat slow to move, Doctor. Far be it from me to seem to blame them—

HOVSTAD. We are going to stir them up in the paper tomorrow, Aslaksen.

ASLAKSEN. But not violently, I trust, Mr. Hovstad. Proceed with moderation, or you will do nothing with them. You may take my advice; I have gathered my experience in the school of life. Well, I must say good-bye, Doctor. You know now that we small tradesmen are at your back at all events, like a solid wall. You have the compact majority on your side, Doctor.

DR. STOCKMANN. I am very much obliged, dear Mr. Aslaksen. (*Shakes hands with him*) Good-bye, good-bye.

ASLAKSEN. Are you going my way, towards the printing-office, Mr. Hovstad?

HOVSTAD. I will come later; I have something to settle up first.

ASLAKSEN. Very well.

(*Bows and goes out;* STOCKMANN *follows him into the hall.*)

HOVSTAD (*as* STOCKMANN *comes in again*). Well, what do you think of that, Doctor? Don't you think it is high time we stirred a little life into all this slackness and vacillation and cowardice?

DR. STOCKMANN. Are you referring to Aslaksen?

HOVSTAD. Yes, I am. He is one of those who are floundering in a bog —decent enough fellow though he may be, otherwise. And most of the people here are in just the same case—see-sawing and edging first to one side and then to the other, so overcome with caution and scruple that they never dare to take any decided step.

DR. STOCKMANN. Yes, but Aslaksen seemed to me so thoroughly well-intentioned.

HOVSTAD. There is one thing I esteem higher than that; and that is for a man to be self-reliant and sure of himself.

DR. STOCKMANN. I think you are perfectly right there.

HOVSTAD. That is why I want to seize this opportunity, and try if I cannot manage to put a little virility into these well-intentioned people for once. The idol of Authority must be shattered in this town. This gross and inexcusable blunder about the water-supply must be brought home to the mind of every municipal voter.

DR. STOCKMANN. Very well; if you are of opinion that it is for the good of the community, so be it. But not until I have had a talk with my brother.

HovsTAD. Anyway, I will get a leading article ready; and if the Mayor refuses to take the matter up—

DR. STOCKMANN. How can you suppose such a thing possible?

HovsTAD. It is conceivable. And in that case—

DR. STOCKMANN. In that case I promise you—. Look here, in that case you may print my report—every word of it.

HovsTAD. May I? Have I your word for it?

DR. STOCKMANN (giving him the MS.). Here it is; take it with you. It can do no harm for you to read it through, and you can give it me back later on.

HovsTAD. Good, good! That is what I will do. And now good-bye, Doctor.

DR. STOCKMANN. Good-bye, good-bye. You will see everything will run quite smoothly, Mr. Hovstad—quite smoothly.

HovsTAD. Hm!—we shall see. (Bows and goes out.)

DR. STOCKMANN (opens the dining-room door and looks in). Katherine! Oh, you are back, Petra?

PETRA (coming in). Yes, I have just come from the school.

MRS. STOCKMANN (coming in). Has he not been here yet?

DR. STOCKMANN. Peter? No. But I have had a long talk with Hovstad. He is quite excited about my discovery. I find it has a much wider bearing than I at first imagined. And he has put his paper at my disposal if necessity should arise.

MRS. STOCKMANN. Do you think it will?

DR. STOCKMANN. Not for a moment. But at all events it makes me feel proud to know that I have the liberal-minded independent press on my side. Yes, and—just imagine—I have had a visit from the Chairman of the Householders' Association!

MRS. STOCKMANN. Oh! What did he want?

DR. STOCKMANN. To offer me his support too. They will support me in a body if it should be necessary. Katherine—do you know what I have got behind me?

MRS. STOCKMANN. Behind you? No, what have you got behind you?

DR. STOCKMANN. The compact majority.

MRS. STOCKMANN. Really? Is that a good thing for you, Thomas?

DR. STOCKMANN. I should think it was a good thing. (Walks up and down rubbing his hands.) By Jove, it's a fine thing to feel this bond of brotherhood between oneself and one's fellow-citizens!

PETRA. And to be able to do so much that is good and useful, father!

DR. STOCKMANN. And for one's own native town into the bargain, my child!

MRS. STOCKMANN. That was a ring at the bell.

DR. STOCKMANN. It must be he, then. (A knock is heard at the door.) Come in!

PETER STOCKMANN (*comes in from the hall*). Good morning.

DR. STOCKMANN. Glad to see you, Peter!

MRS. STOCKMANN. Good morning, Peter. How are you?

PETER STOCKMANN. So so, thank you. (*To* DR. STOCKMANN) I received from you yesterday, after office-hours, a report dealing with the condition of the water at the Baths.

DR. STOCKMANN. Yes. Have you read it?

PETER STOCKMANN. Yes, I have.

DR. STOCKMANN. And what have you to say to it?

PETER STOCKMANN (*with a sidelong glance*). Hm!—

MRS. STOCKMANN. Come along, Petra.

(*She and* PETRA *go into the room on the left.*)

PETER STOCKMANN (*after a pause*). Was it necessary to make all these investigations behind my back?

DR. STOCKMANN. Yes, because until I was absolutely certain about it—

PETER STOCKMANN. Then you mean that you are absolutely certain now?

DR. STOCKMANN. Surely you are convinced of that.

PETER STOCKMANN. Is it your intention to bring this document before the Baths Committee as a sort of official communication?

DR. STOCKMANN. Certainly. Something must be done in the matter—and that quickly.

PETER STOCKMANN. As usual, you employ violent expressions in your report. You say, amongst other things, that what we offer visitors in our Baths is a permanent supply of poison.

DR. STOCKMANN. Well, can you describe it any other way, Peter? Just think—water that is poisonous, whether you drink it or bathe in it! And this we offer to the poor sick folk who come to us trustfully and pay us at an exorbitant rate to be made well again!

PETER STOCKMANN. And your reasoning leads you to this conclusion, that we must build a sewer to draw off the alleged impurities from Mölledal and must relay the water-conduits.

DR. STOCKMANN. Yes. Do you see any other way out of it? I don't.

PETER STOCKMANN. I made a pretext this morning to go and see the town engineer, and, as if only half seriously, broached the subject of these proposals as a thing we might perhaps have to take under consideration some time later on.

DR. STOCKMANN. Some time later on!

PETER STOCKMANN. He smiled at what he considered to be my extravagance, naturally. Have you taken the trouble to consider what your proposed alterations would cost? According to the information I obtained, the expenses would probably mount up to fifteen or twenty thousand pounds.

DR. STOCKMANN. Would it cost so much?

PETER STOCKMANN. Yes; and the worst part of it would be that the work would take at least two years.

DR. STOCKMANN. Two years? Two whole years?

PETER STOCKMANN. At least. And what are we to do with the Baths in the meantime? Close them? Indeed we should be obliged to. And do you suppose any one would come near the place after it had got about that the water was dangerous?

DR. STOCKMANN. Yes, but, Peter, that is what it is.

PETER STOCKMANN. And all this at this juncture—just as the Baths are beginning to be known. There are other towns in the neighbourhood with qualifications to attract visitors for bathing purposes. Don't you suppose they would immediately strain every nerve to divert the entire stream of strangers to themselves? Unquestionably they would; and then where should we be? We should probably have to abandon the whole thing, which has cost us so much money—and then you would have ruined your native town.

DR. STOCKMANN. I—should have ruined—!

PETER STOCKMANN. It is simply and solely through the Baths that the town has before it any future worth mentioning. You know that just as well as I.

DR. STOCKMANN. But what do you think ought to be done, then?

PETER STOCKMANN. Your report has not convinced me that the condition of the water at the Baths is as bad as you represent it to be.

DR. STOCKMANN. I tell you it is even worse!—or at all events it will be in summer, when the warm weather comes.

PETER STOCKMANN. As I said, I believe you exaggerate the matter considerably. A capable physician ought to know what measures to take—he ought to be capable of preventing injurious influences or of remedying them if they become obviously persistent.

DR. STOCKMANN. Well? What more?

PETER STOCKMANN. The water-supply for the Baths is now an established fact, and in consequence must be treated as such. But probably the Committee, at its discretion, will not be disinclined to consider the question of how far it might be possible to introduce certain improvements consistently with a reasonable expenditure.

DR. STOCKMANN. And do you suppose that I will have anything to do with such a piece of trickery as that?

PETER STOCKMANN. Trickery!!

DR. STOCKMANN. Yes, it would be a trick—a fraud, a lie, a downright crime towards the public, towards the whole community!

PETER STOCKMANN. I have not, as I remarked before, been able to convince myself that there is actually any imminent danger.

DR. STOCKMANN. You have! It is impossible that you should not be convinced. I know I have represented the facts absolutely truthfully and fairly. And you know it very well, Peter, only you won't acknowledge it. It was owing to your action that both the Baths and the water-conduits were built where they are; and that is what you won't acknowledge—that damnable blunder of yours. Pooh!—do you suppose I don't see through you?

PETER STOCKMANN. And even if that were true? If I perhaps guard my reputation somewhat anxiously, it is in the interests of the town. Without moral authority I am powerless to direct public affairs as seems, to my judgment, to be best for the common good. And on that account—and for various other reasons, too—it appears to me to be a matter of importance that your report should not be delivered to the Committee. In the interests of the public, you must withhold it. Then, later on, I will raise the question and we will do our best, privately; but nothing of this unfortunate affair—not a single word of it—must come to the ears of the public.

DR. STOCKMANN. I am afraid you will not be able to prevent that now, my dear Peter.

PETER STOCKMANN. It must and shall be prevented.

DR. STOCKMANN. It is no use, I tell you. There are too many people that know about it.

PETER STOCKMANN. That know about it? Who? Surely you don't mean those fellows on the "People's Messenger"?

DR. STOCKMANN. Yes, they know. The liberal-minded independent press is going to see that you do your duty.

PETER STOCKMANN (after a short pause). You are an extraordinarily independent man, Thomas. Have you given no thought to the consequences this may have for yourself?

DR. STOCKMANN. Consequences?—for me?

PETER STOCKMANN. For you and yours, yes.

DR. STOCKMANN. What the deuce do you mean?

PETER STOCKMANN. I believe I have always behaved in a brotherly way to you—have always been ready to oblige or to help you?

DR. STOCKMANN. Yes, you have, and I am grateful to you for it.

PETER STOCKMANN. There is no need. Indeed, to some extent I was forced to do so—for my own sake. I always hoped that, if I helped to improve your financial position, I should be able to keep some check on you.

DR. STOCKMANN. What!! Then it was only for your own sake—!

PETER STOCKMANN. Up to a certain point, yes. It is painful for a man in an official position to have his nearest relative compromising himself time after time.

DR. STOCKMANN. And do you consider that I do that?

PETER STOCKMANN. Yes, unfortunately, you do, without even being aware of it. You have a restless, pugnacious, rebellious disposition. And then there is that disastrous propensity of yours to want to write about every sort of possible and impossible thing. The moment an idea comes into your head, you must needs go and write a newspaper article or a whole pamphlet about it.

DR. STOCKMANN. Well, but is it not the duty of a citizen to let the public share in any new ideas he may have?

PETER STOCKMANN. Oh, the public doesn't require any new ideas. The public is best served by the good, old-established ideas it already has.

DR. STOCKMANN. And that is your honest opinion?

PETER STOCKMANN. Yes, and for once I must talk frankly to you. Hitherto I have tried to avoid doing so, because I know how irritable you are; but now I must tell you the truth, Thomas. You have no conception what an amount of harm you do yourself by your impetuosity. You complain of the authorities, you even complain of the government—you are always pulling them to pieces; you insist that you have been neglected and persecuted. But what else can such a cantankerous man as you expect?

DR. STOCKMANN. What next! Cantankerous, am I?

PETER STOCKMANN. Yes, Thomas, you are an extremely cantankerous man to work with—I know that to my cost. You disregard everything that you ought to have consideration for. You seem completely to forget that it is me you have to thank for your appointment here as medical officer to the Baths—

DR. STOCKMANN. I was entitled to it as a matter of course!—I and nobody else! I was the first person to see that the town could be made into a flourishing watering-place, and I was the only one who saw it at that time. I had to fight single-handed in support of the idea for many years; and I wrote and wrote—

PETER STOCKMANN. Undoubtedly. But things were not ripe for the scheme then—though, of course, you could not judge of that in your out-of-the-way corner up north. But as soon as the opportune moment came I—and the others—took the matter into our hands—

DR. STOCKMANN. Yes, and made this mess of all my beautiful plan. It is pretty obvious now what clever fellows you were!

PETER STOCKMANN. To my mind the whole thing only seems to mean that you are seeking another outlet for your combativeness. You want to pick a quarrel with your superiors—an old habit of yours. You cannot put up with any authority over you. You look askance at anyone who occupies a superior official position; you regard him as a personal enemy, and then any stick is good enough to beat him with. But now I have called your attention to the fact that the town's interests are at stake—and, incidentally, my own too. And therefore I must tell you, Thomas, that you will find me inexorable with regard to what I am about to require you to do.

DR. STOCKMANN. And what is that?

PETER STOCKMANN. As you have been so indiscreet as to speak of this delicate matter to outsiders, despite the fact that you ought to have treated it as entirely official and confidential, it is obviously impossible to hush it up now. All sorts of rumours will get about directly, and everybody who has a grudge against us will take care to embellish these rumours. So it will be necessary for you to refute them publicly.

Dr. Stockmann. I! How? I don't understand.

Peter Stockmann. What we shall expect is that, after making further investigations, you will come to the conclusion that the matter is not by any means as dangerous or as critical as you imagined in the first instance.

Dr. Stockmann. Oho!—so that is what you expect!

Peter Stockmann. And, what is more, we shall expect you to make public profession of your confidence in the Committee and in their readiness to consider fully and conscientiously what steps may be necessary to remedy any possible defects.

Dr. Stockmann. But you will never be able to do that by patching and tinkering at it—never! Take my word for it, Peter; I mean what I say, as deliberately and emphatically as possible.

Peter Stockmann. As an officer under the Committee, you have no right to any individual opinion.

Dr. Stockmann (amazed). No right?

Peter Stockmann. In your official capacity, no. As a private person, it is quite another matter. But as a subordinate member of the staff of the Baths, you have no right to express any opinion which runs contrary to that of your superiors.

Dr. Stockmann. This is too much! I, a doctor, a man of science, have no right to—!

Peter Stockmann. The matter in hand is not simply a scientific one. It is a complicated matter, and has its economic as well as its technical side.

Dr. Stockmann. I don't care what it is! I intend to be free to express my opinion on any subject under the sun.

Peter Stockmann. As you please—but not on any subject concerning the Baths. That we forbid.

Dr. Stockmann (shouting). You forbid—! You! A pack of—

Peter Stockmann. I forbid it—I, your chief; and if I forbid it, you have to obey.

Dr. Stockmann (controlling himself). Peter—if you were not my brother—

Petra (throwing open the door). Father, you shan't stand this!

Mrs. Stockmann (coming in after her). Petra, Petra!

Peter Stockmann. Oh, so you have been eavesdropping.

Mrs. Stockmann. You were talking so loud, we couldn't help—

Petra. Yes, I was listening.

Peter Stockmann. Well, after all, I am very glad—

Dr. Stockmann (going up to him). You were saying something about forbidding and obeying?

Peter Stockmann. You obliged me to take that tone with you.

Dr. Stockmann. And so I am to give myself the lie, publicly?

Peter Stockmann. We consider it absolutely necessary that you should make some such public statement as I have asked for.

Dr. Stockmann. And if I do not—obey?

PETER STOCKMANN. Then we shall publish a statement ourselves to reassure the public.

DR. STOCKMANN. Very well; but in that case I shall use my pen against you. I stick to what I save said; I will show that I am right and that you are wrong. And what will you do then?

PETER STOCKMANN. Then I shall not be able to prevent your being dismissed.

DR. STOCKMANN. What—?

PETRA. Father—dismissed!

MRS. STOCKMANN. Dismissed!

PETER STOCKMANN. Dismissed from the staff of the Baths. I shall be obliged to propose that you shall immediately be given notice, and shall not be allowed any further participation in the Baths' affairs.

DR. STOCKMANN. You would dare to do that!

PETER STOCKMANN. It is you that are playing the daring game.

PETRA. Uncle, that is a shameful way to treat a man like father!

MRS. STOCKMANN. Do hold your tongue, Petra!

PETER STOCKMANN (*looking at* PETRA). Oh, so we volunteer our opinions already, do we? Of course. (*To* MRS. STOCKMANN) Katherine, I imagine you are the most sensible person in this house. Use any influence you may have over your husband, and make him see what this will entail for his family as well as—

DR. STOCKMANN. My family is my own concern and nobody else's!

PETER STOCKMANN. —for his own family, as I was saying, as well as for the town he lives in.

DR. STOCKMANN. It is I who have the real good of the town at heart! I want to lay bare the defects that sooner or later must come to the light of day. I will show whether I love my native town.

PETER STOCKMANN. You, who in your blind obstinacy want to cut off the most important source of the town's welfare?

DR. STOCKMANN. The source is poisoned, man! Are you mad? We are making our living by retailing filth and corruption! The whole of our flourishing municipal life derives its sustenance from a lie!

PETER STOCKMANN. All imagination—or something even worse. The man who can throw out such offensive insinuations about his native town must be an enemy of our community.

DR. STOCKMANN (*going up to him*). Do you dare to—!

MRS. STOCKMANN (*throwing herself between them*). Thomas!

PETRA (*catching her father by the arm*). Don't lose your temper, father!

PETER STOCKMANN. I will not expose myself to violence. Now you have had a warning; so reflect on what you owe to yourself and your family. Good-bye. (*Goes out.*)

DR. STOCKMANN (*walking up and down*). Am I to put up with such treatment as this? In my own house, Katherine! What do you think of that!

MRS. STOCKMANN. Indeed it is both shameful and absurd, Thomas—

PETRA. If only I could give uncle a piece of my mind—

DR. STOCKMANN. It is my own fault. I ought to have flown out at him long ago!—shown my teeth!—bitten! To hear him call me an enemy to our community! Me! I shall not take that lying down, upon my soul!

MRS. STOCKMANN. But, dear Thomas, your brother has power on his side—

DR. STOCKMANN. Yes, but I have right on mine, I tell you.

MRS. STOCKMANN. Oh yes, right—right. What is the use of having right on your side if you have not got might?

PETRA. Oh, mother—how can you say such a thing!

DR. STOCKMANN. Do you imagine that in a free country it is no use having right on your side? You are absurd, Katherine. Besides, haven't I got the liberal-minded, independent press to lead the way, and the compact majority behind me? That is might enough, I should think!

MRS. STOCKMANN. But, good heavens, Thomas, you don't mean to—?

DR. STOCKMANN. Don't mean to what?

MRS. STOCKMANN. To set yourself up in opposition your brother.

DR. STOCKMANN. In God's name, what else do you suppose I should do but take my stand on right and truth?

PETRA. Yes, I was just going to say that.

MRS. STOCKMANN. But it won't do you any earthly good. If they won't do it, they won't.

DR. STOCKMANN. Oho, Katherine! Just give me time, and you will see how I will carry the war into their camp.

MRS. STOCKMANN. Yes, you carry the war into their camp, and you get your dismissal—that is what you will do.

DR. STOCKMANN. In any case I shall have done my duty towards the public—towards the community. I, who am called its enemy!

MRS. STOCKMANN. But towards your family, Thomas? Towards your own home! Do you think that is doing your duty towards those you have to provide for?

PETRA. Ah, don't think always first of us, mother.

MRS. STOCKMANN. Oh, it is easy for you to talk; you are able to shift for yourself, if need be. But remember the boys, Thomas; and think a little, too, of yourself, and of me—

DR. STOCKMANN. I think you are out of your senses, Katherine! If I were to be such a miserable coward as to go on my knees to Peter and his damned crew, do you suppose I should ever know an hour's peace of mind all my life afterwards?

MRS. STOCKMANN. I don't know anything about that; but God preserve us from the peace of mind we shall have, all the same, if you go on defying him! You will find yourself again without the means of subsistence, with no income to count upon. I should think we had had enough of that in the old days. Remember that, Thomas; think what that means.

DR. STOCKMANN (*collecting himself with a struggle and clenching his fist*). And this is what this slavery can bring upon a free, honorable man! Isn't it horrible, Katherine?

MRS. STOCKMANN. Yes, it is sinful to treat you so, it is perfectly true. But, good heavens, one has to put up with so much injustice in this world.— There are the boys, Thomas! Look at them! What is to become of them? Oh, no, no, you can never have the heart—.

(EJLIF *and* MORTEN *have come in while she was speaking, with their school books in their hands.*)

DR. STOCKMANN. The boys—! (*Recovers himself suddenly.*) No, even if the whole world goes to pieces, I will never bow my neck to this yoke! (*Goes towards his room.*)

MRS. STOCKMANN (*following him*). Thomas—what are you going to do!

DR. STOCKMANN (*at his door*). I mean to have the right to look my sons in the face when they are grown men. (*Goes into his room.*)

MRS. STOCKMANN (*bursting into tears*). God help us all!

PETRA. Father is splendid! He will not give in.

(*The boys look on in amazement;* PETRA *signs to them not to speak.*)

ACT III

SCENE. *The editorial office of the* People's Messenger. *The entrance door is on the left-hand side of the back wall; on the right-hand side is another door with glass panels through which the printing-room can be seen. Another door in the right-hand wall. In the middle of the room is a large table covered with papers, newspapers and books. In the foreground on the left a window, before which stand a desk and a high stool. There are a couple of easy chairs by the table, and other chairs standing along the wall. The room is dingy and uncomfortable; the furniture is old, the chairs stained and torn. In the printing-room the compositors are seen at work, and a printer is working a hand-press.* HOVSTAD *is sitting at the desk, writing.* BILLING *comes in from the right with* DR. STOCKMANN's *manuscript in his hand.*

BILLING. Well, I must say!

HOVSTAD (*still writing*). Have you read it through?

BILLING (*laying the MS. on the desk*). Yes, indeed I have.

HOVSTAD. Don't you think the Doctor hits them pretty hard?

BILLING. Hard? Bless my soul, he's crushing! Every word falls like— how shall I put it?—like the blow of a sledgehammer.

HOVSTAD. Yes, but they are not the people to throw up the sponge at the first blow.

BILLING. That is true; and for that reason we must strike blow upon blow until the whole of this aristocracy tumbles to pieces. As I sat in there reading this, I almost seemed to see a revolution in being.

HOVSTAD (*turning round*). Hush!—Speak so that Aslaksen cannot hear you.

BILLING (*lowering his voice*). Aslaksen is a chicken-hearted chap, a coward; there is nothing of the man in him. But this time you will insist on your own way, won't you? You will put the Doctor's article in?

HOVSTAD. Yes, and if the Mayor doesn't like it—

BILLING. That will be the devil of a nuisance.

HOVSTAD. Well, fortunately we can turn the situation to good account, whatever happens. If the Mayor will not fall in with the Doctor's project, he will have all the small tradesmen down on him—the whole of the Householders' Association and the rest of them. And if he does fall in with it, he will fall out with the whole crowd of large shareholders in the Baths, who up to now have been his most valuable supporters—

BILLING. Yes, because they will certainly have to fork out a pretty penny—

HOVSTAD. Yes, you may be sure they will. And in this way the ring will be broken up, you see, and then in every issue of the paper we will enlighten the public on the Mayor's incapability on one point and another, and make it clear that all the positions of trust in the town, the whole control of municipal affairs, ought to be put in the hands of the Liberals.

BILLING. That is perfectly true! I see it coming—I see it coming; we are on the threshold of a revolution!

(*A knock is heard at the door.*)

HOVSTAD. Hush! (*Calls out*) Come in! (DR. STOCKMANN *comes in by the street door.* HOVSTAD *goes to meet him.*) Ah, it is you, Doctor! Well?

DR. STOCKMANN. You may set to work and print it, Mr. Hovstad!

HOVSTAD. Has it come to that, then?

BILLING. Hurrah!

DR. STOCKMANN. Yes, print away. Undoubtedly it has come to that Now they must take what they got. There is going to be a fight in the town, Mr. Billing!

BILLING. War to the knife, I hope! We will get our knives to their throats, Doctor!

DR. STOCKMANN. This article is only a beginning. I have already got four or five more sketched out in my head. Where is Aslaksen?

BILLING (*calls into the printing-room*). Aslaksen, just come here for a minute!

HOVSTAD. Four or five more articles, did you say? On the same subject?

Dr. Stockmann. No—far from it, my dear fellow. No, they are about quite another matter. But they all spring from the question of the water-supply and the drainage. One thing leads to another, you know. It is like beginning to pull down an old house, exactly.

Billing. Upon my soul, it's true; you find you are not done till you have pulled all the old rubbish down.

Aslaksen (*coming in*). Pulled down? You are not thinking of pulling down the Baths surely, Doctor?

Hovstad. Far from it, don't be afraid.

Dr. Stockmann. No, we meant something quite different. Well, what do you think of my article, Mr. Hovstad?

Hovstad. I think it is simply a masterpiece—

Dr. Stockmann. Do you really think so? Well, I am very pleased, very pleased.

Hovstad. It is so clear and intelligible. One need have no special knowledge to understand the bearing of it. You will have every enlightened man on your side.

Aslaksen. And every prudent man too, I hope?

Billing. The prudent and the imprudent—almost the whole town.

Aslaksen. In that case we may venture to print it.

Dr. Stockmann. I should think so!

Hovstad. We will put it in to-morrow morning.

Dr. Stockmann. Of course—you must not lose a single day. What I wanted to ask you, Mr. Aslaksen, was if you would supervise the printing of it yourself.

Aslaksen. With pleasure.

Dr. Stockmann. Take care of it as if it were a treasure! No misprints —every word is important. I will look in again a little later; perhaps you will be able to let me see a proof. I can't tell you how eager I am to see it in print, and see it burst upon the public—

Billing. Burst upon them—yes, like a flash of lightning!

Dr. Stockmann. —and to have it submitted to the judgment of my intelligent fellow-townsmen. You cannot imagine what I have gone through to-day. I have been threatened first with one thing and then with another; they have tried to rob me of my most elementary rights as a man—

Billing. What! Your rights as a man!

Dr. Stockmann. —they have tried to degrade me, to make a coward of me, to force me to put personal interests before my most sacred convictions—

Billing. That is too much—I'm damned if it isn't.

Hovstad. Oh, you mustn't be surprised at anything from that quarter.

Dr. Stockmann. Well, they will get the worst of it with me; they may assure themselves of that. I shall consider the "People's Messenger" my sheet-anchor now, and every single day I will bombard them with one article after another, like bomb-shells—

ASLAKSEN. Yes, but—

BILLING. Hurrah!—it is war, it is war!

DR. STOCKMANN. I shall smite them to the ground—I shall crush them —I shall break down all their defences, before the eyes of the honest public! That is what I shall do!

ASLAKSEN. Yes, but in moderation, Doctor—proceed with moderation—

BILLING. Not a bit of it, not a bit of it! Don't spare the dynamite!

DR. STOCKMANN. Because it is not merely a question of water-supply and drains now, you know. No—it is the whole of our social life that we have got to purify and disinfect—

BILLING. Spoken like a deliverer!

DR. STOCKMANN. All the incapables must be turned out, you understand—and that in every walk of life! Endless vistas have opened themselves to my mind's eye to-day. I cannot see it all quite clearly yet, but I shall in time. Young and vigorous standard-bearers—those are what we need and must seek, my friends; we must have new men in command at all our outposts.

BILLING. Hear, hear!

DR. STOCKMANN. We only need to stand by one another, and it will all be perfectly easy. The revolution will be launched like a ship that runs smoothly off the stocks. Don't you think so?

HOVSTAD. For my part I think we have now a prospect of getting the municipal authority into the hands where it should lie.

ASLAKSEN. And if only we proceed with moderation, I cannot imagine that there will be any risk.

DR. STOCKMANN. Who the devil cares whether there is any risk or not! What I am doing, I am doing in the name of truth and for the sake of my conscience.

HOVSTAD. You are a man who deserves to be supported, Doctor.

ASLAKSEN. Yes, there is no denying that the Doctor is a true friend to the town—a real friend to the community, that he is.

BILLING. Take my word for it, Aslaksen, Dr. Stockmann is a friend of the people.

ASLAKSEN. I fancy the Householders' Association will make use of that expression before long.

DR. STOCKMANN (affected, grasps their hands). Thank you, thank you, my dear staunch friends. It is very refreshing to me to hear you say that; my brother called me something quite different. By Jove, he shall have it back, with interest! But now I must be off to see a poor devil—. I will come back, as I said. Keep a very careful eye on the manuscript, Aslaksen, and don't for worlds leave out any of my notes of exclamation! Rather put one or two more in! Capital, capital! Well, good-bye for the present—good-bye, good-bye!

(*They show him to the door, and bow him out.*)

Hovstad.   He may prove an invaluably useful man to us.

Aslaksen.   Yes, so long as he confines himself to this matter of the Baths. But if he goes farther afield, I don't think it would be advisable to follow him.

Hovstad.   Hm!—that all depends—

Billing.   You are so infernally timid, Aslaksen!

Aslaksen.   Timid? Yes, when it is a question of the local authorities, I am timid, Mr. Billing; it is a lesson I have learnt in the school of experience, let me tell you. But try me in higher politics, in matters that concern the government itself, and then see if I am timid.

Billing.   No, you aren't, I admit. But this is simply contradicting yourself.

Aslaksen.   I am a man with a conscience, and that is the whole matter. If you attack the government, you don't do the community any harm, anyway; those fellows pay no attention to attacks, you see—they go on just as they are, in spite of them. But *local* authorities are different; they *can* be turned out, and then perhaps you may get an ignorant lot into office who may do irreparable harm to the householders and everybody else.

Hovstad.   But what of the education of citizens by self-government—don't you attach any importance to that?

Aslaksen.   When a man has interests of his own to protect, he cannot think of everything, Mr. Hovstad.

Hovstad.   Then I hope I shall never have interests of my own to protect!

Billing.   Hear, hear!

Aslaksen (*with a smile*).   Hm! (*Points to the desk*) Mr. Sheriff Stensgaard was your predecessor at that editorial desk.

Billing (*spitting*).   Bah! That turncoat.

Hovstad.   I am not a weathercock—and never will be.

Aslaksen.   A politician should never be too certain of anything, Mr. Hovstad. And as for you, Mr. Billing, I should think it is time for you to be taking in a reef or two in your sails, seeing that you are applying for the post of secretary to the Bench.

Billing.   I—!

Hovstad.   Are you, Billing?

Billing.   Well, yes—but you must clearly understand I am doing it only to annoy the bigwigs.

Aslaksen.   Anyhow, it is no business of mine. But if I am to be accused of timidity and of inconsistency in my principles, this is what I want to point out: my political past is an open book. I have never changed, except perhaps to become a little more moderate, you see. My heart is still with the people; but I don't deny that my reason has a certain bias towards the authorities— the local ones, I mean. (*Goes into the printing-room.*)

BILLING. Oughtn't we to try and get rid of him, Hovstad?

HOVSTAD. Do you know anyone else who will advance the money for our paper and printing bill?

BILLING. It is an infernal nuisance that we don't possess some capital to trade on.

HOVSTAD (*sitting down at his desk*). Yes, if we only had that, then—

BILLING. Suppose you were to apply to Dr. Stockmann?

HOVSTAD (*turning over some papers*). What is the use? He has got nothing.

BILLING. No, but he has got a warm man in the background, old Morten Kiil—"the Badger," as they call him.

HOVSTAD (*writing*). Are you so sure *he* has got anything?

BILLING. Good Lord, of course he has! And some of it must come to the Stockmanns. Most probably he will do something for the children, at all events.

HOVSTAD (*turning half round*). Are you counting on that?

BILLING. Counting on it? Of course I am not counting on anything.

HOVSTAD. That is right. And I should not count on the secretaryship to the Bench either, if I were you; for I can assure you—you won't get it.

BILLING. Do you think I am not quite aware of that? My object is precisely *not* to get it. A slight of that kind stimulates a man's fighting power—it is like getting a supply of fresh bile—and I am sure one needs that badly enough in a hole-and-corner place like this, where it is so seldom anything happens to stir one up.

HOVSTAD (*writing*). Quite so, quite so.

BILLING. Ah, I shall be heard of yet!—Now I shall go and write the appeal to the Householders' Association. (*Goes into the room on the right.*)

HOVSTAD (*sitting at his desk, biting his penholder, says slowly*). Hm!— that's it, is it? (*A knock is heard*) Come in! (PETRA *comes in by the outer door.* HOVSTAD *gets up.*) What, you!—here?

PETRA. Yes, you must forgive me—

HOVSTAD (*pulling a chair forward*). Won't you sit down?

PETRA. No, thank you, I must go again in a moment.

HOVSTAD. Have you come with a message from your father, by any chance?

PETRA. No, I have come on my own account. (*Takes a book out of her coat pocket*) Here is the English story.

HOVSTAD. Why have you brought it back?

PETRA. Because I am not going to translate it.

HOVSTAD. But you promised me faithfully—

PETRA. Yes, but then I had not read it. I don't suppose you have read it either?

HOVSTAD. No, you know quite well I don't understand English; but—

PETRA. Quite so. That is why I wanted to tell you that you must find something else. (*Lays the book on the table*) You can't use this for the "People's Messenger."

HOVSTAD. Why not?

PETRA. Because it conflicts with all your opinions.

HOVSTAD. Oh, for that matter—

PETRA. You don't understand me. The burden of this story is that there is a supernatural power that looks after the so-called good people in this world and makes everything happen for the best in their case—while all the so-called bad people are punished.

HOVSTAD. Well, but that is all right. That is just what our readers want.

PETRA. And are you going to be the one to give it to them? For myself, I do not believe a word of it. You know quite well that things do not happen so in reality.

HOVSTAD. You are perfectly right; but an editor cannot always act as he would prefer. He is often obliged to bow to the wishes of the public in unimportant matters. Politics are the most important thing in life—for a newspaper, anyway; and if I want to carry my public with me on the path that leads to liberty and progress, I must not frighten them away. If they find a moral tale of this sort in the serial at the bottom of the page, they will be all the more ready to read what is printed above it; they feel more secure, as it were.

PETRA. For shame! You would never go and set a snare like that for your readers; you are not a spider!

HOVSTAD (*smiling*). Thank you for having such a good opinion of me. No; as a matter of fact that is Billing's idea and not mine.

PETRA. Billing's!

HOVSTAD. Yes; anyway he propounded that theory here one day. And it is Billing who is so anxious to have that story in the paper; I don't know anything about the book.

PETRA. But how can Billing, with his emancipated views—

HOVSTAD. Oh, Billing is a many-sided man. He is applying for the post of secretary to the Bench, too, I hear.

PETRA. I don't believe it, Mr. Hovstad. How could he possibly bring himself to do such a thing?

HOVSTAD. Ah, you must ask him that.

PETRA. I should never have thought it of him.

HOVSTAD (*looking more closely at her*). No? Does it really surprise you so much?

PETRA. Yes. Or perhaps not altogether. Really, I don't quite know—

HOVSTAD. We journalists are not much worth, Miss Stockmann.

PETRA. Do you really mean that?

HOVSTAD. I think so sometimes.

PETRA. Yes, in the ordinary affairs of everyday life, perhaps; I can understand that. But now, when you have taken a weighty matter in hand—

HOVSTAD. This matter of your father's, you mean?

PETRA. Exactly. It seems to me that now you must feel you are a man worth more than most.

HOVSTAD. Yes, to-day I do feel something of that sort.

PETRA. Of course you do, don't you? It is a splendid vocation you have chosen—to smooth the way for the march of unappreciated truths, and new and courageous lines of thought. If it were nothing more than because you stand fearlessly in the open and take up the cause of an injured man—

HOVSTAD. Especially when that injured man is—ahem!—I don't rightly know how to—

PETRA. When that man is so upright and so honest, you mean?

HOVSTAD (more gently). Especially when he is your father, I meant.

PETRA (suddenly checked). That?

HOVSTAD. Yes, Petra—Miss Petra.

PETRA. Is it that, that is first and foremost with you? Not the matter itself? Not the truth?—not my father's big generous heart?

HOVSTAD. Certainly—of course—that too.

PETRA. No, thank you; you have betrayed yourself, Mr. Hovstad, and now I shall never trust you again in anything.

HOVSTAD. Can you really take it so amiss in me that it is mostly for your sake—?

PETRA. What I am angry with you for, is for not having been honest with my father. You talked to him as if the truth and the good of the community were what lay nearest to your heart. You have made fools of both my father and me. You are not the man you made yourself out to be. And that I shall never forgive you—never!

HOVSTAD. You ought not to speak so bitterly, Miss Petra—least of all now.

PETRA. Why not now, especially?

HOVSTAD. Because your father cannot do without my help.

PETRA (looking him up and down). Are you that sort of man too? For shame!

HOVSTAD. No, no, I am not. This came upon me so unexpectedly— you must believe that.

PETRA. I know what to believe. Good-bye.

ASLAKSEN (coming from the printing-room, hurriedly and with an air of mystery). Damnation, Hovstad!—(Sees PETRA) Oh, this is awkward—

PETRA. There is the book; you must give it to some one else. (Goes towards the door.)

HOVSTAD (*following her*). But, Miss Stockmann—

PETRA. Good-bye. (*Goes out.*)

ASLAKSEN. I say—Mr. Hovstad—

HOVSTAD. Well, well!—what is it?

ASLAKSEN. The Mayor is outside in the printing-room.

HOVSTAD. The Mayor, did you say?

ASLAKSEN. Yes, he wants to speak to you. He came in by the back door—didn't want to be seen, you understand.

HOVSTAD. What can he want? Wait a bit—I will go myself. (*Goes to the door of the printing-room, opens it, bows and invites* PETER STOCKMANN *in*) Just see, Aslaksen, that no one—

ASLAKSEN. Quite so. (*Goes into the printing-room.*)

PETER STOCKMANN. You did not expect to see me here, Mr. Hovstad.

HOVSTAD. No, I confess I did not.

PETER STOCKMANN (*looking round*). You are very snug in here—very nice indeed.

HOVSTAD. Oh—

PETER STOCKMANN. And here I come, without any notice, to take up your time!

HOVSTAD. By all means, Mr. Mayor. I am at your service. But let me relieve you of your— (*Takes* STOCKMANN'S *hat and stick and puts them on a chair.*) Won't you sit down?

PETER STOCKMANN (*sitting down by the table*). Thank you. (HOVSTAD *sits down.*) I have had an extremely annoying experience to-day, Mr. Hovstad.

HOVSTAD. Really? Ah well, I expect with all the various business you have to attend to—

PETER STOCKMANN. The Medical Officer of the Baths is responsible for what happened to-day.

HOVSTAD. Indeed? The Doctor?

PETER STOCKMANN. He has addressed a kind of report to the Baths Committee on the subject of certain supposed defects in the Baths.

HOVSTAD. Has he indeed?

PETER STOCKMANN. Yes—has he not told you? I thought he said—

HOVSTAD. Ah, yes—it is true he did mention something about—

ASLAKSEN (*coming from the printing-room*). I ought to have that copy—

HOVSTAD (*angrily*). Ahem!—there it is on the desk.

ASLAKSEN (*taking it*). Right.

PETER STOCKMANN. But look there—that is the thing I was speaking of!

ASLAKSEN. Yes, that is the Doctor's article, Mr. Mayor.

HOVSTAD. Oh, is *that* what you were speaking about?

PETER STOCKMANN. Yes, that is it. What do you think of it?

HOVSTAD. Oh, I am only a layman—and I have only taken a very cursory glance at it.

PETER STOCKMANN. But you are going to print it?

HOVSTAD. I cannot very well refuse a distinguished man—

ASLAKSEN. I have nothing to do with editing the paper, Mr. Mayor—

PETER STOCKMANN. I understand.

ASLAKSEN. I merely print what is put into my hands.

PETER STOCKMANN. Quite so.

ASLAKSEN. And so I must— (*Moves off towards the printing-room.*)

PETER STOCKMANN. No, but wait a moment, Mr. Aslaksen. You will allow me, Mr. Hovstad?

HOVSTAD. If you please, Mr. Mayor.

PETER STOCKMANN. You are a discreet and thoughtful man, Mr. Aslaksen.

ASLAKSEN. I am delighted to hear you think so, sir.

PETER STOCKMANN. And a man of very considerable influence.

ASLAKSEN. Chiefly among the small tradesmen, sir.

PETER STOCKMANN. The small tax-payers are the majority—here as everywhere else.

ASLAKSEN. That is true.

PETER STOCKMANN. And I have no doubt you know the general trend of opinion among them, don't you?

ASLAKSEN. Yes, I think I may say I do, Mr. Mayor.

PETER STOCKMANN. Yes. Well, since there is such a praiseworthy spirit of self-sacrifice among the less wealthy citizens of our town—

ASLAKSEN. What?

HOVSTAD. Self-sacrifice?

PETER STOCKMANN. It is pleasing evidence of a public-spirited feeling, extremely pleasing evidence. I might almost say I hardly expected it. But you have a closer knowledge of public opinion than I.

ASLAKSEN. But, Mr. Mayor—

PETER STOCKMANN. And indeed it is no small sacrifice that the town is going to make.

HOVSTAD. The town?

ASLAKSEN. But I don't understand. Is it the Baths—?

PETER STOCKMANN. At a provisional estimate, the alterations that the Medical Officer asserts to be desirable will cost somewhere about twenty thousand pounds.

ASLAKSEN. That is a lot of money, but—

PETER STOCKMANN. Of course it will be necessary to raise a municipal loan.

HOVSTAD (*getting up*). Surely you never mean that the town must pay—?

ASLAKSEN. Do you mean that it must come out of the municipal funds? —out of the ill-filled pockets of the small tradesmen?

PETER STOCKMANN. Well, my dear Mr. Aslaksen, where else is the money to come from?

ASLAKSEN. The gentlemen who own the Baths ought to provide that.

PETER STOCKMANN. The proprietors of the Baths are not in a position to incur any further expense.

ASLAKSEN. Is that absolutely certain, Mr. Mayor?

PETER STOCKMANN. I have satisfied myself that it is so. If the town wants these very extensive alterations, it will have to pay for them.

ASLAKSEN. But, damn it all—I beg your pardon—this is quite another matter, Mr. Hovstad!

HOVSTAD. It is, indeed.

PETER STOCKMANN. The most fatal part of it is that we shall be obliged to shut the Baths for a couple of years.

HOVSTAD. Shut them? Shut them altogether?

ASLAKSEN. For two years?

PETER STOCKMANN. Yes, the work will take as long as that—at least.

ASLAKSEN. I'm damned if we will stand that, Mr. Mayor! What are we householders to live upon in the meantime?

PETER STOCKMANN. Unfortunately, that is an extremely difficult question to answer, Mr. Aslaksen. But what would you have us do? Do you suppose we shall have a single visitor in the town, if we go about proclaiming that our water is polluted, that we are living over a plague spot, that the entire town—

ASLAKSEN. And the whole thing is merely imagination?

PETER STOCKMANN. With the best will in the world, I have not been able to come to any other conclusion.

ASLAKSEN. Well then I must say it is absolutely unjustifiable of Dr. Stockman—I beg your pardon, Mr. Mayor—

PETER STOCKMANN. What you say is lamentably true, Mr. Aslaksen. My brother has, unfortunately, always been a headstrong man.

ASLAKSEN. After this, do you mean to give him your support, Mr. Hovstad?

HOVSTAD. Can you suppose for a moment that I—?

PETER STOCKMANN. I have drawn up a short *résumé* of the situation as it appears from a reasonable man's point of view. In it I have indicated how certain possible defects might suitably be remedied without outrunning the resources of the Baths Committee.

HOVSTAD. Have you got it with you, Mr. Mayor?

PETER STOCKMANN (*fumbling in his pocket*). Yes, I brought it with me in case you should—

ASLAKSEN. Good Lord, there he is!

PETER STOCKMANN. Who? My brother?

HOVSTAD. Where? Where?

ASLAKSEN. He has just gone through the printing-room.

PETER STOCKMANN. How unlucky! I don't want to meet him here, and I had still several things to speak to you about.

HOVSTAD (*pointing to the door on the right*). Go in there for the present.

PETER STOCKMANN. But—?

HOVSTAD. You will only find Billing in there.

ASLAKSEN. Quick, quick, Mr. Mayor—he is just coming.

PETER STOCKMANN. Yes, very well; but see that you get rid of him quickly. (*Goes out through the door on the right, which* ASLAKSEN *opens for him and shuts after him.*)

HOVSTAD. Pretend to be doing something, Aslaksen.

(*Sits down and writes.* ASLAKSEN *begins foraging among a heap of newspapers that are lying on a chair.*)

DR. STOCKMANN (*coming in from the printing-room*). Here I am again. (*Puts down his hat and stick.*)

HOVSTAD (*writing*). Already, Doctor? Hurry up with what we were speaking about, Aslaksen. We are very pressed for time to-day.

DR. STOCKMANN (*to* ASLAKEN). No proof for me to see yet, I hear.

ASLAKSEN (*without turning round*). You couldn't expect it yet, Doctor.

DR. STOCKMANN. No, no; but I am impatient, as you can understand. I shall not know a moment's peace of mind till I see it in print.

HOVSTAD. Hm!—it will take a good while yet, won't it, Aslaksen?

ASLAKSEN. Yes, I am almost afraid it will.

DR. STOCKMANN. All right, my dear friends; I will come back. I do not mind coming back twice if necessary. A matter of such great importance —the welfare of the town at stake—it is no time to shirk trouble. (*Is just going, but stops and comes back.*) Look here—there is one thing more I want to speak to you about.

HOVSTAD. Excuse me, but could it not wait till some other time?

DR. STOCKMANN. I can tell you in half a dozen words. It is only this. When my article is read to-morrow and it is realised that I have been quietly working the whole winter for the welfare of the town—

HOVSTAD. Yes, but, Doctor —

DR. STOCKMANN. I know what you are going to say. You don't see how on earth it was any more than my duty—my obvious duty as a citizen. Of course it wasn't; I know that as well as you. But my fellow-citizens, you know—! Good Lord, think of all the good souls who think so highly of me—!

ASLAKSEN. Yes, our townsfolk have had a very high opinion of you so far, Doctor.

DR. STOCKMANN. Yes, and that is just why I am afraid they—. Well, this is the point; when this reaches them, especially the poorer classes, and sounds in their ears like a summons to take the town's affairs into their own hands for the future—

HOVSTAD (getting up). Ahem! Doctor, I won't conceal from you the fact—

DR. STOCKMANN. Ah!—I knew there was something in the wind! But I won't hear a word of it. If anything of that sort is being set on foot—

HOVSTAD. Of what sort?

DR. STOCKMANN. Well, whatever it is—whether it is a demonstration in my honour, or a banquet, or a subscription list for some presentation to me—whatever it is, you must promise me solemnly and faithfully to put a stop to it. You too, Mr. Aslaksen; do you understand?

HOVSTAD. You must forgive me, Doctor, but sooner or later we must tell you the plain truth—

(He is interrupted by the entrance of MRS. STOCKMANN, who comes in from the street door.)

MRS. STOCKMANN (seeing her husband). Just as I thought!

HOVSTAD (going towards her). You too, Mrs. Stockmann?

DR. STOCKMANN. What on earth do you want here, Katherine?

MRS. STOCKMANN. I should think you know very well what I want.

HOVSTAD. Won't you sit down? Or perhaps—

MRS. STOCKMANN. No, thank you; don't trouble. And you must not be offended at my coming to fetch my husband; I am the mother of three children, you know.

DR. STOCKMANN. Nonsense!—we know all about that.

MRS. STOCKMANN. Well, one would not give you credit for much thought for your wife and children to-day; if you had had that, you would not have gone and dragged us all into misfortune.

DR. STOCKMANN. Are you out of your senses, Katherine! Because a man has a wife and children, is he not to be allowed to proclaim the truth— is he not to be allowed to be an actively useful citizen—is he not to be allowed to do a service to his native town!

MRS. STOCKMANN. Yes, Thomas—in reason.

ASLAKSEN. Just what I say. Moderation is everything.

MRS. STOCKMANN. And that is why you wrong us, Mr. Hovstad, in enticing my husband away from his home and making a dupe of him in all this.

HOVSTAD. I certainly am making a dupe of no one—

DR. STOCKMANN. Making a dupe of me! Do you suppose I should allow myself to be duped!

MRS. STOCKMANN. It is just what you do. I know quite well you have more brains than anyone in the town, but you are extremely easily duped, Thomas. (To HOVSTAD) Please to realise that he loses his post at the Baths if you print what he has written—

ASLAKSEN. What!

HOVSTAD. Look here, Doctor—

DR. STOCKMANN (*laughing*). Ha—ha!—just let them try! No, no—they will take good care not to. I have got the compact majority behind me, let me tell you!

MRS. STOCKMANN. Yes, that is just the worst of it—your having any such horrid thing behind you.

DR. STOCKMANN. Rubbish, Katherine!—Go home and look after your house and leave me to look after the community. How can you be so afraid, when I am so confident and happy? (*Walks up and down, rubbing his hands.*) Truth and the People will win the fight, you may be certain! I see the whole of the broad-minded middle class marching like a victorious army—! (*Stops beside a chair*) What the deuce is that lying there?

ASLAKSEN. Good Lord!

HOVSTAD. Ahem!

DR. STOCKMANN. Here we have the topmost pinnacle of authority! (*Takes the Mayor's official hat carefully between his finger-tips and holds it up in the air.*)

MRS. STOCKMANN. The Mayor's hat!

DR. STOCKMANN. And here is the staff of office too. How in the name of all that's wonderful—?

HOVSTAD. Well, you see—

DR. STOCKMANN. Oh, I understand. He has been here trying to talk you over. Ha—ha!—he made rather a mistake there! And as soon as he caught sight of me in the printing-room—. (*Bursts out laughing.*) Did he run away, Mr. Aslaksen?

ASLAKSEN (*hurriedly*). Yes, he ran away, Doctor.

DR. STOCKMANN. Ran away without his stick or his—. Fiddlesticks! Peter doesn't run away and leave his belongings behind him. But what the deuce have you done with him? Ah!—in there, of course. Now you shall see, Katherine.

MRS. STOCKMANN. Thomas—please don't—!

ASLAKSEN. Don't be rash, Doctor.

(DR. STOCKMANN *has put on the Mayor's hat and taken his stick in his hand. He goes up to the door, opens it and stands with his hand to his hat at the salute.* PETER STOCKMANN *comes in, red with anger.* BILLING *follows him.*)

PETER STOCKMANN. What does this tomfoolery mean?

DR. STOCKMANN. Be respectful, my good Peter. I am the chief authority in the town now. (*Walks up and down.*)

MRS. STOCKMANN (*almost in tears*). Really, Thomas!

PETER STOCKMANN (*following him about*). Give me my hat and stick.

DR. STOCKMANN (*in the same tone as before*). If you are chief constable, let me tell you that I am the Mayor—I am the master of the whole town, please understand!

PETER STOCKMANN. Take off my hat, I tell you. Remember it is part of an official uniform.

DR. STOCKMANN. Pooh! Do you think the newly awakened lionhearted people are going to be frightened by an official hat? There is going to be a revolution in the town to-morrow, let me tell you. You thought you could turn me out; but now I shall turn you out—turn you out of all your various offices. Do you think I cannot? Listen to me. I have triumphant social forces behind me. Hovstad and Billing will thunder in the "People's Messenger," and Aslaksen will take the field at the head of the whole Householders' Association—

ASLAKSEN. That I won't, Doctor.

DR. STOCKMANN. Of course you will—

PETER STOCKMANN. Ah!—may I ask then if Mr. Hovstad intends to join this agitation?

HOVSTAD. No, Mr. Mayor.

ASLAKSEN. No, Mr. Hovstad is not such a fool as to go and ruin his paper and himself for the sake of an imaginary grievance.

DR. STOCKMANN (looking round him). What does this mean?

HOVSTAD. You have represented your case in a false light, Doctor, and therefore I am unable to give you my support.

BILLING. And after what the Mayor was so kind as to tell me just now, I—

DR. STOCKMANN. A false light! Leave that part of it to me. Only print my article; I am quite capable of defending it.

HOVSTAD. I am not going to print it. I cannot and will not and dare not print it.

DR. STOCKMANN. You dare not? What nonsense!—you are the editor; and an editor controls his paper, I suppose!

ASLAKSEN. No, it is the subscribers, Doctor.

PETER STOCKMANN. Fortunately, yes.

ASLAKSEN. It is public opinion—the enlightened public—householders and people of that kind; they control the newspapers.

DR. STOCKMANN (composedly). And I have all these influences against me?

ASLAKSEN. Yes, you have. It would mean the absolute ruin of the community if your article were to appear.

DR. STOCKMANN. Indeed.

PETER STOCKMANN. My hat and stick, if you please. (DR. STOCKMANN takes off the hat and lays it on the table with the stick. PETER STOCKMANN takes them up.) Your authority as mayor has come to an untimely end.

DR. STOCKMANN. We have not got to the end yet. (To HOVSTAD)

Then it is quite impossible for you to print my article in the "People's Messenger"?

HOVSTAD. Quite impossible—out of regard for your family as well.

MRS. STOCKMANN. You need not concern yourself about his family, thank you, Mr. Hovstad.

PETER STOCKMANN (*taking a paper from his pocket*). It will be sufficient, for the guidance of the public, if this appears. It is an official statement. May I trouble you?

HOVSTAD (*taking the paper*). Certainly; I will see that it is printed.

DR. STOCKMANN. But not mine. Do you imagine that you can silence me and stifle the truth! You will not find it so easy as you suppose. Mr. Aslaksen, kindly take my manuscript at once and print it as a pamphlet—at my expense. I will have four hundred copies—no, five—six hundred.

ASLAKSEN. If you offered me its weight in gold, I could not lend my press for any such purpose, Doctor. It would be flying in the face of public opinion. You will not get it printed anywhere in the town.

DR. STOCKMANN. Then give it me back.

HOVSTAD (*giving him the MS.*). Here it is.

DR. STOCKMANN (*taking his hat and stick*). It shall be made public all the same. I will read it out at a mass meeting of the townspeople. All my fellow-citizens shall hear the voice of truth!

PETER STOCKMANN. You will not find any public body in the town that will give you the use of their hall for such a purpose.

ASLAKSEN. Not a single one, I am certain.

BILLING. No, I'm damned if you will find one.

MRS. STOCKMANN. But this is too shameful! Why should every one turn against you like that?

DR. STOCKMANN (*angrily*). I will tell you why. It is because all the men in this town are old women—like you; they all think of nothing but their families, and never of the community.

MRS. STOCKMANN (*putting her arm into his*). Then I will show them that an—an old woman can be a man for once. I am going to stand by you, Thomas!

DR. STOCKMANN. Bravely said, Katherine! It shall be made public—as I am a living soul! If I can't hire a hall, I shall hire a drum, and parade the town with it and read it at every street-corner.

PETER STOCKMANN. You are surely not such an arrant fool as that!

DR. STOCKMANN. Yes, I am.

ASLAKSEN. You won't find a single man in the whole town to go with you.

BILLING. No, I'm damned if you will.

MRS. STOCKMANN. Don't give in, Thomas. I will tell the boys to go with you.

DR. STOCKMANN. That is a splendid idea!

Mrs. Stockmann. Morten will be delighted; and Ejlif will do whatever he does.

Dr. Stockmann. Yes, and Petra!—and you too, Katherine!

Mrs. Stockmann. No, I won't do that; but I will stand at the window and watch you, that's what I will do.

Dr. Stockmann (puts his arms round her and kisses her). Thank you, my dear! Now you and I are going to try a fall, my fine gentlemen! I am going to see whether a pack of cowards can succeed in gagging a patriot who wants to purify society!

(He and his wife go out by the street door.)

Peter Stockmann (shaking his head seriously). Now he has sent her out of her senses, too.

ACT IV

Scene. A big old-fashioned room in Captain Horster's house. At the back folding-doors, which are standing open, lead to an ante-room. Three windows in the left-hand wall. In the middle of the opposite wall a platform has been erected. On this is a small table with two candles, a water-bottle and glass, and a bell. The room is lit by lamps placed between the windows. In the foreground on the left there is a table with candles and a chair. To the right is a door and some chairs standing near it. The room is nearly filled with a crowd of townspeople of all sorts, a few women and schoolboys being amongst them. People are still streaming in from the back, and the room is soon filled.

1st Citizen (meeting another). Hullo, Lamstad! You here too?

2nd Citizen. I go to every public meeting, I do.

3rd Citizen. Brought your whistle too, I expect!

2nd Citizen. I should think so. Haven't you?

3rd Citizen. Rather! And old Evensen said he was going to bring a cow-horn, he did.

2nd Citizen. Good old Evensen!

(Laughter among the crowd.)

4th Citizen (coming up to them). I say, tell me what is going on here to-night.

2nd Citizen. Dr. Stockmann is going to deliver an address attacking the Mayor.

4th Citizen. But the Mayor is his brother.

1st Citizen. That doesn't matter; Dr. Stockmann's not the chap to be afraid.

3RD CITIZEN. But he is in the wrong; it said so in the "People's Messenger."

2ND CITIZEN. Yes, I expect he must be in the wrong this time, because neither the Householders' Association nor the Citizens' Club would lend him their hall for his meeting.

1ST CITIZEN. He couldn't even get the loan of the hall at the Baths.

2ND CITIZEN. No, I should think not.

A MAN (in another part of the crowd). I say—who are we to back up in this?

ANOTHER MAN (beside him). Watch Aslaksen, and do as he does.

BILLING (pushing his way through the crowd, with a writing-case under his arm). Excuse me, gentlemen—do you mind letting me through? I am reporting for the "People's Messenger." Thank you very much! (He sits down at the table on the left.)

A WORKMAN. Who was that?

2ND WORKMAN. Don't you know him? It's Billing, who writes for Aslaksen's paper.

(CAPTAIN HORSTER brings in MRS. STOCKMANN and PETRA through the door on the right. EJLIF and MORTEN follow them in.)

HORSTER. I thought you might all sit here; you can slip out easily from here, if things get too lively.

MRS. STOCKMANN. Do you think there will be a disturbance?

HORSTER. One can never tell—with such a crowd. But sit down, and don't be uneasy.

MRS. STOCKMANN (sitting down). It was extremely kind of you to offer my husband the room.

HORSTER. Well, if nobody else would—

PETRA (who has sat down beside her mother). And it was a plucky thing to do, Captain Horster.

HORSTER. Oh, it is not such a great matter as all that.

(HOVSTAD and ASLAKSEN make their way through the crowd.)

ASLAKSEN (going up to HORSTER). Has the Doctor not come yet?

HORSTER. He is waiting in the next room.

(Movement in the crowd by the door at the back.)

HOVSTAD. Look—here comes the Mayor!

BILLING. Yes, I'm damned if he hasn't come after all!

(PETER STOCKMANN makes his way gradually through the crowd, bows courteously and takes up a position by the wall on the left. Shortly afterwards DR. STOCKMANN comes in by the right-hand door. He is dressed in a *black frock-coat, with a white tie. There is a little feeble applause, which is hushed down. Silence is obtained.*)

DR. STOCKMANN (*in an undertone*). How do you feel, Katherine?

MRS. STOCKMANN. All right, thank you. (*Lowering her voice*) Be sure not to lose your temper, Thomas.

DR. STOCKMANN. Oh, I know how to control myself. (*Looks at his watch, steps on to the platform and bows.*) It is a quarter past—so I will begin. (*Takes his MS. out of his pocket.*)

ASLAKSEN. I think we ought to elect a chairman first.

DR. STOCKMANN. No, it is quite unnecessary.

SOME OF THE CROWD. Yes—yes!

PETER STOCKMANN. I certainly think, too, that we ought to have a chairman.

DR. STOCKMANN. But I have called this meeting to deliver a lecture, Peter.

PETER STOCKMANN. Dr. Stockmann's lecture may possibly lead to a considerable conflict of opinion.

VOICES IN THE CROWD. A chairman! A chairman!

HOVSTAD. The general wish of the meeting seems to be that a chairman should be elected.

DR. STOCKMANN (*restraining himself*). Very well—let the meeting have its way.

ASLAKSEN. Will the Mayor be good enough to undertake the task?

THREE MEN (*clapping their hands*). Bravo! Bravo!

PETER STOCKMANN. For various reasons, which you will easily understand, I must beg to be excused. But fortunately we have amongst us a man who I think will be acceptable to you all. I refer to the President of the Householders' Association, Mr. Aslaksen.

SEVERAL VOICES. Yes—Aslaksen! Bravo Aslaksen!

(DR. STOCKMANN *takes up his MS. and walks up and down the platform.*)

ASLAKSEN. Since my fellow-citizens choose to entrust me with this duty, I cannot refuse. (*Loud applause.* ASLAKSEN *mounts the platform.*)

BILLING (*writing*). "Mr. Aslaksen was elected with enthusiasm."

ASLAKSEN. And now, as I am in this position, I should like to say a few brief words. I am a quiet and peaceable man, who believes in discreet moderation, and—and—in moderate discretion. All my friends can bear witness to that.

SEVERAL VOICES. That's right! That's right, Aslaksen!

ASLAKSEN. I have learnt in the school of life and experience that moderation is the most valuable virtue a citizen can possess—

PETER STOCKMANN. Hear, hear!

Aslaksen. —And moreover that discretion and moderation are what enable a man to be of most service to the community. I would therefore suggest to our esteemed fellow-citizen, who has called this meeting, that he should strive to keep strictly within the bounds of moderation.

A Man (*by the door*). Three cheers for the Moderation Society!

A Voice. Shame!

Several Voices. Sh!—Sh!

Aslaksen. No interruptions, gentlemen, please! Does anyone wish to make any remarks?

Peter Stockmann. Mr. Chairman.

Aslaksen. The Mayor will address the meeting.

Peter Stockmann. In consideration of the close relationship in which, as you all know, I stand to the present Medical Officer of the Baths, I should have preferred not to speak this evening. But my official position with regard to the Baths and my solicitude for the vital interests of the town compel me to bring forward a motion. I venture to presume that there is not a single one of our citizens present who considers it desirable that unreliable and exaggerated accounts of the sanitary condition of the Baths and the town should be spread abroad.

Several Voices. No, no! Certainly not! We protest against it!

Peter Stockmann. Therefore I should like to propose that the meeting should not permit the Medical Officer either to read or to comment on his proposed lecture.

Dr. Stockmann (*impatiently*). Not permit—! What the devil—!

Mrs. Stockmann (*coughing*). Ahem!—ahem!

Dr. Stockmann (*collecting himself*). Very well. Go ahead!

Peter Stockmann. In my communication to the "People's Messenger," I have put the essential facts before the public in such a way that every fair-minded citizen can easily form his own opinion. From it you will see that the main result of the Medical Officer's proposals—apart from their constituting a vote of censure on the leading men of the town—would be to saddle the ratepayers with an unnecessary expenditure of at least some thousands of pounds.

(*Sounds of disapproval among the audience, and some cat-calls.*)

Aslaksen (*ringing his bell*). Silence, please, gentlemen! I beg to support the Mayor's motion. I quite agree with him that there is something behind this agitation started by the Doctor. He talks about the Baths; but it is a revolution he is aiming at—he wants to get the administration of the town put into new hands. No one doubts the honesty of the Doctor's intentions—no one will suggest that there can be any two opinions as to that. I myself am a believer in self-government for the people, provided it does not fall too heavily on the ratepayers. But that would be the case here; and that is why I will see Dr. Stockmann damned—I beg your pardon—before

I go with him in the matter. You can pay too dearly for a thing sometimes; that is my opinion.

(*Loud applause on all sides.*)

HOVSTAD. I, too, feel called upon to explain my position. Dr. Stockmann's agitation appeared to be gaining a certain amount of sympathy at first, so I supported it as impartially as I could. But presently we had reason to suspect that we had allowed ourselves to be misled by misrepresentation of the state of affairs—

DR. STOCKMANN. Misrepresentation—!

HOVSTAD. Well, let us say a not entirely trustworthy representation. The Mayor's statement has proved that. I hope no one here has any doubt as to my liberal principles; the attitude of the "People's Messenger" towards important political questions is well known to every one. But the advice of experienced and thoughtful men has convinced me that in purely local matters a newspaper ought to proceed with a certain caution.

ASLAKSEN. I entirely agree with the speaker.

HOVSTAD. And, in the matter before us, it is now an undoubted fact that Dr. Stockmann has public opinion against him. Now, what is an editor's first and most obvious duty, gentlemen? Is it not to work in harmony with his readers? Has he not received a sort of tacit mandate to work persistently and assiduously for the welfare of those whose opinions he represents? Or is it possible I am mistaken in that?

VOICES (*from the crowd*). No, no! You are quite right!

HOVSTAD. It has cost me a severe struggle to break with a man in whose house I have been lately a frequent guest—a man who till to-day has been able to pride himself on the undivided goodwill of his fellow-citizens—a man whose only, or at all events whose essential, failing is that he is swayed by his heart rather than his head.

A FEW SCATTERED VOICES. That is true! Bravo, Stockmann!

HOVSTAD. But my duty to the community obliged me to break with him. And there is another consideration that impels me to oppose him, and, as far as possible, to arrest him on the perilous course he has adopted; that is, consideration for his family—

DR. STOCKMANN. Please stick to the water-supply and drainage!

HOVSTAD. —consideration, I repeat, for his wife and his children for whom he has made no provision.

MORTEN. Is that us, mother?

MRS. STOCKMANN. Hush!

ASLAKSEN. I will now put the Mayor's proposition to the vote.

DR. STOCKMANN. There is no necessity! To-night I have no intention of dealing with all that filth down at the Baths. No; I have something quite different to say to you.

PETER STOCKMANN (*aside*). What is coming now?

A Drunken Man (*by the entrance door*). I am a ratepayer! And therefore I have a right to speak too! And my entire—firm—inconceivable opinion is—

A Number of Voices. Be quiet, at the back there!

Others. He is drunk! Turn him out! (*They turn him out.*)

Dr. Stockmann. Am I allowed to speak?

Aslaksen (*ringing his bell*). Dr. Stockmann will address the meeting.

Dr. Stockmann. I should like to have seen anyone, a few days ago, dare to attempt to silence me as has been done to-night! I would have defended my sacred rights as a man, like a lion! But now it is all one to me; I have something of even weightier importance to say to you.

(*The crowd presses nearer to him,* Morten Kiil *conspicuous among them.*)

Dr. Stockmann (*continuing*). I have thought and pondered a great deal, these last few days—pondered over such a variety of things that in the end my head seemed too full to hold them—

Peter Stockmann (*with a cough*). Ahem!

Dr. Stockmann. —but I got them clear in my mind at last, and then I saw the whole situation lucidly. And that is why I am standing here to-night. I have a great revelation to make to you, my fellow-citizens! I will impart to you a discovery of a far wider scope than the trifling matter that our water-supply is poisoned and our medicinal Baths are standing on pestiferous soil.

A Number of Voices (*shouting*). Don't talk about the Baths! We won't hear you! None of that!

Dr. Stockmann. I have already told you that what I want to speak about is the great discovery I have made lately—the discovery that all the sources of our *moral* life are poisoned and that the whole fabric of our civic community is founded on the pestiferous soil of falsehood.

Voices of Disconcerted Citizens. What is that he says?

Peter Stockmann. Such an insinuation—!

Aslaksen (*with his hand on his bell*). I call upon the speaker to moderate his language.

Dr. Stockmann. I have always loved my native town as a man only can love the home of his youthful days. I was not old when I went away from here; and exile, longing and memories cast, as it were, an additional halo over both the town and its inhabitants. (*Some clapping and applause.*) And there I stayed, for many years, in a horrible hole far away up north. When I came into contact with some of the people that lived scattered about among the rocks, I often thought it would have been more service to the poor half-starved creatures if a veterinary doctor had been sent up there, instead of a man like me. (*Murmurs among the crowd.*)

Billing (*laying down his pen*). I'm damned if I have ever heard—!

HOVSTAD. It is an insult to a respectable population!

DR. STOCKMANN. Wait a bit! I do not think anyone will charge me with having forgotten my native town up there. I was like one of the eider-ducks brooding on its nest, and what I hatched was—the plans for these Baths. (*Applause and protests.*) And then when fate at last decreed for me the great happiness of coming home again—I assure you, gentlemen, I thought I had nothing more in the world to wish for. Or rather, there was one thing I wished for—eagerly, untiringly, ardently—and that was to be able to be of service to my native town and the good of the community.

PETER STOCKMANN (*looking at the ceiling*). You chose a strange way of doing it—ahem!

DR. STOCKMANN. And so, with my eyes blinded to the real facts, I revelled in happiness. But yesterday morning—no, to be precise, it was yesterday afternoon—the eyes of my mind were opened wide, and the first thing I realised was the colossal stupidity of the authorities—.

(*Uproar, shouts and laughter.* MRS. STOCKMANN *coughs persistently.*)

PETER STOCKMANN. Mr. Chairman!

ASLAKSEN (*ringing his bell*). By virtue of my authority—!

DR. STOCKMANN. It is a petty thing to catch me up on a word, Mr. Aslaksen. What I mean is only that I got scent of the unbelievable piggish-ness our leading men had been responsible for down at the Baths. I can't stand leading men at any price!—I have had enough of such people in my time. They are like billy-goats in a young plantation; they do mischief everywhere. They stand in a free man's way, whichever way he turns, and what I should like best would be to see them exterminated like any other vermin—. (*Uproar.*)

PETER STOCKMANN. Mr. Chairman, can we allow such expressions to pass?

ASLAKSEN (*with his hand on his bell*). Doctor—!

DR. STOCKMANN. I cannot understand how it is that I have only now acquired a clear conception of what these gentry are, when I had almost daily before my eyes in this town such an excellent specimen of them—my brother Peter—slow-witted and hide-bound in prejudice—.

(*Laughter, uproar and hisses.* MRS. STOCKMANN *sits coughing assidu-ously.* ASLAKSEN *rings his bell violently.*)

THE DRUNKEN MAN (*who has got in again*). Is it me he is talking about? My name's Petersen, all right—but devil take me if I—

ANGRY VOICES. Turn out that drunken man! Turn him out. (*He is turned out again.*)

PETER STOCKMANN. Who was that person?

1ST CITIZEN. I don't know who he is, Mr. Mayor.

2ND CITIZEN. He doesn't belong here.

3RD CITIZEN. I expect he is a navvy from over at (*the rest is inaudible*).

ASLAKSEN. He had obviously had too much beer.—Proceed, Doctor; but please strive to be moderate in your language.

DR. STOCKMANN. Very well, gentlemen, I will say no more about our leading men. And if anyone imagines, from what I have just said, that my object is to attack these people this evening, he is wrong—absolutely wide of the mark. For I cherish the comforting conviction that these parasites— all these venerable relics of a dying school of thought—are most admirably paving the way for their own extinction; they need no doctor's help to hasten their end. Nor is it folk of that kind who constitute the most pressing danger to the community. It is not they who are most instrumental in poisoning the sources of our moral life and infecting the ground on which we stand. It is not they who are the most dangerous enemies of truth and freedom amongst us.

SHOUTS (*from all sides*). Who then? Who is it? Name! Name!

DR. STOCKMANN. You may depend upon it I shall name them! That is precisely the great discovery I made yesterday. (*Raises his voice.*) The most dangerous enemy of truth and freedom amongst us is the compact majority— yes, the damned compact Liberal majority—that is it! Now you know!

(*Tremendous uproar. Most of the crowd are shouting, stamping and hissing. Some of the older men among them exchange stolen glances and seem to be enjoying themselves. MRS. STOCKMANN gets up, looking anxious. EJLIF and MORTEN advance threateningly upon some schoolboys who are playing pranks. ASLAKSEN rings his bell and begs for silence. HOVSTAD and BILLING both talk at once, but are inaudible. At last quiet is restored.*)

ASLAKSEN. As chairman, I call upon the speaker to withdraw the ill-considered expressions he has just used.

DR. STOCKMANN. Never, Mr. Aslaksen! It is the majority in our community that denies me my freedom and seeks to prevent my speaking the truth.

HOVSTAD. The majority always has right on its side.

BILLING. And truth too, by God!

DR. STOCKMANN. The majority *never* has right on its side. Never, I say! That is one of these social lies against which an independent, intelligent man must wage war. Who is it that constitute the majority of the population in a country? Is it the clever folk or the stupid? I don't imagine you will dispute the fact that at present the stupid people are in an absolutely overwhelming majority all the world over. But, good Lord!—you can never pretend that it is right that the stupid folk should govern the clever ones! (*Uproar and cries.*) Oh, yes—you can shout me down, I know! but you cannot answer me. The majority has *might* on its side—unfortunately; but *right* it has *not*. I am in the right—I and a few other scattered individuals. The minority is always in the right. (*Renewed uproar.*)

HOVSTAD. Aha!—so Dr. Stockmann has become an aristocrat since the day before yesterday!

DR. STOCKMANN. I have already said that I don't intend to waste a word on the puny, narrow-chested, short-winded crew whom we are leaving astern. Pulsating life no longer concerns itself with them. I am thinking of the few, the scattered few amongst us, who have absorbed new and vigorous truths. Such men stand, as it were, at the outposts, so far ahead that the compact majority has not yet been able to come up with them; and there they are fighting for truths that are too newly-born into the world of consciousness to have any considerable number of people on their side as yet.

HOVSTAD. So the Doctor is a revolutionary now!

DR. STOCKMANN. Good heavens—of course I am, Mr. Hovstad! I propose to raise a revolution against the lie that the majority has the monopoly of the truth. What sort of truths are they that the majority usually supports? They are truths that are of such advanced age that they are beginning to break up. And if a truth is as old as that, it is also in a fair way to become a lie, gentlemen. (*Laughter and mocking cries.*) Yes, believe me or not, as you like; but truths are by no means as long-lived as Methuselah—as some folk imagine. A normally constituted truth lives, let us say, as a rule seventeen or eighteen, or at most twenty years; seldom longer. But truths as aged as that are always worn frightfully thin, and nevertheless it is only then that the majority recognises them and recommends them to the community as wholesome moral nourishment. There is no great nutritive value in that sort of fare, I can assure you; and, as a doctor, I ought to know. These "majority truths" are like last year's cured meat—like rancid, tainted ham; and they are the origin of the moral scurvy that is rampant in our communities.

ASLAKSEN. It appears to me that the speaker is wandering a long way from his subject.

PETER STOCKMANN. I quite agree with the Chairman.

DR. STOCKMANN. Have you gone clean out of your senses, Peter? I am sticking as closely to my subject as I can; for my subject is precisely this, that it is the masses, the majority—this infernal compact majority—that poisons the sources of our moral life and infects the ground we stand on.

HOVSTAD. And all this because the great, broad-minded majority of the people is prudent enough to show deference only to well-ascertained and well-approved truths?

DR. STOCKMANN. Ah, my good Mr. Hovstad, don't talk nonsense about well-ascertained truths! The truths of which the masses now approve are the very truths that the fighters at the outposts held to in the days of our grandfathers. We fighters at the outposts nowadays no longer approve of them; and I do not believe there is any other well-ascertained truth except this, that no community can live a healthy life if it is nourished only on such old marrowless truths.

HOVSTAD. But instead of standing there using vague generalities, it would be interesting if you would tell us what these old marrowless truths are, that we are nourished on. (*Applause from many quarters.*)

DR. STOCKMANN. Oh, I could give you a whole string of such abominations; but to begin with I will confine myself to one well-approved truth, which at bottom is a foul lie, but upon which nevertheless Mr. Hovstad and the "People's Messenger" and all the "Messenger's" supporters are nourished.

HOVSTAD. And that is—?

DR. STOCKMANN. That is, the doctrine you have inherited from your forefathers and proclaim thoughtlessly far and wide—the doctrine that the public, the crowd, the masses are the essential part of the population—that they constitute the People—that the common folk, the ignorant and incomplete element in the community, have the same right to pronounce judgment and to approve, to direct and to govern, as the isolated, intellectually superior personalities in it.

BILLING. Well, damn me if ever I—

HOVSTAD (*at the same time, shouting out*). Fellow-citizens, take good note of that!

A NUMBER OF VOICES (*angrily*). Oho!—we are not the People! Only the superior folks are to govern, are they!

A WORKMAN. Turn the fellow out, for talking such rubbish!

ANOTHER. Out with him!

ANOTHER (*calling out*). Blow your horn, Evensen! (*A horn is blown loudly, amidst hisses and an angry uproar.*)

DR. STOCKMANN (*when the noise has somewhat abated*). Be reasonable! Can't you stand hearing the voice of truth for once? I don't in the least expect you to agree with me all at once; but I must say I did expect Mr. Hovstad to admit I was right, when he had recovered his composure a little. He claims to be a freethinker—

VOICES (*in murmurs of astonishment*). Freethinker, did he say? Is Hovstad a freethinker?

HOVSTAD (*shouting*). Prove it, Dr. Stockmann! When have I said so in print?

DR. STOCKMANN (*reflecting*). No, confound it, you are right!—you have never had the courage to. Well, I won't put you in a hole, Mr. Hovstad. Let us say it is I that am the freethinker, then. I am going to prove to you, scientifically, that the "People's Messenger" leads you by the nose in a shameful manner when it tells you that you—that the common people, the crowd, the masses are the real essence of the People. That is only a newspaper lie, I tell you! The common people are nothing more than the raw material of which a People is made. (*Groans, laughter and uproar.*) Well, isn't that the case? Isn't there an enormous difference between a well-bred and an ill-bred strain of animals? Take, for instance, a common barn-door hen. What sort of eating do you get from a shrivelled-up old scrag of a fowl like that? Not much, do you! And what sort of eggs does it lay? A fairly good crow or a raven can lay pretty nearly as good an egg. But take a well-bred Spanish or Japanese hen, or a good pheasant or a turkey—then you will see the difference. Or take the case of dogs, with whom we humans are on such intimate terms. Think first of an ordinary common cur—I mean one of the horrible, coarse-haired, low-bred curs that do nothing but run about the streets and befoul the walls of the houses. Compare one of these curs with a poodle whose sires for many generations have been bred in a gentleman's house, where they have had the best of food and had the opportunity of hearing soft voices and music. Do you not think that the poodle's brain is developed to quite a different degree from that of the cur? Of course it is. It is puppies of well-bred poodles like that, that showmen train to do incredibly clever tricks—things that a common cur could never learn to do even if it stood on its head. (*Uproar and mocking cries.*)

A CITIZEN (*calls out*).   Are you going to make out we are dogs, now?

ANOTHER CITIZEN.   We are not animals, Doctor!

DR. STOCKMANN.   Yes, but bless my soul, we *are*, my friend! It is true we are the finest animals anyone could wish for; but, even amongst us, exceptionally fine animals are rare. There is a tremendous difference between poodle-men and cur-men. And the amusing part of it is, that Mr. Hovstad quite agrees with me as long as it is a question of four-footed animals—

HOVSTAD.   Yes, it is true enough as far as they are concerned.

DR. STOCKMANN.   Very well. But as soon as I extend the principle and apply it to two-legged animals, Mr. Hovstad stops short. He no longer dares to think independently, or to pursue his ideas to their logical conclusion; so he turns the whole theory upside down and proclaims in the "People's Messenger" that it is the barn-door hens and street curs that are the finest specimens in the menagerie. But that is always the way, as long as a man retains the traces of common origin and has not worked his way up to intellectual distinction.

HOVSTAD.   I lay no claim to any sort of distinction. I am the son of humble countryfolk, and I am proud that the stock I come from is rooted deep among the common people he insults.

VOICES.   Bravo, Hovstad! Bravo! Bravo!

DR. STOCKMANN.   The kind of common people I mean are not only to be found low down in the social scale; they crawl and swarm all around us—even in the highest social positions. You have only to look at your own fine, distinguished Mayor! My brother Peter is every bit as plebeian as anyone that walks in two shoes— (*Laughter and hisses.*)

PETER STOCKMANN.   I protest against personal allusions of this kind.

DR. STOCKMANN (*imperturbably*).   —and that, not because he is, like myself, descended from some old rascal of a pirate from Pomerania or thereabouts—because that is who we are descended from—

PETER STOCKMANN. An absurd legend. I deny it!

DR. STOCKMANN. —but because he thinks what his superiors think and holds the same opinions as they. People who do that are, intellectually speaking, common people; and that is why my magnificent brother Peter is in reality so very far from any distinction—and consequently also so far from being liberal-minded.

PETER STOCKMANN. Mr. Chairman—!

HOVSTAD. So it is only the distinguished men that are liberal-minded in this country? We are learning something quite new! (*Laughter.*)

DR. STOCKMANN. Yes, that is part of my new discovery too. And another part of it is that broad-mindedness is almost precisely the same thing as morality. That is why I maintain that it is absolutely inexcusable in the "People's Messenger" to proclaim, day in and day out, the false doctrine that it is the masses, the crowd, the compact majority that have the monopoly of broad-mindedness and morality—and that vice and corruption and every kind of intellectual depravity are the result of culture, just as all the filth that is draining into our Baths is the result of the tanneries up at Mölledal! (*Uproar and interruptions.* DR. STOCKMANN *is undisturbed, and goes on, carried away by his ardour, with a smile.*) And yet this same "People's Messenger" can go on preaching that the masses ought to be elevated to higher conditions of life! But, bless my soul, if the "Messenger's" teaching is to be depended upon, this very raising up the masses would mean nothing more or less than setting them straightway upon the paths of depravity! Happily the theory that culture demoralises is only an old falsehood that our forefathers believed in and we have inherited. No, it is ignorance, poverty, ugly conditions of life that do the devil's work! In a house which does not get aired and swept every day—my wife Katherine maintains that the floor ought to be scrubbed as well, but that is a debatable question—in such a house, let me tell you, people will lose within two or three years the power of thinking or acting in a moral manner. Lack of oxygen weakens the conscience. And there must be a plentiful lack of oxygen in very many houses in this town, I should think, judging from the fact that the whole compact majority can be unconscientious enough to wish to build the town's prosperity on a quagmire of falsehood and deceit.

ASLAKSEN. We cannot allow such a grave accusation to be flung at a citizen community.

A CITIZEN. I move that the Chairman direct the speaker to sit down.

VOICES (*angrily*). Hear, hear! Quite right! Make him sit down!

DR. STOCKMANN (*losing his self-control*). Then I will go and shout the truth at every street corner! I will write it in other towns' newspapers! The whole country shall know what is going on here!

HOVSTAD. It almost seems as if Dr. Stockmann's intention were to ruin the town.

DR. STOCKMANN. Yes, my native town is so dear to me that I would rather ruin it than see it flourishing upon a lie.

ASLAKSEN. This is really serious.

(*Uproar and cat-calls.* MRS. STOCKMANN *coughs, but to no purpose; her husband does not listen to her any longer.*)

HOVSTAD (*shouting above the din*). A man must be a public enemy to wish to ruin a whole community!

DR. STOCKMANN (*with growing fervour*). What does the destruction of a community matter, if it lives on lies! It ought to be razed to the ground, I tell you! All who live by lies ought to be exterminated like vermin! You will end by infecting the whole country; you will bring about such a state of things that the whole country will deserve to be ruined. And if things come to that pass, I shall say from the bottom of my heart: Let the whole country perish, let all these people be exterminated!

VOICES (*from the crowd*). That is talking like an out-and-out enemy of the people!

BILLING. There sounded the voice of the people, by all that's holy!

THE WHOLE CROWD (*shouting*). Yes, yes! He is an enemy of the people! He hates his country! He hates his own people!

ASLAKSEN. Both as a citizen and as an individual, I am profoundly disturbed by what we have had to listen to. Dr. Stockmann has shown himself in a light I should never have dreamed of. I am unhappily obliged to subscribe to the opinion which I have just heard my estimable fellow-citizens utter; and I propose that we should give expression to that opinion in a resolution. I propose a resolution as follows: "This meeting declares that it considers Dr. Thomas Stockmann, Medical Officer of the Baths, to be an enemy of the people."

(*A storm of cheers and applause. A number of men surround the* DOCTOR *and hiss him.* MRS. STOCKMANN *and* PETRA *have got up from their seats.* MORTEN *and* EJLIF *are fighting the other schoolboys for hissing; some of their elders separate them.*)

DR. STOCKMANN (*to the men who are hissing him*). Oh, you fools! I tell you that—

ASLAKSEN (*ringing his bell*). We cannot hear you now, Doctor. A formal vote is about to be taken; but, out of regard for personal feelings, it shall be by ballot and not verbal. Have you any clean paper, Mr. Billings?

BILLING. I have both blue and white here.

ASLAKSEN (*going to him*). That will do nicely; we shall get on more quickly that way. Cut it up into small strips—yes, that's it. (*To the meeting.*) Blue means no; white means yes. I will come round myself and collect votes.

(PETER STOCKMANN *leaves the hall.* ASLAKSEN *and one or two others go round the room with the slips of paper in their hats.*)

1ST CITIZEN (*to* HOVSTAD). I say, what has come to the Doctor? What are we to think of it?

HOVSTAD. Oh, you know how headstrong he is.

2ND CITIZEN (*to* BILLING). Billing, you go to their house—have you ever noticed if the fellow drinks?

BILLING. Well I'm hanged if I know what to say. There are always spirits on the table when you go.

3RD CITIZEN. I rather think he goes quite off his head sometimes.

1ST CITIZEN. I wonder if there is any madness in his family?

BILLING. I shouldn't wonder if there were.

4TH CITIZEN. No, it is nothing more than sheer malice; he wants to get even with somebody for something or other.

BILLING. Well certainly he suggested a rise in his salary on one occasion lately, and did not get it.

THE CITIZENS (*together*). Ah!— then it is easy to understand how it is!

THE DRUNKEN MAN (*who has got amongst the audience again*). I want a blue one, I do! And I want a white one too!

VOICES. It's that drunken chap again! Turn him out!

MORTEN KIIL (*going up to* DR. STOCKMANN). Well, Stockmann, do you see what these monkey tricks of yours lead to?

DR. STOCKMANN. I have done my duty.

MORTEN KIIL. What was that you said about the tanneries at Mölledal?

DR. STOCKMANN. You heard well enough. I said they were the source of all the filth.

MORTEN KIIL. My tannery too?

DR. STOCKMANN. Unfortunately your tannery is by far the worst.

MORTEN KIIL. Are you going to put that in the papers?

DR. STOCKMANN. I shall conceal nothing.

MORTEN KIIL. That may cost you dear, Stockmann. (*Goes out.*)

A STOUT MAN (*going up to* CAPTAIN HORSTER, *without taking any notice of the ladies*). Well, Captain, so you lend your house to enemies of the people?

HORSTER. I imagine I can do what I like with my own possessions, Mr. Vik.

THE STOUT MAN. Then you can have no objection to my doing the same with mine.

HORSTER. What do you mean, sir?

THE STOUT MAN. You shall hear from me in the morning. (*Turns his back on him and moves off.*)

PETRA. Was that not your owner, Captain Horster?

HORSTER. Yes, that was Mr. Vik the ship-owner.

ASLAKSEN (*with the voting-papers in his hands, gets up on to the platform and rings his bell*). Gentlemen, allow me to announce the result. By the votes of very one here except one person—

A YOUNG MAN. That is the drunk chap!

ASLAKSEN. By the votes of every one here except a tipsy man, this meeting of citizens declares Dr. Thomas Stockmann to be an enemy of the people. (*Shouts and applause.*) Three cheers for our ancient and honourable citizen community! (*Renewed applause.*) Three cheers for our able and energetic Mayor, who has so loyally suppressed the promptings of family feeling! (*Cheers.*) The meeting is dissolved. (*Gets down.*)

BILLING. Three cheers for the Chairman!

THE WHOLE CROWD. Three cheers for Aslaksen! Hurrah!

DR. STOCKMANN. My hat and coat, Petra! Captain, have you room on your ship for passengers to the New World?

HORSTER. For you and yours we will make room, Doctor.

DR. STOCKMANN (*as PETRA helps him into his coat*). Good. Come, Katherine! Come, boys!

MRS. STOCKMANN (*in an undertone*). Thomas, dear, let us go out by the back way.

DR. STOCKMANN. No back ways for me, Katherine. (*Raising his voice.*) You will hear more of this enemy of the people, before he shakes the dust off his shoes upon you! I am not so forgiving as a certain Person; I do not say: "I forgive you, for ye know not what ye do."

ASLAKSEN (*shouting*). That is a blasphemous comparison, Dr. Stockmann!

BILLING. It is, by God! It's dreadful for an earnest man to listen to.

A COARSE VOICE. Threatens us now, does he!

OTHER VOICES (*excitedly*). Let's go and break his windows! Duck him in the fjord!

ANOTHER VOICE. Blow your horn, Evensen! Pip, pip!

(*Horn-blowing, hisses and wild cries. DR. STOCKMANN goes out through the hall with his family, HORSTER elbowing a way for them.*)

THE WHOLE CROWD (*howling after them as they go*). Enemy of the People! Enemy of the People!

BILLING (*as he puts his papers together*). Well, I'm damned if I go and drink toddy with the Stockmanns to-night!

(*The crowd press towards the exit. The uproar continues outside; shouts of "Enemy of the People!" are heard from without.*)

ACT V

SCENE. DR. STOCKMANN's *study. Bookcases, and cabinets containing specimens, line the walls. At the back is a door leading to the hall; in the foreground on the left, a door leading to the sitting-room. In the right-hand wall are two windows, of which all the panes are broken. The* DOCTOR'S *desk, littered with books and papers, stands in the middle of the room, which is in disorder. It is morning.* DR. STOCKMANN *in dressing-gown, slippers and a smoking-cap, is bending down and raking with an umbrella under one of the cabinets. After a little while he rakes out a stone.*

DR. STOCKMANN (*calling through the open sitting-room door*). Katherine, I have found another one.

MRS. STOCKMANN (*from the sitting-room*). Oh, you will find a lot more yet, I expect.

DR. STOCKMANN (*adding the stone to a heap of others on the table*). I shall treasure these stones as relics. Ejlif and Morten shall look at them every day, and when they are grown up they shall inherit them as heirlooms. (*Rakes about under a bookcase.*) Hasn't—what the deuce is her name—the girl, you know—hasn't she been to fetch the glazier yet?

MRS. STOCKMANN (*coming in*). Yes, but he said he didn't know if he would be able to come to-day.

DR. STOCKMANN. You will see he won't dare to come.

MRS. STOCKMANN. Well, that is just what Randine thought—that he didn't dare to, on account of the neighbours. (*Calls into the sitting-room.*) What is it you want, Randine? Give it to me. (*Goes in, and comes out again directly.*) Here is a letter for you, Thomas.

DR. STOCKMANN. Let me see it. (*Opens and reads it.*) Ah!—of course.

MRS. STOCKMANN. Who is it from?

DR. STOCKMANN. From the landlord. Notice to quit.

MRS. STOCKMANN. Is it possible? Such a nice man—

DR. STOCKMANN (*looking at the letter*). Does not dare do otherwise, he says. Doesn't like doing it, but dares not do otherwise—on account of his fellow-citizens—out of regard for public opinion. Is in a dependent position—dares not offend certain influential men—

MRS. STOCKMANN. There, you see, Thomas!

DR. STOCKMANN. Yes, yes, I see well enough; the whole lot of them in the town are cowards; not a man among them dares do anything for fear of the others (*Throws the letter on to the table.*) But it doesn't matter to us, Katherine. We are going to sail away to the New World, and—

MRS. STOCKMANN. But, Thomas, are you sure we are well advised to take this step?

DR. STOCKMANN. Are you suggesting that I should stay here, where they have pilloried me as an enemy of the people—branded me—broken my windows! And just look here, Katherine—they have torn a great rent in my black trousers too!

MRS. STOCKMANN. Oh, dear—and they are the best pair you have got!

DR. STOCKMANN. You should never wear your best trousers when you go out to fight for freedom and truth. It is not that I care so much about the trousers, you know; you can always sew them up again for me. But that the common herd should dare to make this attack on me, as if they were my equals—that is what I cannot, for the life of me, swallow!

Mrs. Stockmann. There is no doubt they have behaved very ill to you, Thomas; but is that sufficient reason for our leaving our native country for good and all?

Dr. Stockmann. If we went to another town, do you suppose we should not find the common people just as insolent as they are here? Depend upon it, there is not much to choose between them. Oh, well, let the curs snap—that is not the worst part of it. The worst is that, from one end of this country to the other, every man is the slave of his Party. Although, as far as that goes, I daresay it is not much better in the free West either; the compact majority, and liberal public opinion, and all that infernal old bag of tricks are probably rampant there too. But there things are done on a larger scale, you see. They may kill you, but they won't put you to death by slow torture. They don't squeeze a free man's soul in a vice, as they do here. And, if need be, one can live in solitude. (*Walks up and down.*) If only I knew where there was a virgin forest or a small South Sea island for sale, cheap—

Mrs. Stockmann. But think of the boys, Thomas.

Dr. Stockmann (*standing still*). What a strange woman you are, Katherine! Would you prefer to have the boys grow up in a society like this? You saw for yourself last night that half the population are out of their minds; and if the other half have not lost their senses, it is because they are mere brutes, with no sense to lose.

Mrs. Stockmann. But, Thomas dear, the imprudent things you said had something to do with it, you know.

Dr. Stockmann. Well, isn't what I said perfectly true? Don't they turn every idea topsy-turvy? Don't they make a regular hotch-potch of right and wrong? Don't they say that the things I know are true, are lies? The craziest part of it all is the fact of these "liberals," men of full age, going about in crowds imagining that they are the broad-minded party! Did you ever hear anything like it, Katherine!

Mrs. Stockmann. Yes, yes, it's mad enough of them, certainly; but— (Petra *comes in from the sitting-room*). Back from school already?

Petra. Yes. I have been given notice of dismissal.

Mrs. Stockmann. Dismissal?

Dr. Stockmann. You too?

Petra. Mrs. Busk gave me my notice; so I thought it was best to go at once.

Dr. Stockmann. You were perfectly right, too!

Mrs. Stockmann. Who would have thought Mrs. Busk was a woman like that!

Petra. Mrs. Busk isn't a bit like that, mother; I saw quite plainly how it hurt her to do it. But she didn't dare do otherwise, she said; and so I got my notice.

DR. STOCKMANN (*laughing and rubbing his hands*). She didn't dare do otherwise, either! It's delicious!

MRS. STOCKMANN. Well, after the dreadful scenes last night—

PETRA. It was not only that. Just listen to this, father!

DR. STOCKMANN. Well?

PETRA. Mrs. Busk showed me no less than three letters she received this morning—

DR. STOCKMANN. Anonymous, I suppose?

PETRA. Yes.

DR. STOCKMANN. Yes, because they didn't dare to risk signing their names, Katherine!

PETRA. And two of them were to the effect that a man who has been our guest here, was declaring last night at the Club that my views on various subjects are extremely emancipated—

DR. STOCKMANN. You did not deny that, I hope?

PETRA. No, you know I wouldn't. Mrs. Busk's own views are tolerably emancipated, when we are alone together; but now that this report about me is being spread, she dare not keep me on any longer.

MRS. STOCKMANN. And some one who had been a guest of ours! That shows you the return you get for your hospitality, Thomas!

DR. STOCKMANN. We won't live in such a disgusting hole any longer. Pack up as quickly as you can, Katherine; the sooner we can get away, the better.

MRS. STOCKMANN. Be quiet—I think I hear some one in the hall. See who it is, Petra.

PETRA (*opening the door*). Oh, it's you, Captain Horster! Do come in.

HORSTER (*coming in*). Good morning. I thought I would just come in and see how you were.

DR. STOCKMANN (*shaking his hand*). Thanks—that is really kind of you.

MRS. STOCKMANN. And thank you, too, for helping us through the crowd, Captain Horster.

PETRA. How did you manage to get home again?

HORSTER. Oh, somehow or other. I am fairly strong, and there is more sound than fury about these folk.

DR. STOCKMANN. Yes, isn't their swinish cowardice astonishing? Look here, I will show you something! There are all the stones they have thrown through my windows. Just look at them! I'm hanged if there are more than two decently large bits of hardstone in the whole heap; the rest are nothing but gravel—wretched little things. And yet they stood out there bawling and swearing that they would do me some violence; but as for *doing* anything—you don't see much of that in this town.

HORSTER. Just as well for you this time, doctor!

DR. STOCKMANN. True enough. But it makes one angry all the same; because if some day it should be a question of a national fight in real earnest, you will see that public opinion will be in favour of taking to one's heels, and the compact majority will turn tail like a flock of sheep, Captain Horster. That is what is so mournful to think of; it gives me so much concern, that—. No, devil take it, it is ridiculous to care about it! They have called me an enemy of the people, so an enemy of the people let me be!

MRS. STOCKMANN. You will never be that, Thomas.

DR. STOCKMANN. Don't swear to that, Katherine. To be called an ugly name may have the same effect as a pin-scratch in the lung. And that hateful name—I can't get quit of it. It is sticking here in the pit of my stomach, eating into me like a corrosive acid. And no magnesia will remove it.

PETRA. Bah—you should only laugh at them, father.

HORSTER. They will change their minds some day, Doctor.

MRS. STOCKMANN. Yes, Thomas, as sure as you are standing here.

DR. STOCKMANN. Perhaps, when it is too late. Much good may it do them! They may wallow in their filth then and rue the day when they drove a patriot into exile. When do you sail, Captain Horster?

HORSTER. Hm!—that was just what I had come to speak about—

DR. STOCKMANN. Why, has anything gone wrong with the ship?

HORSTER. No; but what has happened is that I am not to sail in it.

PETRA. Do you mean that you have been dismissed from your command?

HORSTER (smiling). Yes, that's just it.

PETRA. You too.

MRS. STOCKMANN. There, you see, Thomas!

DR. STOCKMANN. And that for the truth's sake! Oh, if I had thought such a thing possible—

HORSTER. You mustn't take it to heart; I shall be sure to find a job with some ship-owner or other, elsewhere.

DR. STOCKMANN. And that is this man Vik—a wealthy man, independent of every one and everything—! Shame on him!

HORSTER. He is quite an excellent fellow otherwise; he told me himself he would willingly have kept me on, if only he had dared—

DR. STOCKMANN. But he didn't dare? No, of course not.

HORSTER. It is not such an easy matter, he said, for a party man—

DR. STOCKMANN. The worthy man spoke the truth. A party is like a sausage machine; it mashes up all sorts of heads together into the same mince-meat—fatheads and blockheads, all in one mash!

MRS. STOCKMANN. Come, come, Thomas dear!

PETRA (to HORSTER). If only you had not come home with us, things might not have come to this pass.

HORSTER. I do not regret it.

PETRA (*holding out her hand to him*). Thank you for that!

HORSTER (*to* DR. STOCKMANN). And so what I came to say was that if you are determined to go away, I have thought of another plan—

DR. STOCKMANN. That's splendid!—if only we can get away at once.

MRS. STOCKMANN. Hush—wasn't that some one knocking?

PETRA. That is uncle, surely.

DR. STOCKMANN. Aha! (*Calls out.*) Come in!

MRS. STOCKMANN. Dear Thomas, promise me definitely—

(PETER STOCKMANN *comes in from the hall.*)

PETER STOCKMANN. Oh, you are engaged. In that case, I will—

DR. STOCKMANN. No, no, come in.

PETER STOCKMANN. But I wanted to speak to you alone.

MRS. STOCKMANN. We will go into the sitting-room in the meanwhile.

HORSTER. And I will look in again later.

DR. STOCKMANN. No, go in there with them, Captain Horster; I want to hear more about—

HORSTER. Very well, I will wait, then. (*He follows* MRS. STOCKMANN *and* PETRA *into the sitting-room.*)

DR. STOCKMANN. I daresay you find it rather draughty here to-day. Put your hat on.

PETER STOCKMANN. Thank you, if I may. (*Does so.*) I think I caught cold last night; I stood and shivered—

DR. STOCKMANN. Really? I found it warm enough.

PETER STOCKMANN. I regret that it was not in my power to prevent those excesses last night.

DR. STOCKMANN. Have you anything particular to say to me besides that?

PETER STOCKMANN (*taking a big letter from his pocket*). I have this document for you, from the Baths Committee.

DR. STOCKMANN. My dismissal?

PETER STOCKMANN. Yes, dating from to-day. (*Lays the letter on the table.*) It gives us pain to do it; but, to speak frankly, we dared not do otherwise on account of public opinion.

DR. STOCKMANN (*smiling*). Dared not? I seem to have heard that word before, to-day.

PETER STOCKMANN. I must beg you to understand your position clearly. For the future you must not count on any practice whatever in the town.

DR. STOCKMANN. Devil take the practice! But why are you so sure of that?

PETER STOCKMANN. The Householders' Association is circulating a list from house to house. All right-minded citizens are being called upon to give up employing you; and I can assure you that not a single head of a family will risk refusing his signature. They simply dare not.

Dr. Stockmann.   No, no; I don't doubt it. But what then?

Peter Stockmann.   If I might advise you, it would be best to leave the place for a little while—

Dr. Stockmann.   Yes, the propriety of leaving the place *has* occurred to me.

Peter Stockmann.   Good. And then, when you have had six months to think things over, if, after mature consideration, you can persuade yourself to write a few words of regret, acknowledging your error—

Dr. Stockmann.   I might have my appointment restored to me, do you mean?

Peter Stockmann.   Perhaps. It is not at all impossible.

Dr. Stockmann.   But what about public opinion, then? Surely you would not dare to do it on account of public feeling.

Peter Stockmann.   Public opinion is an extremely mutable thing. And, to be quite candid with you, it is a matter of great importance to us to have some admission of that sort from you in writing.

Dr. Stockmann.   Oh, that's what you are after, is it! I will just trouble you to remember what I said to you lately about foxy tricks of that sort!

Peter Stockmann.   Your position was quite different then. At that time you had reason to suppose you had the whole town at your back—

Dr. Stockmann.   Yes, and now I feel I have the whole town *on* my back—(*flaring up*) I would not do it if I had the devil and his dam on my back—! Never—never, I tell you!

Peter Stockmann.   A man with a family has no right to behave as you do. You have no right to do it, Thomas.

Dr. Stockmann.   I have no right! There is only one single thing in the world a free man has no right to do. Do you know what that is?

Peter Stockmann.   No.

Dr. Stockmann.   Of course you don't, but I will tell you. A free man has no right to soil himself with filth; he has no right to behave in a way that would justify his spitting in his own face.

Peter Stockmann.   This sort of thing sounds extremely plausible, of course; and if there were no other explanation for your obstinacy—. But as it happens that there is.

Dr. Stockmann.   What do you mean?

Peter Stockmann.   You understand very well what I mean. But, as your brother and as a man of discretion, I advise you not to build too much upon expectations and prospects that may so very easily fail you.

Dr. Stockmann.   What in the world is all this about?

Peter Stockmann.   Do you really ask me to believe that you are ignorant of the terms of Mr. Kiil's will?

Dr. Stockmann.   I know that the small amount he possesses is to go to an institution for indigent old work-people. How does that concern me?

PETER STOCKMANN. In the first place, it is by no means a small amount that is in question. Mr. Kiil is a fairly wealthy man.

DR. STOCKMANN. I had no notion of that!

PETER STOCKMANN. Hm!—hadn't you really? Then I suppose you had no notion, either, that a considerable portion of his wealth will come to your children, you and your wife having a life-rent of the capital. Has he never told you so?

DR. STOCKMANN. Never, on my honour! Quite the reverse; he has consistently done nothing but fume at being so unconscionably heavily taxed. But are you perfectly certain of this, Peter?

PETER STOCKMANN. I have it from an absolutely reliable source.

DR. STOCKMANN. Then, thank God, Katherine is provided for—and the children too! I must tell her this at once— (Calls out.) Katherine, Katherine!

PETER STOCKMANN (restraining him). Hush, don't say a word yet!

MRS. STOCKMANN (opening the door). What is the matter?

DR. STOCKMANN. Oh, nothing, nothing; you can go back. (She shuts the door. DR. STOCKMANN walks up and down in his excitement.) Provided for!—Just think of it, we are all provided for! And for life! What a blessed feeling it is to know one is provided for!

PETER STOCKMANN. Yes, but that is just exactly what you are not. Mr. Kiil can alter his will any day he likes.

DR. STOCKMANN. But he won't do that, my dear Peter. The "Badger" is much too delighted at my attack on you and your wise friends.

PETER STOCKMANN (starts and looks intently at him). Ah, that throws a light on various things.

DR. STOCKMANN. What things?

PETER STOCKMANN. I see that the whole thing was a combined manoeuvre on your part and his. These violent, reckless attacks that you have made against the leading men of the town, under the pretence that it was in the name of truth—

DR. STOCKMANN. What about them?

PETER STOCKMANN. I see that they were nothing else than the stipulated price for that vindictive old man's will.

DR. STOCKMANN (almost speechless). Peter—you are the most disgusting plebeian I have ever met in all my life.

PETER STOCKMANN. All is over between us. Your dismissal is irrevocable—we have a weapon against you now. (Goes out.)

DR. STOCKMANN. For shame! For shame! (Calls out.) Katherine, you must have the floor scrubbed after him! Let—what's her name—devil take it, the girl who has always got soot on her nose—

MRS. STOCKMANN (in the sitting-room). Hush, Thomas, be quiet!

PETRA (coming to the door). Father, grandfather is here, asking if he may speak to you alone.

DR. STOCKMANN. Certainly he may. (*Going to the door.*) Come in, Mr. Kiil. (MORTEN KIIL *comes in.* DR. STOCKMANN *shuts the door after him.*) What can I do for you? Won't you sit down?

MORTEN KIIL. I won't sit. (*Looks around.*) You look very comfortable here to-day, Thomas.

DR. STOCKMANN. Yes, don't we!

MORTEN KIIL. Very comfortable—plenty of fresh air. I should think you have got enough to-day of that oxygen you were talking about yesterday. Your conscience must be in splendid order to-day, I should think.

DR. STOCKMANN. It is.

MORTEN KIIL. So I should think. (*Taps his chest.*) Do you know what I have got here?

DR. STOCKMANN. A good conscience, too, I hope.

MORTEN KIIL. Bah!—No, it is something better than that. (*He takes a thick pocket-book from his breast-pocket, opens it, and displays a packet of papers.*)

DR. STOCKMANN (*looking at him in astonishment*). Shares in the Baths?

MORTEN KIIL. They were not difficult to get to-day.

DR. STOCKMANN. And you have been buying—?

MORTEN KIIL. As many as I could pay for.

DR. STOCKMANN. But, my dear Mr. Kiil—consider the state of the Baths' affairs!

MORTEN KIIL. If you behave like a reasonable man, you can soon set the Baths on their feet again.

DR. STOCKMANN. Well, you can see for yourself that I have done all I can, but—. They are all mad in this town!

MORTEN KIIL. You said yesterday that the worst of this pollution came from my tannery. If that is true, then my grandfather and my father before me, and I myself, for many years past, have been poisoning the town like three destroying angels. Do you think I am going to sit quiet under that reproach?

DR. STOCKMANN. Unfortunately, I am afraid you will have to.

MORTEN KIIL. No, thank you. I am jealous of my name and reputation. They call me "the Badger," I am told. A badger is a kind of pig, I believe; but I am not going to give them the right to call me that. I mean to live and die a clean man.

DR. STOCKMANN. And how are you going to set about it?

MORTEN KIIL. You shall cleanse me, Thomas.

DR. STOCKMANN. I!

MORTEN KIIL. Do you know what money I have bought these shares with? No, of course you can't know—but I will tell you. It is the money that Katherine and Petra and the boys will have when I am gone. Because I have been able to save a little bit after all, you know.

DR. STOCKMANN (*flaring up*). And you have gone and taken Katherine's money for *this!*

MORTEN KIIL. Yes, the whole of the money is invested in the Baths now. And now I just want to see whether you are quite stark, staring mad, Thomas! If you still make out that these animals and other nasty things of that sort come from my tannery, it will be exactly as if you were to flay broad strips of skin from Katherine's body, and Petra's, and the boys'; and no decent man would do that—unless he were mad.

DR. STOCKMANN (*walking up and down*). Yes, but I *am* mad; I *am* mad!

MORTEN KIIL. You cannot be so absurdly mad as all that, when it is a question of your wife and children.

DR. STOCKMANN (*standing still in front of him*). Why couldn't you consult me about it, before you went and bought all that trash?

MORTEN KIIL. What is done cannot be undone.

DR. STOCKMANN (*walks about uneasily*). If only I were not so certain about it—! But I am absolutely convinced that I am right.

MORTEN KIIL (*weighing the pocket-book in his hand*). If you stick to your mad idea, this won't be worth much, you know. (*Puts the pocket-book in his pocket.*)

DR. STOCKMANN. But, hang it all! it might be possible for science to discover some prophylactic, I should think—or some antidote of some kind—

MORTEN KIIL. To kill these animals, do you mean?

DR. STOCKMANN. Yes, or to make them innocuous.

MORTEN KIIL. Couldn't you try some rat's-bane?

DR. STOCKMANN. Don't talk nonsense! They all say it is only imagination, you know. Well, let it go at that! Let them have their own way about it! Haven't the ignorant, narrow-minded curs reviled me as an enemy of the people?—and haven't they been ready to tear the clothes off my back too?

MORTEN KIIL. And broken all your windows to pieces!

DR. STOCKMANN. And then there is my duty to my family. I must talk it over with Katherine; she is great on those things.

MORTEN KIIL. That is right; be guided by a reasonable woman's advice.

DR. STOCKMANN (*advancing towards him*). To think you could do such a preposterous thing! Risking Katherine's money in this way, and putting me in such a horribly painful dilemma! When I look at you, I think I see the devil himself—.

MORTEN KIIL. Then I had better go. But I must have an answer from you before two o'clock—yes or no. If it is no, the shares go to a charity, and that this very day.

DR. STOCKMANN. And what does Katherine get?

MORTEN KIIL. Not a halfpenny. (*The door leading to the hall opens, and* HOVSTAD *and* ASLAKSEN *make their apeparance.*) Look at those two!

DR. STOCKMANN (*staring at them*). What the devil!—have *you* actually the face to come into my house?

HOVSTAD. Certainly.

ASLAKSEN. We have something to say to you, you see.

MORTEN KIIL (*in a whisper*). Yes or no—before two o'clock.

ASLAKSEN (*glancing at* HOVSTAD). Aha!

(MORTEN KIIL *goes out.*)

DR. STOCKMANN. Well, what do you want with me? Be brief.

HOVSTAD. I can quite understand that you are annoyed with us for our attitude at the meeting yesterday—

DR. STOCKMANN. Attitude, do you call it? Yes, it was a charming attitude! I call it weak, womanish—damnably shameful!

HOVSTAD. Call it what you like, we could not do otherwise.

DR. STOCKMANN. You *dared* not do otherwise—isn't that it?

HOVSTAD. Well, if you like to put it that way.

ASLAKSEN. But why did you not let us have word of it beforehand?— just a hint to Mr. Hovstad or to me?

DR. STOCKMANN. A hint? Of what?

ASLAKSEN. Of what was behind it all.

DR. STOCKMANN. I don't understand you in the least.

ASLAKSEN (*with a confidential nod*). Oh, yes, you do, Dr. Stockmann.

HOVSTAD. It is no good making a mystery of it any longer.

DR. STOCKMANN (*looking first at one of them and then at the other*). What the devil do you both mean?

ASLAKSEN. May I ask if your father-in-law is not going round the town buying up all the shares in the Baths?

DR. STOCKMANN. Yes, he has been buying Baths' shares to-day; but—

ASLAKSEN. It would have been more prudent to get some one else to do it—some one less nearly related to you.

HOVSTAD. And you should not have let your name appear in the affair. There was no need for anyone to know that the attack on the Baths came from you. You ought to have consulted me, Dr. Stockmann.

DR. STOCKMANN (*looks in front of him; then a light seems to dawn on him and he says in amazement*). Are such things conceivable? Are such things possible?

ASLAKSEN (*with a smile*). Evidently they are. But it is better to use a little *finesse,* you know.

HOVSTAD. And it is much better to have several persons in a thing of that sort; because the responsibility of each individual is lessened, when there are others with him.

DR. STOCKMANN (*composedly*). Come to the point, gentlemen. What do you want?

ASLAKSEN. Perhaps Mr. Hovstad had better—

HOVSTAD. No, you tell him, Aslaksen.

ASLAKSEN. Well, the fact is that, now we know the bearings of the whole affair, we think we might venture to put the "People's Messenger" at your disposal.

DR. STOCKMANN. Do you dare do that now? What about public opinion? Are you not afraid of a storm breaking upon our heads?

HOVSTAD. We will try to weather it.

ASLAKSEN. And you must be ready to go off quickly on a new tack, Doctor. As soon as your invective has done its work—

DR. STOCKMANN. Do you mean, as soon as my father-in-law and I have got hold of the shares at a low figure?

HOVSTAD. Your reasons for wishing to get the control of the Baths are mainly scientific, I take it.

DR. STOCKMANN. Of course; it was for scientific reasons that I persuaded the old "Badger" to stand in with me in the matter. So we will tinker at the conduit-pipes a little, and dig up a little bit of the shore, and it shan't cost the town a sixpence. That will be all right—eh?

HOVSTAD. I think so—if you have the "People's Messenger" behind you.

ASLAKSEN. The Press is a power in a free community, Doctor.

DR. STOCKMANN. Quite so. And so is public opinion. And you, Mr. Aslaksen—I suppose you will be answerable for the Householders' Association?

ASLAKSEN. Yes, and for the Temperance Society. You may rely on that.

DR. STOCKMANN. But, gentlemen—I really am ashamed to ask the question—but, what return do you—?

HOVSTAD. We should prefer to help you without any return whatever, believe me. But the "People's Messenger" is in rather a shaky condition; it doesn't go really well; and I should be very unwilling to suspend the paper now, when there is so much work to do here in the political way.

DR. STOCKMANN. Quite so; that would be a great trial to such a friend of the people as you are. (*Flares up.*) But I am an enemy of the people, remember! (*Walks about the room.*) Where have I put my stick? Where the devil is my stick?

HOVSTAD. What's that?

ASLAKSEN. Surely you never mean—?

DR. STOCKMANN (*standing still*). And suppose I don't give you a single penny of all I get out of it? Money is not very easy to get out of us rich folk, please to remember!

HOVSTAD. And you please to remember that this affair of the shares can be represented in two ways!

DR. STOCKMANN. Yes, and you are just the man to do it. If I don't come to the rescue of the "People's Messenger," you will certainly take an evil view of the affair; you will hunt me down, I can well imagine—pursue me—try to throttle me as a dog does a hare.

HOVSTAD.   It is a natural law; every animal must fight for its own livelihood.

ASLAKSEN.   And get its food where it can, you know.

DR. STOCKMANN (*walking about the room*).   Then you go and look for yours in the gutter; because I am going to show you which is the strongest animal of us three! (*Finds an umbrella and brandishes it above his head.*) Ah, now—!

HOVSTAD.   You are surely not going to use violence!

ASLAKSEN.   Take care what you are doing with that umbrella.

DR. STOCKMANN.   Out of the window with you, Mr. Hovstad!

HOVSTAD (*edging to the door*).   Are you quite mad!

DR. STOCKMANN.   Out of the window, Mr. Aslaksen! Jump, I tell you! You will have to do it, sooner or later.

ASLAKSEN (*running round the writing-table*).   Moderation, Doctor—I am a delicate man—I can stand so little— (*Calls out.*) Help, help!

(MRS. STOCKMANN, PETRA *and* HORSTER *come in from the sitting-room.*)

MRS. STOCKMANN.   Good gracious, Thomas! What is happening?

DR. STOCKMANN (*brandishing the umbrella*).   Jump out, I tell you! Out into the gutter!

HOVSTAD.   An assault on an unoffending man! I call you to witness, Captain Horster. (*Hurries out through the hall.*)

ASLAKSEN (*irresolutely*).   If only I knew the way about here—. (*Steals out through the sitting-room.*)

MRS. STOCKMANN (*holding her husband back*).   Control yourself, Thomas!

DR. STOCKMANN (*throwing down the umbrella*).   Upon my soul, they have escaped after all.

MRS. STOCKMANN.   What did they want you to do?

DR. STOCKMANN.   I will tell you later on; I have something else to think about now. (*Goes to the table and writes something on a calling-card.*) Look there, Katherine; what is written there?

MRS. STOCKMANN.   Three big No's; what does that mean?

DR. STOCKMANN.   I will tell you that too, later on. (*Holds out the card to* PETRA.) There, Petra; tell sooty-face to run over to the "Badger's" with that, as quickly as she can. Hurry up!

(PETRA *takes the card and goes out to the hall.*)

DR. STOCKMANN.   Well, I think I have had a visit from every one of the devil's messengers to-day! But now I am going to sharpen my pen till they can feel its point; I shall dip it in venom and gall; I shall hurl my ink-pot at their heads!

MRS. STOCKMANN.   Yes, but we are going away, you know, Thomas.

(PETRA *comes back.*)

DR. STOCKMANN. Well?

PETRA. She has gone with it.

DR. STOCKMANN. Good.—Going away, did you say? No, I'll be hanged if we are going away! We are going to stay where we are, Katherine!

PETRA. Stay here?

MRS. STOCKMANN. Here, in the town?

DR. STOCKMANN. Yes, here. This is the field of battle—this is where the fight will be. This is where I shall triumph! As soon as I have had my trousers sewn up I shall go out and look for another house. We must have a roof over our heads for the winter.

HORSTER. That you shall have in my house.

DR. STOCKMANN. Can I?

HORSTER. Yes, quite well. I have plenty of room, and I am almost never at home.

MRS. STOCKMANN. How good of you, Captain Horster!

PETRA. Thank you!

DR. STOCKMANN (*grasping his hand*). Thank you, thank you! That is one trouble over! Now I can set to work in earnest at once. There is an endless amount of things to look through here, Katherine! Luckily I shall have all my time at my disposal; because I have been dismissed from the Baths, you know.

MRS. STOCKMANN (*with a sigh*). Oh, yes, I expected that.

DR. STOCKMANN. And they want to take my practice away from me, too. Let them! I have got the poor people to fall back upon, anyway—those that don't pay anything; and, after all, they need me most, too. But, by Jove, they will have to listen to me; I shall preach to them in season and out of season, as it says somewhere.

MRS. STOCKMANN. But, dear Thomas, I should have thought events had showed you what use it is to preach.

DR. STOCKMANN. You are really ridiculous, Katherine. Do you want me to let myself be beaten off the field by public opinion and the compact majority and all that devilry? No, thank you! And what I want to do is so simple and clear and straightforward. I only want to drum into the heads of these curs the fact that the liberals are the most insidious enemies of freedom—that party programmes strangle every young and vigorous truth—that considerations of expediency turn morality and justice upside down—and that they will end by making life here unbearable. Don't you think, Captain Horster, that I ought to be able to make people understand that?

HORSTER. Very likely; I don't know much about such things myself.

DR. STOCKMANN. Well, look here—I will explain! It is the party leaders that must be exterminated. A party leader is like a wolf, you see—like a voracious wolf. He requires a certain number of smaller victims to prey upon every year, if he is to live. Just look at Hovstad and Aslaksen! How many smaller victims have they not put an end to—or at any rate maimed and mangled until they are fit for nothing except to be householders or subscribers to the "People's Messenger"! (*Sits down on the edge of the table.*) Come here, Katherine—look how beautifully the sun shines to-day! And this lovely spring air I am drinking in!

Mrs. Stockmann. Yes, if only we could live on sunshine and spring air, Thomas.

Dr. Stockmann. Oh, you will have to pinch and save a bit—then we shall get along. That gives me very little concern. What is much worse is that I know of no one who is liberal-minded and high-minded enough to venture to take up my work after me.

Petra. Don't think about that, father; you have plenty of time before you.—Hullo, here are the boys already!

(Ejlif *and* Morten *come in from the sitting-room.*)

Mrs. Stockmann. Have you got a holiday?

Morten. No; but we were fighting with the other boys between lessons—

Ejlif. That isn't true; it was the other boys were fighting with us.

Morten. Well, and then Mr. Rörlund said we had better stay at home for a day or two.

Dr. Stockmann (*snapping his fingers and getting up from the table*). I have it! I have it, by Jove! You shall never set foot in the school again!

The Boys. No more school!

Mrs. Stockmann. But, Thomas—

Dr. Stockmann. Never, I say. I will educate you myself; that is to say, you shan't learn a blessed thing—

Morten. Hooray!

Dr. Stockmann. —but I will make liberal-minded and high-minded men of you. You must help me with that, Petra.

Petra. Yes, father, you may be sure I will.

Dr. Stockmann. And my school shall be in the room where they insulted me and called me an enemy of the people. But we are too few as we are; I must have at least twelve boys to begin with.

Mrs. Stockmann. You will certainly never get them in this town.

Dr. Stockmann. We shall. (*To the boys.*) Don't you know any street urchins—regular ragamuffins—?

Morten. Yes, father, I know lots!

Dr. Stockmann. That's capital! Bring me some specimens of them. I am going to experiment with curs, just for once; there may be some exceptional heads amongst them.

Morten. And what are we going to do, when you have made liberal-minded and high-minded men of us?

DR. STOCKMANN. Then you shall drive all the wolves out of the country, my boys!

(EJLIF *looks rather doubtful about it;* MORTEN *jumps about crying* "Hurrah!")

MRS. STOCKMANN. Let us hope it won't be the wolves that will drive you out of the country, Thomas.

DR. STOCKMANN. Are you out of your mind, Katherine? Drive me out! Now—when I am the strongest man in the town!

MRS. STOCKMANN. The strongest—now?

DR. STOCKMANN. Yes, and I will go so far as to say that now I am the strongest man in the whole world.

MORTEN. I say!

DR. STOCKMANN (*lowering his voice*). Hush! You mustn't say anything about it yet; but I have made a great discovery.

MRS. STOCKMANN. Another one?

DR. STOCKMANN. Yes. (*Gathers them round him, and says confidentially*) It is this, let me tell you—that the strongest man in the world is he who stands most alone.

MRS. STOCKMANN (*smiling and shaking her head*). Oh, Thomas, Thomas!

PETRA (*encouragingly, as she grasps her father's hands*). Father!

QUESTIONS

1. Dr. Stockmann and his brother are early established as character foils. In what different ways are they contrasted? How does each help to bring out the character of the other?

2. Is Dr. Stockmann's desire to publish the truth about the Baths purely altruistic? Why is he so happy to learn, in Act I, that the Baths are polluted? Is he in any respect like his brother?

3. How astute is Dr. Stockmann in foreseeing the consequences of his discovery? in judging the characters of other people? How would you characterize him as a political man? Trace the stages of his political education. What does he learn in Act II? in Act III? in Act IV? in Act V? To what degree does he change during the course of the play?

4. Morten Kiil says, in Act II, "It is better never to trust anybody; you may find you have been made a fool of before you know where you are." In what respects are Kiil and Dr. Stockmann character foils? Who is shrewder? Who is more admirable?

5. Which of the following adjectives can be accurately applied to Dr. Stockmann's impromptu speech in Act IV: *courageous, intemperate, arrogant, foolish, large-minded, wise?* Support your answer.

6. What purpose is served by the characterization of Dr. Stockmann, in Act I, as a man who likes good things—roast beef, hot toddy, good company?

7. How are we to take Dr. Stockmann's discovery at the end of the play: "the strongest man in the world is he who stands most alone." In terms of the play, is it true?

8. It has been said that "Politics makes strange bedfellows." In this play, what are the respective alignments and relationships between Dr. Stockmann, Peter Stockmann, Hovstad and Billing, and Aslaksen (a) after Dr. Stockmann announces his discovery, (b) at the end of the play? What interests are represented by each of these men?

9. In Act III, Dr. Stockmann asks his wife, "Because a man has a wife and children is he not allowed to tell the truth?" The question poses a real moral dilemma. What answer does Peter Stockmann make to it? What answer to it is implied by the play? Is Dr. Stockmann the only character put under pressure by threats against another member of his family?

10. Evaluate, in terms of the action of the play, Dr. Stockmann's assertion that "The most dangerous enemy to truth and freedom . . . is the compact majority." What other assertions does he make about majorities? Is this play antidemocratic in theme? Why or why not?

11. Hovstad expresses at least three attitudes toward the function of a newspaper: (a) that "truth should be the first consideration" (Act II), (b) that a newspaper should carry the public "on the path that leads to liberty and progress" (Act III), and (c) that "an editor's first and most obvious duty" is "to work in harmony with his readers" (Act IV). In what order does Hovstad honor these three principles? In what order does Ibsen, as judged by the action of the play, rank them?

12. Of Dr. Stockmann's principal antagonists—Peter Stockmann, Hovstad, Billing, Aslaksen, Morton Kiil—which is the most powerful? Which is the second most powerful? Which is most corrupt? What are the chief characterizing qualities of each?

13. Where do Mrs. Stockmann's loyalties lie? Does she change during the course of the play? Is she more, or less, far-sighted than her husband?

14. Mark each of the following statements made by characters in the play as true or false. If the statement is false, explain whether its falseness springs from misjudgment, lack of self-knowledge, or an out-and-out lie: (a) DR. STOCKMANN: "I shall smite them to the ground—I shall crush them—I shall break down all their defenses before the eyes of the honest public!" (Act III). (b) HOVSTAD: "I am not a weathercock—and never will be" (Act III). (c) BILLING (of his application for the post of secretary to the Bench): "You must clearly understand I am doing it only to annoy the bigwigs. . . . My object is precisely *not* to get it" (Act III). (d) HOVSTAD (of the idea that an editor is often obliged to bow to the wishes of the public in unimportant matters): "No; as a matter of fact, that is Billing's idea and not

DIMENSIONS OF DRAMA

IMAGINATIVE LITERATURE: SECOND EDITION

SHAPING COLLEGE WRITING: SECOND EDITION

AT THE REQUEST OF: Michael J. Jones

Jan. 25 - 1973   THE COLLEGE DEPARTMENT

mine. . . . And it is Billing who is so anxious to have that story in the paper" (Act III). (e) ASLAKSEN: "I have nothing to do with editing the paper, Mr. Mayor" (Act III). (f) PETER STOCKMANN: "The proprietors of the Baths are not in a position to incur any further expense" (Act III). (g) DR. STOCK-MANN (in reply to his wife's injunction "Be sure not to lose your temper, Thomas"): "Oh, I know how to control myself" (Act IV). (h) PETER STOCKMANN: "In my communication to the *People's Messenger* I have put the essential facts before the public in such a way that every fair-minded citizen can easily form his own opinion" (Act IV).

15. What advantage does Ibsen's realistic technique have for his particular subject matter? How does he make clear that a character is speaking differently from what he thinks or feels? Or does he always? What would the effect on the tone of the play have been, had Ibsen used asides?

Federico García Lorca

BLOOD WEDDING

CHARACTERS

THE MOTHER	LEONARDO
THE BRIDE	THE BRIDEGROOM
THE MOTHER-IN-LAW	THE BRIDE'S FATHER
LEONARDO'S WIFE	THE MOON
THE SERVANT WOMAN	DEATH (as a BEGGAR WOMAN)
THE NEIGHBOR WOMAN	WOODCUTTERS
YOUNG GIRLS	YOUNG MEN

ACT ONE

SCENE I

A room painted yellow.

BRIDEGROOM (*entering*). Mother.

MOTHER. What?

BRIDEGROOM. I'm going.

MOTHER. Where?

BRIDEGROOM. To the vineyard. (*He starts to go.*)

MOTHER. Wait.

BRIDEGROOM. You want something?

MOTHER. Your breakfast, son.

BRIDEGROOM. Forget it. I'll eat grapes. Give me the knife.

MOTHER. What for?

BRIDEGROOM (*laughing*). To cut the grapes with.

MOTHER (*muttering as she looks for the knife*). Knives, knives. Cursed be all knives, and the scoundrel who invented them.

BRIDEGROOM. Let's talk about something else.

BLOOD WEDDING Translated by James Graham-Lujan and Richard L. O'Connell. Copyright 1945 by James Graham-Lujan and Richard L. O'Connell. From *Three Tragedies* by Federico García Lorca. Copyright 1947, 1955 by New Directions Publishing Corporation. Reprinted by permission of New Directions Publishing Corporation. First performed in 1933.

MOTHER. And guns and pistols and the smallest little knife—and even hoes and pitchforks.

BRIDEGROOM. All right.

MOTHER. Everything that can slice a man's body. A handsome man, full of young life, who goes out to the vineyards or to his own olive groves—his own because he's inherited them . . .

BRIDEGROOM (*lowering his head*). Be quiet.

MOTHER. . . . and then that man doesn't come back. Or if he does come back it's only for someone to cover him over with a palm leaf or a plate of rock salt so he won't bloat. I don't know how you dare carry a knife on your body—or how I let this serpent (*she takes a knife from a kitchen chest*) stay in the chest.

BRIDEGROOM. Have you had your say?

MOTHER. If I lived to be a hundred I'd talk of nothing else. First your father; to me he smelled like a carnation and I had him for barely three years. Then your brother. Oh, is it right—how can it be—that a small thing like a knife or a pistol can finish off a man—a bull of a man? No, I'll never be quiet. The months pass and the hopelessness of it stings in my eyes and even to the roots of my hair.

BRIDEGROOM (*forcefully*). Let's quit this talk!

MOTHER. No. No. Let's not quit this talk. Can anyone bring me your father back? Or your brother? Then there's the jail. What do they mean, jail? They eat there, smoke there, play music there! My dead men choking with weeds, silent, turning to dust. Two men like two beautiful flowers. The killers in jail, carefree, looking at the mountains.

BRIDEGROOM. Do you want me to go kill them?

MOTHER. No . . . If I talk about it it's because . . . Oh, how can I help talking about it, seeing you go out that door? It's . . . I don't like you to carry a knife. It's just that . . . that I wish you wouldn't go out to the fields.

BRIDEGROOM (*laughing*). Oh, come now!

MOTHER. I'd like it if you were a woman. Then you wouldn't be going out to the arroyo now and we'd both of us embroider flounces and little woolly dogs.

BRIDEGROOM (*he puts his arm around his mother and laughs*). Mother, what if I should take you with me to the vineyards?

MOTHER. What would an old lady do in the vineyards? Were you going to put me down under the young vines?

BRIDEGROOM (*lifting her in his arms*). Old lady, old lady—you little old, little old lady!

MOTHER. Your father, he used to take me. That's the way with men of good stock; good blood. Your grandfather left a son on every corner. That's what I like. Men, men; wheat, wheat.

BRIDEGROOM. And I, Mother?

MOTHER. You, what?

BRIDEGROOM. Do I need to tell you again?

MOTHER (*seriously*). Oh!

BRIDEGROOM. Do you think it's bad?

MOTHER. No.

BRIDEGROOM. Well, then?

MOTHER. I don't really know. Like this, suddenly, it always surprises me. I know the girl is good. Isn't she? Well-behaved. Hard working. Kneads her bread, sews her skirts, but even so when I say her name I feel as though someone had hit me on the forehead with a rock.

BRIDEGROOM. Foolishness.

MOTHER. More than foolishness. I'll be left alone. Now only you are left me—I hate to see you go.

BRIDEGROOM. But you'll come with us.

MOTHER. No. I can't leave your father and brother here alone. I have to go to them every morning and if I go away it's possible one of the Félix family, one of the killers, might die—and they'd bury him next to ours. And that'll never happen! Oh, no! That'll never happen! Because I'd dig them out with my nails and, all by myself, crush them against the wall.

BRIDEGROOM (*sternly*). There you go again.

MOTHER. Forgive me. (*pause*) How long have you known her?

BRIDEGROOM. Three years. I've been able to buy the vineyard.

MOTHER. Three years. She used to have another sweetheart, didn't she?

BRIDEGROOM. I don't know. I don't think so. Girls have to look at what they'll marry.

MOTHER. Yes. I looked at nobody. I looked at your father, and when they killed him I looked at the wall in front of me. One woman with one man, and that's all.

BRIDEGROOM. You know my girl's good.

MOTHER. I don't doubt it. All the same, I'm sorry not to have known what her mother was like.

BRIDEGROOM. What difference does it make now?

MOTHER (*looking at him*). Son.

BRIDEGROOM. What is it?

MOTHER. That's true! You're right! When do you want me to ask for her?

BRIDEGROOM (*happily*). Does Sunday seem all right to you?

MOTHER (*seriously*). I'll take her the bronze earrings, they're very old —and you buy her . . .

BRIDEGROOM. You know more about that . . .

MOTHER. . . . you buy her some open-work stockings—and for you, two suits—three! I have no one but you now!

BRIDEGROOM. I'm going. Tomorrow I'll go see her.

MOTHER. Yes, yes—and see if you can make me happy with six grandchildren—or as many as you want, since your father didn't live to give them to me.

BRIDEGROOM. The first-born for you!

MOTHER. Yes, but have some girls. I want to embroider and make lace, and be at peace.

BRIDEGROOM. I'm sure you'll love my wife.

MOTHER. I'll love her. (*She starts to kiss him but changes her mind.*) Go on. You're too big now for kisses. Give them to your wife. (*Pause. To herself*) When she is your wife.

BRIDEGROOM. I'm going.

MOTHER. And that land around the little mill—work it over. You've not taken good care of it.

BRIDEGROOM. You're right. I will.

MOTHER. God keep you.

(*The son goes out. The* MOTHER *remains seated—her back to the door. A* NEIGHBOR WOMAN *with a 'kerchief on her head appears in the door.*)

Come in.

NEIGHBOR. How are you?

MOTHER. Just as you see me.

NEIGHBOR. I came down to the store and stopped in to see you. We live so far away!

MOTHER. It's twenty years since I've been up to the top of the street.

NEIGHBOR. You're looking well.

MOTHER. You think so?

NEIGHBOR. Things happen. Two days ago they brought in my neighbor's son with both arms sliced off by the machine. (*She sits down.*)

MOTHER. Rafael?

NEIGHBOR. Yes. And there you have him. Many times I've thought your son and mine are better off where they are—sleeping, resting—not running the risk of being left helpless.

MOTHER. Hush. That's all just something thought up—but no consolation.

NEIGHBOR (*sighing*). Ay!

MOTHER (*sighing*). Ay!

(*Pause.*)

NEIGHBOR (*sadly*). Where's your son?

MOTHER. He went out.

NEIGHBOR. He finally bought the vineyard!

MOTHER. He was lucky.

NEIGHBOR. Now he'll get married.

MOTHER (*as though reminded of something, she draws her chair near the* NEIGHBOR). Listen.

NEIGHBOR (*in a confidential manner*). Yes. What is it?

MOTHER. You know my son's sweetheart?

NEIGHBOR. A good girl!

MOTHER. Yes, but . . .

NEIGHBOR. But who knows her really well? There's nobody. She lives out there alone with her father—so far away—fifteen miles from the nearest house. But she's a good girl. Used to being alone.

MOTHER. And her mother?

NEIGHBOR. Her mother I *did* know. Beautiful. Her face glowed like a saint's—but I never liked her. She didn't love her husband.

MOTHER (*sternly*). Well, what a lot of things certain people know!

NEIGHBOR. I'm sorry. I didn't mean to offend—but it's true. Now, whether she was decent or not nobody said. That wasn't discussed. She was haughty.

MOTHER. There you go again!

NEIGHBOR. You asked me.

MOTHER. I wish no one knew anything about them—either the live one or the dead one—that they were like two thistles no one even names but cuts off at the right moment.

NEIGHBOR. You're right. Your son is worth a lot.

MOTHER. Yes—a lot. That's why I look after him. They told me the girl had a sweetheart some time ago.

NEIGHBOR. She was about fifteen. He's been married two years now—to a cousin of hers, as a matter of fact. But nobody remembers about their engagement.

MOTHER. How do you remember it?

NEIGHBOR. Oh, what questions you ask!

MOTHER. We like to know all about the things that hurt us. Who was the boy?

NEIGHBOR. Leonardo.

MOTHER. What Leonardo?

NEIGHBOR. Leonardo Félix.

MOTHER. Félix!

NEIGHBOR. Yes, but—how is Leonardo to blame for anything? He was eight years old when those things happened.

MOTHER. That's true. But I hear that name—Félix—and it's all the same. (*Muttering*) Félix, a slimy mouthful. (*She spits.*) It makes me spit—spit so I won't kill!

NEIGHBOR. Control yourself. What good will it do?

MOTHER. No good. But you see how it is.

NEIGHBOR. Don't get in the way of your son's happiness. Don't say anything to him. You're old. So am I. It's time for you and me to keep quiet.

MOTHER. I'll say nothing to him.

NEIGHBOR (*kissing her*). Nothing.

MOTHER (*calmly*). Such things . . . !

NEIGHBOR. I'm going. My men will soon be coming in from the fields.

MOTHER. Have you ever known such a hot sun?

NEIGHBOR. The children carrying water out to the reapers are black with it. Goodbye, woman.

MOTHER. Goodbye. (*The* MOTHER *starts toward the door at the left. Halfway there she stops and slowly crosses herself.*)

SCENE II

A room painted rose with copperware and wreaths of common flowers. In the center of the room is a table with a tablecloth. It is morning.

LEONARDO'S MOTHER-IN-LAW *sits in one corner holding a child in her arms and rocking it. His* WIFE *is in the other corner mending stockings.*

MOTHER-IN-LAW. Lullaby, my baby
once there was a big horse
who didn't like water.
The water was black there
under the branches.
When it reached the bridge
it stopped and it sang.
Who can say, my baby,
what the stream holds
with its long tail
in its green parlor?

WIFE (*softly*). Carnation, sleep and dream,
the horse won't drink from the stream.

MOTHER-IN-LAW. My rose, asleep now lie,
the horse is starting to cry.
His poor hooves were bleeding,
his long mane was frozen,
and deep in his eyes
stuck a silvery dagger.
Down he went to the river,
Oh, down he went down!
And his blood was running,
Oh, more than the water.

WIFE. Carnation, sleep and dream,
the horse won't drink from the stream.

MOTHER-IN-LAW. My rose, asleep now lie,
the horse is starting to cry.

WIFE. He never did touch

the dank river shore
though his muzzle was warm
and with silvery flies.
So, to the hard mountains
he could only whinny
just when the dead stream
covered his throat.
Ay-y-y, for the big horse
who didn't like water!
Ay-y-y, for the snow-wound
big horse of the dawn!

  MOTHER-IN-LAW. Don't come in! Stop him
and close up the window
with branches of dreams
and a dream of branches

  WIFE. My baby is sleeping.

  MOTHER-IN-LAW. My baby is quiet.

  WIFE. Look, horse, my baby
has him a pillow.

  MOTHER-IN-LAW. His cradle is metal.

  WIFE. His quilt a fine fabric.

  MOTHER-IN-LAW. Lullaby, my baby.

  WIFE. Ay-y-y, for the big horse
who didn't like water!

  MOTHER-IN-LAW. Don't come near, don't come in!
Go away to the mountains
and through the grey valleys,
that's where your mare is.

  WIFE (*looking at the baby*). My baby is sleeping.

  MOTHER-IN-LAW. My baby is resting.

  WIFE (*softly*). Carnation, sleep and dream,
The horse won't drink from the stream.

  MOTHER-IN-LAW (*getting up, very softly*). My rose, asleep now lie
for the horse is starting to cry.

  (*She carries the child out. LEONARDO enters.*)

  LEONARDO. Where's the baby?

  WIFE. He's sleeping.

  LEONARDO. Yesterday he wasn't well. He cried during the night.

  WIFE. Today he's like a dahlia. And you? Were you at the black-smith's?

  LEONARDO. I've just come from there. Would you believe it? For more than two months he's been putting new shoes on the horse and they're always coming off. As far as I can see he pulls them off on the stones.

WIFE. Couldn't it just be that you use him so much?

LEONARDO. No. I almost never use him.

WIFE. Yesterday the neighbors told me they'd seen you on the far side of the plains.

LEONARDO. Who said that?

WIFE. The women who gather capers. It certainly surprised me. Was it you?

LEONARDO. No. What would I be doing there, in that wasteland?

WIFE. That's what I said. But the horse was streaming sweat.

LEONARDO. Did you see him?

WIFE. No. Mother did.

LEONARDO. Is she with the baby?

WIFE. Yes. Do you want some lemonade?

LEONARDO. With good cold water.

WIFE. And then you didn't come to eat!

LEONARDO. I was with the wheat weighers. They always hold me up.

WIFE (*very tenderly, while she makes the lemonade*). Did they pay you a good price?

LEONARDO. Fair.

WIFE. I need a new dress and the baby a bonnet with ribbons.

LEONARDO (*getting up*). I'm going to take a look at him.

WIFE. Be careful. He's asleep.

MOTHER-IN-LAW (*coming in*). Well! Who's been racing the horse that way? He's down there, worn out, his eyes popping from their sockets as though he'd come from the ends of the earth.

LEONARDO (*acidly*). I have.

MOTHER-IN-LAW. Oh, excuse me! He's your horse.

WIFE (*timidly*). He was at the wheat buyers.

MOTHER-IN-LAW. He can burst for all of me!

(*She sits down. Pause.*)

WIFE. Your drink. Is it cold?

LEONARDO. Yes.

WIFE. Did you hear they're going to ask for my cousin?

LEONARDO. When?

WIFE. Tomorrow. The wedding will be within a month. I hope they're going to invite us.

LEONARDO (*gravely*). I don't know.

MOTHER-IN-LAW. His mother, I think, wasn't very happy about the match.

LEONARDO. Well, she may be right. She's a girl to be careful with.

WIFE. I don't like to have you thinking bad things about a good girl.

MOTHER-IN-LAW (*meaningfully*). If he does, it's because he knows her. Didn't you know he courted her for three years?

Leonardo. But I left her. (*To his* Wife.) Are you going to cry now? Quit that! (*He brusquely pulls her hands away from her face.*) Let's go see the baby.

(*They go in with their arms around each other. A* Girl *appears. She is happy. She enters running.*)

Girl. Señora.

Mother-in-Law. What is it?

Girl. The groom came to the store and he's bought the best of everything they had.

Mother-in-Law. Was he alone?

Girl. No. With his mother. Stern, tall. (*She imitates her.*) And such extravagance!

Mother-in-Law. They have money.

Girl. And they bought some open-work stockings! Oh, such stockings! A woman's dream of stockings! Look: a swallow here (*she points to her ankle*) a ship here (*she points to her calf*) and here (*she points to her thigh*) a rose!

Mother-in-Law. Child!

Girl. A rose with the seeds and the stem! Oh! All in silk.

Mother-in-Law. Two rich families are being brought together.

(Leonardo *and his* Wife *appear.*)

Girl. I came to tell you what they're buying.

Leonardo (*loudly*). We don't care.

Wife. Leave her alone.

Mother-in-Law. Leonardo, it's not that important.

Girl. Please excuse me. (*She leaves, weeping.*)

Mother-in-Law. Why do you always have to make trouble with people?

Leonardo. I didn't ask for your opinion. (*He sits down.*)

Mother-in-Law. Very well.

(*Pause.*)

Wife (*to* Leonardo). What's the matter with you? What idea've you got boiling there inside your head? Don't leave me like this, not knowing anything.

Leonardo. Stop that.

Wife. No. I want you to look at me and tell me.

Leonardo. Let me alone. (*He rises.*)

Wife. Where are you going, love?

Leonardo (*sharply*). Can't you shut up?

Mother-in-Law (*energetically, to her daughter*). Be quiet!

(Leonardo *goes out.*)

The baby! (*She goes into the bedroom and comes out again with the baby in her arms. The* WIFE *has remained standing, unmoving.*)

MOTHER-IN-LAW. His poor hooves were bleeding,
his long mane was frozen,
and deep in his eyes
stuck a silvery dagger.
Down he went to the river,
Oh, down he went down!
And his blood was running,
Oh, more than the water.

WIFE (*turning slowly, as though dreaming*). Carnation, sleep and dream,
the horse is drinking from the stream.

MOTHER-IN-LAW. My rose, asleep now lie
the horse is starting to cry.

WIFE. Lullaby, my baby.

MOTHER-IN-LAW. Ay-y-y, for the big horse
who didn't like water!

WIFE (*dramatically*). Don't come near, don't come in!
Go away to the mountains!
Ay-y-y, for the snow-wound,
big horse of the dawn!

MOTHER-IN-LAW (*weeping*). My baby is sleeping . . .

WIFE (*weeping, as she slowly moves closer*). My baby is resting . . .

MOTHER-IN-LAW. Carnation, sleep and dream,
the horse won't drink from the stream.

WIFE (*weeping, and leaning on the table*). My rose, asleep now lie,
the horse is starting to cry.

SCENE III

Interior of the cave where the BRIDE *lives. At the back is a cross of large rose colored flowers. The round doors have lace curtains with rose colored ties. Around the walls, which are of a white and hard material, are round fans, blue jars, and little mirrors.*

SERVANT. Come right in . . .

(*She is very affable, full of humble hypocrisy. The* BRIDEGROOM *and his* MOTHER *enter. The* MOTHER *is dressed in black satin and wears a lace mantilla; the* BRIDEGROOM *in black corduroy with a great golden chain.*)

Won't you sit down? They'll be right here.

(*She leaves. The* MOTHER *and son are left sitting motionless as statues. Long pause.*)

MOTHER. Did you wear the watch?

BRIDEGROOM. Yes. (*He takes it out and looks at it.*)

MOTHER. We have to be back on time. How far away these people live!

BRIDEGROOM. But this is good land.

MOTHER. Good; but much too lonesome. A four-hour trip and not one house, not one tree.

BRIDEGROOM. This is the wasteland.

MOTHER. Your father would have covered it with trees.

BRIDEGROOM. Without water?

MOTHER. He would have found some. In the three years we were married he planted ten cherry trees, (*remembering*) those three walnut trees by the mill, a whole vineyard and a plant called Jupiter which had scarlet flowers—but it dried up.

(*Pause.*)

BRIDEGROOM (*referring to the* BRIDE). She must be dressing.

(*The* BRIDE's FATHER *enters. He is very old, with shining white hair. His head is bowed. The* MOTHER *and the* BRIDEGROOM *rise. They shake hands in silence.*)

FATHER. Was it a long trip?

MOTHER. Four hours.

(*They sit down.*)

FATHER. You must have come the longest way.

MOTHER. I'm too old to come along the cliffs by the river.

BRIDEGROOM. She gets dizzy.

(*Pause.*)

FATHER. A good hemp harvest.

BRIDEGROOM. A really good one.

FATHER. When I was young this land didn't even grow hemp. We've had to punish it, even weep over it, to make it give us anything useful.

MOTHER. But now it does. Don't complain. I'm not here to ask you for anything.

FATHER (*smiling*). You're richer than I. Your vineyards are worth a fortune. Each young vine a silver coin. But—do you know?—what bothers me is that our lands are separated. I like to have everything together. One thorn I have in my heart, and that's the little orchard there, stuck in between my fields—and they won't sell it to me for all the gold in the world.

BRIDEGROOM. That's the way it always is.

FATHER. If we could just take twenty teams of oxen and move your vineyards over here, and put them down on the hillside, how happy I'd be!

MOTHER. But why?

FATHER. What's mine is hers and what's yours is his. That's why. Just to see it all together. How beautiful it is to bring things together!

BRIDEGROOM. And it would be less work.

MOTHER. When I die, you could sell ours and buy here, right alongside.

FATHER. Sell, sell? Bah! Buy, my friend, buy everything. If I had had sons I would have bought all this mountainside right up to the part with the stream. It's not good land, but strong arms can make it good, and since no people pass by, they don't steal your fruit and you can sleep in peace.

(*Pause.*)

MOTHER. You know what I'm here for.

FATHER. Yes.

MOTHER. And?

FATHER. It seems all right to me. They have talked it over.

MOTHER. My son has money and knows how to manage it.

FATHER. My daughter too.

MOTHER. My son is handsome. He's never known a woman. His good name cleaner than a sheet spread out in the sun.

FATHER. No need to tell you about my daughter. At three, when the morning star shines, she prepares the bread. She never talks: soft as wool, she embroiders all kinds of fancy work and she can cut a strong cord with her teeth.

MOTHER. God bless her house.

FATHER. May God bless it.

(*The* SERVANT *appears with two trays. One with drinks and the other with sweets.*)

MOTHER (*to the son*). When would you like the wedding?

BRIDEGROOM. Next Thursday.

FATHER. The day on which she'll be exactly twenty-two years old.

MOTHER. Twenty-two! My oldest son would be that age if he were alive. Warm and manly as he was, he'd be living now if men hadn't invented knives.

FATHER. One mustn't think about that.

MOTHER. Every minute. Always a hand on your breast.

FATHER. Thursday, then? Is that right?

BRIDEGROOM. That's right.

FATHER. You and I and the bridal couple will go in a carriage to the church which is very far from here; the wedding party on the carts and horses they'll bring with them.

MOTHER. Agreed.

(*The* SERVANT *passes through.*)

FATHER. Tell her she may come in now. (*To the* MOTHER) I shall be much pleased if you like her.

(*The* BRIDE *appears. Her hands fall in a modest pose and her head is bowed.*)

MOTHER. Come here. Are you happy?

BRIDE. Yes, señora.

FATHER. You shouldn't be so solemn. After all, she's going to be your mother.

BRIDE. I'm happy. I've said "yes" because I wanted to.

MOTHER. Naturally. (*She takes her by the chin.*) Look at me.

FATHER. She resembles my wife in every way.

MOTHER. Yes? What a beautiful glance! Do you know what it is to be married, child?

BRIDE (*seriously*). I do.

MOTHER. A man, some children and a wall two yards thick for everything else.

BRIDEGROOM. Is anything else needed?

MOTHER. No. Just that you all live—that's it! Live long!

BRIDE. I'll know how to keep my word.

MOTHER. Here are some gifts for you.

BRIDE. Thank you.

FATHER. Shall we have something?

MOTHER. Nothing for me. (*To the son*) But you?

BRIDEGROOM. Yes, thank you.

(*He takes one sweet, the* BRIDE *another.*)

FATHER (*to the* BRIDEGROOM). Wine?

MOTHER. He doesn't touch it.

FATHER. All the better.

(*Pause. All are standing.*)

BRIDEGROOM (*to the* BRIDE). I'll come tomorrow.

BRIDE. What time?

BRIDEGROOM. Five.

BRIDE. I'll be waiting for you.

BRIDEGROOM. When I leave your side I feel a great emptiness, and something like a knot in my throat.

BRIDE. When you are my husband you won't have it any more.

BRIDEGROOM. That's what I tell myself.

MOTHER. Come. The sun doesn't wait. (*To the* FATHER) Are we agreed on everything?

FATHER. Agreed.

MOTHER (*to the* SERVANT). Goodbye, woman.

SERVANT. God go with you!

(*The* MOTHER *kisses the* BRIDE *and they begin to leave in silence.*)

MOTHER (*at the door*). Goodbye, daughter.

(*The* BRIDE *answers with her hand.*)

FATHER. I'll go out with you.

(*They leave.*)

SERVANT. I'm bursting to see the presents.

BRIDE (*sharply*). Stop that!

SERVANT. Oh, child, show them to me.

BRIDE. I don't want to.

SERVANT. At least the stockings. They say they're all open work. Please!

BRIDE. I said no.

SERVANT. Well, my Lord. All right then. It looks as if you didn't want to get married.

BRIDE (*biting her hand in anger*). Ay-y-y!

SERVANT. Child, child! What's the matter with you? Are you sorry to give up your queen's life? Don't think of bitter things. Have you any reason to? None. Let's look at the presents. (*She takes the box.*)

BRIDE (*holding her by the wrists*). Let go.

SERVANT. Ay-y-y, girl!

BRIDE. Let go, I said.

SERVANT. You're stronger than a man.

BRIDE. Haven't I done a man's work? I wish I were.

SERVANT. Don't talk like that.

BRIDE. Quiet, I said. Let's talk about something else.

(*The light is fading from the stage. Long pause.*)

SERVANT. Did you hear a horse last night?

BRIDE. What time?

SERVANT. Three.

BRIDE. It might have been a stray horse—from the herd.

SERVANT. No. It carried a rider.

BRIDE. How do you know?

SERVANT. Because I saw him. He was standing by your window. It shocked me greatly.

BRIDE. Maybe it was my fiancé. Sometimes he comes by at that time.

SERVANT. No.

BRIDE. You saw him?

SERVANT. Yes.

BRIDE. Who was it?

SERVANT. It was Leonardo.

BRIDE (*strongly*). Liar! You liar! Why should he come here?

SERVANT. He came.

BRIDE. Shut up! Shut your cursed mouth.

(*The sound of a horse is heard.*)

SERVANT (*at the window*). Look. Lean out. Was it Leonardo.

BRIDE. It was!

ACT TWO

SCENE I

The entrance hall of the BRIDE's *house. A large door in the back. It is night. The* BRIDE *enters wearing ruffled white petticoats full of laces and embroidered bands, and a sleeveless white bodice. The* SERVANT *is dressed the same way.*

SERVANT. I'll finish combing your hair out here.

BRIDE. It's too warm to stay in there.

SERVANT. In this country it doesn't even cool off at dawn.

(*The* BRIDE *sits on a low chair and looks into a little hand mirror. The* SERVANT *combs her hair.*)

BRIDE. My mother came from a place with lots of trees—from a fertile country.

SERVANT. And she was so happy!

BRIDE. But she wasted away here.

SERVANT. Fate.

BRIDE. As we're all wasting away here. The very walls give off heat. Ay-y-y! Don't pull so hard.

SERVANT. I'm only trying to fix this wave better. I want it to fall over your forehead.

(*The* BRIDE *looks at herself in the mirror.*)

How beautiful you are! Ay-y-y! (*She kisses her passionately.*)

BRIDE (*seriously*). Keep right on combing.

SERVANT (*combing*). Oh, lucky you—going to put your arms around a man; and kiss him; and feel his weight.

BRIDE. Hush.

SERVANT. And the best part will be when you'll wake up and you'll feel him at your side and when he caresses your shoulders with his breath, like a little nightingale's feather.

BRIDE (*sternly*). Will you be quiet.

SERVANT. But, child! What *is* a wedding? A wedding is just that and nothing more. Is it the sweets—or the bouquets of flowers? No. It's a shining bed and a man and a woman.

BRIDE. But you shouldn't talk about it.

SERVANT. Oh, *that's* something else again. But fun enough too.

BRIDE. Or bitter enough.

SERVANT. I'm going to put the orange blossoms on from here to here, so the wreath will shine out on top of your hair. (*She tries on the sprigs of orange blossom.*)

BRIDE (*looking at herself in the mirror*). Give it to me. (*She takes the wreath, looks at it and lets her head fall in discouragement.*)

SERVANT. Now what's the matter?

BRIDE. Leave me alone.

SERVANT. This is no time for you to start feeling sad. (*Encouragingly*) Give me the wreath.

(*The* BRIDE *takes the wreath and hurls it away.*)

Child! You're just asking God to punish you, throwing the wreath on the floor like that. Raise your head! Don't you want to get married? Say it. You can still withdraw.

(*The* BRIDE *rises.*)

BRIDE. Storm clouds. A chill wind that cuts through my heart. Who hasn't felt it?

SERVANT. You love your sweetheart, don't you?

BRIDE. I love him.

SERVANT. Yes, yes. I'm sure you do.

BRIDE. But this is a very serious step.

SERVANT. You've got to take it.

BRIDE. I've already given my word.

SERVANT. I'll put on the wreath.

BRIDE (*she sits down*). Hurry. They should be arriving by now.

SERVANT. They've already been at least two hours on the way.

BRIDE. How far is it from here to the church?

SERVANT. Five leagues by the stream, but twice that by the road.

(*The* BRIDE *rises and the* SERVANT *grows excited as she looks at her.*)

SERVANT. Awake, O Bride, awaken,
On your wedding morning waken!
The world's rivers may all
Bear along your bridal Crown!

BRIDE (*smiling*). Come now.

SERVANT (*enthusiastically kissing her and dancing around her*). Awake,
with the fresh bouquet
of flowering laurel.
Awake,
by the trunk and branch
of the laurels!

(*The banging of the front door latch is heard.*)

BRIDE. Open the door! That must be the first guests.

(*She leaves. The* SERVANT *opens the door.*)

SERVANT (*in astonishment*). You!
LEONARDO. Yes, me. Good morning.
SERVANT. The first one!
LEONARDO. Wasn't I invited?
SERVANT. Yes.
LEONARDO. That's why I'm here.
SERVANT. Where's your wife?
LEONARDO. I came on my horse. She's coming by the road.
SERVANT. Didn't you meet anyone?
LEONARDO. I *passed* them on my horse.
SERVANT. You're going to kill that horse with so much racing.
LEONARDO. When he dies, he's dead!

(*Pause.*)

SERVANT. Sit down. Nobody's up yet.
LEONARDO. Where's the bride?
SERVANT. I'm just on my way to dress her.
LEONARDO. The bride! She ought to be happy!
SERVANT (*changing the subject*). How's the baby?
LEONARDO. What baby?
SERVANT. Your son.
LEONARDO (*remembering, as though in a dream*). Ah!
SERVANT. Are they bringing him?
LEONARDO. No.

(*Pause. Voices sing distantly.*)

VOICES. Awake, O Bride, awaken,
On your wedding morning waken!
LEONARDO. Awake, O Bride, awaken,
On your wedding morning waken!
SERVANT. It's the guests. They're still quite a way off.
LEONARDO. The bride's going to wear a big wreath, isn't she? But it
ought not to be so large. One a little smaller would look better on her. Has

the groom already brought her the orange blossom that must be worn on the breast?

BRIDE (*appearing, still in petticoats and wearing the wreath*). He brought it.

SERVANT (*sternly*). Don't come out like that.

BRIDE. What does it matter? (*Seriously*) Why do you ask if they brought the orange blossom? Do you have something in mind?

LEONARDO. Nothing. What would I have in mind? (*Drawing near her*) You, you know me; you know I don't. Tell me so. What have I ever meant to you? Open your memory, refresh it. But two oxen and an ugly little hut are almost nothing. That's the thorn.

BRIDE. What have you come here to do?

LEONARDO. To see your wedding.

BRIDE. Just as I saw yours!

LEONARDO. Tied up by you, done with your two hands. Oh, they can kill me but they can't spit on me. But even money, which shines so much, spits sometimes.

BRIDE. Liar!

LEONARDO. I don't want to talk. I'm hot-blooded and I don't want to shout so all these hills will hear me

BRIDE. My shouts would be louder.

SERVANT. You'll have to stop talking like this. (*To the* BRIDE) You don't have to talk about what's past. (*The* SERVANT *looks around uneasily at the doors.*)

BRIDE. She's right. I shouldn't even talk to you. But it offends me to the soul that you come here to watch me, and spy on my wedding, and ask about the orange blossom with something on your mind. Go and wait for your wife at the door.

LEONARDO. But, can't you and I even talk?

SERVANT (*with rage*). No! No, you can't talk.

LEONARDO. Ever since I got married I've been thinking night and day about whose fault it was, and every time I think about it, out comes a new fault to eat up the old one; but always there's a fault left!

BRIDE. A man with a horse knows a lot of things and can do a lot to ride roughshod over a girl stuck out in the desert. But I have my pride. And that's why I'm getting married. I'll lock myself in with my husband and then I'll have to love him above everyone else.

LEONARDO. Pride won't help you a bit. (*He draws near to her.*)

BRIDE. Don't come near me!

LEONARDO. To burn with desire and keep quiet about it is the greatest punishment we can bring on ourselves. What good was pride to me—and not seeing you, and letting you lie awake night after night? No good! It only served to bring the fire down on me! You think that time heals and walls hide things, but it isn't true, it isn't true! When things get that deep inside you there isn't anybody can change them.

BRIDE (*trembling*). I can't listen to you. I can't listen to your voice. It's as though I'd drunk a bottle of anise and fallen asleep wrapped in a quilt of roses. It pulls me along, and I know I'm drowning—but I go on down.

SERVANT (*seizing* LEONARDO *by the lapels*). You've got to go right now!

LEONARDO. This is the last time I'll ever talk to her. Don't you be afraid of anything.

BRIDE. And I know I'm crazy and I know my breast rots with longing; but here I am—calmed by hearing him, by just seeing him move his arms.

LEONARDO. I'd never be at peace if I didn't tell you these things. I got married. Now you get married.

SERVANT. But she *is* getting married!

(*Voices are heard singing, nearer.*)

VOICES. Awake, O Bride, awaken,
On your wedding morning waken!

BRIDE. Awake, O Bride, awaken, (*She goes out, running toward her room.*)

SERVANT. The people are here now. (*To* LEONARDO) Don't you come near her again.

LEONARDO. Don't worry. (*He goes out to the left. Day begins to break.*)

FIRST GIRL (*entering*). Awake, O Bride, awaken,
the morning you're to marry;
sing round and dance round;
balconies a wreath must carry.

VOICES. Bride, awaken!

SERVANT (*creating enthusiasm*). Awake,
with the green bouquet
of love in flower.
Awake,
by the trunk and the branch
of the laurels!

SECOND GIRL (*entering*). Awake,
with her long hair,
snowy sleeping gown,
patent leather boots with silver—
her forehead jasmines crown.

SERVANT. Oh, shepherdess,
the moon begins to shine!

FIRST GIRL. Oh, gallant,
leave your hat beneath the vine!

FIRST YOUNG MAN (*entering, holding his hat on high*). Bride, awaken,
for over the fields

the wedding draws nigh
with trays heaped with dahlias
and cakes piled high.

VOICES. Bride, awaken!

SECOND GIRL. The bride
has set her white wreath in place
and the groom
ties it on with a golden lace.

SERVANT. By the orange tree,
sleepless the bride will be.

THIRD GIRL (*entering*). By the citron vine,
gifts from the groom will shine.

(*Three* GUESTS *come in.*)

FIRST YOUTH. Dove, awaken!
In the dawn
shadowy bells are shaken.

GUEST. The bride, the white bride
today a maiden,
tomorrow a wife.

FIRST GIRL. Dark one, come down
trailing the train of your silken gown.

GUEST. Little dark one, come down,
cold morning wears a dewy crown.

FIRST GUEST. Awaken, wife, awake,
orange blossoms the breezes shake.

SERVANT. A tree I would embroider her
with garnet sashes wound,
And on each sash a cupid,
with "Long Live" all around.

VOICES. Bride, awaken.

FIRST YOUTH. The morning you're to marry!

GUEST. The morning you're to marry
how elegant you'll seem;
worthy, mountain flower,
of a captain's dream.

FATHER (*entering*) A captain's wife
the groom will marry.
He comes with his oxen the treasure to carry!

THIRD GIRL. The groom
is like a flower of gold.
When he walks,
blossoms at his feet unfold.

SERVANT. Oh, my lucky girl!

SECOND YOUTH. Bride, awaken.
SERVANT. Oh, my elegant girl!
FIRST GIRL. Through the windows
hear the wedding shout.
SECOND GIRL. Let the bride come out.
FIRST GIRL. Come out, come out!
SERVANT. Let the bells
ring and ring out clear!
FIRST YOUTH. For here she comes!
For now she's near!
SERVANT. Like a bull, the wedding
is arising here!

(*The* BRIDE *appears. She wears a black dress in the style of 1900, with a bustle and large train covered with pleated gauzes and heavy laces. Upon her hair, brushed in a wave over her forehead, she wears an orange blossom wreath. Guitars sound. The* GIRLS *kiss the* BRIDE.)

THIRD GIRL. What scent did you put on your hair?
BRIDE (*laughing*). None at all.
SECOND GIRL (*looking at her dress*). This cloth is what you can't get.
FIRST YOUTH. Here's the groom!
BRIDEGROOM. Salud!
FIRST GIRL (*putting a flower behind his ear*). The groom
is like a flower of gold.
SECOND GIRL. Quiet breezes
from his eyes unfold.

(*The* GROOM *goes to the* BRIDE.)

BRIDE. Why did you put on those shoes?
BRIDEGROOM. They're gayer than the black ones.
LEONARDO'S WIFE (*entering and kissing the* BRIDE). Salud!

(*They all speak excitedly.*)

LEONARDO (*entering as one who performs a duty*). The morning you're
to marry
We give you a wreath to wear.
LEONARDO'S WIFE. So the fields may be made happy
with the dew dropped from your hair!
MOTHER (*to the* FATHER). Are those people here, too?
FATHER. They're part of the family. Today is a day of forgiveness!
MOTHER. I'll put up with it, but I don't forgive.
BRIDEGROOM. With your wreath, it's a joy to look at you!
BRIDE. Let's go to the church quickly.
BRIDEGROOM. Are you in a hurry?

BRIDE. Yes. I want to be your wife right now so that I can be with you alone, not hearing any voice but yours.

BRIDEGROOM. That's what I want!

BRIDE. And not seeing any eyes but yours. And for you to hug me so hard, that even though my dead mother should call me, I wouldn't be able to draw away from you.

BRIDEGROOM. My arms are strong. I'll hug you for forty years without stopping.

BRIDE (*taking his arm, dramatically*). Forever!

FATHER. Quick now! Round up the teams and carts! The sun's already out.

MOTHER. And go along carefully! Let's hope nothing goes wrong.

(*The great door in the background opens.*)

SERVANT (*weeping*). As you set out from your house, oh, maiden white, remember you leave shining with a star's light.

FIRST GIRL. Clean of body, clean of clothes from her home to church she goes.

(*They start leaving.*)

SECOND GIRL. Now you leave your home for the church!

SERVANT. The wind sets flowers on the sands.

THIRD GIRL. Ah, the white maid!

SERVANT. Dark winds are the lace of her mantilla.

(*They leave. Guitars, castanets and tambourines are heard.* LEONARDO *and his* WIFE *are left alone.*)

WIFE. Let's go.

LEONARDO. Where?

WIFE. To the church. But not on your horse. You're coming with me.

LEONARDO. In the cart?

WIFE. Is there anything else?

LEONARDO. I'm not the kind of man to ride in a cart.

WIFE. Nor I the wife to go to a wedding without her husband. I can't stand any more of this!

LEONARDO. Neither can I!

WIFE. And why do you look at me that way? With a thorn in each eye.

LEONARDO. Let's go!

WIFE. I don't know what's happening. But I think, and I don't want to think. One thing I do know. I'm already cast off by you. But I have a son. And another coming. And so it goes. My mother's fate was the same. Well, I'm not moving from here.

(*Voices outside.*)

VOICES. As you set out from your home
and to the church go
remember you leave shining
with a star's glow.
WIFE (*weeping*). Remember you leave shining
with a star's glow!
I left my house like that too. They could have stuffed the whole countryside in my mouth. I was that trusting.
LEONARDO (*rising*). Let's go!
WIFE. But you with me!
LEONARDO. Yes. (*pause*) Start moving!

(*They leave.*)

VOICES. As you set out from your home
and to the church go,
remember you leave shining
with a star's glow.

SCENE II

The exterior of the BRIDE'S *Cave Home, in white gray and cold blue tones. Large cactus trees. Shadowy and silver tones. Panoramas of light tan tablelands, everything hard like a landscape in popular ceramics.*

SERVANT (*arranging glasses and trays on a table*). A-turning,
the wheel was a-turning
and the water was flowing,
for the wedding night comes.
May the branches part
and the moon be arrayed
at her white balcony rail.
(*In a loud voice*) Set out the tablecloths! (*In a pathetic voice*)
A-singing,
bride and groom were singing
and the water was flowing
for their wedding night comes.
Oh, rime-frost, flash!—
and almonds bitter
fill with honey!

(*In a loud voice*) Get the wine ready! (*In a poetic tone*)
Elegant girl,
most elegant in the world,
see the way the water is flowing,
for your wedding night comes.
Hold your skirts close in
under the bridegroom's wing
and never leave your house,
for the Bridegroom is a dove
with his breast a firebrand
and the fields wait for the whisper
of spurting blood.
A-turning
the wheel was a-turning
and the water was flowing
and your wedding night comes.
Oh, water, sparkle!

MOTHER (*entering*).   At last!

FATHER.   Are we the first ones?

SERVANT.   No. Leonardo and his wife arrived a while ago. They drove
like demons. His wife got here dead with fright. They made the trip as
though they'd come on horseback.

FATHER.   That one's looking for trouble. He's not of good blood.

MOTHER.   What blood would you expect him to have? His whole
family's blood. It comes down from his great grandfather, who started in
killing, and it goes on down through the whole evil breed of knife wielding
and false smiling men.

FATHER.   Let's leave it at that!

SERVANT.   But how can she leave it at that?

MOTHER.   It hurts me to the tips of my veins. On the forehead of all
of them I see only the hand with which they killed what was mine. Can
you really see me? Don't I seem mad to you? Well, it's the madness of not
having shrieked out all my breast needs to. Always in my breast there's a
shriek standing tiptoe that I have to beat down and hold in under my shawls.
But the dead are carried off and one has to keep still. And then, people find
fault. (*She removes her shawl.*)

FATHER.   Today's not the day for you to be remembering these things.

MOTHER.   When the talk turns on it, I have to speak. And more so today. Because today I'm left alone in my house.

FATHER.   But with the expectation of having someone with you.

MOTHER.   That's my hope: grandchildren.

(*They sit down.*)

FATHER.   I want them to have a lot of them. This land needs hands that aren't hired. There's a battle to be waged against weeds, the thistles, the big rocks that come from one doesn't know where. And those hands have to be the owner's, who chastises and dominates, who makes the seeds grow. Lots of sons are needed.

MOTHER. And some daughters! Men are like the wind! They're forced to handle weapons. Girls never go out into the street.

FATHER (*happily*). I think they'll have both.

MOTHER. My son will cover her well. He's of good seed. His father could have had many sons with me.

FATHER. What I'd like is to have all this happen in a day. So that right away they'd have two or three boys.

MOTHER. But it's not like that. It takes a long time. That's why it's so terrible to see one's own blood spilled out on the ground. A fountain that spurts for a minute, but costs us years. When I got to my son, he lay fallen in the middle of the street. I wet my hands with his blood and licked them with my tongue—because it was my blood. You don't know what that's like. In a glass and topaze shrine I'd put the earth moistened by his blood.

FATHER. Now you must hope. My daughter is wide-hipped and your son is strong.

MOTHER. That's why I'm hoping.

(*They rise.*)

FATHER. Get the wheat trays ready!

SERVANT. They're all ready.

LEONARDO's WIFE (*entering*). May it be for the best!

MOTHER. Thank you.

LEONARDO. Is there going to be a celebration?

FATHER. A small one. People can't stay long.

SERVANT. Here they are!

(GUESTS *begin entering in gay groups. The* BRIDE *and* BRIDEGROOM *come in arm-in-arm.* LEONARDO *leaves.*)

BRIDEGROOM. There's never been a wedding with so many people!

BRIDE (*sullen*). Never.

FATHER. It was brilliant.

MOTHER. Whole branches of families came.

BRIDEGROOM. People who never went out of the house.

MOTHER. Your father sowed well, and now you're reaping it.

BRIDEGROOM. There were cousins of mine whom I no longer knew.

MOTHER. All the people from the seacoast.

BRIDEGROOM (*happily*). They were frightened of the horses.

(*They talk.*)

MOTHER (*to the* BRIDE). What are you thinking about?

BRIDE. I'm not thinking about anything.

MOTHER. Your blessings weigh heavily.

(*Guitars are heard.*)

BRIDE. Like lead.

MOTHER (*stern*). But they shouldn't weigh so. Happy as a dove you ought to be.

BRIDE. Are you staying here tonight?

MOTHER. No. My house is empty.

BRIDE. You ought to stay!

FATHER (*to the* MOTHER). Look at the dance they're forming. Dances of the far away seashore.

(LEONARDO *enters and sits down. His* WIFE *stands rigidly behind him.*)

MOTHER. They're my husband's cousins. Stiff as stones at dancing.

FATHER. It makes me happy to watch them. What a change for this house! (*He leaves.*)

BRIDEGROOM (*to the* BRIDE). Did you like the orange blossom?

BRIDE (*looking at him fixedly*). Yes.

BRIDEGROOM. It's all of wax. It will last forever. I'd like you to have had them all over your dress.

BRIDE. No need of that.

(LEONARDO *goes off to the right.*)

FIRST GIRL. Let's go and and take out your pins.

BRIDE (*to the* BRIDEGROOM). I'll be right back.

LEONARDO'S WIFE. I hope you'll be happy with my cousin!

BRIDEGROOM. I'm sure I will.

LEONARDO'S WIFE. The two of you here; never going out; building a home. I wish I could live far away like this, too!

BRIDEGROOM. Why don't you buy land? The mountainside is cheap and children grow up better.

LEONARDO'S WIFE. We don't have any money. And at the rate we're going . . . !

BRIDEGROOM. Your husband is a good worker.

LEONARDO'S WIFE. Yes, but he likes to fly around too much; from one thing to another. He's not a patient man.

SERVANT. Aren't you having anything? I'm going to wrap up some wine cakes for your mother. She likes them so much.

BRIDEGROOM. Put up three dozen for her.

LEONARDO'S WIFE. No, no. A half-dozen's enough for her!

BRIDEGROOM. But today's a day!

LEONARDO'S WIFE (*to the* SERVANT). Where's Leonardo?

BRIDEGROOM. He must be with the guests.

LEONARDO'S WIFE.   I'm going to go sec. (*She leaves.*)
SERVANT (*looking off at the dance*).   That's beautiful there.
BRIDEGROOM.   Aren't you dancing?
SERVANT.   No one will ask me.

(*Two* GIRLS *pass across the back of the stage; during this whole scene the background should be an animated crossing of figures.*)

BRIDEGROOM (*happily*).   They just don't know anything. Lively old girls like you dance better than the young ones.
SERVANT.   Well! Are you tossing me a compliment, boy? What a family yours is! Men among men! As a little girl I saw your grandfather's wedding. What a figure! It seemed as if a mountain were getting married.
BRIDEGROOM.   I'm not as tall.
SERVANT.   But there's the same twinkle in your eye. Where's the girl?
BRIDEGROOM.   Taking off her wreath.
SERVANT.   Ah! Look. For midnight, since you won't be sleeping, I have prepared ham for you, and some large glasses of old wine. On the lower shelf of the cupboard. In case you need it.
BRIDEGROOM (*smiling*).   I won't be eating at midnight.
SERVANT (*slyly*).   If not you, maybe the bride. (*She leaves.*)
FIRST YOUTH (*entering*).   You've got to come have a drink with us!
BRIDEGROOM.   I'm waiting for the bride.
SECOND YOUTH.   You'll have her at dawn!
FIRST YOUTH.   That's when it's best!
SECOND YOUTH.   Just for a minute.
BRIDEGROOM.   Let's go.

(*They leave. Great excitement is heard. The* BRIDE *enters. From the opposite side two* GIRLS *come running to meet her.*)

FIRST GIRL.   To whom did you give the first pin; me or this one?
BRIDE.   I don't remember.
FIRST GIRL.   To me, you gave it to me here.
SECOND GIRL.   To me, in front of the altar.
BRIDE (*uneasily, with a great inner struggle*).   I don't know anything about it.
FIRST GIRL.   It's just that I wish you'd . . .
BRIDE (*interrupting*).   Nor do I care. I have a lot to think about.
SECOND GIRL.   Your pardon.

(LEONARDO *crosses at the rear of the stage.*)

BRIDE (*she sees* LEONARDO).   And this is an upsetting time.
FIRST GIRL.   We wouldn't know anything about that!
BRIDE.   You'll know about it when your time comes. This step is a very hard one to take.

FIRST GIRL. Has she offended you?

BRIDE. No. You must pardon me.

SECOND GIRL. What for? But *both* the pins are good for getting married, aren't they?

BRIDE. Both of them.

FIRST GIRL. Maybe now one will get married before the other.

BRIDE. Are you so eager?

SECOND GIRL (*shyly*). Yes.

BRIDE. Why?

FIRST GIRL. Well . . .

(*She embraces the* SECOND GIRL. *Both go running off. The* BRIDEGROOM *comes in very slowly and embraces the* BRIDE *from behind.*)

BRIDE (*in sudden fright*). Let go of me!

BRIDEGROOM. Are you frightened of me?

BRIDE. Ay-y-y! It's you?

BRIDEGROOM. Who else would it be? (*pause*) Your father or me.

BRIDE. That's true!

BRIDEGROOM. Of course, your father would have hugged you more gently.

BRIDE (*darkly*). Of course!

BRIDEGROOM (*embracing her strongly and a little bit brusquely*). Because he's old.

BRIDE (*curtly*). Let me go!

BRIDEGROOM. Why? (*He lets her go.*)

BRIDE. Well . . . the people. They can see us.

(*The* SERVANT *crosses at the back of the stage again without looking at the* BRIDE *and* BRIDEGROOM.)

BRIDEGROOM. What of it? It's consecrated now.

BRIDE. Yes, but let me be . . . Later.

BRIDEGROOM. What's the matter with you? You look frightened!

BRIDE. I'm all right. Don't go.

(LEONARDO'S WIFE *enters.*)

LEONARDO'S WIFE. I don't mean to intrude . . .

BRIDEGROOM. What is it?

LEONARDO'S WIFE. Did my husband come through here?

BRIDEGROOM. No.

LEONARDO'S WIFE. Because I can't find him, and his horse isn't in the stable either.

BRIDEGROOM (*happily*). He must be out racing it.

(*The* WIFE *leaves, troubled. The* SERVANT *enters.*)

SERVANT. Aren't you two proud and happy with so many good wishes?

BRIDEGROOM. I wish it were over with. The bride is a little tired.

SERVANT. That's no way to act, child.

BRIDE. It's as though I'd been struck on the head.

SERVANT. A bride from these mountains must be strong. (*To the* BRIDEGROOM) You're the only one who can cure her, because she's yours (*She goes running off.*)

BRIDEGROOM (*embracing the* BRIDE). Let's go dance a little. (*He kisses her.*)

BRIDE (*worried*). No. I'd like to stretch out on my bed a little.

BRIDEGROOM. I'll keep you company.

BRIDE. Never! With all these people here? What would they say? Let me be quiet for a moment.

BRIDEGROOM. Whatever you say! But don't be like that tonight!

BRIDE (*at the door*). I'll be better tonight.

BRIDEGROOM. That's what I want.

(*The* MOTHER *appears.*)

MOTHER. Son.

BRIDEGROOM. Where've you been?

MOTHER. Out there—in all that noise. Are you happy?

BRIDEGROOM. Yes.

MOTHER. Where's your wife?

BRIDEGROOM. Resting a little. It's a bad day for brides!

MOTHER. A bad day? The only good one. To me it was like coming into my own.

(*The* SERVANT *enters and goes toward the* BRIDE's *room.*)

Like the breaking of new ground; the planting of new trees.

BRIDEGROOM. Are you going to leave?

MOTHER. Yes. I ought to be at home.

BRIDEGROOM. Alone.

MOTHER. Not alone. For my head is full of things: of men, and fights.

BRIDEGROOM. But now the fights are no longer fights.

(*The* SERVANT *enters quickly; she disappears at the rear of the stage, running.*)

MOTHER. While you live, you have to fight.

BRIDEGROOM. I'll always obey you!

MOTHER. Try to be loving with your wife, and if you see she's acting foolish or touchy, caress her in a way that will hurt her a little: a strong hug, a bite and then a soft kiss. Not so she'll be angry, but just so she'll feel you're the man, the boss, the one who gives orders. I learned that from your father. And since you don't have him, I have to be the one to tell you about these strong defenses.

BRIDEGROOM. I'll always do as you say.

FATHER (*entering*). Where's my daughter?

BRIDEGROOM. She's inside.

(*The* FATHER *goes to look for her.*)

FIRST GIRL. Get the bride and groom! We're going to dance a round!

FIRST YOUTH (*to the* BRIDEGROOM). You're going to lead it.

FATHER (*entering*). She's not there.

BRIDEGROOM. No?

FATHER. She must have gone up to the railing.

BRIDEGROOM. I'll go see! (*He leaves. A hubbub of excitement and guitars is heard.*)

FIRST GIRL. They've started it already! (*She leaves.*)

BRIDEGROOM (*entering*). She isn't there.

MOTHER (*uneasily*). Isn't she?

FATHER. But where could she have gone?

SERVANT (*entering*). But where's the girl, where is she?

MOTHER (*seriously*). That we don't know.

(*The* BRIDEGROOM *leaves. Three* GUESTS *enter.*)

FATHER (*dramatically*). But, isn't she in the dance?

SERVANT. She's not in the dance.

FATHER (*with a start*). There are a lot of people. Go look!

SERVANT. I've already looked.

FATHER (*tragically*). Then where is she?

BRIDEGROOM (*entering*). Nowhere. Not anywhere.

MOTHER (*to the* FATHER). What does this mean? Where is your daughter?

(LEONARDO'S WIFE *enters.*)

LEONARDO'S WIFE. They've run away! They've run away! She and Leonardo. On the horse. With their arms around each other, they rode off like a shooting star!

FATHER. That's not true! Not my daughter!

MOTHER. Yes, your daughter! Spawn of a wicked mother, and he, he too. But now she's my son's wife!

BRIDEGROOM (*entering*). Let's go after them! Who has a horse?

MOTHER. Who has a horse? Right away! Who has a horse? I'll give him all I have—my eyes, my tongue even . . .

VOICE. Here's one.

MOTHER (*to the* SON). Go! After them! (*He leaves with two young men.*) No. Don't go. Those people kill quickly and well . . . but yes, run, and I'll follow!

FATHER. It couldn't be my daughter. Perhaps she's thrown herself in the well.

MOTHER. Decent women throw themselves in water; not that one! But now she's my son's wife. Two groups. There are two groups here. (*They all enter.*) My family and yours. Everyone set out from here. Shake the dust from your heels! We'll go help my son. (*The people separate into two groups.*) For he has his family: his cousins from the sea, and all who came from inland. Out of here! On all roads. The hour of blood has come again. Two groups! You with yours and I with mine. After them! After them!

ACT THREE

SCENE 1

A forest. It is nighttime. Great moist tree trunks. A dark atmosphere. Two violins are heard. Three WOODCUTTERS *enter.*

FIRST WOODCUTTER. And have they found them?

SECOND WOODCUTTER. No. But they're looking for them everywhere.

THIRD WOODCUTTER. They'll find them.

SECOND WOODCUTTER. Sh-h-h!

THIRD WOODCUTTER. What?

SECOND WOODCUTTER. They seem to be coming closer on all the roads at once.

FIRST WOODCUTTER. When the moon comes out they'll see them.

SECOND WOODCUTTER. They ought to let them go.

FIRST WOODCUTTER. The world is wide. Everybody can live in it.

THIRD WOODCUTTER. But they'll kill them.

SECOND WOODCUTTER. You have to follow your passion. They did right to run away.

FIRST WOODCUTTER. They were deceiving themselves but at the last blood was stronger.

THIRD WOODCUTTER. Blood!

FIRST WOODCUTTER. You have to follow the path of your blood.

SECOND WOODCUTTER. But blood that sees the light of day is drunk up by the earth.

FIRST WOODCUTTER. What of it? Better dead with the blood drained away than alive with it rotting.

THIRD WOODCUTTER. Hush!

FIRST WOODCUTTER. What? Do you hear something?

THIRD WOODCUTTER. I hear the crickets, the frogs, the night's ambush.

FIRST WOODCUTTER. But not the horse.

THIRD WOODCUTTER. No.

FIRST WOODCUTTER. By now he must be loving her.

SECOND WOODCUTTER. Her body for him; his body for her.

THIRD WOODCUTTER. They'll find them and they'll kill them.

FIRST WOODCUTTER. But by then they'll have mingled their bloods. They'll be like two empty jars, like two dry arroyos.

SECOND WOODCUTTER. There are many clouds and it would be easy for the moon not to come out.

THIRD WOODCUTTER. The bridegroom will find them with or without the moon. I saw him set out. Like a raging star. His face the color of ashes. He looked the fate of all his clan.

FIRST WOODCUTTER. His clan of dead men lying in the middle of the street.

SECOND WOODCUTTER. There you have it!

THIRD WOODCUTTER. You think they'll be able to break through the circle?

SECOND WOODCUTTER. It's hard to. There are knives and guns for ten leagues 'round.

THIRD WOODCUTTER. He's riding a good horse.

SECOND WOODCUTTER. But he's carrying a woman.

FIRST WOODCUTTER. We're close by now.

SECOND WOODCUTTER. A tree with forty branches. We'll soon cut it down.

THIRD WOODCUTTER. The moon's coming out now. Let's hurry.

(*From the left shines a brightness.*)

FIRST WOODCUTTER. O rising moon!
Moon among the great leaves.

SECOND WOODCUTTER. Cover the blood with jasmines!

FIRST WOODCUTTER. O lonely moon!
Moon among the great leaves.

SECOND WOODCUTTER. Silver on the bride's face.

THIRD WOODCUTTER. O evil moon!
Leave for their love a branch in shadow.

FIRST WOODCUTTER. O sorrowing moon!
Leave for their love a branch in shadow.

(*They go out. The* MOON *appears through the shining brightness at the left. The* MOON *is a young woodcutter with a white face. The stage takes on an intense blue radiance.*)

MOON. Round swan in the river
and a cathedral's eye,
false dawn on the leaves,
they'll not escape; these things am I!
Who is hiding? And who sobs

in the thornbrakes of the valley?
The moon sets a knife
abandoned in the air
which being a leaden threat
yearns to be blood's pain.
Let me in! I come freezing
down to walls and windows!
Open roofs, open breasts
where I may warm myself!
I'm cold! My ashes
of somnolent metals
seek the fire's crest
on mountains and streets.
But the snow carries me
upon its mottled back
and pools soak me
in their water, hard and cold.
But this night there will be
red blood for my cheeks,
and for the reeds that cluster
at the wide feet of the wind.
Let there be neither shadow nor bower,
and then they can't get away!
O let me enter a breast
where I may get warm!
A heart for me!
Warm! That will spurt
over the mountains of my chest;
let me come in, oh let me! (*To the branches*)
I want no shadows. My rays
must get in everywhere,
even among the dark trunks I want
the whisper of gleaming lights,
so that this night there will be
sweet blood for my cheeks,
and for the reeds that cluster
at the wide feet of the wind.
Who is hiding? Out, I say!
No! They will not get away!
I will light up the horse
with a fever bright as diamonds.

(*He disappears among the trunks, and the stage goes back to its dark lighting. An* OLD WOMAN *comes out completely covered by thin green cloth.*

She is barefooted. Her face can barely be seen among the folds. This character does not appear in the cast.)

BEGGAR WOMAN. That moon's going away, just when they's near.
They won't get past here. The river's whisper
and the whispering tree trunks will muffle
the torn flight of their shrieks.
It has to be here, and soon. I'm worn out.
The coffins are ready, and white sheets
wait on the floor of the bedroom
for heavy bodies with torn throats.
Let not one bird awake, let the breeze,
gathering their moans in her skirt,
fly with them over black tree tops
or bury them in soft mud. (*Impatiently!*)
Oh, that moon! That moon!

(*The* MOON *appears. The intense blue light returns.*)

MOON. They're coming. One band through the ravine and the other
along the river. I'm going to light up the boulders. What do you need?
BEGGAR WOMAN. Nothing.
MOON. The wind blows hard now, with a double edge.
BEGGAR WOMAN. Light up the waistcoat and open the buttons; the
knives will know the path after that.
MOON. But let them be a long time a-dying. So the blood
will slide its delicate hissing between my fingers.
Look how my ashen valleys already are waking
in longing for this fountain of shuddering gushes!
BEGGAR WOMAN. Let's not let them get past the arroyo. Silence!
MOON. There they come! (*He goes. The stage is left dark.*)
BEGGAR WOMAN. Quick! Lots of light! Do you hear me? They can't
get away!

(*The* BRIDEGROOM *and the* FIRST YOUTH *enter. The* BEGGAR WOMAN
sits down and covers herself with her cloak.)

BRIDEGROOM. This way.
FIRST YOUTH. You won't find them.
BRIDEGROOM (*angrily*). Yes, I'll find them.
FIRST YOUTH. I think they've taken another path.
BRIDEGROOM. No. Just a moment ago I felt the galloping.
FIRST YOUTH. It could have been another horse.
BRIDEGROOM (*intensely*). Listen to me. There's only one horse in the
whole world, and this one's it. Can't you understand that? If you're going
to follow me, follow me without talking.

FIRST YOUTH. It's only that I want to . . .

BRIDEGROOM. Be quiet. I'm sure of meeting them there. Do you see this arm? Well, it's not my arm. It's my brother's arm, and my father's, and that of all the dead ones in my family. And it has so much strength that it can pull this tree up by the roots, if it wants to. And let's move on, because here I feel the clenched teeth of all my people in me so that I can't breathe easily.

BEGGAR WOMAN (*whining*). Ay-y-y!

FIRST YOUTH. Did you hear that?

BRIDEGROOM. You go that way and then circle back.

FIRST YOUTH. This is a hunt.

BRIDEGROOM. A hunt. The greatest hunt there is.

(*The* YOUTH *goes off. The* BRIDEGROOM *goes rapidly to the left and stumbles over the* BEGGAR WOMAN, *Death*.)

BEGGAR WOMAN. Ay-y-y!

BRIDEGROOM. What do you want?

BEGGAR WOMAN. I'm cold.

BRIDEGROOM. Which way are you going?

BEGGAR WOMAN (*always whining like a beggar*). Over there, far away . . .

BRIDEGROOM. Where are you from?

BEGGAR WOMAN. Over there . . . very far away.

BRIDEGROOM. Have you seen a man and a woman running away on a horse?

BEGGAR WOMAN (*awakening*). Wait a minute . . . (*She looks at him*.) Handsome young man. (*She rises*.) But you'd be much handsomer sleeping.

BRIDEGROOM. Tell me; answer me. Did you see them?

BEGGAR WOMAN. Wait a minute . . . What broad shoulders! How would you like to be laid out on them and not have to walk on the soles of your feet which are so small?

BRIDEGROOM (*shaking her*). I asked you if you saw them! Have they passed through here?

BEGGAR WOMAN (*energetically*). No. They haven't passed; but they're coming from the hill. Don't you hear them?

BRIDEGROOM. No.

BEGGAR WOMAN. Do you know the road?

BRIDEGROOM. I'll go, whatever it's like!

BEGGAR WOMAN. I'll go along with you. I know this country.

BRIDEGROOM (*impatiently*). Well, let's go! Which way?

BEGGAR WOMAN (*dramatically*). This way!

(*They go rapidly out. Two violins, which represent the forest, are heard distantly. The* WOODCUTTERS *return. They have their axes on their shoulders. They move slowly among the tree trunks.*)

FIRST WOODCUTTER. O rising death!
Death among the great leaves.
SECOND WOODCUTTER. Don't open the gush of blood!
FIRST WOODCUTTER. O lonely death!
Death among the dried leaves.
THIRD WOODCUTTER. Don't lay flowers over the wedding!
SECOND WOODCUTTER. O sad death!
Leave for their love a green branch.
FIRST WOODCUTTER. O evil death!
Leave for their love a branch of green!

(*They go out while they are talking.* LEONARDO *and the* BRIDE *appear.*)

LEONARDO. Hush!
BRIDE. From here I'll go on alone.
You go now! I want you to turn back.
LEONARDO. Hush, I said!
BRIDE. With your teeth, with your hands, anyway you can,
take from my clean throat
the metal of this chain,
and let me live forgotten
back there in my house in the ground.
And if you don't want to kill me
as you would kill a tiny snake,
set in my hands, a bride's hands,
the barrel of your shotgun.
Oh, what lamenting, what fire,
sweeps upward through my head!
What glass splinters are stuck in my tongue!
LEONARDO. We've taken the step now; hush!
because they're close behind us,
and I must take you with me.
BRIDE. Then it must be by force!
LEONARDO. By force? Who was it first
went down the stairway?
BRIDE. I went down it.
LEONARDO. And who was it put
a new bridle on the horse?
BRIDE. I myself did it. It's true.
LEONARDO. And whose were the hands
strapped spurs to my boots?
BRIDE. The same hands, these that are yours,
but which when they see you would like
to break the blue branches
and sunder the purl of your veins.
I love you! I love you! But leave me!

FEDERICO GARCÍA LORCA 165

For if I were able to kill you
I'd wrap you 'round in a shroud
with the edges bordered in violets.
Oh, what lamenting, what fire,
sweeps upward through my head!
  LEONARDO. What glass splinters are stuck in my tongue!
Because I tried to forget you
and put a wall of stone
between your house and mine.
It's true. You remember?
And when I saw you in the distance
I threw sand in my eyes.
But I was riding a horse
and the horse went straight to your door.
And the silver pins of your wedding
turned my red blood black.
And in me our dream was choking
my flesh with its poisoned weeds.
Oh, it isn't my fault—
the fault is the earth's—
and this fragrance that you exhale
from your breasts and your braids.
  BRIDE. Oh, how untrue! I want
from you neither bed nor food,
yet there's not a minute each day
that I don't want to be with you,
because you drag me, and I come,
then you tell me to go back
and I follow you,
like chaff blown on the breeze.
I have left a good, honest man,
and all his people,
with the wedding feast half over
and wearing my bridal wreath.
But you are the one will be punished.
and that I don't want to happen.
Leave me alone now! You run away!
There is no one who will defend you.
  LEONARDO. The birds of early morning
are calling among the trees.
The night is dying
on the stone's ridge.
Let's go to a hidden corner
where I may love you forever,
for to me the people don't matter,

nor the venom they throw on us. (*He embraces her strongly.*)

BRIDE.   And I'll sleep at your feet,
to watch over your dreams.
Naked, looking over the fields,
as though I were a bitch.
Because that's what I am! Oh, I look at you
and your beauty sears me.

LEONARDO.   Fire is stirred by fire.
The same tiny flame
will kill two wheat heads together.
Let's go!

BRIDE.   Where are you taking me?

LEONARDO.   Where they cannot come,
these men who surround us.
Where I can look at you!

BRIDE (*sarcastically*).   Carry me with you from fair to fair,
a shame to clean women,
so that people will see me
with my wedding sheets
on the breeze like banners.

LEONARDO.   I, too, would want to leave you
if I thought as men should.
But wherever you go, I go.
You're the same. Take a step. Try.
Nails of moonlight have fused
my waist and your chains.

(*This whole scene is violent, full of great sensuality.*)

BRIDE.   Listen!

LEONARDO.   They're coming.

BRIDE.   Run!
It's fitting that I should die here,
with water over my feet,
with thorns upon my head.
And fitting the leaves should mourn me,
a woman lost and virgin.

LEONARDO.   Be quiet. Now they're appearing.

BRIDE.   Go now!

LEONARDO.   Quiet. Don't let them hear us.

(*The* BRIDE *hesitates.*)

BRIDE.   Both of us!

LEONARDO (*embracing her*).
                    Any way you want!
If they separate us, it will be

because I am dead.

BRIDE.   And I dead too.

(*They go out in each other's arms. The* MOON *appears very slowly. The stage takes on a strong blue light. The two violins are heard. Suddenly two long, ear-splitting shrieks are heard, and the music of the two violins is cut short. At the second shriek the* BEGGAR WOMAN *appears and stands with her back to the audience. She opens her cape and stands in the center of the stage like a great bird with immense wings. The* MOON *halts. The curtain comes down in absolute silence.*)

SCENE II

THE FINAL SCENE. *A white dwelling with arches and thick walls. To the right and left, are white stairs. At the back, a great arch and a wall of the same color. The floor also should be shining white. This simple dwelling should have the monumental feeling of a church. There should not be a single gray nor any shadow, not even what is necessary for perspective.*

Two GIRLS *dressed in dark blue are winding a red skein.*

FIRST GIRL.   Wool, red wool,
what would you make?
SECOND GIRL.   Oh, jasmine for dresses,
fine wool like glass.
At four o'clock born,
at ten o'clock dead.
A thread from this wool yarn,
a chain 'round your feet
a knot that will tighten
the bitter white wreath.
LITTLE GIRL (*singing*).   Were you at the wedding?
FIRST GIRL.   No.
LITTLE GIRL.   Well, neither was I!
What could have happened
'midst the shoots of the vineyards?
What could have happened
'neath the branch of the olive?
What really happened
that no one came back?
Were you at the wedding?
SECOND GIRL.   We told you once, no.
LITTLE GIRL (*leaving*).   Well, neither was I!
SECOND GIRL.   Wool, red wool,
what would you sing?
FIRST GIRL.   Their wounds turning waxen

balm-myrtle for pain.
Asleep in the morning,
and watching at night.
LITTLE GIRL (*in the doorway*).   And then, the thread stumbled
on the flinty stones,
but mountains, blue mountains,
are letting it pass.
Running, running, running,
and finally to come
to stick in a knife blade,
to take back the bread. (*She goes out.*)
SECOND GIRL. Wool, red wool,
what would you tell?
FIRST GIRL. The lover is silent,
crimson the groom,
at the still shoreline
I saw them laid out. (*She stops and looks at the skein.*)
LITTLE GIRL (*appearing in the doorway*).   Running, running, running,
the thread runs to here.
All covered with clay
I feel them draw near.
Bodies stretched stiffly
in ivory sheets!

(*The* WIFE *and* MOTHER-IN-LAW *of* LEONARDO *appear. They are anguished.*)

FIRST GIRL. Are they coming yet?
MOTHER-IN-LAW (*harshly*). We don't know.
SECOND GIRL. What can you tell us about the wedding?
FIRST GIRL. Yes, tell me.
MOTHER-IN-LAW (*curtly*). Nothing.
LEONARDO'S WIFE. I want to go back and find out all about it.
MOTHER-IN-LAW (*sternly*). You, back to your house.
Brave and alone in your house.
To grow old and to weep.
But behind closed doors.
Never again. Neither dead nor alive.
We'll nail up our windows
and let rains and nights
fall on the bitter weeds.
LEONARDO'S WIFE. What could have happened?
MOTHER-IN-LAW. It doesn't matter what.
Put a veil over your face.
Your children are yours,

that's all. On the bed
put a cross of ashes
where his pillow was. (*They go out.*)

BEGGAR WOMAN (*at the door*).   A crust of bread, little girls.

LITTLE GIRL.   Go away!

(*The* GIRLS *huddle close together.*)

BEGGAR WOMAN.   Why?

LITTLE GIRL.   Because you whine; go away!

FIRST GIRL.   Child!

BEGGAR WOMAN.   I might have asked for your eyes! A cloud
of birds is following me. Will you have one?

LITTLE GIRL.   I want to get away from here!

SECOND GIRL (*to the* BEGGAR WOMAN).   Don't mind her!

FIRST GIRL.   Did you come by the road through the arroyo?

BEGGAR WOMAN.   I came that way!

FIRST GIRL (*timidly*).   Can I ask you something?

BEGGAR WOMAN.   I saw them: they'll be here soon; two torrents
still at last, among the great boulders,
two men at the horse's feet.

FIRST GIRL.   Hush, old woman, hush!

BEGGAR WOMAN.   Crushed flowers for eyes, and their teeth
Two dead men in the night's splendor. (*With pleasure*) Dead, yes, dead.
two fistfuls of hard-frozen snow.
Both of them fell, and the Bride returns
with bloodstains on her skirt and hair.
And they come covered with two sheets
carried on the shoulders of two tall boys.
That's how it was; nothing more. What was fitting.
Over the golden flower, dirty sand.

(*She goes. The* GIRLS *bow their heads and start going out rhythmically.*)

FIRST GIRL.   Dirty sand.

SECOND GIRL.   Over the golden flower.

LITTLE GIRL.   Over the golden flower
they're bringing the dead from the arroyo.
Dark the one,
dark the other.
What shadowy nightingale flies and weeps
over the golden flower!

(*She goes. The stage is left empty. The* MOTHER *and a* NEIGHBOR *woman appear. The* NEIGHBOR *is weeping.*)

MOTHER.   Hush.

NEIGHBOR. I can't.

MOTHER. Hush, I said. (*At the door*) Is there nobody here? (*She puts her hands to her forehead.*) My son ought to answer me. But now my son is an armful of shrivelled flowers. My son is a fading voice beyond the mountains now. (*With rage, to the* NEIGHBOR) Will you shut up? I want no wailing in this house. Your tears are only tears from your eyes, but when I'm alone mine will come—from the soles of my feet, from my roots—burning more than blood.

NEIGHBOR. You come to my house; don't you stay here.

MOTHER. I want to be here. Here. In peace. They're all dead now: and at midnight I'll sleep, sleep without terror of guns or knives. Other mothers will go to their windows, lashed by rain, to watch for their sons' faces. But not I. And of my dreams I'll make a cold ivory dove that will carry camellias of white frost to the graveyard. But no; not graveyard, not graveyard: the couch of earth, the bed that shelters them and rocks them in the sky (*A woman dressed in black enters, goes toward the right, and there kneels. To the* NEIGHBOR) Take your hands from your face. We have terrible days ahead. I want to see no one. The earth and I. My grief and I. And these four walls. Ay-y-y! Ay-y-y! (*She sits down, overcome.*)

NEIGHBOR. Take pity on yourself!

MOTHER (*pushing back her hair*). I must be calm. (*She sits down.*) Because the neighbor women will come and I don't want them to see me so poor. So poor! A woman without even one son to hold to her lips.

(*The* BRIDE *appears. She is without her wreath and wears a black shawl.*)

NEIGHBOR (*with rage, seeing the* BRIDE). Where are you going?

BRIDE. I'm coming here.

MOTHER (*to the* NEIGHBOR). Who is it?

NEIGHBOR. Don't you recognize her?

MOTHER. That's why I asked who it was. Because I don't want to recognize her, so I won't sink my teeth in her throat. You snake! (*She moves wrathfully on the* BRIDE, *then stops. To the* NEIGHBOR) Look at her! There she is, and she's crying, while I stand here calmly and don't tear her eyes out. I don't understand myself. Can it be I didn't love my son? But, where's his good name? Where is it now? Where is it? (*She beats the* BRIDE, *who drops to the floor.*)

NEIGHBOR. For God's sake! (*She tries to separate them.*)

BRIDE (*to the* NEIGHBOR). Let her; I came here so she'd kill me and they'd take me away with them. (*To the* MOTHER) But not with her hands; with grappling hooks, with a sickle—and with force—until they break on my bones. Let her! I want her to know I'm clean, that I may be crazy, but that they can bury me without a single man ever having seen himself in the whiteness of my breasts.

MOTHER. Shut up, shut up; what do I care about that?

BRIDE. Because I ran away with the other one; I ran away! (*With anguish*) You would have gone, too. I was a woman burning with desire, full of sores inside and out, and your son was a little bit of water from which I hoped for children, land, health; but the other one was a dark river, choked with brush, that brought near me the undertone of its rushes and its whispered song. And I went along with your son who was like a little boy of cold water—and the other sent against me hundreds of birds who got in my way and left white frost on my wounds, my wounds of a poor withered woman, of a girl caressed by fire. I didn't want to; remember that! I didn't want to. Your son was my destiny and I have not betrayed him, but the other one's arm dragged me along like the pull of the sea, like the head toss of a mule, and he would have dragged me always, always, always—even if I were an old woman and all your son's sons held me by the hair!

(*A* NEIGHBOR *enters.*)

MOTHER. She is not to blame; nor am I! (*Sarcastically*) Who is, then? It's a delicate, lazy, sleepless woman who throws away an orange blossom wreath and goes looking for a piece of bed warmed by another woman!

BRIDE. Be still! Be still! Take your revenge on me; here I am! See how soft my throat is; it would be less work for you than cutting a dahlia in your garden. But never that! Clean, clean as a new-born little girl. And strong enough to prove it to you. Light the fire. Let's stick our hands in; you, for your son, I, for my body. *You'll* draw yours out first.

(*Another* NEIGHBOR *enters.*)

MOTHER. But what does your good name matter to me? What does your death matter to me? What does anything about anything matter to me? Bléssed be the wheat stalks, because my sons are under them; bléssed be the rain, because it wets the face of the dead. Bléssed be God, who stretches us out together to rest.

(*Another* NEIGHBOR *enters.*)

BRIDE. Let me weep with you.
MOTHER. Weep. But at the door.

(*The* GIRL *enters. The* BRIDE *stays at the door. The* MOTHER *is at the center of the stage.*)

LEONARDO'S WIFE (*entering and going to the left*). He was a beautiful horseman,
now he's a heap of snow.
He rode to fairs and mountains
and women's arms.
Now, the night's dark moss

crowns his forehead.

MOTHER.   A sunflower to your mother,
a mirror of the earth.
Let them put on your breast
the cross of bitter rosebay;
and over you a sheet
of shining silk;
between your quiet hands
let water form its lament.

WIFE.   Ay-y-y, four gallant boys
come with tired shoulders!

BRIDE.   Ay-y-y, four gallant boys
carry death on high!

MOTHER.   Neighbors.

LITTLE GIRL (*at the door*).   They're bringing them now.

MOTHER.   It's the same thing.
Always the cross, the cross.

WOMEN.   Sweet nails,
cross adored,
sweet name
of Christ our Lord.

BRIDE.   May the cross protect both the quick and the dead.

MOTHER.   Neighbors: with a knife,
with a little knife,
on their appointed day, between two and three,
these two men killed each other for love.
With a knife,
with a tiny knife
that barely fits the hand,
but that slides in clean
through the astonished flesh
and stops at the place
where trembles, enmeshed,
the dark root of a scream.

BRIDE.   And this is a knife,
a tiny knife
that barely fits the hand;
fish without scales, without river,
so that on their appointed day, between two and three,
with this knife,
two men are left stiff,
with their lips turning yellow.

MOTHER.   And it barely fits the hand
but it slides in clean

through the astonished flesh
and stops there, at the place
where trembles enmeshed
the dark root of a scream.

(*The* NEIGHBORS, *kneeling on the floor, sob.*)

QUESTIONS

1. Who is the protagonist of this tragedy—the mother? the bridegroom? Leonardo Félix? the bride? Why is only one of the characters given a name?

2. The external conflicts of the play are strong. In which characters are there also internal conflicts? What forces conflict in each? What are the two chief conflicting forces in the play? Does the play favor one force over the other?

3. Reconstruct the past history of Leonardo and the bride. Why did they not marry? Why did Leonardo marry someone else?

4. Reconstruct the past history of the bride's mother and father. Of what importance is this material to the play? Why is it included?

5. Explain the motivations in or attitudes toward the marriage of each of the following: the mother, the father, the servant, the bridegroom, the bride, Leonardo.

6. The setting of the play is a district in rural Spain. How much does the play reveal about the customs, mores, and culture of this society? What do you learn about its economy, family relationships, courtship and marriage customs, morality, and religious beliefs?

7. Where does the play place responsibility for the tragedy? What force or forces does the play assert to be dominant in human life? Could the tragedy have been averted?

8. The language of the play consists of prose dialogue, verse dialogue, and song. At what points is verse dialogue used? Why? What function is served by the songs? Are the three kinds of language sharply separated, or do they blend into each other? Compare the quality of the prose dialogue with that in Ibsen's play. What function does language serve in each play?

9. Contrast the directions in this play regarding settings with those in Ibsen's play. How do you explain the difference? What purpose do the settings serve in each play?

10. In Act II, Scene 2, the wedding celebration, there is a great deal of coming and going, entering and exiting, by all the characters. Does this serve a utilitarian or a poetic purpose? Explain. Contrast with the use of exits and entrances in Act III of Ibsen's play.

11. What function is served by the three woodcutters in Act III, Scene 1? In what scenes do other characters serve a similar purpose?

12. Does the personification of the moon in Act III come as a shock? Why or why not? What would have happened to Ibsen's play had a similar scene been introduced into it?

13. In the scene in the forest, García Lorca directs the use of two violins. For what effect? Would background music be appropriate for Ibsen's play?

14. Why is the beggar woman not listed in the cast of characters? Since she is identified as death only in a stage direction, which the audience would not see, how is her role made clear? Could an audience identify it?

15. What symbolic meanings are suggested by each of the following? (a) the lullaby about the big horse (Act I, Scene 2), (b) the fact that the bride lives in a cave house, (c) Leonardo's horse, (d) blood, (e) the moon, (f) the red skein (Act III, Scene 2).

CHAPTER THREE

Tragedy and Comedy

The two masks of drama—one with the corners of its mouth turned down, the other with the corners of its mouth turned up—are familiar everywhere. Derived from masks actually worn by the actors in ancient Greek plays, they symbolize the two principal modes of drama. Indeed, just as life gravitates between tears and laughter, they seem to imply that all drama is divided between tragedy and comedy.

But drama is an ancient literary form; in its development from the beginnings to the present it has produced a rich variety of plays. Can all these plays be classified under two terms? If our answer to this question is Yes, we must define the terms very broadly. If our answer is No, then how many terms do we need, and where do we stop? Polonius, in *Hamlet,* says of a visiting troupe of players that they can act either "tragedy, comedy, history, pastoral, pastoral-comical, historical-pastoral, tragical-historical, tragical-comical-historical-pastoral, scene individable, or poem unlimited." Like Polonius himself, his list seems ridiculous. Moreover, even if we adopted these terms, and more, could we be sure that they would accurately classify all plays or that a new play, written tomorrow, would not demand a totally new category?

The discussion that follows proceeds on four assumptions. First, perfect definitions and an airtight system of classification are impossible. There exist no views of tragedy and comedy that have not been challenged and no classification system that unequivocally provides for all examples. Second, it is quite unnecessary that we classify each play we read or see. The most important questions to ask about a play are not "Is this a tragedy?" or "Is this a comedy?" but "Does this play furnish an enjoyable, valid, and significant experience?" Third, the quality of experience furnished by a play, however, may be partially dependent on our perception of its relationship to earlier literary forms, and therefore familiarity with traditional notions of tragedy and comedy is important for our understanding and appreciation of plays. Many of the conventions used in specific plays have been determined by the kind of play the author felt himself to be writing. Other plays have been written in deliberate defiance of these conventions. Fourth, whether or not tragedy and comedy be taken as the two all-inclusive dramatic modes, they are certainly, as symbolized by the masks, the two principal ones, and useful points, therefore, from which to begin discussion.

The popular distinctions between comedy and tragedy are fairly simple: comedy is funny; tragedy is sad. Comedy has a happy ending, tragedy an unhappy one. The typical ending for comedy is a marriage; the typical ending for tragedy is a death. There is some truth in these notions, but only some. Some plays called comedies make no attempt to be funny. Successful tragedies, though they involve suffering and sadness, do not leave the spectator depressed. Some funny plays have sad endings: they send the viewer away with a lump in the throat. A few plays usually classified as tragedies do not have unhappy endings but conclude with the protagonist's triumph. In short, the popular distinctions are unreliable. Though we need not entirely abandon them, we must take a more complex view. Let us begin with tragedy.

The first great theorist of dramatic art was Aristotle, whose discussion of tragedy in *Poetics* has dominated critical thought ever since. A very brief summary of Aristotle's view will be helpful.

A tragedy, so Aristotle wrote, is the imitation in dramatic form of an action that is serious and complete, with incidents arousing pity and fear wherewith it effects a catharsis of such emotions. The language used is pleasurable and throughout is appropriate to the situation in which it is used. The chief characters are noble personages ("better than ourselves," says Aristotle), and the actions they perform are noble actions. The plot involves a change in the protagonist's fortune, in which he falls from happiness to misery. The protagonist is not a perfectly good man nor yet a bad man; his misfortune is brought upon him not by vice and depravity but by some error of judgment. A good tragic plot has organic unity: the events follow not just *after* one another but *because* of one another. The best tragic plots involve a reversal (a change from one state of things within the play to its opposite) or a discovery (a change from ignorance to knowledge) or both.

In the account that follows, we will not attempt to delineate the boundaries of tragedy nor necessarily to describe it at its greatest. Instead, we will describe a common understanding of tragedy as a point of departure for further discussion. Nor shall we enter into the endless controversies over what Aristotle meant by "catharsis" or over which of his statements are meant to apply to all tragedies and which only to the best ones. The important thing is that Aristotle had important insights into the nature of some of the greatest tragedies and that, rightly or wrongly interpreted, his conceptions are the basis for a kind of archetypal notion of tragedy that has dominated critical thought. What are the central features of that archetype?

1. The tragic hero is a man of noble stature. He has a greatness about him. He is not an ordinary man but one of outstanding quality. In Greek and in Shakespearean tragedy, he is usually a prince or a king. We may, if we wish, set down this predilection of former times for kings as tragic heroes as an undemocratic prejudice that regarded some men to be of nobler "blood" than others—pre-eminent by virtue of their aristocratic birth. But it is only partially that. We may with equal validity regard the hero's kingship as the symbol rather than as the cause of his greatness. He is great not primarily by virtue of his kingship but by his possession of extraordinary powers, by qualities of passion or aspiration or nobility of mind. The tragic hero's kingship is also a symbol of his initial good fortune, the mark of his high position. If the hero's fall is to arouse in us the emotions of pity and fear, it must be a fall from a height.

2. Though the tragic hero is pre-eminently great, he is not perfect. Combined with his strength, there is usually a weakness. Aristotle says that his fall is caused by "some error of judgment," and probably he meant no more than that. Critical tradition, however, has most frequently interpreted this error of judgment as a flaw in character—the so-called tragic flaw. With all his great qualities, the tragic hero is usually afflicted with some fault of character such as inordinate ambition, quickness to anger, a tendency to jealousy, or overweening pride. This flaw in his character leads to his downfall.

3. The hero's downfall, therefore, is partially his own fault, the result of his own free choice, not the result of pure accident or villainy or some overriding malignant fate. Accident, villainy, or fate may contribute to the downfall but only as cooperating agents: they are not alone responsible. The combination of the hero's greatness and his responsibility for his own downfall is what entitles us to describe his down-

fall as tragic rather than as merely pathetic. In common speech these two adjectives are often confused. If a father of ten children is accidentally killed at a street corner, the event, strictly speaking, is pathetic, not tragic. When a weak man succumbs to his weakness and comes to a bad end, the event should be called pathetic, not tragic. The tragic event involves a fall from greatness, brought about, at least partially, by the agent's free action.

4. Nevertheless, the hero's misfortune is not wholly deserved. The punishment exceeds the crime. We do not come away from tragedy with the feeling that "He got what he had coming to him" but rather with the sad sense of a waste of human potential. For what most impresses us about the tragic hero is not his weakness but his greatness. He is, in a sense, "larger than life," or, as Aristotle said, "better than ourselves." He reveals to us the dimensions of human possibility. He is a person mainly admirable, and his fall therefore fills us with pity and fear.

5. Yet the tragic fall is not pure loss. Though it may result in the protagonist's death, it involves, before his death, some increase in awareness, some gain in self-knowledge—as Aristotle puts it, some "discovery" —a change from ignorance to knowledge. On the level of plot, the discovery may be merely learning the truth about some fact or situation of which the protagonist was ignorant, but on the level of character it is accompanied or followed by a significant insight, a fuller self-knowledge, an increase not only in knowledge but in wisdom. Not unusually this increase in wisdom involves some sort of reconciliation with the universe or with the protagonist's situation. He exits not cursing his fate but accepting it and acknowledging that it is to some degree just.

6. Though it arouses solemn emotions—pity and fear, says Aristotle, but compassion and awe might be better terms—tragedy, when well performed, does not leave its audience in a state of depression. Though we cannot be sure what Aristotle meant by his term catharsis, some sort of emotional release at the end is a common experience of those who witness great tragedies on the stage. They have been greatly moved by pity, fear, and associated emotions, but they are not left emotionally beaten down or dejected. Instead, there may be a feeling almost of exhilaration. This feeling is a response to the tragic action. With the fall of the hero and his gain in wisdom or self-knowledge, there is, besides the appalling sense of human waste, a fresh recognition of human greatness, a sense that human life has unrealized potentialities. Though the hero may be defeated, he at least has dared greatly, and he gains understanding from his defeat.

Is the comic mask laughing or smiling? The question is more important than may at first appear, for usually we laugh *at* someone but smile *with* someone. The laugh expresses recognition of some absurdity in human behavior; the smile expresses pleasure in someone's company or good fortune.

The comic mask may be interpreted both ways. Comedy, Northrop Frye has said, lies between satire and romance. Historically, there have been two chief kinds of comedy—scornful comedy and romantic comedy, laughing comedy and smiling comedy. Of the two, scornful or satiric comedy is the oldest and probably still the most dominant.

The most essential difference between tragedy and comedy, particularly scornful comedy, is in their depiction of human nature. Where tragedy emphasizes human greatness, comedy delineates human weakness. Where tragedy celebrates human freedom, comedy points up human limitation. Wherever men fail to measure up to their own resolutions or to their own self-conceptions, wherever they are guilty of hypocrisy, vanity, or folly, wherever they fly in the face of good sense and rational behavior, comedy exhibits their absurdity and invites us to laugh at them. Where tragedy tends to say, with Shakespeare's Hamlet, "What a piece of work is man! how noble in reason! how infinite in faculty! in form and moving how express and admirable! in action how like an angel! in apprehension how like a god!" comedy says, with Shakespeare's Puck, "Lord, what fools these mortals be!"

Because comedy exposes human folly, its function is partly critical and corrective. Where tragedy challenges us with a vision of human possibility, comedy reveals to us a spectacle of human ridiculousness that it makes us want to avoid. No doubt, we should not exaggerate this function of comedy. We go to the theater primarily for enjoyment, not to receive lessons in personality or character development. Nevertheless, laughter may be educative at the same time that it is enjoyable. The comedies of Aristophanes and Molière, of Ben Jonson and Congreve, are, first of all, good fun, but, secondly, they are antidotes for human folly.

Romantic or smiling comedy, as opposed to scornful comedy, and as exemplified by many plays of Shakespeare—*As You Like It, Twelfth Night, The Merchant of Venice, The Tempest,* for instance—puts its emphasis upon sympathetic rather than ridiculous characters. These characters—likeable, not given up to folly or vanity—are placed in various kinds of difficulties from which, at the end of the play, they are rescued, attaining their ends or having their good fortunes restored. Though

different from the protagonists of scornful comedy, however, these characters are not the commanding or lofty figures that tragic heroes are.
They are sensible and good rather than noble, aspiring, and grand. They
do not strike us with awe as the tragic hero does. They do not so chal-
lengingly test the limits of human possibility. In short, they move in a
smaller world. Romantic comedies, therefore, do not occupy a different
universe from satiric comedies; they simply lie at opposite sides of the
same territory. The romantic comedy, moreover, though its protagonists
are sympathetic, has usually a number of lesser characters whose folly
is held up to ridicule. The satiric comedy, on the other hand, frequently
has minor characters—often a pair of young lovers—who are sympathetic
and likeable. The difference between the two kinds of comedy may be
only a matter of whether we laugh at the primary or at the secondary
characters.

There are other differences between comedy and tragedy. The norms
of comedy are primarily social. Where tragedy tends to isolate the tragic
hero and emphasize his uniqueness, comedy puts its protagonists always
in the midst of a group and emphasizes their commonness. Where the
tragic hero possesses an overpowering individuality, so that his play is
often named after him (for example, *Oedipus Rex, Othello*), the comic
protagonist tends to be a type, and his play is often named for the type
(for example, *The Misanthrope, The Brute*). We judge the tragic hero
by absolute moral standards, by how far he soars above society. We judge
the comic protagonist by social standards, by how well he adjusts to
society and conforms to the expectations of the group.

Finally, comic plots are less likely than tragic plots to exhibit the
high degree of organic unity—of logical cause-and-effect progression—
that Aristotle required of tragedy. Plausibility, in fact, is not usually the
central characteristic of a comic plot. Unlikely coincidences, improbable
disguises, mistaken identities—these are the stuff of which comedy is
made; and, as long as they make us laugh and, at at the same time,
help to illuminate human nature and human folly, we need not greatly
care. Not that plausibility is no longer important—only that other things
are more important, and these other things are often achieved by the
most outrageous violations of probability.

Particularly is this true as regards the comic ending. Conventionally,
comedies have a happy ending, but the emphasis here is on *conventionally*. The happy ending is, indeed, a *convention* of comedy, which is to
say that a comedy ends happily because comedies end happily—that is
the nature of the form—not necessarily because a happy ending is a

plausible outcome of the events that have preceded. The greatest masters of comedy—Aristophanes, Shakespeare, Molière—have often been extremely arbitrary in the manner in which they achieved their endings. The accidental discovery of a lost will, rescue by an act of divine intervention (*deus ex machina*), the sudden reform of a mean-spirited person into a friendly person—such devices have been used by the greatest comic writers. And, even where the ending is achieved more plausibly, comedy asks us to forget for the time being that in actuality life has no endings, except for death. Marriage, which provides the ending for so many comedies, is really a beginning. The marriage agreement at the end of Chekhov's play *The Brute* delights us because the reversal from the beginning has been so complete. We need not mar our delight by asking how long a marriage between such opposite and obstinate temperaments is likely to be happy.

And now, though we do not wish to imitate the folly of Polonius, it is well that we learn two additional terms: melodrama and farce. In the two-part classification suggested by the two symbolic masks, melodrama belongs with tragedy and farce with comedy, but the differences are sufficient to make the two new terms useful.

Melodrama, like tragedy, attempts to arouse feelings of fear and pity, but it does so ordinarily through cruder means. The conflict is an over-simplified one between good and evil depicted in terms of black and white. Plot is emphasized at the expense of characterization. Sensational incidents provide the staple of the plot. The young mother and her baby are evicted into a howling storm by the villain holding the mortgage. The heroine is tied to the railroad tracks as the express train approaches. Most important, good finally triumphs over evil, and the ending is happy. Typically, at the end, the hero marries the heroine; villainy is foiled or crushed. Melodrama may, of course, have different degrees of power and subtlety; it is not always as crude as its crudest examples. But, in it, moral issues are typically over-simplified, and good is finally triumphant. Melodrama does not provide the complex insights of tragedy. It is typically escapist rather than interpretive.

Farce, more consistently than comedy, is aimed at arousing explosive laughter. But again the means are cruder. The conflicts are violent and usually at the physical level. Plot is emphasized at the expense of characterization, improbable situations and coincidence at the expense of articulated plot. Absurdity replaces plausibility. Coarse wit, practical jokes, and physical action are staples. Characters trip over benches, insult each other, run into walls, knock each other down, get into brawls. Performed with gusto, farce may be hilariously funny. Psychologically, it may boost our spirits and purge us of hostility and aggression. In content, however, like melodrama, it is escapist rather than interpretive.

Now we have four classifications—tragedy, comedy, melodrama, farce—the latter two as appendages of the former. But none of these classifications is rigid. They blend into each other and are incapable of exact definition. If we take them over-seriously, the tragic mask may laugh, and the comic mask weep.

TOPICS FOR DISCUSSION

1. *An Enemy of the People* has been referred to, by at least one critic, as "a satiric comedy." Is this an accurate description? How does the play differ from comedy as popularly conceived? Does it have a happy ending? Is Dr. Stockmann the kind of hero you would most expect to find in satiric comedy, romantic comedy, or tragedy? Why?

2. How does *Blood Wedding* differ from an Aristotelian tragedy?

3. *Everyman* is often referred to as a tragedy. In what respects does it resemble the classical conception of tragedy? (See page 177). In what respects does it differ?

Sophocles

OEDIPUS REX

The plots of Greek tragedies were based on legends with which Greek audiences were more or less familiar (as American audiences, for example, would be familiar with the major events in a historical play based on the life of Lincoln). These plays often owed much of their impact to the audience's previous knowledge of the characters and their fate, for it enabled the playwright to make powerful use of dramatic irony and allusion. Much of the audience's delight, in addition, came from seeing how the playwright worked out the details of the story. The purpose of this introductory note is therefore to supply such information as the play's first audiences might be presumed to have had.

Because of a prophecy that their new son would kill his father, Laius and Jocasta, King and Queen of Thebes, gave their infant to a shepherd with orders that he be left on a mountainside to die. The shepherd, however, after having pinned the babe's ankles together, took pity on him and gave him instead to a Corinthian shepherd. This shepherd in turn presented him to Polybus and Merope, King and Queen of Corinth, who, childless, adopted him as their own. The child was given the name Oedipus ('Swollen-foot") because of the injury to his ankles.

When grown to manhood at Polybus' court, Oedipus was accused by a drunken guest of not being his father's son. Though reassured by Polybus and Merope, he was still disturbed and traveled to consult the Delphic oracle. The oracle, without answering the question about his parentage, prophesied that Oedipus would kill his father and beget children by his mother. Horrified, resolved to avert this fate, Oedipus determined never to return to Corinth. Traveling from Delphi, he came to a place where three roads met and was ordered off the road by a man in a chariot. Blows were exchanged, and Oedipus killed the man and four of his attendants. Later, on the outskirts of Thebes, he encountered the Sphinx, a monster with the head of a woman, wings of an eagle, and body of a lion, which was terrorizing Thebes by slaying all who failed to answer its riddle ("What goes on four legs in the morning, two legs at noon, and three legs in the evening?"). When Oedipus correctly

OEDIPUS REX by Sophocles. An English Version by Dudley Fitts and Robert Fitzgerald, copyright, 1949, by Harcourt Brace Jovanovich, Inc., and reprinted with their permission.

answered the riddle ("Man, for he crawls as an infant, walks erect as a man, and uses a staff in old age"), the Sphinx destroyed herself. As a reward, Oedipus was named King of Thebes to replace the recently slain Laius and was given the hand of Jocasta in marriage. With her, he ruled Thebes successfully for some years and had four children—two sons and two daughters. Then the city was afflicted by a plague. It is at this point that the action of the play begins.

The play was first performed in Athens about 430 B.C. In the present version, the translators use spellings for the proper names that are closer to the original Greek than the more familiar Anglicized spellings used in this note.

CHARACTERS

OEDIPUS, *King of Thebes, supposed son of Polybos and Meropê, King and Queen of Corinth*
IOKASTÊ, *wife of Oedipus and widow of the late King Laïos*
KREON, *brother of Iokastê, a prince of Thebes*
TEIRESIAS, *a blind seer who serves Apollo*
PRIEST
MESSENGER, *from Corinth*
SHEPHERD, *former servant of Laïos*
SECOND MESSENGER, *from the palace*
CHORUS OF THEBAN ELDERS
CHORAGOS, *leader of the Chorus*
ANTIGONE *and* ISMENE, *young daughters of Oedipus and Iokastê. They appear in the Éxodos but do not speak.*
SUPPLIANTS, GUARDS, SERVANTS

THE SCENE. *Before the palace of* OEDIPUS, *King of Thebes. A central door and two lateral doors open onto a platform which runs the length of the façade. On the platform, right and left, are altars; and three steps lead down into the orchêstra, or chorus-ground. At the beginning of the action these steps are crowded by suppliants who have brought branches and chaplets of olive leaves and who sit in various attitudes of despair.* OEDIPUS *enters.*

PROLOGUE

OEDIPUS. My children, generations of the living
In the line of Kadmos,[1] nursed at his ancient hearth:
Why have you strewn yourselves before these altars
In supplication, with your boughs and garlands?
The breath of incense rises from the city   5

[1] Kadmos: founder of Thebes.

With a sound of prayer and lamentation.

                            Children,

I would not have you speak through messengers,
And therefore I have come myself to hear you—
I, Oedipus, who bear the famous name.
(*To a* PRIEST) You, there, since you are eldest in the company,   10
Speak for them all, tell me what preys upon you,
Whether you come in dread, or crave some blessing:
Tell me, and never doubt that I will help you
In every way I can; I should be heartless
Were I not moved to find you suppliant here.   15

    PRIEST.   Great Oedipus, O powerful king of Thebes!
You see how all the ages of our people
Cling to your altar steps: here are boys
Who can barely stand alone, and here are priests
By weight of age, as I am a priest of God,   20
And young men chosen from those yet unmarried;
As for the others, all that multitude,
They wait with olive chaplets in the squares,
At the two shrines of Pallas, and where Apollo
Speaks in the glowing embers.

                          Your own eyes   25
Must tell you: Thebes is tossed on a murdering sea
And can not lift her head from the death surge.
A rust consumes the buds and fruits of the earth;
The herds are sick; children die unborn,
And labor is vain. The god of plague and pyre   30
Raids like detestable lightning through the city,
And all the house of Kadmos is laid waste,
All emptied, and all darkened: Death alone
Battens upon the misery of Thebes.

You are not one of the immortal gods, we know;   35
Yet we have come to you to make our prayer
As to the man surest in mortal ways
And wisest in the ways of God. You saved us
From the Sphinx, that flinty singer, and the tribute
We paid to her so long; yet you were never   40
Better informed than we, nor could we teach you:
A god's touch, it seems, enabled you to help us.

Therefore, O mighty power, we turn to you:
Find us our safety, find us a remedy,
Whether by counsel of the gods or of men.   45
A king of wisdom tested in the past
Can act in a time of troubles, and act well.

Noblest of men, restore
Life to your city! Think how all men call you
Liberator for your boldness long ago;   50
Ah, when your years of kingship are remembered,
Let them not say *We rose, but later fell*—
Keep the State from going down in the storm!
Once, years ago, with happy augury,
You brought us fortune; be the same again!   55
No man questions your power to rule the land:
But rule over men, not over a dead city!
Ships are only hulls, high walls are nothing,
When no life moves in the empty passageways.

    OEDIPUS.   Poor children! You may be sure I know   60
All that you longed for in your coming here.
I know that you are deathly sick; and yet,
Sick as you are, not one is as sick as I.
Each of you suffers in himself alone
His anguish, not another's; but my spirit   65
Groans for the city, for myself, for you.

I was not sleeping, you are not waking me.
No, I have been in tears for a long while
And in my restless thought walked many ways.
In all my search I found one remedy,   70
And I have adopted it: I have sent Kreon,
Son of Menoikeus, brother of the queen,
To Delphi, Apollo's place of revelation,
To learn there, if he can,
What act or pledge of mine may save the city.   75
I have counted the days, and now, this very day,
I am troubled, for he has overstayed his time.
What is he doing? He has been gone too long.
Yet whenever he comes back, I should do ill
Not to take any action the god orders.   80

    PRIEST.   It is a timely promise. At this instant
They tell me Kreon is here.

    OEDIPUS.   O Lord Apollo!
May his news be fair as his face is radiant!

    PRIEST.   Good news, I gather! he is crowned with bay,
The chaplet is thick with berries.

    OEDIPUS.   We shall soon know;   85
He is near enough to hear us now.

    (*Enter* KREON.)

               O prince:

Brother: son of Menoikeus:
What answer do you bring us from the god?
KREON.   A strong one. I can tell you, great afflictions
Will turn out well, if they are taken well.   90
    OEDIPUS.   What was the oracle? These vague words
Leave me still hanging between hope and fear.
    KREON.   Is it your pleasure to hear me with all these
Gathered around us? I am prepared to speak,
But should we not go in?
    OEDIPUS.   Speak to them all,   95
It is for them I suffer, more than for myself.
    KREON.   Then I will tell you what I heard at Delphi.
In plain words
The god commands us to expel from the land of Thebes
An old defilement we are sheltering.   100
It is deathly thing, beyond cure;
We must not let it feed upon us longer.
    OEDIPUS.   What defilement? How shall we rid ourselves of it?
    KREON.   By exile or death, blood for blood. It was
Murder that brought the plague-wind on the city.   105
    OEDIPUS.   Murder of whom? Surely the god has named him?
    KREON.   My lord: Laïos once ruled this land,
Before you came to govern us.
    OEDIPUS.   I know;
I learned of him from others; I never saw him.
    KREON.   He was murdered; and Apollo commands us now   110
To take revenge upon whoever killed him.
    OEDIPUS.   Upon whom? Where are they? Where shall we find a clue
To solve that crime, after so many years?
    KREON.   Here in this land, he said. Search reveals
Things that escape an inattentive man.   115
    OEDIPUS.   Tell me: Was Laïos murdered in his house,
Or in the fields, or in some foreign country?
    KREON.   He said he planned to make a pilgrimage.
He did not come home again.
    OEDIPUS.   And was there no one,
No witness, no companion, to tell what happened?   120
    KREON.   They were all killed but one, and he got away
So frightened that he could remember one thing only.
    OEDIPUS.   What was the one thing? One may be the key
To everything, if we resolve to use it.
    KREON.   He said that a band of highwaymen attacked them,   125
Outnumbered them, and overwhelmed the king.
    OEDIPUS.   Strange, that a highwayman should be so daring—
Unless some faction here bribed him to do it.

KREON. We thought of that. But after Laïos' death
New troubles arose and we had no avenger.   130
    OEDIPUS. What troubles could prevent your hunting down the killers?
    KREON. The riddling Sphinx's song
Made us deaf to all mysteries but her own.
    OEDIPUS. Then once more I must bring what is dark to light.
It is most fitting that Apollo shows,   135
As you do, this compunction for the dead.
You shall see how I stand by you, as I should,
Avenging this country and the god as well,
And not as though it were for some distant friend,
But for my own sake, to be rid of evil.   140
Whoever killed King Laïos might—who knows?—
Lay violent hands even on me—and soon.
I act for the murdered king in my own interest.

Come, then, my children: leave the altar steps,
Lift up your olive boughs!
                  One of you go   145
And summon the people of Kadmos to gather here.
I will do all that I can; you may tell them that.

    (*Exit a* PAGE.)

So, with the help of God,
We shall be saved—or else indeed we are lost.
    PRIEST. Let us rise, children. It was for this we came,   150
And now the king has promised it.
Phoibos[1] has sent us an oracle; may he descend
Himself to save us and drive out the plague.

    (*Exeunt* OEDIPUS *and* KREON *into the palace by the central door. The*
PRIEST *and the* SUPPLIANTS *disperse R and L. After a short pause the*
CHORUS *enters the* orchêstra.)

PÁRODOS[2]

STROPHE 1
    CHORUS. What is God singing in his profound
Delphi of gold and shadow?   155
What oracle for Thebes, the sunwhipped city?
Fear unjoints me, the roots of my heart tremble.

    [1]Phoibos: Apollo.

    [2]Parados: the song or ode chanted by the chorus on their entry. It is accompanied by dancing and music played on a flute. The chorus, in this play, represents elders of the city of Thebes. They remain on stage (on a level lower than the principal actors) for the remainder of the play. The choral odes and dances serve

Now I remember, O Healer, your power, and wonder:
Will you send doom like a sudden cloud, or weave it
Like nightfall of the past?   160
Speak to me, tell me, O
Child of golden Hope, immortal Voice.

ANTISTROPHE 1
Let me pray to Athenê, the immortal daughter of Zeus,
And to Artemis her sister
Who keeps her famous throne in the market ring,   165
And to Apollo, archer from distant heaven—
O gods, descend! Like three streams leap against
The fires of our grief, the fires of darkness;
Be swift to bring us rest!
As in the old time from the brilliant house   170
Of air you stepped to save us, come again!

STROPHE 2
Now our afflictions have no end,
Now all our stricken host lies down
And no man fights off death with his mind;
The noble plowland bears no grain,   175
And groaning mothers can not bear—
See, how our lives like birds take wing,
Like sparks that fly when a fire soars,
To the shore of the god of evening.

ANTISTROPHE 2
The plague burns on, it is pitiless,   180
Though pallid children laden with death
Lie unwept in the stony ways,
And old gray women by every path
Flock to the strand about the altars
There to strike their breasts and cry   185
Worship of Phoibos in wailing prayers:
Be kind, God's golden child!

STROPHE 3
There are no swords in this attack by fire,
No shields, but we are ringed with cries.

---

to separate one scene from another (there was no curtain in Greek theater) as well
as to comment on the action, reinforce the emotion, and interpret the situation.
The chorus also performs dance movements during certain portions of the scenes
themselves. *Strophe* and *antistrophe* are terms denoting the movement and counter-
movement of the chorus from one side of their playing area to the other. When
the chorus participates in dialogue with the other characters, their lines are
spoken by the Choragos, their leader.

Send the besieger plunging from our homes   190
Into the vast sea-room of the Atlantic
Or into the waves that foam eastward of Thrace—
For the day ravages what the night spares—
Destroy our enemy, lord of the thunder!
Let him be riven by lightning from heaven!   195

ANTISTROPHE 3
Phoibos Apollo, stretch the sun's bowstring,
That golden cord, until it sing for us,
Flashing arrows in heaven!
                 Artemis, Huntress,
Race with flaring lights upon our mountains!
O scarlet god, O golden-banded brow,   200
O Theban Bacchos in a storm of Maenads,

    (*Enter* OEDIPUS, *C.*)

Whirl upon Death, that all the Undying hate!
Come with blinding torches, come in joy!

SCENE I

    OEDIPUS. Is this your prayer? It may be answered. Come,
Listen to me, act as the crisis demands,   205
And you shall have relief from all these evils.

Until now I was a stranger to this tale,
As I had been a stranger to the crime.
Could I track down the murderer without a clue?
But now, friends,   210
As one who became a citizen after the murder,
I make this proclamation to all Thebans:
If any man knows by whose hand Laïos, son of Labdakos,
Met his death, I direct that man to tell me everything,
No matter what he fears for having so long withheld it.   215
Let it stand as promised that no further trouble
Will come to him, but he may leave the land in safety.

Moreover: If anyone knows the murderer to be foreign,
Let him not keep silent: he shall have his reward from me.
However, if he does conceal it; if any man   220
Fearing for his friend or for himself disobeys this edict,
Hear what I propose to do:

I solemnly forbid the people of this country,
Where power and throne are mine, ever to receive that man

Or speak to him, no matter who he is, or let him   225
Join in sacrifice, lustration, or in prayer.
I decree that he be driven from every house,
Being, as he is, corruption itself to us: the Delphic
Voice of Apollo has pronounced this revelation.
Thus I associate myself with the oracle   230
And take the side of the murdered king.

As for the criminal, I pray to God—
Whether it be a lurking thief, or one of a number—
I pray that that man's life be consumed in evil and wretchedness.
And as for me, this curse applies no less   235
If it should turn out that the culprit is my guest here,
Sharing my hearth.
                          You have heard the penalty.
I lay it on you now to attend to this
For my sake, for Apollo's, for the sick
Sterile city that heaven has abandoned.   240
Suppose the oracle had given you no command:
Should this defilement go uncleansed for ever?
You should have found the murderer: your king,
A noble king, had been destroyed!
                          Now I,
Having the power that he held before me,   245
Having his bed, begetting children there
Upon his wife, as he would have, had he lived—
Their son would have been my children's brother,
If Laïos had had luck in fatherhood!
(And now his bad fortune has struck him down)—   250
I say I take the son's part, just as though
I were his son, to press the fight for him
And see it won! I'll find the hand that brought
Death to Labdakos' and Polydoros' child,
Heir of Kadmos' and Agenor's line.[1]   255
And as for those who fail me,
May the gods deny them the fruit of the earth,
Fruit of the womb, and may they rot utterly!
Let them be wretched as we are wretched, and worse!

For you, for loyal Thebans, and for all   260
Who find my actions right, I pray the favor
Of justice, and of all the immortal gods.
          CHORAGOS.   Since I am under oath, my lord, I swear

----

[1] Labdakos, Polydoros, Kadmos, and Agenor: father, grandfather, great-grandfather, and great-great-grandfather of Laïos.

I did not do the murder, I can not name
The murderer. Phoibos ordained the search;   265
Why did he not say who the culprit was?
    OEDIPUS.   An honest question. But no man in the world
Can make the gods do more than the gods will.
    CHORAGOS.   There is an alternative, I think—
    OEDIPUS.   Tell me.
Any or all, you must not fail to tell me.   270
    CHORAGOS.   A lord clairvoyant to the lord Apollo,
As we all know, is the skilled Teiresias.
One might learn much about this from him, Oedipus.
    OEDIPUS.   I am not wasting time:
Kreon spoke of this, and I have sent for him—   275
Twice, in fact; it is strange that he is not here.
    CHORAGOS.   The other matter—that old report—seems useless.
    OEDIPUS.   What was that? I am interested in all reports.
    CHORAGOS.   The king was said to have been killed by highwaymen.
    OEDIPUS.   I know. But we have no witnesses to that.   280
    CHORAGOS.   If the killer can feel a particle of dread,
Your curse will bring him out of hiding!
    OEDIPUS.   No.
The man who dared that act will fear no curse.

(*Enter the blind seer* TEIRESIAS, *led by a* PAGE.)

    CHORAGOS.   But there is one man who may detect the criminal.
This is Teiresias, this is the holy prophet   285
In whom, alone of all men, truth was born.
    OEDIPUS.   Teiresias: seer: student of mysteries,
Of all that's taught and all that no man tells,
Secrets of Heaven and secrets of the earth:
Blind though you are, you know the city lies   290
Sick with plague; and from this plague, my lord,
We find that you alone can guard or save us.

Possibly you did not hear the messengers?
Apollo, when we sent to him,
Sent us back word that this great pestilence   295
Would lift, but only if we established clearly
The identity of those who murdered Laïos.
They must be killed or exiled.
                         Can you use
Birdflight[2] or any art of divination

2 Birdflight: Prophets predicted the future or divined the unknown by observing the flight of birds.

To purify yourself, and Thebes, and me   300
From this contagion? We are in your hands.
There is no fairer duty
Than that of helping others in distress.

    TEIRESIAS.   How dreadful knowledge of the truth can be
When there's no help in truth! I knew this well,   305
But did not act on it: else I should not have come.

    OEDIPUS.   What is troubling you? Why are your eyes so cold?

    TEIRESIAS.   Let me go home. Bear your own fate, and I'll
Bear mine. It is better so: trust what I say.

    OEDIPUS.   What you say is ungracious and unhelpful   310
To your native country. Do not refuse to speak.

    TEIRESIAS.   When it comes to speech, your own is neither temperate
Nor opportune. I wish to be more prudent.

    OEDIPUS.   In God's name, we all beg you—

    TEIRESIAS.   You are all ignorant.
No; I will never tell you what I know.   315
Now it is my misery; then, it would be yours.

    OEDIPUS.   What! You do know something, and will not tell us?
You would betray us all and wreck the State?

    TEIRESIAS.   I do not intend to torture myself, or you.
Why persist in asking? You will not persuade me.   320

    OEDIPUS.   What a wicked old man you are! You'd try a stone's
Patience! Out with it! Have you no feeling at all?

    TEIRESIAS.   You call me unfeeling. If you could only see
The nature of your own feelings . . .

    OEDIPUS.   Why,
Who would not feel as I do? Who could endure   325
Your arrogance toward the city?

    TEIRESIAS.   What does it matter?
Whether I speak or not, it is bound to come.

    OEDIPUS.   Then, if "it" is bound to come, you are bound to tell me.

    TEIRESIAS.   No, I will not go on. Rage as you please.

    OEDIPUS.   Rage? Why not!
                      And I'll tell you what I think: 330
You planned it, you had it done, you all but
Killed him with your own hands: if you had eyes,
I'd say the crime was yours, and yours alone.

    TEIRESIAS.   So? I charge you, then,
Abide by the proclamation you have made: 335
From this day forth
Never speak again to these men or to me;
You yourself are the pollution of this country.

    OEDIPUS.   You dare say that! Can you possibly think you have

Some way of going free, after such insolence?   340
TEIRESIAS. I have gone free. It is the truth sustains me.
OEDIPUS. Who taught you shamelessness? It was not your craft.
TEIRESIAS. You did. You made me speak. I did not want to.
OEDIPUS. Speak what? Let me hear it again more clearly.
TEIRESIAS. Was it not clear before? Are you tempting me?   345
OEDIPUS. I did not understand it. Say it again.
TEIRESIAS. I say that you are the murderer whom you seek.
OEDIPUS. Now twice you have spat out infamy. You'll pay for it!
TEIRESIAS. Would you care for more? Do you wish to be really angry?
OEDIPUS. Say what you will. Whatever you say is worthless.   350
TEIRESIAS. I say you live in hideous shame with those
Most dear to you. You can not see the evil.
OEDIPUS. Can you go on babbling like this for ever?
TEIRESIAS. I can, if there is power in truth.
OEDIPUS.   There is:
But not for you, not for you,   355
You sightless, witless, senseless, mad old man!
TEIRESIAS. You are the madman. There is no one here
Who will not curse you soon, as you curse me.
OEDIPUS. You child of total night! I would not touch you;
Neither would any man who sees the sun.   360
TEIRESIAS. True: it is not from you my fate will come.
That lies within Apollo's competence,
As it is his concern.
OEDIPUS.   Tell me, who made
These fine discoveries? Kreon? or someone else?
TEIRESIAS. Kreon is no threat. You weave your own doom.   365
OEDIPUS. Wealth, power, craft of statesmanship!
Kingly position, everywhere admired!
What savage envy is stored up against these,
If Kreon, whom I trusted, Kreon my friend,
For this great office which the city once   370
Put in my hands unsought—if for this power
Kreon desires in secret to destroy me!

He has bought this decrepit fortune teller, this
Collector of dirty pennies, this prophet fraud—
Why, he is no more clairvoyant than I am!
                                              Tell us: 375
Has your mystic mummery ever approached the truth?
When that hellcat the Sphinx was performing here,
What help were you to these people?
Her magic was not for the first man who came along:

It demanded a real exorcist. Your birds— 380
What good were they? or the gods, for the matter of that?
But I came by,
Oedipus, the simple man, who knows nothing—
I thought it out for myself, no birds helped me!
And this is the man you think you can destroy, 385
That you may be close to Kreon when he's king!
Well, you and your friend Kreon, it seems to me,
Will suffer most. If you were not an old man,
You would have paid already for your plot.

    CHORAGOS.   We can not see that his words or yours 390
Have been spoken except in anger, Oedipus,
And of anger we have no need. How to accomplish
The god's will best: that is what most concerns us.

    TEIRESIAS.   You are a king. But where argument's concerned
I am your man, as much a king as you. 395
I am not your servant, but Apollo's.
I have no need of Kreon or Kreon's name.

Listen to me. You mock my blindness, do you?
But I say that you, with both your eyes, are blind:
You can not see the wretchedness of your life, 400
Nor in whose house you live, no, nor with whom.
Who are your father and mother? Can you tell me?
You do not even know the blind wrongs
That you have done them, on earth and in the world below.
But the double lash of your parents' curse will whip you 405
Out of this land some day, with only night
Upon your precious eyes.
Your cries then—where will they not be heard?
What fastness of Kithairon³ will not echo them?
And that bridal-descant of yours—you'll know it then, 410
The song they sang when you came here to Thebes
And found your misguided berthing.
All this, and more, that you can not guess at now,
Will bring you to yourself among your children.

Be angry, then. Curse Kreon. Curse my words. 415
I tell you, no man that walks upon the earth
Shall be rooted out more horribly than you.

    OEDIPUS.   Am I to bear this from him?—Damnation
Take you! Out of this place! Out of my sight!

    TEIRESIAS.   I would not have come at all if you had not asked me. 420

³ Kithairon: the mountain where Oedipus was taken to be exposed as an
infant.

OEDIPUS. Could I have told that you'd talk nonsense, that
You'd come here to make a fool of yourself, and of me?
TEIRESIAS. A fool? Your parents thought me sane enough.
OEDIPUS. My parents again!—Wait: who were my parents?
TEIRESIAS. This day will give you a father, and break your heart. 425
OEDIPUS. Your infantile riddles! Your damned abracadabra!
TEIRESIAS. You were a great man once at solving riddles.
OEDIPUS. Mock me with that if you like; you will find it true.
TEIRESIAS. It was true enough. It brought about your ruin.
OEDIPUS. But if it saved this town?
TEIRESIAS (to the PAGE).   Boy, give me your hand. 430
OEDIPUS. Yes, boy; lead him away.

                              —While you are here
We can do nothing. Go; leave us in peace.
TEIRESIAS. I will go when I have said what I have to say.
How can you hurt me? And I tell you again:
The man you have been looking for all this time,   435
The damned man, the murderer of Laïos,
That man is in Thebes. To your mind he is foreign-born,
But it will soon be shown that he is a Theban,
A revelation that will fail to please.

                    A blind man,
Who has his eyes now; a penniless man, who is rich now;   440
And he will go tapping the strange earth with his staff.
To the children with whom he lives now he will be
Brother and father—the very same; to her
Who bore him, son and husband—the very same
Who came to his father's bed, wet with his father's blood.   445

Enough. Go think that over.
If later you find error in what I have said,
You may say that I have no skill in prophecy.

(*Exit* TEIRESIAS, *led by his* PAGE. OEDIPUS *goes into the palace.*)

ODE I

STROPHE 1
CHORUS.   The Delphic stone of prophecies
Remembers ancient regicide   450
And a still bloody hand.
That killer's hour of flight has come.
He must be stronger than riderless
Coursers of untiring wind,
For the son[1] of Zeus armed with his father's thunder   455

    [1] son: Apollo.

Leaps in lightning after him;
And the Furies hold his track, the sad Furies.

ANTISTROPHE 1
Holy Parnassos'[2] peak of snow
Flashes and blinds that secret man,
That all shall hunt him down: 460
Though he may roam the forest shade
Like a bull gone wild from pasture
To rage through glooms of stone.
Doom comes down on him; flight will not avail him;
For the world's heart calls him desolate,   465
And the immortal voices follow, for ever follow.

STROPHE 2
But now a wilder thing is heard
From the old man skilled at hearing Fate in the wing-beat of a bird.
Bewildered as a blown bird, my soul hovers and can not find
Foothold in this debate, or any reason or rest of mind.   470
But no man ever brought—none can bring
Proof of strife between Thebes' royal house,
Labdakos' line, and the son of Polybos;
And never until now has any man brought word
Of Laïos' dark death staining Oedipus the King.   475

ANTISTROPHE 2
Divine Zeus and Apollo hold
Perfect intelligence alone of all tales ever told;
And well though this diviner works, he works in his own night;
No man can judge that rough unknown or trust in second sight,
For wisdom changes hands among the wise.   480
Shall I believe my great lord criminal
At a raging word that a blind old man let fall?
I saw him, when the carrion woman[3] faced him of old,
Prove his heroic mind. These evil words are lies.

SCENE II

    KREON.   Men of Thebes: 485
I am told that heavy accusations
Have been brought against me by King Oedipus.

I am not the kind of man to bear this tamely.

If in these present difficulties

    [2] Parnassos: mountain sacred to Apollo.
    [3] woman: the Sphinx.

He holds me accountable for any harm to him 490
Through anything I have said or done—why, then,
I do not value life in this dishonor.
It is not as though this rumor touched upon
Some private indiscretion. The matter is grave.
The fact is that I am being called disloyal 495
To the State, to my fellow citizens, to my friends.
    CHORAGOS.   He may have spoken in anger, not from his mind.
    KREON.   But did you not hear him say I was the one
Who seduced the old prophet into lying?
    CHORAGOS.   The thing was said; I do not know how seriously. 500
    KREON.   But you were watching him! Were his eyes steady?
Did he look like a man in his right mind?
    CHORAGOS.   I do not know.
I can not judge the behavior of great men.
But here is the king himself.

    (*Enter* OEDIPUS.)

    OEDIPUS.   So you dared come back.
Why? How brazen of you to come to my house, 505
You murderer!
              Do you think I do not know
That you plotted to kill me, plotted to steal my throne?
Tell me, in God's name: am I coward, a fool,
That you should dream you could accomplish this?
A fool who could not see your slippery game? 510
A coward, not to fight back when I saw it?
You are the fool, Kreon, are you not? hoping
Without support or friends to get a throne?
Thrones may be won or bought: you could do neither.
    KREON.   Now listen to me. You have talked; let me talk, too. 515
You can not judge unless you know the facts.
    OEDIPUS.   You speak well: there is one fact; but I find it hard
To learn from the deadliest enemy I have.
    KREON.   That above all I must dispute with you.
    OEDIPUS.   That above all I will not hear you deny. 520
    KREON.   If you think there is anything good in being stubborn
Against all reason, then I say you are wrong.
    OEDIPUS.   If you think a man can sin against his own kind.
And not be punished for it, I say you are mad.
    KREON.   I agree. But tell me: What have I done to you? 525
    OEDIPUS.   You advised me to send for that wizard, did you not?
    KREON.   I did. I should do it again.
    OEDIPUS.   Very well. Now tell me:

How long has it been since Laïos—
    KREON.   What of Laïos?
    OEDIPUS.   Since he vanished in that onset by the road?
    KREON.   It was long ago, a long time.
    OEDIPUS.   And this prophet,   530
Was he practicing here then?
    KREON.   He was; and with honor, as now.
    OEDIPUS.   Did he speak of me at that time?
    KREON.   He never did,
At least, not when I was present.
    OEDIPUS.   But . . . the enquiry?
I suppose you held one?
    KREON.   We did, but we learned nothing.
    OEDIPUS.   Why did the prophet not speak against me then?   535
    KREON.   I do not know; and I am the kind of man
Who holds his tongue when he has no facts to go on.
    OEDIPUS.   There's one fact that you know, and you could tell it.
    KREON.   What fact is that? If I know it, you shall have it.
    OEDIPUS.   If he were not involved with you, he could not say   540
That it was I who murdered Laïos.
    KREON.   If he says that, you are the one that knows it!—
But now it is my turn to question you.
    OEDIPUS.   Put your questions. I am no murderer.
    KREON.   First, then: You married my sister?
    OEDIPUS.   I married your sister. 545
    KREON.   And you rule the kingdom equally with her?
    OEDIPUS.   Everything that she wants she has from me.
    KREON.   And I am the third, equal to both of you?
    OEDIPUS.   That is why I call you a bad friend.
    KREON.   No. Reason it out, as I have done.   550
Think of this first: Would any sane man prefer
Power, with all a king's anxieties,
To that same power and the grace of sleep?
Certainly not I.
I have never longed for the king's power—only his rights.   555
Would any wise man differ from me in this?
As matters stand, I have my way in everything
With your consent, and no responsibilities.
If I were king, I should be a slave to policy.

How could I desire a scepter more   560
Than what is now mine—untroubled influence?
No, I have not gone mad; I need no honors,
Except those with the perquisites I have now.

I am welcome everywhere; every man salutes me,
And those who want your favor seek my ear,   565
Since I know how to manage what they ask.
Should I exchange this ease for that anxiety?
Besides, no sober mind is treasonable.
I hate anarchy
And never would deal with any man who likes it.   570
Test what I have said. Go to the priestess
At Delphi, ask if I quoted her correctly.
And as for this other thing: if I am found
Guilty of treason with Teiresias,
Then sentence me to death. You have my word   575
It is a sentence I should cast my vote for—
But not without evidence!
                    You do wrong
When you take good men for bad, bad men for good.
A true friend thrown aside—why, life itself
Is not more precious!
                    In time you will know this well: 580
For time, and time alone, will show the just man,
Though scoundrels are discovered in a day.
    CHORAGOS.   This is well said, and a prudent man would ponder it.
Judgments too quickly formed are dangerous.
    OEDIPUS.   But is he not quick in his duplicity?   585
And shall I not be quick to parry him?
Would you have me stand still, hold my peace, and let
This man win everything, through my inaction?
    KREON.   And you want—what is it, then? To banish me?
    OEDIPUS.   No, not exile. It is your death I want,   590
So that all the world may see what treason means.
    KREON.   You will persist, then? You will not believe me?
    OEDIPUS.   How can I believe you?
    KREON.   Then you are a fool.
    OEDIPUS.   To save myself?
    KREON.   In justice, think of me.
    OEDIPUS.   You are evil incarnate.
    KREON.   But suppose that you are wrong? 595
    OEDIPUS.   Still I must rule.
    KREON.   But not if you rule badly.
    OEDIPUS.   O city, city!
    KREON.   It is my city, too!
    CHORAGOS.   Now, my lords, be still. I see the queen,
Iokastê, coming from her palace chambers;
And it is time she came, for the sake of you both.   600

This dreadful quarrel can be resolved through her.

(*Enter* IOKASTÊ.)

IOKASTÊ.   Poor foolish men, what wicked din is this?
With Thebes sick to death, is it not shameful
That you should rake some private quarrel up?
(*To* OEDIPUS) Come into the house.
                                            —And you, Kreon, go now: 605
Let us have no more of this tumult over nothing.
     KREON.   Nothing? No, sister: what your husband plans for me
Is one of two great evils: exile or death.
     OEDIPUS.   He is right.
                              Why, woman I have caught him squarely
Plotting against my life.
     KREON.   No! Let me die   610
Accurst if ever I have wished you harm!
     IOKASTÊ.   Ah, believe it, Oedipus!
In the name of the gods, respect this oath of his
For my sake, for the sake of these people here!

STROPHE 1
     CHORAGOS.   Open your mind to her, my lord. Be ruled by her, I beg
          you!   615
     OEDIPUS.   What would you have me do?
     CHORAGOS.   Respect Kreon's word. He has never spoken like a fool,
And now he has sworn an oath.
     OEDIPUS.   You know what you ask?
     CHORAGOS.   I do.
     OEDIPUS.   Speak on, then.
     CHORAGOS.   A friend so sworn should not be baited so,   620
In blind malice, and without final proof.
     OEDIPUS.   You are aware, I hope, that what you say
Means death for me, or exile at the least.

STROPHE 2
     CHORAGOS.   No, I swear by Helios, first in Heaven!
May I die friendless and accurst,   625
The worst of deaths, if ever I meant that!
                    It is the withering fields
                         That hurt my sick heart:
                    Must we bear all these ills,
                         And now your bad blood as well?   630
     OEDIPUS.   Then let him go. And let me die, if I must,
Or be driven by him in shame from the land of Thebes.

It is your unhappiness, and not his talk,
That touches me.
                    As for him—
Wherever he goes, hatred will follow him.   635
    KREON.   Ugly in yielding, as you were ugly in rage!
Natures like yours chiefly torment themselves.
    OEDIPUS.   Can you not go? Can you not leave me?
    KREON.   I can.
You do not know me; but the city knows me,
And in its eyes I am just, if not in yours. (*Exit* KREON.)   640

ANTISTROPHE 1
    CHORAGOS.   Lady Iokastê, did you not ask the King to go to his
      chambers?
    IOKASTÊ.   First tell me what has happened.
    CHORAGOS.   There was suspicion without evidence; yet it rankled
As even false charges will.
    IOKASTÊ.   On both sides?
    CHORAGOS.   On both.
    IOKASTÊ.   But what was said?   645
    CHORAGOS.   Oh let it rest, let it be done with!
Have we not suffered enough?
    OEDIPUS.   You see to what your decency has brought you:
You have made difficulties where my heart saw none.

ANTISTROPHE 2
    CHORAGOS.   Oedipus, it is not once only I have told you—   650
You must know I should count myself unwise
To the point of madness, should I now forsake you—
      You, under whose hand,
        In the storm of another time,
      Our dear land sailed out free.   655
      But now stand fast at the helm!
    IOKASTÊ.   In God's name, Oedipus, inform your wife as well:
Why are you so set in this hard anger?
    OEDIPUS.   I will tell you, for none of these men deserves
My confidence as you do. It is Kreon's work,   660
His treachery, his plotting against me.
    IOKASTÊ.   Go on, if you can make this clear to me.
    OEDIPUS.   He charges me with the murder of Laïos.
    IOKASTÊ.   Has he some knowledge? Or does he speak from hearsay?
    OEDIPUS.   He would not commit himself to such a charge,   665
But he has brought in that damnable soothsayer
To tell his story.
    IOKASTÊ.   Set your mind at rest.

If it is a question of soothsayers, I tell you
That you will find no man whose craft gives knowledge
Of the unknowable.
                        Here is my proof: 670

An oracle was reported to Laïos once
(I will not say from Phoibos himself, but from
His appointed ministers, at any rate)
That his doom would be death at the hands of his own son—
His son, born of his flesh and of mine!   675

Now, you remember the story: Laïos was killed
By marauding strangers where three highways meet;
But his child had not been three days in this world
Before the king had pierced the baby's ankles
And left him to die on a lonely mountainside.   680

Thus, Apollo never caused that child
To kill his father, and it was not Laïos' fate
To die at the hands of his son, as he had feared.
This is what prophets and prophecies are worth!
Have no dread of them.
                        It is God himself   685
Who can show us what he wills, in his own way.
    OEDIPUS. How strange a shadowy memory crossed my mind,
Just now while you were speaking; it chilled my heart.
    IOKASTÊ. What do you mean? What memory do you speak of?
    OEDIPUS. If I understand you, Laïos was killed   690
At a place where three roads meet.
    IOKASTÊ.   So it was said;
We have no later story.
    OEDIPUS.   Where did it happen?
    IOKASTÊ. Phokis, it is called: at a place where the Theban Way
Divides into the roads toward Delphi and Daulia.
    OEDIPUS. When?   695
    IOKASTÊ. We had the news not long before you came
And proved the right to your succession here.
    OEDIPUS. Ah, what net has God been weaving for me?
    IOKASTÊ. Oedipus! Why does this trouble you?
    OEDIPUS.   Do not ask me yet.
First, tell me how Laïos looked, and tell me
How old he was.
    IOKASTÊ.   He was tall, his hair just touched   700
With white; his form was not unlike your own.
    OEDIPUS. I think that I myself may be accurst

By my own ignorant edict.

IOKASTÊ.   You speak strangely.
It makes me tremble to look at you, my king.

OEDIPUS.   I am not sure that the blind man can not see.   705
But I should know better if you were to tell me—

IOKASTÊ.   Anything—though I dread to hear you ask it.

OEDIPUS.   Was the king lightly escorted, or did he ride
With a large company, as a ruler should?

IOKASTÊ.   There were five men with him in all: one was a
    herald.   710
And a single chariot, which he was driving.

OEDIPUS.   Alas, that makes it plain enough!

                                        But who—
Who told you how it happened?

IOKASTÊ.   A household servant,
The only one to escape.

OEDIPUS.   And is he still
A servant of ours?

IOKASTÊ.   No; for when he came back at last   715
And found you enthroned in the place of the dead king,
He came to me, touched my hand with his, and begged
That I would send him away to the frontier district
Where only the shepherds go—
As far away from the city as I could send him.   720
I granted his prayer; for although the man was a slave,
He had earned more than this favor at my hands.

OEDIPUS.   Can he be called back quickly?

IOKASTÊ.   Easily.
But why?

OEDIPUS.   I have taken too much upon myself
Without enquiry; therefore I wish to consult him.   725

IOKASTÊ.   Then he shall come.

                          But am I not one also
To whom you might confide these fears of yours?

OEDIPUS.   That is your right; it will not be denied you,
Now least of all; for I have reached a pitch
Of wild foreboding. Is there anyone   730
To whom I should sooner speak?

Polybos of Corinth is my father.
My mother is a Dorian: Meropê.
I grew up chief among the men of Corinth
Until a strange thing happened—   735
Not worth my passion, it may be, but strange.

At a feast, a drunken man maundering in his cups
Cries out that I am not my father's son![1]

I contained myself that night, though I felt anger
And a sinking heart. The next day I visited   740
My father and mother, and questioned them. They stormed,
Calling it all the slanderous rant of a fool;
And this relieved me. Yet the suspicion
Remained always aching in my mind;
I knew there was talk; I could not rest;   745
And finally, saying nothing to my parents,
I went to the shrine at Delphi.

The god dismissed my question without reply;
He spoke of other things.
                            Some were clear,
Full of wretchedness, dreadful, unbearable: 750
As, that I should lie with my own mother, breed
Children from whom all men would turn their eyes;
And that I should be my father's murderer.

I heard all this, and fled. And from that day
Corinth to me was only in the stars   755
Descending in that quarter of the sky,
As I wandered farther and farther on my way
To a land where I should never see the evil
Sung by the oracle. And I came to this country
Where, so you say, King Laïos was killed.   760

I will tell you all that happened there, my lady.

There were three highways
Coming together at a place I passed;
And there a herald came towards me, and a chariot
Drawn by horses, with a man such as you describe   765
Seated in it. The groom leading the horses
Forced me off the road at his lord's command;
But as this charioteer lurched over towards me
I struck him in my rage. The old man saw me
And brought his double goad down upon my head   770
As I came abreast.
                    He was paid back, and more!

[1] not my father's son: Oedipus perhaps interprets this as an allegation that
he is a bastard, the son of Meropê but not of Polybos. The implication, at any
rate, is that he is not of royal birth, not the legitimate heir to the throne of
Corinth.

Swinging my club in this right hand I knocked him
Out of his car, and he rolled on the ground.
                                    I killed him.

I killed them all.
Now if that stranger and Laïos were—kin,   775
Where is a man more miserable than I?
More hated by the gods? Citizen and alien alike
Must never shelter me or speak to me—
I must be shunned by all.
                        And I myself
Pronounced this malediction upon myself!   780

Think of it: I have touched you with these hands,
These hands that killed your husband. What defilement!

Am I all evil, then? It must be so,
Since I must flee from Thebes, yet never again
See my own countrymen, my own country,   785
For fear of joining my mother in marriage
And killing Polybos, my father.
                            Ah,
If I was created so, born to this fate,
Who could deny the savagery of God?

O holy majesty of heavenly powers!   790
May I never see that day! Never!
Rather let me vanish from the race of men
Than know the abomination destined me!
    CHORAGOS.   We too, my lord, have felt dismay at this.
But there is hope: you have yet to hear the shepherd.   795
    OEDIPUS.   Indeed, I fear no other hope is left me.
    IOKASTÊ.   What do you hope from him when he comes?
    OEDIPUS.   This much:
If his account of the murder tallies with yours,
Then I am cleared.
    IOKASTÊ.   What was it that I said
Of such importance?
    OEDIPUS.   Why, "marauders," you said,   800
Killed the king, according to this man's story.
If he maintains that still, if there were several,
Clearly the guilt is not mine: I was alone.
But if he says one man, singlehanded, did it,
Then the evidence all points to me.   805
    IOKASTÊ.   You may be sure that he said there were several;
And can he call back that story now? He can not.

The whole city heard it as plainly as I.
But suppose he alters some detail of it:
He can not ever show that Laïos' death   810
Fulfilled the oracle: for Apollo said
My child was doomed to kill him; and my child—
Poor baby!—it was my child that died first.

No. From now on, where oracles are concerned,
I would not waste a second thought on any.   815
    OEDIPUS.   You may be right.
                                But come: let someone go
For the shepherd at once. This matter must be settled.
    IOKASTÊ.   I will send for him.
I would not wish to cross you in anything,
And surely not in this.—Let us go in.   820

   (*Exeunt into the palace.*)

ODE II

STROPHE 1
    CHORUS.   Let me be reverent in the ways of right,
Lowly the paths I journey on;
Let all my words and actions keep
The laws of the pure universe
From highest Heaven handed down.   825
For Heaven is their bright nurse,
Those generations of the realms of light;
Ah, never of mortal kind were they begot,
Nor are they slaves of memory, lost in sleep:
Their Father is greater than Time, and ages not.   830

ANTISTROPHE 1
The tyrant is a child of Pride
Who drinks from his great sickening cup
Recklessness and vanity,
Until from his high crest headlong
He plummets to the dust of hope.   835
That strong man is not strong.
But let no fair ambition be denied;
May God protect the wrestler for the State
In government, in comely policy,
Who will fear God, and on His ordinance wait.   840

STROPHE 2
Haughtiness and the high hand of disdain
Tempt and outrage God's holy law;

And any mortal who dares hold
No immortal Power in awe
Will be caught up in a net of pain: 845
The price for which his levity is sold.
Let each man take due earnings, then,
And keep his hands from holy things,
And from blasphemy stand apart—
Else the crackling blast of heaven   850
Blows on his head, and on his desperate heart.
Though fools will honor impious men,
In their cities no tragic poet sings.

ANTISTROPHE 2
Shall we lose faith in Delphi's obscurities,
We who have heard the world's core   855
Discredited, and the sacred wood
Of Zeus at Elis praised no more?
The deeds and the strange prophecies
Must make a pattern yet to be understood.
Zeus, if indeed you are lord of all,   860
Throned in light over night and day,
Mirror this in your endless mind:
Our masters call the oracle
Words on the wind, and the Delphic vision blind!
Their hearts no longer know Apollo,   865
And reverence for the gods has died away.

SCENE III

Enter IOKASTÊ.

IOKASTÊ.   Princes of Thebes, it has occurred to me
To visit the altars of the gods, bearing
These branches as a suppliant, and this incense.
Our king is not himself: his noble soul   870
Is overwrought with fantasies of dread,
Else he would consider
The new prophecies in the light of the old.
He will listen to any voice that speaks disaster,
And my advice goes for nothing.

(*She approaches the altar, R.*)

                              To you, then, Apollo,   875
Lycéan lord, since you are nearest, I turn in prayer.
Receive these offerings, and grant us deliverance

From defilement. Our hearts are heavy with fear
When we see our leader distracted, as helpless sailors
Are terrified by the confusion of their helmsman.   880

  (*Enter* MESSENGER.)

  MESSENGER.   Friends, no doubt you can direct me:
Where shall I find the house of Oedipus,
Or, better still, where is the king himself?
  CHORAGOS.   It is this very place, stranger; he is inside.
This is his wife and mother of his children.   885
  MESSENGER.   I wish her happiness in a happy house,
Blest in all the fulfillment of her marriage.
  IOKASTÊ.   I wish as much for you: your courtesy
Deserves a like good fortune. But now, tell me:
Why have you come? What have you to say to us?   890
  MESSENGER.   Good news, my lady, for your house and your husband.
  IOKASTÊ.   What news? Who sent you here?
  MESSENGER.   I am from Corinth.
The news I bring ought to mean joy for you,
Though it may be you will find some grief in it.
  IOKASTÊ.   What is it? How can it touch us in both ways?   895
  MESSENGER.   The word is that the people of the Isthmus
Intend to call Oedipus to be their king.
  IOKASTÊ.   But old King Polybos—is he not reigning still?
  MESSENGER.   No. Death holds him in his sepulchre.
  IOKASTÊ.   What are you saying? Polybos is dead?   900
  MESSENGER.   If I am not telling the truth, may I die myself.
  IOKASTÊ (*to a* MAIDSERVANT).   Go in, go quickly; tell this to your
master.

O riddlers of God's will, where are you now!
This was the man whom Oedipus, long ago,
Feared so, fled so, in dread of destroying him—   905
But it was another fate by which he died.

  (*Enter* OEDIPUS, C.)

  OEDIPUS.   Dearest Iokasté, why have you sent for me?
  IOKASTÊ.   Listen to what this man says, and then tell me
What has become of the solemn prophecies.
  OEDIPUS.   Who is this man? What is his news for me?   910
  IOKASTÊ.   He has come from Corinth to announce your father's death!
  OEDIPUS.   Is it true, stranger? Tell me in your own words.
  MESSENGER.   I can not say it more clearly: the king is dead.
  OEDIPUS.   Was it by treason? Or by an attack of illness?

MESSENGER. A little thing brings old men to their rest.   915
OEDIPUS. It was sickness, then?
MESSENGER.   Yes, and his many years.
OEDIPUS. Ah!
Why should a man respect the Pythian hearth,[1] or
Give heed to the birds that jangle above his head?
They prophesied that I should kill Polybos,   920
Kill my own father; but he is dead and buried,
And I am here—I never touched him, never,
Unless he died of grief for my departure,
And thus, in a sense, through me. No. Polybos
Has packed the oracles off with him underground.   925
They are empty words.
    IOKASTÊ.   Had I not told you so?
OEDIPUS. You had; it was my faint heart that betrayed me.
IOKASTÊ. From now on never think of those things again.
OEDIPUS. And yet—must I not fear my mother's bed?
IOKASTÊ. Why should anyone in this world be afraid,   930
Since Fate rules us and nothing can be foreseen?
A man should live only for the present day.

Have no more fear of sleeping with your mother:
How many men, in dreams, have lain with their mothers!
No reasonable man is troubled by such things.   935
    OEDIPUS. That is true; only—
If only my mother were not still alive!
But she is alive. I can not help my dread.
    IOKASTÊ. Yet this news of your father's death is wonderful.
OEDIPUS. Wonderful. But I fear the living woman.   940
MESSENGER. Tell me, who is this woman that you fear?
OEDIPUS. It is Meropê, man; the wife of King Polybos.
MESSENGER. Meropê? Why should you be afraid of her?
OEDIPUS. An oracle of the gods, a dreadful saying.
MESSENGER. Can you tell me about it or are you sworn to silence? 945
OEDIPUS. I can tell you, and I will.
Apollo said through his prophet that I was the man
Who should marry his own mother, shed his father's blood
With his own hands. And so, for all these years
I have kept clear of Corinth, and no harm has come—   950
Though it would have been sweet to see my parents again.
    MESSENGER. And is this the fear that drove you out of Corinth?
OEDIPUS. Would you have me kill my father?
MESSENGER.   As for that

[1] Pythian hearth: Delphi.

You must be reassured by the news I gave you.

OEDIPUS.   If you could reassure me, I would reward you.   955

MESSENGER.   I had that in mind, I will confess: I thought
I could count on you when you returned to Corinth.

OEDIPUS.   No: I will never go near my parents again.

MESSENGER.   Ah, son, you still do not know what you are doing—

OEDIPUS.   What do you mean? In the name of God tell me!   960

MESSENGER.   —if these are your reasons for not going home.

OEDIPUS.   I tell you, I fear the oracle may come true.

MESSENGER.   And guilt may come upon you through your parents?

OEDIPUS.   That is the dread that is always in my heart.

MESSENGER.   Can you not see that all your fears are groundless?   965

OEDIPUS.   Groundless? Am I not my parents' son?

MESSENGER.   Polybos was not your father.

OEDIPUS.   Not my father?

MESSENGER.   No more your father than the man speaking to you.

OEDIPUS.   But you are nothing to me!

MESSENGER.   Neither was he.

OEDIPUS.   Then why did he call me son?

MESSENGER.   I will tell you: 970
Long ago he had you from my hands, as a gift.

OEDIPUS.   Then how could he love me so, if I was not his?

MESSENGER.   He had no children, and his heart turned to you.

OEDIPUS.   What of you? Did you buy me? Did you find me by chance?

MESSENGER.   I came upon you in the woody vales of Kithairon.   975

OEDIPUS.   And what were you doing there?

MESSENGER.   Tending my flocks.

OEDIPUS.   A wandering shepherd?

MESSENGER.   But your savior, son, that day.

OEDIPUS.   From what did you save me?

MESSENGER.   Your ankles should tell you that.

OEDIPUS.   Ah, stranger, why do you speak of that childhood pain?

MESSENGER.   I pulled the skewer that pinned your feet together.   980

OEDIPUS.   I have had the mark as long as I can remember.

MESSENGER.   That was why you were given the name you bear.

OEDIPUS.   God! Was it my father or my mother who did it?
Tell me!

MESSENGER.   I do not know. The man who gave you to me
Can tell you better than I.   985

OEDIPUS.   It was not you that found me, but another?

MESSENGER.   It was another shepherd gave you to me.

OEDIPUS.   Who was he? Can you tell me who he was?

MESSENGER.   I think he was said to be one of Laïos' people.

OEDIPUS.   You mean the Laïos who was king here years ago?   990

MESSENGER. Yes; King Laïos; and the man was one of his herdsmen.
OEDIPUS. Is he still alive? Can I see him?
MESSENGER.   These men here
Know best about such things.
OEDIPUS.   Does anyone here
Know this shepherd that he is talking about?
Have you seen him in the fields, or in the town?   995
If you have, tell me. It is time things were made plain.
    CHORAGOS. I think the man he means is that same shepherd
You have already asked to see. Iokastê perhaps
Could tell you something.
OEDIPUS.   Do you know anything
About him, Lady? Is he the man we have summoned?   1000
Is that the man this shepherd means?
    IOKASTÊ.   Why think of him?
Forget this herdsman. Forget it all.
This talk is a waste of time.
OEDIPUS.   How can you say that,
When the clues to my true birth are in my hands?
    IOKASTÊ. For God's love, let us have no more questioning!   1005
Is your life nothing to you?
My own is pain enough for me to bear.
    OEDIPUS. You need not worry. Suppose my mother a slave,
And born of slaves: no baseness can touch you.
    IOKASTÊ. Listen to me, I beg you: do not do this thing!   1010
    OEDIPUS. I will not listen; the truth must be made known.
    IOKASTÊ. Everything that I say is for your own good!
    OEDIPUS.   My own good
Snaps my patience, then; I want none of it.
    IOKASTÊ. You are fatally wrong! May you never learn who you are!
    OEDIPUS. Go, one of you, and bring the shepherd here.   1015
Let us leave this woman to brag of her royal name.
    IOKASTÊ. Ah, miserable!
That is the only word I have for you now.
That is the only word I can ever have. (*Exit into the palace.*)
    CHORAGOS. Why has she left us, Oedipus? Why has she gone   1020
In such a passion of sorrow? I fear this silence:
Something dreadful may come of it.
    OEDIPUS.   Let it come!
However base my birth, I must know about it.
The Queen, like a woman, is perhaps ashamed
To think of my low origin. But I   1025
Am a child of Luck; I can not be dishonored.
Luck is my mother; the passing months, my brothers,

Have seen me rich and poor.
                    If this is so,
How could I wish that I were someone else?
How could I not be glad to know my birth?   1030

ODE III

STROPHE

CHORUS. If ever the coming time were known
To my heart's pondering,
Kithairon, now by Heaven I see the torches
At the festival of the next full moon,
And see the dance, and hear the choir sing   1035
A grace to your gentle shade:
Mountain where Oedipus was found,
O mountain guard of a noble race!
May the god[1] who heals us lend his aid,
And let that glory come to pass   1040
For our king's cradling-ground.

ANTISTROPHE

Of the nymphs that flower beyond the years,
Who bore you,[2] royal child,
To Pan of the hills or the timberline Apollo,
Cold in delight where the upland clears,   1045
Or Hermês for whom Kyllenê's heights are piled?
Or flushed as evening cloud,
Great Dionysos, roamer of mountains,
He—was it he who found you there,
And caught you up in his own proud   1050
Arms from the sweet god-ravisher
Who laughed by the Muses' fountains?

SCENE IV

OEDIPUS. Sirs: though I do not know the man,
I think I see him coming, this shepherd we want:
He is old, like our friend here, and the men   1055
Bringing him seem to be servants of my house.
But you can tell, if you have ever seen him.

(*Enter* SHEPHERD *escorted by* SERVANTS.)

[1] god: Apollo.
[2] Who bore you: The chorus is suggesting that perhaps Oedipus is the son
of one of the immortal nymphs and of a god—Pan, Apollo, Hermes, or Dionysos.
The "sweet god-ravisher" (line 1051) is the presumed mother.

CHORAGOS. I know him, he was Laïos' man. You can trust him.

OEDIPUS. Tell me first, you from Corinth: is this the shepherd
We were discussing?

MESSENGER. This is the very man.   1060

OEDIPUS (to SHEPHERD). Come here. No, look at me. You must answer
Everything I ask.—You belonged to Laïos?

SHEPHERD. Yes: born his slave, brought up in his house.

OEDIPUS. Tell me: what kind of work did you do for him?

SHEPHERD. I was a shepherd of his, most of my life.   1065

OEDIPUS. Where mainly did you go for pasturage?

SHEPHERD. Sometimes Kithairon, sometimes the hills near-by.

OEDIPUS. Do you remember ever seeing this man out there?

SHEPHERD. What would he be doing there? This man?

OEDIPUS. This man standing here. Have you ever seen him before? 1070

SHEPHERD. No. At least, not to my recollection.

MESSENGER. And that is not strange, my lord. But I'll refresh
His memory: he must remember when we two
Spent three whole seasons together, March to September,
On Kithairon or thereabouts. He had two flocks;   1075
I had one. Each autumn I'd drive mine home
And he would go back with his to Laïos' sheepfold.—
Is this not true, just as I have described it?

SHEPHERD. True, yes; but it was all so long ago.

MESSENGER. Well, then: do you remember, back in those days, 1080
That you gave me a baby boy to bring up as my own?

SHEPHERD. What if I did? What are you trying to say?

MESSENGER. King Oedipus was once that little child.

SHEPHERD. Damn you, hold your tongue!

OEDIPUS.   No more of that!
It is your tongue needs watching, not this man's.   1085

SHEPHERD. My king, my master, what is it I have done wrong?

OEDIPUS. You have not answered his question about the boy.

SHEPHERD. He does not know . . . He is only making trouble . . .

OEDIPUS. Come, speak plainly, or it will go hard with you.

SHEPHERD. In God's name, do not torture an old man!   1090

OEDIPUS. Come here, one of you; bind his arms behind him.

SHEPHERD. Unhappy king! What more do you wish to learn?

OEDIPUS. Did you give this man the child he speaks of?

SHEPHERD.   I did.
And I would to God I had died that very day.

OEDIPUS. You will die now unless you speak the truth.   1095

SHEPHERD. Yet if I speak the truth, I am worse than dead.

OEDIPUS (to ATTENDANT). He intends to draw it out, apparently—

SHEPHERD.   No! I have told you already that I gave him the boy.

OEDIPUS.   Where did you get him? From your house? From somewhere else?

SHEPHERD.   Not from mine, no. A man gave him to me.   1100

OEDIPUS.   Is that man here? Whose house did he belong to?

SHEPHERD.   For God's love, my king, do not ask me any more!

OEDIPUS.   You are a dead man if I have to ask you again.

SHEPHERD.   Then . . . Then the child was from the palace of Laïos.

OEDIPUS.   A slave child? or a child of his own line?   1105

SHEPHERD.   Ah, I am on the brink of dreadful speech!

OEDIPUS.   And I of dreadful hearing. Yet I must hear.

SHEPHERD.   If you must be told, then . . .

                                            They said it was Laïos' child;
But it is your wife who can tell you about that.

OEDIPUS.   My wife!—Did she give it to you?

SHEPHERD.   My lord, she did.   1110

OEDIPUS.   Do you know why?

SHEPHERD.   I was told to get rid of it.

OEDIPUS.   Oh heartless mother!

SHEPHERD.   But in dread of prophecies . . .

OEDIPUS.   Tell me.

SHEPHERD.   It was said that the boy would kill his own father.

OEDIPUS.   Then why did you give him over to this old man?

SHEPHERD.   I pitied the baby, my king,   1115
And I thought that this man would take him far away
To his own country.

                    He saved him—but for what a fate!
For if you are what this man says you are,
No man living is more wretched than Oedipus.

OEDIPUS.   Ah God!   1120
It was true!
            All the prophecies!
                                —Now,
O Light, may I look on you for the last time!
I, Oedipus,
Oedipus, damned in his birth, in his marriage damned,
Damned in the blood he shed with his own hand! (*He rushes into the
palace.*)   1125

ODE IV

STROPHE 1

CHORUS.   Alas for the seed of men.
What measure shall I give these generations

That breathe on the void and are void
And exist and do not exist?
Who bears more weight of joy   1130
Than mass of sunlight shifting in images,
Or who shall make his thought stay on
That down time drifts away?
Your splendor is all fallen.
O naked brow of wrath and tears,   1135
O change of Oedipus!
I who saw your days call no man blest—
Your great days like ghósts góne.

ANTISTROPHE 1

That mind was a strong bow.
Deep, how deep you drew it then, hard archer,   1140
At a dim fearful range,
And brought dear glory down!
You overcame the stranger[1]—
The virgin with her hooking lion claws—
And though death sang, stood like a tower   -   1145
To make pale Thebes take heart.
Fortress against our sorrow!
True king, giver of laws,
Majestic Oedipus!
No prince in Thebes had ever such renown,   1150
No prince won such grace of power.

STROPHE 2

And now of all men ever known
Most pitiful is this man's story:
His fortunes are most changed, his state
Fallen to a low slave's   1155
Ground under bitter fate.
O Oedipus, most royal one!
The great door[2] that expelled you to the light
Gave at night—ah, gave night to your glory:
As to the father, to the fathering son.   1160
All understood too late.
How could that queen whom Laïos won,
The garden that he harrowed at his height,
Be silent when that act was done?

[1] stranger: the Sphinx.
[2] door: Iokastê's womb.

ANTISTROPHE 2

But all eyes fail before time's eye,   1165
All actions come to justice there.
Though never willed, though far down the deep past,
Your bed, your dread sirings,
Are brought to book at last.
Child by Laïos doomed to die,   1170
Then doomed to lose that fortunate little death,
Would God you never took breath in this air
That with my wailing lips I take to cry:
For I weep the world's outcast.
I was blind, and now I can tell why: 1175
Asleep, for you had given ease of breath
To Thebes, while the false years went by.

EXODOS[1]

Enter, from the palace, SECOND MESSENGER.

SECOND MESSENGER.   Elders of Thebes, most honored in this land,
What horrors are yours to see and hear, what weight
Of sorrow to be endured, if, true to your birth,   1180
You venerate the line of Labdakos!
I think neither Istros nor Phasis, those great rivers,
Could purify this place of all the evil
It shelters now, or soon must bring to light—
Evil not done unconsciously, but willed.   1185

The greatest griefs are those we cause ourselves.
    CHORAGOS.   Surely, friend, we have grief enough already;
What new sorrow do you mean?
    SECOND MESSENGER.   The queen is dead.
    CHORAGOS.   O miserable queen! But at whose hand?
    SECOND MESSENGER.   Her own.
The full horror of what happened you can not know,   1190
For you did not see it; but I, who did, will tell you
As clearly as I can how she met her death.

When she had left us,
In passionate silence, passing through the court,
She ran to her apartment in the house,   1195
Her hair clutched by the fingers of both hands.
She closed the doors behind her; then, by that bed
Where long ago the fatal son was conceived—

1 Exodos: final scene.

That son who should bring about his father's death—
We heard her call upon Laïos, dead so many years,   1200
And heard her wail for the double fruit of her marriage,
A husband by her husband, children by her child.

Exactly how she died I do not know:
For Oedipus burst in moaning and would not let us
Keep vigil to the end: it was by him   1205
As he stormed about the room that our eyes were caught.
From one to another of us he went, begging a sword,
Hunting the wife who was not his wife, the mother
Whose womb had carried his own children and himself.
I do not know: it was none of us aided him,   1210
But surely one of the gods was in control!
For with a dreadful cry
He hurled his weight, as though wrenched out of himself,
At the twin doors: the bolts gave, and he rushed in.
And there we saw her hanging, her body swaying   1215
From the cruel cord she had noosed about her neck.
A great sob broke from him, heartbreaking to hear,
As he loosed the rope and lowered her to the ground.

I would blot out from my mind what happened next!
For the king ripped from her gown the golden brooches   1220
That were her ornament, and raised them, and plunged them down
Straight into his own eyeballs, crying, "No more,
No more shall you look on the misery about me,
The horrors of my own doing! Too long you have known
The faces of those whom I should never have seen,   1225
Too long been blind to those for whom I was searching!
From this hour, go in darkness!" And as he spoke,
He struck at his eyes—not once, but many times;
And the blood spattered his beard,
Bursting from his ruined sockets like red hail.   1230

So from the unhappiness of two this evil has sprung,
A curse on the man and woman alike. The old
Happiness of the house of Labdakos
Was happiness enough: where is it today?
It is all wailing and ruin, disgrace, death—all   1235
The misery of mankind that has a name—
And it is wholly and for ever theirs.
        CHORAGOS.   Is he in agony still? Is there no rest for him?
        SECOND MESSENGER.   He is calling for someone to open the doors wide
So that all the children of Kadmos may look upon   1240

His father's murderer, his mother's—no,
I can not say it!
                    And then he will leave Thebes,
Self-exiled, in order that the curse
Which he himself pronounced may depart from the house
He is weak, and there is none to lead him,   1245
So terrible is his suffering.
                    But you will see:
Look, the doors are opening; in a moment
You will see a thing that would crush a heart of stone.

(*The central door is opened;* OEDIPUS, *blinded, is led in.*)

CHORAGOS.   Dreadful indeed for men to see.
Never have my own eyes   1250
Looked on a sight so full of fear.

Oedipus!
What madness came upon you, what daemon
Leaped on your life with heavier
Punishment than a mortal man can bear?   1255
No: I can not even
Look at you, poor ruined one.
And I would speak, question, ponder,
If I were able. No.
You make me shudder.   1260
        OEDIPUS.   God. God.
Is there a sorrow greater?
Where shall I find harbor in this world?
My voice is hurled far on a dark wind.
What has God done to me?   1265
        CHORAGOS.   Too terrible to think of, or to see.

STROPHE 1
        OEDIPUS.   O cloud of night,
Never to be turned away: night coming on,
I can not tell how: night like a shroud!
My fair winds brought me here.
                            O God. Again   1270
The pain of the spikes where I had sight,
The flooding pain
Of memory, never to be gouged out.
        CHORAGOS.   This is not strange.
You suffer it all twice over, remorse in pain,   1275
Pain in remorse.

ANTISTROPHE 1

OEDIPUS.   Ah dear friend
Are you faithful even yet, you alone?
Are you still standing near me, will you stay here,
Patient, to care for the blind?

                 The blind man!   1280
Yet even blind I know who it is attends me,
By the voice's tone—
Though my new darkness hide the comforter.
    CHORAGOS.   Oh fearful act!
What god was it drove you to rake black   1285
Night across your eyes?

STROPHE 2

OEDIPUS.   Apollo. Apollo. Dear
Children, the god was Apollo.
He brought my sick, sick fate upon me.
But the blinding hand was my own!   1290
How could I bear to see
When all my sight was horror everywhere?
    CHORAGOS.   Everywhere; that is true.
    OEDIPUS.   And now what is left?
Images? Love? A greeting even,   1295
Sweet to the senses? Is there anything?
Ah, no, friends: lead me away.
Lead me away from Thebes.
               Lead the great wreck
And hell of Oedipus, whom the gods hate.
    CHORAGOS.   Your misery, you are not blind to that.   1300
Would God you had never found it out!

ANTISTROPHE 2

OEDIPUS.   Death take the man who unbound
My feet on that hillside
And delivered me from death to life! What life?
If only I had died,   1305
This weight of monstrous doom
Could not have dragged me and my darlings down.
    CHORAGOS.   I would have wished the same.
    OEDIPUS.   Oh never to have come here
With my father's blood upon me! Never   1310
To have been the man they call his mother's husband!
Oh accurst! Oh child of evil,
To have entered that wretched bed—

the selfsame one!

More primal than sin itself, this fell to me.

    CHORAGOS.   I do not know what words to offer you.   1315
You were better dead than alive and blind.

    OEDIPUS.   Do not counsel me any more. This punishment
That I have laid upon myself is just.
If I had eyes,
I do not know how I could bear the sight   1320
Of my father, when I came to the house of Death,
Or my mother: for I have sinned against them both
So vilely that I could not make my peace
By strangling my own life.
Or do you think my children,
Born as they were born, would be sweet to my eyes?   1325
Ah never, never! Nor this town with its high walls,
Nor the holy images of the gods.
For I,
Thrice miserable!—Oedipus, noblest of all the line
Of Kadmos, have condemned myself to enjoy
These things no more, by my own malediction   1330
Expelling that man whom the gods declared
To be a defilement in the house of Laïos.
After exposing the rankness of my own guilt,
How could I look men frankly in the eyes?
No, I swear it,   1335
If I could have stifled my hearing at its source,
I would have done it and made all this body
A tight cell of misery, blank to light and sound:
So I should have been safe in my dark mind
Beyond external evil.
Ah Kithairon!   1340
Why did you shelter me? When I was cast upon you,
Why did I not die? Then I should never
Have shown the world my execrable birth.

Ah Polybos! Corinth, city that I believed
The ancient seat of my ancestors: how fair   1345
I seemed, your child! And all the while this evil
Was cancerous within me!
For I am sick
In my own being, sick in my origin.

O three roads, dark ravine, woodland and way
Where three roads met: you, drinking my father's blood,   1350
My own blood, spilled by my own hand: can you remember

The unspeakable things I did there, and the things
I went on from there to do?
                  O marriage, marriage!
The act that engendered me, and again the act
Performed by the son in the same bed—
                       Ah, the net   1355
Of incest, mingling fathers, brothers, sons,
With brides, wives, mothers: the last evil
That can be known by men: no tongue can say
How evil!
         No. For the love of God, conceal me
Somewhere far from Thebes; or kill me; or hurl me   1360
Into the sea, away from men's eyes for ever.

Come, lead me. You need not fear to touch me.
Of all men, I alone can bear this guilt.

   (*Enter* KREON.)

    CHORAGOS.   Kreon is here now. As to what you ask,
He may decide the course to take. He only   1365
Is left to protect the city in your place.
    OEDIPUS.   Alas, how can I speak to him? What right have I
To beg his courtesy whom I have deeply wronged?
    KREON.   I have not come to mock you, Oedipus,
Or to reproach you, either. (*To* ATTENDANTS)
              —You, standing there: 1370
If you have lost all respect for man's dignity,
At least respect the flame of Lord Helios:
Do not allow this pollution to show itself
Openly here, an affront to the earth
And Heaven's rain and the light of day. No, take him   1375
Into the house as quickly as you can.
For it is proper
That only the close kindred see his grief.
    OEDIPUS.   I pray you in God's name, since your courtesy
Ignores my dark expectation, visiting   1380
With mercy this man of all men most execrable:
Give me what I ask—for your good, not for mine.
    KREON.   And what is it that you turn to me begging for?
    OEDIPUS.   Drive me out of this country as quickly as may be
To a place where no human voice can ever greet me.   1385
    KREON.   I should have done that before now—only,
God's will had not been wholly revealed to me.
    OEDIPUS.   But his command is plain: the parricide
Must be destroyed. I am that evil man.

KREON. That is the sense of it, yes; but as things are,   1390
We had best discover clearly what is to be done.
    OEDIPUS. You would learn more about a man like me?
    KREON. You are ready now to listen to the god.
    OEDIPUS. I will listen. But it is to you
That I must turn for help. I beg you, hear me.   1395

The woman in there—
Give her whatever funeral you think proper:
She is your sister.
                    —But let me go, Kreon!
Let me purge my father's Thebes of the pollution
Of my living here, and go out to the wild hills,   1400
To Kithairon, that has won such fame with me,
The tomb my mother and father appointed for me,
And let me die there, as they willed I should.
And yet I know
Death will not ever come to me through sickness   1405
Or in any natural way: I have been preserved
For some unthinkable fate. But let that be.

As for my sons, you need not care for them.
They are men, they will find some way to live.
But my poor daughters, who have shared my table,   1410
Who never before have been parted from their father—
Take care of them, Kreon; do this for me.

And will you let me touch them with my hands
A last time, and let us weep together?
Be kind, my lord,   1415
Great prince, be kind!
                    Could I but touch them,
They would be mine again, as when I had my eyes.

    (*Enter* ANTIGONE *and* ISMENE, *attended.*)

Ah, God!
Is it my dearest children I hear weeping?
Has Kreon pitied me and sent my daughters?   1420
    KREON. Yes, Oedipus: I knew that they were dear to you
In the old days, and know you must love them still.
    OEDIPUS. May God bless you for this—and be a friendlier
Guardian to you than he has been to me!

Children, where are you?   1425
Come quickly to my hands: they are your brother's—
Hands that have brought your father's once clear eyes

To this way of seeing—
                    Ah dearest ones,
I had neither sight nor knowledge then, your father
By the woman who was the source of his own life!   1430
And I weep for you—having no strength to see you—,
I weep for you when I think of the bitterness
That men will visit upon you all your lives.
What homes, what festivals can you attend
Without being forced to depart again in tears?   1435
And when you come to marriageable age,
Where is the man, my daughters, who would dare
Risk the bane that lies on all my children?
Is there any evil wanting? Your father killed
His father; sowed the womb of her who bore him;   1440
Engendered you at the fount of his own existence!
That is what they will say of you.

                              Then, whom
Can you ever marry? There are no bridegrooms for you,
And your lives must wither away in sterile dreaming.

O Kreon, son of Menoikeus!   1445
You are the only father my daughters have,
Since we, their parents, are both of us gone for ever.
They are your own blood: you will not let them
Fall into beggary and loneliness;
You will keep them from the miseries that are mine!   1450
Take pity on them; see, they are only children,
Friendless except for you. Promise me this,
Great prince, and give me your hand in token of it.

        (KREON *clasps his right hand.*)

Children:
I could say much, if you could understand me,   1455
But as it is, I have only this prayer for you:
Live where you can, be as happy as you can—
Happier, please God, than God has made your father.
        KREON.   Enough. You have wept enough. Now go within.
        OEDIPUS.   I must; but it is hard.
        KREON.   Time eases all things.   1460
        OEDIPUS.   You know my mind, then?
        KREON.   Say what you desire.
        OEDIPUS.   Send me from Thebes!
        KREON.   God grant that I may!

OEDIPUS.   But since God hates me . . .
KREON.   No, he will grant your wish.
OEDIPUS.   You promise?
KREON.   I can not speak beyond my knowledge.
OEDIPUS.   Then lead me in.
KREON.   Come now, and leave your children. 1465
OEDIPUS.   No! Do not take them from me!
KREON.   Think no longer
That you are in command here, but rather think
How, when you were, you served your own destruction.

(*Exeunt into the house all but the* CHORUS; *the* CHORAGOS *chants direct-ly to the audience.*)

CHORAGOS.   Men of Thebes: look upon Oedipus.

This is the king who solved the famous riddle   1470
And towered up, most powerful of men.
No mortal eyes but looked on him with envy,
Yet in the end ruin swept over him.

Let every man in mankind's frailty
Consider his last day; and let none   1475
Presume on his good fortune until he find
Life, at his death, a memory without pain.

QUESTIONS

1. The oracles had prophesied that Oedipus would kill his father and beget children by his mother. Is Oedipus therefore *made* to do these things? Is the play premised on the notion that Oedipus is bound or free—the puppet of fate or the creator of his own fate? Or some of each?

2. In what ways is Oedipus shown to be a person of extraordinary stature? Consider both his life before the play begins and his actions during the course of the play. What is Oedipus' primary motivation throughout the play? What characters try to dissuade him from pursuing that motivation? How do his subjects regard him?

3. What errors in judgment does Oedipus make? Are these errors grounded in weakness of character? If so, what are his weaknesses of character? (Do not answer this question too quickly. Respectable critics have differed sharply, not only over the identification of Oedipus' "flaw," but, indeed, over whether he has one.)

4. Is any common pattern of behavior exhibited in Oedipus' encounters with Laïos, with Teiresias, and with Kreon? Is there any justification for his anger with Teiresias? for his suspicion of Kreon? Why?

5. Oedipus' original question, "Who killed Laïos?" soon turns into the question "Who am I?" On the level of plot, the answer is "Son of Laïos and Iokastê, father's murderer, mother's husband." What is the answer at the level of character—that is, in a psychological or philosophical sense?

6. What philosophical issues are raised by Iokastê's judgment on the oracles (Scene 2)? How does the chorus respond to her judgment? How does the play resolve these issues?

7. Why does Oedipus blind himself? Is this an act of weakness or of strength? Why does he ask Kreon to drive him from Thebes? Does he feel that his fate has been just or unjust? Is his suffering, in fact, deserved? partially deserved? undeserved?

8. There is a good deal in the play about seeing and blindness. What purpose does this serve? How is Oedipus contrasted with Teiresias? How does Oedipus at the beginning of the play contrast with Oedipus at the end? Why is his blinding himself dramatically appropriate?

9. In what sense may Oedipus be regarded as a better man, though a less fortunate one, at the end of the play than at the beginning? What has he gained from his experience?

10. Some critics have suggested that Oedipus' answer to the Sphinx's riddle was incomplete—that the answer should have been not just man but Oedipus himself—and that Oedipus was as ignorant of the whole truth here as he is when he lays his curse in Scene 1 on the murderer of Laïos. Does this suggestion make sense? On how many legs does Oedipus walk at the end of the play?

11. If the answer to the Sphinx's riddle is not just man but Oedipus himself, may the answer to Oedipus' question "Who am I?" pertain not only to Oedipus but also to man, or at least to civilized Western man? What characteristics of Oedipus as an individual are also characteristics of man in the Western world? Is Sophocles writing only about Oedipus the king, or is he saying something about man's presumed place and his real place in the universe?

12. What purposes are served by the appearance of Antigone and Ismene in the Exodos?

13. What purposes does the chorus serve in the play? Whom does it speak for? Comment on the function of each of the four Odes.

14. What does the final speech of the Choragos tell us about human life?

15. A central formal feature of the play is its use of dramatic irony. Point out speeches by Oedipus, especially in the Prologue and Scene 1, that have a different or a larger meaning for the audience than for Oedipus himself.

16. The plot of *Oedipus Rex* has been called one of the most perfect dramatic plots ever devised. Why is it admired? What are its outstanding characteristics?

William Shakespeare

OTHELLO

CHARACTERS

DUKE OF VENICE
BRABANTIO, *a Senator*
OTHER SENATORS
GRATIANO, *brother to Brabantio*
LODOVICO, *kinsman to Brabantio*
OTHELLO, *a noble Moor in the service of the Venetian state*
CASSIO, *his lieutenant*
IAGO, *his ancient*
MONTANO, *Othello's predecessor in the government of Cyprus*
RODERIGO, *a Venetian gentleman*
CLOWN, *servant to Othello*
DESDEMONA, *daughter to Brabantio and wife to Othello*
EMILIA, *wife to Iago*
BIANCA, *mistress to Cassio*
SAILOR, MESSENGER, HERALD, OFFICERS, GENTLEMEN, MUSICIANS, *and* ATTENDANTS

SCENE. *Venice; a seaport in Cyprus.*

ACT I

SCENE I. Venice. A street.

Enter RODERIGO *and* IAGO.

RODERIGO.   Tush, never tell me. I take it much unkindly
That thou, Iago, who hast had my purse
As if the strings were thine, shouldst know of this.
IAGO.   'Sblood, but you will not hear me.
If ever I did dream of such a matter,   5
Abhor me.
RODERIGO.   Thou told'st me thou didst hold him in thy hate.
IAGO.   Despise me if I do not. Three great ones of the city,
In personal suit to make me his Lieutenant,
Off-capped to him. And, by the faith of man,   10
I know my price, I am worth no worse a place.
But he, as loving his own pride and purposes,

Evades them, with a bombast circumstance
Horribly stuffed with epithets of war.
And, in conclusion,   15
Nonsuits° my mediators, for, "Certes," says he,
"I have already chose my officer."
And what was he?
Forsooth, a great arithmetician,°
One Michael Cassio, a Florentine,   20
A fellow almost damned in a fair wife,°
That never set a squadron in the field,
Nor the division of a battle knows
More than a spinster, unless the bookish theoric,
Wherein the toged Consuls° can propose   25
As masterly as he—mere prattle without practice
Is all his soldiership. But he, sir, had the election.
And I, of whom his eyes had seen the proof
At Rhodes, at Cyprus, and on other grounds
Christian and heathen, must be beleed° and calmed   30
By debitor and creditor. This countercaster,°
He, in good time,° must his Lieutenant be,
And I—God bless the mark!—his Moorship's Ancient.°
    RODERIGO.   By Heaven, I rather would have been his hangman.
    IAGO.   Why, there's no remedy. 'Tis the course of service,   35
Preferment goes by letter and affection,
And not by old gradation,° where each second
Stood heir to the first. Now, sir, be judge yourself
Whether I in any just term am affined°
To love the Moor.
    RODERIGO.   I would not follow him, then.   40
    IAGO.   Oh, sir, content you,
I follow him to serve my turn upon him.
We cannot all be masters, nor all masters
Cannot be truly followed. You shall mark

---

16. Nonsuits: rejects the petition of.   19. arithmetician: Contemporary books
on military tactics are full of elaborate diagrams and numerals to explain military
formations. Cassio is a student of such books.   21. almost . . . wife: A much-
disputed phrase. There is an Italian proverb, "You have married a fair wife? You
are damned." If Iago has this in mind, he means by almost that Cassio is about
to marry.   25. toged Consuls: councilors in togas [L.P.].   30. beleed: placed
on the lee (or unfavorable) side.   31. countercaster: calculator (repeating the
idea of arithmetician). Counters were used in making calculations.   32. in . . .
time: A phrase expressing indignation.   33. Ancient: ensign, the third officer in
the company of which Othello is Captain and Cassio Lieutenant.   36–37. Preferment . . . gradation: promotion comes through private recommendation and
favoritism and not by order of seniority.   39. affined: tied by affection.

Many a duteous and knee-crooking knave   45
That doting on his own obsequious bondage
Wears out his time, much like his master's ass,
For naught but provender, and when he's old, cashiered.
Whip me such honest knaves. Others there are
Who, trimmed in forms and visages of duty,   50
Keep yet their hearts attending on themselves,
And throwing but shows of service on their lords
Do well thrive by them, and when they have lined their coats
Do themselves homage. These fellows have some soul,
And such a one do I profess myself. For, sir,   55
It is as sure as you are Roderigo,
Were I the Moor, I would not be Iago.
In following him, I follow but myself.
Heaven is my judge, not I for love and duty,
But seeming so, for my peculiar° end.   60
For when my outward action doth demonstrate
The native act and figure of my heart
In compliment extern, 'tis not long after
But I will wear my heart upon my sleeve
For daws to peck at. I am not what I am.   65
    RODERIGO.   What a full fortune does the thick-lips owe°
If he can carry 't thus!°
    IAGO.   Call up her father,
Rouse him. Make after him, poison his delight,
Proclaim him in the streets. Incense her kinsmen,
And though he in a fertile climate dwell,   70
Plague him with flies. Though that his joy be joy,
Yet throw such changes of vexation on 't
As it may lose some color.
    RODERIGO.   Here is her father's house, I'll call aloud.
    IAGO.   Do, with like timorous° accent and dire yell   75
As when, by night and negligence, the fire
Is spied in populous cities.
    RODERIGO.   What ho, Brabantio! Signior Brabantio, ho!
    IAGO.   Awake! What ho, Brabantio! Thieves! Thieves! Thieves!
Look to your house, your daughter and your bags!°   80
Thieves! Thieves!

(BRABANTIO *appears above, at a window.*)

    BRABANTIO.   What is the reason of this terrible summons?
What is the matter there?

60. peculiar: personal [L.P.]. **66. owe:** own. **67. carry't thus:** i.e., bring off
this marriage. **75. timorous:** terrifying. **80. bags:** moneybags.

RODERIGO. Signior, is all your family within?

IAGO. Are your doors locked?

BRABANTIO. Why, wherefore ask you this? 85

IAGO. 'Zounds, sir, you're robbed. For shame, put on your gown,
Your heart is burst, you have lost half your soul.
Even now, now, very now, an old black ram
Is tupping your white ewe. Arise, arise,
Awake the snorting° citizens with the bell, 90
Or else the Devil° will make a grandsire of you.
Arise, I say.

BRABANTIO. What, have you lost your wits?

RODERIGO. Most reverend signior, do you know my voice?

BRABANTIO. Not I. What are you?

RODERIGO. My name is Roderigo.

BRABANTIO. The worser welcome. 95
I have charged thee not to haunt about my doors.
In honest plainness thou hast heard me say
My daughter is not for thee, and now, in madness,
Being full of supper and distempering draughts,
Upon malicious bravery° dost thou come 100
To start° my quiet.

RODERIGO. Sir, sir, sir—

BRABANTIO. But thou must needs be sure
My spirit and my place have in them power
To make this bitter to thee.

RODERIGO. Patience, good sir.

BRABANTIO. What tell'st thou me of robbing? This is Venice, 105
My house is not a grange.°

RODERIGO. Most grave Brabantio,
In simple and pure soul I come to you.

IAGO. 'Zounds, sir, you are one of those that will not serve God if the
Devil bid you. Because we come to do you service and you think we are
ruffians, you'll have your daughter covered with a Barbary° horse, 110
you'll have your nephews° neigh to you, you'll have coursers for cousins,°
and jennets° for germans.°

BRABANTIO. What profane wretch art thou?

IAGO. I am one, sir, that comes to tell you your daughter and the Moor
are now making the beast with two backs. 115

BRABANTIO. Thou art a villain.

IAGO. You are—a Senator.

---

90. snorting: snoring. 91. Devil: The Devil in old pictures and woodcuts was
represented as black. 100. bravery: defiance. 101. start: startle. 106. grange:
lonely farm. 110. Barbary: Moorish. 111. nephews: grandsons. cousins: near
relations. 112. jennets: Moorish ponies. germans: kinsmen.

BRABANTIO. This thou shalt answer. I know thee, Roderigo.
RODERIGO.   Sir, I will answer anything. But I beseech you
If 't be your pleasure and most wise consent,
As partly I find it is, that your fair daughter,   120
At this odd-even° and dull watch o' the night,
Transported with no worse nor better guard
But with a knave of common hire, a gondolier,
To the gross clasps of a lascivious Moor—
If this be known to you, and your allowance,°   125
We then have done you bold and saucy wrongs.
But if you know not this, my manners tell me
We have your wrong rebuke. Do not believe
That from the sense of all civility
I thus would play and trifle with your reverence.   130
Your daughter, if you have not given her leave,
I say again, hath made a gross revolt,
Tying her duty, beauty, wit, and fortunes
In an extravagant° and wheeling° stranger
Of here and everywhere. Straight satisfy yourself.   135
If she be in her chamber or your house,
Let loose on me the justice of the state
For thus deluding you.
        BRABANTIO.   Strike on the tinder,° ho!
Give me a taper!° Call up all my people!
This accident is not unlike my dream.   140
Belief of it oppresses me already.
Light, I say! Light!

        (*Exit above.*)

        IAGO.   Farewell, for I must leave you.
It seems not meet, nor wholesome to my place,°
To be produced—as if I stay I shall—   145
Against the Moor. For I do know the state,
However this may gall him with some check,
Cannot with safety cast° him. For he's embarked
With such loud reason to the Cyprus wars,
Which even now stand in act, that, for their souls,   150
Another of his fathom they have none
To lead their business. In which regard,
Though I do hate him as I do Hell pains,

121. **odd-even**: about midnight. 125. **your allowance**: by your permission.
134. **extravagant**: vagabond. **wheeling**: wandering. 138. **tinder**: the primitive
method of making fire, used before the invention of matches. 139. **taper**: candle.
144. **place**: i.e., as Othello's officer. 148. **cast**: dismiss from service.

Yet for necessity of present life
I must show out a flag and sign of love,   155
Which is indeed but sign. That you shall surely find him,
Lead to the Sagittary° the raisèd search,
And there will I be with him. So farewell. (*Exit*.)

(*Enter, below,* BRABANTIO, *in his nightgown, and* SERVANTS
with torches.)

BRABANTIO.   It is too true an evil. Gone she is,
And what's to come of my despisèd time   160
Is naught but bitterness. Now, Roderigo,
Where didst thou see her? Oh, unhappy girl!
With the Moor, say'st thou? Who would be a father!
How didst thou know 'twas she? Oh, she deceives me
Past thought! What said she to you? Get more tapers.   165
Raise all my kindred. Are they married, think you?
RODERIGO.   Truly, I think they are.
BRABANTIO.   Oh Heaven! How got she out? Oh, treason of the blood!
Fathers, from hence trust not your daughters' minds
By what you see them act. Are there not charms°   170
By which the property° of youth and maidhood
May be abused?° Have you not read, Roderigo,
Of some such thing?
RODERIGO.   Yes, sir, I have indeed.
BRABANTIO.   Call up my brother. Oh, would you had had her!
Some one way, some another. Do you know   175
Where we may apprehend her and the Moor?
RODERIGO.   I think I can discover him, if you please
To get good guard and go along with me.
BRABANTIO.   Pray you, lead on. At every house I'll call,
I may command° at most. Get weapons, ho!   180
And raise some special officers of night.
On, good Roderigo, I'll deserve your pains.°

(*Exeunt*.)

SCENE II. *Another street.*

Enter OTHELLO, IAGO, *and* ATTENDANTS *with torches.*

---

157. Sagittary: presumably some building in Venice, not identified, used as a
meeting place for the Council.   **170. charms:** magic spells.   **171. property:**
nature.   **172. abused:** deceived.   **180. command:** find supporters.   **182. deserve
. . . pains:** reward your labor.

IAGO.   Though in the trade of war I have slain men,
Yet do I hold it very stuff o' the conscience
To do no contrivèd murder. I lack iniquity
Sometimes to do me service. Nine or ten times
I had thought to have yerked him here under the ribs.   5
OTHELLO.   'Tis better as it is.
IAGO.   Nay, but he prated
And spoke such scurvy and provoking terms
Against your honor
That, with the little godliness I have,
I did full hard forbear him. But I pray you, sir,   10
Are you fast married? Be assured of this,
That the Magnifico is much beloved,
And hath in his effect a voice potential
As double as° the Duke's. He will divorce you,
Or put upon you what restraint and grievance   15
The law, with all his might to enforce it on,
Will give him cable.
OTHELLO.   Let him do his spite.
My services which I have done the signiory°
Shall outtongue his complaints. 'Tis yet to know—
Which, when I know that boasting is an honor,   20
I shall promulgate—I fetch my life and being
From men of royal siege, and my demerits°
May speak unbonneted to as proud a fortune
As this that I have reached. For know, Iago,
But that I love the gentle Desdemona,   25
I would not my unhousèd° free condition
Put into circumscription and confine
For the sea's worth. But look! What lights come yond?
IAGO.   Those are the raisèd father and his friends.
You were best go in.
OTHELLO.   Not I, I must be found.   30
My parts, my title, and my perfect° soul
Shall manifest me rightly. Is it they?
IAGO.   By Janus, I think no.

(*Enter* CASSIO, *and certain* OFFICERS *with torches.*)

OTHELLO.   The servants of the Duke, and my Lieutenant.
The goodness of the night upon you, friends!   35
What is the news?

13–14. potential . . . as: twice as powerful as.   **18. signiory:** state of Venice.
22. demerits: deserts.   **26. unhousèd:** unmarried.   **31. perfect:** ready.

CASSIO. The Duke does greet you, General
And he requires your haste-posthaste appearance,
Even on the instant.
OTHELLO. What is the matter, think you?
CASSIO. Something from Cyprus, as I may divine.
It is a business of some heat. The galleys   40
Have sent a dozen sequent messengers
This very night at one another's heels,
And many of the consuls, raised and met,
Are at the Duke's already. You have been hotly called for
When, being not at your lodging to be found,   45
The Senate hath sent about three several° quests
To search you out.
OTHELLO. 'Tis well I am found by you.
I will but spend a word here in the house
And go with you. (Exit.)
CASSIO. Ancient, what makes he here?
IAGO. Faith, he tonight hath boarded a land carrack.°   50
If it prove lawful prize, he's made forever.
CASSIO. I do not understand.
IAGO. He's married.
CASSIO. To who?

(Re-enter OTHELLO.)

IAGO. Marry, to—Come, Captain, will you go?
OTHELLO. Have with you.
CASSIO. Here comes another troop to seek for you.
IAGO. It is Brabantio. General, be advised,   55
He comes to bad intent.

(Enter BRABANTIO, RODERIGO, and OFFICERS with torches and
weapons.)

OTHELLO. Holloa! Stand there!
RODERIGO. Signior, it is the Moor.
BRABANTIO. Down with him, thief!

(They draw on both sides.)

IAGO. You, Roderigo! Come, sir, I am for you.
OTHELLO. Keep up° your bright swords, for the dew will rust them.
Good signior, you shall more command with years   60
Than with your weapons.

46. several: separate.   50. carrack: the largest type of Spanish merchant ship.
59. Keep up: sheathe.

BRABANTIO.   O thou foul thief, where hast thou stowed my daughter?
Damned as thou art, thou hast enchanted her.
For I'll refer me to all things of sense
If she in chains of magic were not bound,   65
Whether a maid so tender, fair, and happy,
So opposite to marriage that she shunned
The wealthy curlèd darlings of our nation,
Would ever have, to incur a general mock,
Run from her guardage° to the sooty bosom   70
Of such a thing as thou, to fear, not to delight.
Judge me the world if 'tis not gross in sense
That thou hast practiced on her with foul charms,
Abused her delicate youth with drugs or minerals
That weaken motion.° I'll have 't disputed on,°   75
'Tis probable, and palpable to thinking.
I therefore apprehend and do attach° thee
For an abuser of the world, a practicer
Of arts inhibited and out of warrant.°
Lay hold upon him. If he do resist,   80
Subdue him at his peril.
      OTHELLO.   Hold your hands,
Both you of my inclining and the rest.
Were it my cue to fight, I should have known it
Without a prompter. Where will you that I go
To answer this your charge?
      BRABANTIO.   To prison, till fit time   85
Of law and course of direct session
Call thee to answer.
      OTHELLO.   What if I do obey?
How may the Duke be therewith satisfied,
Whose messengers are here about my side
Upon some present business of the state   90
To bring me to him?
      FIRST OFFICER.   'Tis true, most worthy signior.
The Duke's in Council, and your noble self
I am sure is sent for.
      BRABANTIO.   How! The Duke in Council!
In this time of the night! Bring him away.
Mine's not an idle cause. The Duke himself,   95
Or any of my brothers of the state,
Cannot but feel this wrong as 'twere their own.

70. **guardage:** guardianship.   75. **motion:** sense.   **disputed on:** argued in the
law courts [L.P.].   77. **attach:** arrest.   79. **inhibited** . . . **warrant:** forbidden and
illegal [L.P.].

For if such actions may have passage free,
Bondslaves and pagans shall our statesmen be.

(*Exeunt.*)

SCENE III. *A council chamber.*

The DUKE *and* SENATORS *sitting at a table,* OFFICERS *attending.*

DUKE.   There is no composition° in these news°
That gives them credit.
FIRST SENATOR.   Indeed they are disproportioned.
My letters say a hundred and seven galleys.
DUKE.   And mine, a hundred and forty.
SECOND SENATOR.   And mine, two hundred.
But though they jump not on a just account°—   5
As in these cases, where the aim reports,°
'Tis oft with difference—yet do they all confirm
A Turkish fleet, and bearing up to Cyprus.
DUKE.   Nay, it is possible enough to judgment.
I do not so secure me in the error,°   10
But the main article° I do approve
In fearful° sense.
SAILOR (*within*).   What ho! What ho! What ho!
FIRST OFFICER.   A messenger from the galleys.

(*Enter* SAILOR.)
DUKE.   Now, what's the business
SAILOR.   The Turkish preparation makes for Rhodes.
So was I bid report here to the state.   15
By Signior Angelo.
DUKE.   How say you by this change?
FIRST SENATOR.   This cannot be,
By no assay of reason. 'Tis a pageant
To keep us in false gaze. When we consider
The importancy of Cyprus to the Turk,   20
And let ourselves again but understand
That as it more concerns the Turk than Rhodes,
So may he with more facile question bear it,°

---

1. **composition:** agreement. **news:** reports.   **5. jump . . . account:** do not agree
with an exact estimate.   **6. aim reports:** i.e., intelligence reports of an enemy's
intention often differ in the details.   **10. I . . . error:** I do not consider myself
free from danger, because the reports may not all be accurate.   **11. main article:**
general report.   **12. fearful:** to be feared.   **23. with . . . it:** take it more easily.

For that it stands not in such warlike brace
But altogether lacks the abilities   25
That Rhodes is dressed in—if we make thought of this,
We must not think the Turk is so unskillful
To leave that latest which concerns him first,
Neglecting an attempt of ease and gain
To wake and wage a danger profitless.   30
    Duke. Nay, in all confidence, he's not for Rhodes.
    First Officer. Here is more news.

    (Enter a Messenger.)

    Messenger. The Ottomites,° Reverend and Gracious,
Steering with due course toward the isle of Rhodes,
Have there injointed° them with an after-fleet.°   35
    First Senator. Aye, so I thought. How many, as you guess?
    Messenger. Of thirty sail. And now they do restem°
Their backward course, bearing with frank appearance
Their purposes toward Cyprus. Signior Montano,
Your trusty and most valiant servitor,   40
With his free duty recommends° you thus,
And prays you to believe him.
    Duke. 'Tis certain then for Cyprus.
Marcus Luccicos, is not he in town?
    First Senator. He's now in Florence.   45
    Duke. Write from us to him, post-posthaste dispatch.
    First Senator. Here comes Brabantio and the valiant Moor.

    (Enter Brabantio, Othello, Iago, Roderigo, and Officers.)

    Duke. Valiant Othello, we must straight employ you
Against the general enemy Ottoman.
(To Brabantio) I did not see you. Welcome, gentle signior,   50
We lacked your counsel and your help tonight.
    Brabantio. So did I yours. Good your Grace, pardon me,
Neither my place nor aught I heard of business
Hath raised me from my bed, nor doth the general care
Take hold on me. For my particular° grief   55
Is of so floodgate and o'erbearing nature
That it engluts and swallows other sorrows,
And it is still itself.
    Duke.   Why, what's the matter?
    Brabantio. My daughter! Oh, my daughter!

---

33. Ottomites: Turks.   **35. injointed:** joined. **after-fleet:** second fleet.   **37. restem:** steer again.   **41. recommends:** advises [L.P.].   **55. particular:** personal.

ALL. Dead?

BRABANTIO. Aye, to me.

She is abused, stol'n from me and corrupted 60
By spells and medicines bought of mountebanks.
For nature so preposterously to err,
Being not deficient, blind, or lame of sense,
Sans witchcraft could not.

DUKE. Whoe'er he be that in this foul proceeding 65
Hath thus beguiled your daughter of herself
And you of her, the bloody book of law
You shall yourself read in the bitter letter
After your own sense—yea, though our proper° son
Stood in your action.

BRABANTIO. Humbly I thank your Grace. 70
Here is the man, this Moor, whom now, it seems,
Your special mandate for the state affairs
Hath hither brought.

ALL. We are very sorry for 't.

DUKE (to OTHELLO). What in your own part can you say to this?

BRABANTIO. Nothing but this is so. 75

OTHELLO. Most potent, grave, and reverend signiors,
My very noble and approved good masters,
That I have ta'en away this old man's daughter,
It is most true—true, I have married her.
The very head and front of my offending 80
Hath this extent, no more. Rude am I in my speech,
And little blest with the soft phrase of peace,
For since these arms of mine had seven years' pith
Till now some nine moons wasted, they have used
Their dearest action in the tented field. 85
And little of this great world can I speak,
More than pertains to feats of broil and battle,
And therefore little shall I grace my cause
In speaking for myself. Yet, by your gracious patience,
I will a round unvarnished tale deliver 90
Of my whole course of love—what drugs, what charms,
What conjuration and what mighty magic—
For such proceeding I am charged withal—
I won his daughter.

BRABANTIO. A maiden never bold,
Of spirit so still and quiet that her motion 95
Blushed at herself, and she—in spite of nature,

69. **proper:** own.

Of years, of country, credit,° everything—
To fall in love with what she feared to look on!
It is a judgment maimed and most imperfect
That will confess perfection so could err   100
Against all rules of nature, and must be driven
To find out practices of cunning Hell
Why this should be. I therefore vouch again
That with some mixtures powerful o'er the blood,
Or with some dram conjured to this effect,   105
He wrought upon her.
   Duke.   To vouch this is no proof
Without more certain and more overt test
Than these thin habits and poor likelihoods
Of modern seeming do prefer against him.
   First Senator. But, Othello, speak.   110
Did you by indirect and forcèd courses
Subdue and poison this young maid's affections?
Or came it by request, and such fair question
As soul to soul affordeth?
   Othello.   I do beseech you
Send for the lady to the Sagittary,   115
And let her speak of me before her father.
If you do find me foul in her report,
The trust, the office I do hold of you,
Not only take away, but let your sentence
Even fall upon my life.
   Duke.   Fetch Desdemona hither.   120
   Othello. Ancient, conduct them, you best know the place.

(*Exeunt* Iago *and* Attendants.)

And till she come, as truly as to Heaven
I do confess the vices of my blood,
So justly to your grave ears I'll present
How I did thrive in this fair lady's love   125
And she in mine.
   Duke. Say it, Othello.
   Othello. Her father loved me, oft invited me,
Still questioned me the story of my life
From year to year, the battles, sieges, fortunes,
That I have passed.   130
I ran it through, even from my boyish days
To the very moment that he bade me tell it.

97. **credit**: reputation.

Wherein I spake of most disastrous chances,
Of moving accidents by flood and field,
Of hairbreadth 'scapes i' the imminent deadly breach,   135
Of being taken by the insolent foe
And sold to slavery, of my redemption thence,
And portance in my travels' history.
Wherein of antres° vast and deserts idle,
Rough quarries, rocks, and hills whose heads touch heaven,   140
It was my hint to speak—such was the process.
And of the cannibals that each other eat,
The anthropophagi,° and men whose heads
Do grow beneath their shoulders. This to hear
Would Desdemona seriously incline.   145
But still the house affairs would draw her thence,
Which ever as she could with haste dispatch,
She'd come again, and with a greedy ear
Devour up my discourse. Which I observing,
Took once a pliant hour and found good means   150
To draw from her a prayer of earnest heart
That I would all my pilgrimage dilate,
Whereof by parcels she had something heard,
But not intentively. I did consent,
And often did beguile her of her tears   155
When I did speak of some distressful stroke
That my youth suffered. My story being done,
She gave me for my pains a world of sighs.
She swore, in faith, 'twas strange, 'twas passing strange,
'Twas pitiful, 'twas wondrous pitiful.   160
She wished she had not heard it, yet she wished
That Heaven had made her° such a man. She thanked me,
And bade me, if I had a friend that loved her,
I should but teach him how to tell my story
And that would woo her. Upon this hint I spake.   165
She loved me for the dangers I had passed,
And I loved her that she did pity them.
This only is the witchcraft I have used.
Here comes the lady, let her witness it.

　　(*Enter* DESDEMONA, IAGO, *and* ATTENDANTS.)

　　DUKE.　I think this tale would win my daughter too.   170
Good Brabantio,
Take up this mangled matter at the best.°

---

139. antres: caves.　　**143. anthropophagi:** cannibals.　　**162. her:** for her.　　**172.**
Take . . . best: make the best settlement you can of this confused business.

Men do their broken weapons rather use
Than their bare hands.

    BRABANTIO.   I pray you hear her speak.
If she confess that she was half the wooer, 175
Destruction on my head if my bad blame
Light on the man! Come hither, gentle mistress.
Do you perceive in all this noble company
Where most you owe obedience?

    DESDEMONA.   My noble Father,
I do perceive here a divided duty. 180
To you I am bound for life and education,
My life and education both do learn me
How to respect you, you are the lord of duty,
I am hitherto your daughter. But here's my husband,
And so much duty as my mother showed 185
To you, preferring you before her father
So much I challenge that I may profess
Due to the Moor my lord.

    BRABANTIO.   God be with you! I have done.
Please it your Grace, on to the state affairs.
I had rather to adopt a child than get° it. 190
Come hither, Moor.
I here do give thee that with all my heart
Which, but thou hast already, with all my heart
I would keep from thee. For your sake, jewel,
I am glad at soul I have no other child, 195
For thy escape would teach me tyranny,
To hang clogs on them. I have done, my lord.

    DUKE.   Let me speak like yourself, and lay a sentence°
Which, as a grise° or step, may help these lovers
Into your favor. 200
When remedies are past, the griefs are ended
By seeing the worst, which late on hopes depended.
To mourn a mischief that is past and gone
Is the next way to draw new mischief on.
What cannot be preserved when fortune takes, 205
Patience her injury a mockery makes.
The robbed that smiles steals something from the thief.
He robs himself that spends a bootless grief.

    BRABANTIO.   So let the Turk of Cyprus us beguile,
We lose it not so long as we can smile. 210
He bears the sentence well that nothing bears

---

190. get: beget.   **198. sentence:** proverbial saying.   **199. grise:** degree.

But the free comfort which from thence he hears.
But he bears both the sentence and the sorrow
That, to pay grief, must of poor patience borrow.
These sentences, to sugar or to gall,   215
Being strong on both sides, are equivocal.
But words are words. I never yet did hear
That the bruised heart was piercèd through the ear.
I humbly beseech you, proceed to the affairs of state.
    DUKE. The Turk with a most mighty preparation makes for   220
Cyprus. Othello, the fortitude of the place is best known to you, and though
we have there a substitute° of most allowed sufficiency, yet opinion, a
sovereign mistress of effects, throws a more safer voice on you. You must
therefore be content to slubber° the gloss of your new fortunes with this
more stubborn and boisterous expedition.   225
    OTHELLO. The tyrant custom, most grave Senators,
Hath made the flinty and steel couch of war
My thrice-driven bed of down. I do agnize°
A natural and prompt alacrity
I find in hardness, and do undertake   230
These present wars against the Ottomites.
Most humbly therefore bending to your state,
I crave fit disposition for my wife,
Due reference of place and exhibition,°
With such accommodation and besort°   235
As levels with her breeding.
    DUKE.   If you please,
Be 't at her father's.
    BRABANTIO.   I'll not have it so.
    OTHELLO. Nor I.
    DESDEMONA.   Nor I. I would not there reside,
To put my father in impatient thoughts
By being in his eye. Most gracious Duke,   240
To my unfolding lend your prosperous° ear,
And let me find a charter in your voice
To assist my simpleness.
    DUKE. What would you, Desdemona?
    DESDEMONA. That I did love the Moor to live with him,   245
My downright violence and storm of fortunes
May trumpet to the world. My heart's subdued
Even to the very quality° of my lord.
I saw Othello's visage in his mind,

222. substitute: deputy commander. 224. slubber: tarnish. 228. agnize: confess. 234. exhibition: allowance. 235. besort: attendants. 241. prosperous: favorable. 248. quality: profession.

And to his honors and his valiant parts   250
Did I my soul and fortunes consecrate.
So that, dear lords, if I be left behind,
A moth of peace, and he go to the war,
The rites for which I love him are bereft me,
And I a heavy interim shall support   255
By his dear absence. Let me go with him.
    OTHELLO.   Let her have your voices.
Vouch with me, Heaven, I therefore beg it not
To please the palate of my appetite,
Nor to comply with heat—the young affects   260
In me defunct°—and proper satisfaction,
But to be free and bounteous to her mind.°
And Heaven defend your good souls, that you think
I will your serious and great business scant
For she is with me. No, when light-winged toys   265
Of feathered Cupid seel° with wanton dullness
My speculative and officed instruments,°
That my disports° corrupt and taint my business,
Let housewives make a skillet of my helm,
And all indign° and base adversities   270
Make head against my estimation!°
    DUKE.   Be it as you shall privately determine,
Either for her stay or going. The affair cries haste,
And speed must answer 't. You must hence tonight.
    DESDEMONA.   Tonight, my lord?
    DUKE.   This night.
    OTHELLO.   With all my heart.   275
    DUKE.   At nine i' the morning here we'll meet again.
Othello, leave some officer behind,
And he shall our commission bring to you,
With such things else of quality and respect
As doth import you.
    OTHELLO.   So please your Grace, my Ancient,   280
A man he is of honesty and trust.
To his conveyance I assign my wife,
With what else needful your good grace shall think
To be sent after me.
    DUKE.   Let it be so.

260–61. young . . . defunct: in me the passion of youth is dead. 262. to . . .
mind: Othello repeats Desdemona's claim that this is a marriage of minds. 266.
seel: close up. 267. speculative . . . instruments: powers of sight and action;
i.e., my efficiency as your general. 268. disports: amusements. 270. indign:
unworthy. 271. estimation: reputation.

Good night to everyone. (*To* BRABANTIO) And, noble signior,   285
If virtue no delighted beauty lack,
Your son-in-law is far more fair than black.
FIRST SENATOR.   Adieu, brave Moor. Use Desdemona well.
BRABANTIO.   Look to her, Moor, if thou hast eyes to see.
She has deceived her father, and may thee.   290

(*Exeunt* DUKE, SENATORS, OFFICERS, *etc.*)

OTHELLO.   My life upon her faith! Honest Iago,
My Desdemona must I leave to thee.
I prithee, let thy wife attend on her,
And bring them after in the best advantage.
Come, Desdemona, I have but an hour   295
Of love, of worldly matters and direction,
To spend with thee. We must obey the time.

(*Exeunt* OTHELLO *and* DESDEMONA.)

RODERIGO.   Iago!
IAGO.   What say'st thou, noble heart?
RODERIGO.   What will I do, thinkest thou?   300
IAGO.   Why, go to bed and sleep.
RODERIGO.   I will incontinently° drown myself.
IAGO.   If thou dost, I shall never love thee after. Why, thou silly gentle-
man!
RODERIGO.   It is silliness to live when to live is torment, and then   305
have we a prescription to die when death is our physician.
IAGO.   Oh, villainous! I have looked upon the world for four times
seven years, and since I could distinguish betwixt a benefit and an injury
I never found man that knew how to love himself. Ere I would say I would
drown myself for the love of a guinea hen, I would change my human-   310
ity with a baboon.
RODERIGO.   What should I do? I confess it is my shame to be so found,
but it is not in my virtue to amend it.
IAGO.   Virtue! A fig! 'Tis in ourselves that we are thus or thus. Our
bodies are gardens, to the which our wills are gardeners. So that if we   315
will plant nettles or sow lettuce, set hyssop and weed up thyme, supply it
with one gender of herbs or distract it with many, either to have it sterile with
idleness or manured with industry—why, the power and corrigible° authority
of this lies in our wills. If the balance of our lives had not one scale of
reason to poise another of sensuality, the blood and baseness of our   320
natures would conduct us to most preposterous conclusions. But we have reason to cool our raging motions, our carnal stings, our unbitted lusts, whereof

302. **incontinently:** immediately.   318. **corrigible:** correcting, directing.

I take this that you call love to be a sect or scion.°
RODERIGO. It cannot be.
IAGO. It is merely a lust of the blood and a permission of the will. 325
Come, be a man. Drown thyself! Drown cats and blind puppies. I have pro-
fessed me thy friend, and I confess me knit to thy deserving with cables of
perdurable toughness. I could never better stead thee than now. Put money
in thy purse, follow thou the wars, defeat thy favor with an usurped beard°—
I say put money in thy purse. It cannot be that Desdemona should 330
long continue her love to the Moor—put money in thy purse—nor he his
to her. It was a violent commencement, and thou shalt see an answerable
sequestration°—put but money in thy purse. These Moors and changeable
in their wills.—Fill thy purse with money. The food that to him now is as
luscious as locusts shall be to him shortly as bitter as coloquintida. 335
She must change for youth. When she is sated with his body, she will find
the error of her choice. She must have change, she must—therefore put
money in thy purse. If thou wilt needs damn thyself, do it a more delicate way than drowning. Make all the money thou canst. If sanctimony and
a frail vow betwixt an erring° barbarian and a supersubtle Venetian be 340
not too hard for my wits and all the tribe of Hell, thou shalt enjoy her—
therefore make money. A pox of drowning thyself! It is clean out of the way.
Seek thou rather to be hanged in compassing thy joy than to be drowned
and go without her.
RODERIGO. Wilt thou be fast to my hopes if I depend on the issue? 345
IAGO. Thou art sure of me. Go, make money. I have told thee often,
and I retell thee again and again, I hate the Moor. My cause is hearted,°
thine hath no less reason. Let us be conjunctive in our revenge against him.
If thou canst cuckold him thou dost thyself a pleasure, me a sport. There
are many events in the womb of time, which will be delivered. 350
Traverse, go, provide thy money. We will have more of this tomorrow.
Adieu.
RODERIGO. Where shall we meet i' the morning?
IAGO. At my lodging.
RODERIGO. I'll be with thee betimes. 355
IAGO. Go to, farewell. Do you hear, Roderigo?
RODERIGO. What say you?
IAGO. No more of drowning, do you hear?
RODERIGO. I am changed. I'll go sell all my land. (*Exit.*)
IAGO. Thus do I ever make my fool my purse, 360
For I mine own gained knowledge should profane

323. **sect or scion:** Both words mean a slip taken from a tree and planted to
produce a new growth. 329. **defeat . . . beard:** disguise your face by growing
a beard. 332–33. **answerable sequestration:** corresponding separation; i.e., reaction. 339. **Make . . . canst:** turn all you can into ready cash. 340. **erring:**
vagabond. 347. **hearted:** heartfelt.

If I would time expend with such a snipe
But for my sport and profit. I hate the Moor,
And it is thought abroad that 'twixt my sheets
He has done my office. I know not if 't be true,   365
But I for mere suspicion in that kind
Will do as if for surety. He holds me well,
The better shall my purpose work on him.
Cassio's a proper° man. Let me see now,
To get his place, and to plume up my will   370
In double knavery—How, how?—Let's see.—
After some time, to abuse Othello's ear
That he is too familiar with his wife.
He hath a person and a smooth dispose
To be suspected,° framed to make women false.   375
The Moor is of a free and open nature
That thinks men honest that but seem to be so,
And will as tenderly be led by the nose
As asses are.
I have 't. It is engendered. Hell and night   380
Must bring this monstrous birth to the world's light. (*Exit.*)

ACT II

SCENE I. A seaport in Cyprus. An open place near the wharf.
Enter MONTANO *and two* GENTLEMEN.

MONTANO.   What from the cape can you discern at sea?
FIRST GENTLEMAN.   Nothing at all. It is a high-wrought flood.
I cannot 'twixt the heaven and the main
Descry a sail.
      MONTANO.   Methinks the wind hath spoke aloud at land,   5
A fuller blast ne'er shook our battlements.
If it hath ruffianed so upon the sea,
What ribs of oak, when mountains melt on them,
Can hold the mortise? What shall we hear of this?
      SECOND GENTLEMAN.   A segregation° of the Turkish fleet.   10
For do but stand upon the foaming shore,
The chidden billow seems to pelt the clouds,
The wind-shaked surge, with high and monstrous mane,
Seems to cast water on the burning Bear,
And quench the guards of the ever-fixèd Pole.   15
I never did like molestation view

369. proper: handsome.   **374–75. He . . . suspected:** an easy way with him that
is naturally suspected.
    Act II, Sc. i: 10. segregation: separation.

On the enchafèd flood.

MONTANO.   If that the Turkish fleet
Be not ensheltered and embayed, they are drowned.
It is impossible to bear it out.

(*Enter a* THIRD GENTLEMAN.)

THIRD GENTLEMAN.   News, lads! Our wars are done.   20
The desperate tempest hath so banged the Turks
That their designment halts. A noble ship of Venice
Hath seen a grievous wreck and sufferance°
On most part of their fleet.
MONTANO.   How! Is this true?
THIRD GENTLEMAN.   The ship is here put in,   25
A Veronesa. Michael Cassio,
Lieutenant to the warlike Moor Othello,
Is come on shore, the Moor himself at sea,
And is in full commission here for Cyprus.
MONTANO.   I am glad on 't. 'Tis a worthy governor.   30
THIRD GENTLEMAN.   But this same Cassio, though he speak of comfort
Touching the Turkish loss, yet he looks sadly
And prays the Moor be safe, for they were parted
With foul and violent tempest.
MONTANO.   Pray Heavens he be,
For I have served him, and the man commands   35
Like a full soldier. Let's to the seaside, ho!
As well to see the vessel that's come in
As to throw out our eyes for brave Othello,
Even till we make the main and the aerial blue
An indistinct regard.
THIRD GENTLEMAN.   Come, let's do so.   40
For every minute is expectancy
Of more arrivance.

(*Enter* CASSIO.)

CASSIO.   Thanks, you the valiant of this warlike isle
That so approve the Moor! Oh, let the heavens
Give him defense against the elements,   45
For I have lost him on a dangerous sea.
MONTANO.   Is he well shipped?
CASSIO.   His bark is stoutly timbered, and his pilot
Of very expert and approved allowance.
Therefore my hopes, not surfeited to death,   50
Stand in bold cure.

23. **sufferance:** damage.

(A cry within: "A sail, a sail, a sail!" Enter a FOURTH GENTLEMAN.)

CASSIO.   What noise?

FOURTH GENTLEMAN.   The town is empty. On the brow o' the sea
Stand ranks of people, and they cry "A sail!"

CASSIO.   My hopes do shape him for the governor.   55

(Guns heard.)

SECOND GENTLEMAN.   They do discharge their shot of courtesy.
Our friends, at least.

CASSIO.   I pray you, sir, go forth,
And give us truth who 'tis that is arrived.

SECOND GENTLEMAN.   I shall. *(Exit.)*

MONTANO.   But, good Lieutenant, is your General wived?   60

CASSIO.   Most fortunately. He hath achieved a maid
That paragons description and wild fame,
One that excels the quirks of blazoning pens
And in the essential vesture of creation
Does tire the ingener. °

(Re-enter SECOND GENTLEMAN.)

                     How now! Who has put in?   65

SECOND GENTLEMAN.   'Tis one Iago, Ancient to the General.

CASSIO.   He has had most favorable and happy speed.
Tempests themselves, high seas, and howling winds,
The guttered rocks, and congregated sands,
Traitors ensteeped to clog the guiltless keel,   70
As having sense of beauty, do omit
Their mortal nature, letting go safely by
The divine Desdemona.

MONTANO.   What is she?

CASSIO.   She that I spake of, our great Captain's captain,
Left in the conduct of the bold Iago,   75
Whose footing here anticipates our thoughts
A sennight's speed. Great Jove, Othello guard,
And swell his sail with thine own powerful breath,
That he may bless this bay with his tall ship,
Make love's quick pants in Desdemona's arms,   80
Give renewed fire to our extincted spirits,
And bring all Cyprus comfort.

(Enter DESDEMONA, EMILIA, IAGO, RODERIGO, *and* ATTENDANTS.)

63–65. One . . . ingener: one that is too good for the fancy phrases (*quirks*) of
painting pens (i.e., poets) and in her absolute perfection wearies the artist (i.e., the
painter). (Cassio is full of gallant phrases and behavior, in contrast to Iago's bluntness.) **ingener:** inventor.

Oh, behold,
The riches of the ship is come on shore!
Ye men of Cyprus, let her have your knees.
Hail to thee, lady! And the grace of Heaven,   85
Before, behind thee, and on every hand,
Enwheel thee round!
    DESDEMONA.   I thank you, valiant Cassio.
What tidings can you tell me of my lord?
    CASSIO.   He is not yet arrived, nor know I aught
But that he's well and will be shortly here.   90
    DESDEMONA.   Oh, but I fear—How lost you company?
    CASSIO.   The great contention of the sea and skies
Parted our fellowship.—But hark! A sail.

(*A cry within: "A sail, a sail!" Guns heard.*)

    SECOND GENTLEMAN.   They give their greeting to the citadel.
This likewise is a friend.
    CASSIO.   See for the news.   95

(*Exit* GENTLEMAN.)

Good Ancient, you are welcome. (*To* EMILIA) Welcome, mistress.
Let it not gall your patience, good Iago,
That I extend my manners. 'Tis my breeding
That gives me this bold show of courtesy. (*Kissing her.*)
    IAGO.   Sir, would she give you so much of her lips   100
As of her tongue she oft bestows on me,
You'd have enough.
    DESDEMONA.   Alas, she has no speech.
    IAGO.   In faith, too much,
I find it still when I have list° to sleep.
Marry, before your ladyship, I grant,   105
She puts her tongue a little in her heart
And chides with thinking.
    EMILIA.   You have little cause to say so.
    IAGO.   Come on, come on. You are pictures° out of doors,
Bells° in your parlors, wildcats in your kitchens,   110
Saints in your injuries,° devils being offended,
Players in your housewifery, and housewives in your beds.
    DESDEMONA.   Oh, fie upon thee, slanderer!
    IAGO.   Nay, it is true, or else I am a Turk.
You rise to play, and go to bed to work.   115

---

104. list: desire.   109. pictures: i.e., painted and dumb.   110. Bells: i.e., ever
clacking.   111. Saints . . . injuries: saints when you hurt anyone else.

EMILIA.   You shall not write my praise.
IAGO.   No, let me not.
DESDEMONA.   What wouldst thou write of me if thou shouldst praise me?
IAGO.   O gentle lady, do not put me to 't,
For I am nothing if not critical.
DESDEMONA.   Come on, assay.°—There's one gone to the harbor?   120
IAGO.   Aye, madam.
DESDEMONA.   I am not merry, but I do beguile
The thing I am by seeming otherwise.
Come, how wouldst thou praise me?
IAGO.   I am about it, but indeed my invention   125
Comes from my pate as birdlime does from frieze°—
It plucks out brains and all. But my Muse labors,
And thus she is delivered.
If she be fair and wise, fairness and wit,
The one's for use, the other useth it.   130
DESDEMONA.   Well praised! How if she be black and witty?
IAGO.   If she be black, and thereto have a wit,
She'll find a white° that shall her blackness fit.
DESDEMONA.   Worse and worse.
EMILIA.   How if fair and foolish?   135
IAGO.   She never yet was foolish that was fair,
For even her folly helped her to an heir.
DESDEMONA.   These are old fond paradoxes to make fools laugh i' the
alehouse. What miserable praise hast thou for her that's foul and foolish?
IAGO.   There's none so foul, and foolish thereunto,   140
But does foul pranks which fair and wise ones do.
DESDEMONA.   Oh, heavy ignorance! Thou praisest the worst best. But
what praise couldst thou bestow on a deserving woman indeed, one that in
the authority of her merit did justly put on the vouch of very malice
itself?°   145
IAGO.   She that was ever fair and never proud,
Had tongue at will° and yet was never loud,
Never lacked gold and yet went never gay,
Fled from her wish and yet said "Now I may."
She that, being angered, her revenge being nigh,   150
Bade her wrong stay and her displeasure fly.
She that in wisdom never was so frail
To change the cod's head for the salmon's tail.°

120. assay: try.   125–26. my . . . frieze: my literary effort (*invention*) is as hard
to pull out of my head as frieze (cloth with a nap) stuck to birdlime.   133. white:
with a pun on *wight* (l. 156), man, person.   143–45. one . . . itself: one so deserving that even malice would declare her good.   147. tongue . . . will: a ready
flow of words.   153. To . . . tail: to prefer the tail end of a good thing to the head
of a poor thing.

She could think and ne'er disclose her mind,
See suitors following and not look behind.   155
She was a wight, if ever such wight were—
DESDEMONA.   To do what?
IAGO.   To suckle fools and chronicle small beer.°
DESDEMONA.   Oh, most lame and impotent conclusion! Do not learn
of him, Emilia, though he be thy husband. How say you, Cassio? Is   160
he not a most profane and liberal° counselor?
CASSIO.   He speaks home, madam. You may relish him more in the
soldier than in the scholar.
IAGO (aside).   He takes her by the palm. Aye, well said, whisper. With
as little a web as this will I ensnare as great a fly as Cassio. Aye, smile   165
upon her, do, I will gyve thee in thine own courtship. You say true, 'tis so
indeed. If such tricks as these strip you out of your Lieutenantry, it had
been better you had not kissed your three fingers° so oft, which now
again you are most apt to play the sir° in. Very good, well kissed! An excellent courtesy! 'Tis so indeed. Yet again your fingers to your lips?   170
Would they were clyster pipes° for your sake! (Trumpet within.) The Moor!
I know the trumpet.
CASSIO.   'Tis truly so.
DESDEMONA.   Let's meet him and receive him.
CASSIO.   Lo where he comes!   175

(Enter OTHELLO and ATTENDANTS.)

OTHELLO.   O my fair warrior!°
DESDEMONA.   My dear Othello!
OTHELLO.   It gives me wonder great as my content
To see you here before me. O my soul's joy!
If after every tempest come such calms,
May the winds blow till they have wakened death!   180
And let the laboring bark climb hills of seas
Olympus-high, and duck again as low
As Hell's from Heaven! If it were now to die,
'Twere now to be most happy, for I fear
My soul hath her content so absolute   185
That not another comfort like to this
Succeeds in unknown fate.
DESDEMONA.   The Heavens forbid
But that our loves and comforts should increase,
Even as our days do grow!

---

158. chronicle . . . beer: write a whole history about trifles (*small beer* thin drink).
161. liberal: gross.   **168. kissed . . . fingers:** a gesture of gallantry.   **169. play
. . . sir:** act the fine gentleman.   **171. clyster pipes:** an enema syringe.   **176.
warrior:** because she is a soldier's wife.

OTHELLO.   Amen to that, sweet powers!
I cannot speak enough of this content.   190
It stops me here,° it is too much of joy.
And this, and this, the greatest discords be (*Kissing her*)
That e'er our hearts shall make!
    IAGO (*aside*).   Oh, you are well tuned now,
But I'll set down the pegs° that make this music,
As honest as I am.
    OTHELLO.   Come, let us to the castle.   195
News, friends. Our wars are done, the Turks are drowned.
How does my old acquaintance of this isle?
Honey, you shall be well desired in Cyprus,
I have found great love amongst them. O my sweet,
I prattle out of fashion, and I dote   200
In mine own comforts. I prithee, good Iago,
Go to the bay and disembark my coffers.°
Bring thou the master° to the citadel.
He is a good one, and his worthiness
Does challenge much respect. Come, Desdemona,   205
Once more well met at Cyprus.

    (*Exeunt all but* IAGO *and* RODERIGO.)

    IAGO.   Do thou meet me presently at the harbor. Come hither. If thou
beest valiant—as they say base men being in love have then a nobility
in their natures more than is native to them—list me. The Lieutenant tonight watches on the court of guard. First, I must tell thee this. Desde-   210
mona is directly in love with him.
    RODERIGO.   With him! Why, 'tis not possible.
    IAGO.   Lay thy finger thus,° and let thy soul be instructed. Mark me
with what violence she first loved the Moor, but for bragging and telling her
fantastical lies. And will she love him still for prating? Let not thy dis-   215
creet heart think it. Her eye must be fed, and what delight shall she have to
look on the Devil? When the blood is made dull with the act of sport, there
should be, again to inflame it and to give satiety a fresh appetite, love-
liness in favor,° sympathy in years, manners, and beauties, all which the
Moor is defective in. Now, for want of these required conveniences,   220
her delicate tenderness will find itself abused, begin to heave the gorge, dis-
relish and abhor the Moor. Very nature will instruct her in it and compel her
to some second choice. Now, sir, this granted—as it is a most pregnant and
unforced position°—who stands so eminently in the degree of this fortune

191. here: i.e., in the heart.   194. set . . . pegs: i.e., make you sing in a different
key. A stringed instrument was tuned by the pegs.   202. coffers: trunks.   203.
master: captain of the ship.   213. thus: i.e., on the lips.   219. favor: face.
223–24. pregnant . . . position: very significant and probable argument.

as Cassio does? A knave very voluble, no further conscionable° than   225
in putting on the mere form of civil and humane seeming° for the better
compassing of his salt° and most hidden loose affection? Why, none, why,
none. A slipper° and subtle knave, a finder-out of occasions, that has an
eye can stamp and counterfeit advantages,° though true advantage never
present itself. A devilish knave! Besides, the knave is handsome, young,   230
and hath all those requisites in him that folly and green minds look after. A
pestilent complete knave, and the woman hath found him already.

RODERIGO.   I cannot believe that in her. She's full of most blest
condition.°

IAGO.   Blest fig's-end!° The wine she drinks is made of grapes. If   235
she had been blest, she would never have loved the Moor. Blest pudding!
Didst thou not see her paddle with the palm of his hand? Didst not mark that?

RODERIGO.   Yes, that I did, but that was just courtesy.

IAGO.   Lechery, by this hand, an index and obscure prologue to the
history of lust and foul thoughts. They met so near with their lips that   240
their breaths embraced together. Villainous thoughts, Roderigo! When these
mutualities so marshal the way, hard at hand comes the master and main exercise, the incorporate° conclusion. Pish! But, sir, be you ruled by me. I
have brought you from Venice. Watch you tonight. For the command, I'll
lay't upon you. Cassio knows you not. I'll not be far from you. Do you   245
find some occasion to anger Cassio, either by speaking too loud, or tainting°
his discipline, or from what other curse you please which the time shall more
favorably minister.

RODERIGO.   Well.

IAGO.   Sir, he is rash and very sudden in choler,° and haply may   250
strike at you. Provoke him, that he may, for even out of that will I cause these
of Cyprus to mutiny, whose qualification shall come into no true taste again
but by the displanting of Cassio. So shall you have a shorter journey
to your desires by the means I shall then have to prefer° them, and the
impediment most profitably removed without the which there were   255
no expectation of our prosperity.

RODERIGO.   I will do this, if I can bring it to any opportunity.

IAGO.   I warrant thee. Meet me by and by at the citadel. I must
fetch his necessaries ashore. Farewell.

RODERIGO.   Adieu. (*Exit.*)   260

IAGO.   That Cassio loves her, I do well believe it.
That she loves him, 'tis apt and of great credit.
The Moor, howbeit that I endure him not,
Is of a constant, loving, noble nature,

---

225. no . . . conscionable: who has no more conscience.   **226. humane seeming:**
courteous appearance.   **227. salt:** lecherous.   **228. slipper:** slippery.   **229.**
stamp . . . advantages: forge false opportunities.   **234. condition:** disposition.
235. fig's-end: nonsense [L.P.].   **243. incorporate:** bodily.   **246. tainting:** dis-
paraging.   **250. choler:** anger.   **254. prefer:** promote.

And I dare think he'll prove to Desdemona   265
A most dear husband. Now, I do love her too,
Not out of absolute lust, though peradventure
I stand accountant for as great a sin.
But partly led to diet° my revenge
For that I do suspect the lusty Moor   270
Hath leaped into my seat. The thought whereof
Doth like a poisonous mineral gnaw my inwards.
And nothing can or shall content my soul
Till I am evened with him, wife for wife.
At least into a jealousy so strong
Or failing so, yet that I put the Moor   275
That judgment cannot cure. Which thing to do,
If this poor trash of Venice, whom I trash
For his quick hunting,° stand the putting-on,
I'll have our Michael Cassio on the hip,   280
Abuse him to the Moor in the rank garb°—
For I fear Cassio with my nightcap too—
Make the Moor thank me, love me, and reward me
For making him egregiously an ass
And practicing upon his peace and quiet   285
Even to madness. 'Tis here, but yet confused.
Knavery's plain face is never seen till used. (*Exit.*)

SCENE II. *A street.*

Enter a HERALD *with a proclamation,* PEOPLE *following.*

HERALD. It is Othello's pleasure, our noble and valiant General, that
upon certain tidings now arrived, importing the mere perdition° of the
Turkish fleet, every man put himself into triumph°—some to dance, some
to make bonfires, each man to what sport and revels his addiction leads him.
For, besides these beneficial news, it is the celebration of his nuptial.   5
So much was his pleasure should be proclaimed. All offices° are open, and
there is full liberty of feasting from this present hour of five till the bell have
told eleven. Heaven bless the isle of Cyprus and our noble General Othello!

(*Exeunt.*)

SCENE III. *A hall in the castle.*

Enter OTHELLO, DESDEMONA, CASSIO, *and* ATTENDANTS.

269. diet: feed. 278-79. trash . . . hunting: hold back from outrunning the
pack. [L.P.]. 281. rank garb: gross manner; i.e., by accusing him of being
Desdemona's lover.
    Sc. ii. 2. mere perdition: absolute destruction. 3. triumph: celebrate. 6. of-
fices: the kitchen and buttery—i.e., free food and drink for all.

OTHELLO.   Good Michael, look you to the guard tonight.
Let's teach ourselves that honorable stop,
Not to outsport discretion.
CASSIO.   Iago hath direction what to do,
But notwithstanding with my personal eye   5
Will I look to 't.
OTHELLO.   Iago is most honest.
Michael, good night. Tomorrow with your earliest
Let me have speech with you. Come, my dear love,
The purchase made, the fruits are to ensue—
That profit's yet to come 'tween me and you.   10
Good night.

(*Exeunt* OTHELLO, DESDEMONA, *and* ATTENDANTS. *Enter* IAGO.)

CASSIO.   Welcome, Iago. We must to the watch.
IAGO.   Not this hour, Lieutenant, 'tis not yet ten o' the clock. Our
General cast° us thus early for the love of his Desdemona, who let us not
therefore blame. He hath not yet made wanton the night with her, and   15
she is sport for Jove.
CASSIO.   She's a most exquisite lady.
IAGO.   And, I'll warrant her, full of game
CASSIO.   Indeed she's a most fresh and delicate creature.
IAGO.   What an eye she has! Methinks it sounds a parley to provo-   20
cation.
CASSIO.   An inviting eye, and yet methinks right modest.
IAGO.   And when she speaks, is it not an alarum to love?
CASSIO.   She is indeed perfection.
IAGO.   Well, happiness to their sheets! Come, Lieutenant, I have a   25
stoup of wine, and here without are a brace of Cyprus gallants that would
fain have a measure to the health of black Othello.
CASSIO.   Not tonight, good Iago. I have very poor and unhappy brains
for drinking. I could well wish courtesy would invent some other custom of
entertainment.   30
IAGO.   Oh, they are our friends. But one cup—I'll drink for you.
CASSIO.   I have drunk but one cup tonight, and that was craftily quali-
fied too, and behold what innovation it makes here. I am unfortunate in the
infirmity, and dare not task my weakness with any more.
IAGO.   What, man! 'Tis a night of revels. The gallants desire it.   35
CASSIO.   Where are they?
IAGO.   Here at the door. I pray you call them in.
CASSIO.   I'll do 't, but it dislikes me. (*Exit.*)
IAGO.   If I can fasten but one cup upon him,

14. **cast:** dismissed.

With that which he hath drunk tonight already 40
He'll be as full of quarrel and offense
As my young mistress' dog. Now my sick fool Roderigo,
Whom love hath turned almost the wrong side out,
To Desdemona hath tonight caroused
Potations pottle-deep, and he's to watch. 45
Three lads of Cyprus, noble swelling spirits
That hold their honors in a wary distance,°
The very elements° of this warlike isle,
Have I tonight flustered with flowing cups,
And they watch too. Now, 'mongst this flock of drunkards, 50
Am I to put our Cassio in some action
That may offend the isle. But here they come.
If consequence do but approve my dream,
My boat sails freely, both with wind and stream.

(*Re-enter* Cassio, *with him* Montano *and* Gentlemen, Servants *following with wine.*)

Cassio. 'Fore God, they have given me a rouse already. 55
Montano. Good faith, a little one—not past a pint, as I am a soldier.
Iago. Some wine, ho! (*Sings*)
  "And let me the cannikin clink, clink,
  And let me the cannikin clink.
  A soldier's a man, 60
  A life's but a span.°
  Why, then let a soldier drink."
Some wine, boys!
Cassio. 'Fore God, an excellent song.
Iago. I learned it in England, where indeed they are most potent 65
in potting.° Your Dane, your German, and your swag-bellied Hollander—
Drink, ho!—are nothing to your English.
Cassio. Is your Englishman so expert in his drinking?
Iago. Why, he drinks you with facility your Dane dead drunk, he
sweats not to overthrow your Almain, he gives your Hollander a vomit° 70
ere the next pottle can be filled.
Cassio. To the health of our General!
Montano. I am for it, Lieutenant, and I'll do you justice.
Iago. O sweet England! (*Sings*)
  "King Stephen was a worthy peer, 75
  His breeches cost him but a crown.

47. hold . . . distance: "have a chip on their shoulders." 48. very elements: typical specimens. 61. span: lit., the measure between the thumb and little finger of the outstretched hand; about 9 inches. 66. potting: drinking. 70. gives . . . vomit: drinks as much as will make a Dutchman throw up.

He held them sixpence all too dear,
 With that he called the tailor lown.°

"He was a wight of high renown,
 And thou art but of low degree.   80
'Tis pride that pulls the country down.
 Then take thine auld cloak about thee."
Some wine, ho!

CASSIO. Why, this is a more exquisite song than the other.

IAGO. Will you hear 't again?   85

CASSIO. No, for I hold him to be unworthy of his place that does those things. Well, God's above all, and there be souls must be saved and there be souls must not be saved.

IAGO. It's true, good Lieutenant.

CASSIO. For mine own part—no offense to the General, nor any 90 man of quality—I hope to be saved.

IAGO. And so do I too, Lieutenant.

CASSIO. Aye, but, by your leave, not before me. The Lieutenant is to be saved before the Ancient. Let's have no more of this, let's to our affairs. God forgive us our sins! Gentlemen, let's look to our business. 95 Do not think, gentlemen, I am drunk. This is my Ancient, this is my right hand and this is my left. I am not drunk now, I can stand well enough and speak well enough.

ALL. Excellent well.

CASSIO. Why, very well, then, you must not think then that I am 100 drunk. (*Exit.*)

MONTANO. To the platform, masters. Come, let's set the watch.

IAGO. You see this fellow that is gone before.
He is a soldier fit to stand by Caesar
And give direction. And do but see his vice.   105
'Tis to his virtue a just equinox,
The one as long as the other. 'Tis pity of him.
I fear the trust Othello puts him in
On some odd time of his infirmity
Will shake this island.

MONTANO.   But is he often thus?   110

IAGO. 'Tis evermore the prologue to his sleep.
He'll watch the horologe a double set,°
If drink rock not his cradle.

MONTANO.   It were well
The General were put in mind of it.
Perhaps he sees it not, or his good nature   115

---

78. **lown:** lout. 112. **watch . . . set:** stay awake the clock twice round.

Prizes the virtue that appears in Cassio
And looks not on his evils. Is not this true?

(*Enter* RODERIGO.)

IAGO (*aside to him*).   How now, Roderigo! I pray you, after the Lieutenant. Go.

(*Exit* RODERIGO.)

MONTANO.   And 'tis great pity that the noble Moor   120
Should hazard such a place as his own second
With one of an ingraft infirmity.
It were an honest action to say
So to the Moor.
IAGO.   Not I, for this fair island.
I do love Cassio well, and would do much   125
To cure him of this evil—But, hark! What noise?

(*A cry within: "Help! Help!" Re-enter* CASSIO, *driving in* RODERIGO.)

CASSIO.   'Zounds! You rogue! You rascal!
MONTANO.   What's the matter, Lieutenant?
CASSIO.   A knave teach me my duty!
But I'll beat the knave into a wicker bottle.
RODERIGO.   Beat me!   130
CASSIO.   Dost thou prate, rogue? (*Striking* RODERIGO.)
MONTANO.   Nay, good Lieutenant, (*staying him*)
I pray you, sir, hold your hand.
CASSIO.   Let me go, sir,
Or I'll knock you o'er the mazzard.
MONTANO.   Come, come, you're drunk.
CASSIO.   Drunk!

(*They fight.*)

IAGO (*aside to* RODERIGO).   Away, I say. Go out and cry a mutiny.   135

(*Exit* RODERIGO.)

Nay, good Lieutenant! God's will, gentlemen!
Help, ho!—Lieutenant—sir—Montano—sir—
Help, masters!—Here's a goodly watch indeed!

(*A bell rings.*)

Who's that that rings the bell?—Diablo, ho!
The town will rise. God's will, Lieutenant, hold—   140
You will be shamed forever.

(*Re-enter* OTHELLO *and* ATTENDANTS.)

OTHELLO.   What is the matter here?
MONTANO.   'Zounds, I bleed still, I am hurt to the death. (*Faints.*)
OTHELLO.   Hold, for your lives!
IAGO.   Hold, ho! Lieutenant—sir—Montano—gentlemen—
Have you forgot all sense of place and duty?   145
Hold! The General speaks to you. Hold, hold, for shame!
OTHELLO.   Why, how now, ho! From whence ariseth this?
Are we turned Turks, and to ourselves do that
Which Heaven hath forbid the Ottomites?
For Christian shame, put by this barbarous brawl.   150
He that stirs next to carve for his own rage
Holds his soul light, he dies upon his motion.
Silence that dreadful bell. It frights the isle
From her propriety. What is the matter, masters?
Honest Iago, that look'st dead with grieving,   155
Speak, who began this? On thy love, I charge thee.
IAGO.   I do not know. Friends all but now, even now,
In quarter and in terms like bride and groom
Devesting them for bed. And then, but now,
As if some planet had unwitted men,   160
Swords out, and tilting one at other's breast
In opposition bloody. I cannot speak
Any beginning to this peevish odds,
And would in action glorious I had lost
Those legs that brought me to a part of it!   165
OTHELLO.   How comes it, Michael, you are thus forgot?°
CASSIO.   I pray you, pardon me, I cannot speak.
OTHELLO.   Worthy Montano, you were wont be civil.
The gravity and stillness of your youth
The world hath noted, and your name is great   170
In mouths of wisest censure.° What's the matter
That you unlace your reputation thus,
And spend your rich opinion° for the name
Of a night brawler? Give me answer to it.
MONTANO.   Worthy Othello, I am hurt to danger.   175
Your officer, Iago, can inform you—
While I spare speech, which something now offends me—
Of all that I do know. Nor know I aught
By me that's said or done amiss this night,
Unless self-charity° be sometimes a vice,   180

---

166. are . . . forgot: have so forgotten yourself. **171. censure:** judgment.
173. opinion: reputation [L.P.].   **180. self-charity:** love for oneself.

And to defend ourselves it be a sin
When violence assails us.
    OTHELLO.   Now, by Heaven,
My blood begins my safer guides to rule,
And passion, having my best judgment collied,°
Assays to lead the way. If I once stir,   185
Or do but lift this arm, the best of you
Shall sink in my rebuke. Give me to know
How this foul rout began, who set it on,
And he that is approved° in this offense,
Though he had twinned with me, both at a birth,   190
Shall lose me. What! In a town of war,
Yet wild, the people's hearts brimful of fear,
To manage private and domestic quarrel,
In night, and on the court and guard of safety!
'Tis monstrous. Iago, who began 't?   195
    MONTANO.   If partially affined, or leagued in office,
Thou dost deliver more or less than truth,
Thou art no soldier.
    IAGO.   Touch me not so near.
I had rather have this tongue cut from my mouth
Than it should do offense to Michael Cassio.   200
Yet I persuade myself to speak the truth
Shall nothing wrong him. Thus it is, General.
Montano and myself being in speech,
There comes a fellow crying out for help,
And Cassio following him with determined sword   205
To execute upon him. Sir, this gentleman
Steps in to Cassio and entreats his pause.
Myself the crying fellow did pursue,
Lest by his clamor—as it so fell out—
The town might fall in fright. He, swift of foot,   210
Outran my purpose, and I returned the rather
For that I heard the clink and fall of swords,
And Cassio high in oath, which till tonight
I ne'er might say before. When I came back—
For this was brief—I found them close together,   215
At blow and thrust, even as again they were
When you yourself did part them.
More of this matter cannot I report.
But men are men, the best sometimes forget
Though Cassio did some little wrong to him,   220

184. **collied:** darkened.   189. **approved:** proved guilty.

As men in rage strike those that wish them best,
Yet surely Cassio, I believe, received
From him that fled some strange indignity,
Which patience could not pass.

OTHELLO.   I know, Iago,
Thy honesty and love doth mince this matter,   225
Making it light to Cassio. Cassio, I love thee,
But never more be officer of mine.

(*Re-enter* DESDEMONA, *attended.*)

Look, if my gentle love be not raised up!
I'll make thee an example.

DESDEMONA.   What's the matter?

OTHELLO. All's well now, sweeting. Come away to   230
bed. (*To* MONTANO, *who is led off*)
Sir, for your hurts, myself will be your surgeon.
Lead him off.
Iago, look with care about the town,
And silence those whom this vile brawl distracted.
Come, Desdemona. 'Tis the soldiers' life   235
To have their balmy slumbers waked with strife.

(*Exeunt all but* IAGO *and* CASSIO.)

IAGO. What, are you hurt, Lieutenant?

CASSIO. Aye, past all surgery.

IAGO. Marry, Heaven forbid!

CASSIO. Reputation, reputation, reputation! Oh, I have lost my   240
reputation! I have lost the immortal part of myself, and what remains is
bestial. My reputation, Iago, my reputation!

IAGO. As I am an honest man, I thought you had received some bodily
wound. There is more sense in that than in reputation. Reputation is an idle
and most false imposition, oft got without merit and lost without   245
deserving. You have lost no reputation at all unless you repute yourself
such a loser. What, man! There are ways to recover the General again. You
are but now cast in his mood,° a punishment more in policy° than in malice
—even so as one would beat his offenseless dog to affright an imperious
lion.° Sue to him again and he's yours.   250

CASSIO. I will rather sue to be despised than to deceive so good a
commander with so slight, so drunken, and so indiscreet an officer. Drunk?
And speak parrot?° And squabble? Swagger? Swear? And discourse fustian

248. cast . . . mood: dismissed because he is in a bad mood. in policy: i.e., because he must appear to be angry before the Cypriots. 249–50. even . . . lion:
a proverb meaning that when the lion sees the dog beaten, he will know what is
coming to him. 253. speak parrot: babble.

with one's own shadow? O thou invisible spirit of wine, if thou has no
name to be known by, let us call thee devil!   255

IAGO. What was he that you followed with your sword? What had he
done to you?

CASSIO. I know not.

IAGO. Is 't possible?

CASSIO. I remember a mass of things, but nothing distinctly—a   260
quarrel, but nothing wherefore. Oh God, that men should put an enemy in
their mouths to steal away their brains! That we should, with joy, pleasance,
revel, and applause, transform ourselves into beasts!

IAGO. Why, but you are now well enough. How came you thus
recovered?   265

CASSIO. It hath pleased the devil drunkenness to give place to the devil
wrath. One unperfectness shows me another, to make me frankly despise
myself.

IAGO. Come, you are too severe a moraler. As the time, the place, and
the condition of this country stands, I could heartily wish this had not   270
befallen. But since it is as it is, mend it for your own good.

CASSIO. I will ask him for my place again, he shall tell me I am a
drunkard! Had I as many mouths as Hydra, such an answer would stop them
all. To be now a sensible man, by and by a fool, and presently a beast! Oh,
strange! Every inordinate cup is unblest, and the ingredient is a   275
devil.

IAGO. Come, come, good wine is a good familiar creature, if it be well
used. Exclaim no more against it. And, good Lieutenant, I think you think
I love you.

CASSIO. I have well approved it, sir. I drunk!   280

IAGO. You or any man living may be drunk at some time, man. I'll tell
you what you shall do. Our General's wife is now the General. I may say
so in this respect, for that he hath devoted and given up himself to the
contemplation, mark, and denotement of her parts and graces. Confess
yourself freely to her, importune her help to put you in your place   285
again. She is of so free, so kind, so apt, so blessed a disposition, she holds
it a vice in her goodness not to do more than she is requested. This broken
joint between you and her husband entreat her to splinter° and, my fortunes against any lay° worth naming, this crack of your love shall grow
stronger than it was before.   290

CASSIO. You advise me well.

IAGO. I protest, in the sincerity of love and honest kindness.

CASSIO. I think it freely, and betimes in the morning I will beseech
the virtuous Desdemona to undertake for me. I am desperate of my fortunes
if they check me here.   295

288. splinter: put in splints. 289. lay: bet.

IAGO. You are in the right. Good night, Lieutenant, I must to the watch.

CASSIO. Good night, honest Iago. (*Exit.*)

IAGO. And what's he then that says I play the villain?
When this advice is free I give and honest,   300
Probal° to thinking, and indeed the course
To win the Moor again? For 'tis most easy
The inclining Desdemona to subdue
In any honest suit. She's framed as fruitful
As the free elements. And then for her   305
To win the Moor, were 't to renounce his baptism,
All seals and symbols of redeemèd sin,
His soul is so enfettered to her love
That she may make, unmake, do what she list,
Even as her appetite shall play the god   310
With his weak function.° How am I then a villain
To counsel Cassio to this parallel course,
Directly to his good? Divinity of Hell!
When devils will the blackest sins put on,
They do suggest at first with heavenly shows,   315
As I do now. For whiles this honest fool
Plies Desdemona to repair his fortunes,
And she for him pleads strongly to the Moor,
I'll pour this pestilence into his ear,
That she repeals° him for her body's lust.   320
And by how much she strives to do him good,
She shall undo her credit with the Moor.
So will I turn her virtue into pitch,
And out of her own goodness make the net
That shall enmesh them all.

(*Enter* RODERIGO.)

                                        How now, Roderigo!   325

RODERIGO. I do follow here in the chase, not like a hound that hunts but one that fills up the cry. My money is almost spent, I have been tonight exceedingly well cudgeled, and I think the issue will be I shall have so much experience for my pains and so, with no money at all and a little more wit, return again to Venice.   330

IAGO. How poor are they that have not patience!
What wound did ever heal but by degrees?
Thou know'st we work by wit and not by witchcraft,
And wit depends on dilatory Time.

301. **Probal:** probable.   310. **function:** intelligence.   320. **repeals:** calls back.

Does't not go well? Cassio hath beaten thee,   335
And thou by that small hurt hast cashiered Cassio.
Though other things grow fair against the sun,
Yet fruits that blossom first will first be ripe.
Content thyself awhile. By the mass, 'tis morning.
Pleasure and action make the hours seem short.   340
Retire thee, go where thou art billeted.
Away, I say. Thou shalt know more hereafter.
Nay, get thee gone.

   (*Exit* RODERIGO.)

             Two things are to be done:
My wife must move for Cassio to her mistress,
I'll set her on,   345
Myself the while to draw the Moor apart
And bring him jump when he may Cassio find
Soliciting his wife. Aye, that's the way.
Dull not device by coldness and delay. (*Exit.*)

ACT III

SCENE I. *Before the castle.*

Enter CASSIO *and some* MUSICIANS.

CASSIO. Masters, play here, I will content your pains°—
Something that's brief, and bid "Good morrow, General."°

   (*Music. Enter* CLOWN.)

CLOWN. Why, masters, have your instruments been in Naples, that
they speak i' the nose thus?
FIRST MUSICIAN. How, sir, how?   5
CLOWN. Are these, I pray you, wind instruments?
FIRST MUSICIAN. Aye, marry are they, sir.
CLOWN. Oh, thereby hangs a tail.
FIRST MUSICIAN. Whereby hangs a tale, sir?
CLOWN. Marry, sir, by many a wind instrument that I know.   10
But, masters, here's money for you. And the General so likes your music
that he desires you, for love's sake, to make no more noise with it.
FIRST MUSICIAN. Well, sir, we will not.

---

1. content . . . pains: reward your labor. 2. bid . . . General: It was a common
custom to play or sing a song beneath the bedroom window of a distinguished
guest or of a newly wedded couple on the morning after their wedding night.

CLOWN. If you have any music that may not be heard, to 't again.
But, as they say, to hear music the General does not greatly care.   15
FIRST MUSICIAN. We have none such, sir.
CLOWN. Then put up your pipes in your bag, for I'll away. Go,
vanish into air, away!

(*Exeunt* MUSICIANS.)

CASSIO. Dost thou hear, my honest friend?
CLOWN. No, I hear not your honest friend, I hear you.   20
CASSIO. Prithee keep up thy quillets.° There's a poor piece of gold
for thee. If the gentlewoman that attends the General's wife be stirring, tell
her there's one Cassio entreats her a little favor of speech. Wilt thou do this?
CLOWN. She is stirring, sir. If she will stir hither, I shall seem to
notify unto her.   25
CASSIO. Do, good my friend.

(*Exit* CLOWN. *Enter* IAGO.)

                              In happy time, Iago.
IAGO. You have not been abed, then?
CASSIO. Why, no, the day had broke
Before we parted. I have made bold, Iago,
To send in to your wife. My suit to her   30
Is that she will to virtuous Desdemona
Procure me some access.
IAGO.   I'll send her to you presently,
And I'll devise a mean to draw the Moor
Out of the way, that your convérse and business
May be more free.   35
CASSIO. I humbly thank you for 't.

(*Exit* IAGO.)

                              I never knew
A Florentine more kind and honest.

(*Enter* EMILIA.)

EMILIA. Good morrow, good Lieutenant. I am sorry
For your displeasure, but all will sure be well.
The General and his wife are talking of it,   40
And she speaks for you stoutly. The Moor replies
That he you hurt is of great fame in Cyprus
And great affinity,° and that in wholesome wisdom
He might not but refuse you. But he protests he loves you,

21. keep . . . quillets: put away your wisecracks.   43. affinity: kindred.

And needs no other suitor but his likings   45
To take the safest occasion by the front
To bring you in again.
    CASSIO.   Yet I beseech you
If you think fit, or that it may be done,
Give me advantage of some brief discourse
With Desdemona alone.
    EMILIA.   Pray you, come in.   50
I will bestow you where you shall have time
To speak your bosom freely.
    CASSIO.   I am much bound to you.

(Exeunt.)

SCENE II. *A room in the castle.*

Enter OTHELLO, IAGO, *and* GENTLEMEN.

OTHELLO.   These letters give, Iago, to the pilot,
And by him do my duties to the Senate.
That done, I will be walking on the works.
Repair there to me.
    IAGO.   Well, my good lord, I'll do 't.
OTHELLO.   This fortification, gentlemen, shall we see 't?   5
GENTLEMEN.   We'll wait upon your lordship.

(Exeunt.)

SCENE III. *The garden of the castle.*

Enter DESDEMONA, CASSIO, *and* EMILIA.

DESDEMONA.   Be thou assured, good Cassio, I will do
All my abilities in thy behalf.
    EMILIA.   Good madam, do. I warrant it grieves my husband
As if the case were his.
    DESDEMONA.   Oh, that's an honest fellow. Do not doubt, Cassio,   5
But I will have my lord and you again
As friendly as you were.
    CASSIO.   Bounteous madam,
Whatever shall become of Michael Cassio,
He's never anything but your true servant.
    DESDEMONA.   I know 't. I thank you. You do love my lord.   10
You have known him long, and be you well assured

He shall in strangeness stand no farther off
Than in a politic distance.°
    CASSIO.   Aye, but, lady,
That policy may either last so long,
Or feed upon such nice and waterish diet,   15
Or breed itself so out of circumstance,
That, I being absent and my place supplied,
My General will forget my love and service.
    DESDEMONA.   Do not doubt° that. Before Emilia here
I give thee warrant of thy place.° Assure thee,   20
If I do vow a friendship, I'll perform it
To the last article. My lord shall never rest.
I'll watch him tame and talk him out of patience,
His bed shall seem a school, his board a shrift.°
I'll intermingle every thing he does   25
With Cassio's suit. Therefore be merry, Cassio,
For thy solicitor shall rather die
Than give thy cause away.

       (Enter OTHELLO and IAGO, at a distance.)

    EMILIA.   Madam, here comes my lord.
    CASSIO.   Madam, I'll take my leave.   30
    DESDEMONA.   Nay, stay and hear me speak.
    CASSIO.   Madam, not now. I am very ill at ease,
Unfit for mine own purposes.
    DESDEMONA.   Well, do your discretion.

       (Exit CASSIO.)

    IAGO.   Ha! I like not that.   35
    OTHELLO.   What dost thou say?
    IAGO.   Nothing, my lord. Or if—I know not what.
    OTHELLO.   Was not that Cassio parted from my wife?
    IAGO.   Cassio, my lord! No, sure, I cannot think it,
That he would steal away so guilty-like,   40
Seeing you coming.
    OTHELLO.   I do believe 'twas he.
    DESDEMONA.   How now, my lord!
I have been talking with a suitor here,
A man that languishes in your displeasure.
    OTHELLO.   Who is 't you mean?   45

12–13. He . . . distance: i.e., his apparent coldness to you shall only be so much
as his official position demands for reasons of policy. **19. doubt:** fear. **20. give
. . . place:** guarantee that you will be restored to your position. **24. shrift:** place
of confession [L.P.].

DESDEMONA. Why, your Lieutenant, Cassio. Good my lord,
If I have any grace or power to move you,
His present reconciliation take.°
For if he be not one that truly loves you,
That errs in ignorance and not in cunning,   50
I have no judgment in an honest face.
I prithee call him back.
OTHELLO.   Went he hence now?
DESDEMONA.   Aye, sooth, so humbled
That he hath left part of his grief with me,
To suffer with him. Good love, call him back.   55
OTHELLO.   Not now, sweet Desdemona, some other time.
DESDEMONA.   But shall 't be shortly?
OTHELLO.   The sooner, sweet, for you.
DESDEMONA.   Shall 't be tonight at supper?
OTHELLO.   No, not tonight.
DESDEMONA.   Tomorrow dinner then?
OTHELLO.   I shall not dine at home.
I meet the captains at the citadel.   60
DESDEMONA.   Why, then tomorrow night or Tuesday morn,
On Tuesday noon, or night, on Wednesday morn.
I prithee name the time, but let it not
Exceed three days. In faith, he's penitent,
And yet his trespass, in our common reason—   65
Save that, they say, the wars must make examples
Out of their best—is not almost° a fault
To incur a private check.° When shall he come?
Tell me, Othello. I wonder in my soul
What you would ask me that I should deny,   70
Or stand so mammering° on. What! Michael Cassio,
That came a-wooing with you, and so many a time
When I have spoke of you dispraisingly
Hath ta'en your part—to have so much to do
To bring him in! Trust me, I could do much—   75
OTHELLO.   Prithee, no more. Let him come when he will.
I will deny thee nothing.
DESDEMONA.   Why, this is not a boon.
'Tis as I should entreat you wear your gloves,
Or feed on nourishing dishes, or keep you warm,
Or sue to you to do a peculiar profit   80
To your own person. Nay, when I have a suit

48. His . . . take: accept his immediate apology and forgive him.   67. almost:
hardly.   68. check: rebuke.   71. mammering: hesitating.

Wherein I mean to touch your love indeed,
It shall be full of poise and difficult weight,
And fearful to be granted.
OTHELLO.   I will deny thee nothing.
Whereon I do beseech thee grant me this,   85
To leave me but a little to myself.
DESDEMONA.   Shall I deny you? No. Farewell, my lord.
OTHELLO.   Farewell, my Desdemona. I'll come to thee straight.
DESDEMONA.   Emilia, come. Be as your fancies teach you.
Whate'er you be, I am obedient.   90

(*Exeunt* DESDEMONA *and* EMILIA.)

OTHELLO.   Excellent wretch! Perdition catch my soul
But I do love thee! And when I love thee not,
Chaos is come again.
IAGO.   My noble lord—
OTHELLO.   What dost thou say, Iago?
IAGO.   Did Michael Cassio, when you wooed my lady,   95
Know of your love?
OTHELLO.   He did, from first to last. Why dost thou ask?
IAGO.   But for a satisfaction of my thought,
No further harm.
OTHELLO.   Why of thy thought, Iago?
IAGO.   I did not think he had been acquainted with her.   100
OTHELLO.   Oh yes, and went between us very oft.
IAGO. Indeed!
OTHELLO.   Indeed! Aye, indeed. Discern'st thou aught in that?
Is he not honest?
IAGO.   Honest, my lord!
OTHELLO.   Honest! Aye, honest.
IAGO.   My lord, for aught I know.   105
OTHELLO.   What dost thou think?
IAGO.   Think, my lord!
OTHELLO.   Think, my lord! By Heaven, he echoes me
As if there were some monster in his thought
Too hideous to be shown. Thou dost mean something.
I heard thee say even now thou likedst not that   110
When Cassio left my wife. What didst not like?
And when I told thee he was of my counsel
In my whole course of wooing, thou criedst "Indeed!"
And didst contract and purse thy brow together
As if thou then hadst shut up in thy brain   115
Some horrible conceit. If thou dost love me,
Show me thy thought.
IAGO.   My lord, you know I love you.

OTHELLO. I think thou dost,
And for I know thou'rt full of love and honesty
And weigh'st thy words before thou givest them breath,   120
Therefore these stops of thine fright me the more.
For such things in a false disloyal knave
Are tricks of custom, but in a man that's just
They're close delations,° working from the heart,
That passion cannot rule.
IAGO.   For Michael Cassio,   125
I dare be sworn I think that he is honest.
OTHELLO.   I think so too.
IAGO.   Men should be what they seem,
Or those that be not, would they might seem none!°
OTHELLO.   Certain, men should be what they seem.
IAGO.   Why, then I think Cassio's an honest man.   130
OTHELLO.   Nay, yet there's more in this.
I prithee speak to me as to thy thinkings,
As thou dost ruminate, and give thy worst of thoughts
The worst of words.
IAGO.   Good my lord, pardon me.
Though I am bound to every act of duty,   135
I am not bound to that all slaves are free to.
Utter my thoughts? Why, say they are vile and false,
As where's that palace whereinto foul things
Sometimes intrude not? Who has a breast so pure
But some uncleanly apprehensions   140
Keep leets° and law days, and in session sit
With meditations lawful?
OTHELLO.   Thou dost conspire against thy friend, Iago,
If thou but think'st him wronged and makest his ear
A stranger to thy thoughts.
IAGO.   I do beseech you—   145
Though I perchance am vicious in my guess,
As, I confess, it is my nature's plague
To spy into abuses, and oft my jealousy°
Shapes faults that are not—that your wisdom yet,
From one that so imperfectly conceits,°   150
Would take no notice, nor build yourself a trouble
Out of his scattering and unsure observance.°
It were not for your quiet nor your good,

---

124. close delations: concealed accusations.   **128. seem none:** i.e., not seem to be
honest men.   **141. leets:** courts.   **148. jealousy:** suspicion.   **150. conceits:** con-
ceives.   **152. observance:** observation.

Nor for my manhood, honesty, or wisdom,
To let you know my thoughts.
    OTHELLO.   What dost thou mean?   155
    IAGO. Good name in man and woman, dear my lord,
Is the immediate jewel of their souls.
Who steals my purse steals trash—'tis something, nothing,
'Twas mine, 'tis his, and has been slave to thousands—
But he that filches from me my good name   160
Robs me of that which not enriches him
And makes me poor indeed.
    OTHELLO. By Heaven, I'll know thy thoughts.
    IAGO. You cannot if my heart were in your hand,
Nor shall not whilst 'tis in my custody.   165
    OTHELLO. Ha!
    IAGO.   Oh, beware, my lord, of jealousy.
It is the green-eyed monster which doth mock
The meat it feeds on. That cuckold lives in bliss
Who, certain of his fate, loves not his wronger.°
But, oh, what damnèd minutes tells he o'er   170
Who dotes, yet doubts, suspects, yet strongly loves!
    OTHELLO. Oh, misery!
    IAGO. Poor and content is rich, and rich enough,
But riches fineless° is as poor as winter
To him that ever fears he shall be poor.   175
Good Heaven, the souls of all my tribe defend
From jealousy!
    OTHELLO. Why, why is this?
Think'st thou I'd make a life of jealousy,
To follow still the changes of the moon
With fresh suspicions? No, to be once in doubt   180
Is once to be resolved.° Exchange me for a goat
When I shall turn the business of my soul
To such exsufflicate and blown surmises,
Matching thy inference.° 'Tis not to make me jealous
To say my wife is fair, feeds well, loves company,   185
Is free of speech, sings, plays, and dances well.
Where virtue is, these are more virtuous.
Nor from mine own weak merits will I draw

168–69. That . . . wronger: i.e., the cuckold who hates his wife and knows her
falseness is not tormented by suspicious jealousy. **174. fineless:** limitless.
180–81. to . . . resolved: whenever I find myself in doubt I at once seek out the
truth. **182–84. When . . . inference:** when I shall allow that which concerns
me most dearly to be influenced by such trifling suggestions as yours. **exsufflicate:**
blown up like a bubble.

The smallest fear or doubt of her revolt,
For she had eyes, and chose me. No, Iago,   190
I'll see before I doubt, when I doubt, prove,
And on the proof, there is no more but this—
Away at once with love or jealousy!
    IAGO.   I am glad of it, for now I shall have reason
To show the love and duty that I bear you   195
With franker spirit. Therefore, as I am bound,
Receive it from me. I speak not yet of proof.
Look to your wife. Observe her well with Cassio.
Wear your eye thus, not jealous nor secure.
I would not have your free and noble nature   200
Out of self-bounty° be abused, look to 't.
I know our country disposition well.
In Venice° they do let Heaven see the pranks
They dare not show their husbands. Their best conscience
Is not to leave 't undone, but keep 't unknown.   205
    OTHELLO.   Dost thou say so?
    IAGO.   She did deceive her father, marrying you,
And when she seemed to shake and fear your looks,
She loved them most.
    OTHELLO.   And so she did.
    IAGO.   Why, go to, then.
She that so young could give out such a seeming   210
To seel° her father's eyes up close as oak—
He thought 'twas witchcraft—but I am much to blame.
I humbly do beseech you of your pardon
For too much loving you.
    OTHELLO.   I am bound to thee forever.
    IAGO.   I see this hath a little dashed your spirits.   215
    OTHELLO.   Not a jot, not a jot.
    IAGO.   I' faith, I fear it has.
I hope you will consider what is spoke
Comes from my love, but I do see you're moved.
I am to pray you not to strain my speech
To grosser issues nor to larger reach   220
Than to suspicion.
    OTHELLO.   I will not.
    IAGO.   Should you do so, my lord,
My speech should fall into such vile success
As my thoughts aim not at. Cassio's my worthy friend.—

201. self-bounty: natural goodness. 203. In Venice: Venice was notorious for its
loose women; the Venetian courtesans were among the sights of Europe and
were much commented upon by travelers. 211. seel: blind.

My lord, I see you're moved.

OTHELLO.   No, not much moved.   225
I do not think but Desdemona's honest.°
    IAGO.   Long live she so! And long live you to think so!
    OTHELLO.   And yet, how nature erring from itself—
    IAGO.   Aye, there's the point. As—to be bold with you—
Not to affect° many proposed matches   230
Of her own clime, complexion, and degree,
Whereto we see in all things nature tends°—
Foh! One may smell in such a will most rank,°
Foul disproportion, thoughts unnatural.
But pardon me. I do not in position   235
Distinctly speak of her, though I may fear
Her will, recoiling to her better judgment,
May fall to match° you with her country forms,°
And happily° repent.
    OTHELLO.   Farewell, farewell.
If more thou dost perceive, let me know more.   240
Set on thy wife to observe. Leave me, Iago.
    IAGO (going).   My lord, I take my leave.
    OTHELLO.   Why did I marry? This honest creature doubtless
Sees and knows more, much more, than he unfolds.
    IAGO (returning).   My lord, I would I might entreat your   245
        honor
To scan this thing no further. Leave it to time.
Though it be fit that Cassio have his place,
For sure he fills it up with great ability,
Yet if you please to hold him off awhile,
You shall by that perceive him and his means.   250
Note if your lady strain his entertainment°
With any strong or vehement importunity—
Much will be seen in that. In the meantime,
Let me be thought too busy in my fears—
As worthy cause I have to fear I am—   255
And hold her free, I do beseech your Honor.
    OTHELLO.   Fear not my government.°
    IAGO.   I once more take my leave. (*Exit.*)
    OTHELLO.   This fellow's of exceeding honesty,

226. honest: When applied to Desdemona, "honest" means "chaste," but applied
to Iago it has the modern meaning of "open and sincere."   230. affect: be inclined to.   232. in . . . tends: i.e., a woman naturally marries a man of her own
country, color, and rank.   233. will . . . rank: desire most lustful.   238. match:
compare. country forms: the appearance of her countrymen; i.e., white men.
239. happily: haply, by chance.   251. strain . . . entertainment: urge you to
receive him.   257. government: self-control.

And knows all qualities, with a learned spirit,   260
Of human dealings. If I do prove her haggard,
Though that her jesses were my dear heartstrings,
I'd whistle her off and let her down the wind
To prey at fortune.° Haply, for I am black
And have not those soft parts of conversation   265
That chamberers° have, or for I am declined
Into the vale of years—yet that's not much—
She's gone, I am abused, and my relief
Must be to loathe her. Oh, curse of marriage,
That we can call these delicate creatures ours,   270
And not their appetites! I had rather be a toad
And live upon the vapor of a dungeon
Than keep a corner in the thing I love
For others' uses. Yet, 'tis the plague of great ones,
Prerogatived are they less than the base.   275
'Tis destiny unshunnable, like death.
Even then this forkèd plague° is fated to us
When we do quicken.° Desdemona comes.

(*Re-enter* DESDEMONA *and* EMILIA.)

If she be false, oh, then Heaven mocks itself!
I'll not believe 't.
  DESDEMONA. How now, my dear Othello!   280
Your dinner, and the generous° islanders
By you invited, do attend your presence.
  OTHELLO. I am to blame.
  DESDEMONA.   Why do you speak so faintly?
Are you not well?
  OTHELLO. I have a pain upon my forehead here.   285
  DESDEMONA. Faith, that's with watching,° 'twill away again.
Let me but bind it hard, within this hour
It will be well.
  OTHELLO. Your napkin° is too little,

(*He puts the handkerchief from him, and she drops it.*)

Let it alone. Come, I'll go in with you.
  DESDEMONA. I am very sorry that you are not well.   290

261–64. If . . . fortune: Othello keeps up the imagery of falconry throughout.
He means: If I find that she is wild, I'll whistle her off the game and let her go
where she will, for she's not worth keeping. **haggard:** a wild hawk. **jesses:** the
straps attached to a hawk's legs. **266. chamberers:** playboys. **277. forkèd
plague:** i.e., to be a cuckold. **278. quicken:** stir in our mother's womb. **281.
generous:** noble [L.P.]. **286. watching:** lack of sleep. **288. napkin:** handkerchief.

(*Exeunt* OTHELLO *and* DESDEMONA.)

EMILIA.   I am glad I have found this napkin.
This was her first remembrance from the Moor.
My wayward° husband hath a hundred times
Wooed me to steal it, but she so loves the token,
For he conjured° her she should ever keep it,   295
That she reserves it evermore about her
To kiss and talk to. I'll have the work ta'en out,°
And give 't Iago. What he will do with it
Heaven knows, not I.
I nothing but to please his fantasy.°   300

(*Re-enter* IAGO.)

IAGO.   How now! What do you here alone?
EMILIA.   Do not you chide, I have a thing for you.
IAGO.   A thing for me? It is a common thing—
EMILIA.   Ha!
IAGO.   To have a foolish wife.   305
EMILIA.   Oh, is that all? What will you give me now
For that same handkerchief?
IAGO.   What handkerchief?
EMILIA.   What handkerchief!
Why, that the Moor first gave to Desdemona,
That which so often you did bid me steal.   310
IAGO.   Hast stol'n it from her?
EMILIA.   No, faith, she let it drop by negligence,
And, to the advantage, I being here took 't up.
Look, here it is.
IAGO.   A good wench. Give it me.
EMILIA.   What will you do with 't, that you have been so earnest 315
To have me filch it?
IAGO (*snatching it*).   Why, what's that to you?
EMILIA.   If 't be not for some purpose of import,
Give 't me again. Poor lady, she'll run mad
When she shall lack it.   320
IAGO.   Be not acknown on 't,° I have use for it.
Go, leave me.

(*Exit* EMILIA.)

I will in Cassio's lodging lose this napkin,
And let him find it. Trifles light as air

293. wayward: unaccountable.   295. conjured: begged with an oath.   297. work
. . . out: pattern copied.   300. fantasy: whim.   321. Be . . . 't: know nothing
about it.

Are to the jealous confirmations strong 325
As proofs of Holy Writ. This may do something.
The Moor already changes with my poison.
Dangerous conceits are in their natures poisons,
Which at the first are scarce found to distaste,
But with a little act upon the blood 330
Burn like the mines of sulphur. I did say so.°
Look where he comes!

  (*Re-enter* OTHELLO.)

      Not poppy,° nor mandragora,°
Nor all the drowsy syrups of the world,
Shall ever medicine thee to that sweet sleep
Which thou owedst° yesterday,
  OTHELLO.   Ha! Ha! False to me? 335
  IAGO. Why, how now, General! No more of that.
  OTHELLO. Avaunt! Be gone! Thou hast set me on the rack.
I swear 'tis better to be much abused
Than but to know 't a little.
  IAGO.   How now, my lord!
  OTHELLO. What sense had I of her stol'n hours of lust? 340
I saw 't not, thought it not, it harmed not me.
I slept the next night well, was free and merry.
I found not Cassio's kisses on her lips.
He that is robbed, not wanting° what is stol'n,
Let him not know 't and he's not robbed at all. 345
  IAGO. I am sorry to hear this.
  OTHELLO. I had been happy if the general camp,
Pioners° and all, had tasted her sweet body,
So I had nothing known. Oh, now forever
Farewell the tranquil mind! Farewell content! 350
Farewell the plumèd troop and the big wars
That make ambition virtue! Oh, farewell,
Farewell the neighing steed and the shrill trump,
The spirit-stirring drum, the ear-piercing fife,
The royal banner and all quality, 355
Pride, pomp, and circumstance of glorious war!
And, O you mortal engines, whose rude throats
The immortal Jove's dread clamors counterfeit,
Farewell! Othello's occupation's gone!

---

331. I . . . so: As Iago says this, Othello is seen approaching, with all the signs
of his agitation outwardly visible. **332. poppy:** opium. **mandragora:** called also
mandrake, a root used as a drug to bring sleep. **335. owedst:** owned. **344. wanting:** missing. **348. Pioners:** pioneers, the lowest type of soldier.

IAGO. Is 't possible, my lord? 360
OTHELLO. Villain, be sure thou prove my love a whore,
Be sure of it, give me the ocular proof.
Or by the worth of man's eternal soul,
Thou hadst been better have been born a dog
Than answer my waked wrath!
IAGO. Is 't come to this? 365
OTHELLO. Make me to see 't, or at the least so prove it
That the probation° bear no hinge nor loop
To hang a doubt on, or woe upon thy life!
IAGO. My noble lord—
OTHELLO. If thou dost slander her and torture me, 370
Never pray more, abandon all remorse.°
On horror's head horrors accumulate,
Do deeds to make Heaven weep, all earth amazed,
For nothing canst thou to damnation add
Greater than that.
IAGO. Oh, grace! Oh, Heaven defend me! 375
Are you a man? Have you a soul or sense?
God be wi' you, take mine office. O wretched fool,
That livest to make thine honesty a vice!
O monstrous world! Take note, take note, O world,
To be direct and honest is not safe. 380
I thank you for this profit, and from hence
I'll love no friend, sith° love breeds such offense.
OTHELLO. Nay, stay. Thou shouldst be honest.
IAGO. I should be wise, for honesty's a fool,
And loses that it works for.
OTHELLO. By the world, 385
I think my wife be honest, and think she is not.
I think that thou art just, and think thou art not.
I'll have some proof. Her name, that was as fresh
As Dian's° visage, is now begrimed and black
As mine own face. If there be cords, or knives, 390
Poison, or fire, or suffocating streams,
I'll not endure it. Would I were satisfied!
IAGO. I see, sir, you are eaten up with passion.
I do repent me that I put it to you.
You would be satisfied?
OTHELLO. Would! Nay, I will. 395
IAGO. And may, but, how? How satisfied, my lord?

367. prob⁻tion: proof. 371. remorse: pity. 382. sith: since. 389. Dian:
Diana, goddess of chastity.

Would you, the supervisor,° grossly gape on?
Behold her topped?
    OTHELLO.   Death and damnation! Oh!
    IAGO.   It were a tedious difficulty, I think,
To bring them to that prospect. Damn them then,   400
If ever mortal eyes do see them bolster°
More than their own! What then? How then?
What shall I say? Where's satisfaction?
It is impossible you should see this,
Were they as prime° as goats, as hot as monkeys,   405
As salt° as wolves in pride,° and fools as gross
As ignorance made drunk. But yet I say
If imputation° and strong circumstances,
Which lead directly to the door of truth,
Will give you satisfaction, you may have 't.   410
    OTHELLO.   Give me a living reason she's disloyal.
    IAGO.   I do not like the office.
But sith I am entered in this cause so far,
Pricked to 't by foolish honesty and love,
I will go on. I lay with Cassio lately,   415
And being troubled with a raging tooth,
I could not sleep.
There are a kind of men so loose of soul
That in their sleeps will mutter their affairs.
One of this kind is Cassio.   420
In sleep I heard him say "Sweet Desdemona,
Let us be wary, let us hide our loves."
And then, sir, would he gripe° and wring my hand,
Cry "O sweet creature!" and then kiss me hard,
As if he plucked up kisses by the roots   425
That grew upon my lips. Then laid his leg
Over my thigh, and sighed and kissed, and then
Cried "Cursed fate that gave thee to the Moor!"
    OTHELLO.   Oh, monstrous! Monstrous!
    IAGO.   Nay, this was but his dream.
    OTHELLO.   But this denoted a foregone conclusion.   430
'Tis a shrewd doubt,° though it be but a dream.
    IAGO.   And this may help to thicken other proofs
That do demónstrate thinly.
    OTHELLO.   I'll tear her all to pieces.

---

397. supervisor: looker-on. 401. bolster: sleep together. 405. prime: lustful.
406. salt: eager. pride: in heat. 408. imputation: probability. 423. gripe: grip.
431. shrewd doubt: bitter suspicion.

IAGO. Nay, but be wise. Yet we see nothing done.
She may be honest yet. Tell me but this: 435
Have you not sometimes seen a handkerchief
Spotted with strawberries in your wife's hand?
OTHELLO. I gave her such a one, 'twas my first gift.
IAGO. I know not that. But such a handkerchief—
I am sure it was your wife's—did I today 440
See Cassio wipe his beard with.
OTHELLO.   If it be that—
IAGO. If it be that, or any that was hers,
It speaks against her with the other proofs.
OTHELLO. Oh, that the slave had forty thousand lives!
One is too poor, too weak, for my revenge. 445
Now do I see 'tis true. Look here, Iago,
All my fond love thus do I blow to Heaven—
'Tis gone.
Arise, black Vengeance, from thy hollow cell!
Yield up, O Love, thy crown and hearted throne 450
To tyrannous hate! Swell, bosom, with thy fraught,°
For 'tis of aspics'° tongues!
IAGO.   Yet be content.
OTHELLO. Oh, blood, blood, blood!
IAGO. Patience, I say. Your mind perhaps may change.
OTHELLO. Never, Iago. Like to the Pontic Sea, 455
Whose icy current and compulsive course
Ne'er feels retiring ebb but keeps due on
To the Propontic and the Hellespont;
Even so my bloody thoughts, with violent pace,
Shall ne'er look back, ne'er ebb to humble love, 460
Till that capable° and wide revenge
Swallow them up. Now, by yond marble Heaven,
In the due reverence of a sacred vow (Kneels.)
I here engage my words.
IAGO.   Do not rise yet. (Kneels.)
Witness, you ever burning lights above, 465
You elements that clip° us round about,
Witness that here Iago doth give up
The execution of his wit, hands, heart,
To wronged Othello's service! Let him command,
And to obey shall be in me remorse,° 470

---

451. fraught: freight.   **452. aspics':** asps'.   **461. capable:** comprehensive.   **466.
clip:** embrace.   **470. remorse:** solemn obligation.

What bloody business ever.

(*They rise.*)

OTHELLO.   I greet thy love,
Not with vain thanks, but with acceptance bounteous,
And will upon the instant put thee to 't.
Within these three days let me hear thee say
That Cassio's not alive.   475
  IAGO.   My friend is dead. 'Tis done at your request.
But let her live.
  OTHELLO.   Damn her, lewd minx! Oh, damn her!
Come, go with me apart. I will withdraw,
To furnish me with some swift means of death   480
For the fair devil. Now art thou my Lieutenant.
  IAGO.   I am your own forever.

(*Exeunt.*)

SCENE IV. *Before the castle.*

Enter DESDEMONA, EMILIA, *and* CLOWN.

DESDEMONA.   Do you know, sirrah, where Lieutenant Cassio lies?
CLOWN.   I dare not say he lies anywhere.
DESDEMONA.   Why, man?
CLOWN.   He's a soldier, and for one to say a soldier lies is stabbing.
DESDEMONA.   Go to. Where lodges he?   5
CLOWN.   To tell you where he lodges is to tell you where I lie.
DESDEMONA.   Can anything be made of this?
CLOWN.   I know not where he lodges, and for me to devise a lodging,
and say he lies here or he lies there, were to lie in mine own throat.
DESDEMONA.   Can you inquire him out and be edified by report?°   10
CLOWN.   I will catechize the world for him; that is, make questions
and by them answer.
DESDEMONA.   Seek him, bid him come hither. Tell him I have moved
my lord on his behalf and hope all will be well.
CLOWN.   To do this is within the compass of man's wit, and there-   15
fore I will attempt the doing it. (*Exit.*)
DESDEMONA.   Where should I lose that handkerchief, Emilia?
EMILIA.   I know not, madam.
DESDEMONA.   Believe me, I had rather have lost my purse
Full of crusados. And, but my noble Moor   20
Is true of mind and made of no such baseness
As jealous creatures are, it were enough

10. **edified . . . report:** enlightened by the information. Desdemona speaks with
mock pomposity.

To put him to ill thinking.

EMILIA.   Is he not jealous?

DESDEMONA.   Who, he? I think the sun where he was born
Drew all such humors from him.

EMILIA.   Look where he comes.   25

DESDEMONA.   I will not leave him now till Cassio
Be called to him.

(*Enter* OTHELLO.)

                    How is 't with you, my lord?

OTHELLO.   Well, my good lady. (*Aside*) Oh, hardness to dissemble!
How do you, Desdemona?

DESDEMONA.   Well, my good lord.

OTHELLO.   Give me your hand. This hand is moist,°my lady.   30

DESDEMONA.   It yet has felt no age nor known no sorrow.

OTHELLO.   This argues fruitfulness and liberal heart.
Hot, hot, and moist—this hand of yours requires
A sequester from liberty, fasting and prayer,
Much castigation, exercise devout.   35
For here's a young and sweating devil here,
That commonly rebels. 'Tis a good hand,
A frank one.

DESDEMONA.   You may indeed say so,
For 'twas that hand that gave away my heart.

OTHELLO.   A liberal° hand. The hearts of old gave hands,   40
But our new heraldry is hands, not hearts. °

DESDEMONA.   I cannot speak of this. Come now, your promise.

OTHELLO.   What promise, chuck?°

DESDEMONA.   I have sent to bid Cassio come speak with you.

OTHELLO.   I have a salt and sorry rheum offends me.   45
Lend me thy handkerchief.

DESDEMONA.   Here, my lord.

OTHELLO.   That which I gave you.

DESDEMONA.   I have it not about me.

OTHELLO.   Not?

DESDEMONA.   No indeed, my lord.

OTHELLO.   That's a fault. That handkerchief
Did an Egyptian to my mother give.   50
She was a charmer, and could almost read
The thoughts of people. She told her while she kept it

30. moist: a hot moist palm was believed to show desire.   **40. liberal:** over-
generous.   **40–41. The . . . hearts:** once love and deeds went together, but now it
is all deeds (i.e., faithlessness) and no love.   **43. chuck:** a term of affection, but
not the kind of word with which a person of Othello's dignity would normally
address his wife. He is beginning to treat her with contemptuous familiarity.

'Twould make her amiable and subdue my father
Entirely to her love, but if she lost it
Or made a gift of it, my father's eye   55
Should hold her loathed and his spirits should hunt
After new fancies. She dying gave it me,
And bid me, when my fate would have me wive,
To give it her. I did so. And take heed on 't,
Make it a darling like your precious eye.   60
To lose 't or give 't away were such perdition
As nothing else could match.
DESDEMONA.   It 't possible?
OTHELLO.   'Tis true. There's magic in the web of it.
A sibyl that had numbered in the world
The sun to course two hundred compasses   65
In her prophetic fury sewed the work.
The worms were hallowed that did breed the silk,
And it was dyed in mummy which the skillful
Conserved° of maidens' hearts.
DESDEMONA.   Indeed! Is 't true?
OTHELLO.   Most veritable, therefore look to 't well.   70
DESDEMONA.   Then would to God that I had never seen 't.
OTHELLO.   Ha! Wherefore?
DESDEMONA.   Why do you speak so startlingly and rash?
OTHELLO.   Is 't lost? Is 't gone? Speak, is it out o' the way?
DESDEMONA.   Heaven bless us!   75
OTHELLO.   Say you?
DESDEMONA.   It is not lost, but what an if it were?
OTHELLO.   How!
DESDEMONA.   I say it is not lost.
OTHELLO.   Fetch 't, let me see it.
DESDEMONA.   Why, so I can, sir, but I will not now.   80
This is a trick to put me from my suit.
Pray you let Cassio be received again.
OTHELLO.   Fetch me the handkerchief. My mind misgives.
DESDEMONA.   Come, come,
You'll never meet a more sufficient man.   85
OTHELLO.   The handkerchief!
DESDEMONA.   I pray talk me of Cassio.
OTHELLO.   The handkerchief!
DESDEMONA.   A man that all his time
Hath founded his good fortunes on your love,
Shared dangers with you—

69. **Conserved:** prepared.

OTHELLO. The handkerchief! 90
DESDEMONA. In sooth, you are to blame.
OTHELLO. Away! (*Exit.*)
EMILIA. Is not this man jealous?
DESDEMONA. I ne'er saw this before.
Sure there's some wonder in this handkerchief. 95
I am most unhappy in the loss of it.
EMILIA. 'Tis not a year or two shows us a man.°
They are all but stomachs and we all but food.
They eat us hungerly, and when they are full
They belch us. Look you, Cassio and my husband. 100

(*Enter* CASSIO *and* IAGO.)

IAGO. There is no other way, 'tis she must do 't.
And, lo, the happiness!° Go and impórtune her.
DESDEMONA. How now, good Cassio! What's the news with you?
CASSIO. Madam, my former suit. I do beseech you
That by your virtuous means I may again 105
Exist, and be a member of his love
Whom I with all the office of my heart
Entirely honor. I would not be delayed.
If my offense be of such mortal kind
That nor my service past nor present sorrows 110
Nor purposed merit in futurity
Can ransom me into his love again,
But to know so must be my benefit.
So shall I clothe me in a forced content
And shut myself up in some other course 115
To Fortune's alms.
DESDEMONA. Alas, thrice-gentle Cassio!
My advocation° is not now in tune.
My lord is not my lord, nor should I know him
Were he in favor° as in humor altered.
So help me every spirit sanctified, 120
As I have spoken for you all my best
And stood within the blank° of his displeasure
For my free speech! You must awhile be patient.
What I can do I will, and more I will
Than for myself I dare. Let that suffice you. 125

97. 'Tis . . . man: it does not take a couple of years for us to discover the nature of a man; i.e., he soon shows his real nature. 102. And . . . happiness: what good luck, here she is. 117. advocation: advocacy. 119. favor: face [L.P.]. 122. blank: aim.

IAGO. Is my lord angry?
EMILIA.   He went hence but now,
And certainly in strange unquietness.
IAGO.   Can he be angry? I have seen the cannon
When it hath blown his ranks into the air,
And, like the Devil, from his very arm   130
Puffed his own brother, and can he be angry?
Something of moment then. I will go meet him.
There's matter in 't indeed if he be angry.
DESDEMONA.   I prithee do so.

(*Exit* IAGO.)

                              Something sure of state,
Either from Venice, or some unhatched practice   135
Made demonstrable here in Cyprus to him,
Hath puddled his clear spirit. And in such cases
Men's natures wrangle with inferior things,
Though great ones are their object. 'Tis even so,
For let our finger ache and it indues   140
Our other healthful members even to that sense
Of pain. Nay, we must think men are not gods,
Nor of them look for such observancy
As fits the bridal.° Beshrew me much, Emilia,
I was, unhandsome warrior° as I am,   145
Arraigning his unkindness with my soul,
But now I find I had suborned the witness,°
And he's indicted falsely.
EMILIA.   Pray Heaven it be state matters, as you think,
And no conception nor no jealous toy°   150
Concerning you.
DESDEMONA.   Alas the day, I never gave him cause!
EMILIA.   But jealous souls will not be answered so.
They are not ever jealous for the cause,
But jealous for they are jealous 'Tis a monster   155
Begot upon itself, born on itself.
DESDEMONA.   Heaven keep that monster from Othello's mind!
EMILIA.   Lady, amen.
DESDEMONA.   I will go seek him. Cassio, walk hereabout.
If I do find him fit, I'll move your suit,   160
And seek to effect it to my uttermost.

144. **bridal:** honeymoon.   145. **unhandsome warrior:** clumsy soldier. Desdemona
continually thinks of herself as Othello's companion in arms. Cf. I.iii249 ff.
147. **suborned . . . witness:** corrupted the evidence; i.e., it is my fault, not his.
150. **jealous toy:** silly suspicion.

CASSIO. I humbly thank your ladyship.

(*Exeunt* DESDEMONA *and* EMILIA. *Enter* BIANCA.)

BIANCA. Save you, friend Cassio!
CASSIO.   What make you from home?
How is it with you, my most fair Bianca?
I' faith, sweet love, I was coming to your house.   165
BIANCA. And I was going to your lodging, Cassio.
What, keep a week away? Seven days and nights?
Eightscore eight hours? And lovers' absent hours,
More tedious than the dial eightscore times?
Oh, weary reckoning!
CASSIO.   Pardon me, Bianca.   170
I have this while with leaden thoughts been pressed,
But I shall in a more continuate time
Strike off this score of absence. Sweet Bianca,

(*Giving her* DESDEMONA'S *handkerchief*)

Take me this work out.
BIANCA.   O' Cassio, whence came this?
This is some token from a newer friend.   175
To the felt absence now I feel a cause.
Is 't come to this? Well, well.
CASSIO.   Go to, woman!
Throw your vile guesses in the Devil's teeth,
From whence you have them. You are jealous now
That this is from some mistress, some remembrance.   180
No, by my faith, Bianca.
BIANCA.   Why, whose is it?
CASSIO. I know not, sweet. I found it in my chamber.
I like the work well. Ere it be demanded—
As like enough it will—I'd have it copied.
Take it, and do 't, and leave me for this time.   185
BIANCA. Leave you! Wherefore?
CASSIO. I do attend here on the General,
And think it no addition,° nor my wish,
To have him see me womaned.°
BIANCA.   Why, I pray you?
CASSIO. Not that I love you not.
BIANCA.   But that you do not love me.   190
I pray you bring me on the way a little,
And say if I shall see you soon at night.

188. addition: honor. **189. womaned:** with a girl.

CASSIO. 'Tis but a little way that I can bring you,
For I attend here. But I'll see you soon.
BIANCA. 'Tis very good, I must be circumstanced.°   195
(*Exeunt.*)

ACT IV

SCENE I. Cyprus. Before the castle.

Enter OTHELLO *and* IAGO.

IAGO. Will you think so?
OTHELLO.   Think so, Iago!
IAGO.   What,
To kiss in private?
OTHELLO. An unauthorized kiss.
IAGO. Or to be naked with her friend in bed
An hour or more, not meaning any harm?
OTHELLO. Naked in bed, Iago, and not mean harm!   5
It is hypocrisy against the Devil.
They that mean virtuously and yet do so,
The Devil their virtue tempts and they tempt Heaven.
IAGO. So they do nothing, 'tis a venial° slip.
But if I give my wife a handkerchief—   10
OTHELLO. What then?
IAGO. Why, then, 'tis hers, my lord, and being hers,
She may, I think, bestow 't on any man.
OTHELLO. She is protectress of her honor too.
May she give that?   15
IAGO. Her honor is an essence that's not seen.
They have it very oft that have it not.
But for the handkerchief—
OTHELLO. By Heaven, I would most gladly have forgot it.
Thou said'st—oh, it comes o'er my memory,   20
As doth the raven o'er the infected house,°
Boding to all—he had my handkerchief.
IAGO. Aye, what of that?
OTHELLO.   That's not so good now.
IAGO.   What,
If I had said I had seen him do you wrong?
Or heard him say—as knaves be such abroad,   25

---

195. circumstanced: put off.
    Act iv, Sc. 1. 9. venial: pardonable. 21. As . . . house: i.e., as a bird of
prey waits for its victim to die.

Who having, by their own importunate suit,
Or voluntary dotage of some mistress,
Convincèd or supplied° them, cannot choose
But they must blab—
OTHELLO.   Hath he said anything?
IAGO.   He hath, my lord, but be you well assured,   30
No more, than he'll unswear.
OTHELLO.   What hath he said?
IAGO.   Faith, that he did—I know not what he did.
OTHELLO.   What? What?
IAGO.   Lie—
OTHELLO.   With her?
IAGO.   With her, on her, what you will.
OTHELLO.   Lie° with her! Lie on her!—We say lie on her when   35
they belie her.—Lie with her! 'Zounds, that's fulsome!° Handkerchief—
confessions—handkerchief!—To confess, and be hanged for his labor. First
to be hanged, and then to confess. I tremble at it. Nature would not invest
herself in such shadowing passion without some instruction.° It is not
words that shake me thus. Pish! Noses, ears, and lips. Is 't possible?—   40
Confess?—Handkerchief?—Oh, devil! (*Falls in a trance.*)
IAGO.   Work on,
My medicine, work! Thus credulous fools are caught,
And many worthy and chaste dames even thus,
All guiltless, meet reproach. What ho! My lord!   45
My lord, I say! Othello!

(*Enter* CASSIO.)

How now, Cassio!
CASSIO.   What's the matter?
IAGO.   My lord is fall'n into an epilepsy.
This is his second fit, he had one yesterday.
CASSIO.   Rub him about the temples.
IAGO.   No, forbear,   50
The lethargy° must have his quiet course.
If not, he foams at mouth and by and by
Breaks out to savage madness. Look, he stirs.
Do you withdraw yourself a little while,
He will recover straight. When he is gone,   55
I would on great occasion speak with you.

(*Exit* CASSIO.)

28. **Convincèd or supplied**: overcome or satisfied their desires. **35–41. Lie . . .
devil**: Othello breaks into incoherent muttering before he falls down in a fit.
36. fulsome: disgusting. **38–39. Nature . . . instruction**: nature would not fill
me with such overwhelming emotion unless there was some cause. **51. lethargy**:
epileptic fit.

How is it, General? Have you not hurt your head?°
OTHELLO. Dost thou mock me?
IAGO. I mock you! No, by Heaven.
Would you would bear your fortune like a man!
OTHELLO. A hornèd man's a monster and a beast. 60
IAGO. There's many a beast, then, in a populous city,
And many a civil monster.
OTHELLO. Did he confess it?
IAGO. Good sir, be a man.
Think every bearded fellow that's but yoked°
May draw with you.° There's millions now alive 65
That nightly lie in those unproper beds
Which they dare swear peculiar.° Your case is better.
Oh, 'tis the spite of Hell, the Fiend's archmock,
To lip° a wanton in a secure couch°
And to suppose her chaste! No, let me know, 70
And knowing what I am, I know what she shall be.
OTHELLO. Oh, thou art wise, 'tis certain.
IAGO. Stand you awhile apart,
Confine yourself but in a patient list.°
Whilst you were here o'erwhelmèd with your grief—
A passion most unsuiting such a man— 75
Cassio came hither. I shifted him away,
And laid good 'scuse upon your ecstasy,°
Bade him anon return and here speak with me,
The which he promisèd. Do but encave yourself,
And mark the fleers, the gibes, and notable scorns, 80
That dwell in every region of his face.
For I will make him tell the tale anew,
Where, how, how oft, how long ago, and when
He hath and is again to cope° your wife.
I say but mark his gesture. Marry, patience, 85
Or I shall say you are all in all in spleen,
And nothing of a man.
OTHELLO. Dost thou hear, Iago?
I will be found most cunning in my patience,
But—dost thou hear?—most bloody.
IAGO. That's not amiss,
But yet keep time in all. Will you withdraw? 90

57. Have . . . head: With brutal cynicism Iago asks whether Othello is suffering
from cuckold's headache. 64. yoked: married. 65. draw . . . you: be your yoke
fellow 66–67. That . . . peculiar: that lie nightly in beds which they believe
are their own but which others have shared. 69. lip: kiss. secure couch: lit.,
a carefree bed; i.e., a bed which has been used by the wife's lover, but secretly.
73. patient list: confines of patience. 77. ecstasy: fit. 84. cope: encounter.

(OTHELLO *retires*.)

Now will I question Cassio of Bianca,
A housewife° that by selling her desires
Buys herself bread and clothes. It is a creature
That dotes on Cassio, as 'tis the strumpet's plague
To beguile many and be beguiled by one.   95
He, when he hears of her, cannot refrain
From the excess of laughter. Here he comes.

(*Re-enter* CASSIO.)

As he shall smile, Othello shall go mad,
And his unbookish° jealousy must construe
Poor Cassio's smiles, gestures, and light behavior   100
Quite in the wrong. How do you now, Lieutenant?
CASSIO. The worser that you give me the addition°
Whose want even kills me.
IAGO. Ply Desdemona well, and you are sure on 't.
Now, if this suit lay in Bianca's power,   105
How quickly should you speed!
CASSIO.   Alas, poor caitiff!°
OTHELLO. Look how he laughs already!
IAGO. I never knew a woman love man so.
CASSIO. Alas, poor rogue! I think, i' faith, she loves me.
OTHELLO. Now he denies it faintly and laughs it out.   110
IAGO. Do you hear, Cassio?
OTHELLO.   Now he impórtunes him
To tell it o'er. Go to. Well said, well said.
IAGO. She gives it out that you shall marry her.
Do you intend it?
CASSIO. Ha, ha, ha!   115
OTHELLO. Do you triumph, Roman?° Do you triumph?
CASSIO. I marry her! What, a customer! I prithee bear some charity
to my wit. Do not think it so unwholesome. Ha, ha, ha!
OTHELLO. So, so, so, so. They laugh that win.
IAGO. Faith, the cry goes that you shall marry her.   120
CASSIO. Prithee say true.
IAGO. I am a very villain else.
OTHELLO. Have you scored° me? Well.
CASSIO. This is the monkey's own giving out. She is persuaded I

---

92. **housewife**: hussy.   99. **unbookish**: unlearned.   102. **addition**: title (Lieutenant) which he has lost.   106. **caitiff**: wretch.   116. **triumph, Roman**: The
word "triumph" suggests "Roman" because the Romans celebrated their victories
with triumphs, elaborate shows, and processions.   123. **scored**: marked, as with
a blow from a whip.

will marry her out of her own love and flattery, not out of my promise.   125
OTHELLO. Iago beckons me, now he begins the story.
CASSIO. She was here even now. She haunts me in every place. I was the other day talking on the sea bank with certain Venetians, and thither comes the bauble, and, by this hand, she falls me thus about my neck—   130
OTHELLO. Crying "O dear Cassio!" as it were. His gesture imports it.
CASSIO. So hangs and lolls and weeps upon me, so hales and pulls me. Ha, ha, ha!
OTHELLO. Now he tells how she plucked him to my chamber. Oh, I see that nose of yours, but not that dog I shall throw it to.   135
CASSIO. Well, I must leave her company.
IAGO. Before me!° Look where she comes.
CASSIO. 'Tis such another fitchew!° Marry, a perfumed one.

(*Enter* BIANCA.)

What do you mean by this haunting of me?
BIANCA. Let the Devil and his dam haunt you! What did you   140
mean by that same handkerchief you gave me even now? I was a fine fool to take it. I must take out the work? A likely piece of work, that you should find it in your chamber and not know who left it there! This is some minx's token, and I must take out the work? There, give it your hobbyhorse. Wheresoever you had it, I'll take out no work on 't.   145
CASSIO. How now, my sweet Bianca! How now! How now!
OTHELLO. By Heaven, that should be my handkerchief!
BIANCA. An° you'll come to supper tonight, you may. An you will not, come when you are next prepared for. (*Exit.*)
IAGO. After her, after her.
CASSIO. Faith, I must, she'll rail i' the street else.   150
IAGO. Will you sup there?
CASSIO. Faith, I intend so.
IAGO. Well, I may chance to see you, for I would very fain speak with you.
CASSIO. Prithee, come, will you?   155
IAGO. Go to. Say no more.

(*Exit* CASSIO.)

OTHELLO (*advancing*). How shall I murder him, Iago?
IAGO. Did you perceive how he laughed at his vice?
OTHELLO. Oh, Iago!
IAGO. And did you see the handkerchief?   160
OTHELLO. Was that mine?
IAGO. Yours, by this hand. And to see how he prizes the foolish

137. **Before me:** by my soul.   138. **fitchew:** polecat.   148. **An:** if.

woman your wife! She gave it him, and he hath given it his whore.

OTHELLO. I would have him nine years a-killing. A fine woman!
A fair woman! A sweet woman!   165

IAGO. Nay, you must forget that.

OTHELLO. Aye, let her rot, and perish, and be damned tonight, for
she shall not live. No, my heart is turned to stone, I strike it and it hurts
my hand. Oh, the world hath not a sweeter creature. She might lie by an
emperor's side, and command him tasks.   170

IAGO. Nay, that's not your way.°

OTHELLO. Hang her! I do but say what she is, so delicate with her
needle, an admirable musician—oh, she will sing the savageness out of a
bear—of so high and plenteous wit and invention—

IAGO. She's the worse for all this.   175

OTHELLO. Oh, a thousand thousand times. And then, of so gentle a
condition!

IAGO. Aye, too gentle.

OTHELLO. Nay, that's certain. But yet the pity of it, Iago! O Iago, the
pity of it, Iago!   180

IAGO. If you are so fond over her iniquity, give her patent to offend,
for if it touch not you, it comes near nobody.

OTHELLO. I will chop her into messes. Cuckold me!

IAGO. Oh, 'tis foul in her.

OTHELLO. With mine officer!   185

IAGO. That's fouler.

OTHELLO. Get me some poison, Iago, this night. I'll not expostulate
with her, lest her body and beauty unprovide my mind again. This night, Iago.

IAGO. Do it not with poison, strangle her in her bed, even the bed she
hath contaminated.   190

OTHELLO. Good, good. The justice of it pleases. Very good.

IAGO. And for Cassio, let me be his undertaker.°
You shall hear more by midnight.

OTHELLO. Excellent good. (A trumpet within.) What trumpet is that
same?

IAGO. Something from Venice, sure. 'Tis Lodovico   195
Come from the Duke. And see, your wife is with him.

(Enter LODOVICO, DESDEMONA, and ATTENDANTS.)

LODOVICO. God save the worthy General!

OTHELLO.   With all my heart, sir.

LODOVICO. The Duke and Senators of Venice greet you. (Gives him a
letter.)

171. Nay . . . way: i.e., don't get soft thoughts about her. 192. be . . . undertaker: undertake to manage his business. In Shakespeare's plays the word does
not mean "mortician."

OTHELLO. I kiss the instrument of their pleasures. (*Opens the letter,*
and reads.)   200
DESDEMONA. And what's the news, good Cousin Lodovico?
IAGO. I am very glad to see you, signior.
Welcome to Cyprus.
LODOVICO. I thank you. How does Lieutenant Cassio?
IAGO. Lives, sir.   205
DESDEMONA. Cousin, there's fall'n between him and my lord
An unkind breach, but you shall make all well.
OTHELLO. Are you sure of that?
DESDEMONA. My lord?
OTHELLO (*reads*). "This fail you not to do, as you will—"   210
LODOVICO. He did not call, he's busy in the paper.
Is there division 'twixt my lord and Cassio?
DESDEMONA. A most unhappy one. I would do much
To atone° them, for the love I bear to Cassio.
OTHELLO. Fire and brimstone!
DESDEMONA.   My lord?
OTHELLO.   Are you wise?°   215
DESDEMONA. What, is he angry?
LODOVICO.   Maybe the letter moved him,
For, as I think, they do command him home,
Deputing Cassio in his government.
DESDEMONA. By my troth, I am glad on 't.
OTHELLO   Indeed!
DESDEMONA.   My lord?
OTHELLO. I am glad to see you mad.
DESDEMONA.   Why, sweet Othello?   220
OTHELLO. Devil! (*Striking her.*)
DESDEMONA. I have not deserved this.
LODOVICO. My lord, this would not be believed in Venice.
Though I should swear I saw 't. 'Tis very much.
Make her amends, she weeps.
OTHELLO.   O devil, devil!   225
If that the earth could teem with a woman's tears,
Each drop she falls would prove a crocodile.°
Out of my sight!
DESDEMONA. I will not stay to offend you. (*Going.*)
LODOVICO. Truly, an obedient lady.
I do beseech your lordship, call her back.   230

214. atone: reconcile.   215. Are . . . wise: i.e., in saying you bear love to Cassio.
226–27. If . . . crocodile: If the earth could breed from woman's tears, each tear
that she lets fall would become a crocodile. It was believed that the crocodile would
cry and sob to attract the sympathetic passer-by, who was then snapped up.

OTHELLO. Mistress!
DESDEMONA. My lord?
OTHELLO. What would you with her, sir?
LODOVICO.   Who, I, my lord?
OTHELLO. Aye, you did wish that I would make her turn.
Sir, she can turn and turn, and yet go on   235
And turn again. And she can weep, sir, weep.
And she's obedient, as you say, obedient,
Very obedient. Proceed you in your tears.
Concerning this, sir—oh, well-painted passion!°—
I am commanded home. Get you away.   240
I'll send for you anon. Sir, I obey the mandate,
And will return to Venice. Hence, avaunt!

    (*Exit* DESDEMONA.)

Cassio shall have my place. And, sir, tonight,
I do entreat that we may sup together.
You are welcome, sir, to Cyprus. Goats and monkeys! (*Exit.*)   245
    LODOVICO. Is this the noble Moor whom our full Senate
Call all-in-all sufficient? This the nature
Whom passion could not shake? Whose solid virtue
The shot of accident nor dart of chance
Could neither graze nor pierce?
    IAGO.   He is much changed.   250
    LODOVICO. Are his wits safe? Is he not light of brain?
    IAGO. He's that he is. I may not breathe my censure°
What he might be. If what he might he is not,
I would to Heaven he were!
    LODOVICO.   What, strike his wife!
    IAGO. Faith, that was not so well, yet would I knew   255
That stroke would prove the worst!
    LODOVICO.   Is it his use?
Or did the letters work upon his blood,
And new-create this fault?
    IAGO.   Alas, alas!
It is not honesty in me to speak
What I have seen and known. You shall observe him,   260
And his own courses will denote him so
That I may save my speech. Do but go after,
And mark how he continues.
    LODOVICO. I am sorry that I am deceived in him.

    (*Exeunt.*)

239. well-painted passion: emotion [L.P.].   **252. censure:** opinion [L.P.].

SCENE II. *A room in the castle.*

Enter OTHELLO *and* EMILIA.

OTHELLO. You have seen nothing, then?
EMILIA. Nor ever heard, nor ever did suspect.
OTHELLO. Yes, you have seen Cassio and she together.
EMILIA. But then I saw no harm, and then I heard
Each syllable that breath made up between them. 5
OTHELLO. What, did they never whisper?
EMILIA.   Never, my lord.
OTHELLO. Nor send you out o' the way?
EMILIA. Never.
OTHELLO. To fetch her fan, her gloves, her mask, nor nothing?
EMILIA. Never, my lord. 10
OTHELLO. That's strange.
EMILIA. I durst, my lord, to wager she is honest,
Lay down my soul at stake. If you think other,
Remove your thought, it doth abuse your bosom.
If any wretch have put this in your head, 15
Let Heaven requite it with the serpent's curse!
For if she be not honest, chaste, and true,
There's no man happy, the purest of their wives
Is foul as slander.
OTHELLO.   Bid her come hither. Go.

(*Exit* EMILIA.)

She says enough. Yet she's a simple bawd 20
That cannot say as much. This is a subtle whore,
A closet lock and key of villainous secrets.
And yet she'll kneel and pray, I have seen her do 't.

(*Enter* DESDEMONA *with* EMILIA.)

DESDEMONA. My lord, what is your will?
OTHELLO.   Pray, chuck, come hither.
DESDEMONA. What is your pleasure?
OTHELLO,   Let me see your eyes. 25
Look in my face.
DESDEMONA. What horrible fancy's this?
OTHELLO (*to* EMILIA). Some of your function,° mistress.
Leave procreants alone and shut the door,
Cough, or cry hem, if anybody come.

27. **Some . . . function:** get about your business; i.e., prostitution. Othello pretends that Emilia is keeper of a brothel and Desdemona one of the women.

Your mystery,° your mystery. Nay, dispatch.   30

(*Exit* EMILIA.)

    DESDEMONA.   Upon my knees, what doth your speech import?
I understand a fury in your words,
But not the words.
    OTHELLO.   Why, what art thou?
    DESDEMONA.   Your wife, my lord, your true and loyal wife.
    OTHELLO.   Come, swear it, damn thyself,   35
Lest, being like one of Heaven,° the devils themselves
Should fear to seize thee. Therefore be double-damned.
Swear thou art honest.
    DESDEMONA.   Heaven doth truly know it.
    OTHELLO.   Heaven truly knows that thou art false as Hell.
    DESDEMONA.   To whom, my lord? With whom? How am I false?   40
    OTHELLO.   O Desdemona! Away! Away! Away!
    DESDEMONA.   Alas the heavy day! Why do you weep?
Am I the motive of these tears, my lord?
If haply you my father do suspect
An instrument of this your calling-back,   45
Lay not your blame on me. If you have lost him,
Why, I have lost him too.
    OTHELLO.   Had it pleased Heaven
To try me with affliction, had they rained
All kinds of sores and shames on my bare head,
Steeped me in poverty to the very lips,   50
Given to captivity me and my utmost hopes,
I should have found in some place of my soul
A drop of patience. But, alas, to make me
A fixèd figure for the time of scorn
To point his slow unmoving finger at!   55
Yet could I bear that too, well, very well.
But there where I have garnered up my heart,
Where either I must live or bear no life,
The fountain from the which my current runs
Or else dries up—to be discarded thence!   60
Or keep it as a cistern for foul toads
To knot and gender in! Turn thy complexion there,
Patience, thou young and rose-lipped cherubin—
Aye, there, look grim as Hell!
    DESDEMONA.   I hope my noble lord esteems me honest.   65

30. **mystery**: profession.   **36. being . . . Heaven**: because you look like an angel.

OTHELLO. Oh, aye, as summer flies are in the shambles,°
That quicken even with blowing.° O thou weed,
Who art so lovely fair and smell'st so sweet
That the sense aches at thee, would thou hadst ne'er been born!
DESDEMONA. Alas, what ignorant sin have I committed?   70
OTHELLO. Was this fair paper,° this most goodly book,
Made to write "whore" upon? What committed!
Committed! O thou public commoner!°
I should make very forges of my cheeks
That would to cinders burn up modesty   75
Did I but speak thy deeds. What committed!
Heaven stops the nose at it, and the moon winks.
The bawdy wind, that kisses all it meets,
Is hushed within the hollow mine of earth
And will not hear it. What committed!   80
Impudent strumpet!
DESDEMONA. By Heaven, you do me wrong.
OTHELLO. Are not you a strumpet?
DESDEMONA.   No, as I am a Christian.
If to preserve this vessel for my lord
From any other foul unlawful touch
Be not to be a strumpet, I am none.   85
OTHELLO. What, not a whore?
DESDEMONA.   No, as I shall be saved.
OTHELLO. Is 't possible?
DESDEMONA. Oh, Heaven forgive us!
OTHELLO.   I cry you mercy, then.
I took you for that cunning whore of Venice
That married with Othello. (Raising his voice) You, mistress,   90
That have the office opposite to Saint Peter,
And keep the gate of Hell!

      (Re-enter EMILIA.)

                    You, you, aye, you!
We have done our course, there's money for your pains.
I pray you turn the key, and keep our counsel. (Exit.)
EMILIA. Alas, what does this gentleman conceive?   95
How do you, madam? How do you, my good lady?
DESDEMONA. Faith, half-asleep.
EMILIA. Good madam, what's the matter with my lord?
DESDEMONA. With who?

66. shambles: slaughterhouse. 67. quicken . . . blowing: come to life as soon
as the eggs are laid. 71. fair paper: i.e., her white body. 73. public commoner:
one who offers herself to all comers.

EMILIA. Why, with my lord, madam.   100
DESDEMONA. Who is thy lord?
EMILIA.   He that is yours, sweet lady.
DESDEMONA. I have none. Do not talk to me, Emilia.
I cannot weep, nor answer have I none
But what should go by water.° Prithee tonight
Lay on my bed my wedding sheets. Remember,   105
And call thy husband hither.
EMILIA.   Here's a change indeed! (*Exit.*)
DESDEMONA. 'Tis meet I should be used so, very meet.
How have I been behaved that he might stick
The small'st opinion on my least misuse?°

   (*Re-enter* EMILIA *with* IAGO.)

IAGO. What is your pleasure, madam? How is 't with you?   110
DESDEMONA. I cannot tell. Those that do teach young babes
Do it with gentle means and easy tasks.
He might have chid me so, for, in good faith,
I am a child to chiding.
IAGO.   What's the matter, lady?
EMILIA. Alas, Iago, my lord hath so bewhored her,   115
Thrown such despite and heavy terms upon her,
As true hearts cannot bear.
DESDEMONA. Am I that name, Iago?
IAGO.   What name, fair lady?
DESDEMONA. Such as she says my lord did say I was.
EMILIA. He called her whore. A beggar in his drink   120
Could not have laid such terms upon his callet.°
IAGO. Why did he so?
DESDEMONA. I do not know. I am sure I am none such.
IAGO. Do not weep, do not weep. Alas the day!
EMILIA. Hath she forsook so many noble matches,   125
Her father and her country and her friends,
To be called whore? Would it not make one weep?
DESDEMONA. It is my wretched fortune.
IAGO.   Beshrew him for 't!
How comes this trick upon him?
DESDEMONA.   Nay, Heaven doth know.
EMILIA. I will be hanged if some eternal villain,   130
Some busy and insinuating rogue,
Some cogging, cozening slave, to get some office,

---

104. go . . . water: be expressed in tears. **109. misuse:** mistake. **121. callet:**
moll.

Have not devised this slander. I'll be hanged else.

IAGO.   Fie, there is no such man, it is impossible.

DESDEMONA.   If any such there be, Heaven pardon him!   135

EMILIA.   A halter pardon him! And Hell gnaw his bones!
Why should he call her whore? Who keeps her company?
What place? What time? What form? What likelihood?
The Moor's abused by some most villainous knave,
Some base notorious knave, some scurvy fellow.   140
O Heaven, that such companions° Thou'dst unfold,°
And put in every honest hand a whip
To lash the rascals naked through the world
Even from the east to the west!

IAGO.   Speak withindoor.°

EMILIA.   Oh, fie upon them! Some such squire he was   145
That turned your wit the seamy side without,
And made you to suspect me with the Moor.

IAGO.   You are a fool. Go to.°

DESDEMONA.   O good Iago,
What shall I do to win my lord again?
Good friend, go to him, for, by this light of Heaven,   150
I know not how I lost him. Here I kneel.
If e'er my will did trespass 'gainst his love
Either in discourse of thought or actual deed,
Or that mine eyes, mine ears, or any sense
Delighted them in any other form,   155
Or that I do not yet, and ever did,
And ever will, though he do shake me off
To beggarly divorcement, love him dearly,
Comfort forswear me! Unkindness may do much,
And his unkindness may defeat my life,   160
But never taint my love. I cannot say "whore,"
It doth abhor me now I speak the word.
To do the act that might the addition° earn
Not the world's mass of vanity° could make me.

IAGO.   I pray you be content, 'tis but his humor.   165
The business of the state does him offense,
And he does chide with you.

DESDEMONA.   If 'twere no other—

IAGO.   'Tis but so, I warrant. (*Trumpets within.*)
Hark how these instruments summon to supper!
The messengers of Venice stay the meat.°   170

141. companions: low creatures. unfold: bring to light.   144. Speak withindoor:
don't shout so loud that all the street will hear you.   148. Go to: an expression
of derision.   163. addition: title.   164. vanity: i.e., riches.   170. meat: serving
of supper.

Go in, and weep not, all things shall be well.

(*Exeunt* DESDEMONA *and* EMILIA. *Enter* RODERIGO.)

How now, Roderigo!

RODERIGO. I do not find that thou dealest justly with me.

IAGO. What in the contrary?

RODERIGO. Every day thou daffest me with some device, Iago,   175
and rather, as it seems to me now, keepest from me all conveniency than
suppliest me with the least advantage of hope. I will indeed no longer endure
it, nor am I yet persuaded to put up in peace what already I have foolishly
suffered.

IAGO. Will you hear me, Roderigo?   180

RODERIGO. Faith, I have heard too much, for your words and performances are no kin together.

IAGO. You charge me most unjustly.

RODERIGO. With naught but truth. I have wasted myself out of my
means. The jewels you have had from me to deliver to Desdemona   185
would half have corrupted a votarist.° You have told me she hath received
them, and returned me expectations and comforts of sudden respect and
acquaintance, but I find none.

IAGO. Well, go to, very well.

RODERIGO. Very well! Go to! I cannot go to, man, nor 'tis not   190
very well. By this hand, I say 'tis very scurvy, and begin to find myself
fopped in it.

IAGO. Very well.

RODERIGO. I tell you 'tis not very well. I will make myself known to
Desdemona. If she will return me my jewels, I will give over my suit   195
and repent my unlawful solicitation. If not, assure yourself I will seek
satisfaction of you.

IAGO. You have said now.°

RODERIGO. Aye, and said nothing but what I protest intendment of
doing.   200

IAGO. Why, now I see there's mettle in thee, and even from this instant
do build on thee a better opinion than ever before. Give me thy hand,
Roderigo. Thou hast taken against me a most just exception, but yet I
protest I have dealt most directly in thy affair.

RODERIGO. It hath not appeared.   205

IAGO. I grant indeed it hath not appeared, and your suspicion is not
without wit and judgment. But, Roderigo, if thou hast that in thee indeed
which I have greater reason to believe now than ever—I mean purpose,
courage, and valor—this night show it. If thou the next night following

---

186. votarist: nun.   **198. You . . . now:** or in modern slang, "Oh yeah."

enjoy not Desdemona, take me from this world with treachery and   210
devise engines° for my life.

RODERIGO.   Well, what is it? Is it within reason and compass?

IAGO.   Sir, there is especial commission come from Venice to depute
Cassio in Othello's place.

RODERIGO.   Is that true? Why, then Othello and Desdemona   215
return again to Venice.

IAGO.   Oh, no. He goes into Mauritania, and takes away with him the
fair Desdemona, unless his abode be lingered here by some accident. Wherein
none can be so determinate as the removing of Cassio.

RODERIGO.   How do you mean, "removing of" him?   220

IAGO.   Why, by making him uncapable of Othello's place, knocking
out his brains.

RODERIGO.   And that you would have me to do?

IAGO.   Aye, if you dare do yourself a profit and a right. He sups tonight
with a harlotry,° and thither will I go to him. He knows not yet of his   225
honorable fortune. If you will watch his going thence, which I will fashion
to fall out between twelve and one, you may take him at your pleasure.
I will be near to second your attempt, and he shall fall between us. Come,
stand not amazed at it, but go along with me. I will show you such a
necessity in his death that you shall think yourself bound to put it on   230
him. It is now high suppertime, and the night grows to waste. About it.

RODERIGO.   I will hear further reason for this.

IAGO.   And you shall be satisfied.

(*Exeunt.*)

SCENE III. *Another room in the castle.*

Enter OTHELLO, LODOVICO, DESDEMONA, EMILIA, *and* ATTENDANTS.

LODOVICO.   I do beseech you, sir, trouble yourself no further.

OTHELLO.   Oh, pardon me, 'twill do me good to walk.

LODOVICO.   Madam, good night. I humbly thank your ladyship.

DESDEMONA.   Your Honor is most welcome.

OTHELLO.   Will you walk, sir?
Oh—Desdemona—   5

DESDEMONA.   My lord?

OTHELLO.   Get you to bed on the instant, I will be returned forthwith.
Dismiss your attendant there. Look it be done.

DESDEMONA.   I will, my lord.

(*Exeunt* OTHELLO, LODOVICO, *and* ATTENDANTS.)

---

211. engines: instruments of torture.   **225. harlotry:** harlot.

EMILIA.   How goes it now? He looks gentler than he did.   10
DESDEMONA.   He says he will return incontinent.°
He hath commanded me to go to bed,
And bade me to dismiss you. ,
EMILIA.   Dismiss me!
DESDEMONA.   It was his bidding, therefore, good Emilia,
Give me my nightly wearing, and adieu.   15
We must not now displease him.
EMILIA.   I would you had never seen him!
DESDEMONA.   So would not I. My love doth so approve him
That even his stubbornness, his checks, his frowns—
Prithee, unpin me—have grace and favor in them.   20
EMILIA.   I have laid those sheets you bade me on the bed.
DESDEMONA.   All's one. Good faith, how foolish are our minds!
If I do die before thee, prithee shroud me
In one of those same sheets.
EMILIA.   Come, come, you talk.
DESDEMONA.   My mother had a maid called Barbara.   25
She was in love, and he she loved proved mad
And did forsake her. She had a song of "willow"°—
An old thing 'twas, but it expressed her fortune,
And she died singing it. That song tonight
Will not go from my mind. I have much to do   30
But to go hang my head all at one side
And sing it like poor Barbara. Prithee, dispatch.
EMILIA.   Shall I go fetch your nightgown?
DESDEMONA.   No, unpin me here.
This Lodovico is a proper man.
EMILIA.   A very handsome man.   35
DESDEMONA.   He speaks well.
EMILIA.   I know a lady in Venice would have walked barefoot to
Palestine for a touch of his nether lip.
DESDEMONA (singing).
        "The poor soul sat sighing by a sycamore tree,
            Sing all a green willow.   40
        Her hand on her bosom, her head on her knee,
            Sing willow, willow, willow.
        The fresh streams ran by her, and murmured her moans,
            Sing willow, willow, willow.
        Her salt tears fell from her, and softened the stones—"   45
Lay by these—(singing)
                "Sing willow, willow, willow"

---

11. incontinent: immediately.   27. willow: the emblem of the forlorn lover.

Prithee, hie thee, he'll come anon.—(*singing*)
　　"Sing all a green willow must be my garland.
　　Let nobody blame him, his scorn I approve—"　　50
Nay, that's not next. Hark! Who is 't that knocks?
EMILIA.　It's the wind.
DESDEMONA (*singing*).
　　"I called my love false love, but what said he then?
　　　Sing willow, willow, willow.
　　If I court moe° women, you'll couch with moe men."　　55
So get thee gone, good night. Mine eyes do itch.
Doth that bode weeping?
EMILIA.　　　　　　'Tis neither here nor there.
DESDEMONA.　I have heard it said so. Oh, these men, these men!
Dost thou in conscience think—tell me, Emilia—
That there be women do abuse their husbands　　60
In such gross kind?
EMILIA.　　　　There be some such, no question.
DESDEMONA.　Wouldst thou do such a deed for all the world?
EMILIA.　Why, would not you?
DESDEMONA.　　　　　　No, by this heavenly light!
EMILIA.　Nor I neither by this heavenly light. I might do 't as well i' the
dark.　　65
DESDEMONA.　Wouldst thou do such a deed for all the world?
EMILIA.　The world's a huge thing. It is a great price
For a small vice.
DESDEMONA.　In troth, I think thou wouldst not.
EMILIA.　In troth, I think I should, and undo 't when I had done.　　70
Marry, I would not do such a thing for a joint ring,° nor for measures of
lawn,° nor for gowns, petticoats, nor caps, nor any petty exhibition;° but
for the whole world—why, who would not make her husband a cuckold to
make him a monarch? I should venture Purgatory for 't.
DESDEMONA.　Beshrew me if I would do such a wrong　　75
For the whole world.
EMILIA.　Why, the wrong is but a wrong i' the world, and having the
world for your labor, 'tis a wrong in your own world and you might quickly
make it right.
DESDEMONA.　I do not think there is any such woman.　　80
EMILIA.　Yes, a dozen, and as many to the vantage as would store the
world they played for. But I do think it is their husbands' faults

---

55. moe: more.　71–72. joint ring: ring made in two pieces, a lover's gift.
measures of lawn: lengths of finest lawn, or as a modern woman would say,
"sheer nylon." petty exhibition: small allowance of money.

If wives do fall. Say that they slack their duties
And pour our treasures into foreign laps,   85
Or else break out in peevish jealousies,
Throwing restraint upon us, or say they strike us,
Or scant our former having in despite,°
Why, we have galls,° and though we have some grace,
Yet have we some revenge. Let husbands know   90
Their wives have sense like them. They see and smell
And have their palates both for sweet and sour,
As husbands have. What is it that they do
When they change us for others? Is it sport?
I think it is. And doth affection breed it?   95
I think it doth. Is 't frailty that thus errs?
It is so too. And have not we affections,
Desires for sport, and frailty, as men have?
Then let them use us well. Else let them know
The ills we do, their ills instruct us so.   100
    DESDEMONA.   Good night, good night. Heaven me such uses send,
Not to pick bad from bad, but by bad mend!

    (*Exeunt.*)

ACT V

SCENE I. Cyprus. A street.

Enter IAGO *and* RODERIGO.

    IAGO.   Here, stand behind this bulk, straight will he come.
Wear thy good rapier bare, and put it home.
Quick, quick, fear nothing, I'll be at thy elbow.
It makes us, or it mars us. Think on that,
And fix most firm thy resolution.   5
    RODERIGO.   Be near at hand, I may miscarry in 't.
    IAGO.   Here, at thy hand. Be bold, and take thy stand. (*Retires.*)
    RODERIGO.   I have no great devotion to the deed,
And yet he hath given me satisfying reasons.
'Tis but a man gone. Forth, my sword. He dies.   10
    IAGO.   I have rubbed this young quat° almost to the sense,°
And he grows angry. Now, whether he kill Cassio,
Or Cassio him, or each do kill the other,

---

88. scant . . . despite: for spite cut down our allowance.   **89. galls:** bile, the cause
of bitterness.
    Act V, Sc. i. 11. quat: pimple. **sense:** quick.

Every way makes my gain. Live Roderigo,
He calls me to a restitution large   15
Of gold and jewels that I bobbed from him
As gifts to Desdemona.
It must not be. If Cassio do remain,
He hath a daily beauty in his life
That makes me ugly,° and besides, the Moor   20
May unfold me to him. There stand I in much peril.
No, he must die. Be 't so. I hear him coming.

(*Enter* CASSIO.)

RODERIGO.   I know his gait, 'tis he. Villain, thou diest! (*Makes a pass
at* CASSIO.)
CASSIO.   That thrust had been mine enemy indeed
But that my coat is better than thou know'st.   25
I will make proof of thine. (*Draws, and wounds* RODERIGO.)
RODERIGO.   Oh, I am slain!

(IAGO *from behind wounds* CASSIO *in the leg, and exit.*)

CASSIO.   I am maimed for ever. Help, ho! Murder! Murder! (*Falls.*)

(*Enter* OTHELLO.)

OTHELLO.   The voice of Cassio. Iago keeps his word.
RODERIGO.   Oh, villain that I am!
OTHELLO.   It is even so.
CASSIO.   Oh, help, ho! Light! A surgeon!   30
OTHELLO.   'Tis he. O brave Iago, honest and just,
That hast such noble sense of thy friend's wrong!
Thou teachest me. Minion,° your dear lies dead,
And your unblest fate hies. Strumpet, I come!
Forth of my heart those charms, thine eyes, are blotted.   35
Thy bed lust-stained shall with lust's blood be spotted. (*Exit.*)

(*Enter* LODOVICO *and* GRATIANO.)

CASSIO.   What ho! No watch?° No passage?° Murder! Murder!
GRATIANO.   'Tis some mischance, the cry is very direful.
CASSIO.   Oh, help!
LODOVICO.   Hark!   40
RODERIGO.   Oh, wretched villain!
LODOVICO.   Two or three groan. It is a heavy° night.
These may be counterfeits. Let's think 't unsafe

19–20. He . . . ugly: by comparison with him I am a poor thing. Iago is conscious
of his lack of social graces.   33. Minion: darling, in a bad sense.   37. watch:
police. No passage: nobody passing.   42. heavy: thick.

To come in to the cry without more help.

RODERIGO. Nobody come? Then shall I bleed to death.   45
LODOVICO. Hark!

(Re-enter IAGO, with a light.)

GRATIANO. Here's one comes in his shirt, with light and weapons.
IAGO. Who's there? Whose noise is this that cries on murder?
LODOVICO. We do not know.
IAGO.   Did not you hear a cry?
CASSIO. Here, here! For Heaven's sake, help me!
IAGO.   What's the matter? 50
GRATIANO. This is Othello's Ancient, as I take it.
LODOVICO. The same indeed, a very valiant fellow.
IAGO. What are you here that cry so grievously?
CASSIO. Iago? Oh, I am spoiled, undone by villains! Give me some
help.   55
IAGO. Oh me, Lieutenant! What villains have done this?
CASSIO. I think that one of them is hereabout,
And cannot make away.
IAGO.   Oh, treacherous villains!
(To LODOVICO *and* GRATIANO) What are you there?
Come in and give some help.
RODERIGO.   Oh, help me here!   60
CASSIO. That's one of them.
IAGO.   Oh, murderous slave! Oh, villain! *(Stabs*
RODERIGO.)
RODERIGO. Oh, damned Iago! Oh, inhuman dog!
IAGO. Kill men i' the dark! Where be these bloody thieves?
How silent is this town! Ho! Murder! Murder!
What may you be? Are you of good or evil?   65
LODOVICO. As you shall prove us, praise us.
IAGO. Signior Lodovico?
LODOVICO. He, sir.
IAGO. I cry you mercy. Here's Cassio hurt by villains.
GRATIANO. Cassio!   70
IAGO. How is 't, brother?
CASSIO. My leg is cut in two.
IAGO.   Marry, Heaven forbid!
Light, gentlemen. I'll bind it with my shirt.

(Enter BIANCA.)

BIANCA. What is the matter, ho? Who is 't that cried?
IAGO. Who is 't that cried!   75

BIANCA. Oh, my dear Cassio! My sweet Cassio! Oh, Cassio, Cassio, Cassio!

IAGO. Oh, notable strumpet, Cassio, may you suspect
Who they should be that have thus mangled you?

CASSIO. No.

GRATIANO. I am sorry to find you thus. I have been to seek you.   80

IAGO. Lend me a garter. So. Oh, for a chair,
To bear him easily hence!

BIANCA. Alas, he faints! Oh, Cassio, Cassio, Cassio!

IAGO. Gentlemen all, I do suspect this trash
To be a party in this injury.   85
Patience awhile, good Cassio. Come, come,
Lend me a light. Know we this face or no?
Alas, my friend and my dear countryman
Roderigo? No—yes, sure. Oh Heaven! Roderigo.

GRATIANO. What, of Venice?   90

IAGO. Even he, sir. Did you know him?

GRATIANO.   Know him! Aye.

IAGO. Signior Gratiano? I cry you gentle pardon.
These bloody accidents must excuse my manners,
That so neglected you.

GRATIANO.   I am glad to see you.

IAGO. How do you, Cassio? Oh, a chair, a chair!   95

GRATIANO. Roderigo!

IAGO. He, he, 'tis he. (A chair brought in) Oh, that's well said, the chair.
Some good man bear him carefully from hence.
I'll fetch the General's surgeon. (To BIANCA) For you, mistress,
Save you your labor. He that lies slain here, Cassio,   100
Was my dear friend. What malice was between you?

CASSIO. None in the world, nor do I know the man.

IAGO (to BIANCA). What, look you pale? Oh, bear him out o' the air.

(CASSIO and RODERIGO are borne off.)

Stay you, good gentlemen. Look you pale, mistress?
Do you perceive the gastness of her eye?   105
Nay, if you stare, we shall hear more anon.
Behold her well, I pray you look upon her.
Do you see, gentlemen? Nay, guiltiness will speak,
Though tongues were out of use.

(Enter EMILIA.)

EMILIA. 'Las, what's the matter? What's the matter, husband?   110

IAGO. Cassio hath here been set on in the dark

By Roderigo, and fellows that are 'scaped.
He's almost slain, and Roderigo dead.
EMILIA.   Alas, good gentlemen! Alas, good Cassio!
IAGO.   This is the fruit of whoring. Prithee, Emilia,   115
Go know of Cassio where he supped tonight.
What, do you shake at that?
BIANCA.   He supped at my house, but I therefore shake not.
IAGO.   Oh, did he so? I charge you, go with me.
EMILIA.   Fie, fie upon thee, strumpet!   120
BIANCA.   I am no strumpet, but of life as honest
As you that thus abuse me.
EMILIA.   As I! Foh! Fie upon thee!
IAGO.   Kind gentlemen, let's go see poor Cassio dressed.°
Come, mistress, you must tell 's another tale.
Emilia, run you to the citadel,   125
And tell my lord and lady what hath happed!
Will you go on? I pray. (*Aside*) This is the night
That either makes me or fordoes me quite.

   (*Exeunt.*)

   SCENE II. *A bedchamber in the castle.* DESDEMONA *in bed asleep, a
light burning.*

   Enter OTHELLO.

   OTHELLO.   It is the cause,° it is the cause, my soul.
Let me not name it to you, you chaste stars!
It is the cause. Yet I'll not shed her blood,
Nor scar that whiter skin of hers than snow
And smooth as monumental alabaster.   5
Yet she must die, else she'll betray more men.
Put out the light, and then put out the light.
If I quench thee, thou flaming minister,°
I can again thy former light restore,
Should I repent me. But once put out thy light,   10
Thou cunning'st° pattern of excelling nature,
I know not where is that Promethean heat
That can thy light relume. When I have plucked the rose,

---

123. dressed: i.e., his wound dressed.
   Sc. ii. 1. It . . . cause: The meaning of the opening lines of this speech has
been much discussed. The *cause* is Desdemona's supposed faithlessness; Othello,
at this moment, sees himself as embodied vengeance, the venger of man betrayed
by woman.   **8. minister:** servant.   **11. cunning'st:** most skillfully made.

I cannot give it vital growth again,
It needs must wither. I'll smell it on the tree. (*Kissing her*)   15
Ah, balmy breath, that dost almost persuade
Justice to break her sword! One more, one more.
Be thus when thou art dead, and I will kill thee,
And love thee after. One more, and this the last.
So sweet was ne'er so fatal. I must weep,   20
But they are cruel tears. This sorrow's heavenly,
It strikes where it doth love. She wakes.
    DESDEMONA. Who's there? Othello?
    OTHELLO.   Aye, Desdemona.
    DESDEMONA. Will you come to bed, my lord?
    OTHELLO. Have you prayed tonight, Desdemona?   25
    DESDEMONA. Aye, my lord.
    OTHELLO. If you bethink yourself of any crime
Unreconciled as yet to Heaven and grace,
Solicit for it straight.
    DESDEMONA. Alas, my lord, what may you mean by that?   30
    OTHELLO. Well, do it, and be brief. I will walk by.
I would not kill thy unpreparèd spirit.
No, Heaven forfend! I would not kill thy soul.
    DESDEMONA. Talk you of killing?
    OTHELLO. Aye, I do.
    DESDEMONA.   Then Heaven have mercy on me!   35
    OTHELLO. Amen, with all my heart!
    DESDEMONA. If you say so, I hope you will not kill me.
    OTHELLO. Hum!
    DESDEMONA. And yet I fear you, for you are fatal then
When your eyes roll so. Why I should fear I know not,   40
Since guiltiness I know not, but yet I feel I fear.
    OTHELLO. Think on thy sins.
    DESDEMONA.   They are loves I bear to you.
    OTHELLO. Aye, and for that thou diest.
    DESDEMONA. That death's unnatural that kills for loving.
Alas, why gnaw you so your nether lip?   45
Some bloody passion shakes your very frame.
These are portents, but yet I hope, I hope,
They do not point on me.
    OTHELLO.   Peace, and be still!
    DESDEMONA. I will so. What's the matter?
    OTHELLO. That handkerchief which I so loved and gave thee   50
Thou gavest to Cassio.
    DESDEMONA.   No, by my life and soul!

Send for the man, and ask him.

OTHELLO.   Sweet soul, take heed,
Take heed of perjury, thou art on thy deathbed.

DESDEMONA.   Aye, but not yet to die.

OTHELLO.   Yes, presently.°
Therefore confess thee freely of thy sin,   55
For to deny each article with oath
Cannot remove nor choke the strong conception
That I do groan withal. Thou art to die.

DESDEMONA.   Then Lord have mercy on me!

OTHELLO.   I say amen.

DESDEMONA.   And have you mercy too! I never did   60
Offend you in my life, never loved Cassio
But with such general warranty of Heaven
As I might love. I never gave him token.

OTHELLO.   By Heaven, I saw my handkerchief in 's hand.
O perjured woman! Thou dost stone° my heart,   65
And makest me call what I intend to do
A murder, which I thought a sacrifice.
I saw the handkerchief.

DESDEMONA.   He found it, then,
I never gave it him. Send for him hither.
Let him confess a truth.

OTHELLO.   He hath confessed.   70

DESDEMONA.   What, my lord?

OTHELLO.   That he hath used thee.

DESDEMONA.   How? Unlawfully?

OTHELLO.   Aye.

DESDEMONA.   He will not say so.

OTHELLO.   No, his mouth is stopped.
Honest Iago hath ta'en order for 't.   75

DESDEMONA.   Oh, my fear interprets! What, is he dead?

OTHELLO.   Had all his hairs been lives, my great revenge
Had stomach for them all.

DESDEMONA.   Alas, he is betrayed, and I undone!

OTHELLO.   Out, strumpet! Weep'st thou for him to my face?   80

DESDEMONA.   Oh, banish me, my lord, but kill me not!

OTHELLO.   Down, strumpet!

DESDEMONA.   Kill me tomorrow, let me live tonight!

OTHELLO.   Nay, if you strive—

DESDEMONA.   But half an hour!

OTHELLO.   Being done, there is no pause.   85

---

54. presently: at once.   **65. stone:** turn to stone.

DESDEMONA. But while I say one prayer!

OTHELLO.   It is too late. (*He stifles her.*)

EMILIA (*within*). My lord, my lord! What ho! My lord, my lord!

OTHELLO. What noise is this? Not dead? Not yet quite dead?

I that am cruel am yet merciful,

I would not have thee linger in thy pain.   90

So, so.

EMILIA (*within*). What ho! My lord, my lord!

OTHELLO.   Who's there?

EMILIA (*within*). Oh, good my lord, I would speak a word with you!

OTHELLO. Yes, 'tis Emilia. By and by. She's dead.

'Tis like she comes to speak of Cassio's death.   95

The noise was here. Ha! No more moving?

Still as the grave. Shall she come in? Were 't good?

I think she stirs again. No. What's best to do?

If she come in, she'll sure speak to my wife.

My wife! My wife! My wife! I have no wife.   100

Oh, insupportable! Oh, heavy hour!

Methinks it should be now a huge eclipse

Of sun and moon, and that the affrighted globe

Should yawn° at alteration.

EMILIA (*within*).   I do beseech you

That I may speak with you, O good my lord!   105

OTHELLO. I had forgot thee. Oh, come in, Emilia.

Soft, by and by. Let me the curtains° draw.

Where art thou? (*Unlocks the door.*)

(*Enter* EMILIA.)

                What's the matter with thee now?

EMILIA. Oh, my good lord, yonder 's foul murders done!

OTHELLO. What, now?   110

EMILIA. But now, my lord.

OTHELLO. It is the very error of the moon.

She comes more nearer earth than she was wont

And makes men mad.

EMILIA. Cassio, my lord, hath killed a young Venetian   115

Called Roderigo.

OTHELLO. Roderigo killed!

And Cassio killed!

EMILIA.   No, Cassio is not killed.

OTHELLO. Not Cassio killed! Then murder's out of tune,

---

104. yawn: gape [L.P.]. **107. curtains:** i.e., of the bed.

And sweet revenge grows harsh.

DESDEMONA.   Oh, falsely, falsely murdered!

EMILIA.   Alas, what cry is that?   120

OTHELLO.   That! What?

EMILIA.   Out and alas! That was my lady's voice.

Help! Help, ho! Help! O lady, speak again!

Sweet Desdemona! O sweet mistress, speak!

DESDEMONA.   A guiltless death I die.   125

EMILIA.   Oh, who hath done this deed?

DESDEMONA.   Nobody, I myself. Farewell.

Commend me to my kind lord. Oh, farewell! (*Dies.*)

OTHELLO.   Why, how should she be murdered?

EMILIA.   Alas, who knows?   130

OTHELLO.   You heard her say herself it was not I.

EMILIA.   She said so. I must needs report the truth.

OTHELLO.   She's like a liar gone to burning Hell.

'Twas I that killed her.

EMILIA.   Oh, the more angel she,

And you the blacker devil!   135

OTHELLO.   She turned to folly, and she was a whore.

EMILIA.   Thou dost belie her, and thou art a devil.

OTHELLO.   She was false as water.

EMILIA.   Thou art rash as fire to say

That she was false. Oh, she was heavenly true!

OTHELLO.   Cassio did top her, ask thy husband else.   140

Oh, I were damned beneath all depth in Hell

But that I did proceed upon just grounds

To this extremity. Thy husband knew it all.

EMILIA.   My husband!

OTHELLO.   Thy husband.   145

EMILIA.   That she was false to wedlock?

OTHELLO.   Aye, with Cassio. Nay, had she been true,

If Heaven would make me such another world

Of one entire and perfect chrysolite,

I'd not have sold her for it.   150

EMILIA.   My husband!

OTHELLO.   Aye, 'twas he that told me first.

An honest man he is, and hates the slime

That sticks on filthy deeds.

EMILIA.   My husband!

OTHELLO.   What needs this iteration, woman? I say thy husband.

EMILIA.   Oh, mistress, villainy hath made mocks with love!   155

My husband say that she was false!

OTHELLO.   He, woman.

I say thy husband. Dost understand the word?
My friend, thy husband, honest, honest Iago.
    EMILIA. If he say so, may his pernicious soul
Rot half a grain a day! He lies to the heart.   160
She was too fond of her most filthy bargain.
    OTHELLO. Ha!
    EMILIA. Do thy worst.
This deed of thine is no more worthy Heaven
Than thou wast worthy her.
    OTHELLO.   Peace, you were best.   165
    EMILIA. Thou hast not half that power to do me harm
As I have to be hurt. O gull! O dolt!
As ignorant as dirt! Thou hast done a deed—
I care not for thy sword, I'll make thee known,
Though I lost twenty lives. Help! Help, ho! Help!   170
The Moor hath killed my mistress! Murder! Murder!

    (*Enter* MONTANO, GRATIANO, IAGO, *and others.*)

    MONTANO. What is the matter? How now, General!
    EMILIA. Oh, are you come, Iago? You have done well,
That men must lay their murders on your neck.
    GRATIANO. What is the matter?   175
    EMILIA. Disprove this villain, if thou be'st a man.
He says thou told'st him that his wife was false.
I know thou didst not, thou'rt not such a villain.
Speak, for my heart is full.
    IAGO. I told him what I thought, and told no more   180
Than what he found himself was apt and true.
    EMILIA. But did you ever tell him she was false?
    IAGO. I did.
    EMILIA. You told a lie, an odious, damnèd lie,
Upon my soul, a lie, a wicked lie!   185
She false with Cassio! Did you say with Cassio?
    IAGO. With Cassio, mistress. Go to, charm your tongue.°
    EMILIA. I will not charm my tongue, I am bound to speak.
My mistress here lies murdered in her bed.
    ALL. Oh, Heavens forfend!   190
    EMILIA. And your reports have set the murder on.
    OTHELLO. Nay, stare not, masters. It is true indeed.
    GRATIANO. 'Tis a strange truth.
    MONTANO. Oh, monstrous act!
    EMILIA.   Villainy, villainy, villainy!

187. **charm . . . tongue:** be silent.

I think upon 't. I think I smell 't. Oh, villainy! 195
I thought so then.° I'll kill myself for grief.
Oh, villainy, villainy!
    IAGO. What, are you mad? I charge you, get you home.
    EMILIA. Good gentlemen, let me have leave to speak.
'Tis proper I obey him, but not now. 200
Perchance, Iago, I will ne'er go home.
    OTHELLO. Oh! Oh! Oh! (*Falling on the bed.*)
    EMILIA.   Nay, lay thee down and roar,
For thou hast killed the sweetest innocent
That e'er did lift up eye.
    OTHELLO (*rising*). Oh, she was foul!
I scarce did know you, Uncle. There lies your niece, 205
Whose breath indeed these hands have newly stopped.
I know this act shows horrible and grim.
    GRATIANO. Poor Desdemona! I am glad thy father's dead.
Thy match was mortal to him, and pure grief
Shore his old thread in twain. Did he live now, 210
This sight would make him do a desperate turn—
Yea, curse his better angel from his side,
And fall to reprobation.°
    OTHELLO. 'Tis pitiful, but yet Iago knows
That she with Cassio hath the act of shame 215
A thousand times committed. Cassio confessed it.
And she did gratify his amorous works
With that recognizance and pledge of love
Which I first gave her, I saw it in his hand.
It was a handkerchief, an antique token 220
My father gave my mother.
    EMILIA. Oh, Heaven! Oh, heavenly powers!
    IAGO. 'Zounds! Hold your peace.
    EMILIA.   'Twill out, 'twill out. I peace!
No, I will speak as liberal as the north.°
Let Heaven and men and devils, let them all, 225
All, all, cry shame against me, yet I'll speak.
    IAGO. Be wise, and get you home.
    EMILIA.   I will not.

(IAGO *offers to stab* EMILIA.)

    GRATIANO.   Fie!
Your sword upon a woman!

---

196. I . . . then: i.e., I suspected this earlier—as for example when Iago took the handkerchief. **213. reprobation:** damnation; i.e., by self-murder. **224. liberal . . . north:** as freely as the north wind, which is loud and bitter.

EMILIA.   O thou dull Moor! That handkerchief thou speak'st of
I found by fortune and did give my husband,   230
For often with a solemn earnestness,
More than indeed belonged to such a trifle,
He begged of me to steal it.
    IAGO.   Villainous whore!
    EMILIA.   She give it Cassio! No, alas, I found it,
And I did give 't my husband.
    IAGO.   Filth, thou liest!   235
    EMILIA.   By Heaven, I do not, I do not, gentlemen.
Oh, murderous coxcomb! What should such a fool
Do with so good a wife?
    OTHELLO.   Are there no stones° in Heaven
But what serve for the thunder? Precious villain!

(*He runs at* IAGO. IAGO, *from behind, stabs* EMILIA, *and exit.*)

    GRATIANO.   The woman falls. Sure, he hath killed his wife.   240
    EMILIA.   Aye, aye. Oh, lay me by my mistress' side.
    GRATIANO.   He's gone, but his wife's killed.
    MONTANO.   'Tis a notorious villain. Take you this weapon,
Which I have here recovered from the Moor.
Come, guard the door without, let him not pass,   245
But kill him rather. I'll after that same villain,
For 'tis a damnèd slave.

(*Exeunt all but* OTHELLO *and* EMILIA.)

    OTHELLO.   I am not valiant neither.
But every puny whipster gets my sword.
But why should honor outlive honesty?
Let it go all.
    EMILIA.   What did thy song bode, lady?   250
Hark, canst thou hear me? I will play the swan,
And die in music. (*Singing.*)
                    "Willow, willow, willow."
Moor, she was chaste. She loved thee, cruel Moor,
So come my soul to bliss as I speak true.
So speaking as I think, I die, I die. (*Dies.*)   255
    OTHELLO.   I have another weapon in this chamber.
It is a sword of Spain, the ice brook's temper.—
Oh, here it is. Uncle, I must come forth.
    GRATIANO (*within*).   If thou attempt it, it will cost thee dear.
Thou hast no weapon, and perforce must suffer.   260

238. stones: thunderbolts.

OTHELLO.   Look in upon me then, and speak with me,
Or, naked° as I am, I will assault thee.

(*Re-enter* GRATIANO.)

GRATIANO.   What is the matter?
OTHELLO.   Behold, I have a weapon,
A better never did itself sustain
Upon a soldier's thigh. I have seen the day   265
That with this little arm and this good sword
I have made my way through more impediments
Than twenty times your stop. But, oh, vain boast!
Who can control his fate? 'Tis not so now.
Be not afraid, though you do see me weaponed.   270
Here is my journey's end, here is my butt°
And very sea mark of my utmost sail.
Do you go back dismayed? 'Tis a lost fear.
Man but a rush° against Othello's breast,
And he retires. Where should Othello go?   275
Now, how dost thou look now? O ill-starred wench!
Pale as thy smock! When we shall meet at compt,°
This look of thine will hurl my soul from Heaven
And fiends will snatch at it. Cold, cold, my girl!
Even like thy chastity. Oh, cursèd slave!   280
Whip me, ye devils,
From the possession of this heavenly sight!
Blow me about in winds! Roast me in sulphur!
Wash me in steep-down gulfs of liquid fire!
O Desdemona! Desdemona! Dead!   285
Oh! Oh! Oh!

(*Enter* LODOVICO, MONTANO, CASSIO *carried in a chair,
and* OFFICERS *with* IAGO, *prisoner.*)

LODOVICO.   Where is this rash and most unfortunate man?
OTHELLO.   That's he that was Othello. Here I am.
LODOVICO.   Where is that viper? Bring the villain forth.
OTHELLO.   I look down toward his feet,° but that's a fable.   290
If that thou be'st a devil, I cannot kill thee. (*Wounds* IAGO.)
LODOVICO.   Wrench his sword from him.
IAGO.   I bleed, sir, but not killed.
OTHELLO.   I am not sorry neither. I'd have thee live,
For, in my sense, 'tis happiness to die.

262. naked: unarmed.   271. butt: aim.   274. Man . . . rush: attack with only
a reed.   277. compt: account; i.e., the Day of Judgment.   290. toward . . . feet:
i.e., to see if he has the cloven hoof of a devil.

LODOVICO.   O thou Othello, that wert once so good,   295
Fall'n in the practice° of a damnèd slave,
What shall be said to thee?
OTHELLO.   Why, anything.
An honorable murderer, if you will,
For naught did I in hate, but all in honor.
LODOVICO.   This wretch hath part confessed his villainy.   300
Did you and he consent in Cassio's death?
OTHELLO.   Aye.
CASSIO.   Dear General, I never gave you cause.
OTHELLO.   I do believe it, and I ask your pardon.
Will you, I pray, demand that demidevil   305
Why he hath thus ensnared my soul and body?
IAGO.   Demand me nothing. What you know, you know.
From this time forth I never will speak word.
LODOVICO.   What, not to pray?
GRATIANO.   Torments will ope your lips.
OTHELLO.   Well, thou dost best.   310
LODOVICO.   Sir, you shall understand what hath befall'n,
Which, as I think, you know not. Here is a letter
Found in the pocket of the slain Roderigo,
And here another. The one of them imports
The death of Cassio to be undertook   315
By Roderigo.
OTHELLO.   Oh, villain!
CASSIO.   Most heathenish and most gross!
LODOVICO.   Now here's another discontented paper,
Found in his pocket too. And this, it seems,
Roderigo meant to have sent this damnèd villain   320
But that, belike, Iago in the interim
Came in and satisfied him.
OTHELLO.   Oh, the pernicious caitiff!
How came you, Cassio, by that handkerchief
That was my wife's?
CASSIO.   I found it in my chamber.
And he himself confessed but even now   325
That there he dropped it for a special purpose
Which wrought to his desire.
OTHELLO.   O fool! Fool! Fool!
CASSIO.   There is besides in Roderigo's letter
How he upbraids Iago, that he made him
Brave° me upon the watch, whereon it came   330

296. Fall'n . . . practice: destroyed by the plotting.   **330. Brave:** insult.

That I was cast.° And even but now he spake
After long seeming dead, Iago hurt him,
Iago set him on.
    LODOVICO.   You must forsake this room, and go with us.
Your power and your command is taken off,   335
And Cassio rules in Cyprus. For this slave,
If there be any cunning cruelty
That can torment him much and hold him long,°
It shall be his. You shall close prisoner rest
Till that the nature of your fault be known   340
To the Venetian state. Come, bring away.
    OTHELLO.   Soft you, a word or two before you go.
I have done the state some service, and they know 't.
No more of that. I pray you, in your letters,
When you shall these unlucky deeds relate,   345
Speak of me as I am, nothing extenuate,
Nor set down aught in malice. Then must you speak
Of one that loved not wisely but too well,
Of one not easily jealous, but, being wrought,
Perplexed in the extreme, of one whose hand,   350
Like the base Indian, threw a pearl away
Richer than all his tribe—of one whose subdued eyes,
Albeit unusèd to the melting mood,
Drop tears as fast as the Arabian trees
Their medicinal gum. Set you down this,   355
And say besides that in Aleppo once,
Where a malignant and a turbaned Turk
Beat a Venetian and traduced the state,
I took by the throat the circumcisèd dog
And smote him, thus. (*Stabs himself.*)   360
    LODOVICO.   Oh, bloody period!
    GRATIANO.   All that's spoke is marred.
    OTHELLO.   I kissed thee ere I killed thee. No way but this,
Killing myself, to die upon a kiss. (*Falls on the bed, and dies.*)
    CASSIO.   This did I fear, but thought he had no weapon.
For he was great of heart.   365
    LODOVICO (*to* IAGO).   O Spartan° dog,
More fell° than anguish, hunger, or the sea!
Look on the tragic loading of this bed,
This is thy work. The object poisons sight,
Let it be hid.° Gratiano, keep the house,   370

331. cast: dismissed.   **338. long:** i.e., in dying.   **366. Spartan:** i.e., hardhearted.
367. fell: cruel.   **370. Let . . . hid:** At these words the curtains are closed across
the inner stage (or chamber, if this scene was acted aloft), concealing all three
bodies.

And seize upon the fortunes of the Moor,
For they succeed on you. To you, Lord Governor,
Remains the censure of this hellish villain,
The time, the place, the torture.
Oh, enforce it!   375
Myself will straight aboard, and to the state
This heavy act with heavy heart relate.

(*Exeunt.*)

QUESTIONS

1. In what ways is Othello, in the first two acts, shown to be a person of extraordinary quality?

2. Is Othello a person jealous "by nature"? Does he show any disposition to jealousy in the first two acts? What does he say about himself in his final soliloquy? Would he make a good comic hero? (There has been much critical controversy over the psychological probability of Othello's being roused so quickly to such a high pitch of jealousy in Act III. Some have explained it by attributing a predisposition to jealousy in Othello; others have attributed it to the almost superhuman Machiavellian cleverness of Iago, which would have taken in any husband. In general, however, Shakespeare was less interested in psychological consistency and the subtle tracing of motivation—which are modern interests—than he was in theatrical effectiveness and the orchestration of emotions. Perhaps the question we should properly ask is not "How probable is Othello's jealousy?" but "How vital and effective has Shakespeare rendered it?")

3. Who is more naturally suspicious of human nature—Othello or Iago?

4. Is something of Othello's nobility manifested even in the scale of his jealousy? How does he respond to his conviction that Desdemona has been unfaithful to him? Would a lesser man have responded in the same way? Why or why not?

5. How does Othello's final speech reestablish his greatness?

6. What are Iago's motivations in his actions toward Othello, Cassio, and Roderigo? What is his philosophy? How does his technique of handling Roderigo differ from his technique in handling Othello and Cassio? Why?

7. In rousing Othello's suspicions against Desdemona (III, iii) Iago uses the same technique, in part, that he had used with Othello in inculpating Cassio (II, iii) and that he later uses with Lodovico in inculpating Othello (IV, ii). What is this technique? Why is it effective?

8. What opinions of Iago, before his exposure, are expressed by Othello, Desdemona, Cassio, and Lodovico? Is Othello the only one taken in by him? Does his own wife think him capable of villainy?

9. Though Othello is the protagonist, the majority of the soliloquies and asides are given to Iago. Why?

10. The difference between Othello and Desdemona that Iago plays on most is that of color, and, reading the play today, we may be tempted to see the play as being centrally about race relations. However, only one other character, besides Othello, makes much of this difference in color. Which one? Is this character sympathetically portrayed? What attitude toward Othello himself, and his marriage, is taken by the Duke, Cassio, Lodovico, Emilia, Desdemona herself? What differences between Othello and Desdemona, besides color, are used by Iago to undermine Othello's confidence in Desdemona's fidelity? What differences does Othello himself take into account?

11. What are Desdemona's principal character traits? In what ways are she and Emilia character foils? Is she entirely discreet in pleading Cassio's case to Othello? Why or why not? Why does she lie about the handkerchief (III, iv)?

12. Like Sophocles in *Oedipus Rex*, Shakespeare makes extensive use of dramatic irony in this play. Point out effective examples.

13. Unlike *Oedipus Rex* and *Blood Wedding*, *Othello* utilizes comedy. For what purposes is it used? What larger difference in effect between *Othello* and these other tragedies does this use of comedy contribute to?

14. As much responsible as any other quality for the original popularity and continued vitality of *Othello* is its poetry. What are some of the prominent characteristics of that poetry (language, imagery, rhythm)? What speeches are particularly memorable or effective? Though most of the play is written in blank verse, some passages are written in rhymed iambic pentameter couplets and others in prose. Can you suggest any reasons for Shakespeare's use of these other mediums?

15. How would the effect of the play have been different if Othello had died *before* discovering Desdemona's innocence?

Molière

THE MISANTHROPE

CHARACTERS

ALCESTE, *in love with Célimène*
PHILINTE, *Alceste's friend*
ORONTE, *in love with Célimène*
CÉLIMÈNE, *Alceste's beloved*
ELIANTE, *Célimène's cousin*
ARSINOÉ, *a friend of Célimène's*
ACASTE ⎱ *marquesses*
CLITANDRE ⎰
BASQUE, *Célimène's servant*
A GUARD *of the Marshalsea*
DUBOIS, *Alceste's valet*

The scene throughout is in Célimène's house at Paris.

ACT I

SCENE I

PHILINTE. Now, what's got into you?
ALCESTE (*seated*).   Kindly leave me alone.
PHILINTE. Come, come, what is it? This lugubrious tone . . .
ALCESTE. Leave me, I said; you spoil my solitude.
PHILINTE. Oh, listen to me, now, and don't be rude.
ALCESTE. I choose to be rude, Sir, and to be hard of hearing.   5
PHILINTE. These ugly moods of yours are not endearing;
Friends though we are, I really must insist . . .

ALCESTE (*abruptly rising*).   Friends? Friends, you say? Well, cross me
off your list.
I've been your friend till now, as you well know;
But after what I saw a moment ago   10
I tell you flatly that our ways must part.
I wish no place in a dishonest heart.
    PHILINTE.   Why, what have I done, Alceste? Is this quite just?
    ALCESTE.   My God, you ought to die of self-disgust.
I call your conduct inexcusable, Sir,   15
And every man of honor will concur.
I see you almost hug a man to death,
Exclaim for joy until you're out of breath,
And supplement these loving demonstrations
With endless offers, vows, and protestations;   20
Then when I ask you "Who was that?" I find
That you can barely bring his name to mind!
Once the man's back is turned, you cease to love him,
And speak with absolute indifference of him!
By God, I say it's base and scandalous   25
To falsify the heart's affections thus;
If I caught myself behaving in such a way,
I'd hang myself for shame, without delay.
    PHILINTE.   It hardly seems a hanging matter to me;
I hope that you will take it graciously   30
If I extend myself a slight reprieve,
And live a little longer, by your leave.
    ALCESTE.   How dare you joke about a crime so grave?
    PHILINTE.   What crime? How else are people to behave?
    ALCESTE.   I'd have them be sincere, and never part   35
With any word that isn't from the heart.
    PHILINTE.   When someone greets us with a show of pleasure,
It's but polite to give him equal measure,
Return his love the best that we know how,
And trade him offer for offer, vow for vow.   40
    ALCESTE.   No, no, this formula you'd have me follow,
However fashionable, is false and hollow,
And I despise the frenzied operations
Of all these barterers of protestations,
These lavishers of meaningless embraces,   45
These utterers of obliging commonplaces,
Who court and flatter everyone on earth
And praise the fool no less than the man of worth.
Should you rejoice that someone fondles you,
Offers his love and service, swears to be true,   50

And fills your ears with praises of your name,
When to the first damned fop he'll say the same?
No, no: no self-respecting heart would dream
Of prizing so promiscuous an esteem;
However high the praise, there's nothing worse 55
Than sharing honors with the universe.
Esteem is founded on comparison:
To honor all men is to honor none.
Since you embrace this indiscriminate vice,
Your friendship comes at far too cheap a price; 60
I spurn the easy tribute of a heart
Which will not set the worthy man apart:
I choose, Sir, to be chosen; and in fine,
The friend of mankind is no friend of mine.
    PHILINTE.   But in polite society, custom decrees 65
That we show certain outward courtesies . . .
    ALCESTE.   Ah, no! we should condemn with all our force
Such false and artificial intercourse.
Let men behave like men; let them display
Their inmost hearts in everything they say; 70
Let the heart speak, and let our sentiments
Not mask themselves in silly compliments.
    PHILINTE.   In certain cases it would be uncouth
And most absurd to speak the naked truth;
With all respect for your exalted notions, 75
It's often best to veil one's true emotions.
Wouldn't the social fabric come undone
If we were wholly frank with everyone?
Suppose you met with someone you couldn't bear;
Would you inform him of it then and there? 80
    ALCESTE.   Yes.
    PHILINTE.   Then you'd tell old Emilie it's pathetic
The way she daubs her features with cosmetic
And plays the gay coquette at sixty-four?
    ALCESTE.   I would.
    PHILINTE.   And you'd call Dorilas a bore,
And tell him every ear at court is lame 85
From hearing him brag about his noble name?
    ALCESTE.   Precisely.
    PHILINTE.   Ah, you're joking.
    ALCESTE.   *Au contraire:*
In this regard there's none I'd choose to spare.
All are corrupt; there's nothing to be seen
In court or town but aggravates my spleen. 90

I fall into deep gloom and melancholy
When I survey the scene of human folly,
Finding on every hand base flattery,
Injustice, fraud, self-interest, treachery . . .
Ah, it's too much; mankind has grown so base,   95
I mean to break with the whole human race.
   PHILINTE. This philosophic rage is a bit extreme;
You've no idea how comical you seem;
Indeed, we're like those brothers in the play
Called *School for Husbands*, one of whom was prey . . .[1]   100
   ALCESTE. Enough, now! None of your stupid similes.
   PHILINTE. Then let's have no more tirades, if you please.
The world won't change, whatever you say or do;
And since plain speaking means so much to you,
I'll tell you plainly that by being frank   105
You've earned the reputation of a crank,
And that you're thought ridiculous when you rage
And rant against the manners of the age.
   ALCESTE. So much the better; just what I wish to hear.
No news could be more grateful to my ear.   110
All men are so detestable in my eyes,
I should be sorry if they thought me wise.
   PHILINTE. Your hatred's very sweeping, is it not?
   ALCESTE. Quite right: I hate the whole degraded lot.
   PHILINTE. Must all poor human creatures be embraced,   115
Without distinction, by your vast distaste?
Even in these bad times, there are surely a few . . .
   ALCESTE. No, I include all men in one dim view:
Some men I hate for being rogues; the others
I hate because they treat the rogues like brothers,   120
And, lacking a virtuous scorn for what is vile,
Receive the villain with a complaisant smile.
Notice how tolerant people choose to be
Toward that bold rascal who's at law with me.
His social polish can't conceal his nature;   125
One sees at once that he's a treacherous creature;
No one could possibly be taken in
By those soft speeches and that sugary grin.

    [1] *School . . . prey: School for Husbands* is an earlier play by Molière. The
chief characters are two brothers, one of whom, puritanical and suspicious, mis-
trusts the fashions and customs of the world, shuts up his ward and fiancée to
keep her from infection by them, and is outwitted and betrayed by her. The
other, more amiable and easy going, allows his ward a free reign and is rewarded
with her love.

The whole world knows the shady means by which
The low-brow's grown so powerful and rich,   130
And risen to a rank so bright and high
That virtue can but blush, and merit sigh.
Whenever his name comes up in conversation,
None will defend his wretched reputation;
Call him knave, liar, scoundrel, and all the rest,   135
Each head will nod, and no one will protest.
And yet his smirk is seen in every house,
He's greeted everywhere with smiles and bows,
And when there's any honor that can be got
By pulling strings, he'll get it, like as not.   140
My God! It chills my heart to see the ways
Men come to terms with evil nowadays;
Sometimes, I swear, I'm moved to flee and find
Some desert land unfouled by humankind.
    PHILINTE.   Come, let's forget the follies of the times   145
And pardon mankind for its petty crimes;
Let's have an end of rantings and of railings,
And show some leniency toward human failings.
This world requires a pliant rectitude;
Too stern a virtue makes one stiff and rude;   150
Good sense views all extremes with detestation,
And bids us to be noble in moderation.
The rigid virtues of the ancient days
Are not for us; they jar with all our ways
And ask of us too lofty a perfection.   155
Wise men accept their times without objection,
And there's no greater folly, if you ask me,
Than trying to reform society.
Like you, I see each day a hundred and one
Unhandsome deeds that might be better done,   160
But still, for all the faults that meet my view,
I'm never known to storm and rave like you.
I take men as they are, or let them be,
And teach my soul to bear their frailty;
And whether in court or town, whatever the scene,   165
My phlegm's as philosophic as your spleen.
    ALCESTE.   This phlegm which you so eloquently commend,
Does nothing ever rile it up, my friend?
Suppose some man you trust should treacherously
Conspire to rob you of your property,   170
And do his best to wreck your reputation?
Wouldn't you feel a certain indignation?

PHILINTE.   Why, no. These faults of which you so complain
Are part of human nature, I maintain,
And it's no more a matter for disgust   175
That men are knavish, selfish and unjust,
Than that the vulture dines upon the dead,
And wolves are furious, and apes ill-bred.
PHILINTE.   Shall I see myself betrayed, robbed, torn to bits,
And not . . . Oh, let's be still and rest our wits.   180
Enough of reasoning, now. I've had my fill.
PHILINTE.   Indeed, you would do well, Sir, to be still.
Rage less at your opponent, and give some thought
To how you'll win this lawsuit that he's brought.
ALCESTE.   I assure you I'll do nothing of the sort.   185
PHILINTE.   Then who will plead your case before the court?
ALCESTE.   Reason and right and justice will plead for me.
PHILINTE.   Oh, Lord. What judges do you plan to see?
ALCESTE.   Why, none. The justice of my cause is clear.
PHILINTE.   Of course, man; but there's politics to fear . . .   190
ALCESTE.   No, I refuse to lift a hand. That's flat.
I'm either right, or wrong.
PHILINTE.   Don't count on that.
ALCESTE.   No, I'll do nothing.
PHILINTE.   Your enemy's influence
Is great, you know . . .
ALCESTE.   That makes no difference.
PHILINTE.   It will; you'll see.
ALCESTE.   Must honor bow to guile?   195
If so, I shall be proud to lose the trial.
PHILINTE.   Oh, really . . .
ALCESTE.   I'll discover by this case
Whether or not men are sufficiently base
And impudent and villainous and perverse
To do me wrong before the universe.   200
PHILINTE.   What a man!
ALCESTE.   Oh, I could wish, whatever the cost,
Just for the beauty of it, that my trial were lost.
PHILINTE.   If people heard you talking so, Alceste,
They'd split their sides. Your name would be a jest.
ALCESTE.   So much the worse for jesters.
PHILINTE.   May I enquire   205
Whether this rectitude you so admire,
And these hard virtues you're enamored of
Are qualities of the lady whom you love?
It much surprises me that you, who seem

To view mankind with furious disesteem,　　　　　　210
Have yet found something to enchant your eyes
Amidst a species which you so despise.
And what is more amazing, I'm afraid,
Is the most curious choice your heart has made.
The honest Eliante is fond of you,　　　　　　　215
Arsinoé, the prude, admires you too;
And yet your spirit's been perversely led
To choose the flighty Célimène instead,
Whose brittle malice and coquettish ways
So typify the manners of our days.　　　　　　　220
How is it that the traits you most abhor
Are bearable in this lady you adore?
Are you so blind with love that you can't find them?
Or do you contrive, in her case, not to mind them?
　　ALCESTE.　My love for that young widow's not the kind　　225
That can't perceive defects; no, I'm not blind.
I see her faults, despite my ardent love,
And all I see I fervently reprove.
And yet I'm weak; for all her falsity,
That woman knows the art of pleasing me,　　　　230
And though I never cease complaining of her,
I swear I cannot manage not to love her.
Her charm outweighs her faults; I can but aim
To cleanse her spirit in my love's pure flame.
　　PHILINTE.　That's no small task; I wish you all success.　　235
You think then that she loves you?
　　ALCESTE.　　　　　　　　Heavens, yes!
I wouldn't love her did she not love me.
　　PHILINTE.　Well, if her taste for you is plain to see,
Why do these rivals cause you such despair?
　　ALCESTE.　True love, Sir, is possessive, and cannot bear　　240
To share with all the world. I'm here today
To tell her she must send that mob away.
　　PHILINTE.　If I were you, and had your choice to make,
Eliante, her cousin, would be the one I'd take;
That honest heart, which cares for you alone,　　　245
Would harmonize far better with your own.
　　ALCESTE.　True, true: each day my reason tells me so;
But reason doesn't rule in love, you know.
　　PHILINTE.　I fear some bitter sorrow is in store;
This love . . .

SCENE II[2]

ORONTE (*to Alceste*).   The servants told me at the door   250
That Eliante and Célimène were out,
But when I heard, dear Sir, that you were about,
I came to say, without exaggeration,
That I hold you in the vastest admiration,
And that it's always been my dearest desire   255
To be the friend of one I so admire.
I hope to see my love of merit requited,
And you and I in friendship's bond united.
I'm sure you won't refuse—if I may be frank—
A friend of my devotedness—and rank. (*During this speech of*   260
ORONTE'S, ALCESTE *is abstracted, and seems unaware that he is being
spoken to. He only breaks off his reverie when* ORONTE *says*)
It was for you, if you please, that my words were intended.
    ALCESTE.   For me, Sir?
    ORONTE.   Yes, for you. You're not offended?
    ALCESTE.   By no means. But this much surprises me . . .
The honor comes most unexpectedly . . .
    ORONTE.   My high regard should not astonish you;   265
The whole world feels the same. It is your due.
    ALCESTE.   Sir . . .
    ORONTE.   Why, in all the State there isn't one
Can match your merits; they shine, Sir, like the sun.
    ALCESTE.   Sir . . .
    ORONTE.   You are higher in my estimation
Than all that's most illustrious in the nation.   270
    ALCESTE.   Sir . . .
    ORONTE.   If I lie, may heaven strike me dead!
To show you that I mean what I have said,
Permit me, Sir, to embrace you most sincerely,
And swear that I will prize our friendship dearly.
Give me your hand. And now, Sir, if you choose,   275
We'll make our vows.
    ALCESTE.   Sir . . .
    ORONTE.   What! You refuse?
    ALCESTE.   Sir, it's a very great honor you extend:

² Scene II: In English and in most modern plays, a scene is a continuous section of the action in one setting, and acts are not usually divided into scenes unless
there is a shift in setting or a shift in time. In older French drama, however, a
scene is any portion of the play involving one group of characters, and a new
scene begins, without interruption of the action, whenever any important character enters or exits.

But friendship is a sacred thing, my friend;
It would be profanation to bestow
The name of friend on one you hardly know.   280
All parts are better played when well-rehearsed;
Let's put off friendship, and get acquainted first.
We may discover it would be unwise
To try to make our natures harmonize.
    ORONTE.   By heaven! You're sagacious to the core;   285
This speech has made me admire you even more.
Let time, then, bring us closer day by day;
Meanwhile, I shall be yours in every way.
If, for example, there should be anything
You wish at court, I'll mention it to the King.   290
I have his ear, of course; it's quite well known
That I am much in favor with the throne.
In short, I am your servant. And now, dear friend,
Since you have such fine judgment, I intend
To please you, if I can, with a small sonnet   295
I wrote not long ago. Please comment on it,
And tell me whether I ought to publish it.
    ALCESTE.   You must excuse me, Sir; I'm hardly fit
To judge such matters.
    ORONTE.   Why not?
    ALCESTE.   I am, I fear,
Inclined to be unfashionably sincere.   300
    ORONTE.   Just what I ask; I'd take no satisfaction
In anything but your sincere reaction.
I beg you not to dream of being kind.
    ALCESTE.   Since you desire it, Sir, I'll speak my mind.
    ORONTE.   *Sonnet*. It's a sonnet . . . *Hope* . . . The poem's addressed 305
To a lady who wakened hopes within my breast.
Hope . . . this is not the pompous sort of thing,
Just modest little verses, with a tender ring.
    ALCESTE.   Well, we shall see.
    ORONTE.   *Hope* . . . I'm anxious to hear
Whether the style seems properly smooth and clear,   310
And whether the choice of words is good or bad.
    ALCESTE.   We'll see, we'll see.
    ORONTE.   Perhaps I ought to add
That it took me only a quarter-hour to write it.
    ALCESTE.   The time's irrelevant, Sir: kindly recite it.
    ORONTE (*reading*).   Hope comforts us awhile, t'is true,   315
               Lulling our cares with careless laughter,
               And yet such joy is full of rue,

My Phyllis, if nothing follows after.

PHILINTE. I'm charmed by this already; the style's delightful.

ALCESTE (*sotto voce, to* PHILINTE). How can you say that? Why, the thing is frightful.   320

ORONTE.   Your fair face smiled on me awhile,
                 But was it kindness so to enchant me?
                 'Twould have been fairer not to smile,
                 If hope was all you meant to grant me.

PHILINTE. What a clever thought! How handsomely you phrase it! 325

ALCESTE (*sotto voce, to* PHILINTE). You know the thing is trash. How dare you praise it?

ORONTE.   If it's to be my passion's fate
                 Thus everlastingly to wait,
                 Then death will come to set me free:
                 For death is fairer than the fair;   330
                 Phyllis, to hope is to despair
                 When one must hope eternally.

PHILINTE. The close is exquisite—full of feeling and grace.

ALCESTE (*sotto voce, aside*). Oh, blast the close; you'd better close your face

Before you send your lying soul to hell.   335

PHILINTE. I can't remember a poem I've liked so well.

ALCESTE (*sotto voce, aside*). Good Lord!

ORONTE (*to* PHILINTE).   I fear you're flattering me a bit.

PHILINTE. Oh, no!

ALCESTE (*sotto voce, aside*). What else d'you call it, you hypocrite?

ORONTE (*to* ALCESTE). But you, Sir, keep your promise now: don't shrink

From telling me sincerely what you think.   340

ALCESTE. Sir, these are delicate matters; we all desire

To be told that we've the true poetic fire.
But once, to one whose name I shall not mention,
I said, regarding some verse of his invention,
That gentlemen should rigorously control   345
That itch to write which often afflicts the soul;
That one should curb the heady inclination
To publicize one's little avocation;
And that in showing off one's works of art
One often plays a very clownish part.   350

ORONTE. Are you suggesting in a devious way

That I ought not . . .

ALCESTE.   Oh, that I do not say.

Further, I told him that no fault is worse
Than that of writing frigid, lifeless verse,
And that the merest whisper of such a shame   355

Suffices to destroy a man's good name.
    ORONTE.   D'you mean to say my sonnet's dull and trite?
    ALCESTE.   I don't say that. But I went on to cite
Numerous cases of once-respected men
Who came to grief by taking up the pen.   360
    ORONTE.   And am I like them? Do I write so poorly?
    ALCESTE.   I don't say that. But I told this person, "Surely
You're under no necessity to compose;
Why you should wish to publish, heaven knows.
There's no excuse for printing tedious rot   365
Unless one writes for bread, as you do not.
Resist temptation, then, I beg of you;
Conceal your pastimes from the public view;
And don't give up, on any provocation,
Your present high and courtly reputation,   370
To purchase at a greedy printer's shop
The name of silly author and scribbling fop."
These were the points I tried to make him see.
    ORONTE.   I sense that they are also aimed at me;
But now—about my sonnet—I'd like to be told . . .   375
    ALCESTE.   Frankly, that sonnet should be pigeonholed.
You've chosen the worst models to imitate.
The style's unnatural. Let me illustrate:

> For example, Your fair face smiled on me awhile,
> Followed by, 'Twould have been fairer not to smile!   380
> Or this: such joy is full of rue;
> Or this: For death is fairer than the fair;
> Or, Phyllis, to hope is to despair
>   When one must hope eternally!

This artificial style, that's all the fashion,   385
Has neither taste, nor honesty, nor passion;
It's nothing but a sort of wordy play,
And nature never spoke in such a way.
What, in this shallow age, is not debased?
Our fathers, though less refined, had better taste;   390
I'd barter all that men admire today
For one old love-song I shall try to say:

> If the King had given me for my own
> Paris, his citadel,
> And I for that must leave alone   395
> Her whom I love so well,
> I'd say then to the Crown,

Take back your glittering town;
My darling is more fair, I swear,
My darling is more fair.   400

The rhyme's not rich, the style is rough and old,
But don't you see that it's the purest gold
Beside the tinsel nonsense now preferred,
And that there's passion in its every word?

If the King had given me for my own   405
Paris, his citadel,
And I for that must leave alone
Her whom I love so well,
I'd say then to the Crown,
Take back your glittering town;   410
My darling is more fair, I swear,
My darling is more fair.

There speaks a loving heart. (*To* PHILINTE) You're laughing, eh?
Laugh on, my precious wit. Whatever you say,
I hold that song's worth all the bibelots   415
That people hail today with ah's and oh's.
  ORONTE.   And I maintain my sonnet's very good.
  ALCESTE.   It's not at all surprising that you should.
You have your reasons; permit me to have mine
For thinking that you cannot write a line.   420
  ORONTE.   Others have praised my sonnet to the skies.
  ALCESTE.   I lack their art of telling pleasant lies.
  ORONTE.   You seem to think you've got no end of wit.
  ALCESTE.   To praise your verse, I'd need still more of it.
  ORONTE.   I'm not in need of your approval, Sir.   425
  ALCESTE.   That's good; you couldn't have it if you were.
  ORONTE.   Come now, I'll lend you the subject of my sonnet;
I'd like to see you try to improve upon it.
  ALCESTE.   I might, by chance, write something just as shoddy;
But then I wouldn't show it to everybody.   430
  ORONTE.   You're most opinionated and conceited.
  ALCESTE.   Go find your flatterers, and be better treated.
  ORONTE.   Look here, my little fellow, pray watch your tone.
  ALCESTE.   My great big fellow, you'd better watch your own.
  PHILINTE (*stepping between them*).   Oh, please, please, gentlemen!
This will never do.   435
  ORONTE.   The fault is mine, and I leave the field to you.
I am your servant, Sir, in every way.
  ALCESTE.   And I, Sir, am your most abject valet.

SCENE III

PHILINTE. Well, as you see, sincerity in excess
Can get you into a very pretty mess;   440
Oronte was hungry for appreciation . . .
    ALCESTE. Don't speak to me.
    PHILINTE.   What?
    ALCESTE.   No more conversation.
    PHILINTE. Really, now . . .
    ALCESTE.   Leave me alone.
    PHILINTE.   If I . . .
    ALCESTE.   Out of my sight!
    PHILINTE. But what . . .
    ALCESTE.   I won't listen.
    PHILINTE.   But . . .
    ALCESTE.   Silence!
    PHILINTE.   Now, is it polite . . .
    ALCESTE. By heaven, I've had enough. Don't follow me.   445
    PHILINTE. Ah, you're just joking. I'll keep you company.

ACT II

SCENE I

ALCESTE. Shall I speak plainly, Madam? I confess
Your conduct gives me infinite distress,
And my resentment's grown too hot to smother.
Soon, I foresee, we'll break with one another.
If I said otherwise, I should deceive you;   5
Sooner or later, I shall be forced to leave you,
And if I swore that we shall never part,
I should misread the omens of my heart.
    CÉLIMÈNE. You kindly saw me home, it would appear,
So as to pour invectives in my ear.   10
    ALCESTE. I've no desire to quarrel. But I deplore
Your inability to shut the door
On all these suitors who beset you so.
There's what annoys me, if you care to know.
    CÉLIMÈNE. Is it my fault that all these men pursue me?   15
Am I to blame if they're attracted to me?
And when they gently beg an audience,
Ought I to take a stick and drive them hence?
    ALCESTE. Madam, there's no necessity for a stick;
A less responsive heart would do the trick.   20

Of your attractiveness I don't complain;
But those your charms attract, you then detain
By a most melting and receptive manner,
And so enlist their hearts beneath your banner.
It's the agreeable hopes which you excite 25
That keep these lovers round you day and night;
Were they less liberally smiled upon,
That sighing troop would very soon be gone.
But tell me, Madam, why it is that lately
This man Clitandre interests you so greatly? 30
Because of what high merits do you deem
Him worthy of the honor of your esteem?
Is it that your admiring glances linger
On the splendidly long nail of his little finger?
Or do you share the general deep respect 35
For the blond wig he chooses to affect?
Are you in love with his embroidered hose?
Do you adore his ribbons and his bows?
Or is it that this paragon bewitches
Your tasteful eye with his vast German breeches? 40
Perhaps his giggle, or his falsetto voice,
Makes him the latest gallant of your choice?
    CÉLIMÈNE.   You're much mistaken to resent him so.
Why I put up with him you surely know:
My lawsuit's very shortly to be tried, 45
And I must have his influence on my side.
    ALCESTE.   Then lose your lawsuit, Madam, or let it drop;
Don't torture me by humoring such a fop.
    CÉLIMÈNE.   You're jealous of the whole world, Sir.
    ALCESTE.   That's true,
Since the whole world is well-received by you. 50
    CÉLIMÈNE.   That my good nature is so unconfined
Should serve to pacify your jealous mind;
Were I to smile on one, and scorn the rest,
Then you might have some cause to be distressed.
    ALCESTE.   Well, if I mustn't be jealous, tell me, then, 55
Just how I'm better treated than other men.
    CÉLIMÈNE.   You know you have my love. Will that not do?
    ALCESTE.   What proof have I that what you say is true?
    CÉLIMÈNE.   I would expect, Sir, that my having said it
Might give the statement a sufficient credit. 60
    ALCESTE.   But how can I be sure that you don't tell
The selfsame thing to other men as well?
    CÉLIMÈNE.   What a gallant speech! How flattering to me!

What a sweet creature you make me out to be!
Well then, to save you from the pangs of doubt,   65
All that I've said I hereby cancel out;
Now, none but yourself shall make a monkey of you:
Are you content?
    ALCESTE.   Why, why am I doomed to love you?
I swear that I shall bless the blissful hour
When this poor heart's no longer in your power!   70
I make no secret of it: I've done my best
To exorcise this passion from my breast;
But thus far all in vain; it will not go;
It's for my sins that I must love you so.
    CÉLIMÈNE.   Your love for me is matchless, Sir; that's clear.   75
    ALCESTE.   Indeed, in all the world it has no peer;
Words can't describe the nature of my passion,
And no man ever loved in such a fashion.
    CÉLIMÈNE.   Yes, it's a brand-new fashion, I agree:
You show your love by castigating me,   80
And all your speeches are enraged and rude.
I've never been so furiously wooed.
    ALCESTE.   Yet you could calm that fury, if you chose.
Come, shall we bring our quarrels to a close?
Let's speak with open hearts, then, and begin . . .   85

SCENE II

    CÉLIMÈNE.   What is it?
    BASQUE.   Acaste is here.
    CÉLIMÈNE.   Well, send him in.

SCENE III

    ALCESTE.   What! Shall we never be alone at all?
You're always ready to receive a call,
And you can't bear, for ten ticks of the clock,
Not to keep open house for all who knock.   90
    CÉLIMÈNE.   I couldn't refuse him: he'd be most put out.
    ALCESTE.   Surely that's not worth worrying about.
    CÉLIMÈNE.   Acaste would never forgive me if he guessed
That I consider him a dreadful pest.
    ALCESTE.   If he's a pest, why bother with him then?   95
    CÉLIMÈNE.   Heavens! One can't antagonize such men;
Why, they're the chartered gossips of the court,

And have a say in things of every sort.
One must receive them, and be full of charm;
They're no great help, but they can do you harm, 100
And though your influence be ever so great,
They're hardly the best people to alienate.
    ALCESTE.   I see, dear lady, that you could make a case
For putting up with the whole human race;
These friendships that you calculate so nicely . . . 105

SCENE IV

BASQUE.   Madam, Clitandre is here as well.
ALCESTE.   Precisely.
CÉLIMÈNE.   Where are you going?
ALCESTE.   Elsewhere.
CÉLIMÈNE.   Stay.
ALCESTE.   No, no.
CÉLIMÈNE.   Stay, Sir.
ALCESTE.   I can't.
CÉLIMÈNE.   I wish it.
ALCESTE.   No, I must go.
I beg you, Madam, not to press the matter;
You know I have no taste for idle chatter. 110
CÉLIMÈNE.   Stay: I command you.
ALCESTE.   No, I cannot stay.
CÉLIMÈNE.   Very well; you have my leave to go away.

SCENE V

ELIANTE (to CÉLIMÈNE).   The Marquesses have kindly come to call.
Were they announced?
    CÉLIMÈNE.   Yes. Basque, bring chairs for all. (BASQUE
provides the chairs, and exits. To ALCESTE)
You haven't gone?
    ALCESTE.   No; and I shan't depart 115
Till you decide who's foremost in your heart.
    CÉLIMÈNE.   Oh, hush.
    ALCESTE.   It's time to choose; take them, or me.
    CÉLIMÈNE.   You're mad.
    ALCESTE.   I'm not, as you shall shortly see.
    CÉLIMÈNE.   Oh?
    ALCESTE.   You'll decide.
    CÉLIMÈNE.   You're joking now, dear friend.

ALCESTE.   No, no; you'll choose; my patience is at an end.   120
CLITANDRE.   Madam, I come from court, where poor Cléonte
Behaved like a perfect fool, as is his wont.
Has he no friend to counsel him, I wonder,
And teach him less unerringly to blunder?
CÉLIMÈNE.   It's true, the man's a most accomplished dunce;   125
His gauche behavior charms the eye at once;
And every time one sees him, on my word,
His manner's grown a trifle more absurd.
ACASTE.   Speaking of dunces, I've just now conversed
With old Damon, who's one of the very worst;   130
I stood a lifetime in the broiling sun
Before his dreary monologue was done.
CÉLIMÈNE.   Oh, he's a wondrous talker, and has the power
To tell you nothing hour after hour:
If, by mistake, he ever came to the point,   135
The shock would put his jawbone out of joint.
ELIANTE (to PHILINTE).   The conversation takes its usual turn,
And all our dear friends' ears will shortly burn.
CLITANDRE.   Timante's a character, Madam.
CÉLIMÈNE.   Isn't he, though?
A man of mystery from top to toe,   140
Who moves about in a romantic mist
On secret missions which do not exist.
His talk is full of eyebrows and grimaces;
How tired one gets of his momentous faces;
He's always whispering something confidential   145
Which turns out to be quite inconsequential;
Nothing's too slight for him to mystify;
He even whispers when he says "good-by."
ACASTE.   Tell us about Géralde.
CÉLIMÈNE.   That tiresome ass.
He mixes only with the titled class,   150
And fawns on dukes and princes, and is bored
With anyone who's not at least a lord.
The man's obsessed with rank, and his discourses
Are all of hounds and carriages and horses;
He uses Christian names with all the great,   155
And the word Milord, with him, is out of date.
CLITANDRE.   He's very taken with Bélise, I hear.
CÉLIMÈNE.   She is the dreariest company, poor dear.
Whenever she comes to call, I grope about
To find some topic which will draw her out,   160
But, owing to her dry and faint replies,

The conversation wilts, and droops, and dies.
In vain one hopes to animate her face
By mentioning the ultimate commonplace;
But sun or shower, even hail or frost 165
Are matters she can instantly exhaust.
Meanwhile her visit, painful though it is,
Drags on and on through mute eternities,
And though you ask the time, and yawn, and yawn,
She sits there like a stone and won't be gone. 170
    ACASTE.   Now for Adraste.
    CÉLIMÈNE.   Oh, that conceited elf
Has a gigantic passion for himself;
He rails against the court, and cannot bear it
That none will recognize his hidden merit;
All honors given to others give offense 175
To his imaginary excellence.
    CLITANDRE.   What about young Cléon? His house, they say,
Is full of the best society, night and day.
    CÉLIMÈNE.   His cook has made him popular, not he:
It's Cléon's table that people come to see. 180
    ELIANTE.   He gives a splendid dinner, you must admit.
    CÉLIMÈNE.   But must he serve himself along with it?
For my taste, he's a most insipid dish
Whose presence sours the wine and spoils the fish.
    PHILINTE.   Damis, his uncle, is admired no end. 185
What's your opinion, Madam?
    CÉLIMÈNE.   Why, he's my friend.
    PHILINTE.   He seems a decent fellow, and rather clever.
    CÉLIMÈNE.   He works too hard at cleverness, however.
I hate to see him sweat and struggle so
To fill his conversation with bons mots. 190
Since he's decided to become a wit
His taste's so pure that nothing pleases it;
He scolds at all the latest books and plays,
Thinking that wit must never stoop to praise,
That finding fault's a sign of intellect, 195
That all appreciation is abject,
And that by damning everything in sight
One shows oneself in a distinguished light.
He's scornful even of our conversations:
Their trivial nature sorely tries his patience; 200
He folds his arms, and stands above the battle,
And listens sadly to our childish prattle.
    ACASTE.   Wonderful, Madam! You've hit him off precisely.

CLITANDRE. No one can sketch a character so nicely.

ALCESTE. How bravely, Sirs, you cut and thrust at all   205
These absent fools, till one by one they fall:
But let one come in sight, and you'll at once
Embrace the man you lately called a dunce,
Telling him in a tone sincere and fervent
How proud you are to be his humble servant.   210

CLITANDRE. Why pick on us? Madame's been speaking, Sir,
And you should quarrel, if you must, with her.

ALCESTE. No, no, by God, the fault is yours, because
You lead her on with laughter and applause,
And make her think that she's the more delightful   215
The more her talk is scandalous and spiteful.
Oh, she would stoop to malice far, far less
If no such claque approved her cleverness.
It's flatterers like you whose foolish praise
Nourishes all the vices of these days.   220

PHILINTE. But why protest when someone ridicules
Those you'd condemn, yourself, as knaves or fools?

CÉLIMÈNE. Why, Sir? Because he loves to make a fuss.
You don't expect him to agree with us,
When there's an opportunity to express   225
His heaven-sent spirit of contrariness?
What other people think, he can't abide;
Whatever they say, he's on the other side;
He lives in deadly terror of agreeing;
'Twould make him seem an ordinary being.   230
Indeed, he's so in love with contradiction,
He'll turn against his most profound conviction
And with a furious eloquence deplore it,
If only someone else is speaking for it.

ALCESTE. Go on, dear lady, mock me as you please;   235
You have your audience in ecstasies.

PHILINTE. But what she says is true: you have a way
Of bridling at whatever people say;
Whether they praise or blame, your angry spirit
Is equally unsatisfied to hear it.   240

ALCESTE. Men, Sir, are always wrong, and that's the reason
That righteous anger's never out of season;
All that I hear in all their conversation
Is flattering praise or reckless condemnation.

CÉLIMÈNE. But . . .

ALCESTE.   No, no, Madam, I am forced to state   245
That you have pleasures which I deprecate,

And that these others, here, are much to blame
For nourishing the faults which are your shame.
    CLITANDRE.   I shan't defend myself, Sir; but I vow
I'd thought this lady faultless until now.   250
    ACASTE.   I see her charms and graces, which are many;
But as for faults, I've never noticed any.
    ALCESTE.   I see them, Sir; and rather than ignore them,
I strenuously criticize her for them.
The more one loves, the more one should object   255
To every blemish, every least defect.
Were I this lady, I would soon get rid
Of lovers who approved of all I did,
And by their slack indulgence and applause
Endorsed my follies and excused my flaws.   260
    CÉLIMÈNE.   If all hearts beat according to your measure,
The dawn of love would be the end of pleasure;
And love would find its perfect consummation
In ecstasies of rage and reprobation.
    ELIANTE.   Love, as a rule, affects men otherwise,   265
And lovers rarely love to criticize.
They see their lady as a charming blur,
And find all things commendable in her.
If she has any blemish, fault, or shame,
They will redeem it by a pleasing name.   270
The pale-faced lady's lily-white, perforce;
The swarthy one's a sweet brunette, of course;
The spindly lady has a slender grace;
The fat one has a most majestic pace;
The plain one, with her dress in disarray,   275
They classify as *beauté négligée;*
The hulking one's a goddess in their eyes,
The dwarf, a concentrate of Paradise;
The haughty lady has a noble mind;
The mean one's witty, and the dull one's kind;   280
The chatterbox has liveliness and verve,
The mute one has a virtuous reserve.
So lovers manage, in their passion's cause,
To love their ladies even for their flaws.
    ALCESTE.   But I still say . . .
    CÉLIMÈNE.   I think it would be nice   285
To stroll around the gallery once or twice.
What! You're not going, Sirs?
    CLITANDRE and ACASTE.   No, Madam, no.
    ALCESTE.   You seem to be in terror lest they go.

Do what you will, Sirs; leave, or linger on,
But I shan't go till after you are gone.   290
    ACASTE.   I'm free to linger, unless I should perceive
Madame is tired, and wishes me to leave.
    CLITANDRE.   And as for me, I needn't go today
Until the hour of the King's *coucher*.
    CÉLIMÈNE (*to* ALCESTE).   You're joking, surely?
    ALCESTE.   Not in the least;
we'll see   295
Whether you'd rather part with them, or me.

SCENE VI

    BASQUE (*to* ALCESTE).   Sir, there's a fellow here who bids me state
That he must see you, and that it can't wait.
    ALCESTE.   Tell him that I have no such pressing affairs.
    BASQUE.   It's a long tailcoat that this fellow wears,   300
With gold all over.
    CÉLIMÈNE (*to* ALCESTE).   You'd best go down and see.
Or—have him enter.

SCENE VII

    ALCESTE (*confronting the guard*).   Well, what do you want with me?
Come in, Sir.
    GUARD.   I've a word, Sir, for your ear.
    ALCESTE.   Speak it aloud, Sir; I shall strive to hear.
    GUARD.   The Marshals have instructed me to say   305
You must report to them without delay.
    ALCESTE.   Who? Me, Sir?
    GUARD.   Yes, Sir; you.
    ALCESTE.   But what do they want?
    PHILINTE (*to* ALCESTE).   To scotch your silly quarrel with Oronte.
    CÉLIMÈNE (*to* PHILINTE).   What quarrel?
    PHILINTE.   Oronte and he have fallen
out
Over some verse he spoke his mind about;   310
The Marshals wish to arbitrate the matter.
    ALCESTE.   Never shall I equivocate or flatter!
    PHILINTE.   You'd best obey their summons; come, let's go.
    ALCESTE.   How can they mend our quarrel, I'd like to know?
Am I to make a cowardly retraction,   315
And praise those jingles to his satisfaction?

I'll not recant; I've judged that sonnet rightly.
It's bad.
  PHILINTE. But you might say so more politely. . . .
  ALCESTE. I'll not back down; his verses make me sick.
  PHILINTE. If only you could be more politic!   320
But come, let's go.
  ALCESTE.   I'll go, but I won't unsay
A single word.
  PHILINTE. Well, let's be on our way.
  ALCESTE. Till I am ordered by my lord the King
To praise that poem, I shall say the thing
Is scandalous, by God, and that the poet   325
Ought to be hanged for having the nerve to show it. (*To* CLITANDRE *and*
ACASTE, *who are laughing*)
By heaven, Sirs, I really didn't know
That I was being humorous.
  CÉLIMÈNE.   Go, Sir, go;
Settle your business.
  ALCESTE.   I shall, and when I'm through,
I shall return to settle things with you.   330

ACT III

SCENE I

  CLITANDRE. Dear Marquess, how contented you appear;
All things delight you, nothing mars your cheer.
Can you, in perfect honesty, declare
That you've a right to be so debonair?
  ACASTE. By Jove, when I survey myself, I find   5
No cause whatever for distress of mind.
I'm young and rich; I can in modesty
Lay claim to an exalted pedigree;
And owing to my name and my condition
I shall not want for honors and position.   10
Then as to courage, that most precious trait,
I seem to have it, as was proved of late
Upon the field of honor, where my bearing,
They say, was very cool and rather daring.
I've wit, of course; and taste in such perfection   15
That I can judge without the least reflection,
And at the theater, which is my delight,
Can make or break a play on opening night,

And lead the crowd in hisses or bravos,
And generally be known as one who knows.   20
I'm clever, handsome, gracefully polite;
My waist is small, my teeth are strong and white;
As for my dress, the world's astonished eyes
Assure me that I bear away the prize.
I find myself in favor everywhere,   25
Honored by men, and worshiped by the fair;
And since these things are so, it seems to me
I'm justified in my complacency.
    CLITANDRE. Well, if so many ladies hold you dear,
Why do you press a hopeless courtship here?   30
    ACASTE. Hopeless, you say? I'm not the sort of fool
That likes his ladies difficult and cool.
Men who are awkward, shy, and peasantish
May pine for heartless beauties, if they wish,
Grovel before them, bear their cruelties,   35
Woo them with tears and sighs and bended knees,
And hope by dogged faithfulness to gain
What their poor merits never could obtain.
For men like me, however, it makes no sense
To love on trust, and foot the whole expense.   40
Whatever any lady's merits be,
I think, thank God, that I'm as choice as she;
That if my heart is kind enough to burn
For her, she owes me something in return;
And that in any proper love affair   45
The partners must invest an equal share.
    CLITANDRE. You think, then, that our hostess favors you?
    ACASTE. I've reason to believe that that is true.
    CLITANDRE. How did you come to such a mad conclusion?
You're blind, dear fellow. This is sheer delusion.   50
    ACASTE. All right, then: I'm deluded and I'm blind.
    CLITANDRE. Whatever put the notion in your mind?
    ACASTE. Delusion.
    CLITANDRE.   What persuades you that you're right?
    ACASTE. I'm blind.
    CLITANDRE.   But have you any proofs to cite?
    ACASTE. I tell you I'm deluded.
    CLITANDRE.   Have you, then,   55
Received some secret pledge from Célimène?
    ACASTE. Oh, no: she scorns me.
    CLITANDRE.   Tell me the truth, I beg.

ACASTE. She just can't bear me.

CLITANDRE.   Ah, don't pull my leg.
Tell me what hope she's given you, I pray.

ACASTE. I'm hopeless, and it's you who win the day.   60
She hates me thoroughly, and I'm so vexed
I mean to hang myself on Tuesday next.

CLITANDRE. Dear Marquess, let us have an armistice
And make a treaty. What do you say to this?
If ever one of us can plainly prove   65
That Célimène encourages his love,
The other must abandon hope, and yield,
And leave him in possession of the field.

ACASTE. Now, there's a bargain that appeals to me;
With all my heart, dear Marquess, I agree.   70
But hush.

SCENE II

CÉLIMÈNE. Still here?

CLITANDRE.   'Twas love that stayed our feet.

CÉLIMÈNE. I think I heard a carriage in the street.
Whose is it? D'you know?

SCENE III

BASQUE.   Arsinoé is here,
Madame.

CÉLIMÈNE. Arsinoé, you say? Oh, dear.

BASQUE. Eliante is entertaining her below.   75

CÉLIMÈNE. What brings the creature here, I'd like to know?

ACASTE. They say she's dreadfully prudish, but in fact
I think her piety . . .

CÉLIMÈNE.   It's all an act.
At heart she's worldly, and her poor success
In snaring men explains her prudishness.   80
It breaks her heart to see the beaux and gallants
Engrossed by other women's charms and talents,
And so she's always in a jealous rage
Against the faulty standards of the age.
She lets the world believe that she's a prude   85
To justify her loveless solitude,
And strives to put a brand of moral shame
On all the graces that she cannot claim.

But still she'd love a lover; and Alceste
Appears to be the one she'd love the best.   90
His visits here are poison to her pride;
She seems to think I've lured him from her side;
And everywhere, at court or in the town,
The spiteful, envious woman runs me down.
In short, she's just as stupid as can be,   95
Vicious and arrogant in the last degree,
And . . .

SCENE IV

CÉLIMÈNE.   Ah! What happy chance has brought you here?
I've thought about you ever so much, my dear.
  ARSINOÉ.   I've come to tell you something you should know.
  CÉLIMÈNE.   How good of you to think of doing so!   100

(CLITANDRE *and* ACASTE *go out, laughing.*)

SCENE V

ARSINOÉ.   It's just as well those gentlemen didn't tarry.
  CÉLIMÈNE.   Shall we sit down?
  ARSINOÉ.   That won't be necessary.
Madam, the flame of friendship ought to burn
Brightest in matters of the most concern,
And as there's nothing which concerns us more   105
Than honor, I have hastened to your door
To bring you, as your friend, some information
About the status of your reputation.
I visited, last night, some virtuous folk,
And, quite by chance, it was of you they spoke;   110
There was, I fear, no tendency to praise
Your light behavior and your dashing ways.
The quantity of gentlemen you see
And your by now notorious coquetry
Were both so vehemently criticized   115
By everyone, that I was much surprised.
Of course, I needn't tell you where I stood;
I came to your defense as best I could,
Assured them you were harmless, and declared
Your soul was absolutely unimpaired.   120
But there are some things, you must realize,

One can't excuse, however hard one tries,
And I was forced at last into conceding
That your behavior, Madam, is misleading,
That it makes a bad impression, giving rise   125
To ugly gossip and obscene surmise,
And that if you were more *overtly* good,
You wouldn't be so much misunderstood.
Not that I think you've been unchaste—no! no!
The saints preserve me from a thought so low!   130
But mere good conscience never did suffice:
One must avoid the outward show of vice.
Madam, you're too intelligent, I'm sure,
To think my motives anything but pure
In offering you this counsel—which I do   135
Out of a zealous interest in you.
    CÉLIMÈNE. Madam, I haven't taken you amiss;
I'm very much obliged to you for this;
And I'll at once discharge the obligation
By telling you about *your* reputation.   140
You've been so friendly as to let me know
What certain people say of me, and so
I mean to follow your benign example
By offering you a somewhat similar sample.
The other day, I went to an affair   145
And found some most distinguished people there
Discussing piety, both false and true.
The conversation soon came round to you.
Alas! Your prudery and bustling zeal
Appeared to have a very slight appeal.   150
Your affectation of a grave demeanor,
Your endless talk of virtue and of honor,
The aptitude of your suspicious mind
For finding sin where there is none to find,
Your towering self-esteem, that pitying face   155
With which you contemplate the human race,
Your sermonizings and your sharp aspersions
On people's pure and innocent diversions—
All these were mentioned, Madam, and, in fact,
Were roundly and concertedly attacked.   160
"What good," they said, "are all these outward shows,
When everything belies her pious pose?
She prays incessantly; but then, they say,
She beats her maids and cheats them of their pay;
She shows her zeal in every holy place,   165

But still she's vain enough to paint her face;
She holds that naked statues are immoral,
But with a naked *man* she'd have no quarrel."
Of course, I said to everybody there
That they were being viciously unfair; 170
But still they were disposed to criticize you,
And all agreed that someone should advise you
To leave the morals of the world alone,
And worry rather more about your own.
They felt that one's self-knowledge should be great 175
Before one thinks of setting others straight;
That one should learn the art of living well
Before one threatens other men with hell,
And that the Church is best equipped, no doubt,
To guide our souls and root our vices out. 180
Madam, you're too intelligent, I'm sure,
To think my motives anything but pure
In offering you this counsel—which I do
Out of a zealous interest in you.
        ARSINOÉ.   I dared not hope for gratitude, but I 185
Did not expect so acid a reply;
I judge, since you've been so extremely tart,
That my good counsel pierced you to the heart.
        CÉLIMÈNE.   Far from it, Madam. Indeed, it seems to me
We ought to trade advice more frequently. 190
One's vision of oneself is so defective
That it would be an excellent corrective.
If you are willing, Madam, let's arrange
Shortly to have another frank exchange
In which we'll tell each other, *entre nous,* 195
What you've heard tell of me, and I of you.
        ARSINOÉ.   Oh, people never censure you, my dear;
It's me they criticize. Or so I hear.
        CÉLIMÈNE.   Madam, I think we either blame or praise
According to our taste and length of days. 200
There is a time of life for coquetry,
And there's a season, too, for prudery.
When all one's charms are gone, it is, I'm sure,
Good strategy to be devout and pure:
It makes one seem a little less forsaken. 205
Some day, perhaps, I'll take the road you've taken:
Time brings all things. But I have time aplenty,
And see no cause to be a prude at twenty.
        ARSINOÉ.   You give your age in such a gloating tone

That one would think I was an ancient crone;   210
We're not so far apart, in sober truth,
That you can mock me with a boast of youth!
Madam, you baffle me. I wish I knew
What moves you to provoke me as you do.
    CÉLIMÈNE. For my part, Madam, I should like to know   215
Why you abuse me everywhere you go.
Is it my fault, dear lady, that your hand
Is not, alas, in very great demand?
If men admire me, if they pay me court
And daily make me offers of the sort   220
You'd dearly love to have them make to you,
How can I help it? What would you have me do?
If what you want is lovers, please feel free
To take as many as you can from me.
    ARSINOÉ. Oh, come. D'you think the world is losing sleep   225
Over that flock of lovers which you keep,
Or that we find it difficult to guess
What price you pay for their devotedness?
Surely you don't expect us to suppose
Mere merit could attract so many beaux?   230
It's not your virtue that they're dazzled by;
Nor is it virtuous love for which they sigh.
You're fooling no one, Madam; the world's not blind;
There's many a lady heaven has designed
To call men's noblest, tenderest feelings out,   235
Who has no lovers dogging her about;
From which it's plain that lovers nowadays
Must be acquired in bold and shameless ways,
And only pay one court for such reward
As modesty and virtue can't afford.   240
Then don't be quite so puffed up, if you please,
About your tawdry little victories;
Try, if you can, to be a shade less vain,
And treat the world with somewhat less disdain.
If one were envious of your amours,   245
One soon could have a following like yours;
Lovers are no great trouble to collect
If one prefers them to one's self-respect.
    CÉLIMÈNE. Collect them then, my dear; I'd love to see
You demonstrate that charming theory;   250
Who knows, you might . . .
    ARSINOÉ.   Now, Madam, that will do;
It's time to end this trying interview.

My coach is late in coming to your door,
Or I'd have taken leave of you before.
    CÉLIMÈNE. Oh, please don't feel that you must rush away;   255
I'd be delighted, Madam, if you'd stay.
However, lest my conversation bore you,
Let me provide some better company for you;
This gentleman, who comes most apropos,
Will please you more than I could do, I know.   260

SCENE VI

    CÉLIMÈNE. Alceste, I have a little note to write
Which simply must go out before tonight;
Please entertain *Madame;* I'm sure that she
Will overlook my incivility.

SCENE VII

    ARSINOÉ. Well, Sir, our hostess graciously contrives   265
For us to chat until my coach arrives;
And I shall be forever in her debt
For granting me this little tête-à-tête.
We women very rightly give our hearts
To men of noble character and parts,   270
And your especial merits, dear Alceste,
Have roused the deepest sympathy in my breast.
Oh, how I wish they had sufficient sense
At court, to recognize your excellence!
They wrong you greatly, Sir. How it must hurt you   275
Never to be rewarded for your virtue!
    ALCESTE. Why, Madam, what cause have I to feel aggrieved?
What great and brilliant thing have I achieved?
What service have I rendered to the King
That I should look to him for anything?   280
    ARSINOÉ. Not everyone who's honored by the State
Has done great services. A man must wait
Till time and fortune offer him the chance.
Your merit, Sir, is obvious at a glance,
And . . .
    ALCESTE. Ah, forget my merit; I'm not neglected.   285
The court, I think, can hardly be expected
To mine men's souls for merit, and unearth
Our hidden virtues and our secret worth.

ARSINOÉ. *Some* virtues, though, are far too bright to hide;
Yours are acknowledged, Sir, on every side.   290
Indeed, I've heard you warmly praised of late
By persons of considerable weight.
    ALCESTE. This fawning age has praise for everyone,
And all distinctions, Madam, are undone.
All things have equal honor nowadays,   295
And no one should be gratified by praise.
To be admired, one only need exist,
And every lackey's on the honors list.
    ARSINOÉ. I only wish, Sir, that you had your eye
On some position at court, however high;   300
You'd only have to hint at such a notion
For me to set the proper wheels in motion;
I've certain friendships I'd be glad to use
To get you any office you might choose.
    ALCESTE. Madam, I fear that any such ambition   305
Is wholly foreign to my disposition.
The soul God gave me isn't of the sort
That prospers in the weather of a court.
It's all too obvious that I don't possess
The virtues necessary for success.   310
My one great talent is for speaking plain;
I've never learned to flatter or to feign;
And anyone so stupidly sincere
Had best not seek a courtier's career.
Outside the court, I know, one must dispense   315
With honors, privilege, and influence;
But still one gains the right, foregoing these,
Not to be tortured by the wish to please.
One needn't live in dread of snubs and slights,
Nor praise the verse that every idiot writes,   320
Nor humor silly Marquesses, nor bestow
Politic sighs on Madam So-and-So.
    ARSINOÉ. Forget the court, then; let the matter rest.
But I've another cause to be distressed
About your present situation, Sir.   325
It's to your love affair that I refer.
She whom you love, and who pretends to love you,
Is, I regret to say, unworthy of you.
    ALCESTE. Why, Madam! Can you seriously intend
To make so grave a charge against your friend?   330
    ARSINOÉ. Alas, I must. I've stood aside too long
And let that lady do you grievous wrong;

But now my debt to conscience shall be paid:
I tell you that your love has been betrayed.
    ALCESTE.   I thank you, Madam; you're extremely kind.   335
Such words are soothing to a lover's mind.
    ARSINOÉ.   Yes, though she *is* my friend, I say again
You're very much too good for Célimène.
She's wantonly misled you from the start.
    ALCESTE.   You may be right; who knows another's heart?   340
But ask yourself if it's the part of charity
To shake my soul with doubts of her sincerity.
    ARSINOÉ.   Well, if you'd rather be a dupe than doubt her,
That's your affair. I'll say no more about her.
    ALCESTE.   Madam, you know that doubt and vague suspicion   345
Are painful to a man in my position;
It's most unkind to worry me this way
Unless you've some real proof of what you say.
    ARSINOÉ.   Sir, say no more: all doubt shall be removed,
And all that I've been saying shall be proved.   350
You've only to escort me home, and there
We'll look into the heart of this affair.
I've ocular evidence which will persuade you
Beyond a doubt, that Célimène's betrayed you.
Then, if you're saddened by that revelation,   355
Perhaps I can provide some consolation.

ACT IV

SCENE I

    PHILINTE.   Madam, he acted like a stubborn child;
I thought they never would be reconciled;
In vain we reasoned, threatened, and appealed;
He stood his ground and simply would not yield.
The Marshals, I feel sure, have never heard   5
An argument so splendidly absurd
"No, gentlemen," said he, "I'll not retract.
His verse is bad: extremely bad, in fact.
Surely it does the man no harm to know it.
Does it disgrace him, not to be a poet?   10
A gentleman may be respected still,
Whether he writes a sonnet well or ill.
That I dislike his verse should not offend him;
In all that touches honor, I commend him;

He's noble, brave, and virtuous—but I fear 15
He can't in truth be called a sonneteer.
I'll gladly praise his wardrobe; I'll endorse
His dancing, or the way he sits a horse;
But, gentlemen, I cannot praise his rhyme.
In fact, it ought to be a capital crime 20
For anyone so sadly unendowed
To write a sonnet, and read the thing aloud."
At length he fell into a gentler mood
And, striking a concessive attitude,
He paid Oronte the following courtesies: 25
"Sir, I regret that I'm so hard to please,
And I'm profoundly sorry that your lyric
Failed to provoke me to a panegyric."
After these curious words, the two embraced,
And then the hearing was adjourned—in haste. 30
    ELIANTE.   His conduct has been very singular lately;
Still, I confess that I respect him greatly.
The honesty in which he takes such pride
Has—to my mind—its noble, heroic side.
In this false age, such candor seems outrageous; 35
But I could wish that it were more contagious.
    PHILINTE.   What most intrigues me in our friend Alceste
Is the grand passion that rages in his breast.
The sullen humors he's compounded of
Should not, I think, dispose his heart to love; 40
But since they do, it puzzles me still more
That he should choose your cousin to adore.
    ELIANTE.   It does, indeed, belie the theory
That love is born of gentle sympathy,
And that the tender passion must be based 45
On sweet accords of temper and of taste.
    PHILINTE.   Does she return his love, do you suppose?
    ELIANTE.   Ah, that's a difficult question, Sir. Who knows?
How can we judge the truth of her devotion?
Her heart's a stranger to its own emotion. 50
Sometimes it thinks it loves, when no love's there;
At other times it loves quite unaware.
    PHILINTE.   I rather think Alceste is in for more
Distress and sorrow than he's bargained for;
Were he of my mind, Madam, his affection 55
Would turn in quite a different direction,
And we would see him more responsive to
The kind regard which he receives from you.

ELIANTE. Sir, I believe in frankness, and I'm inclined,
In matters of the heart, to speak my mind.   60
I don't oppose his love for her; indeed,
I hope with all my heart that he'll succeed,
And were it in my power, I'd rejoice
In giving him the lady of his choice.
But if, as happens frequently enough   65
In love affairs, he meets with a rebuff—
If Célimène should grant some rival's suit—
I'd gladly play the role of substitute;
Nor would his tender speeches please me less
Because they'd once been made without success.   70
    PHILINTE. Well, Madam, as for me, I don't oppose
Your hopes in this affair; and heaven knows
That in my conversations with the man
I plead your cause as often as I can.
But if those two should marry, and so remove   75
All chance that he will offer you his love,
Then I'll declare my own, and hope to see
Your gracious favor pass from him to me.
In short, should you be cheated of Alceste,
I'd be most happy to be second best.   80
    ELIANTE. Philinte, you're teasing.
    PHILINTE.   Ah, Madam, never fear;
No words of mine were ever so sincere,
And I shall live in fretful expectation
Till I can make a fuller declaration.

SCENE II

    ALCESTE. Avenge me, Madam! I must have satisfaction,   85
Or this great wrong will drive me to distraction!
    ELIANTE. Why, what's the matter? What's upset you so?
    ALCESTE. Madam, I've had a mortal, mortal blow.
If Chaos repossessed the universe,
I swear I'd not be shaken any worse.   90
I'm ruined . . . I can say no more . . . My soul . . .
    ELIANTE. Do try, Sir, to regain your self-control.
    ALCESTE. Just heaven! Why were so much beauty and grace
Bestowed on one so vicious and so base?
    ELIANTE. Once more, Sir, tell us . . .
    ALCESTE.   My world has gone to wrack; 95
I'm—I'm betrayed; she's stabbed me in the back:

Yes, Célimène (who would have thought it of her?)
Is false to me, and has another lover.
    ELIANTE.   Are you quite certain? Can you prove these things?
    PHILINTE.   Lovers are prey to wild imaginings   100
And jealous fancies. No doubt there's some mistake . . .
    ALCESTE.   Mind your own business, Sir, for heaven's sake.
(To ELIANTE) Madam, I have the proof that you demand
Here in my pocket, penned by her own hand.
Yes, all the shameful evidence one could want   105
Lies in this letter written to Oronte—
Oronte! whom I felt sure she couldn't love,
And hardly bothered to be jealous of.
    PHILINTE.   Still, in a letter, appearances may deceive;
This may not be so bad as you believe.   110
    ALCESTE.   Once more I beg you, Sir, to let me be;
Tend to your own affairs; leave mine to me.
    ELIANTE.   Compose yourself; this anguish that you feel . . .
    ALCESTE.   Is something, Madam, you alone can heal.
My outraged heart, beside itself with grief,   115
Appeals to you for comfort and relief.
Avenge me on your cousin, whose unjust
And faithless nature has deceived my trust;
Avenge a crime your pure soul must detest.
    ELIANTE.   But how, Sir?
    ALCESTE.   Madam, this heart within my breast   120
Is yours; pray take it; redeem my heart from her,
And so avenge me on my torturer.
Let her be punished by the fond emotion,
The ardent love, the bottomless devotion,
The faithful worship which this heart of mine   125
Will offer up to yours as to a shrine.
    ELIANTE.   You have my sympathy, Sir, in all you suffer;
Nor do I scorn the noble heart you offer;
But I suspect you'll soon be mollified,
And this desire for vengeance will subside.   130
When some beloved hand has done us wrong
We thirst for retribution—but not for long;
However dark the deed that she's committed,
A lovely culprit's very soon acquitted.
Nothing's so stormy as an injured lover,   135
And yet no storm so quickly passes over.
    ALCESTE.   No, Madam, no—this is no lovers' spat;
I'll not forgive her; it's gone too far for that;
My mind's made up; I'll kill myself before

I waste my hopes upon her any more.   140
Ah, here she is. My wrath intensifies.
I shall confront her with her tricks and lies,
And crush her utterly, and bring you then
A heart no longer slave to Célimène.

SCENE III

ALCESTE (aside).   Sweet heaven, help me to control my passion.   145
CÉLIMÈNE (aside, to ALCESTE).   Oh, Lord. Why stand there
   staring in that fashion?
And what d'you mean by those dramatic sighs,
And that malignant glitter in your eyes?
ALCESTE.   I mean that sins which cause the blood to freeze
Look innocent beside your treacheries;   150
That nothing Hell's or Heaven's wrath could do
Ever produced so bad a thing as you.
CÉLIMÈNE.   Your compliments were always sweet and pretty.
ALCESTE.   Madam, it's not the moment to be witty.
No, blush and hang your head; you've ample reason,   155
Since I've the fullest evidence of your treason.
Ah, this is what my sad heart prophesied;
Now all my anxious fears are verified;
My dark suspicion and my gloomy doubt
Divined the truth, and now the truth is out.   160
For all your trickery, I was not deceived;
It was my bitter stars that I believed.
But don't imagine that you'll go scot-free;
You shan't misuse me with impunity.
I know that love's irrational and blind;   165
I know the heart's not subject to the mind,
And can't be reasoned into beating faster;
I know each soul is free to choose its master;
Therefore had you but spoken from the heart,
Rejecting my attentions from the start,   170
I'd have no grievance, or at any rate
I could complain of nothing but my fate.
Ah, but so falsely to encourage me—
That was a treason and a treachery
For which you cannot suffer too severely,   175
And you shall pay for that behavior dearly.
Yes, now I have no pity, not a shred;
My temper's out of hand; I've lost my head;

Shocked by the knowledge of your double-dealings,
My reason can't restrain my savage feelings; 180
A righteous wrath deprives me of my senses,
And I won't answer for the consequences.
    CÉLIMÈNE.   What does this outburst mean? Will you please
    explain?
Have you, by any chance, gone quite insane? 185
    ALCESTE.   Yes, yes, I went insane the day I fell
A victim to your black and fatal spell,
Thinking to meet with some sincerity
Among the treacherous charms that beckoned me.
    CÉLIMÈNE.   Pooh. Of what treachery can you complain? 190
    ALCESTE.   How sly you are, how cleverly you feign!
But you'll not victimize me any more.
Look: here's a document you've seen before.
This evidence, which I acquired today,
Leaves you, I think, without a thing to say. 195
    CÉLIMÈNE.   Is this what sent you into such a fit?
    ALCESTE.   You should be blushing at the sight of it.
    CÉLIMÈNE.   Ought I to blush? I truly don't see why.
    ALCESTE.   Ah, now you're being bold as well as sly;
Since there's no signature, perhaps you'll claim . . . 200
    CÉLIMÈNE.   I wrote it, whether or not it bears my name.
    ALCESTE.   And you can view with equanimity
This proof of your disloyalty to me!
    CÉLIMÈNE.   Oh, don't be so outrageous and extreme.
    ALCESTE.   You take this matter lightly, it would seem. 205
Was it no wrong to me, no shame to you,
That you should send Oronte this billet-doux?
    CÉLIMÈNE.   Oronte! Who said it was for him?
    ALCESTE.   Why, those
Who brought me this example of your prose.
But what's the difference? If you wrote the letter 210
To someone else, it pleases me no better.
My grievance and your guilt remain the same.
    CÉLIMÈNE.   But need you rage, and need I blush for shame,
If this was written to a *woman* friend?
    ALCESTE.   Ah! Most ingenious. I'm impressed no end; 215
And after that incredible evasion
Your guilt is clear. I need no more persuasion.
How dare you try so clumsy a deception?
D'you think I'm wholly wanting in perception?
Come, come, let's see how brazenly you'll try 220
To bolster up so palpable a lie:
Kindly construe this ardent closing section

As nothing more than sisterly affection!
Here, let me read it. Tell me, if you dare to,
That this is for a woman . . .
    CÉLIMÈNE.   I don't care to.   225
What right have you to badger and berate me,
And so highhandedly interrogate me?
    ALCESTE.   Now, don't be angry; all I ask of you
Is that you justify a phrase or two . . .
    CÉLIMÈNE.   No, I shall not. I utterly refuse,   230
And you may take those phrases as you choose.
    ALCESTE.   Just show me how this letter could be meant
For a woman's eyes, and I shall be content.
    CÉLIMÈNE.   No, no, it's for Oronte; you're perfectly right.
I welcome his attentions with delight,   235
I prize his character and his intellect,
And everything is just as you suspect.
Come, do your worst now; give your rage free rein;
But kindly cease to bicker and complain.
    ALCESTE (aside).   Good God! Could anything be more inhuman? 240
Was ever a heart so mangled by a woman?
When I complain of how she has betrayed me,
She bridles, and commences to upbraid me!
She tries my tortured patience to the limit;
She won't deny her guilt; she glories in it!   245
And yet my heart's too faint and cowardly
To break these chains of passion, and be free,
To scorn her as it should, and rise above
This unrewarded, mad, and bitter love.
(To CÉLIMÈNE) Ah, traitress, in how confident a fashion   250
You take advantage of my helpless passion,
And use my weakness for your faithless charms
To make me once again throw down my arms!
But do at least deny this black transgression;
Take back that mocking and perverse confession;   255
Defend this letter and your innocence,
And I, poor fool, will aid in your defense.
Pretend, pretend, that you are just and true,
And I shall make myself believe in you.
    CÉLIMÈNE.   Oh, stop it. Don't be such a jealous dunce,   260
Or I shall leave off loving you at once.
Just why should I pretend? What could impel me
To stoop so low as that? And kindly tell me
Why, if I loved another, I shouldn't merely
Inform you of it, simply and sincerely!   265
I've told you where you stand, and that admission

Should altogether clear me of suspicion;
After so generous a guarantee,
What right have you to harbor doubts of me?
Since women are (from natural reticence)   270
Reluctant to declare their sentiments,
And since the honor of our sex requires
That we conceal our amorous desires,
Ought any man for whom such laws are broken
To question what the oracle has spoken?   275
Should he not rather feel an obligation
To trust that most obliging declaration?
Enough, now. Your suspicions quite disgust me;
Why should I love a man who doesn't trust me?
I cannot understand why I continue,   280
Fool that I am, to take an interest in you.
I ought to choose a man less prone to doubt,
And give you something to be vexed about.
    ALCESTE.   Ah, what a poor enchanted fool I am;
These gentle words, no doubt, were all a sham;   285
But destiny requires me to entrust
My happiness to you, and so I must.
I'll love you to the bitter end, and see
How false and treacherous you dare to be.
    CÉLIMÈNE.   No, you don't really love me as you ought.   290
    ALCESTE.   I love you more than can be said or thought;
Indeed, I wish you were in such distress
That I might show my deep devotedness.
Yes, I could wish that you were wretchedly poor,
Unloved, uncherished, utterly obscure;   295
That fate had set you down upon the earth
Without possessions, rank, or gentle birth;
Then, by the offer of my heart, I might
Repair the great injustice of your plight;
I'd raise you from the dust, and proudly prove   300
The purity and vastness of my love.
    CÉLIMÈNE.   This is a strange benevolence indeed!
God grant that I may never be in need . . .
Ah, here's Monsieur Dubois, in quaint disguise.

SCENE IV

    ALCESTE.   Well, why this costume? Why those frightened eyes?   305
What ails you?

DUBOIS.   Well, Sir, things are most mysterious.
ALCESTE.   What do you mean?
DUBOIS.   I fear they're very serious.
ALCESTE.   What?
DUBOIS.   Shall I speak more loudly?
ALCESTE.   Yes; speak out.
DUBOIS.   Isn't there someone here, Sir?
ALCESTE.   Speak, you lout!
Stop wasting time.
DUBOIS.   Sir, we must slip away.   310
ALCESTE.   How's that?
DUBOIS.   We must decamp without delay.
ALCESTE.   Explain yourself.
DUBOIS.   I tell you we must fly.
ALCESTE.   What for?
DUBOIS.   We mustn't pause to say good-by.
ALCESTE.   Now what d'you mean by all of this, you clown?
DUBOIS.   I mean, Sir, that we've got to leave this town.   315
ALCESTE.   I'll tear you limb from limb and joint from joint
If you don't come more quickly to the point.
DUBOIS.   Well, Sir, today a man in a black suit,
Who wore a black and ugly scowl to boot,
Left us a document scrawled in such a hand   320
As even Satan couldn't understand.
It bears upon your lawsuit, I don't doubt;
But all hell's devils couldn't make it out.
ALCESTE.   Well, well, go on. What then? I fail to see
How this event obliges us to flee.   325
DUBOIS.   Well, Sir: an hour later, hardly more,
A gentleman who's often called before
Came looking for you in an anxious way.
Not finding you, he asked me to convey
(Knowing I could be trusted with the same)   330
The following message . . . Now, what was his name?
ALCESTE.   Forget his name, you idiot. What did he say?
DUBOIS.   Well, it was one of your friends, Sir, anyway.
He warned you to begone, and he suggested
That if you stay, you may well be arrested.   335
ALCESTE.   What? Nothing more specific? Think, man, think!
DUBOIS.   No, Sir. He had me bring him pen and ink,
And dashed you off a letter which, I'm sure,
Will render things distinctly less obscure.
ALCESTE.   Well—let me have it!
CÉLIMÈNE.   What is this all about?   340

ALCESTE. God knows; but I have hopes of finding out.
How long am I to wait, you blitherer?
    DUBOIS (*after a protracted search for the letter*). I must have left it on
    your table, Sir.
    ALCESTE. I ought to . . .
    CÉLIMÈNE.   No, no, keep your self-control;
Go find out what's behind his rigmarole.   345
    ALCESTE. It seems that fate, no matter what I do,
Has sworn that I may not converse with you;
But, Madam, pray permit your faithful lover
To try once more before the day is over.

ACT V

SCENE I

    ALCESTE. No, it's too much. My mind's made up, I tell you.
    PHILINTE. Why should this blow, however hard, compel you . . .
    ALCESTE. No, no, don't waste your breath in argument;
Nothing you say will alter my intent;
This age is vile, and I've made up my mind   5
To have no further commerce with mankind.
Did not truth, honor, decency, and the laws
Oppose my enemy and approve my cause?
My claims were justified in all men's sight;
I put my trust in equity and right;   10
Yet, to my horror and the world's disgrace,
Justice is mocked, and I have lost my case!
A scoundrel whose dishonesty is notorious
Emerges from another lie victorious!
Honor and right condone his brazen fraud,   15
While rectitude and decency applaud!
Before his smirking face, the truth stands charmed,
And virtue conquered, and the law disarmed!
His crime is sanctioned by a court decree!
And not content with what he's done to me,   20
The dog now seeks to ruin me by stating
That I composed a book now circulating,
A book so wholly criminal and vicious
That even to speak its title is seditious!
Meanwhile Oronte, my rival, lends his credit   25
To the same libelous tale, and helps to spread it!
Oronte! a man of honor and of rank,
With whom I've been entirely fair and frank;

Who sought me out and forced me, willy-nilly,
To judge some verse I found extremely silly;   30
And who, because I properly refused
To flatter him, or see the truth abused,
Abets my enemy in a rotten slander!
There's the reward of honesty and candor!
The man will hate me to the end of time   35
For failing to commend his wretched rhyme!
And not this man alone, but all humanity
Do what they do from interest and vanity;
They prate of honor, truth, and righteousness,
But lie, betray, and swindle nonetheless.   40
Come then: man's villainy is too much to bear;
Let's leave this jungle and this jackal's lair.
Yes! treacherous and savage race of men,
You shall not look upon my face again.
    PHILINTE.   Oh, don't rush into exile prematurely;   45
Things aren't as dreadful as you make them, surely.
It's rather obvious, since you're still at large,
That people don't believe your enemy's charge.
Indeed, his tale's so patently untrue
That it may do more harm to him than you.   50
    ALCESTE.   Nothing could do that scoundrel any harm:
His frank corruption is his greatest charm,
And, far from hurting him, a further shame
Would only serve to magnify his name.
    PHILINTE.   In any case, his bald prevarication   55
Has done no injury to your reputation,
And you may feel secure in that regard.
As for your lawsuit, it should not be hard
To have the case reopened, and contest
This judgment . . .
    ALCESTE.   No, no, let the verdict rest.   60
Whatever cruel penalty it may bring,
I wouldn't have it changed for anything.
It shows the times' injustice with such clarity
That I shall pass it down to our posterity
As a great proof and signal demonstration   65
Of the black wickedness of this generation.
It may cost twenty thousand francs; but I
Shall pay their twenty thousand, and gain thereby
The right to storm and rage at human evil,
And send the race of mankind to the devil.   70

PHILINTE. Listen to me . . .

ALCESTE.   Why? What can you possibly say?
Don't argue, Sir; your labor's thrown away.
Do you propose to offer lame excuses
For men's behavior and the times' abuses?

PHILINTE. No, all you say I'll readily concede: 75
This is a low, dishonest age indeed;
Nothing but trickery prospers nowadays,
And people ought to mend their shabby ways.
Yes, man's a beastly creature; but must we then
Abandon the society of men?   80
Here in the world, each human frailty
Provides occasion for philosophy,
And that is virtue's noblest exercise;
If honesty shone forth from all men's eyes,
If every heart were frank and kind and just,   85
What could our virtues do but gather dust
(Since their employment is to help us bear
The villainies of men without despair)?
A heart well-armed with virtue can endure . . .

ALCESTE. Sir, you're a matchless reasoner, to be sure;   90
Your words are fine and full of cogency;
But don't waste time and eloquence on me.
My reason bids me go, for my own good.
My tongue won't lie and flatter as it should;
God knows what frankness it might next commit,   95
And what I'd suffer on account of it.
Pray let me wait for Célimène's return
In peace and quiet. I shall shortly learn,
By her response to what I have in view,
Whether her love for me is feigned or true.   100

PHILINTE. Till then, let's visit Eliante upstairs.

ALCESTE. No, I am too weighed down with somber cares.
Go to her, do; and leave me with my gloom
Here in the darkened corner of this room.

PHILINTE. Why, that's no sort of company, my friend;   105
I'll see if Eliante will not descend.

SCENE II

ORONTE. Yes, Madam, if you wish me to remain
Your true and ardent lover, you must deign
To give me some more positive assurance.

All this suspense is quite beyond endurance.   110
If your heart shares the sweet desires of mine,
Show me as much by some convincing sign;
And here's the sign I urgently suggest:
That you no longer tolerate Alceste,
But sacrifice him to my love, and sever   115
All your relations with the man forever.
    CÉLIMÈNE.   Why do you suddenly dislike him so?
You praised him to the skies not long ago.
    ORONTE.   Madam, that's not the point. I'm here to find
Which way your tender feelings are inclined.   120
Choose, if you please, between Alceste and me,
And I shall stay or go accordingly.
    ALCESTE (*emerging from the corner*).   Yes, Madam, choose; this gentle-
    man's demand
Is wholly just, and I support his stand.
I too am true and ardent; I too am here   125
To ask you that you make your feelings clear.
No more delays, now; no equivocation;
The time has come to make your declaration.
    ORONTE.   Sir, I've no wish in any way to be
An obstacle to your felicity.   130
    ALCESTE.   Sir, I've no wish to share her heart with you;
That may sound jealous, but at least it's true.
    ORONTE.   If, weighing us, she leans in your direction . . .
    ALCESTE.   If she regards you with the least affection . . .
    ORONTE.   I swear I'll yield her to you there and then.   135
    ALCESTE.   I swear I'll never see her face again.
    ORONTE.   Now, Madam, tell us what we've come to hear.
    ALCESTE.   Madam, speak openly and have no fear.
    ORONTE.   Just say which one is to remain your lover.
    ALCESTE.   Just name one name, and it will all be over.   140
    ORONTE.   What! Is it possible that you're undecided?
    ALCESTE.   What! Can your feelings possibly be divided?
    CÉLIMÈNE.   Enough: this inquisition's gone too far·
How utterly unreasonable you are!
Not that I couldn't make the choice with ease;   145
My heart has no conflicting sympathies;
I know full well which one of you I favor,
And you'd not see me hesitate or waver.
But how can you expect me to reveal
So cruelly and bluntly what I feel?   150
I think it altogether too unpleasant

To choose between two men when both are present;
One's heart has means more subtle and more kind
Of letting its affections be divined,
Nor need one be uncharitably plain   155
To let a lover know he loves in vain.
    ORONTE.   No, no, speak plainly; I for one can stand it.
I beg you to be frank.
    ALCESTE.   And I demand it.
The simple truth is what I wish to know,
And there's no need for softening the blow.   160
You've made an art of pleasing everyone,
But now your days of coquetry are done:
You have no choice now, Madam, but to choose,
For I'll know what to think if you refuse;
I'll take your silence for a clear admission   165
That I'm entitled to my worst suspicion.
    ORONTE.   I thank you for this ultimatum, Sir,
And I may say I heartily concur.
    CÉLIMÈNE.   Really, this foolishness is very wearing:
Must you be so unjust and overbearing?   170
Haven't I told you why I must demur?
Ah, here's Eliante; I'll put the case to her.

SCENE III

    CÉLIMÈNE.   Cousin, I'm being persecuted here
By these two persons, who, it would appear,
Will not be satisfied till I confess   175
Which one I love the more, and which the less,
And tell the latter to his face that he
Is henceforth banished from my company.
Tell me, has ever such a thing been done?
    ELIANTE.   You'd best not turn to me; I'm not the one   180
To back you in a matter of this kind:
I'm all for those who frankly speak their mind.
    ORONTE.   Madam, you'll search in vain for a defender.
    ALCESTE.   You're beaten, Madam, and may as well surrender.
    ORONTE.   Speak, speak, you must; and end this awful strain.   185
    ALCESTE.   Or don't, and your position will be plain.
    ORONTE.   A single word will close this painful scene.
    ALCESTE.   But if you're silent, I'll know what you mean.

ACASTE (*to Célimène*).   Madam, with all due deference, we two
Have come to pick a little bone with you.   190
    CLITANDRE (*to* ORONTE *and* ALCESTE).   I'm glad you're present, Sirs;
        as you'll soon learn,
Our business here is also your concern.
    ARSINOÉ (*to Célimène*).   Madam, I visit you so soon again
Only because of these two gentlemen,
Who came to me indignant and aggrieved   195
About a crime too base to be believed.
Knowing your virtue, having such confidence in it,
I couldn't think you guilty for a minute,
In spite of all their telling evidence;
And, rising above our little difference,   200
I've hastened here in friendship's name to see
You clear yourself of this great calumny.
    ACASTE.   Yes, Madam, let us see with what composure
You'll manage to respond to this disclosure.
You lately sent Clitandre this tender note.   205
    CLITANDRE.   And this one, for Acaste, you also wrote.
    ACASTE (*to* ORONTE *and* ALCESTE).   You'll recognize this
        writing Sirs, I think;
The lady is so free with pen and ink
That you must know it all too well, I fear.
But listen: this is something you should hear.   210

    "How absurd you are to condemn my lightheartedness
in society, and to accuse me of being happiest in the company of
others. Nothing could be more unjust; and if you do not come
to me instantly and beg pardon for saying such a thing, I shall
never forgive you as long as I live. Our big bumbling friend   215
the Viscount . . ."

What a shame that he's not here.

    "Our big bumbling friend the Viscount, whose name
stands first in your complaint, is hardly a man to my
taste; and ever since the day I watched him spend three-   220
quarters of an hour spitting into a well, so as to make
circles in the water, I have been unable to think highly
of him. As for the little Marquess . . ."

In all modesty, gentlemen, that is I.

    "As for the little Marquess, who sat squeezing my   225

hand for such a long while yesterday, I find him in all
respects the most trifling creature alive; and the only
things of value about him are his cape and his sword.
As for the man with the green ribbons . . ."

(*To* ALCESTE) It's your turn now, Sir.   230

"As for the man with the green ribbons, he amuses
me now and then with his bluntness and his bearish ill-
humor; but there are many times indeed when I think
him the greatest bore in the world. And as for the sonneteer . . ."   235

(*To* ORONTE) Here's your helping.

"And as for the sonneteer, who has taken it into his
head to be witty, and insists on being an author in the
teeth of opinion, I simply cannot be bothered to listen to
him, and his prose wearies me quite as much as his   240
poetry. Be assured that I am not always so well-enter-
tained as you suppose; that I long for your company,
more than I dare to say, at all these entertainments to
which people drag me; and that the presence of those
one loves is true and perfect seasoning to all one's   245
pleasures."

CLITANDRE.   And now for me.

"Clitandre, whom you mention, and who so pesters
me with his saccharine speeches, is the last man on earth
for whom I could feel any affection. He is quite mad to   250
suppose that I love him, and so are you, to doubt that
you are loved. Do come to your senses; exchange your
suppositions for his; and visit me as often as possible,
to help me bear the annoyance of his unwelcome attentions."   255

It's a sweet character that these letters show,
And what to call it, Madam, you well know.
Enough. We're off to make the world acquainted
With this sublime self-portrait that you've painted.
    ACASTE.   Madam, I'll make you no farewell oration;   260
No, you're not worthy of my indignation.
Far choicer hearts than yours, as you'll discover,
Would like this little Marquess for a lover.

SCENE V

ORONTE.   So! After all those loving letters you wrote,
You turn on me like this, and cut my throat!   265
And your dissembling, faithless heart, I find,
Has pledged itself by turns to all mankind!
How blind I've been! But now I clearly see;
I thank you, Madam, for enlightening me.
My heart is mine once more, and I'm content;   270
The loss of it shall be your punishment.
(*To* ALCESTE) Sir, she is yours; I'll seek no more to stand
Between your wishes and this lady's hand.

SCENE VI

ARSINOÉ (*to* CÉLIMÈNE).   Madam, I'm forced to speak. I'm far too
stirred
To keep my counsel, after what I've heard.   275
I'm shocked and staggered by your want of morals.
It's not my way to mix in others' quarrels;
But really, when this fine and noble spirit,
This man of honor and surpassing merit,
Laid down the offering of his heart before you,   280
How *could* you . . .
ALCESTE.   Madam, permit me, I implore you,
To represent myself in this debate.
Don't bother, please, to be my advocate.
My heart, in any case, could not afford
To give your services their due reward;   285
And if I chose, for consolation's sake,
Some other lady, t'would not be you I'd take.
ARSINOÉ.   What makes you think you could, Sir? And how dare you
Imply that I've been trying to ensnare you?
If you can for a moment entertain   290
Such flattering fancies, you're extremely vain.
I'm not so interested as you suppose
In Célimène's discarded gigolos.
Get rid of that absurd illusion, do.
Women like me are not for such as you.   295
Stay with this creature, to whom you're so attached;
I've never seen two people better matched.

ALCESTE (*to* CÉLIMÈNE).   Well, I've been still throughout this exposé,
Till everyone but me has said his say.
Come, have I shown sufficient self-restraint?   300
And may I now . . .
    CÉLIMÈNE.   Yes, make your just complaint.
Reproach me freely, call me what you will;
You've every right to say I've used you ill.
I've wronged you, I confess it; and in my shame
I'll make no effort to escape the blame.   305
The anger of those others I could despise;
My guilt toward you I sadly recognize.
Your wrath is wholly justified, I fear;
I know how culpable I must appear,
I know all things bespeak my treachery,   310
And that, in short, you've grounds for hating me.
Do so; I give you leave.
    ALCESTE.   Ah, traitress—how,
How should I cease to love you, even now?
Though mind and will were passionately bent
On hating you, my heart would not consent.   315
(*To* ELIANTE *and* PHILINTE) Be witness to my madness, both of you;
See what infatuation drives one to;
But wait; my folly's only just begun,
And I shall prove to you before I'm done
How strange the human heart is, and how far   320
From rational we sorry creatures are.
(*To* CÉLIMÈNE) Woman, I'm willing to forget your shame,
And clothe your treacheries in a sweeter name;
I'll call them youthful errors, instead of crimes,
And lay the blame on these corrupting times.   325
My one condition is that you agree
To share my chosen fate, and fly with me
To that wild, trackless solitary place
In which I shall forget the human race.
Only by such a course can you atone   330
For those atrocious letters; by that alone
Can you remove my present horror of you,
And make it possible for me to love you.
    CÉLIMÈNE.   What! *I* renounce the world at my young age,
And die of boredom in some hermitage?   335
    ALCESTE.   Ah, if you really loved me as you ought,
You wouldn't give the world a moment's thought;

Must you have me, and all the world beside?
CÉLIMÈNE.   Alas, at twenty one is terrified
Of solitude. I fear I lack the force   340
And depth of soul to take so stern a course.
But if my hand in marriage will content you,
Why, there's a plan which I might well consent to,
And . . .
    ALCESTE.   No, I detest you now. I could excuse
Everything else, but since you thus refuse   345
To love me wholly, as a wife should do,
And see the world in me, as I in you,
Go! I reject your hand, and disenthrall
My heart from your enchantments, once for all.

SCENE VIII

    ALCESTE (to ELIANTE).   Madam, your virtuous beauty has no peer, 350
Of all this world, you only are sincere;
I've long esteemed you highly, as you know;
Permit me ever to esteem you so,
And if I do not now request your hand,
Forgive me, Madam, and try to understand.   355
I feel unworthy of it; I sense that fate
Does not intend me for the married state,
That I should do you wrong by offering you
My shattered heart's unhappy residue,
And that in short . . .
    ELIANTE.   Your argument's well taken: 360
Nor need you fear that I shall feel forsaken.
Were I to offer him this hand of mine,
Your friend Philinte, I think, would not decline.
    PHILINTE.   Ah, Madam, that's my heart's most cherished goal,
For which I'd gladly give my life and soul.   365
    ALCESTE (to ELIANTE and PHILINTE).   May you be true to all you
        now profess,
And so deserve unending happiness.
Meanwhile, betrayed and wronged in everything,
I'll flee this bitter world where vice is king,
And seek some spot unpeopled and apart   370
Where I'll be free to have an honest heart.
    PHILINTE.   Come, Madam, let's do everything we can
To change the mind of this unhappy man.

QUESTIONS

1. How does the argument between Alceste and Philinte in the opening scene state the play's major thematic conflict? Which of the two philosophies expressed is the more idealistic? Which more realistic? Is either or are both of them extreme?

2. What are the attitudes of Célimène, Eliante, and Arsinoé toward Alceste? Do they respect him? Why or why not?

3. *The Misanthrope* is generally acknowledged to be one of the world's greatest comedies, but, at the same time, it is an atypical one, both in its hero and in its ending. In what ways does Alceste approach the stature of a tragic hero? What characteristic does he share with Oedipus? In what way is the ending unlike a comic ending?

4. Alceste is in conflict with social convention, with social injustice, and with Célimène. Does he discriminate between them as to their relative importance? Discuss.

5. Are there any indications in the opening scene that the motivations behind Alceste's hatred of social convention are not as unmixed as he thinks them?

6. Alceste declares himself not blind to Célimène's faults. Is he blind in any way about his relationship with Célimène? If so, what does his blindness spring from?

7. What do Alceste's reasons for refusing to appeal his law suit (Act V, Scene i) and his wish that Célimène were "Unloved, uncherished, utterly obscure" so that he might raise her "from the dust" (Act IV, Scene iii) tell us about his character?

8. What are Célimène's good qualities? What are her bad ones? In what ways are she and Alceste foils? Might Célimène have been redeemed had Alceste been able to accept her without taking her from society?

9. How is the gossip session between Acaste, Clitandre, and Célimène (Act II, Scene v) a double-edged satire? Which of Célimène's satirical portraits is the finest? How accurate is Célimène's portrait of Alceste himself?

10. Which is the more scathingly satirized—Alceste, or the society in which he lives? Why?

11. What character in the play most nearly represents a desirable norm of social behavior? Why?

12. What characteristics keep Alceste from being a tragic hero? What keeps the ending from being a tragic ending?

13. The verse of Molière's play is quite different in kind and quality from García Lorca's. Insofar as they can be judged in translation, what are the major differences? What relation is there between the poetic style of each play and its subject matter?

14. Compare *The Misanthrope* and *An Enemy of the People* as plays dealing with conflict between an individual and his society. How are the characters of Alceste and Dr. Stockmann similar? How are they different? Which is portrayed by his creator with the greater sympathy? Why?

15. Are politeness and hypocrisy the same thing? If not, distinguish between them.

George Bernard Shaw
CANDIDA

ACT I

A *fine morning in October 1894 in the north east quarter of London, a vast district miles away from the London of Mayfair and St. James's, and much less narrow, squalid, fetid and airless in its slums. It is strong in unfashionable middle class life: wide-streeted; myriad-populated; well served with ugly iron urinals, Radical clubs, and tram lines carrying a perpetual stream of yellow cars; enjoying in its main thoroughfares the luxury of grass-grown "front gardens" untrodden by the foot of man save as to the path from the gate to the hall door; blighted by a callously endured monotony of miles and miles of unlovely brick houses, black iron railings, stony pavements, slated roofs, and respectably ill dressed or disreputably worse dressed people, quite accustomed to the place, and mostly plodding uninterestedly about somebody else's work. The little energy and eagerness that crop up shew themselves in cockney cupidity and business "push." Even the policemen and the chapels are not infrequent enough to break the monotony. The sun is shining cheerfully: there is no fog; and though the smoke effectually prevents anything, whether faces and hands or bricks and mortar, from looking fresh and clean, it is not hanging heavily enough to trouble a Londoner.*

This desert of unattractiveness has its oasis. Near the outer end of the Hackney Road is a park of 217 acres, fenced in, not by railings, but by a wooden paling, and containing plenty of greensward, trees, a lake for bathers, flower beds which are triumphs of the admired cockney art of carpet gardening, and a sandpit, originally imported from the seaside for the delight of children, but speedily deserted on its becoming a natural vermin preserve for all the petty fauna of Kingsland, Hackney, and Hoxton. A bandstand, an unfurnished forum for religious, anti-religious, and political orators, cricket pitches, a gymnasium, and an old fashioned stone kiosk are among its attractions. Wherever the prospect is bounded by trees or rising green grounds, it is a pleasant place. Where the ground stretches flat to the grey palings, with bricks and mortar, sky signs, crowded chimneys and smoke beyond, the prospect makes it desolate and sordid.

The best view of Victoria Park is commanded by the front window of St. Dominic's Parsonage, from which not a brick is visible. The parsonage is semi-detached, with a front garden and a porch. Visitors go up the flight of steps to the porch: tradespeople and members of the family go down by a door under the steps to the basement, with a breakfast room, used for all meals, in front, and the kitchen at the back. Upstairs, on the level of the hall door, is the drawingroom, with its large plate glass window looking out

CANDIDA   Reprinted by permission of the Society of Authors, as Agent for the Bernard Shaw Estate. First performed in 1895.

on the park. In this, the only sittingroom that can be spared from the children and the family meals, the parson, the REVEREND JAMES MAVOR MORELL, *does his work. He is sitting in a strong round backed revolving chair at the end of a long table, which stands across the window, so that he can cheer himself with a view of the park over his left shoulder. At the opposite end of the table, adjoining it, is a little table only half as wide as the other, with a typewriter on it. His typist is sitting at this machine, with her back to the window. The large table is littered with pamphlets, journals, letters, nests of drawers, an office diary, postage scales and the like. A spare chair for visitors having business with the parson is in the middle, turned to his end. Within reach of his hand is a stationery case, and a photograph in a frame. The wall behind him is fitted with bookshelves, on which an adept eye can measure the parson's casuistry and divinity by Maurice's Theological Essays and a complete set of Browning's poems, and the reformer's politics by a yellow backed Progress and Poverty, Fabian Essays, A Dream of John Ball, Marx's Capital, and half a dozen other literary landmarks in Socialism. Facing him on the other side of the room, near the typewriter, is the door. Further down opposite the fireplace, a bookcase stands on a cellaret, with a sofa near it. There is a generous fire burning; and the hearth, with a comfortable armchair and a black japanned flower-painted coal scuttle at one side, a miniature chair for children on the other, a varnished wooden mantelpiece, with neatly moulded shelves, tiny bits of mirror let into the panels, a travelling clock in a leather case (the inevitable wedding present), and on the wall above a large autotype of the chief figure in Titian's Assumption of the Virgin, is very inviting. Altogether the room is the room of a good housekeeper, vanquished, as far as the table is concerned, by an untidy man, but elsewhere mistress of the situation. The furniture, in its ornamental aspect, betrays the style of the advertised "drawingroom suite" of the pushing suburban furniture dealer; but there is nothing useless or pretentious in the room, money being too scarce in the house of an east end parson to be wasted on snobbish trimmings.*

The REVEREND JAMES MAVOR MORELL *is a Christian Socialist clergyman of the Church of England, and an active member of the Guild of St Matthew and the Christian Social Union. A vigorous, genial, popular man of forty, robust and goodlooking, full of energy, with pleasant, hearty, considerate manners, and a sound unaffected voice, which he uses with the clean athletic articulation of a practised orator, and with a wide range and perfect command of expression. He is a first rate clergyman, able to say what he likes to whom he likes, to lecture people without setting himself up against them, to impose his authority on them without humiliating them, and, on occasion, to interfere in their business without impertinence. His well-spring of enthusiasm and sympathetic emotion has never run dry for a moment: he still eats and sleeps heartily enough to win the daily battle between exhaustion and recuperation triumphantly. Withal, a great baby, pardonably vain of his powers and unconsciously pleased with himself. He has a healthy complexion: good forehead, with the brows somewhat blunt, and the eyes bright and eager, mouth resolute but not particularly well cut, and a substantial nose, with the mobile spreading nostrils of the dramatic orator, void, like all his features, of subtlety.*

The typist, MISS PROSERPINE GARNETT, is a brisk little woman of about 30, of the lower middle class, neatly but cheaply dressed in a black merino skirt and a blouse, notably pert and quick of speech, and not very civil in her manner, but sensitive and affectionate. She is clattering away busily at her machine whilst MORELL opens the last of his morning's letters. He realizes its contents with a comic groan of despair.

PROSERPINE.   Another lecture?

MORELL.   Yes. The Hoxton Freedom Group wants me to address them on Sunday morning (*he lays great emphasis on Sunday, this being the unreasonable part of the business*). What are they?

PROSERPINE.   Communist Anarchists, I think.

MORELL.   Just like Anarchists not to know that they cant have a parson on Sunday! Tell them to come to church if they want to hear me: it will do them good. Say I can come on Mondays and Thursdays only. Have you the diary there?

PROSERPINE (*taking up the diary*).   Yes.

MORELL.   Have I any lecture for next Monday?

PROSERPINE (*referring to diary*).   Tower Hamlets Radical Club.

MORELL.   Well, Thursday then?

PROSERPINE.   English Land Restoration League.

MORELL.   What next?

PROSERPINE.   Guild of St Matthew on Monday. Independent Labor Party, Greenwich Branch, on Thursday. Monday, Social-Democratic Federation, Mile End Branch. Thursday, first Confirmation class. (*Impatiently*) Oh, I'd better tell them you cant come. Theyre only half a dozen ignorant and conceited costermongers without five shillings between them.

MORELL (*amused*).   Ah; but you see theyre near relatives of mine.

PROSERPINE (*staring at him*).   Relatives of yours!

MORELL.   Yes: we have the same father—in Heaven.

PROSERPINE (*relieved*).   Oh, is that all?

MORELL (*with a sadness which is a luxury to a man whose voice expresses it so finely*).   Ah, you dont believe it. Everybody says it: nobody believes it: nobody. (*Briskly, getting back to business*) Well, well! Come, Miss Proserpine: cant you find a date for the costers? What about the 25th? That was vacant the day before yesterday.

PROSERPINE (*referring to diary*).   Engaged. The Fabian Society.

MORELL.   Bother the Fabian Society! Is the 28th gone too?

PROSERPINE.   City dinner. Youre invited to dine with the Founders' Company.

MORELL. Thatll do: I'll go to the Hoxton Group of Freedom instead. *(She enters the engagement in silence, with implacable disparagement of the Hoxton Anarchists in every line of her face.* MORELL *bursts open the cover of a copy of* The Church Reformer, *which has come by post, and glances through Mr Stewart Headlam's leader and the Guild of St Matthew news. These proceedings are presently enlivened by the appearance of* MORELL'S *curate, the* REVEREND ALEXANDER MILL, *a young gentleman gathered by* MORELL *from the nearest University settlement, whither he had come from Oxford to give the east end of London the benefit of his university training. He is a conceitedly well intentioned, enthusiastic, immature novice, with nothing positively unbearable about him except a habit of speaking with his lips carefully closed a full half inch from each corner for the sake of a finicking articulation and a set of university vowels, this being his chief means so far of bringing his Oxford refinement (as he calls his habits) to bear on Hackney vulgarity.* MORELL, *whom he has won over by a doglike devotion, looks up indulgently from* The Church Reformer, *and remarks)* Well, Lexy? Late again, as usual!

LEXY. I'm afraid so. I wish I could get up in the morning.

MORELL *(exulting in his own energy).* Ha! Ha! *(Whimsically)* Watch and pray, Lexy: watch and pray.

LEXY. I know. *(Rising wittily to the occasion)* But how can I watch and pray when I am asleep? Isnt that so, Miss Prossy? *(He makes for the warmth of the fire.)*

PROSERPINE *(sharply).* Miss Garnett, if you please.

LEXY. I beg your pardon. Miss Garnett.

PROSERPINE. Youve got to do all the work today.

LEXY *(on the hearth).* Why?

PROSERPINE. Never mind why. It will do you good to earn your supper before you eat it, for once in a way, as I do. Come! dont dawdle. You should have been off on your rounds half an hour ago.

LEXY *(perplexed).* Is she in earnest, Morell?

MORELL *(in the highest spirits: his eyes dancing).* Yes. I am going to dawdle today.

LEXY. You! You dont know how.

MORELL *(rising).* Ha! ha! Dont I? I'm going to have this morning all to myself. My wife's coming back: she's due here at 11.45.

LEXY *(surprised).* Coming back already! with the children? I thought they were to stay to the end of the month.

MORELL. So they are: she's only coming up for two days, to get some flannel things for Jimmy, and to see how we're getting on without her.

LEXY *(anxiously).* But, my dear Morell, if what Jimmy and Fluffy had was scarlatina, do you think it wise—

MORELL. Scarlatina! Rubbish! it was German measles. I brought it into the house myself from the Pycroft Street school. A parson is like a doctor, my boy: he must face infection as a soldier must face bullets. *(He claps* LEXY *manfully on the shoulders.*) Catch the measles if you can, Lexy: she'll nurse you; and what a piece of luck that will be for you! Eh?

LEXY (*smiling uneasily*). It's so hard to understand you about Mrs Morell—

MORELL (*tenderly*). Ah, my boy, get married: get married to a good woman; and then youll understand. Thats a foretaste of what will be best in the Kingdom of Heaven we are trying to establish on earth. That will cure you of dawdling. An honest man feels that he must pay Heaven for every hour of happiness with a good spell of hard unselfish work to make others happy. We have no more right to consume happiness without producing it than to consume wealth without producing it. Get a wife like my Candida; and youll always be in arrear with your repayment. (*He pats* LEXY *affectionately and moves to leave the room.*)

LEXY. Oh, wait a bit: I forgot. (MORELL *halts and turns with the door knob in his hand*) Your father-in-law is coming round to see you.

(MORELL, *surprised and not pleased, shuts the door again, with a complete change of manner.*)

MORELL. Mr. Burgess?

LEXY. Yes. I passed him in the park, arguing with somebody. He asked me to let you know that he was coming.

MORELL (*half incredulous*). But he hasnt called here for three years. Are you sure, Lexy? Youre not joking, are you?

LEXY (*earnestly*). No sir, really.

MORELL (*thoughtfully*). Hm! Time for him to take another look at Candida before she grows out of his knowledge. (*He resigns himself to the inevitable, and goes out.*)

(LEXY *looks after him with beaming worship.* MISS GARNETT, *not being able to shake* LEXY, *relieves her feelings by worrying the typewriter.*)

LEXY. What a good man! What a thorough loving soul he is! (*He takes* MORELL's *place at the table, making himself very comfortable as he takes out a cigaret.*)

PROSERPINE (*impatiently, pulling the letter she has been working at off the typewriter and folding it*). Oh, a man ought to be able to be fond of his wife without making a fool of himself about her.

LEXY (*shocked*). Oh, Miss Prossy!

PROSERPINE (*snatching at the stationery case for an envelope, in which she encloses the letter as she speaks*). Candida here, and Candida there, and Candida everywhere! (*She licks the envelope*) It's enough to drive anyone out of their *senses* (*thumping the envelope to make it stick*) to hear a woman raved about in that absurd manner merely because she's got good hair and a tolerable figure.

LEXY (*with reproachful gravity*). I think her extremely beautiful, Miss

Garnett. (*He takes the photograph up; looks at it; and adds, with even greater impressiveness*) extremely beautiful. How fine her eyes are!

PROSERPINE. Her eyes are not a bit better than mine: now! (*He puts down the photograph and stares austerely at her.*) And you know very well you think me dowdy and second rate enough.

LEXY (*rising majestically*). Heaven forbid that I should think of any of God's creatures in such a way! (*He moves stiffly away from her across the room to the neighborhood of the bookcase.*)

PROSERPINE (*sarcastically*). Thank you. Thats very nice and comforting.

LEXY (*saddened by her depravity.*) I had no idea you had any feeling against Mrs Morell.

PROSERPINE (*indignantly*). I have no feeling against her. She's very nice, very good-hearted: I'm very fond of her, and can appreciate her real qualities far better than any man can. (*He shakes his head sadly. She rises and comes at him with intense pepperiness*) You dont believe me? You think I'm jealous? Oh, what a knowledge of the human heart you have, Mr Lexy Mill! How well you know the weaknesses of Woman, dont you? It must be so nice to be a man and have a fine penetrating intellect instead of mere emotions like us, and to know that the reason we dont share your amorous delusions is that we're all jealous of one another! (*She abandons him with a toss of her shoulders, and crosses to the fire to warm her hands.*)

LEXY. Ah, if you women only had the same clue to Man's strength that you have to his weakness, Miss Prossy, there would be no Woman Question.

PROSERPINE (*over her shoulder, as she stoops, holding her hands to the blaze*). Where did you hear Morell say that? You didnt invent it yourself: youre not clever enough.

LEXY. Thats quite true. I am not ashamed of owing him that, as I owe him so many other spiritual truths. He said it at the annual conference of the Women's Liberal Federation. Allow me to add that though they didnt appreciate it, I, a mere man, did. (*He turns to the bookcase again, hoping that this may leave her crushed.*)

PROSERPINE (*putting her hair straight at a panel of mirror in the mantel-piece*). Well, when you talk to me, give me your own ideas, such as they are, and not his. You never cut a poorer figure than when you are trying to imitate him.

LEXY (*stung*). I try to follow his example, not to imitate him.

PROSERPINE (*coming at him again on her way back to her work*). Yes, you do: you *imitate* him. Why do you tuck your umbrella under your left arm instead of carrying it in your hand like anyone else? Why do you walk with your chin stuck out before you, hurrying along with that eager look in your eyes? you! who never get up before half past nine in the morning. Why do you say "knoaledge" in church, though you always say "knolledge" in private conversation! Bah! do you think I dont know? (*She goes back to the typewriter.*) Here! come and set about your work: weve wasted enough time for one morning. Here's copy of the diary for today. (*She hands him a memorandum.*)

LEXY (*deeply offended*).   Thank you.

(*He takes it and stands at the table with his back to her, reading it. She begins to transcribe her shorthand notes on the typewriter without troubling herself about his feelings*).

(*The door opens; and MR BURGESS enters unannounced. He is a man of sixty, made coarse and sordid by the compulsory selfishness of petty commerce, and later on softened into sluggish bumptiousness by overfeeding and commercial success. A vulgar ignorant guzzling man, offensive and contemptuous to people whose labor is cheap, respectful to wealth and rank, and quite sincere and without rancor or envy in both attitudes. The world has offered him no decently paid work except that of a sweater; and he has become, in consequence, somewhat hoggish. But he has no suspicion of this himself, and honestly regards his commercial prosperity as the inevitable and socially wholesome triumph of the ability, industry, shrewdness, and experience in business of a man who in private is easygoing, affectionate, and humorously convivial to a fault. Corporeally he is podgy, with a snoutish nose in the centre of a flat square face, a dust colored beard with a patch of grey in the centre under his chin, and small watery blue eyes with a plaintively sentimental expression, which he transfers easily to his voice by his habit of pompously intoning his sentences.*)

BURGESS (*stopping on the threshold, and looking round*).   They told me Mr Morell was here.

PROSERPINE (*rising*).   I'll fetch him for you.

BURGESS (*staring disappointedly at her*).   Youre not the same young lady as hused to typewrite for him?

PROSERPINE.   No.

BURGESS (*grumbling on his way to the hearthrug*).   No: she was young-er. (*Miss GARNETT stares at him; then goes out, slamming the door.*) Startin on your rounds, Mr Mill?

LEXY (*folding his memorandum and pocketing it*).   Yes: I must be off presently.

BURGESS (*momentously*).   Dont let me detain you, Mr. Mill. What I come about is *private* between me and Mr Morell.

LEXY (*huffily*).   I have no intention of intruding, I am sure, Mr Burgess. *Good* morning.

BURGESS (*patronizingly*).   Oh, good morning to you.

(*MORELL returns as LEXY is making for the door.*)

MORELL (*to LEXY*).   Off to work?

LEXY. Yes, sir.

MORELL. Take my silk handkerchief and wrap your throat up. Theres a cold wind. Away with you.

(LEXY, *more than consoled for* BURGESS's *rudeness, brightens up and goes out.*)

BURGESS. Spoilin your korates as usu'l, James. Good mornin. When I pay a man, an' 'is livin depens on me, I keep him in 'is place.

MORELL (*rather shortly*). I always keep my curates in their places as my helpers and comrades. If you get as much work out of your clerks and warehousemen as I do out of my curates, you must be getting rich pretty fast. Will you take your old chair. (*He points with curt authority to the armchair beside the fireplace; then takes the spare chair from the table and sits down at an unfamiliar distance from his visitor.*)

BURGESS (*without moving*). Just the same as hever, James!

MORELL. When you last called—it was about three years ago, I think —you said the same thing a little more frankly. Your exact words then were "Just as big a fool as ever, James!"

BURGESS (*soothingly*). Well, praps I did; but (*with conciliatory cheerfulness*) I meant no hoffence by it. A clorgyman is privileged to be a bit of a fool, you know: it's ony becomin in 'is profession that he should. Anyhow, I come here, not to rake up hold differences, but to let bygones be bygones. (*Suddenly becoming very solemn, and approaching* MORELL) James: three years ago, you done me a hill turn. You done me hout of a contrac; an when I gev you arsh words in my natral disappointment, you turned my daughrter again me. Well, Ive come to hact the part of a Kerischin. (*Offering his hand*) I forgive you, James.

MORELL (*starting up*). Confound your impudence!

BURGESS (*retreating, with almost lachrymose deprecation of this treatment*). Is that becomin language for a clorgyman, James? And you so particlar, too!

MORELL (*hotly*). No, sir: it is not becoming language for a clergyman. I used the wrong word. I should have said damn your impudence: thats what St Paul or any honest priest would have said to you. Do you think I have forgotten that tender of yours for the contract to supply clothing to the workhouse?

BURGESS (*in a paroxysm of public spirit*). I hacted in the hinterest of the ratepayers, James. It was the lowest tender: you carnt deny that.

MORELL. Yes, the lowest, because you paid worse wages than any other employer—starvation wages—aye, worse than starvation wages—to the women who made the clothing. Your wages would have driven them to the streets to keep body and soul together. (*Getting angrier and angrier*) Those women were my parishioners. I shamed the Guardians out of accepting your tender: I shamed the ratepayers out of letting them do it: I shamed everybody but you. (*Boiling over*) How dare you, sir, come here and offer to forgive me, and talk about your daughter, and—

BURGESS. Heasy, James! heasy! heasy! Dont git hinto a fluster about nothink. Ive howned I was wrong.

MORELL. Have you? I didnt hear you.

BURGESS. Of course I did. I hown it now. Come: I harsk your pardon for the letter I wrote you. Is that enough?

MORELL (*snapping his fingers*). Thats nothing. Have you raised the wages?

BURGESS (*triumphantly*). Yes.

MORELL. What!

BURGESS (*unctuously*). Ive turned a moddle hemployer. I dont hemploy no women now: theyre all sacked; and the work is done by machinery. Not a man 'as less than sixpence a *hour*; and the skilled ands gits the Trade Union rate. (*Proudly*) What ave you to say to me now?

MORELL (*overwhelmed*). Is it possible! Well, theres more joy in heaven over one sinner that repenteth!—(*Going to* BURGESS *with an explosion of apologetic cordiality*) My dear Burgess: how splendid of you! I most heartily beg your pardon for my hard thoughts. (*Grasping his hand*) And now, dont you feel the better for the change? Come! confess! youre happier. You look happier.

BURGESS (*ruefully*). Well, praps I do. I spose I must, since you notice it. At all events, I git my contrax assepted by the County Council. (*Savagely*) They dussent ave no-think to do with me unless I paid fair wages: curse em for a parcel o meddlin fools!

MORELL (*dropping his hand, utterly discouraged*). So that was why you raised the wages! (*He sits down moodily.*)

BURGESS (*severely, in spreading, mounting tones*). Woy helse should I do it? What does it lead to but drink and huppishness in workin men? (*He seats himself magisterially in the easy chair.*) It's hall very well for you, James: it gits you hinto the papers and makes a great man of you; but you never think of the arm you do, puttin money into the pockets of workin men that they dunno ow to spend, and takin it from people that might be makin a good huse on it.

MORELL (*with a heavy sigh, speaking with cold politeness*). What is your business with me this morning? I shall not pretend to believe that you are here merely out of family sentiment.

BURGESS (*obstinately*). Yes I ham: just family sentiment and nothink helse.

MORELL (*with weary calm*). I dont believe you.

BURGESS (*rising threateningly*). Dont say that to me again, James Mavor Morell.

MORELL (*unmoved*). I'll say it just as often as may be necessary to convince you that it's true. I dont believe you.

BURGESS (*collapsing into an abyss of wounded feeling*). Oh, well, if voure detormined to be hunfriendly, I spose I'd better go. (*He moves reluctantly towards the door.* MORELL *makes no sign. He lingers.*) I didnt hexpect to find a hunforgivin spirit in you, James. (MORELL *still not responding, he takes a few more reluctant steps doorwards. Then he comes back, whining.*) We huseter git on well enough, spite of our different hopinions. Woy are you so changed to me? I give you my word I come here in peeorr [pure] frenliness, not wishin to be hon bad terms with my hown daughrter's usban. Come, James: be a Kerischin, and shake ands. (*He puts his hand sentimentally on* MORELL's *shoulder.*)

MORELL (*looking up at him thoughtfully*). Look here, Burgess. Do you want to be as welcome here as you were before you lost that contract?

BURGESS. I do, James. I do—honest.

MORELL. Then why dont you behave as you did then?

BURGESS (*cautiously removing his hand*). Ow d'y' mean?

MORELL. I'll tell you. You thought me a young fool then.

BURGESS (*coaxingly*). No I didnt, James. I—

MORELL (*cutting him short*). Yes, you did. And I thought you an old scoundrel.

BURGESS (*most vehemently deprecating this gross self-accusation on* MORELL's *part*). No you didnt, James. Now you do yourself a hinjustice.

MORELL. Yes I did. Well, that did not prevent our getting on very well together. God made you what I call a scoundrel as He made me what you call a fool. (*The effect of this observation on* BURGESS *is to remove the keystone of his moral arch. He becomes bodily weak, and, with his eyes fixed on* MORELL *in a helpless stare, puts out his hand apprehensively to balance himself, as if the floor had suddenly sloped under him.* MORELL *proceeds, in the same tone of quiet conviction*) It was not for me to quarrel with His handiwork in the one case more than in the other. So long as you come here honestly as a self-respecting, thorough, convinced scoundrel, justifying your scoundrelism and proud of it, you are welcome. But (*and now* MORELL's *tone becomes formidable; and he rises and strikes the back of the chair for greater emphasis*) I wont have you here snivelling about being a model employer and a converted man when youre only an apostate with your coat turned for the sake of a County Council contract. (*He nods at him to enforce the point; then goes to the hearth-rug, where he takes up a comfortably commanding position with his back to the fire, and continues*) No: I like a man to be true to himself, even in wickedness. Come now: either take your hat and go; or else sit down and give me a good scoundrelly reason for wanting to be friends with me. (BURGESS, *whose emotions have subsided sufficiently to be expressed by a dazed grin, is relieved by this concrete proposition. He ponders it for a moment, and then, slowly and very modestly, sits down in the chair* MORELL *has just left.*) Thats right. Now out with it.

BURGESS (*chuckling in spite of himself*). Well, you orr a queer bird,

James, and no mistake. But (*almost enthusiastically*) one carnt elp likin you: besides, as I said afore, of course one dont take hall a clorgyman says seriously, or the world couldnt go on. Could it now? (*He composes himself for graver discourse, and, turning his eyes on* MORELL, *proceeds with dull seriousness*) Well, I dont mind tellin you, since it's your wish we should be free with one another, that I did think you a bit of a fool once; but I'm beginnin to think that praps I was be'ind the times a bit.

MORELL (*exultant*). Aha! Youre finding that out at last, are you?

BURGESS (*portentously*). Yes: times 'as changed mor'n I could a believed. Five yorr [year] ago, no sensible man would a thought o takin hup with your hidears. I hused to wonder you was let preach at all. Why, I know a clorgyman what 'as bin kep hout of his job for yorrs by the Bishop o London, although the pore feller's not a bit more religious than you are. But today, if hennyone was to horffer to bet me a thousan pound that youll hend by bein a bishop yourself, I dussent take the bet. (*Very impressively*) You and your crew are getting hinfluential: I can see that. Theyll ave to give you somethink someday, if it's honly to stop your mouth. You ad the right instinc arter all, James: the line you took is the payin line in the long run for a man o your sort.

MORELL (*offering his hand with thorough decision*). Shake hands, Burgess. Now youre talking honestly. I dont think theyll make me a bishop; but if they do, I'll introduce you to the biggest jobbers I can get to come to my dinner parties.

BURGESS (*who has risen with a sheepish grin and accepted the hand of friendship*). You will ave your joke, James. Our quarrel's made up now, ain it?

A WOMAN'S VOICE. Say yes, James.

(*Startled, they turn quickly and find that* CANDIDA *has just come in, and is looking at them with an amused maternal indulgence which is her characteristic expression. She is a woman of 33, well built, well nourished, likely, one guesses, to become matronly later on, but now quite at her best, with the double charm of youth and motherhood. Her ways are those of a woman who has found that she can always manage people by engaging their affection, and who does so frankly and instinctively without the smallest scruple. So far, she is like any other pretty woman who is just clever enough to make the most of her sexual attractions for trivially selfish ends; but* CANDIDA'S *serene brow, courageous eyes, and well set mouth and chin signify largeness of mind and dignity of character to ennoble her cunning in the affections. A wise-hearted observer, looking at her, would at once guess that whoever had placed the Virgin of the Assumption over her hearth did so because he fancied some spiritual resemblance between them, and yet would not suspect either her husband or herself of any such idea, or indeed of any concern with the art of Titian.*)

(*Just now she is in bonnet and mantle, carrying a strapped rug with her umbrella stuck through it, a handbag, and a supply of illustrated papers.*)

MORELL (*shocked at his remissness*).   Candida! Why—(*he looks at his watch, and is horrified to find it so late*). My darling! (*Hurrying to her and seizing the rug strap, pouring forth his remorseful regrets all the time*) I intended to meet you at the train. I let the time slip. (*Flinging the rug on the sofa*) I was so engrossed by—(*returning to her*)—I forgot—oh! (*he embraces her with penitent emotion*).

BURGESS (*a little shamefaced and doubtful of his reception*).   How orr you, Candy? (*She, still in* MORELL's *arms, offers him her cheek, which he kisses.*) James and me is come to a nunnerstannin. A honorable unnerstannin. Ain we, James?

MORELL (*impetuously*).   Oh bother your understanding! youve kept me late for Candida. (*With compassionate fervor*) My poor love: how did you manage about the luggage? How—

CANDIDA (*stopping him and disengaging herself*).   There! there! there! I wasnt alone. Eugene has been down with us; and we travelled together.

MORELL (*pleased*).   Eugene!

CANDIDA.   Yes: he's struggling with my luggage, poor boy. Go out, dear, at once; or he'll pay for the cab; and I dont want that. (MORELL *hurries out.* CANDIDA *puts down her handbag; then takes off her mantle and bonnet and puts them on the sofa with the rug, chatting meanwhile.*) Well, papa: how are you getting on at home?

BURGESS.   The ouse aint worth livin in since you left it, Candy. I wish youd come round and give the gurl a talkin to. Who's this Eugene thats come with you?

CANDIDA.   Oh, Eugene's one of James discoveries. He found him sleeping on the Embankment last June. Havnt you noticed our new picture (*pointing to the Virgin*)? He gave us that.

BURGESS (*incredulously*).   Garn! D'you mean to tell me—your hown father—that cab touts or such like, orf the Embankment, buys pictures like that? (*Severely*) Dont deceive me, Candy: it's a 'Igh Church picture; and James chose it hisself.

CANDIDA.   Guess again. Eugene isnt a cab tout.

BURGESS.   Then what is he? (*Sarcastically*) A nobleman, I spose.

CANDIDA (*nodding delightedly*).   Yes. His uncle's a peer! A real live earl.

BURGESS (*not daring to believe such good news*).   No!

CANDIDA.   Yes. He had a seven day bill for £55 in his pocket when James found him on the Embankment. He thought he couldnt get any money for it until the seven days were up; and he was too shy to ask for credit. Oh, he's a dear boy! We are very fond of him.

BURGESS (*pretending to belittle the aristocracy, but with his eyes gleam-*

ing). Hm! I thort you wouldnt git a hearl's nevvy visitin in Victawriar Pawrk unless he were a bit of a flat. (*Looking again at the picture*) Of course I dont old with that picture, Candy; but still it's a 'igh class fust rate work of ort: I can see that. Be sure you hintrodooce me to im, Candy. (*He looks at his watch anxiously*) I can ony stay about two minutes.

(MORELL *comes back with* EUGENE, *whom* BURGESS *contemplates moist-eyed with enthusiasm. He is a strange, shy youth of eighteen, slight, effeminate, with a delicate childish voice, and a hunted tormented expression and shrinking manner that shew the painful sensitiveness of very swift and acute apprehensiveness in youth, before the character has grown to its full strength. Miserably irresolute, he does not know where to stand or what to do. He is afraid of* BURGESS, *and would run away into solitude if he dared; but the very intensity with which he feels a perfectly commonplace position comes from excessive nervous force; and his nostrils, mouth, and eyes betray a fiercely petulant wilfulness, as to the bent of which his brow, already lined with pity, is reassuring. He is so uncommon as to be almost unearthly; and to prosaic people there is something noxious in this unearthliness, just as to poetic people there is something angelic in it. His dress is anarchic. He wears an old blue serge jacket, unbuttoned, over a woollen lawn tennis shirt, with a silk handkerchief for a cravat, trousers matching the jacket, and brown canvas shoes. In these garments he has apparently lain in the heather and waded through the waters; and there is no evidence of his having ever brushed them.*

(*As he catches sight of a stranger on entering, he stops, and edges along the wall on the opposite side of the room.*)

MORELL (*as he enters*).   Come along: you can spare us quarter of an hour at all events. This is my father-in-law. Mr Burgess—Mr Marchbanks.

MARCHBANKS (*nervously backing against the bookcase*).   Glad to meet you, sir.

BURGESS (*crossing to him with great heartiness, whilst* MORELL *joins* CANDIDA *at the fire*).   Glad to meet you, I'm shore, Mr Morchbanks. (*Forcing him to shake hands*) Ow do you find yoreself this weather? Ope you aint lettin James put no foolish ideas into your ed?

MARCHBANKS.   Foolish ideas? Oh, you mean Socialism? No.

BURGESS.   Thats right. (*Again looking at his watch*) Well, I must go now: there's no elp for it. Yore not comin my way, orr you, Mr Morchbanks?

MARCHBANKS.   Which way is that?

BURGESS.   Victawriar Pawrk Station. Theres a city train at 12.25.

MORELL.   Nonsense. Eugene will stay to lunch with us, I expect.

MARCHBANKS (*anxiously excusing himself*).   No—I—I—

BURGESS.   Well, well, I shornt press you: I bet youd rather lunch with Candy. Some night, I ope, youll come and dine with me at my club, the Freeman Founders in Nortn Folgit. Come: say you will!

MARCHBANKS. Thank you, Mr. Burgess. Where is Norton? Down in Surrey, isnt it?

(BURGESS, *inexpressibly tickled, begins to splutter with laughter.*)

CANDIDA (*coming to the rescue*). Youll lose your train, papa, if you dont go at once. Come back in the afternoon and tell Mr Marchbanks where to find the club.

BURGESS (*roaring with glee*). Down in Surrey! Har, har! thats not a bad one. Well, I never met a man as didnt know Nortn Folgit afore. (*Abashed at his own noisiness*) Goodbye, Mr Morchbanks: I know yore too ighbred to take my pleasantry in bad part. (*He again offers his hand.*)

MARCHBANKS (*taking it with a nervous jerk*). Not at all.

BURGESS. Bye, bye, Candy. I'll look in again later on. So long, James.

MORELL. Must you go?

BURGESS. Dont stir. (*He goes out with unabated heartiness.*)

MORELL. Oh, I'll see you off. (*He follows him.*)

(EUGENE *stares after them apprehensively, holding his breath until* BURGESS *disappears.*)

CANDIDA (*laughing*). Well, Eugene? (*He turns with a start, and comes eagerly towards her, but stops irresolutely as he meets her amused look.*) What do you think of my father?

MARCHBANKS. I—I hardly know him yet. He seems to be a very nice old gentleman.

CANDIDA (*with gentle irony*). And youll go to the Freeman Founders to dine with him, wont you?

MARCHBANKS (*miserably, taking it quite seriously*). Yes, if it will please you.

CANDIDA (*touched*). Do you know, you are a very nice boy, Eugene, with all your queerness. If you had laughed at my father I shouldnt have minded; but I like you ever so much better for being nice to him.

MARCHBANKS. Ought I to have laughed? I noticed that he said something funny; but I am so ill at ease with strangers; and I never can see a joke. I'm very sorry. (*He sits down on the sofa, his elbows on his knees and his temples between his fists, with an expression of hopeless suffering.*)

CANDIDA (*bustling him goodnaturedly*). Oh come! You great baby, you! You are worse than usual this morning. Why were you so melancholy as we came along in the cab?

MARCHBANKS. Oh, that was nothing. I was wondering how much I ought to give the cabman. I know it's utterly silly; but you dont know how dreadful such things are to me—how I shrink from having to deal with strange people. (*Quickly and reassuringly*) But it's all right. He beamed all over and touched his hat when Morell gave him two shillings. I was on the point of offering him ten.

(MORELL *comes back with a few letters and newspapers which have come by the midday post.*)

CANDIDA. Oh, James dear, he was going to give the cabman ten shillings! ten shillings for a three minutes drive! Oh dear!

MORELL (*at the table, glancing through the letters*). Never mind her, Marchbanks. The overpaying instinct is a generous one: better than the underpaying instinct, and not so common.

MARCHBANKS (*relapsing into dejection*). No: cowardice, incompetence. Mrs Morell's quite right.

CANDIDA. Of course she is. (*She takes up her hand-bag*) And now I must leave you to James for the present. I suppose you are too much of a poet to know the state a woman finds her house in when she's been away for three weeks. Give me my rug. (EUGENE *takes the strapped rug from the couch, and gives it to her. She takes it in her left hand, having the bag in her right.*) Now hang my cloak across my arm. (*He obeys.*) Now my hat. (*He puts it into the hand which has the bag.*) Now open the door for me. (*He hurries before her and opens the door.*) Thanks. (*She goes out; and* MARCHBANKS *shuts the door.*)

MORELL (*still busy at the table*). Youll stay to lunch, Marchbanks, of course.

MARCHBANKS (*scared*). I mustnt. (*He glances quickly at* MORELL, *but at once avoids his frank look, and adds, with obvious disingenuousness*) I mean I cant.

MORELL. You mean you wont.

MARCHBANKS (*earnestly*). No: I should like to, indeed. Thank you very much. But—but—

MORELL. But—but—but—but—Bosh! If youd like to stay, stay. If youre shy, go and take a turn in the park and write poetry until half past one; and then come in and have a good feed.

MARCHBANKS. Thank you, I should like that very much. But I really mustnt. The truth is, Mrs Morell told me not to. She said she didnt think youd ask me to stay to lunch, but that I was to remember, if you did, that you didnt really want me to. (*Plaintively*) She said I'd understand; but I dont. Please dont tell her I told you.

MORELL (*drolly*). Oh, is that all? Wont my suggestion that you should take a turn in the park meet the difficulty?

MARCHBANKS. How?

MORELL (*exploding good-humoredly*). Why, you duffer—(*But this boisterousness jars himself as well as* EUGENE. *He checks himself*) No: I wont put it in that way. (*He comes to* EUGENE *with affectionate seriousness*) My dear lad: in a happy marriage like ours, there is something very sacred in the return of the wife to her home. (MARCHBANKS *looks quickly at him, half anticipating his meaning.*) An old friend or a truly noble and sympathetic soul is not in the way on such occasions; but a chance visitor is. (*The hunted horror-stricken expression comes out with sudden vividness in* EUGENE's *face as he understands.* MORELL, *occupied with his own thoughts, goes on without noticing this*) Candida thought I would rather not have you here; but she was wrong. I'm very fond of you, my boy; and I should like you to see for yourself what a happy thing it is to be married as I am.

MARCHBANKS. Happy! Your marriage! You think that! You believe that!

MORELL (*buoyantly*). I know it, my lad. Larochefoucauld said that there are convenient marriages but no delightful ones. You dont know the comfort of seeing through and through a thundering liar and rotten cynic like that fellow. Ha! ha! Now, off with you to the park, and write your poem. Half past one, sharp, mind: we never wait for anybody.

MARCHBANKS (*wildly*). No: stop: you shant. I'll force it into the light.

MORELL (*puzzled*). Eh? Force what?

MARCHBANKS. I must speak to you. There is something that must be settled between us.

MORELL (*with a whimsical glance at his watch*). Now?

MARCHBANKS (*passionately*). Now. Before you leave this room. (*He retreats a few steps, and stands as if to bar* MORELL's *way to the door.*)

MORELL (*without moving, and gravely, perceiving now that there is something serious the matter*). I'm not going to leave it, my dear boy: I thought you were. (EUGENE, *baffled by his firm tone, turns his back on him, writhing with anger.* MORELL *goes to him and puts his hand on his shoulder strongly and kindly, disregarding his attempt to shake it off.*) Come: sit down quietly; and tell me what it is. And remember: we are friends, and need not fear that either of us will be anything but patient and kind to the other, whatever we may have to say.

MARCHBANKS (*twisting himself round on him*). Oh, I am not forgetting myself: I am only (*covering his face desperately with his hands*) full of horror. (*Then, dropping his hands, and thrusting his face forward fiercely at* MORELL, *he goes on threateningly*) You shall see whether this is a time for patience and kindness. (MORELL, *firm as a rock, looks indulgently at him.*) Dont look at me in that self-complacent way. You think yourself stronger than I am; but I shall stagger you if you have a heart in your breast.

MORELL (*powerfully confident*). Stagger me, my boy. Out with it.

MARCHBANKS. First—

MORELL. First?

MARCHBANKS. I love your wife.

(MORELL *recoils, and, after staring at him for a moment in utter amazement, bursts into uncontrollable laughter.* EUGENE *is taken aback, but not disconcerted; and he soon becomes indignant and contemptuous.*)

MORELL (*sitting down to have his laugh out*). Why, my dear child, of course you do. Everybody loves her: they cant help it. I like it. But (*looking up jocosely at him*) I say, Eugene: do you think yours is a case to be talked about? Youre under twenty: she's over thirty. Doesnt it look rather too like a case of calf love?

MARCHBANKS (*vehemently*). You dare say that of her! You think that way of the love she inspires! It is an insult to her!

MORELL (*rising quickly, in an altered tone*). To her! Eugene: take care. I have been patient. I hope to remain patient. But there are some things I wont allow. Dont force me to shew you the indulgence I should shew to a child. Be a man.

MARCHBANKS (*with a gesture as if sweeping something behind him*). Oh, let us put aside all that cant. It horrifies me when I think of the doses of it she has had to endure in all the weary years during which you have selfishly and blindly sacrificed her to minister to your self-sufficiency: you! (*turning on him*) who have not one thought—one sense—in common with her.

MORELL (*philosophically*). She seems to bear it pretty well. (*Looking him straight in the face*) Eugene, my boy: you are making a fool of yourself: a very great fool of yourself. Theres a piece of wholesome plain speaking for you. (*He knocks in the lesson with a nod in his old way, and posts himself on the hearth-rug, holding his hands behind him to warm them.*)

MARCHBANKS. Oh, do you think I dont know all that? Do you think that the things people make fools of themselves about are any less real and true than the things they behave sensibly about? (*MORELL's gaze wavers for the first time. He forgets to warm his hands, and stands listening, startled and thoughtful.*) They are more true: they are the only things that are true. You are very calm and sensible and moderate with me because you can see that I am a fool about your wife; just as no doubt that old man who was here just now is very wise over your Socialism, because he sees that you are a fool about it. (*MORELL's perplexity deepens markedly. EUGENE follows up his advantage, plying him fiercely with questions*) Does that prove you wrong? Does your complacent superiority to me prove that *I* am wrong?

MORELL. Marchbanks: some devil is putting these words into your mouth. It is easy—terribly easy—to shake a man's faith in himself. To take advantage of that to break a man's spirit is devil's work. Take care of what you are doing. Take care.

MARCHBANKS (*ruthlessly*). I know. I'm doing it on purpose. I told you I should stagger you.

(*They confront one another threateningly for a moment. Then* MORELL *recovers his dignity.*)

MORELL (*with noble tenderness*). Eugene: listen to me. Some day, I hope and trust, you will be a happy man like me. (*EUGENE chafes intolerantly, repudiating the worth of his happiness.* MORELL, *deeply insulted, con-*

trols himself with fine forbearance, and continues steadily, with great artistic beauty of delivery) You will be married; and you will be working with all your might and valor to make every spot on earth as happy as your own home. You will be one of the makers of the Kingdom of Heaven on earth; and—who knows—you may be a master builder where I am only a humble journeyman; for dont think, my boy, that I cannot see in you, young as you are, promise of higher powers than I can ever pretend to. I well know that it is in the poet that the holy spirit of man—the god within him—is most god like. It should make you tremble to think of that—to think that the heavy burthen and great gift of a poet may be laid upon you.

MARCHBANKS (*unimpressed and remorseless, his boyish crudity of assertion telling sharply against* MORELL's *oratory*). It does not make me tremble. It is the want of it in others that makes me tremble.

MORELL (*redoubling his force of style under the stimulus of his genuine feeling and* EUGENE's *obduracy*). Then help to kindle it in them—in me— not to extinguish it. In the future, when you are as happy as I am, I will be your true brother in the faith. I will help you to believe that God has given us a world that nothing but our own folly keeps from being a paradise. I will help you to believe that every stroke of your work is sowing happiness for the great harvest that all—even the humblest— shall one day reap. And last, but trust me, not least, I will help you to believe that your wife loves you and is happy in her home. We need such help, Marchbanks: we need it greatly and always. There are so many things to make us doubt, if once we let our understanding be troubled. Even at home, we sit as if in camp, encompassed by a hostile army of doubts. Will you play the traitor and let them in on me?

MARCHBANKS (*looking round wildly*). Is it like this for her here always? A woman, with a great soul, craving for reality, truth, freedom; and being fed on metaphors, sermons, stale perorations, mere rhetoric. Do you think a woman's soul can live on your talent for preaching?

MORELL (*stung*). Marchbanks: you make it hard for me to control myself. My talent is like yours insofar as it has any real worth at all. It is the gift of finding words for divine truth.

MARCHBANKS (*impetuously*). It's the gift of the gab, nothing more and nothing less. What has your knack of fine talking to do with the truth, any more than playing the organ has? Ive never been in your church; but Ive been to your political meetings; and Ive seen you do whats called rousing the meeting to enthusiasm: that is, you excited them until they behaved exactly as if they were drunk. And their wives looked on and saw what fools they were. Oh, it's an old story: youll find it in the Bible. I imagine King David, in his fits of enthusiasm, was very like you. (*Stabbing him with the words*) "But his wife despised him in her heart."

MORELL (*wrathfully*). Leave my house. Do you hear? (*He advances on him threateningly.*)

MARCHBANKS (*shrinking back against the couch*). Let me alone. Dont touch me. (MORELL *grasps him powerfully by the lapel of his coat: he cowers down on the sofa and screams passionately*) Stop, Morell: if you strike me, I'll kill myself: I wont bear it. (*Almost in hysterics*) Let me go. Take your hand away.

MORELL (*with slow emphatic scorn*). You little snivelling cowardly whelp. (*He releases him*) Go, before you frighten yourself into a fit.

MARCHBANKS (*on the sofa, gasping, but relieved by the withdrawal of* MORELL's *hand*). I'm not afraid of you: it's you who are afraid of me.

MORELL (*quietly, as he stands over him*). It looks like it, doesnt it?

MARCHBANKS (*with petulant vehemence*). Yes it does. (MORELL *turns away contemptuously.* EUGENE *scrambles to his feet and follows him*) You think because I shrink from being brutally handled—because (*with tears in his voice*) I can do nothing but cry with rage when I am met with violence—because I cant lift a heavy trunk down from the top of a cab like you—because I cant fight you for your wife as a drunken navvy would: all that makes you think I'm afraid of you. But youre wrong. If I havnt got what you call British pluck, I havnt British cowardice either: I'm not afraid of a clergyman's ideas. I'll fight your ideas. I'll rescue her from her slavery to them. I'll pit my own ideas against them. You are driving me out of the house because you darent let her choose between your ideas and mine. You are afraid to let me see her again. (MORELL, *angered, turns suddenly on him. He flies to the door in involuntary dread*) Let me alone, I say. I'm going.

MORELL (*with cold scorn*). Wait a moment: I am not going to touch you: dont be afraid. When my wife comes back she will want to know why you have gone. And when she finds that you are never going to cross our threshold again, she will want to have that explained too. Now I dont wish to distress her by telling her that you have behaved like a blackguard.

MARCHBANKS (*coming back with renewed vehemence*). You shall. You must. If you give any explanation but the true one, you are a liar and a coward. Tell her what I said; and how you were strong and manly, and shook me as a terrier shakes a rat; and how I shrank and was terrified; and how you called me a snivelling little whelp and put me out of the house. If you dont tell her, I will: I'll write it to her.

MORELL (*puzzled*). Why do you want her to know this?

MARCHBANKS (*with lyric rapture*). Because she will understand me, and know that I understand her. If you keep back one word of it from her —if you are not ready to lay the truth at her feet as I am—then you will know to the end of your days that she really belongs to me and not to you. Goodbye. (*Going.*)

MORELL (*terribly disquieted*). Stop: I will not tell her.

MARCHBANKS (*turning near the door*). Either the truth or a lie you must tell her, if I go.

MORELL (*temporizing*). Marchbanks: it is sometimes justifiable—

MARCHBANKS (*cutting him short*). I know: to lie. It will be useless. Goodbye, Mr. Clergyman.

(*As he turns finally to the door, it opens and* CANDIDA *enters in her housekeeping dress.*)

CANDIDA. Are you going, Eugene? (*Looking more observantly at him*) Well, dear me, just look at you, going out into the street in that state! You are a poet, certainly. Look at him, James! (*She takes him by the coat, and brings him forward, shewing him to* MORELL) Look at his collar! Look at his tie! look at his hair! One would think somebody had been throttling you. (EUGENE *instinctively tries to look round at* MORELL; *but she pulls him back*) Here! Stand still. (*She buttons his collar; ties his neckerchief in a bow; and arranges his hair.*) There! Now you look so nice that I think youd better stay to lunch after all, though I told you you mustnt. It will be ready in half an hour. (*She puts a final touch to the bow. He kisses her hand*) Dont be silly.

MARCHBANKS. I want to stay, of course; unless the reverend gentleman your husband has anything to advance to the contrary.

CANDIDA. Shall he stay, James, if he promises to be a good boy and help me to lay the table?

MORELL (*shortly*). Oh yes, certainly: he had better. (*He goes to the table and pretends to busy himself with his papers there.*)

MARCHBANKS (*offering his arm to* CANDIDA). Come and lay the table. (*She takes it. They go to the door together. As they pass out he adds*) I am the happiest of mortals.

MORELL. So was I—an hour ago.

ACT II

The same day later in the afternoon. The same room. The chair for visitors has been replaced at the table. MARCHBANKS, *alone and idle, is trying to find out how the typewriter works. Hearing someone at the door, he steals guiltily away to the window and pretends to be absorbed in the view.* MISS GARNETT, *carrying the notebook in which she takes down* MORELL's *letters in shorthand from his dictation, sits down at the typewriter and sets to work transcribing them, much too busy to notice* EUGENE. *When she begins the second line she stops and stares at the machine. Something wrong evidently.*

PROSERPINE. Bother! You've been meddling with my typewriter, Mr Marchbanks; and theres not the least use in your trying to look as if you hadnt.

MARCHBANKS (*timidly*). I'm very sorry, Miss Garnett. I only tried to make it write. (*Plaintively*) But it wouldnt.

PROSERPINE. Well, youve altered the spacing.

MARCHBANKS (*earnestly*). I assure you I didnt. I didnt indeed. I only turned a little wheel. It gave a sort of click.

PROSERPINE. Oh, now I understand. (*She restores the spacing, talking volubly all the time*) I suppose you thought it was a sort of barrel-organ. Nothing to do but turn the handle, and it would write a beautiful love letter for you straight off, eh?

MARCHBANKS (*seriously*). I suppose a machine could be made to write love letters. Theyre all the same, arnt they?

PROSERPINE (*somewhat indignantly: any such discussion, except by way of pleasantry, being outside her code of manners*) How do I know? Why do you ask me?

MARCHBANKS. I beg your pardon. I thought clever people—people who can do business and write letters and that sort of thing—always had to have love affairs to keep them from going mad.

PROSERPINE (*rising, outraged*). Mr Marchbanks! (*She looks severely at him, and marches majestically to the bookcase.*)

MARCHBANKS (*approaching her humbly*). I hope I havnt offended you. Perhaps I shouldnt have alluded to your love affairs.

PROSERPINE (*plucking a blue book from the shelf and turning sharply on him*). I havnt any love affairs. How dare you say such a thing? The idea! (*She tucks the book under her arm, and is flouncing back to her machine when he addresses her with awakened interest and sympathy.*)

MARCHBANKS. Really! Oh, then you are shy, like me.

PROSERPINE. Certainly I am not shy. What do you mean?

MARCHBANKS (*secretly*). You must be: that is the reason there are so few love affairs in the world. We all go about longing for love: it is the first need of our natures, the first prayer of our hearts; but we dare not utter our longing: we are too shy. (*Very earnestly*) Oh, Miss Garnett, what would you not give to be without fear, without shame—

PROSERPINE (*scandalized*). Well, upon my word!

MARCHBANKS (*with petulant impatience*). Ah, dont say those stupid things to me: they dont deceive me: what use are they? Why are you afraid to be your real self with me? I am just like you.

PROSERPINE. Like me! Pray are you flattering me or flattering yourself? I dont feel quite sure which. (*She again tries to get back to her work.*)

MARCHBANKS (*stopping her mysteriously*). Hush! I go about in search of love; and I find it in unmeasured stores in the bosoms of others. But when I try to ask for it, this horrible shyness strangles me; and I stand dumb, or worse than dumb, saying meaningless things: foolish lies. And I see the affection I am longing for given to dogs and cats and pet birds, because they come and ask it. (*Almost whispering*) It must be asked for: it is like a ghost: it cannot speak unless it is first spoken to. (*At his usual pitch, but with deep melancholy*) All the love in the world is longing to speak; only it dare not, because it is shy! shy! shy! That is the world's tragedy. (*With a deep sigh he sits in the visitors' chair and buries his face in his hands.*)

PROSERPINE (*amazed, but keeping her wits about her: her point of honor in encounters with strange young men*). Wicked people get over that shyness occasionally, dont they?

MARCHBANKS (*scrambling up almost fiercely*). Wicked people means people who have no love: therefore they have no shame. They have the power to ask love because they dont need it: they have the power to offer it because they have none to give. (*He collapses into his seat, and adds, mournfully*) But we, who *have* love, and long to mingle it with the love of others: we cannot utter a word. (*Timidly*) You find that, dont you?

PROSERPINE. Look here: if you dont stop talking like this, I'll leave the room, Mr Marchbanks: I really will. It's not proper.

(*She resumes her seat at the typewriter, opening the blue book and preparing to copy a passage from it.*)

MARCHBANKS (*hopelessly*). Nothing thats worth saying is proper. (*He rises, and wanders about the room in his lost way.*) I cant understand you, Miss Garnett. What am I to talk about?

PROSERPINE (*snubbing him*). Talk about indifferent things. Talk about the weather.

MARCHBANK. Would you talk about indifferent things if a child were by, crying bitterly with hunger?

PROSERPINE. I suppose not.

MARCHBANKS. Well: *I* cant talk about indifferent things with my heart crying out bitterly in its hunger.

PROSERPINE. Then hold your tongue.

MARCHBANKS. Yes: that is what it always comes to. We hold our tongues. Does that stop the cry of your heart? for it does cry: doesnt it? It must, if you have a heart.

PROSERPINE (*suddenly rising with her hand pressed on her heart*). Oh, it's no use trying to work while you talk like that. (*She leaves her little table and sits on the sofa. Her feelings are keenly stirred*) It's no business of yours whether my heart cries or not; but I have a mind to tell you, for all that.

MARCHBANKS. You neednt. I know already that it must.

PROSERPINE. But mind! if you ever say I said so, I'll deny it.

MARCHBANKS (*compassionately*). Yes, I know. And so you havnt the courage to tell him?

PROSERPINE (*bouncing up*). Him! Who?

MARCHBANKS. Whoever he is. The man you love. It might be anybody. The curate, Mr Mill, perhaps.

PROSERPINE (*with disdain*). Mr. Mill!!! A fine man to break my heart about, indeed! I'd rather have you than Mr Mill.

Marchbanks (*recoiling*). No, really: I'm very sorry; but you mustnt think of that. I—

Proserpine (*testily, going to the fire-place and standing at it with her back to him*). Oh, dont be frightened: it's not you. It's not any one particular person.

Marchbanks. I know. You feel that you could love anybody that offered—

Proserpine (*turning, exasperated*). Anybody that offered! No, I do not. What do you take me for?

Marchbanks (*discouraged*). No use. You wont make me real answers: only those things that everybody says. (*He strays to the sofa and sits down disconsolately.*)

Proserpine (*nettled at what she takes to be a disparagement of her manners by an aristocrat*). Oh well, if you want original conversation, youd better go and talk to yourself.

Marchbanks. That is what all poets do: they talk to themselves but out loud; and the world overhears them. But it's horribly lonely not to hear someone else talk sometimes.

Proserpine. Wait until Mr Morell comes. He'll talk to you. (Marchbanks *shudders*) Oh, you neednt make wry faces over him: he can talk better than you. (*With temper*) He'd talk your little head off. (*She is going back angrily to her place, when he, suddenly enlightened, springs up and stops her.*)

Marchbanks. Ah! I understand now.

Proserpine (*reddening*). What do you understand?

Marchbanks. Your secret. Tell me: is it really and truly possible for a woman to love him?

Proserpine (*as if this were beyond all bounds*). Well!!

Marchbanks (*passionately*). No: answer me. I want to know: I *must* know. *I* can't understand it. I can see nothing in him but words, pious resolutions, what people call goodness. You cant love that.

Proserpine (*attempting to snub him by an air of cool propriety*). I simply dont know what youre talking about. I dont understand you.

Marchbanks (*vehemently*). You do. You lie.

Proserpine. Oh!

Marchbanks. You do understand; and you *know*. (*Determined to have an answer*) Is it possible for a woman to love him?

Proserpine (*looking him straight in the face*). Yes. (*He covers his face with his hands*) Whatever is the matter with you! (*He takes down his hands. Frightened at the tragic mask presented to her, she hurries past him at the utmost possible distance, keeping her eyes on his face until he turns from her and goes to the child's chair beside the hearth, where he sits in the deepest dejection. As she approaches the door, it opens and* Burgess *enters. Seeing him, she ejaculates*) Praise heaven! here's somebody (*and feels safe enough to resume her place at her table. She puts a fresh sheet of paper into the typewriter as* BURGESS *crosses to* EUGENE).

BURGESS (*bent on taking care of the distinguished visitor*). Well: so this is the way they leave you to yoreself, Mr Morchbanks. Ive come to keep you company. (MARCHBANKS *looks up at him in consternation, which is quite lost on him.*) James is receivin a deppitation in the dinin room; and Candy is hupstairs heducating of a young stitcher gurl she's hinterested in. (*Condolingly*) You must find it lonesome here with no one but the typist to talk to. (*He pulls round the easy chair, and sits down.*)

PROSERPINE (*highly incensed*). He'll be all right now that he has the advantage of *your* polished conversation: thats one comfort, anyhow. (*She begins to typewrite with clattering asperity.*)

BURGESS (*amazed at her audacity*). Hi was not addressin myself to you, young woman, that I'm awerr of.

PROSERPINE. Did you ever see worse manners, Mr Marchbanks?

BURGESS (*with pompous severity*). Mr Morchbanks is a gentleman, and knows his place, which is more than some people do.

PROSERPINE (*fretfully*). It's well you and I are not ladies and gentlemen: I'd talk to you pretty straight if Mr Marchbanks wasnt here. (*She pulls the letter out of the machine so crossly that it tears.*) There! now I've spoiled this letter! have to be done all over again! Oh, I cant contain myself: silly old fathead!

BURGESS (*rising, breathless with indignation*). Ho! I'm a silly ole fat'ead, am I? Ho, indeed (*gasping*)! Hall right, my gurl! Hall right. You just wait till I tell that to yore hemployer. Youll see. I'll teach you: see if I dont.

PROSERPINE (*conscious of having gone too far*) I—

BURGESS (*cutting her short*). No: youve done it now. No huse a-talkin to me. I'll let you know who I am. (PROSERPINE *shifts her paper carriage with a defiant bang, and disdainfully goes on with her work.*) Dont you take no notice of her, Mr Morchbanks. She's beneath it. (*He loftily sits down again.*)

MARCHBANKS (*miserably nervous and disconcerted*). Hadnt we better change the subject? I—I dont think Miss Garnett meant anything.

PROSERPINE (*with intense conviction*). Oh, didn't I though, *just!*

BURGESS. I wouldnt demean myself to take notice on her.

(*An electric bell rings twice.*)

PROSERPINE (*gathering up her note-book and papers*). Thats for me. (*She hurries out.*)

BURGESS (*calling after her*). Oh, we can spare you. (*Somewhat relieved by the triumph of having the last word, and yet half inclined to try to improve on it, he looks after her for a moment; then subsides into his seat by* EUGENE, *and addresses him very confidentially*) Now we're alone, Mr Morchbanks, let me give you a friendly int that I wouldnt give to heverybody. Ow long ave you known my son-in-law James ere?

MARCHBANKS. I dont know. I never can remember dates. A few months, perhaps.

BURGESS. Ever notice hennythink queer about him?

MARCHBANKS. I dont think so.

BURGESS (*impressively*). No more you wouldnt. Thats the danger on it. Well, he's mad.

MARCHBANKS. Mad!

BURGESS. Mad as a Morch 'are. You take notice on him and youll see.

MARCHBANKS (*uneasily*). But surely that is only because his opinions—

BURGESS (*touching him on the knee with his forefinger, and pressing it to hold his attention*). Thats the same what I hused to think, Mr Morchbanks. Hi thought long enough that it was only his hopinions; though, mind you, hopinions becomes vurry serious things when people takes to hactin on em as e does. But thats not what I go on. (*He looks round to make sure that they are alone, and bends over to* EUGENE's *ear*) What do you think he sez to me this mornin in this very room?

MARCHBANKS. What?

BURGESS. He sez to me—this is as sure as we're setting here now—he sez "I'm a fool," he sez; "and yore a scounderl." Me a scounderl, mind you! And then shook ands with me on it, as if it was to my credit! Do you mean to tell me as that man's sane?

MORELL (*outside, calling to* PROSERPINE *as he opens the door*). Get all their names and addresses, Miss Garnett.

PROSERPINE (*in the distance*). Yes, Mr Morell.

(MORELL *comes in, with the deputation's documents in his hands.*)

BURGESS (*aside to* MARCHBANKS). Yorr he is. Just keep your heye on im and see. (*Rising momentously*) I'm sorry, James, to ave to make a complaint to you. I dont want to do it; but I feel I oughter, as a matter o right and dooty.

MORELL. Whats the matter?

BURGESS. Mr Morchbanks will bear me hout: he was a witness. (*Very solemnly*) Yore young woman so far forgot herself as to call me a silly ole fat'ead.

MORELL (*with tremendous heartiness*). Oh, now, isnt that *exactly* like Prossy? She's so frank: she cant contain herself! Poor Prossy! Ha! ha!

BURGESS (*trembling with rage*). And do you hexpec me to put up with it from the like of er?

MORELL. Pooh, nonsense! you cant take any notice of it. Never mind. (*He goes to the cellaret and puts the papers into one of the drawers.*)

BURGESS. Oh, Hi dont mind. Hi'm above it. But is it *right*? thats what I want to know. Is it right?

MORELL. Thats a question for the Church, not for the laity. Has it done you any harm? thats the question for you, eh? Of course it hasnt. Think no more of it. (*He dismisses the subject by going to his place at the table and setting to work at his correspondence.*)

BURGESS (*aside to* MARCHBANKS). What did I tell you? Mad as a atter. (*He goes to the table and asks, with the sickly civility of a hungry man*) When's dinner, James?

MORELL. Not for a couple of hours yet.

BURGESS (*with plaintive resignation*). Gimme a nice book to read over the fire, will you, James: thur's a good chap.

MORELL. What sort of book? A good one?

BURGESS (*with almost a yell of remonstrance*). Nah-oo! Summat pleasant, just to pass the time. (MORELL *takes an illustrated paper from the table and offers it. He accepts it humbly*) Thank yer, James. (*He goes back to the big chair at the fire, and sits there at his ease, reading.*)

MORELL (*as he writes*). Candida will come to entertain you presently. She has got rid of her pupil. She is filling the lamps.

MARCHBANKS (*starting up in the wildest consternation*). But that will soil her hands. I cant bear that, Morell: it's a shame. I'll go and fill them. (*He makes for the door.*)

MORELL. Youd better not. (MARCHBANKS *stops irresolutely*) She'd only set you to clean my boots, to save me the trouble of doing it myself in the morning.

BURGESS (*with grave disapproval*). Dont you keep a servant now, James?

MORELL. Yes; but she isnt a slave; and the house looks as if I kept three. That means that everyone has to lend a hand. It's not a bad plan: Prossy and I can talk business after breakfast while we're washing up. Washing up's no trouble when there are two people to do it.

MARCHBANKS (*tormentedly*). Do you think every woman is as coarse-grained as Miss Garnett?

BURGESS (*emphatically*). Thats quite right, Mr Morchbanks: thats quite right. She *is* corsegrained.

MORELL (*quietly and significantly*). Marchbanks!

MARCHBANKS. Yes?

MORELL. How many servants does your father keep?

MARCHBANKS (*pettishly*). Oh, I dont know. (*He moves to the sofa, as if to get as far as possible from* MORELL's *questioning, and sits down in great agony of spirit, thinking of the paraffin.*)

MORELL (*very gravely*). So many that you dont know! (*More aggressively*) When theres anything coarsegrained to be done, you just ring the bell and throw it on to somebody else, eh?

MARCHBANKS. Oh, dont torture me. You dont even ring the bell. But your wife's beautiful fingers are dabbling in paraffin oil while you sit here comfortably preaching about it: everlasting preaching! preaching! words! words! words!

BURGESS (*intensely appreciating this retort*). Har, har! Devil a better! (*Radiantly*) Ad you there, James, straight.

(CANDIDA *comes in, well aproned, with a reading lamp trimmed, filled, and ready for lighting. She places it on the table near* MORELL, *ready for use.*)

CANDIDA (*brushing her finger tips together with a slight twitch of her nose*). If you stay with us, Eugene, I think I will hand over the lamps to you.

MARCHBANKS. I will stay on condition that you hand over all the rough work to me.

CANDIDA. Thats very gallant; but I think I should like to see how you do it first. (*Turning to* MORELL) James: youve not been looking after the house properly.

MORELL. What have I done—or not done—my love?

CANDIDA (*with serious vexation*). My own particular pet scrubbing brush has been used for blackleading. (*A heart-breaking wail bursts from* MARCHBANKS. BURGESS *looks round, amazed.* CANDIDA *hurries to the sofa.*) Whats the matter? Are you ill, Eugene?

MARCHBANKS. No: not ill. Only horror! horror! horror! (*He bows his head on his hands.*)

BURGESS (*shocked*). What! Got the orrors, Mr Morchbanks! Oh, thats bad, at your age. You must leave it off grajally.

CANDIDA (*reassured*). Nonsense, papa! It's only poetic horror, isnt it, Eugene (*petting him*)?

BURGESS (*abashed*). Oh, poetic orror, is it? I beg your pordon, I'm shore (*He turns to the fire again, deprecating his hasty conclusion.*)

CANDIDA. What is it, Eugene? the scrubbing brush? (*He shudders*) Well, there! never mind. (*She sits down beside him.*) Wouldnt you like to present me with a nice new one, with an ivory back inlaid with mother-of-pearl?

MARCHBANKS (*softly and musically, but sadly and longingly*). No, not a scrubbing brush, but a boat: a tiny shallop to sail away in, far from the world, where the marble floors are washed by the rain and dried by the sun; where the south wind dusts the beautiful green and purple carpets. Or a chariot! to carry us up into the sky, where the lamps are stars, and dont need to be filled with paraffin oil every day.

MORELL (*harshly*). And where there is nothing to do but be idle, selfish, and useless.

CANDIDA (*jarred*). Oh, James! how could you spoil it all?

MARCHBANKS (*firing up*). Yes, to be idle, selfish, and useless: that is, to be beautiful and free and happy: hasnt every man desired that with all his soul for the woman he loves? Thats my ideal: whats yours, and that of all the dreadful people who live in these hideous rows of houses? Sermons and scrubbing brushes! With you to preach the sermon and your wife to scrub.

CANDIDA (*quaintly*). He cleans the boots, Eugene. You will have to clean them to-morrow for saying that about him.

MARCHBANKS. Oh, dont talk about boots! Your feet should be beautiful on the mountains.

CANDIDA. My feet would not be beautiful on the Hackney Road without boots.

BURGESS (*scandalized*). Come, Candy! dont be vulgar. Mr Morchbanks aint accustomed to it. Youre giving him the orrors again. I mean the poetic ones.

(MORELL *is silent. Apparently he is busy with his letters: really he is puzzling with misgiving over his new and alarming experience that the surer he is of his moral thrusts, the more swiftly and effectively* EUGENE *parries them. To find himself beginning to fear a man whom he does not respect afflicts him bitterly.*)

(MISS GARNETT *comes in with a telegram.*)

PROSERPINE (*handing the telegram to* MORELL). Reply paid. The boy's waiting. (*To* CANDIDA, *coming back to her machine and sitting down*) Maria is ready for you now in the kitchen, Mrs Morell. (CANDIDA *rises.*) The onions have come.

MARCHBANKS (*convulsively*). Onions!

CANDIDA. Yes, onions. Not even Spanish ones: nasty little red onions. You shall help me to slice them. Come along.

(*She catches him by the wrist and runs out, pulling him after her.* BURGESS *rises in consternation, and stands aghast on the hearth-rug, staring after them.*)

BURGESS. Candy didnt oughter andle a hearl's nevvy like that. It's goin too fur with it. Lookee ere, James: do e often git taken queer like that?

MORELL (*shortly, writing a telegram*). I dont know.

BURGESS (*sentimentally*). He talks very pretty. I awlus had a turn for a bit of poetry. Candy takes arter me that-a-way. Huseter make me tell er fairy stories when she was ony a little kiddy not that igh (*indicating a stature of two feet or thereabouts*).

MORELL (*preoccupied*). Ah, indeed. (*He blots the telegram and goes out.*)

PROSERPINE. Used you to make the fairy stories up out of your own head?

(BURGESS, *not deigning to reply, strikes an attitude of the haughtiest disdain on the hearth-rug.*)

PROSERPINE (*calmly*). I should never have supposed you had it in you. By the way, I'd better warn you, since youve taken such a fancy to Mr Marchbanks. He's mad.

BURGESS. Mad! What! Im too!!

PROSERPINE. Mad as a March hare. He did frighten me, I can tell you, just before you came in that time. Havnt you noticed the queer things he says?

BURGESS. So thats what the poetic orrors means. Blame me if it didnt come into my ed once or twyst that he was a bit horff 'is chump! (*He crosses the room to the door, lifting up his voice as he goes.*) Well, this is a pretty sort of asylum for a man to be in, with no one but you to take care of him!

PROSERPINE (*as he passes her*). Yes, what a dreadful thing it would be if anything happened to *you!*

BURGESS (*loftily*). Dont you haddress no remarks to me. Tell your hemployer that Ive gone into the gorden for a smoke.

PROSERPINE (*mocking*). Oh!

(*Before* BURGESS *can retort,* MORELL *comes back.*)

BURGESS (*sentimentally*). Goin for a turn in the gording to smoke, James.

MORELL (*brusquely*). Oh, all right, all right. (BURGESS *goes out pathetically in the character of a weary old man.* MORELL *stands at the table, turning over his papers, and adding, across to* PROSERPINE, *half humorously, half absently*) Well, Miss Prossy, why have you been calling my father-in-law names?

PROSERPINE (*blushing fiery red, and looking quickly up at him, half scared, half reproachful*). I—(*She bursts into tears.*)

MORELL (*with tender gaiety, leaning across the table towards her, and consoling her*). Oh, come! come! come! Never mind, Pross: he *is* a silly old fathead, isn't he?

(*With an explosive sob, she makes a dash at the door, and vanishes, banging it.* MORELL, *shaking his head resignedly, sighs, and goes wearily to his chair, where he sits down and sets to work, looking old and careworn.*

(CANDIDA *comes in. She has finished her household work and taken off the apron. She at once notices his dejected appearance, and posts herself quietly at the visitors' chair, looking down at him attentively. She says nothing.*)

MORELL (*looking up, but with his pen raised ready to resume his work*). Well? Where is Eugene?

CANDIDA. Washing his hands in the scullery under the tap. He will make an excellent cook if he can only get over his dread of Maria.

MORELL (*shortly*). Ha! No doubt. (*He begins writing again.*)

CANDIDA (*going nearer, and putting her hand down softly on his to stop him as she says*). Come here, dear. Let me look at you. (*He drops his pen and yields himself to her disposal. She makes him rise, and brings him a little away from the table, looking at him critically all the time.*) Turn your face to the light. (*She places him facing the window*) My boy is not well. Has he been overworking?

MORELL. Nothing more than usual.

CANDIDA. He looks very pale, and grey, and wrinkled, and old. (*His melancholy deepens; and she attacks it with wilful gaiety*) Here: (*pulling him towards the easy chair*) youve done enough writing for to-day. Leave Prossy to finish it. Come and talk to me.

MORELL. But—

CANDIDA (*insisting*). Yes, I *must* be talked to. (*She makes him sit down, and seats herself on the carpet beside his knee*) Now (*patting his hand*) youre beginning to look better already. Why must you go out every night lecturing and talking? I hardly have one evening a week with you. Of course what you say is all very true; but it does no good: they dont mind what you say to them one little bit. They think they agree with you; but whats the use of their agreeing with you if they go and do just the opposite of what you tell them the moment your back is turned? Look at our congregation at St Dominic's! Why do they come to hear you talking about Christianity every Sunday? Why, just because theyve been so full of business and money-making for six days that they want to forget all about it and have a rest on the seventh; so that they can go back fresh and make money harder than ever! You positively help them at it instead of hindering them.

MORELL (*with energetic seriousness*). You know very well, Candida, that I often blow them up soundly for that. And if there is nothing in their churchgoing but rest and diversion, why dont they try something more amusing? more self-indulgent? There must be some good in the fact that they prefer St Dominic's to worse places on Sundays.

CANDIDA. Oh, the worse places arnt open; and even if they were, they darent be seen going to them. Besides, James dear, you preach so splendidly that it's as good as a play for them. Why do you think the women are so enthusiastic?

MORELL (*shocked*). Candida!

CANDIDA. Oh, I know. You silly boy: you think it's your Socialism and your religion; but if it were that, theyd do what you tell them instead of only coming to look at you. They all have Prossy's complaint.

MORELL. Prossy's complaint! What do you mean, Candida?

CANDIDA. Yes, Prossy, and all the other secretaries you ever had. Why does Prossy condescend to wash up the things, and to peel potatoes and abase herself in all manner of ways for six shillings a week less than she used to get in a city office? She's in love with you, James: thats the reason. Theyre all in love with you. And you are in love with preaching because you do it so beautifully. And you think it's all enthusiasm for the kingdom of Heaven on earth; and so do they. You dear silly!

MORELL. Candida: what dreadful! what soul-destroying cynicism! Are you jesting? Or—can it be?—are you jealous?

CANDIDA (*with curious thoughtfulness*). Yes, I feel a little jealous sometimes.

MORELL (*incredulously*). Of Prossy?

CANDIDA (*laughing*). No, no, no, no. Not jealous *of* anybody. Jealous *for* somebody else, who is not loved as he ought to be.

MORELL. Me?

CANDIDA. You! Why, youre spoiled with love and worship: you get far more than is good for you. No: I mean Eugene.

MORELL (*startled*). Eugene!

CANDIDA. It seems unfair that all the love should go to you, and none to him; although he needs it so much more than you do. (*A convulsive movement shakes him in spite of himself.*) Whats the matter? Am I worrying you?

MORELL (*hastily*). Not at all. (*Looking at her with troubled intensity*) You know that I have perfect confidence in you, Candida.

CANDIDA. You vain thing! Are you so sure of your irresistible attractions?

MORELL. Candida; you are shocking me. I never thought of my attractions. I thought of your goodness, of your purity. That is what I confide in.

CANDIDA. What a nasty uncomfortable thing to say to me! Oh, you are a clergyman, James: a thorough clergyman!

MORELL (*turning away from her, heart-stricken*). So Eugene says.

CANDIDA (*with lively interest, leaning over to him with her arms on his knee*). Eugene's always right. He's a wonderful boy: I have grown fonder and fonder of him all the time I was away. Do you know, James, that though he has not the least suspicion of it himself, he is ready to fall madly in love with me?

MORELL (*grimly*). Oh, he has no suspicion of it himself, hasnt he?

CANDIDA. Not a bit. (*She takes her arms from his knee, and turns thoughtfully, sinking into a more restful attitude with her hands in her lap*) Some day he will know: when he is grown up and experienced, like you. And he will know that I must have known. I wonder what he will think of me then.

MORELL. No evil, Candida. I hope and trust, no evil.

CANDIDA (*dubiously*). That will depend.

MORELL (*bewildered*). Depend!

CANDIDA (*looking at him*). Yes: it will depend on what happens to him. (*He looks vacantly at her.*) Dont you see? It will depend on how he comes to learn what love really is. I mean on the sort of woman who will teach it to him.

MORELL (*quite at a loss*). Yes. No. I dont know what you mean.

CANDIDA (*explaining*).   If he learns it from a good woman, then it will be all right: he will forgive me.

MORELL.   Forgive?

CANDIDA.   But suppose he learns it from a bad woman, as so many men do, especially poetic men, who imagine all women are angels! Suppose he only discovers the value of love when he has thrown it away and degraded himself in his ignorance! Will he forgive me then, do you think?

MORELL.   Forgive you for what?

CANDIDA (*realizing how stupid he is, and a little disappointed, though quite tenderly so*).   Dont you understand? (*He shakes his head. She turns to him again, so as to explain with the fondest intimacy*) I mean, will he forgive me for not teaching him myself? For abandoning him to the bad women for the sake of my goodness, of my purity, as you call it? Ah, James, how little you understand me, to talk of your confidence in my goodness and purity! I would give them both to poor Eugene as willingly as I would give my shawl to a beggar dying of cold, if there were nothing else to restrain me. Put your trust in my love for you, James; for if that went, I should care very little for your sermons: mere phrases that you cheat yourself and others with every day. (*She is about to rise.*)

MORELL.   *His* words!

CANDIDA (*checking herself quickly in the act of getting up*).   Whose words?

MORELL.   Eugene's.

CANDIDA (*delighted*).   He is always right. He understands you; he understands me; he understands Prossy; and you, darling, you understand nothing. (*She laughs, and kisses him to console him. He recoils as if stabbed, and springs up.*)

MORELL.   How can you bear to do that when—Oh, Candida (*with anguish in his voice*) I had rather you had plunged a grappling iron into my heart than given` me that kiss.

CANDIDA (*amazed*).   My dear: whats the matter?

MORELL (*frantically waving her off*).   Dont touch me.

CANDIDA.   James!!!

(*They are interrupted by the entrance of* MARCHBANKS *with* BURGESS, *who stop near the door, staring.*)

MARCHBANKS (*aside to her*).   It is your cruelty. I hate cruelty. It is a horrible thing to see one person make another suffer.

CANDIDA (*petting him ironically*).   Poor boy! have I been cruel? Did I make it slice nasty little red onions?

MARCHBANKS (*earnestly*).   Oh, stop, stop: I dont mean myself. You have made him suffer frightfully. I feel his pain in my own heart. I know that it is not your fault: it is something that must happen; but dont make light of it. I shudder when you torture him and laugh.

CANDIDA (*incredulously*).   *I* torture James! Nonsense, Eugene: how you exaggerate! Silly! (*She rises and goes to the table, a little troubled*) Dont work any more, dear. Come and talk to us.

MORELL (*affectionately but bitterly*). Ah no: I cant talk. I can only preach.

CANDIDA (*caressing his hand*). Well, come and preach.

BURGESS (*strongly remonstrating*). Aw no, Candy. 'Ang it all!

(LEXY MILL *comes in, anxious and important.*)

LEXY (*hastening to shake hands with* CANDIDA). How do you do, Mrs Morell? So glad to see you back again.

CANDIDA. Thank you, Lexy. You know Eugene, dont you?

LEXY. Oh yes. How do you do, Marchbanks?

MARCHBANKS. Quite well, thanks.

LEXY (*to* MORELL). Ive just come from the Guild of St Matthew. They are in the greatest consternation about your telegram.

CANDIDA. What did you telegraph about, James?

LEXY (*to* CANDIDA). He was to have spoken for them tonight. Theyve taken the large hall in Mare Street and spent a lot of money on posters. Morell's telegram was to say he couldnt come. It came on them like a thunderbolt.

CANDIDA (*surprised, and beginning to suspect something wrong*). Given up an engagement to speak!

MARCHBANKS. Is anything the matter?

MORELL (*deadly white, putting an iron constraint on himself*). Nothing but this: that either you were right this morning, or Candida is mad.

BURGESS (*in loudest protest*). What! Candy mad too! Oh, come! come! come! (*He crosses the room to the fireplace, protesting as he goes, and knocks the ashes out of his pipe on the bars.*)

(MORELL *sits down at his table desperately, leaning forward to hide his face, and interlacing his fingers rigidly to keep them steady.*)

CANDIDA (*to* MORELL, *relieved and laughing*). Oh, youre only shocked! Is that all? How conventional all you unconventional people are! (*She sits gaily on the arm of the chair.*)

BURGESS. Come: be'ave yourself, Candy. Whatll Mr Morchbanks think of you?

CANDIDA. This comes of James teaching me to think for myself, and never to hold back out of fear of what other people may think of me. It works beautifully as long as I think the same things as he does. But now! because I have just thought something different! look at him! Just look! (*She points to* MORELL, *greatly amused.*)

(EUGENE *looks, and instantly presses his hand on his heart, as if some pain had shot through it. He sits down on the sofa like a man witnessing a tragedy.*)

BURGESS (*on the hearth-rug*). Well, James, you certnly haint as himpressive lookin as usu'l.

MORELL (*with a laugh which is half a sob*). I suppose not. I beg all your pardons: I was not conscious of making a fuss. (*Pulling himself together*) Well, well, well, well, well! (*He sets to work at his papers again with resolute cheerfulness.*)

CANDIDA (*going to the sofa and sitting beside MARCHBANKS, still in a bantering humor*). Well, Eugene: why are you so sad. Did the onions make you cry?

BURGESS. Fust time in his life, I'll bet. Ain it, Candy?

LEXY (*to MORELL*). They decided to send an urgent telegram to you asking whether you could not change your mind. Have you received it?

MORELL (*with restrained impatience*). Yes, yes: I got it.

LEXY. It was reply paid.

MORELL. Yes, I know. I answered it. I cant go.

CANDIDA. But why, James?

MORELL (*almost fiercely*). Because I dont choose. These people forget that I am a man: they think I am a talking machine to be turned on for their pleasure every evening of my life. May I not have *one* night at home, with my wife, and my friends?

(*They are all amazed at this outburst, except EUGENE. His expression remains unchanged.*)

CANDIDA. Oh, James, you mustnt mind what I said about that. And if you dont go youll have an attack of bad conscience to-morrow.

LEXY (*intimidated, but urgent*). I know, of course, that they make the most unreasonable demands on you. But they have been telegraphing all over the place for another speaker; and they can get nobody but the President of the Agnostic League.

MORELL (*promptly*). Well, an excellent man. What better do they want?

LEXY. But he always insists so powerfully on the divorce of Socialism from Christianity. He will undo all the good we have been doing. Of course you know best; but—(*he shrugs his shoulders and wanders to the hearth beside BURGESS*).

CANDIDA (*coaxingly*). Oh, do go, James. We'll all go.

BURGESS (*grumblingly*). Look 'ere, Candy! I say! Let's stay at home by the fire, comfortable. He wont need to be more'n a couple-o-hour away.

CANDIDA. Youll be just as comfortable at the meeting. We'll all sit on the platform and be great people.

EUGENE (*terrified*). Oh please dont let us go on the platform. No: everyone will stare at us: I couldnt. I'll sit at the back of the room.

CANDIDA.   Dont be afraid. Theyll be too busy looking at James to notice you.

MORELL.   Prossy's complaint, Candida! Eh?

CANDIDA (gaily).   Yes: Prossy's complaint.

BURGESS (mystified).   Prossy's complaint! What are you talkin about, James?

MORELL (not heeding him, rises; goes to the door; and holds it open, calling in a commanding tone).   Miss Garnett.

PROSERPINE (in the distance).   Yes, Mr Morell. Coming.

(They all wait, except BURGESS, who turns stealthily to LEXY.)

BURGESS.   Listen ere, Mr Mill. Whats Prossy's complaint? Whats wrong with er?

LEXY (confidentially).   Well, I dont exactly know; but she spoke very strangely to me this morning. I'm afraid she's a little out of her mind sometimes.

BURGESS (overwhelmed).   Why, it must be catchin! Four in the same ouse!

PROSERPINE (appearing on the threshold).   What is it, Mr Morell?

MORELL.   Telegraph to the Guild of St Matthew that I am coming.

PROSERPINE (surprised).   Dont they expect you?

MORELL (peremptorily).   Do as I tell you.

(PROSERPINE, frightened, sits down at her typewriter, and obeys. MORELL, now unaccountably resolute and forceful, goes across to BURGESS. CANDIDA watches his movements with growing wonder and misgiving.)

MORELL.   Burgess: you dont want to come.

BURGESS.   Oh, dont put it like that, James. It's ony that it aint Sunday, you know.

MORELL.   I'm sorry. I thought you might like to be introduced to the chairman. He's on the Works Committee of the County Council, and has some influence in the matter of contracts. (BURGESS wakes up at once.) Youll come?

BURGESS (with enthusiasm).   Cawrse I'll come, James. Aint it awlus a pleasure to ear you!

MORELL (turning to PROSSY).   I shall want you to take some notes at the meeting, Miss Garnett, if you have no other engagement. (She nods, afraid to speak.) You are coming, Lexy, I suppose?

LEXY.   Certainly.

CANDIDA.   We're all coming, James.

MORELL.   No: you are not coming; and Eugene is not coming. You will stay here and entertain him—to celebrate your return home. (EUGENE rises, breathless.)

CANDIDA. But, James—

MORELL (*authoritatively*). I insist. You do not want to come; and he does not want to come. (CANDIDA *is about to protest.*) Oh, dont concern yourselves: I shall have plenty of people without you: your chairs will be wanted by unconverted people who have never heard me before.

CANDIDA (*troubled*). Eugene: wouldnt you like to come?

MORELL. I should be afraid to let myself go before Eugene: he is so critical of sermons. (*Looking at him*) He knows I am afraid of him: he told me as much this morning. Well, I shall shew him how much afraid I am by leaving him here in your custody, Candida.

MARCHBANKS (*to himself, with vivid feeling*). Thats brave. Thats beautiful.

CANDIDA (*with anxious misgiving*). But—but—Is anything the matter, James? (*Greatly troubled*) I cant understand—

MORELL (*taking her tenderly in his arms and kissing her on the forehead*). Ah, I thought it was *I* who couldnt understand, dear.

ACT III

Past ten in the evening. The curtains are drawn, and the lamps lighted. The typewriter is in its case: the large table has been cleared and tidied: everything indicates that the day's work is over.

CANDIDA *and* MARCHBANKS *are sitting by the fire. The reading lamp is on the mantelshelf above* MARCHBANKS, *who is in the small chair, reading aloud. A little pile of manuscripts and a couple of volumes of poetry are on the carpet beside him.* CANDIDA *is in the easy chair. The poker, a light brass one, is upright in her hand. Leaning back and looking intently at the point of it, with her feet stretched towards the blaze, she is in a waking dream, miles away from her surroundings and completely oblivious of Eugene.*

MARCHBANKS (*breaking off in his recitation*). Every poet that ever lived has put that thought into a sonnet. He must: he cant help it. (*He looks to her for assent, and notices her absorption in the poker*) Havnt you been listening? (*No response*) Mrs Morell!

CANDIDA (*starting*). Eh?

MARCHBANKS. Havnt you been listening?

CANDIDA (*with a guilty excess of politeness*). Oh yes. It's very nice. Go on, Eugene. I'm longing to hear what happens to the angel.

MARCHBANKS (*letting the manuscript drop from his hand to the floor*). I beg your pardon for boring you.

CANDIDA. But you are not boring me, I assure you. *Please* go on. Do, Eugene.

MARCHBANKS. I finished the poem about the angel quarter of an hour ago. Ive read you several things since.

CANDIDA (*remorsefully*). I'm so sorry, Eugene. I think the poker must have hypnotized me. (*She puts it down.*)

MARCHBANKS. It made me horribly uneasy.

CANDIDA. Why didnt you tell me? I'd have put it down at once.

MARCHBANKS. I was afraid of making you uneasy too. It looked as if it were a weapon. If I were a hero of old I should have laid my drawn sword between us. If Morell had come in he would have thought you had taken up the poker because there was no sword between us.

CANDIDA (*wondering*). What? (*With a puzzled glance at him*) I cant quite follow that. Those sonnets of yours have perfectly addled me. Why should there be a sword between us?

MARCHBANKS (*evasively*). Oh, never mind. (*He stoops to pick up the manuscript.*)

CANDIDA. Put that down again, Eugene. There are limits to my appetite for poetry: even your poetry. Youve been reading to me for more than two hours, ever since James went out. I want to talk.

MARCHBANKS (*rising, scared*). No: I mustnt talk. (*He looks round him in his lost way, and adds, suddenly*) I think I'll go out and take a walk in the park. (*He makes for the door.*)

CANDIDA. Nonsense: it's closed long ago. Come and sit down on the hearth-rug, and talk moonshine as you usually do. I want to be amused. Dont you want to?

MARCHBANKS (*half in terror, half enraptured*). Yes.

CANDIDA. Then come along. (*She moves her chair back a little to make room.*)

(*He hesitates; then timidly stretches himself on the hearth-rug, face upwards, and throws back his head across her knees, looking up at her.*)

MARCHBANKS. Oh, Ive been so miserable all the evening, because I was doing right. Now I'm doing wrong; and I'm happy.

CANDIDA (*tenderly amused at him*). Yes: I'm sure you feel a great grown-up wicked deceiver. Quite proud of yourself, arnt you?

MARCHBANKS (*raising his head quickly and turning a little to look round at her*). Take care. I'm ever so much older than you, if you only knew. (*He turns quite over on his knees, with his hands clasped and his arms on her lap, and speaks with growing impulse, his blood beginning to stir.*) May I say some wicked things to you?

CANDIDA (*without the least fear or coldness, and with perfect respect for his passion, but with a touch of her wise-hearted maternal humor*). No. But you may say anything you really and truly feel. Anything at all, no matter what it is. I am not afraid, so long as it is your real self that speaks, and not a mere attitude: a gallant attitude, or a wicked attitude, or even a poetic attitude. I put you on your honor and truth. Now say whatever you want to.

MARCHBANKS (*the eager expression vanishing utterly from his lips and nostrils as his eyes light up with pathetic spirituality*). Oh, now I cant say anything: all the words I know belong to some attitude or other—all except one.

CANDIDA. What one is that?

MARCHBANKS (*softly, losing himself in the music of the name*). Candida, Candida, Candida, Candida, Candida. I must say that now, because you have put me on my honor and truth; and I never think or feel Mrs Morell: it is always Candida.

CANDIDA. Of course. And what have you to say to Candida?

MARCHBANKS. Nothing but to repeat your name a thousand times. Dont you feel that every time is a prayer to you?

CANDIDA. Doesnt it make you happy to be able to pray?

MARCHBANKS. Yes, very happy.

CANDIDA. Well, that happiness is the answer to your prayer. Do you want anything more?

MARCHBANKS. No: I have come into heaven, where want is unknown.

(MORELL *comes in. He halts on the threshold, and takes in the scene at a glance.*)

MORELL (*grave and self-contained*). I hope I dont disturb you.

(CANDIDA *starts up violently, but without the smallest embarrassment, laughing at herself.* EUGENE, *capsized by her sudden movement, recovers himself without rising, and sits on the rug hugging his ankles, also quite unembarrassed.*)

CANDIDA. Oh, James how you startled me! I was so taken up with Eugene that I didnt hear your latchkey. How did the meeting go off? Did you speak well?

MORELL. I have never spoken better in my life.

CANDIDA. That was first rate! How much was the collection?

MORELL. I forgot to ask.

CANDIDA (*to* EUGENE). He must have spoken splendidly, or he would never have forgotten that. (*To* MORELL) Where are all the others?

MORELL. They left long before I could get away: I thought I should never escape. I believe they are having supper somewhere.

CANDIDA (*in her domestic business tone*). Oh, in that case, Maria may go to bed. I'll tell her. (*She goes out to the kitchen.*)

MORELL (*looking sternly down at* MARCHBANKS). Well?

MARCHBANKS (*squatting grotesquely on the hearth-rug, and actually at ease with* MORELL: *even impishly humorous*). Well?

MORELL. Have you anything to tell me?

MARCHBANKS. Only that I have been making a fool of myself here in private whilst you have been making a fool of yourself in public.

MORELL. Hardly in the same way, I think.

MARCHBANKS (*eagerly, scrambling up*). The very, very *very* same way. I have been playing the Good Man. Just like you. When you began your heroics about leaving me here with Candida—

MORELL (*involuntarily*). Candida!

MARCHBANKS. Oh yes: Ive got that far. But dont be afraid. Heroics are infectious: I caught the disease from you. I swore not to say a word in your absence that I would not have said a month ago in your presence.

MORELL. Did you keep your oath?

MARCHBANKS (*suddenly perching himself on the back of the easy chair*). It kept itself somehow until about ten minutes ago. Up to that moment I went on desperately reading to her—reading my own poems—anybody's poems—to stave off a conversation. I was standing outside the gate of Heaven, and refusing to go in. Oh, you cant think how heroic it was, and how uncomfortable! Then—

MORELL (*steadily controlling his suspense*). Then?

MARCHBANKS (*prosaically slipping down into a quite ordinary attitude on the seat of the chair*). Then she couldnt bear being read to any longer.

MORELL. And you approached the gate of Heaven at last?

MARCHBANKS. Yes.

MORELL. Well? (*Fiercely*) Speak, man: have you no feeling for me?

MARCHBANKS (*softly and musically*). Then she became an angel; and there was a flaming sword that turned every way, so that I couldnt go in; for I saw that gate was really the gate of Hell.

MORELL (*triumphantly*). She repulsed you!

MARCHBANKS (*rising in wild scorn*). No, you fool: if she had done that I should never have seen that I was in Heaven already. Repulsed me! You think that would have saved us! virtuous indignation! Oh, you are not worthy to live in the same world with her. (*He turns away contemptuously to the other side of the room.*)

MORELL (*who has watched him quietly without changing his place*). Do you think you make yourself more worthy by reviling me, Eugene?

MARCHBANKS. Here endeth the thousand and first lesson. Morell: I dont think much of your preaching after all: I believe I could do it better myself. The man I want to meet is the man that Candida married.

MORELL. The man that—? Do you mean me?

MARCHBANKS. I dont mean the Reverend James Mavor Morell, moralist and windbag. I mean the real man that the Reverend James must have hidden somewhere inside his black coat: the man that Candida loved. You cant make a woman like Candida love you by merely buttoning your collar at the back instead of in front.

MORELL (*boldly and steadily*). When Candida promised to marry me,

I was the same moralist and windbag you now see. I wore my black coat; and my collar was buttoned behind instead of in front. Do you think she would have loved me any the better for being insincere in my profession?

MARCHBANKS (*on the sofa, hugging his ankles*). Oh, she forgave you, just as she forgives me for being a coward, and a weakling, and what you call a snivelling little whelp and all the rest of it. (*Dreamily*) A woman like that has divine insight: she loves our souls, and not our follies and vanities and illusions, nor our collars and coats, nor any other of the rags and tatters we are rolled up in. (*He reflects on this for an instant; then turns intently to question* MORELL) What I want to know is how you got past the flaming sword that stopped me.

MORELL. Perhaps because I was not interrupted at the end of ten minutes.

MARCHBANKS (*taken aback*). What!

MORELL. Man can climb to the highest summits; but he cannot dwell there long.

MARCHBANKS (*springing up*). It's false: there can he dwell for ever, and there only. It's in the other moments that he can find no rest, no sense of the silent glory of life. Where would you have me spend my moments, if not on the summits?

MORELL. In the scullery, slicing onions and filling lamps.

MARCHBANKS. Or in the pulpit, scrubbing cheap earthenware souls?

MORELL. Yes, that too. It was there that I earned my golden moment, and the right, in that moment, to ask her to love me. I did not take the moment on credit; nor did I use it to steal another man's happiness.

MARCHBANKS (*rather disgustedly, trotting back towards the fireplace*). I have no doubt you conducted the transaction as honestly as if you were buying a pound of cheese. (*He stops on the brink of the hearth-rug, and adds, thoughtfully, to himself, with his back turned to* MORELL) I could only go to her as a beggar.

MORELL (*starting*). A beggar dying of cold! asking for her shawl!

MARCHBANKS (*turning, surprised*). Thank you for touching up my poetry. Yes, if you like: a beggar dying of cold, asking for her shawl.

MORELL (*excitedly*). And she refused. Shall I tell you why she refused? I *can* tell you, on her own authority. It was because of—

MARCHBANKS. She didnt refuse.

MORELL. Not!

MARCHBANKS. She offered me all I chose to ask for: her shawl, her wings, the wreath of stars on her head, the lilies in her hand, the crescent moon beneath her feet—

MORELL (*seizing him*). Out with the truth, man: my wife is my wife: I want no more of your poetic fripperies. I know well that if I have lost her love and you have gained it, no law will bind her.

MARCHBANKS (*quaintly, without fear or resistance*). Catch me by the shirt collar, Morell: she will arrange it for me afterwards as she did this morning. (*With quiet rapture*) I shall feel her hands touch me.

MORELL. You young imp, do you know how dangerous it is to say that to me? Or (*with a sudden misgiving*) has something made you brave?

MARCHBANKS. I'm not afraid now. I disliked you before: that was why I shrank from your touch. But I saw today—when she tortured you—that you love her. Since then I have been your friend: you may strangle me if you like.

MORELL (*releasing him*). Eugene: if that is not a heartless lie—if you have a spark of human feeling left in you—will you tell me what has happened during my absence?

MARCHBANKS. What happened! Why, the flaming sword (MORELL *stamps with impatience*)—Well, in plain prose, I love her so exquisitely that I wanted nothing more than the happiness of being in such love. And before I had time to come down from the highest summits, *you* came in.

MORELL (*suffering deeply*). So it is still unsettled. Still the misery of doubt.

MARCHBANKS. Misery! I am the happiest of men. I desire nothing now but her happiness. (*In a passion of sentiment*) Oh, Morell, let us both give her up. Why should she have to choose between a wretched little nervous disease like me, and a pig-headed parson like you? Let us go on a pilgrimage, you to the east and I to the west, in search of a worthy lover for her: some beautiful archangel with purple wings—

MORELL. Some fiddlestick! Oh, if she is mad enough to leave me for you, who will protect her? who will help her? who will work for her? who will be a father to her children? (*He sits down distractedly on the sofa, with his elbows on his knees and his head propped on his clenched fists.*)

MARCHBANKS (*snapping his fingers wildly*). She does not ask those silly questions. It is she who wants somebody to protect, to help, to work for: somebody to give her children to protect, to help and to work for. Some grown up man who has become as a little child again. Oh, you fool, you fool, you triple fool! I am the man, Morell: I am the man. (*He dances about excitedly, crying*) You don't understand what a woman is. Send for her, Morell: send for her and let her choose between—(*The door opens and* CANDIDA *enters. He stops as if petrified.*)

CANDIDA (*amazed, on the threshold*). What on earth are you at, Eugene?

MARCHBANKS (*oddly*). James and I are having a preaching match; and he is getting the worst of it.

(CANDIDA *looks quickly round at* MORELL. *Seeing that he is distressed, she hurries down to him, greatly vexed.*)

CANDIDA. You have been annoying him. Now I wont have it, Eugene: do you hear? (*She puts her hand on* MORELL's *shoulder, and quite forgets her wifely tact in her anger*) My boy shall not be worried: I will protect him.

MORELL (*rising proudly*). Protect!

CANDIDA (*not heeding him: to* EUGENE). What have you been saying?

MARCHBANKS (*appalled*). Nothing. I—

CANDIDA. Eugene! Nothing?

MARCHBANKS (*piteously*). I mean—I—I'm very sorry. I wont do it again: indeed I wont. I'll let him alone.

MORELL (*indignantly, with an aggressive movement towards* EUGENE). Let me alone! You young—

CANDIDA (*stopping him*). Sh!—no: let me deal with him, James.

MARCHBANKS. Oh, youre not angry with me, are you?

CANDIDA (*severely*). Yes I am: very angry. I have a good mind to pack you out of the house.

MORELL (*taken aback by* CANDIDA's *vigor, and by no means relishing the position of being rescued by her from another man*). Gently, Candida, gently. I am able to take care of myself.

CANDIDA (*petting him*). Yes, dear: of course you are. But you mustnt be annoyed and made miserable.

MARCHBANKS (*almost in tears, turning to the door*). I'll go.

CANDIDA. Oh, you neednt go: I cant turn you out at this time of night. (*Vehemently*) Shame on you! For shame!

MARCHBANKS (*desperately*). But what have I done?

CANDIDA. I know what you have done: as well as if I had been here all the time. Oh, it was unworthy! You are like a child: you cannot hold your tongue.

MARCHBANKS. I would die ten times over sooner than give you a moment's pain.

CANDIDA (*with infinite contempt for this puerility*). Much good your dying would do me!

MORELL. Candida, my dear: this altercation is hardly quite seemly. It is a matter between two men; and I am the right person to settle it.

CANDIDA. Two men! Do you call that a man? (*To* EUGENE) You bad boy!

MARCHBANKS (*gathering a whimsically affectionate courage from the scolding*). If I am to be scolded like a boy, I must make a boy's excuse. He began it. And he's bigger than I am.

CANDIDA (*losing confidence a little as her concern for* MORELL's *dignity takes the alarm*). That cant be true. (*To* MORELL) You didnt begin it, James, did you?

MORELL (*contemptuously*). No.

MARCHBANKS (*indignant*). Oh!

MORELL (*to* EUGENE). *You* began it: this morning. (CANDIDA, *instantly connecting this with his mysterious allusion in the afternoon to something told him by* EUGENE *in the morning, looks at him with quick suspicion.*

GEORGE BERNARD SHAW   413

MORELL *proceeds, with the emphasis of offended superiority*) But your other point is true. I am certainly the bigger of the two, and, I hope, the stronger, Candida. So you had better leave the matter in my hands.

CANDIDA (*again soothing him*). Yes, dear; but—(*troubled*) I dont understand about this morning.

MORELL (*gently snubbing her*). You need not understand, my dear.

CANDIDA. But James, I (*the street bell rings*)—Oh bother! Here they all come. (*She goes out to let them in.*)

MARCHBANKS (*running to* MORELL). Oh, Morell, isnt it dreadful? She's angry with us: she hates me. What shall I do?

MORELL (*with quaint desperation, walking up and down the middle of the room*). Eugene: my head is spinning round. I shall begin to laugh presently.

MARCHBANKS (*following him anxiously*). No, no: she'll think Ive thrown you into hysterics. Dont laugh.

(*Boisterous voices and laughter are heard approaching.* LEXY MILL, *his eyes sparkling, and his bearing denoting unwonted elevation of spirit, enters with* BURGESS, *who is greasy and self-complacent, but has all his wits about him.* MISS GARNETT, *with her smartest hat and jacket on, follows them; but though her eyes are brighter than before, she is evidently a prey to misgiving. She places herself with her back to her typewriting table, with one hand on it to steady herself, passing the other across her forehead as if she were a little tired and giddy.* MARCHBANKS *relapses into shyness and edges away into the corner near the window, where* MORELL'S *books are.*)

LEXY (*exhilarated*). Morell: I *must* congratulate you. (*Grasping his hand*) What a noble, splendid, inspired address you gave us! You surpassed yourself.

BURGESS. So you did, James. It fair kep me awake to the lars' word. Didnt it, Miss Gornett?

PROSERPINE (*worriedly*). Oh, I wasnt minding you: I was trying to make notes. (*She takes out her note-book, and looks at her stenography, which nearly makes her cry.*)

MORELL. Did I go too fast, Pross?

PROSERPINE. Much too fast. You know I cant do more than ninety words a minute. (*She relieves her feelings by throwing her note-book angrily beside her machine, ready for use next morning.*)

MORELL (*soothingly*). Oh well, well, never mind, never mind, never mind. Have you all had supper?

LEXY. Mr Burgess has been kind enough to give us a really splendid supper at the Belgrave.

BURGESS (*with effusive magnanimity*). Dont mention it, Mr Mill. (*Modestly*) Youre arty welcome to my little treat.

PROSERPINE. We had champagne. I never tasted it before. I feel quite giddy.

MORELL (*surprised*). A champagne supper! That was very handsome. Was it my eloquence that produced all this extravagance?

LEXY (*rhetorically*). Your eloquence, and Mr Burgess's goodness of heart. (*With a fresh burst of exhilaration*) And what a very fine fellow the chairman is, Morell! He came to supper with us.

MORELL (*with long drawn significance, looking at* BURGESS). O-o-o-h! the chairman. Now I understand.

(BURGESS *covers with a deprecatory cough a lively satisfaction with his own diplomatic cunning.* LEXY *folds his arms and leans against the head of the sofa in a high-spirited attitude after nearly losing his balance.* CANDIDA *comes in with glasses, lemons, and a jug of hot water on a tray.*)

CANDIDA. Who will have some lemonade? You know our rules: total abstinence. (*She puts the tray on the table, and takes up the lemon squeezer, looking enquiringly round at them.*)

MORELL. No use, dear. Theyve all had champagne. Pross has broken her pledge.

CANDIDA (*to* PROSERPINE). You dont mean to say youve been drinking champagne!

PROSERPINE (*stubbornly*). Yes I do. I'm only a beer teetotaller, not a champagne teetotaller. I don't like beer. Are there any letters for me to answer, Mr Morell?

MORELL. No more to-night.

PROSERPINE. Very well. Goodnight, everybody.

LEXY (*gallantly*). Had I not better see you home, Miss Garnett?

PROSERPINE. No thank you. I shant trust myself with anybody to-night. I wish I hadnt taken any of that stuff. (*She takes uncertain aim at the door; dashes at it; and barely escapes without disaster.*)

BURGESS (*indignantly*). Stuff indeed! That girl dunno what champagne is! Pommery and Greeno at twelve and six a bottle. She took two glasses amost straight horff.

MORELL (*anxious about her*). Go and look after her, Lexy.

LEXY (*alarmed*). But if she should really be—Suppose she began to sing in the street, or anything of that sort.

MORELL. Just so: she may. Thats why youd better see her safely home.

CANDIDA. Do, Lexy: theres a good fellow. (*She shakes his hand and pushes him gently to the door.*)

LEXY. It's evidently my duty to go. I hope it may not be necessary. Goodnight, Mrs Morell. (*To the rest*) Goodnight. (*He goes.* CANDIDA *shuts the door.*)

BURGESS. He was gushin with hextra piety hisself arter two sips. People carnt drink like they huster. (*Bustling across to the hearth*) Well, James: it's time to lock up. Mr Morchbanks: shall I ave the pleasure of your company for a bit o the way ome?

MARCHBANKS (*affrightedly*). Yes: I'd better go. (*He hurries towards the door; but* CANDIDA *places herself before it, barring his way.*)

CANDIDA (*with quiet authority*). You sit down. Youre not going yet.

MARCHBANKS (*quailing*). No: I—I didnt mean to. (*He sits down abjectly on the sofa.*)

CANDIDA. Mr Marchbanks will stay the night with us, papa.

BURGESS. Oh well, I'll say goodnight. So long, James. (*He shakes hands with* MORELL, *and goes over to* EUGENE) Make em give you a night-light by your bed, Mr Morchbanks: itll comfort you if you wake up in the night with a touch of that complaint of yores. Goodnight.

MARCHBANKS. Thank you: I will. Goodnight, Mr. Burgess. (*They shake hands.* BURGESS *goes to the door.*)

CANDIDA (*intercepting* MORELL, *who is following* BURGESS). Stay here, dear: I'll put on papa's coat for him. (*She goes out with* BURGESS.)

MARCHBANKS (*rising and stealing over to* MORELL). Morell: theres going to be a terrible scene. Arnt you afraid?

MORELL. Not in the least.

MARCHBANKS. I never envied you your courage before. (*He puts his hand appealingly on* MORELL'S *forearm*) Stand by me, wont you?

MORELL (*casting him off resolutely*). Each for himself, Eugene. She must choose between us now.

(CANDIDA *returns.* EUGENE *creeps back to the sofa like a guilty schoolboy.*)

CANDIDA (*between them, addressing* EUGENE). Are you sorry?

MARCHBANKS (*earnestly*). Yes. Heartbroken.

CANDIDA. Well then, you are forgiven. Now go off to bed like a good little boy: I want to talk to James about you.

MARCHBANKS (*rising in great consternation*). Oh, I cant do that, Morell. I must be here. I'll not go away. Tell her.

CANDIDA (*her suspicions confirmed*). Tell me what? (*His eyes avoid hers furtively. She turns and mutely transfers the question to* MORELL.)

MORELL (*bracing himself for the catastrophe*). I have nothing to tell her, except (*here his voice deepens to a measured and mournful tenderness*) that she is my greatest treasure on earth—if she is really mine.

CANDIDA (*coldly, offended by his yielding to his orator's instinct and treating her as if she were the audience at the Guild of St Matthew*). I am sure Eugene can say no less, if that is all.

MARCHBANKS (*discouraged*). Morell: she's laughing at us.

MORELL (*with a quick touch of temper*). There is nothing to laugh at. Are you laughing at us, Candida?

CANDIDA (*with quiet anger*). Eugene is very quick-witted, James. I hope I am going to laugh; but I am not sure that I am not going to be very angry. (*She goes to the fireplace, and stands there leaning with her arms on the mantelpiece, and her foot on the fender, whilst* EUGENE *steals to* MORELL *and plucks him by the sleeve.*)

MARCHBANKS (*whispering*). Stop, Morell. Dont let us say anything.

MORELL (*pushing* EUGENE *away without deigning to look at him*). I hope you dont mean that as a threat, Candida.

CANDIDA (*with emphatic warning*). Take care, James. Eugene: I asked you to go. Are you going?

MORELL (*putting his foot down*). He shall not go. I wish him to remain.

MARCHBANKS. I'll go. I'll do whatever you want. (*He turns to the door.*)

CANDIDA. Stop! (*He obeys.*) Didnt you hear James say he wished you to stay? James is master here. Dont you know that?

MARCHBANKS (*flushing with a young poet's rage against tyranny*). By what right is he master?

CANDIDA (*quietly*). Tell him, James.

MORELL (*taken aback*). My dear: I dont know of any right that makes me master. I assert no such right.

CANDIDA (*with infinite reproach*). You dont know! Oh, James! James! (*To* EUGENE, *musingly*) I wonder do you understand, Eugene! (*He shakes his head helplessly, not daring to look at her.*) No: youre too young. Well, I give you leave to stay: to stay and learn. (*She comes away from the hearth and places herself between them*) Now, James! whats the matter? Come: tell me.

MARCHBANKS (*whispering tremulously across to him*). Dont.

CANDIDA. Come. Out with it!

MORELL (*slowly*). I meant to prepare your mind carefully, Candida, so as to prevent misunderstanding.

CANDIDA. Yes, dear: I am sure you did. But never mind: I shant misunderstand.

MORELL. Well—er— (*he hesitates, unable to find the long explanation which he supposed to be available*).

CANDIDA. Well?

MORELL (*blurting it out baldly*). Eugene declares that you are in love with him.

MARCHBANKS (*frantically*). No, no, no, no, never. I did not, Mrs Morell: it's not true. I said I loved you. I said I understood you, and that he couldnt. And it was not after what passed there before the fire that I spoke: it was not, on my word. It was this morning.

CANDIDA (*enlightened*). This morning!

MARCHBANKS. Yes. (*He looks at her, pleading for credence, and then adds simply*) That was what was the matter with my collar.

CANDIDA. Your collar? (*Suddenly taking in his meaning she turns to* MORELL, *shocked*) Oh, James: did you—(*she stops*)?

MORELL (*ashamed*). You know, Candida, that I have a temper to struggle with. And he said (*shuddering*) that you despised me in your heart.

CANDIDA (*turning quickly on* EUGENE). Did you say that?

MARCHBANKS (*terrified*). No.

CANDIDA (*almost fiercely*). Then James has just told me a falsehood. Is that what you mean?

MARCHBANKS. No, no: I—I—(*desperately*) it was David's wife. And it wasnt at home: it was when she saw him dancing before all the people.

MORELL (*taking the cue with a debater's adroitness*). Dancing before all the people, Candida; and thinking he was moving their hearts by his mission when they were only suffering from—Prossy's complaint. (*She is about to protest: he raises his hand to silence her*) Dont try to look indignant, Candida—

CANDIDA. Try!

MORELL (*continuing*). Eugene was right. As you told me a few hours after, he is always right. He said nothing that you did not say better yourself. He is the poet, who sees everything; and I am the poor parson, who understands nothing.

CANDIDA (*remorsefully*). Do you mind what is said by a foolish boy, because I said something like it in jest?

MORELL. That foolish boy can speak with the inspiration of a child and the cunning of a serpent. He has claimed that you belong to him and not to me; and, rightly or wrongly, I have come to fear that it may be true. I will not go about tortured with doubts and suspicions. I will not live with you and keep a secret from you. I will not suffer the intolerable degradation of jealousy. We have agreed—he and I—that you shall choose between us now. I await your decision.

CANDIDA (*slowly recoiling a step, her heart hardened by his rhetoric in spite of the sincere feeling behind it*). Oh! I am to choose, am I? I suppose it is quite settled that I must belong to one or the other.

MORELL (*firmly*). Quite. You must choose definitely.

MARCHBANKS (*anxiously*). Morell: you dont understand. She means that she belongs to herself.

CANDIDA (*turning on him*). I mean that, and a good deal more, Master Eugene, as you will both find out presently. And pray, my lords and masters, what have you to offer for my choice? I am up for auction, it seems. What do you bid, James?

MORELL (*reproachfully*). Cand—(*He breaks down: his eyes and throat fill with tears: the orator becomes a wounded animal*) I can't speak—

CANDIDA (*impulsively going to him*). Ah, dearest—

MARCHBANKS (*in wild alarm*). Stop: it's not fair. You mustnt shew her that you suffer, Morell. I am on the rack too; but I am not crying.

MORELL (*rallying all his forces*).   Yes: you are right. It is not for pity that I am bidding. (*He disengages himself from* CANDIDA.)

CANDIDA (*retreating, chilled*).   I beg your pardon, James: I did not mean to touch you. I am waiting to hear your bid.

MORELL (*with proud humility*).   I have nothing to offer you but my strength for your defence, my honesty for your surety, my ability and industry for your livelihood, and my authority and position for your dignity. That is all it becomes a man to offer to a woman.

CANDIDA (*quite quietly*).   And you, Eugene? What do you offer?

MARCHBANKS.   My weakness. My desolation. My heart's need.

CANDIDA (*impressed*).   Thats a good bid, Eugene. Now I know how to make my choice.

(*She pauses and looks curiously from one to the other, as if weighing them.* MORELL, *whose lofty confidence has changed into heartbreaking dread at* EUGENE's *bid, loses all power of concealing his anxiety.* EUGENE, *strung to the highest tension, does not move a muscle.*)

MORELL (*in a suffocated voice: the appeal bursting from the depths of his anguish*).   Candida!

MARCHBANKS (*aside, in a flash of contempt*).   Coward!

CANDIDA (*significantly*).   I give myself to the weaker of the two.

(EUGENE *divines her meaning at once: his face whitens like steel in a furnace.*)

MORELL (*bowing his head with the calm of collapse*).   I accept your sentence, Candida.

CANDIDA.   Do *you* understand, Eugene?

MARCHBANKS.   Oh, I feel I'm lost. He cannot bear the burden.

MORELL (*incredulously, raising his head and voice with comic abruptness*).   Do you mean *me*, Candida?

CANDIDA (*smiling a little*).   Let us sit and talk comfortably over it like three friends. (*To* MORELL) Sit down, dear. (MORELL, *quite lost, takes the chair from the fireside: the children's chair.*) Bring me that chair, Eugene. (*She indicates the easy chair. He fetches it silently, even with something like cold strength, and places it next* MORELL, *a little behind him. She sits down. He takes the visitor's chair himself, and sits, inscrutable. When they are all settled she begins, throwing a spell of quietness on them by her calm, sane, tender tone*) You remember what you told me about yourself, Eugene: how nobody has cared for you since your old nurse died: how those clever fashionable sisters and successful brothers of yours were your mother's and father's pets: how miserable you were at Eton: how your father is trying to starve you into returning to Oxford: how you have had to live without comfort or welcome or refuge: always lonely, and nearly always disliked and misunderstood, poor boy!

MARCHBANKS (*faithful to the nobility of his lot*). I had my books. I had Nature. And at last I met you.

CANDIDA. Never mind that just at present. Now I want you to look at this other boy here: *my* boy! spoiled from his cradle. We go once a fortnight to see his parents. You should come with us, Eugene, to see the pictures of the hero of that household. James as a baby! the most wonderful of all babies. James holding his first school prize, won at the ripe age of eight! James as the captain of his eleven! James in his first frock coat! James under all sorts of glorious circumstances! You know how strong he is (I hope he didnt hurt you): how clever he is: how happy. (*With deepening gravity*) Ask James's mother and his three sisters what it cost to save James the trouble of doing anything but be strong and clever and happy. Ask *me* what it costs to be James's mother and three sisters and wife and mother to his children all in one. Ask Prossy and Maria how troublesome the house is even when we have no visitors to help us to slice the onions. Ask the tradesmen who want to worry James and spoil his beautiful sermons who it is that puts them off. When there is money to give, he gives it: when there is money to refuse, I refuse it. I build a castle of comfort and indulgence and love for him, and stand sentinel always to keep little vulgar cares out. I make him master here, though he does not know it, and could not tell you a moment ago how it came to be so. (*With sweet irony*) And when he thought I might go away with you, his only anxiety was—what should become of *me!* And to tempt me to stay he offered me (*leaning forward to stroke his hair caressingly at each phrase*) his strength for *my* defence! his industry for my livelihood! his dignity for my position! his—(*relenting*) ah, I am mixing up your beautiful cadences and spoiling them, am I not, darling? (*She lays her cheek fondly against his.*)

MORELL (*quite overcome, kneeling beside her chair and embracing her with boyish ingenuousness*). It's all true, every word. What I am you have made me with the labor of your hands and the love of your heart. You are my wife, my mother, my sisters: you are the sum of all loving care to me.

CANDIDA (*in his arms, smiling, to* EUGENE). Am I *your* mother and sisters to you, Eugene?

MARCHBANKS (*rising with a fierce gesture of disgust*). Ah, never. Out, then, into the night with me!

CANDIDA (*rising quickly*). You are not going like that, Eugene?

MARCHBANKS (*with the ring of a man's voice—no longer a boy's—in the words*). I know the hour when it strikes. I am impatient to do what must be done.

MORELL (*who has also risen*). Candida: dont let him do anything rash.

CANDIDA (*confident, smiling at* EUGENE). Oh, there is no fear. He has learnt to live without happiness.

MARCHBANKS. I no longer desire happiness: life is nobler than that. Parson James: I give you my happiness with both hands. I love you because you have filled the heart of the woman I loved. Goodbye. (*He goes towards the door.*)

CANDIDA. One last word. (*He stops, but without turning to her. She goes to him*) How old are you, Eugene?

MARCHBANKS. As old as the world now. This morning I was eighteen.

CANDIDA. Eighteen! Will you, for my sake, make a little poem out of the two sentences I am going to say to you? And will you promise to repeat it to yourself whenever you think of me?

MARCHBANKS (*without moving*). Say the sentences.

CANDIDA. When I am thirty, she will be forty-five. When I am sixty, she will be seventy-five.

MARCHBANKS (*turning to her*). In a hundred years, we shall be the same age. But I have a better secret than that in my heart. Let me go now. The night outside grows impatient.

CANDIDA. Goodbye. (*She takes his face in her hands; and as he divines her intention and falls on his knees, she kisses his forehead. Then he flies out into the night. She turns to* MORELL, *holding out her arms to him*) Ah, James!

(*They embrace. But they do not know the secret in the poet's heart.*)

QUESTIONS

1. Morell, at the beginning of the play, regards himself, and is regarded by other people, as a strong man. What reasons are there for this? What are the evidences of his strength?

2. What illusions about himself and his marriage is Morell shown to be under during the course of the play? By what stages and by what means is his self-confidence undermined? What does he learn about himself before the end of the play?

3. Marchbanks, at the beginning of the play, seems the weaker of the two main male characters. In what kinds of matters is he weak? Does he have any strengths? What effect does he have on Prossy and Morell? Why?

4. What illusions is Marchbanks under at the beginning of the play? What does he learn about Candida, about marriage, and about himself during the course of the play? What is the significance of his going out alone "into the night" at the end of the play? Are we to feel sorry for him?

5. In the final stage direction, Shaw raises a question for readers that he does not raise for spectators: What is "the secret in the poet's heart"?

6. What kind of person is Candida? What kind of things does she value? What kind of things bore her? On what qualities does she rely for controlling other people? Why is she a good wife for Morell? Would she make a good wife for Marchbanks?

7. Does Marchbanks really come close to winning Candida's affections away from Morell? Does Candida really auction herself off in Act III? Where does the main conflict in the play lie?

8. Who is the strongest character in the play? Why?

9. *Candida* has been frequently admired for its tight dramatic construction. In what ways is the construction effective?

10. One critic has written of *Candida*: "The plot is the same as that of *Othello*, the awakening of doubt in a husband's mind as to the fidelity of his wife." In what other respects is *Candida* like *Othello*? In what important ways is it different? Why is one tragedy and the other comedy? To what extent does *Candida* confirm or fail to confirm the ideas about comedy expressed in the preceding chapter?

11. *The Stronger, An Enemy of the People,* and *Candida* all have something to say about what constitutes strength. Do they say the same thing or different things? Discuss.

Plays for
Further
Reading

Tennessee Williams

THE GLASS MENAGERIE

CHARACTERS

AMANDA WINGFIELD, *the mother, a little woman of great but confused vitality clinging frantically to another time and place. Her characterization must be carefully created, not copied from type. She is not paranoiac, but her life is paranoia. There is much to admire in Amanda, and as much to love and pity as there is to laugh at. Certainly she has endurance and a kind of heroism, and though her foolishness makes her unwittingly cruel at times, there is tenderness in her slight person.*

LAURA WINGFIELD, *her daughter. Amanda, having failed to establish contact with reality, continues to live vitally in her illusions, but Laura's situation is even graver. A childhood illness has left her crippled, one leg slightly shorter than the other, and held in a brace. This defect need not be more than suggested on the stage. Stemming from this, Laura's separation increases till she is like a piece of her own glass collection, too exquisitely fragile to move from the shelf.*

TOM WINGFIELD, *her son and the narrator of the play. A poet with a job in a warehouse. His nature is not remorseless, but to escape from a trap he has to act without pity.*

JIM O'CONNOR, *the gentleman caller, a nice, ordinary, young man.*

SCENE. *An alley in St. Louis.*

Part I. *Preparation for a gentleman caller.*
Part II. *The gentleman calls.*

Time: *Now and the Past.*

SCENE I

    The Wingfield apartment is in the rear of the building, one of those vast hive-like conglomerations of cellular living-units that flower as warty growths in overcrowded urban centers of lower middle-class population and are symptomatic of the impulse of this largest and fundamentally enslaved section of American society to avoid fluidity and differentiation and to exist and function as one interfused mass of automatism.
    The apartment faces an alley and is entered by a fire-escape, a structure

whose name is a touch of accidental poetic truth, for all of these huge buildings are always burning with the slow and implacable fires of human desperation. The fire-escape is included in the set—that is, the landing of it and steps descending from it.

The scene is memory and is therefore nonrealistic. Memory takes a lot of poetic license. It omits some details; others are exaggerated, according to the emotional value of the articles it touches, for memory is seated predominantly in the heart. The interior is therefore rather dim and poetic.

At the rise of the curtain, the audience is faced with the dark, grim rear wall of the Wingfield tenement. This building, which runs parallel to the footlights, is flanked on both sides by dark, narrow alleys which run into murky canyons of tangled clotheslines, garbage cans and the sinister latticework of neighboring fire-escapes. It is up and down these side alleys that exterior entrances and exits are made, during the play. At the end of Tom's opening commentary, the dark tenement wall slowly reveals (by means of a transparency) the interior of the ground floor Wingfield apartment.

Downstage is the living room, which also serves as a sleeping room for Laura, the sofa unfolding to make her bed. Upstage, center, and divided by a wide arch or second proscenium with transparent faded portieres (or second curtain), is the dining room. In an old-fashioned what-not in the living room are seen scores of transparent glass animals. A blown-up photograph of the father hangs on the wall of the living room, facing the audience, to the left of the archway. It is the face of a very handsome young man in a doughboy's First World War cap. He is gallantly smiling, ineluctably smiling, as if to say, "I will be smiling forever."

The audience hears and sees the opening scene in the dining room through both the transparent fourth wall of the building and the transparent gauze portieres of the dining-room arch. It is during this revealing scene that the fourth wall slowly ascends, out of sight. This transparent exterior wall is not brought down again until the very end of the play, during Tom's final speech.

The narrator is an undisguised convention of the play. He takes whatever license with dramatic convention as is convenient to his purposes.

Tom enters dressed as a merchant sailor from alley, stage left, and strolls across the front of the stage to the fire-escape. There he stops and lights a cigarette. He addresses the audience.

Tom.   Yes, I have tricks in my pocket, I have things up my sleeve. But I am the opposite of a stage magician. He gives you illusion that has the appearance of truth. I give you truth in the pleasant disguise of illusion.

To begin with, I turn back time. I reverse it to that quaint period, the thirties, when the huge middle class of America was matriculating in a school for the blind. Their eyes had failed them, or they had failed their eyes, and so they were having their fingers pressed forcibly down on the fiery Braille alphabet of a dissolving economy.

In Spain there was revolution. Here there was only shouting and confusion.

In Spain there was Guernica. Here there were disturbances of labor, sometimes pretty violent, in otherwise peaceful cities such as Chicago, Cleveland, Saint Louis . . .

This is the social background of the play. (*Music.*)

The play is memory.

Being a memory play, it is dimly lighted, it is sentimental, it is not realistic.

In memory everything seems to happen to music. That explains the fiddle in the wings.

I am the narrator of the play, and also a character in it.

The other characters are my mother, Amanda, my sister, Laura, and a gentleman caller who appears in the final scenes.

He is the most realistic character in the play, being an emissary from a world of reality that we were somehow set apart from.

But since I have a poet's weakness for symbols, I am using this character also as a symbol; he is the long delayed but always expected something that we live for.

There is a fifth character in the play who doesn't appear except in this larger-than-life-size photograph over the mantel.

This is our father who left us a long time ago.

He was a telephone man who fell in love with long distances; he gave up his job with the telephone company and skipped the light fantastic out of town . . .

The last we heard of him was a picture post-card from Mazatlan, on the Pacific coast of Mexico, containing a message of two words—

"Hello—Good-bye!" and no address.

I think the rest of the play will explain itself . . .

(AMANDA's *voice becomes audible through the portieres. He divides the portieres and enters the upstage area.* AMANDA *and* LAURA *are seated at a drop-leaf table. Eating is indicated by gestures without food or utensils.* AMANDA *faces the audience.* TOM *and* LAURA *are seated in profile.*)

(*The interior has lit up softly and through the scrim we see* AMANDA *and* LAURA *seated at the table in the upstage area.*)

AMANDA (*calling*). Tom?

TOM. Yes, Mother.

AMANDA. We can't say grace until you come to the table!

TOM. Coming, Mother. (*He bows slightly and withdraws, reappearing a few moments later in his place at the table.*)

AMANDA (*to her son*). Honey, don't *push* with your *fingers.* If you have to push with something, the thing to push with is a crust of bread. And chew—chew! Animals have sections in their stomachs which enable them to digest food without mastication, but human beings are supposed to chew their food before they swallow it down. Eat food leisurely, son, and really enjoy it. A well-cooked meal has lots of delicate flavors that have to be held in the mouth for appreciation. So chew your food and give your salivary glands a chance to function!

(TOM *deliberately lays his imaginary fork down and pushes his chair back from the table.*)

TOM. I haven't enjoyed one bite of this dinner because of your constant directions on how to eat it. It's you that make me rush through meals with your hawk-like attention to every bite I take. Sickening—spoils my appetite—all this discussion of—animals' secretion—salivary glands—mastication!

AMANDA (*lightly*). Temperament like a Metropolitan star! (*He rises and crosses downstage.*) You're not excused from the table.

TOM. I'm getting a cigarette.

AMANDA. You smoke too much.

(LAURA *rises.*)

LAURA. I'll bring in the blanc mange.

(*He remains standing with his cigarette by the portieres during the following.*)

AMANDA (*rising*). No, sister, no, sister—you be the lady this time and I'll be the darky.

LAURA. I'm already up.

AMANDA. Resume your seat, little sister—I want you to stay fresh and pretty—for gentlemen callers!

LAURA. I'm not expecting any gentlemen callers.

AMANDA (*crossing out to kitchenette. Airily*). Sometimes they come when they are least expected! Why, I remember one Sunday afternoon in Blue Mountain—(*enters kitchenette*).

TOM. I know what's coming!

LAURA. Yes. But let her tell it.

TOM. Again?

LAURA. She loves to tell it.

(AMANDA *returns with bowl of dessert.*)

AMANDA. One Sunday afternoon in Blue Mountain—your mother received—*seventeen!*—gentlemen callers! Why, sometimes there weren't chairs enough to accommodate them all. We had to send the nigger over to bring in folding chairs from the parish house.

Tom (*remaining at portieres*).   How did you entertain those gentlemen callers?

Amanda.   I understood the art of conversation!

Tom.   I bet you could talk.

Amanda.   Girls in those days *knew* how to talk, I can tell you.

Tom.   Yes?

Amanda.   They knew how to entertain their gentlemen callers. It wasn't enough for a girl to be possessed of a pretty face and a graceful figure—although I wasn't slighted in either respect. She also needed to have a nimble wit and a tongue to meet all occasions.

Tom.   What did you talk about?

Amanda.   Things of importance going on in the world! Never anything coarse or common or vulgar. (*She addresses* Tom *as though he were seated in the vacant chair at the table though he remains by portieres. He plays this scene as though he held the book.*) My callers were gentlemen—all! Among my callers were some of the most prominent young planters of the Mississippi Delta—planters and sons of planters!

(Tom *motions for music and a spot of light on* Amanda. *Her eyes lift, her face glows, her voice becomes rich and elegiac.*)

There was young Champ Laughlin who later became vice-president of the Delta Planters Bank.

Hadley Stevenson who was drowned in Moon Lake and left his widow one hundred and fifty thousand in Government bonds.

There were the Cutrere brothers, Wesley and Bates. Bates was one of my bright particular beaux! He got in a quarrel with that wild Wainwright boy. They shot it out on the floor of Moon Lake Casino. Bates was shot through the stomach. Died in the ambulance on his way to Memphis. His widow was also well-provided for, came into eight or ten thousand acres, that's all. She married him on the rebound—never loved her—carried my picture on him the night he died!

And there was that boy that every girl in the Delta had set her cap for! That beautiful, brilliant young Fitzhugh boy from Greene County!

Tom.   What did he leave his widow?

Amanda.   He never married! Gracious, you talk as though all of my old admirers had turned up their toes to the daisies!

Tom.   Isn't this the first you've mentioned that still survives?

Amanda.   That Fitzhugh boy went North and made a fortune—came to be known as the Wolf of Wall Street! He had the Midas touch, whatever he touched turned to gold!

And I could have been Mrs. Duncan J. Fitzhugh, mind you! But—I picked your *father!*

Laura (*rising*).   Mother, let me clear the table.

Amanda.   No, dear, you go in front and study your typewriter chart.

Or practice your shorthand a little. Stay fresh and pretty!—It's almost time for our gentlemen callers to start arriving. (*She flounces girlishly toward the kitchenette.*) How many do you suppose we're going to entertain this afternoon?

(TOM *throws down the paper and jumps up with a groan.*)

LAURA (*alone in the dining room*). I don't believe we're going to receive any, Mother.

AMANDA (*reappearing, airily*). What? No one—not one? You must be joking! (LAURA *nervously echoes her laugh. She slips in a fugitive manner through the half-open portieres and draws them gently behind her. A shaft of very clear light is thrown on her face against the faded tapestry of the curtains. Music: "The Glass Menagerie" under faintly. Lightly*) Not one gentleman caller? It can't be true! There must be a flood, there must have been a tornado!

LAURA. It isn't a flood, it's not a tornado, Mother. I'm just not popular like you were in Blue Mountain . . . (TOM *utters another groan.* LAURA *glances at him with a faint, apologetic smile. Her voice catching a little.*) Mother's afraid I'm going to be an old maid.

(*The scene dims out with "Glass Menagerie" music.*)

SCENE II

On the dark stage the screen is lighted with the image of blue roses.
Gradually LAURA'S *figure becomes apparent and the screen goes out.*
The music subsides.
LAURA *is seated in the delicate ivory chair at the small claw-foot table.*
She wears a dress of soft violet material for a kimono—her hair tied back from her forehead with a ribbon.
She is washing and polishing her collection of glass.
AMANDA *appears on the fire-escape steps. At the sound of her ascent,* LAURA *catches her breath, thrusts the bowl of ornaments away and seats herself stiffly before the diagram of the typewriter keyboard as though it held her spellbound.*
Something has happened to AMANDA. *It is written in her face as she climbs to the landing: a look that is grim and hopeless and a little absurd.*
She has on one of those cheap or imitation velvety-looking cloth coats with imitation fur collar. Her hat is five or six years old, one of those dreadful cloche hats that were worn in the late twenties, and she is clasping an enormous black patent-leather pocketbook with nickel clasps and initials. This is her full-dress outfit, the one she usually wears to the D.A.R.
Before entering she looks through the door.

She purses her lips, opens her eyes very wide, rolls them upward and shakes her head.

Then she slowly lets herself in the door. Seeing her mother's expression LAURA *touches her lips with a nervous gesture.*

LAURA. Hello, Mother, I was—

(*She makes a nervous gesture toward the chart on the wall.* AMANDA *leans against the shut door and stares at* LAURA *with a martyred look.*)

AMANDA. Deception? Deception? (*She slowly removes her hat and gloves, continuing the sweet suffering stare. She lets the hat and gloves fall on the floor—a bit of acting.*)

LAURA (*shakily*). How was the D.A.R. meeting? (AMANDA *slowly opens her purse and removes a dainty white handkerchief which she shakes out delicately and delicately touches to her lips and nostrils.*) Didn't you go to the D.A.R. meeting, Mother?

AMANDA (*faintly, almost inaudibly*). —No.—No. (*Then more forcibly*) I did not have the strength—to go to the D.A.R. In fact, I did not have the courage! I wanted to find a hole in the ground and hide myself in it forever! (*She crosses slowly to the wall and removes the diagram of the typewriter keyboard. She holds it in front of her for a second, staring at it sweetly and sorrowfully—then bites her lips and tears it in two pieces.*)

LAURA (*faintly*). Why did you do that, Mother? (AMANDA *repeats the same procedure with the chart of the Gregg Alphabet.*) Why are you—

AMANDA. Why? Why? How old are you, Laura?

LAURA. Mother, you know my age.

AMANDA. I thought that you were an adult; it seems that I was mistaken. (*She crosses slowly to the sofa and sinks down and stares at* LAURA.)

LAURA. Please don't stare at me, Mother.

(AMANDA *closes her eyes and lowers her head. Count ten.*)

AMANDA. What are we going to do, what is going to become of us, what is the future?

(*Count ten.*)

LAURA. Has something happened, Mother? (AMANDA *draws a long breath and takes out the handkerchief again. Dabbing process.*) Mother, has —something happened?

AMANDA. I'll be all right in a minute, I'm just bewildered—(*Count five*)—by life . . .

LAURA. Mother, I wish that you would tell me what's happened!

AMANDA. As you know, I was supposed to be inducted into my office at the D.A.R. this afternoon. But I stopped off at Rubicam's Business College to speak to your teachers about your having a cold and ask them what progress they thought you were making down there.

LAURA. Oh . . .

AMANDA. I went to the typing instructor and introduced myself as your mother. She didn't know who you were. Wingfield, she said. We don't have any such student enrolled at the school!

I assured her she did, that you had been going to classes since early in January.

"I wonder," she said, "if you could be talking about that terribly shy little girl who dropped out of school after only a few days' attendance?"

"No," I said, "Laura, my daughter, has been going to school every day for the past six weeks!"

"Excuse me," she said. She took the attendance book out and there was your name, unmistakably printed, and all the dates you were absent until they decided that you had dropped out of school.

I still said, "No, there must have been some mistake! There must have been some mix-up in the records!"

And she said, "No—I remember her perfectly now. Her hands shook so that she couldn't hit the right keys! The first time we gave a speed-test, she broke down completely—was sick at the stomach and almost had to be carried into the wash-room! After that morning she never showed up any more. We phoned the house but never got any answer—while I was working at Famous and Barr, I suppose, demonstrating those—Oh!"

I felt so weak I could barely keep on my feet!

I had to sit down while they got me a glass of water!

Fifty dollars' tuition, all of our plans—my hopes and ambitions for you— just gone up the spout, just gone up the spout like that.

(LAURA *draws a long breath and gets awkwardly to her feet. She crosses to the victrola and winds it up.*)

What are you doing?

LAURA. Oh! (*She releases the handle and returns to her seat.*)

AMANDA. Laura, where have you been going when you've gone out pretending that you were going to business college?

LAURA. I've just been going out walking.

AMANDA. That's not true.

LAURA. It is. I just went walking.

AMANDA. Walking? Walking? In winter? Deliberately courting pneumonia in that light coat? Where did you walk to, Laura?

LAURA. All sorts of places—mostly in the park.

AMANDA. Even after you'd started catching that cold?

LAURA. It was the lesser of two evils, Mother. I couldn't go back up. I—threw up—on the floor!

AMANDA. From half past seven till after five every day you mean to tell me you walked around in the park, because you wanted to make me think that you were still going to Rubicam's Business College?

LAURA. It wasn't as bad as it sounds. I went inside places to get warmed up.

AMANDA. Inside where?

LAURA. I went in the art museum and the bird-houses at the Zoo. I visited the penguins every day! Sometimes I did without lunch and went to the movies. Lately I've been spending most of my afternoons in the Jewel-box, that big glass house where they raise the tropical flowers.

AMANDA. You did all this to deceive me, just for deception? (LAURA *looks down.*) Why?

LAURA. Mother, when you're disappointed, you get that awful suffering look on your face, like the picture of Jesus' mother in the museum!

AMANDA. Hush!

LAURA. I couldn't face it.

(*Pause. A whisper of strings.*)

AMANDA (*hopelessly fingering the huge pocketbook*). So what are we going to do the rest of our lives? Stay home and watch the parades go by? Amuse ourselves with the glass menagerie, darling? Eternally play those worn-out phonograph records your father left as a painful reminder of him?

We won't have a business career—we've given that up because it gave us nervous indigestion! (*Laughs wearily*) What is there left but dependency all our lives? I know so well what becomes of unmarried women who aren't prepared to occupy a position. I've seen such pitiful cases in the South— barely tolerated spinsters living upon the grudging patronage of sister's husband or brother's wife!—stuck away in some little mouse-trap of a room— encouraged by one in-law to visit another—little birdlike women without any nest—eating the crust of humility all their life!

Is that the future that we've mapped out for ourselves?

I swear it's the only alternative I can think of!

It isn't a very pleasant alternative, is it?

Of course—some girls *do marry.*

(LAURA *twists her hands nervously.*)

Haven't you ever liked some boy?

LAURA. Yes. I liked one once. (*Rises*) I came across his picture a while ago.

AMANDA (*with some interest*). He gave you his picture?

LAURA. No, it's in the year-book.

AMANDA (*disappointed*). Oh—a high-school boy.

LAURA. Yes. His name was Jim. (LAURA *lifts the heavy annual from the claw-foot table.*) Here he is in *The Pirates of Penzance.*

AMANDA (*absently*). The what?

LAURA. The operetta the senior class put on. He had a wonderful voice and we sat across the aisle from each other Mondays, Wednesdays and Fridays in the Aud. Here he is with the silver cup for debating! See his grin?

AMANDA (*absently*).   He must have had a jolly disposition.

LAURA.   He used to call me—Blue Roses.

AMANDA.   Why did he call you such a name as that?

LAURA.   When I had that attack of pleurosis—he asked me what was the matter when I came back. I said pleurosis—he thought that I said Blue Roses! So that's what he always called me after that. Whenever he saw me, he'd holler, "Hello, Blue Roses!" I didn't care for the girl that he went out with. Emily Meisenbach. Emily was the best-dressed girl at Soldan. She never struck me, though, as being sincere . . . It says in the Personal Section—they're engaged. That's—six years ago! They must be married by now.

AMANDA.   Girls that aren't cut out for business careers usually wind up married to some nice man. (*Gets up with a spark of revival.*) Sister, that's what you'll do!

(LAURA *utters a startled, doubtful laugh. She reaches quickly for a piece of glass.*)

LAURA.   But, Mother—

AMANDA.   Yes? (*Crossing to photograph.*)

LAURA (*in a tone of frightened apology*).   I'm—crippled!

AMANDA.   Nonsense! Laura, I've told you never, never to use that word. Why, you're not crippled, you just have a little defect—hardly noticeable, even! When people have some slight disadvantage like that, they cultivate other things to make up for it—develop charm—and vivacity—and—*charm!* That's all you have to do! (*She turns again to the photograph.*) One thing your father had *plenty of*—was *charm!*

(TOM *motions to the fiddle in the wings. The scene fades out with music.*)

SCENE III

TOM *speaks from the fire-escape landing.*

TOM.   After the fiasco at Rubicam's Business College, the idea of getting a gentleman caller for Laura began to play a more and more important part in Mother's calculations.

It became an obsession. Like some archetype of the universal unconscious, the image of the gentleman caller haunted our small apartment . . .

An evening at home rarely passed without some allusion to this image, this spectre, this hope . . .

Even when he wasn't mentioned, his presence hung in Mother's preoccupied look and in my sister's frightened, apologetic manner—hung like a sentence passed upon the Wingfields!

Mother was a woman of action as well as words.

She began to take logical steps in the planned direction.

Late that winter and in the early spring—realizing that extra money would be needed to properly feather the nest and plume the bird—she conducted a vigorous campaign on the telephone, roping in subscribers to one of those magazines for matrons called *The Home-maker's Companion*, the type of journal that features the serialized sublimations of ladies of letters who think in terms of delicate cup-like breasts, slim, tapering waists, rich, creamy thighs, eyes like wood-smoke in autumn, fingers that soothe and caress like strains of music, bodies as powerful as Etruscan sculpture.

(AMANDA *enters with phone on long extension cord. She is spotted in the dim stage.*)

AMANDA.   Ida Scott? This is Amanda Wingfield!
We *missed* you at the D.A.R. last Monday!
I said to myself: She's probably suffering with that sinus condition! How is that sinus condition?
Horrors! Heaven have mercy!—You're a Christian martyr, yes, that's what you are, a Christian martyr!
Well, I just now happened to notice that your subscription to the *Companion's* about to expire! Yes, it expires with the next issue, honey!—just when that wonderful new serial by Bessie Mae Hopper is getting off to such an exciting start. Oh, honey, it's something that you can't miss! You remember how *Gone With the Wind* took everybody by storm? You simply couldn't go out if you hadn't read it. All everybody *talked* was Scarlett O'Hara. Well, this is a book that critics already compare to *Gone With the Wind*. It's the *Gone With the Wind* of the post-World War generation!—What?—Burning?—Oh, honey, don't let them burn, go take a look in the oven and I'll hold the wire! Heavens—I think she's hung up!

(*Before the stage is lighted, the violent voices of* TOM *and* AMANDA *are heard.*
(*They are quarreling behind the portieres. In front of them stands* LAURA *with clenched hands and panicky expression.*
(*A clear pool of light on her figure throughout this scene.*)

TOM.   What in Christ's name am I—
AMANDA (*shrilly*).   Don't you use that—
TOM.   Supposed to do!
AMANDA.   Expression! Not in my—
TOM.   Ohhh!
AMANDA.   Presence! Have you gone out of your senses?
TOM.   I have, that's true, *driven* out!
AMANDA.   What is the matter with you, you—big—big—IDIOT!
TOM.   Look!—I've got *no thing*, no single thing—
AMANDA.   Lower your voice!
TOM.   In my life here that I can call my OWN! Everything is—

AMANDA. Stop that shouting!

TOM. Yesterday you confiscated my books! You had the nerve to—

AMANDA. I took that horrible novel back to the library—yes! That hideous book by that insane Mr. Lawrence. (TOM *laughs wildly.*) I cannot control the output of diseased minds or people who cater to them—(TOM *laughs still more wildly*) BUT I WON'T ALLOW SUCH FILTH BROUGHT INTO MY HOUSE! No, no, no, no, no!

TOM. House, house! Who pays rent on it, who makes a slave of himself to—

AMANDA (*fairly screeching*). Don't you DARE to—

TOM. No, no, I mustn't say things! *I've* got to just—

AMANDA. Let me tell you—

TOM. I don't want to hear any more!

(*He tears the portieres open. The upstage area is lit with a turgid smoky red glow.*

(AMANDA's *hair is in metal curlers and she wears a very old bathrobe, much too large for her slight figure, a relic of the faithless Mr. Wingfield.*

(*An upright typewriter and a wild disarray of manuscripts is on the drop-leaf table. The quarrel was probably precipitated by* AMANDA's *interruption of his creative labor. A chair lying overthrown on the floor.*

(*Their gesticulating shadows are cast on the ceiling by the fiery glow.*)

AMANDA. You *will* hear more, you—

TOM. No, I won't hear more, I'm going out!

AMANDA. You come right back in—

TOM. Out, out, out! Because I'm—

AMANDA. Come back here, Tom Wingfield! I'm not through talking to you!

TOM. Oh, go—

LAURA (*desperately*). —Tom!

AMANDA. You're going to listen, and no more insolence from you! I'm at the end of my patience!

(*He comes back toward her.*)

TOM. What do you think I'm at? Aren't I supposed to have any patience to reach the end of, Mother? I know, I know. It seems unimportant to you, what I'm *doing*—what I *want* to do—having a little *difference* between them! You don't think that—

AMANDA. I think you've been doing things that you're ashamed of. That's why you act like this. I don't believe that you go every night to the movies. Nobody goes to the movies night after night. Nobody in their right minds goes to the movies as often as you pretend to. People don't go to the movies at nearly midnight, and movies don't let out at two A.M. Come in stumbling. Muttering to yourself like a maniac! You get three hours' sleep and then go to work. Oh, I can picture the way you're doing down there. Moping, doping, because you're in no condition.

Tom (*wildly*). No, I'm in no condition!

AMANDA. What right have you got to jeopardize your job? Jeopardize the security of us all? How do you think we'd manage if you were—

Tom. Listen! You think I'm crazy *about* the *warehouse*? (*He bends fiercely toward her slight figure.*) You think I'm in love with the Continental Shoemakers? You think I want to spend fifty-five *years* down there in that *cclotex interior!* with—*fluorescent—tubes!* Look! I'd rather somebody picked up a crowbar and battered out my brains—than go back mornings! I *go!* Every time you come in yelling that God damn "*Rise and Shine!*" "*Rise and Shine!*" I say to myself, "How *lucky dead* people are!" But I get up. I *go!* For sixty-five dollars a month I give up all that I dream of doing and being *ever!* And you say self—*self*'s all I ever think of. Why, listen, if self is what I thought of, Mother, I'd be where he is—GONE! (*Pointing to father's picture*) As far as the system of transportation reaches! (*He starts past her. She grabs his arm.*) Don't grab at me, Mother!

AMANDA. Where are you going?

Tom. I'm going to the *movies!*

AMANDA. I don't believe that lie!

Tom (*crouching toward her, overtowering her tiny figure. She backs away, gasping*). I'm going to opium dens! Yes, opium dens, dens of vice and criminals' hang-outs, Mother. I've joined the Hogan gang, I'm a hired assassin, I carry a tommy-gun in a violin case! I run a string of cat-houses in the Valley! They call me Killer, Killer Wingfield, I'm leading a double-life, a simple, honest warehouse worker by day, by night a dynamic *czar* of the *underworld, Mother*. I go to gambling casinos, I spin away fortunes on the roulette table! I wear a patch over one eye and a false mustache, sometimes I put on green whiskers. On those occasions they call me—*El Diablo!* Oh, I could tell you things to make you sleepless! My enemies plan to dynamite this place. They're going to blow us all sky-high some night! I'll be glad, very happy, and so will you! You'll go up, up on a broomstick, over Blue Mountain with seventeen gentlemen callers! You ugly—babbling old—*witch* . . .

(*He goes through a series of violent, clumsy movements, seizing his overcoat, lunging to the door, pulling it fiercely open. The women watch him, aghast. His arm catches in the sleeve of the coat as he struggles to pull it on. For a moment he is pinioned by the bulky garment. With an outraged groan he tears the coat off again, splitting the shoulder of it, and hurls it across the room. It strikes against the shelf of LAURA's glass collection, there is a tinkle of shattering glass. LAURA cries out as if wounded. Music: "The Glass Menagerie."*)

LAURA (*shrilly*). My glass!—menagerie . . . (*She covers her face and turns away.*)

(*But* AMANDA *is still stunned and stupefied by the "ugly witch" so that she barely notices this occurrence. Now she recovers her speech.*)

AMANDA (*in an awful voice*).   I won't speak to you—until you apologize!

(*She crosses through portieres and draws them together behind her.* TOM *is left with* LAURA. LAURA *clings weakly to the mantel with her face averted.* TOM *stares at her stupidly for a moment. Then he crosses to shelf. Drops awkwardly on his knees to collect the fallen glass, glancing at* LAURA *as if he would speak but couldn't. "The Glass Menagerie" steals in as the scene dims out.*)

SCENE IV

The interior is dark. Faint light in the alley.

A deep-voiced bell in a church is tolling the hour of five as the scene commences.

TOM *appears at the top of the alley. After each solemn boom of the bell in the tower, he shakes a little noise-maker or rattle as if to express the tiny spasm of man in contrast to the sustained power and dignity of the Almighty. This and the unsteadiness of his advance make it evident that he has been drinking.*

As he climbs the few steps to the fire-escape landing, light steals up inside. LAURA *appears in night-dress, observing* TOM'S *empty bed in the front room.*

TOM *fishes in his pockets for door-key, removing a motley assortment of articles in the search, including a perfect shower of movie-ticket stubs and an empty bottle. At last he finds the key, but just as he is about to insert it, it slips from his fingers. He strikes a match and crouches below the door.*

TOM (*bitterly*).   One crack—and it falls through!

(LAURA *opens the door.*)

LAURA.   Tom! Tom, what are you doing?
TOM.   Looking for a door-key.
LAURA.   Where have you been all this time?
TOM.   I have been to the movies.
LAURA.   All this time at the movies?
TOM.   There was a very long program. There was a Garbo picture and a Mickey Mouse and a travelogue and a newsreel and a preview of coming attractions. And there was an organ solo and a collection for the milk-fund—simultaneously—which ended up in a terrible fight between a fat lady and an usher!
LAURA (*innocently*).   Did you have to stay through everything?

Tom. Of course! And, oh, I forgot! There was a big stage show! The headliner on this stage show was Malvolio the Magician. He performed wonderful tricks, many of them, such as pouring water back and forth between pitchers. First it turned to wine and then it turned to beer and then it turned to whiskey. I know it was whiskey it finally turned into because he needed somebody to come up out of the audience to help him, and I came up—both shows! It was Kentucky Straight Bourbon. A very generous fellow, he gave souvenirs. (*He pulls from his back pocket a shimmering rainbow-colored scarf.*) He gave me this. This is his magic scarf. You can have it, Laura. You wave it over a canary cage and you get a bowl of gold-fish. You wave it over the gold-fish bowl and they fly away canaries . . . But the wonderfullest trick of all was the coffin trick. We nailed him into a coffin and he got out of the coffin without removing one nail. (*He has come inside.*) There is a trick that would come in handy for me—get me out of this 2 by 4 situation! (*Flops onto bed and starts removing shoes.*)

Laura. Tom—Shhh!

Tom. What're you shushing me for?

Laura. You'll wake up Mother.

Tom. Goody, goody! Pay 'er back for all those "Rise an' Shines." (*Lies down, groaning*) You know it don't take much intelligence to get yourself into a nailed-up coffin, Laura. But who in hell ever got himself out of one without removing one nail?

(*As if in answer, the father's grinning photograph lights up. Scene dims out.*

(*Immediately following: The church bell is heard striking six. At the sixth stroke the alarm clock goes off in* Amanda's *room, and after a few moments we hear her calling: "Rise and Shine! Rise and Shine! Laura, go tell your brother to rise and shine!"*)

Tom (*sitting up slowly*). I'll rise—but I won't shine.

(*The light increases.*)

Amanda. Laura, tell your brother his coffee is ready.

(Laura *slips into front room.*)

Laura. Tom!—It's nearly seven. Don't make Mother nervous. (*He stares at her stupidly. Beseechingly*) Tom, speak to Mother this morning. Make up with her, apologize, speak to her!

Tom. She won't to me. It's her that started not speaking.

Laura. If you just say you're sorry she'll start speaking.

Tom. Her not speaking—is that such a tragedy?

Laura. Please—please!

Amanda (*calling from kitchenette*). Laura, are you going to do what I asked you to do, or do I have to get dressed and go out myself?

LAURA. Going, going—soon as I get on my coat! (*She pulls on a shapeless felt hat with nervous, jerky movement, pleadingly glancing at* TOM. *Rushes awkwardly for coat. The coat is one of* AMANDA'S, *inaccurately made-over, the sleeves too short for* LAURA.) Butter and what else?

AMANDA (*entering upstage*). Just butter. Tell them to charge it.

LAURA. Mother, they make such faces when I do that.

AMANDA. Sticks and stones can break our bones, but the expression on Mr. Garfinkel's face won't harm us! Tell your brother his coffee is getting cold.

LAURA (*at door*). Do what I asked you, will you, will you, Tom?

(*He looks sullenly away.*)

AMANDA. Laura, go now or just don't go at all!

LAURA (*rushing out*). Going—going!

(*A second later she cries out.* TOM *springs up and crosses to door.* AMANDA *rushes anxiously in.* TOM *opens the door.*)

TOM. Laura?

LAURA. I'm all right. I slipped, but I'm all right.

AMANDA (*peering anxiously after her*). If anyone breaks a leg on those fire-escape steps, the landlord ought to be sued for every cent he possesses! (*She shuts door. Remembers she isn't speaking and returns to other room.*)

(*As* TOM *enters listlessly for his coffee, she turns her back to him and stands rigidly facing the window on the gloomy gray vault of the areaway. Its light on her face with its aged but childish features is cruelly sharp, satirical as a Daumier print.*

(*Music under: "Ave Maria."*

(*TOM glances sheepishly but sullenly at her averted figure and slumps at the table. The coffee is scalding hot; he sips it and gasps and spits it back in the cup. At his gasp,* AMANDA *catches her breath and half turns. Then catches herself and turns back to window.*

(*TOM blows on his coffee, glancing sidewise at his mother. She clears her throat.* TOM *clears his. He starts to rise. Sinks back down again, scratches his head, clears his throat again.* AMANDA *coughs.* TOM *raises his cup in both hands to blow on it, his eyes staring over the rim of it at his mother for several moments. Then he slowly sets the cup down and awkwardly and hesitantly rises from the chair.*)

TOM (*hoarsely*). Mother. I—I apologize, Mother. (*AMANDA draws a quick, shuddering breath. Her face works grotesquely. She breaks into child-like tears.*) I'm sorry for what I said, for everything that I said, I didn't mean it.

AMANDA (*sobbingly*). My devotion has made me a witch and so I make myself hateful to my children!

Tom. *No,* you *don't.*

Amanda. I worry so much, don't sleep, it makes me nervous!

Tom (*gently*). I understand that.

Amanda. I've had to put up a solitary battle all these years. But you're my right-hand bower! Don't fall down, don't fail!

Tom (*gently*). I try, Mother.

Amanda (*with great enthusiasm*). Try and you will succeed! (*The notion makes her breathless.*) Why, you—you're just *full* of natural endowments! Both of my children—they're *unusual* children! Don't you think I know it? I'm so—*proud!* Happy and—feel I've—so much to be thankful for but—Promise me one thing, Son!

Tom. What, Mother?

Amanda. Promise, son, you'll—never be a drunkard!

Tom (*turns to her grinning*). I will never be a drunkard, Mother.

Amanda. That's what frightened me so, that you'd be drinking! Eat a bowl of Purina!

Tom. Just coffee, Mother.

Amanda. Shredded wheat biscuit?

Tom. No. No, Mother, just coffee.

Amanda. You can't put in a day's work on an empty stomach. You've got ten minutes—don't gulp! Drinking too-hot liquids makes cancer of the stomach . . . Put cream in.

Tom. No, thank you.

Amanda. To cool it.

Tom. No! No, thank you, I want it black.

Amanda. I know, but it's not good for you. We have to do all that we can to build ourselves up. In these trying times we live in, all that we have to cling to is—each other . . . That's why it's so important to—Tom, I—I sent out your sister so I could discuss something with you. If you hadn't spoken I would have spoken to you. (*Sits down.*)

Tom (*gently*). What is it, Mother, that you want to discuss?

Amanda. *Laura!*

(Tom *puts his cup down slowly.*
(*Music: "The Glass Menagerie."*)

Tom. —Oh.—Laura . . .

Amanda (*touching his sleeve*). You know how Laura is. So quiet but—still water runs deep! She notices things and I think she—broods about them. (Tom *looks up.*) A few days ago I came in and she was crying.

Tom. What about?

Amanda. You.

Tom. Me?

Amanda. She has an idea that you're not happy here.

Tom. What gave her that idea?

AMANDA. What gives her any idea? However, you do act strangely. I—I'm not criticizing, understand *that!* I know your ambitions do not lie in the warehouse, that like everybody in the whole wide world—you've had to—make sacrifices, but—Tom—Tom—life's not easy, it calls for—Spartan endurance! There's so many things in my heart that I cannot describe to you! I've never told you but I—*loved* your father . . .

TOM (*gently*). I know that, Mother.

AMANDA. And you—when I see you taking after his ways! Staying out late—and—well, you *had* been drinking the night you were in that—terrifying condition! Laura says that you hate the apartment and that you go out nights to get away from it! Is that true, Tom?

TOM. No. You say there's so much in your heart that you can't describe to me. That's true of me, too. There's so much in my heart that I can't describe to *you!* So let's respect each other's—

AMANDA. But, why—*why*, Tom—are you always so *restless?* Where do you go to, nights?

TOM. I—go to the movies.

AMANDA. Why do you go to the movies so much, Tom?

TOM. I go to the movies because—I like adventure. Adventure is something I don't have much of at work, so I go to the movies.

AMANDA. But, Tom, you go to the movies *entirely* too *much!*

TOM. I like a lot of adventure.

(AMANDA *looks baffled, then hurt. As the familiar inquistion resumes he becomes hard and impatient again.* AMANDA *slips back into her querulous attitude toward him.*)

AMANDA. Most young men find adventure in their careers.

TOM. Then most young men are not employed in a warehouse.

AMANDA. The world is full of young men employed in warehouses and offices and factories.

TOM. Do all of them find adventure in their careers?

AMANDA. They do or they do without it! Not everybody has a craze for adventure.

TOM. Man is by instinct a lover, a hunter, a fighter, and none of those instincts are given much play at the warehouse!

AMANDA. Man is by instinct! Don't quote instinct to me! Instinct is something that people have got away from! It belongs to animals! Christian adults don't want it!

TOM. What do Christian adults want, then, Mother?

AMANDA. Superior things! Things of the mind and the spirit! Only animals have to satisfy instincts! Surely your aims are somewhat higher than theirs! Than monkeys—pigs—

TOM. I reckon they're not.

AMANDA. You're joking. However, that isn't what I wanted to discuss.

Tom (*rising*). I haven't much time.

Amanda (*pushing his shoulders*). Sit down.

Tom. You want me to punch in red at the warehouse, Mother?

Amanda. You have five minutes. I want to talk about Laura.

Tom. All right! What about Laura?

Amanda. We have to be making some plans and provisions for her. She's older than you, two years, and nothing has happened. She just drifts along doing nothing. It frightens me terribly how she just drifts along.

Tom. I guess she's the type that people call home girls.

Amanda. There's no such type, and if there is, it's a pity! That is unless the home is hers, with a husband!

Tom. What?

Amanda. Oh, I can see the handwriting on the wall as plain as I see the nose in front of my face! It's terrifying!

More and more you remind me of your father! He was out all hours without explanation!—Then *left! Good-bye!*

And me with the bag to hold. I saw that letter you got from the Merchant Marine. I know what you're dreaming of. I'm not standing here blindfolded.

Very well, then. Then *do* it!

But not till there's somebody to take your place.

Tom. What do you mean?

Amanda. I mean that as soon as Laura has got somebody to take care of her, married, a home of her own, independent—why, then you'll be free to go wherever you please, on land, on sea, whichever way the wind blows you!

But until that time you've got to look out for your sister. I don't say me because I'm old and don't matter! I say for your sister because she's young and dependent.

I put her in business college—a dismal failure! Frightened her so it made her sick at the stomach.

I took her over to the Young People's League at the church. Another fiasco. She spoke to nobody, nobody spoke to her. Now all she does is fool with those pieces of glass and play those worn-out records. What kind of a life is that for a girl to lead?

Tom. What can I do about it?

Amanda. Overcome selfishness!

Self, self, self is all that you ever think of!

(Tom *springs up and crosses to get his coat. It is ugly and bulky. He pulls on a cap with earmuffs.*)

Where is your muffler? Put your wool muffler on!

(*He snatches it angrily from the closet and tosses it around his neck and pulls both ends tight.*)

Tom! I haven't said what I had in mind to ask you.

Tom. I'm too late to—

Amanda (*catching his arm—very importunately. Then shyly*). Down at the warehouse, aren't there some—nice young men?

Tom. No!

Amanda. There *must* be—*some* . . .

Tom. Mother—(*Gesture.*)

Amanda. Find out one that's clean-living—doesn't drink and—ask him out for sister!

Tom. What?

Amanda. For *sister!* To *meet!* Get *acquainted!*

Tom (*stamping to door*). Oh, my go-osh!

Amanda. Will you? (*He opens door. Imploringly*) Will you? (*He starts down.*) Will you? *Will* you, dear?

Tom (*calling back*). yes!

(Amanda *closes the door hesitantly and with a troubled but faintly hopeful expression.*

(*Spot* Amanda *at phone.*)

Amanda. Ella Cartwright? This is Amanda Wingfield!

How are you, honey?

How is that kidney condition? (*Count five.*)

Horrors! (*Count five.*)

You're a Christian martyr, yes, honey, that's what you are, a Christian martyr!

Well, I just now happened to notice in my little red book that your subscription to the *Companion* has just run out! I knew that you wouldn't want to miss out on the wonderful serial starting in this new issue. It's by Bessie Mae Hopper, the first thing she's written since *Honeymoon for Three*.

Wasn't that a strange and interesting story? Well, this one is even lovelier, I believe. It has a sophisticated, society background. It's all about the horsey set on Long Island!

SCENE V

It is early dusk of a spring evening. Supper has just been finished in the Wingfield *apartment.* Amanda *and* Laura *in light-colored dresses are removing dishes from the table, in the upstage area, which is shadowy, their movements formalized almost as a dance or ritual, their moving forms as pale and silent as moths.*

Tom, *in white shirt and trousers, rises from the table and crosses toward the fire-escape.*

Amanda (*as he passes her*). Son, will you do me a favor?

TOM. What?

AMANDA. Comb your hair! You look so pretty when your hair is combed! TOM *slouches on sofa with evening paper. Enormous caption "Franco Triumphs."*) There is only one respect in which I would like you to emulate your father.

TOM. What respect is that?

AMANDA. The care he always took of his appearance. He never allowed himself to look untidy. (*He throws down the paper and crosses to fire-escape.*) Where are you going?

TOM. I'm going out to smoke.

AMANDA. You smoke too much. A pack a day at fifteen cents a pack. How much would that amount to in a month? Thirty times fifteen is how much, Tom? Figure it out and you will be astounded at what you could save. Enough to give you a night-school course in accounting at Washington U! Just think what a wonderful thing that would be for you, Son!

TOM. I'd rather smoke. (*He steps out on landing, letting the screen door slam.*)

AMANDA (*sharply*). I know! That's the tragedy of it . . . (*Alone, she turns to look at her husband's picture.*)

(*Dance music: "All the World Is Waiting for the Sunrise!"*)

TOM (*to the audience*). Across the alley from us was the Paradise Dance Hall. On evenings in spring the windows and doors were open and the music came outdoors. Sometimes the lights were turned out except for a large glass sphere that hung from the ceiling. It would turn slowly about and filter the dusk with delicate rainbow colors. Then the orchestra played a waltz or a tango, something that had a slow and sensuous rhythm. Couples would come outside, to the relative privacy of the alley. You could see them kissing behind ash-pits and telephone poles.

This was the compensation for lives that passed like mine, without any change or adventure.

Adventure and change were imminent in this year. They were waiting around the corner for all these kids.

Suspended in the mist over Berchtesgaden, caught in the folds of Chamberlain's umbrella—

In Spain there was Guernica!

But here there was only hot swing music and liquor, dance halls, bars, and movies, and sex that hung in the gloom like a chandelier and flooded the world with brief, deceptive rainbows . . .

All the world was waiting for bombardments!

(AMANDA *turns from the picture and comes outside.*)

AMANDA (*sighing*). A fire-escape landing's a poor excuse for a porch. (*She spreads a newspaper on a step and sits down, gracefully and demurely as if she were settling into a swing on a Mississippi veranda.*) What are you looking at?

Tom. The moon.

Amanda. Is there a moon this evening?

Tom. It's rising over Garfinkel's Delicatessen.

Amanda. So it is! A little silver slipper of a moon. Have you made a wish on it yet?

Tom. Um-hum.

Amanda. What did you wish for?

Tom. That's a secret.

Amanda. A secret, huh? Well, I won't tell mine either. I will be just as mysterious as you.

Tom. I bet I can guess what yours is.

Amanda. Is my head so transparent?

Tom. You're not a sphinx.

Amanda. No, I don't have secrets. I'll tell you what I wished for on the moon. Success and happiness for my precious children! I wish for that whenever there's a moon, and when there isn't a moon, I wish for it, too.

Tom. I thought perhaps you wished for a gentleman caller.

Amanda. Why do you say that?

Tom. Don't you remember asking me to fetch one?

Amanda. I remember suggesting that it would be nice for your sister if you brought home some nice young man from the warehouse. I think that I've made that suggestion more than once.

Tom. Yes, you have made it repeatedly.

Amanda. Well?

Tom. We are going to have one.

Amanda. *What?*

Tom. A gentleman caller!

(*The annunciation is celebrated with music.* Amanda *rises.*)

Amanda. You mean you have asked some nice young man to come over?

Tom. Yep. I've asked him to dinner.

Amanda. You really did?

Tom. I did!

Amanda. You did, and did he—*accept?*

Tom. He did!

Amanda. Well, well—well, well! That's—lovely!

Tom. I thought that you would be pleased.

Amanda. It's definite, then?

Tom. Very definite.

Amanda. Soon?

Tom. Very soon.

AMANDA. For heaven's sake, stop putting on and tell me some things, will you?

TOM. What things do you want me to tell you?

AMANDA. *Naturally* I would like to know when he's *coming!*

TOM. He's coming tomorrow.

AMANDA. *Tomorrow?*

TOM. Yep. Tomorrow.

AMANDA. But, Tom!

TOM. Yes, Mother?

AMANDA. Tomorrow gives me no time!

TOM. Time for what?

AMANDA. Preparations! Why didn't you phone me at once, as soon as you asked him, the minute that he accepted? Then, don't you see, I could have been getting ready!

TOM. You don't have to make any fuss.

AMANDA. Oh, Tom, Tom, Tom, of course I have to make a fuss! I want things nice, not sloppy! Not thrown together. I'll certainly have to do some fast thinking, won't I?

TOM. I don't see why you have to think at all.

AMANDA. You just don't know. We can't have a gentleman caller in a pig-sty! All my wedding silver has to be polished, the monogrammed table linen ought to be laundered! The windows have to be washed and fresh curtains put up. And how about clothes? We have to *wear* something, don't we?

TOM. Mother, this boy is no one to make a fuss over!

AMANDA. Do you realize he's the first young man we've introduced to your sister?

It's terrible, dreadful, disgraceful that poor little sister has never received a single gentleman caller! Tom, come inside! (*She opens the screen door.*)

TOM. What for?

AMANDA. I want to ask you some things.

TOM. If you're going to make such a fuss, I'll call it off, I'll tell him not to come!

AMANDA. You certainly won't do anything of the kind. Nothing offends people worse than broken engagements. It simply means I'll have to work like a Turk! We won't be brilliant, but we will pass inspection. Come on inside. (TOM *follows, groaning.*) Sit down.

TOM. Any particular place you would like me to sit?

AMANDA. Thank heavens I've got that new sofa! I'm also making payments on a floor lamp I'll have sent out! And put the chintz covers on, they'll brighten things up! Of course I'd hoped to have these walls re-papered . . . What is the young man's name?

TOM. His name is O'Connor.

AMANDA. That, of course, means fish—tomorrow is Friday! I'll have that salmon loaf—with Durkee's dressing! What does he do? He works at the warehouse?

TOM. Of course! How else would I—

AMANDA. Tom, he—doesn't drink?

TOM. Why do you ask me that?

AMANDA. Your father *did!*

TOM. Don't get started on that!

AMANDA. He *does* drink, then?

TOM. Not that I know of!

AMANDA. Make sure, be certain! The last thing I want for my daughter's a boy who drinks!

TOM. Aren't you being a little bit premature? Mr. O'Connor has not yet appeared on the scene!

AMANDA. But will tomorrow. To meet your sister, and what do I know about his character? Nothing! Old maids are better off than wives of drunkards!

TOM. Oh, my God!

AMANDA. Be still!

TOM (*learning forward to whisper*). Lots of fellows meet girls whom they don't marry!

AMANDA. Oh, talk sensibly, Tom—and don't be sarcastic! (*She has gotten a hairbrush.*)

TOM. What are you doing?

AMANDA. I'm brushing that cow-lick down!

What is this young man's position at the warehouse?

TOM (*submitting grimly to the brush and the interrogation*). This young man's position is that of a shipping clerk, Mother.

AMANDA. Sounds to me like a fairly responsible job, the sort of a job *you* would be in if you just had more *get-up.*

What is his salary? Have you any idea?

TOM. I would judge it to be approximately eighty-five dollars a month.

AMANDA. Well—not princely, but—

TOM. Twenty more than I make.

AMANDA. Yes, how well I know! But for a family man, eighty-five dollars a month is not much more than you can just get by on . . .

TOM. Yes, but Mr. O'Connor is not a family man.

AMANDA. He might be, mightn't he? Some time in the future?

TOM. I see. Plans and provisions.

AMANDA. You are the only young man that I know of who ignores the fact that the future becomes the present, the present the past, and the past turns into everlasting regret if you don't plan for it!

TOM. I will think that over and see what I can make of it.

AMANDA. Don't be supercilious with your mother! Tell me some more about this—what do you call him?

TOM. James D. O'Connor. The D. is for Delaney.

AMANDA. Irish on *both* sides! *Gracious!* And doesn't drink?

TOM. Shall I call him up and ask him right this minute?

AMANDA. The only way to find out about those things is to make discreet inquiries at the proper moment. When I was a girl in Blue Mountain and it was suspected that a young man drank, the girl whose attentions he had been receiving, if any girl *was,* would sometimes speak to the minister of his church, or rather her father would if her father was living, and sort of feel him out on the young man's character. That is the way such things are discreetly handled to keep a young woman from making a tragic mistake!

TOM. Then how did you happen to make a tragic mistake?

AMANDA. That innocent look of your father's had everyone fooled!

He *smiled*—the world was *enchanted!*

No girl can do worse than put herself at the mercy of a handsome appearance!

I hope that Mr. O'Connor is not too good-looking.

TOM. No, he's not too good-looking. He's covered with freckles and hasn't too much of a nose.

AMANDA. He's not right-down homely, though?

TOM. Not right-down homely. Just medium homely, I'd say.

AMANDA. Character's what to look for in a man.

TOM. That's what I've always said, Mother.

AMANDA. You've never said anything of the kind and I suspect you would never give it a thought.

TOM. Don't be so suspicious of me.

AMANDA. At least I hope he's the type that's up and coming.

TOM. I think he really goes in for self-improvement.

AMANDA. What reason have you to think so?

TOM. He goes to night school.

AMANDA (*beaming*). Splendid! What does he do, I mean study?

TOM. Radio engineering and public speaking!

AMANDA. Then he has visions of being advanced in the world!

Any young man who studies public speaking is aiming to have an executive job some day!

And radio engineering? A thing for the future!

Both of these facts are very illuminating. Those are the sort of things that a mother should know concerning any young man who comes to call on her daughter. Seriously or—not.

TOM. One little warning. He doesn't know about Laura. I didn't let on that we had dark ulterior motives. I just said, why don't you come and have dinner with us? He said okay and that was the whole conversation.

AMANDA. I bet it was! You're eloquent as an oyster.

However, he'll know about Laura when he gets here. When he sees how lovely and sweet and pretty she is, he'll thank his lucky stars he was asked to dinner.

TOM. Mother, you mustn't expect too much of Laura.

AMANDA. What do you mean?

TOM. Laura seems all those things to you and me because she's ours and we love her. We don't even notice she's crippled any more.

AMANDA. Don't say crippled! You know that I never allow that word to be used!

TOM. But face facts, Mother. She is and—that's not all—

AMANDA. What do you mean "not all"?

TOM. Laura is very different from other girls.

AMANDA. I think the difference is all to her advantage.

TOM. Not quite all—in the eyes of others—strangers—she's terribly shy and lives in a world of her own and those things make her seem a little peculiar to people outside the house.

AMANDA. Don't say peculiar.

TOM. Face the facts. She is.

(*The dance-hall music changes to a tango that has a minor and somewhat ominous tone.*)

AMANDA. In what way is she peculiar—may I ask?

TOM (*gently*). She lives in a world of her own—a world of—little glass ornaments, Mother . . . (*Gets up.* AMANDA *remains holding brush, looking at him, troubled.*) She plays old phonograph records and—that's about all—(*He glances at himself in the mirror and crosses to door.*)

AMANDA (*sharply*). Where are you going?

TOM. I'm going to the movies. (*Out screen door.*)

AMANDA. Not to the movies, every night to the movies! (*Follows quickly to screen door*) I don't believe you always go to the movies! (*He is gone.* AMANDA *looks worriedly after him for a moment. Then vitality and optimism return and she turns from the door. Crossing to portieres*) Laura! Laura!

(LAURA *answers from kitchenette.*)

LAURA. Yes, Mother.

AMANDA. Let those dishes go and come in front! (LAURA *appears with dish towel. Gaily*) Laura, come here and make a wish on the moon!

LAURA (*entering*). Moon—moon?

AMANDA. A little silver slipper of a moon.

Look over your left shoulder, Laura, and make a wish!

(LAURA *looks faintly puzzled as if called out of sleep.* AMANDA *seizes her shoulders and turns her at an angle by the door.*)

Now!
Now, darling, *wish!*
LAURA. What shall I wish for, Mother?
AMANDA (*her voice trembling and her eyes suddenly filling with tears*).
Happiness! Good fortune!

(*The violin rises and the stage dims out.*)

SCENE VI

And so the following evening I brought Jim home to dinner. I had known
Jim slightly in high school. In high school Jim was a hero. He had tremendous Irish good nature and vitality with the scrubbed and polished look of
white chinaware. He seemed to move in a continual spotlight. He was a
star in basketball, captain of the debating club, president of the senior class
and the glee club and he sang the male lead in the annual light operas. He
was always running or bounding, never just walking. He seemed always at
the point of defeating the law of gravity. He was shooting with such velocity
through his adolescence that you would logically expect him to arrive at
nothing short of the White House by the time he was thirty. But Jim
apparently ran into more interference after his graduation from Soldan. His
speed had definitely slowed. Six years after he left high school he was
holding a job that wasn't much better than mine.

He was the only one at the warehouse with whom I was on friendly
terms. I was valuable to him as someone who could remember his former
glory, who had seen him win basketball games and the silver cup in debating. He knew of my secret practice of retiring to a cabinet of the wash-
room to work on poems when business was slack in the warehouse. He called
me Shakespeare. And while the other boys in the warehouse regarded me
with suspicious hostility, Jim took a humorous attitude toward me. Gradually his attitude affected the others, their hostility wore off and they also
began to smile at me as people smile at an oddly fashioned dog who trots
across their path at some distance.

I knew that Jim and Laura had known each other at Soldan, and I had
heard Laura speak admiringly of his voice. I didn't know if Jim remembered
her or not. In high school Laura had been as unobtrusive as Jim had been
astonishing. If he did remember Laura, it was not as my sister, for when I
asked him to dinner, he grinned and said, "You know, Shakespeare, I never
thought of you as having folks!"

He was about to discover that I did . . .

(*Light up stage.*)
(*Friday evening. It is about five o'clock of a late spring evening which
comes "scattering poems in the sky."*)
(*A delicate lemony light is in the Wingfield apartment.*)

(AMANDA *has worked like a Turk in preparation for the gentleman caller. The results are astonishing. The new floor lamp with its rose-silk shade is in place, a colored paper lantern conceals the broken light fixture in the ceiling, new billowing white curtains are at the windows, chintz covers are on chairs and sofa, a pair of new sofa pillows make their initial appearance.*

(*Open boxes and tissue paper are scattered on the floor.*

(LAURA *stands in the middle with lifted arms while* AMANDA *crouches before her, adjusting the hem of the new dress, devout and ritualistic. The dress is colored and designed by memory. The arrangement of* LAURA's *hair is changed; it is softer and more becoming. A fragile, unearthly prettiness has come out in* LAURA: *she is like a piece of translucent glass touched by light, given a momentary radiance, not actual, not lasting.*)

AMANDA (*impatiently*).   Why are you trembling?
LAURA.   Mother, you've made me so nervous!
AMANDA.   How have I made you nervous?
LAURA.   By all this fuss! You make it seem so important!
AMANDA.   I don't understand you, Laura. You couldn't be satisfied with just sitting home, and yet whenever I try to arrange something for you, you seem to resist it. (*She gets up.*)
Now take a look at yourself.
No, wait! Wait just a moment—I have an idea!
LAURA.   What is it now?

(AMANDA *produces two powder puffs which she wraps in handkerchiefs and stuffs in* LAURA's *bosom.*)

LAURA.   Mother, what are you doing?
AMANDA.   They call them "Gay Deceivers"!
LAURA.   I won't wear them!
AMANDA.   You will!
LAURA.   Why should I?
AMANDA.   Because, to be painfully honest, your chest is flat.
LAURA.   You make it seem like we were setting a trap.
AMANDA.   All pretty girls are a trap, a pretty trap, and men expect them to be.
Now look at yourself, young lady. This is the prettiest you will ever be!
I've got to fix myself now! You're going to be surprised by your mother's appearance! (*She crosses through portieres, humming gaily.*)

(LAURA *moves slowly to the long mirror and stares solemnly at herself.*

(*A wind blows the white curtains inward in a slow, graceful motion and with a faint, sorrowful sighing.*)

AMANDA (*off stage*).   It isn't dark enough yet. (*She turns slowly before the mirror with a troubled look.*)

Amanda (*laughing, off*). I'm going to show you something. I'm going to make a spectacular appearance!

Laura. What is it, Mother?

Amanda. Possess your soul in patience—you will see!

Something I've resurrected from that old trunk! Styles haven't changed so terribly much after all . . . (*She parts the portieres.*)

Now just look at your mother! (*She wears a girlish frock of yellowed voile with a blue silk sash. She carries a bunch of jonquils—the legend of her youth is nearly revived. Feverishly*) This is the dress in which I led the cotillion. Won the cakewalk twice at Sunset Hill, wore one spring to the Governor's ball in Jackson!

See how I sashayed around the ballroom, Laura? (*She raises her skirt and does a mincing step around the room.*)

I wore it on Sundays for my gentlemen callers! I had it on the day I met your father—

I had malaria fever all that spring. The change of climate from East Tennessee to the Delta—weakened resistance—I had a little temperature all the time—not enough to be serious—just enough to make me restless and giddy!—Invitations poured in—parties all over the Delta!—"Stay in bed," said Mother, "you have fever!"—but I just wouldn't.—I took quinine but kept on going, going!—Evenings, dances!—Afternoons, long, long rides! Picnics—lovely!—So lovely, that country in May.—All lacy with dogwood, literally flooded with jonquils!—That was the spring I had the craze for jonquils. Jonquils became an absolute obsession. Mother said, "Honey, there's no more room for jonquils." And still I kept on bringing in more jonquils. Whenever, wherever I saw them, I'd say, "Stop! Stop! I see jonquils!" I made the young men help me gather the jonquils! It was a joke, Amanda and her jonquils! Finally there were no more vases to hold them, every available space was filled with jonquils. No vases to hold them? All right, I'll hold them myself! And then I—(*She stops in front of the picture. Music.*) met your father! Malaria fever and jonquils and then—this—boy . . . (*She switches on the rose-colored lamp.*)

I hope they get here before it starts to rain. (*She crosses upstage and places the jonquils in bowl on table.*)

I gave your brother a little extra change so he and Mr. O'Connor could take the service car home.

Laura (*with altered look*). What did you say his name was?

Amanda. O'Connor.

Laura. What is his first name?

Amanda. I don't remember. Oh, yes, I do. It was—Jim!

(Laura *sways slightly and catches hold of a chair.*)

Laura (*faintly*). Not—Jim!

AMANDA. Yes, that was it, it was Jim! I've never known a Jim that wasn't nice!

(*Music: ominous.*)

LAURA. Are you sure his name is Jim O'Connor?

AMANDA. Yes. Why?

LAURA. Is he the one that Tom used to know in high school?

AMANDA. He didn't say so. I think he just got to know him at the warehouse.

LAURA. There was a Jim O'Connor we both knew in high school— (*Then, with effort*) If that is the one that Tom is bringing to dinner—you'll have to excuse me, I won't come to the table.

AMANDA. What sort of nonsense is this?

LAURA. You asked me once if I'd ever liked a boy. Don't you remember I showed you this boy's picture?

AMANDA. You mean the boy you showed me in the year book?

LAURA. Yes, that boy.

AMANDA. Laura, Laura, were you in love with that boy?

LAURA. I don't know, Mother. All I know is I couldn't sit at the table if it was him!

AMANDA. It won't be him! It isn't the least bit likely. But whether it is or not, you will come to the table. You will not be excused.

LAURA. I'll have to be, Mother.

AMANDA. I don't intend to humor your silliness, Laura. I've had too much from you and your brother, both!

So just sit down and compose yourself till they come. Tom has forgotten his key so you'll have to let them in, when they arrive.

LAURA (*panicky*). Oh, Mother—*you* answer the door!

AMANDA (*lightly*). I'll be in the kitchen—busy!

LAURA. Oh, Mother, please answer the door, don't make me do it!

AMANDA (*crossing into kitchenette*). I've got to fix the dressing for the salmon. Fuss, fuss—silliness!—over a gentleman caller!

(*Door swings shut.* LAURA *is left alone.*

(*She utters a low moan and turns off the lamp—sits stiffly on the edge of the sofa, knotting her fingers together.*

(TOM *and* JIM *appear on the fire-escape steps and climb to landing. Hearing their approach,* LAURA *rises with a panicky gesture. She retreats to the portieres.*

(*The doorbell.* LAURA *catches her breath and touches her throat. Low drums.*)

AMANDA (*calling*). Laura, sweetheart! The door!

(LAURA *stares at it without moving.*)

JIM. I think we just beat the rain.

Tom. Uh-huh. (*He rings again, nervously.* Jim *whistles and fishes for a cigarette.*)

Amanda (*very, very gaily*). Laura, that is your brother and Mr. O'Connor! Will you let them in, darling?

(Laura *crosses toward kitchenette door.*)

Laura (*breathlessly*). Mother—you go to the door!

(Amanda *steps out of kitchenette and stares furiously at* Laura. *She points imperiously at the door.*)

Laura. Please, please!

Amanda (*in a fierce whisper*). What is the matter with you, you silly thing?

Laura (*desperately*). Please, you answer it, *please!*

Amanda. I told you I wasn't going to humor you, Laura. Why have you chosen this moment to lose your mind?

Laura. Please, please, please, you go!

Amanda. You'll have to go to the door because I can't!

Laura (*despairingly*). I can't either!

Amanda. *Why?*

Laura. I'm *sick!*

Amanda. I'm sick, too—of your nonsense! Why can't you and your brother be normal people? Fantastic whims and behavior!

(Tom *gives a long ring.*)

Preposterous goings on! Can you give me one reason—(*Calls out lyrically*) Coming! Just one second!—why you should be afraid to open a door? Now you answer it, Laura!

Laura. Oh, oh, oh . . . (*She returns through the portieres. Darts to the victrola and winds it frantically and turns it on.*)

Amanda. Laura Wingfield, you march right to that door!

Laura. Yes—yes, Mother!

(*A faraway, scratchy rendition of "Dardanella" softens the air and gives her strength to move through it. She slips to the door and draws it cautiously open.*

(Tom *enters with the caller,* Jim O'Connor.)

Tom. Laura, this is Jim. Jim, this is my sister, Laura.

Jim (*stepping inside*). I didn't know that Shakespeare had a sister!

Laura (*retreating stiff and trembling from the door*). How—how do you do?

Jim (*heartily extending his hand*). Okay!

(Laura *touches it hesitantly with hers.*)

JIM. Your hand's *cold*, Laura!

LAURA. Yes, well—I've been playing the victrola . . .

JIM. Must have been playing classical music on it! You ought to play a little hot swing music to warm you up!

LAURA. Excuse me—I haven't finished playing the victrola . . . (*She turns awkwardly and hurries into the front room. She pauses a second by the victrola. Then catches her breath and darts through the portieres like a frightened deer.*)

JIM (*grinning*). What was the matter?

TOM. Oh—with Laura? Laura is—terribly shy.

JIM. Shy, huh? It's unusual to meet a shy girl nowadays. I don't believe you ever mentioned you had a sister.

TOM. Well, now you know. I have one. Here is the *Post Dispatch*. You want a piece of it?

JIM. Uh-huh.

TOM. What piece? The comics?

JIM. Sports! (*Glances at it*) Ole Dizzy Dean is on his bad behavior.

TOM (*disinterest*). Yeah? (*Lights cigarette and crosses back to fire-escape door.*)

JIM. Where are *you* going?

TOM. I'm going out on the terrace.

JIM (*goes after him*). You know, Shakespeare—I'm going to sell you a bill of goods!

TOM. What goods?

JIM. A course I'm taking.

TOM. Huh?

JIM. In public speaking! You and me, we're not the warehouse type.

TOM. Thanks—that's good news.

But what has public speaking got to do with it?

JIM. It fits you for—executive positions!

TOM. Awww.

JIM. I tell you it's done a helluva lot for me.

TOM. In what respect?

JIM. In every! Ask yourself what is the difference between you an' me and men in the office down front? Brains?—No!—Ability?—No! Then what? Just one little thing—

TOM. What is that one little thing?

JIM. Primarily it amounts to—social poise! Being able to square up to people and hold your own on any social level!

AMANDA (*off stage*). Tom?

TOM. Yes, Mother?

AMANDA. Is that you and Mr. O'Connor?

TOM. Yes, Mother.

AMANDA. Well, you just make yourselves comfortable in there.

Tom.   Yes, Mother.

Amanda.   Ask Mr. O'Connor if he would like to wash his hands.

Jim.   Aw, no—no—thank you—I took care of that at the warehouse. Tom—

Tom.   Yes?

Jim.   Mr. Mendoza was speaking to me about you.

Tom.   Favorably?

Jim.   What do you think?

Tom.   Well —

Jim.   You're going to be out of a job if you don't wake up.

Tom.   I am waking up—

Jim.   You show no signs.

Tom.   The signs are interior.

I'm planning to change. (*He leans over the rail speaking with quiet exhilaration. The incandescent marquees and signs of the first-run movie houses light his face from across the alley. He looks like a voyager.*) I'm right at the point of committing myself to a future that doesn't include the warehouse and Mr. Mendoza or even a night-school course in public speaking.

Jim.   What are you gassing about?

Tom.   I'm tired of the movies.

Jim.   Movies!

Tom.   Yes, movies! Look at them—(*A wave toward the marvels of Grand Avenue*) All of those glamorous people—having adventures—hogging it all, gobbling the whole thing up! You know what happens? People go to the *movies* instead of *moving!* Hollywood characters are supposed to have all the adventures for everybody in America, while everybody in America sits in a dark room and watches them have them! Yes, until there's a war. That's when adventure becomes available to the masses! *Everyone's* dish, not only Gable's! Then the people in the dark room come out of the dark room to have some adventures themselves—Goody, goody!—It's our turn now, to go to the South Sea Island—to make a safari—to be exotic, far-off!—But I'm not patient. I don't want to wait till then. I'm tired of the *movies* and I am *about* to *move!*

Jim (*incredulously*).   Move?

Tom.   Yes.

Jim.   When?

Tom.   Soon!

Jim.   Where? Where?

(*Theme three music seems to answer the question, while* Tom *thinks it over. He searches among his pockets.*)

Tom.   I'm starting to boil inside. I know I seem dreamy, but inside—well, I'm boiling!—Whenever I pick up a shoe, I shudder a little thinking how short life is and what I am doing!—Whatever that means, I know it doesn't mean shoes—except as something to wear on a traveler's feet! (*Finds paper*) Look—

Jim. What?

Tom. I'm a member.

Jim (*reading*). The Union of Merchant Seamen.

Tom. I paid my dues this month, instead of the light bill.

Jim. You will regret it when they turn the lights off.

Tom. I won't be here.

Jim. How about your mother?

Tom. I'm like my father. The bastard son of a bastard! See how he grins? And he's been absent going on sixteen years!

Jim. You're just talking, you drip. How does your mother feel about it?

Tom. Shhh!—Here comes Mother! Mother is not acquainted with my plans!

Amanda (*enters portieres*). Where are you all?

Tom. On the terrace, Mother.

(*They start inside. She advances to them. Tom is distinctly shocked at her appearance. Even Jim blinks a little. He is making his first contact with girlish Southern vivacity and in spite of the night-school course in public speaking is somewhat thrown off the beam by the unexpected outlay of social charm.*

(*Certain responses are attempted by Jim but are swept aside by Amanda's gay laughter and chatter. Tom is embarrassed but after the first shock Jim reacts very warmly. Grins and chuckles, is altogether won over.*)

Amanda (*coyly smiling, shaking her girlish ringlets*). Well, well, well, so this is Mr. O'Connor. Introductions entirely unnecessary. I've heard so much about you from my boy. I finally said to him, Tom—good gracious!— why don't you bring this paragon to supper? I'd like to meet this nice young man at the warehouse!—Instead of just hearing him sing your praises so much!

I don't know why my son is so stand-offish—that's not Southern behavior!

Let's sit down and—I think we could stand a little more air in here! Tom, leave the door open. I felt a nice fresh breeze a moment ago. Where has it gone to?

Mmm, so warm already! And not quite summer, even. We're going to burn up when summer really gets started.

However, we're having—we're having a very light supper. I think light things are better fo' this time of year. The same as light clothes are. Light clothes an' light food are what warm weather calls fo'. You know our blood gets so thick during th' winter—it takes a while fo' us to *adjust* ou'selves!— when the season changes . . .

It's come so quick this year. I wasn't prepared. All of a sudden—heavens!

Already summer!—I ran to the trunk an' pulled out this light dress—Terribly old! Historical almost! But feels so good—so good an' co-ol, y' know . . .

Tom. Mother—

Amanda. Yes, honey?

Tom. How about—supper?

Amanda. Honey, you go ask Sister if supper is ready! You know that Sister is in full charge of supper!

Tell her you hungry boys are waiting for it.

(*To* Jim) Have you met Laura?

Jim. She—

Amanda. Let you in? Oh, good, you've met already! It's rare for a girl as sweet an' pretty as Laura to be domestic! But Laura is, thank heavens, not only pretty but also very domestic. I'm not at all. I never was a bit. I never could make a thing but angel-food cake. Well, in the South we had so many servants. Gone, gone, gone. All vestige of gracious living! Gone completely! I wasn't prepared for what the future brought me. All of my gentlemen callers were sons of planters and so of course I assumed that I would be married to one and raise my family on a large piece of land with plenty of servants. But man proposes—and woman accepts the proposal!—To vary that old, old saying a little bit—I married no planter! I married a man who worked for the telephone company!—That gallantly smiling gentleman over there! (*Points to the picture*) A telephone man who—fell in love with long-distance!—Now he travels and I don't even know where! But what am I going on for about my—tribulations?

Tell me yours—I hope you don't have any!

Tom?

Tom (*returning*). Yes, Mother?

Amanda. Is supper nearly ready?

Tom. It looks to me like supper is on the table.

Amanda. Let me look—(*She rises prettily and looks through portieres.*) Oh, lovely!—But where is Sister?

Tom. Laura is not feeling well and she says that she thinks she'd better not come to the table.

Amanda. What?—Nonsense!—Laura? Oh, Laura!

Laura (*off stage, faintly*). Yes, Mother.

Amanda. You really must come to the table. We won't be seated until you come to the table!

Come in, Mr. O'Connor. You sit over there, and I'll—

Laura? Laura Wingfield!

You're keeping us waiting, honey! We can't say grace until you come to the table!

(*The back door is pushed weakly open and* Laura *comes in. She is obviously quite faint, her lips trembling, her eyes wide and staring. She moves unsteadily toward the table.*

(Outside a summer storm is coming abruptly. The white curtains billow inward at the windows and there is a sorrowful murmur and deep blue dusk. (LAURA suddenly stumbles—she catches at a chair with a faint moan.)

TOM. Laura!
AMANDA. Laura!

(There is a clap of thunder.)

(Despairingly) Why, Laura, you *are* sick, darling! Tom, help your sister into the living room, dear!
Sit in the living room, Laura—rest on the sofa.
Well!
(To the gentleman caller) Standing over the hot stove made her ill!—I told her that it was just too warm this evening, but—

(TOM comes back in. LAURA is on the sofa.)

Is Laura all right now?
TOM. Yes.
AMANDA. What *is* that? Rain? A nice cool rain has come up! *(She gives the gentleman caller a frightened look.)* I think we may—have grace—now . . .

(TOM looks at her stupidly.)

Tom, honey—you say grace!
TOM. Oh . . .
"For these and all thy mercies—"

(They bow their heads, AMANDA stealing a nervous glance at JIM. In the living room LAURA, stretched on the sofa, clenches her hand to her lips, to hold back a shuddering sob.)

God's Holy Name be praised—

(The scene dims out.)

SCENE VII

A SOUVENIR.

(Half an hour later. Dinner is just being finished in the upstage area which is concealed by the drawn portieres.

(As the curtain rises LAURA is still huddled upon the sofa, her feet drawn under her, her head resting on a pale blue pillow, her eyes wide and myste- riously watchful. The new floor lamp with its shade of rose-colored silk gives a soft, becoming light to her face, bringing out the fragile, unearthly pretti-

ness which usually escapes attention. There is a steady murmur of rain, but it is slackening and stops soon after the scene begins; the air outside becomes pale and luminous as the moon breaks out.

(A moment after the curtain rises, the lights in both rooms flicker and go out.)

JIM.   Hey, there, Mr. Light Bulb!

(AMANDA *laughs nervously.*)

AMANDA.   Where was Moses when the lights went out? Ha-ha. Do you know the answer to that one, Mr. O'Connor?

JIM.   No, Ma'am, what's the answer?

AMANDA.   In the dark!

(JIM *laughs appreciatively.*)

Everybody sit still. I'll light the candles. Isn't it lucky we have them on the table? Where's a match? Which of you gentlemen can provide a match?

JIM.   Here.

AMANDA.   Thank you, sir.

JIM.   Not at all, Ma'am!

AMANDA.   I guess the fuse has burnt out. Mr. O'Connor, can you tell a burnt-out fuse? I know I can't and Tom is a total loss when it comes to mechanics.

(Sound: getting up: voices recede a little to kitchenette.)

Oh, be careful you don't bump into something. We don't want our gentleman caller to break his neck. Now wouldn't that be a fine howdy-do?

JIM.   Ha-ha!

Where is the fuse-box?

AMANDA.   Right here next to the stove. Can you see anything?

JIM.   Just a minute.

AMANDA.   Isn't electricity a mysterious thing?

Wasn't it Benjamin Franklin who tied a key to a kite?

We live in such a mysterious universe, don't we? Some people say that science clears up all the mysteries for us. In my opinion it only creates more!

Have you found it yet?

JIM.   No, Ma'am. All these fuses look okay to me.

AMANDA.   Tom!

TOM.   Yes, Mother?

AMANDA.   That light bill I gave you several days ago. The one I told you we got the notices about?

TOM.   Oh.—Yeah.

AMANDA.   You didn't neglect to pay it by any chance?

TOM.   Why, I—

AMANDA.   Didn't! I might have known it!

JIM.   Shakespeare probably wrote a poem on that light bill, Mrs. Wingfield.

AMANDA.   I might have known better than to trust him with it! There's such a high price for negligence in this world!

JIM.   Maybe the poem will win a ten-dollar prize.

AMANDA.   We'll just have to spend the remainder of the evening in the nineteenth century, before Mr. Edison made the Mazda lamp!

JIM.   Candlelight is my favorite kind of light.

AMANDA.   That shows you're romantic! But that's no excuse for Tom. Well, we got through dinner. Very considerate of them to let us get through dinner before they plunged us into everlasting darkness, wasn't it, Mr. O'Connor?

JIM.   Ha-ha!

AMANDA.   Tom, as a penalty for your carelessness you can help me with the dishes.

JIM.   Let me give you a hand.

AMANDA.   Indeed you will not!

JIM.   I ought to be good for something.

AMANDA.   Good for something? (*Her tone is rhapsodic.*)

You? Why, Mr. O'Connor, nobody, *nobody's* given me this much entertainment in years—as you have!

JIM.   Aw, now, Mrs. Wingfield!

AMANDA.   I'm not exaggerating, not one bit! But Sister is all by her lonesome. You go keep her company in the parlor!

I'll give you this lovely old candelabrum that used to be on the altar at the church of the Heavenly Rest. It was melted a little out of shape when the church burnt down. Lightning struck it one spring. Gypsy Jones was holding a revival at the time and he intimated that the church was destroyed because the Episcopalians gave card parties.

JIM.   Ha-ha.

AMANDA.   And how about you coaxing Sister to drink a little wine? I think it would be good for her! Can you carry both at once?

JIM.   Sure. I'm Superman!

AMANDA.   Now, Thomas, get into this apron!

(*The door of kitchenette swings closed on* AMANDA's *gay laughter; the flickering light approaches the portieres.*

(LAURA *sits up nervously as he enters. Her speech at first is low and breathless from the almost intolerable strain of being alone with a stranger.*

(*In her first speeches in this scene, before* JIM's *warmth overcomes her paralyzing shyness,* LAURA's *voice is thin and breathless as though she has just run up a steep flight of stairs.*

(JIM's *attitude is gently humorous. In playing this scene it should be stressed that while the incident is apparently unimportant, it is to* LAURA *the climax of her secret life.*)

JIM. Hello, there, Laura.

LAURA (*faintly*). Hello. (*She clears her throat.*)

JIM. How are you feeling now? Better?

LAURA. Yes. Yes, thank you.

JIM. This is for you. A little dandelion wine. (*He extends it toward her with extravagant gallantry.*)

LAURA. Thank you.

JIM. Drink it—but don't get drunk!

(*He laughs heartily.* LAURA *takes the glass uncertainly; laughs shyly.*)

Where shall I set the candles?

LAURA. Oh—oh, anywhere . . .

JIM. How about here on the floor? Any objections?

LAURA. No.

JIM. I'll spread a newspaper under to catch the drippings. I like to sit on the floor. Mind if I do?

LAURA. Oh, no.

JIM. Give me a pillow?

LAURA. What?

JIM. A pillow!

LAURA. Oh . . . (*Hands him one quickly.*)

JIM. How about you? Don't you like to sit on the floor?

LAURA. Oh—yes.

JIM. Why don't you, then?

LAURA. I—will.

JIM. Take a pillow!

(LAURA *does. Sits on the other side of the candelabrum.* JIM *crosses his legs and smiles engagingly at her.*)

I can't hardly see you sitting way over there.

LAURA. I can—see you.

JIM. I know, but that's not fair, I'm in the limelight.

(LAURA *moves her pillow closer.*)

Good! Now I can see you! Comfortable?

LAURA. Yes.

JIM. So am I. Comfortable as a cow! Will you have some gum?

LAURA. No, thank you.

JIM. I think that I will indulge, with your permission. (*Musingly unwraps it and holds it up*) Think of the fortune made by the guy that invented the first piece of chewing gum. Amazing, huh? The Wrigley Building is one of the sights of Chicago.—I saw it summer before last when I went up to the Century of Progress. Did you take in the Century of Progress?

LAURA. No, I didn't.

JIM. Well, it was quite a wonderful exposition. What impressed me most was the Hall of Science. Gives you an idea of what the future will be in America, even more wonderful than the present time is! (*Pause. Smiling at her*) Your brother tells me you're shy. Is that right, Laura?

LAURA. I—don't know.

JIM. I judge you to be an old-fashioned type of girl. Well, I think that's a pretty good type to be. Hope you don't think I'm being too personal— do you?

LAURA (*hastily, out of embarrassment*). I believe I *will* take a piece of gum, if you—don't mind. (*Clearing her throat*) Mr. O'Connor, have you— kept up with your singing?

JIM. Singing? Me?

LAURA. Yes. I remember what a beautiful voice you had.

JIM. When did you hear me sing?

(*Voice off stage in the pause*

> O blow, ye winds, heigh-ho,
> A-roving I will go!
> I'm off to my love
> With a boxing glove—
> Ten thousand miles away!*)

JIM. You say you've heard me sing?

LAURA. Oh, yes! Yes, very often . . . I—don't suppose—you remember me—at all?

JIM (*smiling doubtfully*). You know I have an idea I've seen you before. I had that idea soon as you opened the door. It seemed almost like I was about to remember your name. But the name that I started to call you— wasn't a name! And so I stopped myself before I said it.

LAURA. Wasn't it—Blue Roses?

JIM (*springs up. Grinning*). Blue Roses!—My gosh, yes—Blue Roses! That's what I had on my tongue when you opened the door!

Isn't it funny what tricks your memory plays? I didn't connect you with high school somehow or other.

But that's where it was; it was high school. I didn't even know you were Shakespeare's sister!

Gosh, I'm sorry.

LAURA. I didn't expect you to. You—barely knew me!

JIM. But we did have a speaking acquaintance, huh?

LAURA. Yes, we—spoke to each other.

JIM. When did you recognize me?

LAURA. Oh, right away!

JIM. Soon as I came in the door?

LAURA. When I heard your name I thought it was probably you. I knew that Tom used to know you a little in high school. So when you came in the door—
Well, then I was—sure.

JIM. Why didn't you *say* something, then?

LAURA (*breathlessly*). I didn't know what to say, I was—too surprised!

JIM. For goodness' sakes! You know, this sure is funny!

LAURA. Yes! Yes, isn't it, though . . .

JIM. Didn't we have a class in something together?

LAURA. Yes, we did.

JIM. What class was that?

LAURA. It was—singing—Chorus!

JIM. Aw!

LAURA. I sat across the aisle from you in the Aud.

JIM. Aw.

LAURA. Mondays, Wednesdays and Fridays.

JIM. Now I remember—you always came in late.

LAURA. Yes, it was so hard for me, getting upstairs. I had that brace on my leg—it clumped so loud!

JIM. I never heard any clumping.

LAURA (*wincing at the recollection*). To me it sounded like—thunder!

JIM. Well, well, well, I never even noticed.

LAURA. And everybody was seated before I came in. I had to walk in front of all those people. My seat was in the back row. I had to go clumping all the way up the aisle with everyone watching!

JIM. You shouldn't have been self-conscious.

LAURA. I know, but I was. It was always such a relief when the singing started.

JIM. Aw, yes, I've placed you now! I used to call you Blue Roses. How was it that I got started calling you that?

LAURA. I was out of school a little while with pleurosis. When I came back you asked me what was the matter. I said I had pleurosis—you thought I said Blue Roses. That's what you always called me after that!

JIM. I hope you didn't mind.

LAURA. Oh, no—I liked it. You see, I wasn't acquainted with many—people . . .

JIM. As I remember you sort of stuck by yourself.

LAURA. I—I—never have had much luck at—making friends.

JIM. I don't see why you wouldn't.

LAURA. Well, I—started out badly.

JIM. You mean being—

LAURA. Yes, it sort of—stood between me—

JIM. You shouldn't have let it!

LAURA. I know, but it did, and—

JIM. You were shy with people!

LAURA. I tried not to be but never could—

JIM. Overcome it?

LAURA. No, I—I never could!

JIM. I guess being shy is something you have to work out of kind of gradually.

LAURA (*sorrowfully*). Yes—I guess it—

JIM. Takes time!

LAURA. Yes—

JIM. People are not so dreadful when you know them. That's what you have to remember! And everybody has problems, not just you, but practically everybody has got some problems.

You think of yourself as having the only problems, as being the only one who is disappointed. But just look around you and you will see lots of people as disappointed as you are. For instance, I hoped when I was going to high school that I would be further along at this time, six years later, than I am now— You remember that wonderful write-up I had in *The Torch?*

LAURA. Yes! (*She rises and crosses to table.*)

JIM. It said I was bound to succeed in anything I went into! (LAURA *returns with the annual.*) Holy Jeez! *The Torch!*

(*He accepts it reverently. They smile across it with mutual wonder.* LAURA *crouches beside him and they begin to turn through it.* LAURA'S *shyness is dissolving in his warmth.*)

LAURA. Here you are in *The Pirates of Penzance!*

JIM (*wistfully*). I sang the baritone lead in that operetta.

LAURA (*raptly*). So—*beautifully!*

JIM (*protesting*). Aw—

LAURA. Yes, yes—beautifully—beautifully!

JIM. You heard me?

LAURA. All three times!

JIM. No!

LAURA. Yes!

JIM. All three performances?

LAURA (*looking down*). Yes.

JIM. Why?

LAURA. I—wanted to ask you to—autograph my program.

JIM. Why didn't you ask me to?

LAURA. You were always surrounded by your own friends so much that I never had a chance to.

JIM. You should have just—

LAURA. Well, I—thought you might think I was—

JIM. Thought I might think you was—what?

LAURA. Oh—

JIM (*with reflective relish*). I was beleaguered by females in those days.

LAURA. You were terribly popular!

JIM. Yeah—

LAURA. You had such a—friendly way—

JIM. I was spoiled in high school.

LAURA. Everybody—liked you!

JIM. Including you?

LAURA. I—yes, I—I did, too—(*She gently closes the book in her lap.*)

JIM. Well, well, well!—Give me that program, Laura. (*She hands it to him. He signs it with a flourish.*) There you are—better late than never!

LAURA. Oh, I—what a—surprise!

JIM. My signature isn't worth very much right now.

But some day—maybe—it will increase in value!

Being disappointed is one thing and being discouraged is something else.

I am disappointed but I am not discouraged.

I'm twenty-three years old.

How old are you?

LAURA. I'll be twenty-four in June.

JIM. That's not old age!

LAURA. No, but—

JIM. You finished high school?

LAURA (*with difficulty*). I didn't go back.

JIM. You mean you dropped out?

LAURA. I made bad grades in my final examinations. (*She rises and replaces the book and the program. Her voice strained*) How is—Emily Meisenbach getting along?

JIM. Oh, that kraut-head!

LAURA. Why do you call her that?

JIM. That's what she was.

LAURA. You're not still—going with her?

JIM. I never see her.

LAURA. It said in the Personal Section that you were—engaged!

JIM. I know, but I wasn't impressed by that—propaganda!

LAURA. It wasn't—the truth?

JIM. Only in Emily's optimistic opinion!

LAURA. Oh—

(JIM *lights a cigarette and leans indolently back on his elbows smiling at* LAURA *with a warmth and charm which lights her inwardly with altar candles. She remains by the table and turns in her hands a piece of glass to cover her tumult.*)

JIM (*after several reflective puffs on a cigarette*).   What have you done since high school? (*She seems not to hear him.*) Huh? (LAURA *looks up.*) I said what have you done since high school, Laura?

LAURA.   Nothing much.

JIM.   You must have been doing something these six long years.

LAURA.   Yes.

JIM.   Well, then, such as what?

LAURA.   I took a business course at business college—

JIM.   How did that work out?

LAURA.   Well, not very—well—I had to drop out, it gave me—indigestion—

(JIM *laughs gently.*)

JIM.   What are you doing now?

LAURA.   I don't do anything—much. Oh, please don't think I sit around doing nothing! My glass collection takes up a good deal of time. Glass is something you have to take good care of.

JIM.   What did you say—about glass?

LAURA.   Collection I said—I have one—(*She clears her throat and turns away again, acutely shy.*)

JIM (*abruptly*).   You know what I judge to be the trouble with you? Inferiority complex! Know what that is? That's what they call it when someone low-rates himself!

I understand it because I had it, too. Although my case was not so aggravated as yours seems to be. I had it until I took up public speaking, developed my voice, and learned that I had an aptitude for science. Before that time I never thought of myself as being outstanding in any way whatsoever!

Now I've never made a regular study of it, but I have a friend who says I can analyze people better than doctors that make a profession of it. I don't claim that to be necessarily true, but I can sure guess a person's psychology, Laura! (*Takes out his gum*) Excuse me, Laura. I always take it out when the flavor is gone. I'll use this scrap of paper to wrap it in. I know how it is to get it stuck on a shoe.

Yep—that's what I judge to be your principal trouble. A lack of confidence in yourself as a person. You don't have the proper amount of faith in yourself. I'm basing that fact on a number of your remarks and also on certain observations I've made. For instance that clumping you thought was so awful in high school. You say that you even dreaded to walk into class. You see what you did? You dropped out of school, you gave up an education because of a clump, which as far as I know was practically non-existent!

A little physical defect is what you have. Hardly noticeable even! Magnified thousands of times by imagination!

You know what my strong advice to you is? Think of yourself as *superior* in some way!

LAURA. In what way would I think?

JIM. Why, man alive, Laura! Just look about you a little. What do you see? A world full of common people! All of 'em born and all of 'em going to die!

Which of them has one-tenth of your good points! Or mine! Or anyone else's, as far as that goes—Gosh!

Everybody excels in some on thing. Some in many! (*Unconsciously glances at himself in the mirror.*)

All you've got to do is discover in *what!*

Take me, for instance. (*He adjusts his tie at the mirror.*)

My interest happens to lie in electro-dynamics. I'm taking a course in radio engineering at night school, Laura, on top of a fairly responsible job at the warehouse. I'm taking that course and studying public speaking.

LAURA. Ohhhh.

JIM. Because I believe in the future of television! (*Turning back to her.*)

I wish to be ready to go up right along with it. Therefore I'm planning to get in on the ground floor. In fact I've already made the right connections and all that remains is for the industry itself to get under way! Full steam— (*His eyes are starry.*)

Knowledge—Zzzzzp! Money—Zzzzzzp!—Power!

That's the cycle democracy is built on! (*His attitude is convincingly dynamic.* LAURA *stares at him, even her shyness eclipsed in her absolute wonder. He suddenly grins.*)

I guess you think I think a lot of myself!

LAURA. No—o-o-o, I—

JIM. Now how about you? Isn't there something you take more interest in than anything else?

LAURA. Well, I do—as I said—have my glass collection—

(*A peal of girlish laughter from the kitchen.*)

JIM. I'm not right sure I know what you're talking about. What kind of glass is it?

LAURA. Little articles of it, they're ornaments mostly!

Most of them are little animals made out of glass, the tiniest little animals in the world. Mother calls them a glass menagerie!

Here's an example of one, if you'd like to see it!

This one is one of the oldest. It's nearly thirteen.

(*Music: "The Glass Menagerie."*)
(*He stretches out his hand.*)

Oh, be careful—if you breathe, it breaks!

Jim. I'd better not take it. I'm pretty clumsy with things.

Laura. Go on, I trust you with him! (*Places it in his palm.*)
There now—you're holding him gently!
Hold him over the light, he loves the light! You see how the light shines
through him?

Jim. It sure does shine!

Laura. I shouldn't be partial, but he is my favorite one.

Jim. What kind of a thing is this one supposed to be?

Laura. Haven't you noticed the single horn on his forehead?

Jim. A unicorn, huh?

Laura. Mmm-hmmm!

Jim. Unicorns, aren't they extinct in the modern world?

Laura. I know!

Jim. Poor little fellow, he must feel sort of lonesome.

Laura (*smiling*). Well, if he does he doesn't complain about it. He
stays on a shelf with some horses that don't have horns and all of them seem
to get along nicely together.

Jim. How do you know?

Laura (*lightly*). I haven't heard any arguments among them!

Jim (*grinning*). No arguments, huh? Well, that's a pretty good sign!
Where shall I set him?

Laura. Put him on the table. They all like a change of scenery once in
a while!

Jim (*stretching*). Well, well, well, well—
Look how big my shadow is when I stretch!

Laura. Oh, oh, yes—it stretches across the ceiling!

Jim (*crossing to door*). I think it's stopped raining. (*Opens fire-escape
door*) Where does the music come from?

Laura. From the Paradise Dance Hall across the alley.

Jim. How about cutting the rug a little, Miss Wingfield?

Laura. Oh, I—

Jim. Or is your program filled up? Let me have a look at it. (*Grasps
imaginary card*) Why, every dance is taken! I'll just have to scratch some
out. (*Waltz music: "La Golondrina."*) Ahhh, a waltz! (*He executes some
sweeping turns by himself then holds his arms toward* Laura.)

Laura (*breathlessly*). I—can't dance!

Jim. There you go, that inferiority stuff!

Laura. I've never danced in my life!

Jim. Come on, try!

Laura. Oh, but I'd step on you!

Jim. I'm not made out of glass.

Laura. How—how—how do we start?

Jim. Just leave it to me. You hold your arms out a little.

LAURA. Like this?

JIM. A little bit higher. Right. Now don't tighten up, that's the main thing about it—relax.

LAURA (*laughing breathlessly*). It's hard not to.

JIM. Okay.

LAURA. I'm afraid you can't budge me.

JIM. What do you bet I can't? (*He swings her into motion.*)

LAURA. Goodness, yes, you can!

JIM. Let yourself go, now, Laura, just let yourself go.

LAURA. I'm—

JIM. Come on!

LAURA. Trying!

JIM. Not so stiff—Easy does it!

LAURA. I know but I'm—

JIM. Loosen th' backbone! There now, that's a lot better.

LAURA. Am I?

JIM. Lots, lots better! (*He moves her about the room in a clumsy waltz.*)

LAURA. Oh, my!

JIM. Ha-ha!

LAURA. Oh, my goodness!

JIM. Ha-ha-ha! (*They suddenly bump into the table.* JIM *stops.*) What did we hit on?

LAURA. Table.

JIM. Did something fall off it? I think—

LAURA. Yes.

JIM. I hope that it wasn't the little glass horse with the horn!

LAURA. Yes.

JIM. Aw, aw, aw. Is it broken?

LAURA. Now it is just like all the other horses.

JIM. It's lost its—

LAURA. Horn!

It doesn't matter. Maybe it's a blessing in disguise.

JIM. You'll never forgive me. I bet that that was your favorite piece of glass.

LAURA. I don't have favorites much. It's no tragedy, Freckles. Glass breaks so easily. No matter how careful you are. The traffic jars the shelves and things fall off them.

JIM. Still I'm awfully sorry that I was the cause.

LAURA (*smiling*). I'll just imagine he had an operation. The horn was removed to make him feel less—freakish! (*They both laugh.*)

Now he will feel more at home with the other horses, the ones that don't have horns . . .

JIM. Ha-ha, that's very funny! (*Suddenly serious.*)
I'm glad to see that you have a sense of humor.
You know—you're—well—very different!
Surprisingly different from anyone else I know! (*His voice becomes soft and hesitant with a genuine feeling.*)
Do you mind me telling you that?

(LAURA *is abashed beyond speech.*)

I mean it in a nice way . . .

(LAURA *nods shyly, looking away.*)

You make me feel sort of—I don't know how to put it!
I'm usually pretty good at expressing things, but—
This is something that I don't know how to say!

(LAURA *touches her throat and clears it—turns the broken unicorn in her hands.*)

(*Even softer*) Has anyone ever told you that you were pretty?

(*Pause: music.* LAURA *looks up slowly, with wonder, and shakes her head.*)

Well, you are! In a very different way from anyone else.
And all the nicer because of the difference, too. (*His voice becomes low and husky.* LAURA *turns away, nearly faint with the novelty of her emotions.*)
I wish that you were my sister. I'd teach you to have some confidence in yourself. The different people are not like other people, but being different is nothing to be ashamed of. Because other people are not such wonderful people. They're one hundred times one thousand. You're one times one! They walk all over the earth. You just stay here. They're common as—weeds, but—you—well, you're—*Blue Roses!*

(*Music changes.*)

LAURA. But blue is wrong for—roses . . .
JIM. It's right for you!—You're—pretty!
LAURA. In what respect am I pretty?
JIM. In all respects—believe me! Your eyes—your hair—are pretty! Your hands are pretty! (*He catches hold of her hand.*)
You think I'm making this up because I'm invited to dinner and have to be nice. Oh, I could do that! I could put on an act for you, Laura, and say lots of things without being very sincere. But this time I am. I'm talking to you sincerely. I happened to notice you had this inferiority complex that keeps you from feeling comfortable with people. Somebody needs to build your confidence up and make you proud instead of shy and turning away and—blushing—

Somebody—ought to—

Ought to—kiss you, Laura! (*His hand slips slowly up her arm to her shoulder. Music swells tumultuously. He suddenly turns her about and kisses her on the lips. When he releases her,* LAURA *sinks on the sofa with a bright, dazed look.* JIM *backs away and fishes in his pocket for a cigarette.*)

Stumble-john!

(*He lights the cigarette, avoiding her look.*

(*There is a peal of girlish laughter from* AMANDA *in the kitchen.*

(LAURA *slowly raises and opens her hand. It still contains the little broken glass animal. She looks at it with a tender, bewildered expression.*)

Stumble-john!

I shouldn't have done that—That was way off the beam.

You don't smoke, do you?

(*She looks up, smiling, not hearing the question.*

(*He sits beside her a little gingerly. She looks at him speechlessly—waiting.*

(*He coughs decorously and moves a little farther aside as he considers the situation and senses her feelings, dimly, with perturbation.*)

(*Gently*) Would you—care for a—mint?

(*She doesn't seem to hear him but her look grows brighter even.*)

Peppermint—Life-Saver?

My pocket's a regular drug store—wherever I go . . . (*He pops a mint in his mouth. Then gulps and decides to make a clean breast of it. He speaks slowly and gingerly.*)

Laura, you know, if I had a sister like you, I'd do the same thing as Tom. I'd bring out fellows and—introduce her to them. The right type of boys of a type to—appreciate her.

Only—well—he made a mistake about me.

Maybe I've got no call to be saying this. That may not have been the idea in having me over. But what if it was?

There's nothing wrong about that. The only trouble is that in my case— I'm not in a situation to—do the right thing.

I can't take down your number and say I'll phone.

I can't call up next week and—ask for a date.

I thought I had better explain the situation in case you—misunderstood it and—hurt your feelings . . .

(*Pause.*)

(*Slowly, very slowly,* LAURA's *look changes, her eyes returning slowly from his to the ornament in her palm.*

(AMANDA *utters another gay laugh in the kitchen.*)

LAURA (*faintly*). You—won't—call again?

JIM. No, Laura, I can't. (*He rises from the sofa.*)
As I was just explaining, I've—got strings on me.
Laura, I've—been going steady!
I go out all of the time with a girl named Betty. She's a home-girl like you, and Catholic, and Irish, and in a great many ways we—get along fine.
I met her last summer on a moonlight boat trip up the river to Alton, on the *Majestic.*
Well—right away from the start it was—love!

(LAURA *sways slightly forward and grips the arm of the sofa. He fails to notice, now enrapt in his own comfortable being.*)

Being in love has made a new man of me!

(*Leaning stiffly forward, clutching the arm of the sofa,* LAURA *struggles visibly with her storm. But* JIM *is oblivious, she is a long way off.*)

The power of love is really pretty tremendous!
Love is something that—changes the whole world, Laura!

(*The storm abates a little and* LAURA *leans back. He notices her again.*)

It happened that Betty's aunt took sick, she got a wire and had to go to Centralia. So Tom—when he asked me to dinner—I naturally just accepted the invitation, not knowing that you—that he—that I—(*He stops awkwardly.*)
Huh—I'm a stumble-john!

(*He flops back on the sofa.*
(*The holy candles in the altar of* LAURA's *face have been snuffed out. There is a look of almost infinite desolation.*
(JIM *glances at her uneasily.*)

I wish that you would—say something.

(*She bites her lip which was trembling and then bravely smiles. She opens her hand again on the broken glass ornament. Then she gently takes his hand and raises it level with her own. She carefully places the unicorn in the palm of his hand, then pushes his fingers closed upon it.*)

What are you—doing that for? You want me to have him?—Laura? (*She nods.*) What for?

LAURA. A—souvenir . . . (*She rises unsteadily and crouches beside the victrola to wind it up.*)

(*At this moment* AMANDA *rushes brightly back in the front room. She bears a pitcher of fruit punch in an old-fashioned cut-glass pitcher and a plate of macaroons. The plate has a gold border and poppies painted on it.*)

AMANDA.   Well, well, well! Isn't the air delightful after the shower? I've made you children a little liquid refreshment.

(*Turns gaily to the gentleman caller*) Jim, do you know that song about lemonade?

> "Lemonade, lemonade
> Made in the shade and stirred with a spade—
> Good enough for any old maid!"

JIM (*uneasily*).   Ha-ha! No—I never heard it.

AMANDA.   Why, Laura! You look so serious!

JIM.   We were having a serious conversation.

AMANDA.   Good! Now you're better acquainted!

JIM (*uncertainly*).   Ha-ha! Yes.

AMANDA.   You modern young people are much more serious-minded than my generation. I was so gay as a girl!

JIM.   You haven't changed, Mrs. Wingfield.

AMANDA.   Tonight I'm rejuvenated! The gaiety of the occasion, Mr. O'Connor! (*She tosses her head with a pearl of laughter. Spills lemonade.*) Oooo! I'm baptizing myself!

JIM.   Here—let me—

AMANDA (*setting the pitcher down*).   There now. I discovered we had some maraschino cherries. I dumped them in, juice and all!

JIM.   You shouldn't have gone to that trouble, Mrs. Wingfield.

AMANDA.   Trouble, trouble? Why, it was loads of fun!

Didn't you hear me cutting up in the kitchen? I bet your ears were burning! I told Tom how outdone with him I was for keeping you to himself so long a time! He should have brought you over much, much sooner! Well, now that you've found your way, I want you to be a very frequent caller! Not just occasional but all the time.

Oh, we're going to have a lot of gay times together! I see them coming! Mmm, just breathe that air! So fresh, and the moon's so pretty!

I'll skip back out—I know where my place is when young folks are having a—serious conversation!

JIM.   Oh, don't go out, Mrs. Wingfield. The fact of the matter is I've got to be going.

AMANDA.   Going, now? You're joking! Why, it's only the shank of the evening, Mr. O'Connor!

JIM.   Well, you know how it is.

AMANDA.   You mean you're a young workingman and have to keep workingmen's hours. We'll let you off early tonight. But only on the condition that next time you stay later.

What's the best night for you? Isn't Saturday night the best night for you workingmen?

JIM. I have a couple of time-clocks to punch, Mrs. Wingfield. One at morning, another one at night!

AMANDA. My, but you *are* ambitious! You work at night, too?

JIM. No, Ma'am, not work but—Betty! (*He crosses deliberately to pick up his hat. The band at the Paradise Dance Hall goes into a tender waltz.*)

AMANDA. Betty? Betty? Who's—Betty!

(*There is an ominous cracking sound in the sky.*)

JIM. Oh, just a girl. The girl I go steady with! (*He smiles charmingly. The sky falls.*)

AMANDA (*a long-drawn exhalation*). Ohhhh . . . Is it a serious romance, Mr. O'Connor?

JIM. We're going to be married the second Sunday in June.

AMANDA. Ohhhh—how nice!

Tom didn't mention that you were engaged to be married.

JIM. The cat's not out of the bag at the warehouse yet.

You know how they are. They call you Romeo and stuff like that. (*He stops at the oval mirror to put on his hat. He carefully shapes the brim and the crown to give a discreetly dashing effect.*)

It's been a wonderful evening, Mrs. Wingfield. I guess this is what they mean by Southern hospitality.

AMANDA. It really wasn't anything at all.

JIM. I hope it don't seem like I'm rushing off. But I promised Betty I'd pick her up at the Wabash depot, an' by the time I get my jalopy down there her train'll be in. Some women are pretty upset if you keep 'em waiting.

AMANDA. Yes, I know—The tyranny of women!

(*Extends her hand*) Good-bye, Mr. O'Connor.

I wish you luck—and happiness—and success! All three of them, and so does Laura!—Don't you, Laura?

LAURA. Yes!

JIM (*taking her hand*). Good-bye, Laura. I'm certainly going to treasure that souvenir. And don't you forget the good advice I gave you.

(*Raises his voice to a cheery shout*) So long, Shakespeare!

Thanks again, ladies—Good night! (*He grins and ducks jauntily out.*)

(*Still bravely grimacing, AMANDA closes the door on the gentleman caller. Then she turns back to the room with a puzzled expression. She and LAURA don't dare to face each other. LAURA crouches beside the victrola to wind it.*)

AMANDA (*faintly*). Things have a way of turning out so badly.

I don't believe that I would play the victrola.

Well, well—well—

Our gentleman caller was engaged to be married!
Tom!

TOM (*from back*). Yes, Mother?

AMANDA. Come in here a minute. I want to tell you something awfully funny.

TOM (*enters with macaroon and a glass of the lemonade*). Has the gentleman caller gotten away already?

AMANDA. The gentleman caller has made an early departure. What a wonderful joke you played on us!

TOM. How do you mean?

AMANDA. You didn't mention that he was engaged to be married.

TOM. Jim? Engaged?

AMANDA. That's what he just informed us.

TOM. I'll be jiggered! I didn't know about that.

AMANDA. That seems very peculiar.

TOM. What's peculiar about it?

AMANDA. Didn't you call him your best friend down at the warehouse?

TOM. He is, but how did I know?

AMANDA. It seems extremely peculiar that you wouldn't know your best friend was going to be married!

TOM. The warehouse is where I work, not where I know things about people!

AMANDA. You don't know things anywhere! You live in a dream; you manufacture illusions!

(*He crosses to door.*)

Where are you going?

TOM. I'm going to the movies.

AMANDA. That's right, now that you've had us make such fools of ourselves. The effort, the preparations, all the expense! The new floor lamp, the rug, the clothes for Laura! All for what? To entertain some other girl's fiancé!

Go to the movies, go! Don't think about us, a mother deserted, an unmarried sister who's crippled and has no job! Don't let anything interfere with your selfish pleasure!

Just go, go, go—to the movies!

TOM. All right, I will! The more you shout about my selfishness to me the quicker I'll go, and I won't go to the movies!

AMANDA. Go, then! Then go to the moon—you selfish dreamer!

(TOM *smashes his glass on the floor. He plunges out on the fire-escape, slamming the door.* LAURA *screams.*

(*Dance-hall music up.* TOM *goes to the rail and grips it desperately, lifting his face in the chill white moon light penetrating the narrow abyss of the alley.*

TENNESSEE WILLIAMS   477

(TOM's *closing speech is timed with the interior pantomime. The interior scene is played as though viewed through soundproof glass.* AMANDA *appears to be making a comforting speech to* LAURA *who is huddled upon the sofa. Now that we cannot hear the mother's speech, her silliness is gone and she has dignity and tragic beauty.* LAURA's *dark hair hides her face until at the end of the speech she lifts it to smile at her mother.* AMANDA's *gestures are slow and graceful, almost dance-like, as she comforts the daughter. At the end of her speech she glances a moment at the father's picture—then withdraws through the portieres. At close of* TOM's *speech,* LAURA *blows out the candles, ending the play.*)

TOM. I didn't go to the moon, I went much further—for time is the longest distance between two places—

Not long after that I was fired for writing a poem on the lid of a shoe-box.

I left Saint Louis. I descended the steps of this fire-escape for a last time and followed, from then on, in my father's footsteps, attempting to find in motion what was lost in space—

I traveled around a great deal. The cities swept about me like dead leaves, leaves that were brightly colored but torn away from the branches.

I would have stopped, but I was pursued by something.

It always came upon me unawares, taking me altogether by surprise. Perhaps it was a familiar bit of music. Perhaps it was only a piece of transparent glass—

Perhaps I am walking along a street at night, in some strange city, before I have found companions. I pass the lighted window of a shop where perfume is sold. The window is filled with pieces of colored glass, tiny transparent bottles in delicate colors, like bits of a shattered rainbow.

Then all at once my sister touches my shoulder. I turn around and look into her eyes . . .

Oh, Laura, Laura, I tried to leave you behind me, but I am more faithful than I intended to be!

I reach for a cigarette, I cross the street, I run into the movies or a bar, I buy a drink, I speak to the nearest stranger—anything that can blow your candles out!

(LAURA *bends over the candles.*)

—for nowadays the world is lit by lightning! Blow out your candles, Laura —and so good-bye . . .

(*She blows the candles out.*)

Arthur Miller

DEATH OF A SALESMAN

CHARACTERS

WILLY LOMAN	HOWARD WAGNER
LINDA	JENNY
BIFF	STANLEY
HAPPY	MISS FORSYTHE
BERNARD	LETTA
THE WOMAN	CHARLEY
UNCLE BEN	

THE PLACE. *Willy Loman's house and yard and various places he visits in the New York and Boston of today.*

Throughout the play, in the stage directions, left and right mean stage left and stage right.

ACT I

A melody is heard, played upon a flute. It is small and fine, telling of grass and trees and the horizon. The curtain rises.

Before us is the Salesman's house. We are aware of towering, angular shapes behind it, surrounding it on all sides. Only the blue light of the sky falls upon the house and forestage; the surrounding area shows an angry glow of orange. As more light appears, we see a solid vault of apartment houses around the small, fragile-seeming home. An air of the dream clings to the place, a dream rising out of reality. The kitchen at center seems actual enough, for there is a kitchen table with three chairs, and a refrigerator. But no other fixtures are seen. At the back of the kitchen there is a draped entrance, which leads to the living-room. To the right of the kitchen, on a level raised two feet, is a bedroom furnished only with a brass bedstead and a straight chair. On a shelf over the bed a silver athletic trophy stands. A window opens onto the apartment house at the side.

DEATH OF A SALESMAN Copyright 1949 by Arthur Miller. Reprinted by permission of The Viking Press, Inc. First performed in 1949.

*Behind the kitchen, on a level raised six and a half feet, is the boys'
bedroom, at present barely visible. Two beds are dimly seen, and at the
back of the room a dormer window. (This bedroom is above the unseen
living-room.) At the left a stairway curves up to it from the kitchen.*

*The entire setting is wholly or, in some places, partially transparent. The
roof-line of the house is one-dimensional; under and over it we see the apartment buildings. Before the house lies an apron, curving beyond the forestage into the orchestra. This forward area serves as the back yard as well as
the locale of all* WILLY's *imaginings and of his city scenes. Whenever the
action is in the present the actors observe the imaginary wall-lines, entering
the house only through its door at the left. But in the scenes of the past these
boundaries are broken, and characters enter or leave a room by stepping
"through" a wall onto the forestage.*

From the right, WILLY LOMAN, *the Salesman, enters, carrying two large
sample cases. The flute plays on. He hears but is not aware of it. He is past
sixty years of age, dressed quietly. Even as he crosses the stage to the doorway
of the house, his exhaustion is apparent. He unlocks the door, comes into the
kitchen, and thankfully lets his burden down, feeling the soreness of his
palms. A word-sigh escapes his lips—it might be "Oh, boy, oh, boy." He
closes the door, then carries his cases out into the living-room, through the
draped kitchen doorway.*

LINDA, *his wife, has stirred in her bed at the right. She gets out and puts
on a robe, listening. Most often jovial, she has developed an iron repression
of her exceptions to* WILLY's *behavior—she more than loves him, she admires
him, as though his mercurial nature, his temper, his massive dreams and little
cruelties, served her only as sharp reminders of the turbulent longings within
him, longings which she shares but lacks the temperament to utter and follow
to their end.*

LINDA (*hearing* WILLY *outside the bedroom, calls with some trepidation*).
Willy!

WILLY. It's all right. I came back.

LINDA. Why? What happened? (*Slight pause*) Did something happen,
Willly?

WILLY. No, nothing happened.

LINDA. You didn't smash the car, did you?

WILLY (*with casual irritation*). I said nothing happened. Didn't you
hear me?

LINDA. Don't you feel well?

WILLY. I'm tired to the death. (*The flute has faded away. He sits on
the bed beside her, a little numb.*) I couldn't make it. I just couldn't make it,
Linda.

LINDA (*very carefully, delicately*). Where were you all day? You look
terrible.

WILLY. I got as far as a little above Yonkers. I stopped for a cup of coffee. Maybe it was the coffee.

LINDA. What?

WILLY (*after a pause*). I suddenly couldn't drive any more. The car kept going off onto the shoulder, y'know?

LINDA (*helpfully*). Oh. Maybe it was the steering again. I don't think Angelo knows the Studebaker.

WILLY. No, it's me, it's me. Suddenly I realize I'm goin' sixty miles an hour and I don't remember the last five minutes. I'm—I can't seem to—keep my mind to it.

LINDA. Maybe it's your glasses. You never went for your new glasses.

WILLY. No, I see everything. I came back ten miles an hour. It took me nearly four hours from Yonkers.

LINDA (*resigned*). Well, you'll just have to take a rest, Willy, you can't continue this way.

WILLY. I just got back from Florida.

LINDA. But you didn't rest your mind. Your mind is overactive, and the mind is what counts, dear.

WILLY. I'll start out in the morning. Maybe I'll feel better in the morning. (*She is taking off his shoes.*) These goddam arch supports are killing me.

LINDA. Take an aspirin. Should I get you an aspirin? It'll soothe you.

WILLY (*with wonder*). I was driving along, you understand? And I was fine. I was even observing the scenery. You can imagine, me looking at scenery, on the road every week of my life. But it's so beautiful up there, Linda, the trees are so thick, and the sun is warm. I opened the windshield and just let the warm air bathe over me. And then all of a sudden I'm goin' off the road! I'm tellin' ya, I absolutely forgot I was driving. If I'd've gone the other way over the white line I might've killed somebody. So I went on again—and five minutes later I'm dreamin' again, and I nearly—(*He presses two fingers against his eyes.*) I have such thoughts, I have such strange thoughts.

LINDA. Willy, dear. Talk to them again. There's no reason why you can't work in New York.

WILLY. They don't need me in New York. I'm the New England man. I'm vital in New England.

LINDA. But you're sixty years old. They can't expect you to keep traveling every week.

WILLY. I'll have to send a wire to Portland. I'm supposed to see Brown and Morrison tomorrow morning at ten o'clock to show the line. Goddammit, I could sell them! (*He starts putting on his jacket.*)

LINDA (*taking the jacket from him*). Why don't you go down to the place tomorrow and tell Howard you've simply got to work in New York? You're too accommodating, dear.

WILLY. If old man Wagner was alive I'd a been in charge of New York now! That man was a prince, he was a masterful man. But that boy of his, that Howard, he don't appreciate. When I went north the first time, the Wagner Company didn't know where New England was!

LINDA. Why don't you tell those things to Howard, dear?

WILLY (*encouraged*). I will, I definitely will. Is there any cheese?

LINDA. I'll make you a sandwich.

WILLY. No, go to sleep. I'll take some milk. I'll be up right away. The boys in?

LINDA. They're sleeping. Happy took Biff on a date tonight.

WILLY (*interested*). That so?

LINDA. It was so nice to see them shaving together, one behind the other, in the bathroom. And going out together. You notice? The whole house smells of shaving lotion.

WILLY. Figure it out. Work a lifetime to pay off a house. You finally own it, and there's nobody to live in it.

LINDA. Well, dear, life is a casting off. It's always that way.

WILLY. No, no, some people—some people accomplish something. Did Biff say anything after I went this morning?

LINDA. You shouldn't have criticized him, Willy, especially after he just got off the train. You mustn't lose your temper with him.

WILLY. When the hell did I lose my temper? I simply asked him if he was making any money. Is that a criticism?

LINDA. But, dear, how could he make any money?

WILLY (*worried and angered*). There's such an undercurrent in him. He became a moody man. Did he apologize when I left this morning?

LINDA. He was crestfallen, Willy. You know how he admires you. I think if he finds himself, then you'll both be happier and not fight any more.

WILLY. How can he find himself on a farm? Is that a life? A farmhand? In the beginning, when he was young, I thought, well, a young man, it's good for him to tramp around, take a lot of different jobs. But it's more than ten years now and he has yet to make thirty-five dollars a week!

LINDA. He's finding himself, Willy.

WILLY. Not finding yourself at the age of thirty-four is a disgrace!

LINDA. Shh!

WILLY. The trouble is he's lazy, goddammit!

LINDA. Willy, please!

WILLY. Biff is a lazy bum!

LINDA. They're sleeping. Get something to eat. Go on down.

WILLY. Why did he come home? I would like to know what brought him home.

LINDA. I don't know. I think he's still lost, Willy. I think he's very lost.

WILLY. Biff Loman is lost. In the greatest country in the world a young man with such—personal attractiveness, gets lost. And such a hard worker. There's one thing about Biff—he's not lazy.

LINDA. Never.

WILLY (*with pity and resolve*). I'll see him in the morning; I'll have a nice talk with him. I'll get him a job selling. He could be big in no time. My God! Remember how they used to follow him around in high school? When he smiled at one of them their faces lit up. When he walked down the street . . . (*He loses himself in reminiscences.*)

LINDA (*trying to bring him out of it*). Willy, dear, I got a new kind of American-type cheese today. It's whipped.

WILLY. Why do you get American when I like Swiss?

LINDA. I just thought you'd like a change—

WILLY. I don't want a change! I want Swiss cheese. Why am I always being contradicted?

LINDA (*with a covering laugh*). I thought it would be a surprise.

WILLY. Why don't you open a window in here, for God's sake?

LINDA (*with infinite patience*). They're all open, dear.

WILLY. The way they boxed us in here. Bricks and windows, windows and bricks.

LINDA. We should've bought the land next door.

WILLY. The street is lined with cars. There's not a breath of fresh air in the neighborhood. The grass don't grow any more, you can't raise a carrot in the back yard. They should've had a law against apartment houses. Remember those two beautiful elm trees out there? When I and Biff hung the swing between them?

LINDA. Yeah, like being a million miles from the city.

WILLY. They should've arrested the builder for cutting those down. They massacred the neighborhood. (*Lost*) More and more I think of those days, Linda. This time of year it was lilac and wisteria. And then the peonies would come out, and the daffodils. What fragrance in this room!

LINDA. Well, after all, people had to move somewhere.

WILLY. No, there's more people now.

LINDA. I don't think there's more people. I think—

WILLY. There's more people! That's what's ruining this country! Population is getting out of control. The competition is maddening! Smell the stink from that apartment house! And another one on the other side . . . How can they whip cheese?

(*On* WILLY's *last line, Biff and Happy raise themselves up in their beds, listening.*)

LINDA. Go down, try it. And be quiet.

WILLY (*turning to* LINDA, *guiltily*). You're not worried about me, are you, sweetheart?

BIFF. What's the matter?

HAPPY. Listen!

LINDA. You've got too much on the ball to worry about.

WILLY. You're my foundation and my support, Linda.

LINDA. Just try to relax, dear. You make mountains out of molehills.

WILLY. I won't fight with him any more. If he wants to go back to Texas, let him go.

LINDA. He'll find his way.

WILLY. Sure. Certain men just don't get started till later in life. Like Thomas Edison, I think. Or B. F. Goodrich. One of them was deaf. (*He starts for the bedroom doorway.*) I'll put my money on Biff.

LINDA. And Willy—if it's warm Sunday we'll drive in the country. And we'll open the windshield, and take lunch.

WILLY. No, the windshields don't open on the new cars.

LINDA. But you opened it today.

WILLY. Me? I didn't. (*He stops.*) Now isn't that peculiar! Isn't that a remarkable—(*He breaks off in amazement and fright as the flute is heard distantly.*)

LINDA. What, darling?

WILLY. That is the most remarkable thing.

LINDA. What, dear?

WILLY. I was thinking of the Chevvy. (*Slight pause*) Nineteen twenty-eight . . . when I had that red Chevvy—(*Breaks off*) That's funny? I coulda sworn I was driving that Chevvy today.

LINDA. Well, that's nothing. Something must've reminded you.

WILLY. Remarkable. Ts. Remember those days? The way Biff used to simonize that car? The dealer refused to believe there was eighty thousand miles on it. (*He shakes his head.*) Heh! (*To* LINDA) Close your eyes, I'll be right up. (*He walks out of the bedroom.*)

HAPPY (*to* BIFF). Jesus, maybe he smashed up the car again!

LINDA (*calling after* WILLY). Be careful on the stairs, dear! The cheese is on the middle shelf! (*She turns, goes over to the bed, takes his jacket, and goes out of the bedroom.*)

(*Light has risen on the boys' room. Unseen,* WILLY *is heard talking to himself, "Eighty thousand miles," and a little laugh.* BIFF *gets out of bed, comes downstage a bit, and stands attentively.* BIFF *is two years older than his brother* HAPPY, *well built, but in these days bears a worn air and seems less self-assured. He has succeeded less, and his dreams are stronger and less acceptable than* HAPPY's. HAPPY *is tall, powerfully made. Sexuality is like a visible color on him, or a scent that many women have discovered. He, like his brother, is lost, but in a different way, for he has never allowed himself to turn his face toward defeat and is thus more confused and hard-skinned, although seemingly more content.*)

HAPPY (*getting out of bed*). He's going to get his license taken away if he keeps that up. I'm getting nervous about him, y'know, Biff?

BIFF. His eyes are going.

HAPPY. No, I've driven with him. He sees all right. He just doesn't keep his mind on it. I drove into the city with him last week. He stops at a green light and then it turns red and he goes. (*He laughs.*)

BIFF. Maybe he's color-blind.

HAPPY. Pop? Why he's got the finest eye for color in the business. You know that.

BIFF (*sitting down on his bed*). I'm going to sleep.

HAPPY. You're not still sour on Dad, are you, Biff?

BIFF. He's all right, I guess.

WILLY (*underneath them, in the living-room*). Yes, sir, eighty thousand miles—eighty-two thousand!

BIFF. You smoking?

HAPPY (*holding out a pack of cigarettes*). Want one?

BIFF (*taking a cigarette*). I can never sleep when I smell it.

WILLY. What a simonizing job, heh!

HAPPY (*with deep sentiment*). Funny, Biff, y'know? Us sleeping in here again? The old beds. (*He pats his bed affectionately.*) All the talk that went across those two beds, huh? Our whole lives.

BIFF. Yeah. Lotta dreams and plans.

HAPPY (*with a deep and masculine laugh*). About five hundred women would like to know what was said in this room.

(*They share a soft laugh.*)

BIFF. Remember that big Betsy something—what the hell was her name—over on Bushwick Avenue?

HAPPY (*combing his hair*). With the collie dog!

BIFF. That's the one. I got you in there, remember?

HAPPY. Yeah, that was my first time—I think. Boy, there was a pig! (*They laugh, almost crudely.*) You taught me everything I know about women. Don't forget that.

BIFF. I bet you forgot how bashful you used to be. Especially with girls.

HAPPY. Oh, I still am, Biff.

BIFF. Oh, go on.

HAPPY. I just control it, that's all. I think I got less bashful and you got more so. What happened, Biff? Where's the old humor, the old confidence? (*He shakes* BIFF's *knee.* BIFF *gets up and moves restlessly about the room.*) What's the matter?

BIFF. Why does Dad mock me all the time?

HAPPY. He's not mocking you, he—

BIFF. Everything I say there's a twist of mockery on his face. I can't get near him.

HAPPY. He just wants you to make good, that's all. I wanted to talk to you about Dad for a long time, Biff. Something's—happening to him. He —talks to himself.

BIFF. I noticed that this morning. But he always mumbled.

HAPPY. But not so noticeable. It got so embarrassing I sent him to Florida. And you know something? Most of the time he's talking to you.

BIFF. What's he say about me?

HAPPY. I can't make it out.

BIFF. What's he say about me?

HAPPY. I think the fact that you're not settled, that you're still kind of up in the air . . .

BIFF. There's one or two other things depressing him, Happy.

HAPPY. What do you mean?

BIFF. Never mind. Just don't lay it all to me.

HAPPY. But I think if you just got started—I mean—is there any future for you out there?

BIFF. I tell ya, Hap, I don't know what the future is. I don't know—what I'm supposed to want.

HAPPY. What do you mean?

BIFF. Well, I spent six or seven years after high school trying to work myself up. Shipping clerk, salesman, business of one kind or another. And it's a measly manner of existence. To get on that subway on the hot mornings in summer. To devote your whole life to keeping stock, or making phone calls, or selling or buying. To suffer fifty weeks of the year for the sake of a two-week vacation, when all you really desire is to be outdoors, with your shirt off. And always to have to get ahead of the next fella. And still—that's how you build a future.

HAPPY. Well, you really enjoy it on a farm? Are you content out there?

BIFF (with rising agitation). Hap, I've had twenty or thirty different kinds of jobs since I left home before the war, and it always turns out the same. I just realized it lately. In Nebraska when I herded cattle, and the Dakotas, and Arizona, and now in Texas. It's why I came home now, I guess, because I realized it. This farm I work on, it's spring there now, see? And they've got about fifteen new colts. There's nothing more inspiring or—beautiful than the sight of a mare and a new colt. And it's cool there now, see? Texas is cool now, and it's spring. And whenever spring comes to where I am, I suddenly get the feeling, my God, I'm not gettin' anywhere! What the hell am I doing, playing around with horses, twenty-eight dollars a week! I'm thirty-four years old, I oughta be makin' my future. That's when I come running home. And now, I get here, and I don't know what to do with my-self. (After a pause) I've always made a point of not wasting my life, and everytime I come back here I know that all I've done is to waste my life.

HAPPY. You're a poet, you know that, Biff? You're a—you're an idealist!

BIFF. No, I'm mixed up very bad. Maybe I oughta get married. Maybe

I oughta get stuck into something. Maybe that's my trouble. I'm like a boy. I'm not married, I'm not in business, I just—I'm like a boy. Are you content, Hap? You're a success, aren't you? Are you content?

HAPPY.   Hell, no!

BIFF.   Why? You're making money, aren't you?

HAPPY (*moving about with energy, expressiveness*).   All I can do now is wait for the merchandise manager to die. And suppose I get to be merchandise manager? He's a good friend of mine, and he just built a terrific estate on Long Island. And he lived there about two months and sold it, and now he's building another one. He can't enjoy it once it's finished. And I know that's just what I would do. I don't know what the hell I'm workin' for. Sometimes I sit in my apartment—all alone. And I think of the rent I'm paying. And it's crazy. But then, it's what I always wanted. My own apartment, a car, and plenty of women. And still, goddammit, I'm lonely.

BIFF (*with enthusiasm*).   Listen, why don't you come out West with me?

HAPPY.   You and I, heh?

BIFF.   Sure, maybe we could buy a ranch. Raise cattle, use our muscles. Men built like we are should be working out in the open.

HAPPY (*avidly*).   The Loman Brothers, heh?

BIFF (*with vast affection*).   Sure, we'd be known all over the counties!

HAPPY (*enthralled*).   That's what I dream about, Biff. Sometimes I want to just rip my clothes off in the middle of the store and outbox that goddam merchandise manager. I mean I can outbox, outrun, and outlift anybody in that store, and I have to take orders from those common, petty sons-of-bitches till I can't stand it any more.

BIFF.   I'm tellin' you, kid, if you were with me I'd be happy out there.

HAPPY (*enthused*).   See, Biff, everybody around me is so false that I'm constantly lowering my ideals . . .

BIFF.   Baby, together we'd stand up for one another, we'd have someone to trust.

HAPPY.   If I were around you—

BIFF.   Hap, the trouble is we weren't brought up to grub for money. I don't know how to do it.

HAPPY.   Neither can I!

BIFF.   Then let's go!

HAPPY.   The only thing is—what can you make out there?

BIFF.   But look at your friend. Builds an estate and then hasn't the peace of mind to live in it.

HAPPY.   Yeah, but when he walks into the store the waves part in front of him. That's fifty-two thousand dollars a year coming through the revolving door, and I got more in my pinky finger than he's got in his head.

BIFF.   Yeah, but you just said—

HAPPY.   I gotta show some of those pompous, self-important executives over there that Hap Loman can make the grade. I want to walk into the store the way he walks in. Then I'll go with you, Biff. We'll be together yet, I swear. But take those two we had tonight. Now weren't they gorgeous creatures?

BIFF. Yeah, yeah, most gorgeous I've had in years.

HAPPY. I get that any time I want, Biff. Whenever I feel disgusted. The only trouble is, it gets like bowling or something. I just keep knockin' them over and it doesn't mean anything. You still run around a lot?

BIFF. Naa. I'd like to find a girl—steady, somebody with substance.

HAPPY. That's what I long for.

BIFF. Go on! You'd never come home.

HAPPY. I would! Somebody with character, with resistance! Like Mom, y'know? You're gonna call me a bastard when I tell you this. That girl Charlotte I was with tonight is engaged to be married in five weeks. (*He tries on his new hat.*)

BIFF. No kiddin'!

HAPPY. Sure, the guy's in line for the vice-presidency of the store. I don't know what gets into me, maybe I just have an overdeveloped sense of competition or something, but I went and ruined her, and furthermore I can't get rid of her. And he's the third executive I've done that to. Isn't that a crummy characteristic? And to top it all, I go to their weddings! (*Indignantly, but laughing*) Like I'm not supposed to take bribes. Manufacturers offer me a hundred-dollar bill now and then to throw an order their way. You know how honest I am, but it's like this girl, see. I hate myself for it. Because I don't want the girl, and, still, I take it and—I love it!

BIFF. Let's go to sleep.

HAPPY. I guess we didn't settle anything, heh?

BIFF. I just got one idea that I think I'm going to try.

HAPPY. What's that?

BIFF. Remember Bill Oliver?

HAPPY. Sure, Oliver is very big now. You want to work for him again?

BIFF. No, but when I quit he said something to me. He put his arm on my shoulder, and he said, "Biff, if you ever need anything, come to me."

HAPPY. I remember that. That sounds good.

BIFF. I think I'll go to see him. If I could get ten thousand or even seven or eight thousand dollars I could buy a beautiful ranch.

HAPPY. I bet he'd back you. 'Cause he thought highly of you, Biff. I mean, they all do. You're well liked, Biff. That's why I say to come back here, and we both have the apartment. And I'm tellin' you, Biff, any babe you want . . .

BIFF. No, with a ranch I could do the work I like and still be something. I just wonder though. I wonder if Oliver still thinks I stole that carton of basketballs.

HAPPY. Oh, he probably forgot that long ago. It's almost ten years.

You're too sensitive. Anyway, he didn't really fire you.

BIFF. Well, I think he was going to. I think that's why I quit. I was never sure whether he knew or not. I know he thought the world of me, though. I was the only one he'd let lock up the place.

WILLY (*below*). You gonna wash the engine, Biff?

HAPPY. Shh!

(BIFF *looks at* HAPPY, *who is gazing down, listening.* WILLY *is mumbling in the parlor.*)

HAPPY. You hear that?

(*They listen.* WILLY *laughs warmly.*)

BIFF (*growing angry*). Doesn't he know Mom can hear that?

WILLY. Don't get your sweater dirty, Biff!

(*A look of pain crosses* BIFF's *face.*)

HAPPY. Isn't that terrible? Don't leave again, will you? You'll find a job here. You gotta stick around. I don't know what to do about him, it's getting embarrassing.

WILLY. What a simonizing job!

BIFF. Mom's hearing that!

WILLY. No kiddin', Biff, you got a date? Wonderful!

HAPPY. Go on to sleep. But talk to him in the morning, will you?

BIFF (*reluctantly getting into bed*). With her in the house. Brother!

HAPPY (*getting into bed*). I wish you'd have a good talk with him.

(*The light on their room begins to fade.*)

BIFF (*to himself in bed*). That selfish, stupid . . .

HAPPY. Sh . . . Sleep, Biff.

(*Their light is out. Well before they have finished speaking,* WILLY's *form is dimly seen below in the darkened kitchen. He opens the refrigerator, searches in there, and takes out a bottle of milk. The apartment houses are fading out, and the entire house and surroundings become covered with leaves. Music insinuates itself as the leaves appear.*)

WILLY. Just wanna be careful with those girls, Biff, that's all. Don't make any promises. No promises of any kind. Because a girl, y'know, they always believe what you tell 'em, and you're very young, Biff, you're too young to be talking seriously to girls.

(*Light rises on the kitchen.* WILLY, *talking, shuts the refrigerator door and comes downstage to the kitchen table. He pours milk into a glass. He is totally immersed in himself, smiling faintly.*)

WILLY. Too young entirely, Biff. You want to watch your schooling first. Then when you're all set, there'll be plenty of girls for a boy like you.

(*He smiles broadly at a kitchen chair.*) That so? The girls pay for you? (*He laughs.*) Boy, you must really be makin' a hit.

(WILLY *is gradually addressing—physically—a point offstage, speaking through the wall of the kitchen, and his voice has been rising in volume to that of a normal conversation.*)

WILLY. I been wondering why you polish the car so careful. Ha! Don't leave the hubcaps, boys. Get the chamois to the hubcaps. Happy, use newspaper on the windows, it's the easiest thing. Show him how to do it, Biff! You see, Happy? Pad it up, use it like a pad. That's it, that's it, good work. You're doin' all right, Hap. (*He pauses, then nods in approbation for a few seconds, then looks upward.*) Biff, first thing we gotta do when we get time is clip that big branch over the house. Afraid it's gonna fall in a storm and hit the roof. Tell you what. We get a rope and sling her around, and then we climb up there with a couple of saws and take her down. Soon as you finish the car, boys, I wanna see ya. I got a surprise for you, boys.

BIFF (*offstage*). Whatta ya got, Dad?

WILLY. No, you finish first. Never leave a job till you're finished— remember that. (*Looking toward the "big trees"*) Biff, up in Albany I saw a beautiful hammock. I think I'll buy it next trip, and we'll hang it right between those two elms. Wouldn't that be something? Just swingin' there under those branches. Boy, that would be . . .

(*Young* BIFF *and Young* HAPPY *appear from the direction* WILLY *was addressing.* HAPPY *carries rags and a pail of water.* BIFF, *wearing a sweater with a block "S," carries a football.*)

BIFF (*pointing in the direction of the car offstage*). How's that, Pop, professional?

WILLY. Terrific. Terrific job, boys. Good work, Biff.

HAPPY. Where's the surprise, Pop?

WILLY. In the back seat of the car.

HAPPY. Boy! (*He runs off.*)

BIFF. What is it, Dad? Tell me, what'd you buy?

WILLY (*laughing, cuffs him*). Never mind, something I want you to have.

BIFF (*turns and starts off*). What is it, Hap?

HAPPY (*offstage*). It's a punching bag!

BIFF. Oh, Pop!

WILLY. It's got Gene Tunney's signature on it!

(HAPPY *runs onstage with a punching bag.*)

BIFF. Gee, how'd you know we wanted a punching bag?

WILLY. Well, it's the finest thing for the timing.

HAPPY (*lies down on his back and pedals with his feet*). I'm losing weight, you notice, Pop?

WILLY (*to* HAPPY). Jumping rope is good too.

BIFF. Did you see the new football I got?

WILLY (*examining the ball*). Where'd you get a new ball?

BIFF. The coach told me to practice my passing.

WILLY. That so? And he gave you the ball, heh?

BIFF. Well, I borrowed it from the locker room. (*He laughs confidentially.*)

WILLY (*laughing with him at the theft*). I want you to return that.

HAPPY. I told you he wouldn't like it!

BIFF (*angrily*). Well, I'm bringing it back!

WILLY (*stopping the incipient argument, to* HAPPY). Sure, he's gotta practice with a regulation ball, doesn't he? (*To* BIFF) Coach'll probably congratulate you on your initiative!

BIFF. Oh, he keeps congratulating my initiative all the time, Pop.

WILLY. That's because he likes you. If somebody else took that ball there'd be an uproar. So what's the report, boys, what's the report?

BIFF. Where'd you go this time, Dad? Gee, we were lonesome for you.

WILLY (*pleased, puts an arm around each boy and they come down to the apron*). Lonesome, heh?

BIFF. Missed you every minute.

WILLY. Don't say? Tell you a secret, boys. Don't breathe it to a soul. Someday I'll have my own business, and I'll never have to leave home any more.

HAPPY. Like Uncle Charley, heh?

WILLY. Bigger than Uncle Charley! Because Charley is not—liked. He's liked, but he's not—well liked.

BIFF. Where'd you go this time, Dad?

WILLY. Well, I got on the road, and I went north to Providence. Met the Mayor.

BIFF. The Mayor of Providence!

WILLY. He was sitting in the hotel lobby.

BIFF. What'd he say?

WILLY. He said, "Morning!" And I said, "You got a fine city here, Mayor." And then he had coffee with me. And then I went to Waterbury. Waterbury is a fine city. Big clock city, the famous Waterbury clock. Sold a nice bill there. And then Boston—Boston is the cradle of the Revolution. A fine city. And a couple of other towns in Mass., and on to Portland and Bangor and straight home!

BIFF. Gee, I'd love to go with you sometime, Dad.

WILLY. Soon as summer comes.

HAPPY. Promise?

WILLY. You and Hap and I, and I'll show you all the towns. America is full of beautiful towns and fine, upstanding people. And they know me, boys, they know me up and down New England. The finest people. And when I bring you fellas up, there'll be open sesame for all of us, 'cause one thing, boys: I have friends. I can park my car in any street in New England, and the cops protect it like their own. This summer, heh?

BIFF *and* HAPPY (*together*).   Yeah! You bet!

WILLY.   We'll take our bathing suits.

HAPPY.   We'll carry your bags, Pop!

WILLY.   Oh, won't that be something! Me comin' into the Boston stores with you boys carryin' my bags. What a sensation!

(BIFF *is prancing around, practicing passing the ball.*)

WILLY.   You nervous, Biff, about the game?

BIFF.   Not if you're gonna be there.

WILLY.   What do they say about you in school, now that they made you captain?

HAPPY.   There's a crowd of girls behind him everytime the classes change.

BIFF (*taking* WILLY'*s hand*).   This Saturday, Pop, this Saturday—just for you, I'm going to break through for a touchdown.

HAPPY.   You're supposed to pass.

BIFF.   I'm takin' one play for Pop. You watch me, Pop, and when I take off my helmet, that means I'm breakin' out. Then you watch me crash through that line!

WILLY (*kisses* BIFF).   Oh, wait'll I tell this in Boston!

(BERNARD *enters in knickers. He is younger than* BIFF, *earnest and loyal, a worried boy.*)

BERNARD.   Biff, where are you? You're supposed to study with me today.

WILLY.   Hey, looka Bernard. What're you lookin' so anemic about, Bernard?

BERNARD.   He's gotta study, Uncle Willy. He's got Regents next week.

HAPPY (*tauntingly, spinning* BERNARD *around*).   Let's box, Bernard!

BERNARD.   Biff! (*He gets away from* HAPPY.) Listen, Biff, I heard Mr. Birnbaum say that if you don't start studyin' math he's gonna flunk you, and you won't graduate. I heard him!

WILLY.   You better study with him, Biff. Go ahead now.

BERNARD.   I heard him!

BIFF.   Oh, Pop, you didn't see my sneakers! (*He holds up a foot for* WILLY *to look at.*)

WILLY.   Hey, that's a beautiful job of printing!

BERNARD (*wiping his glasses*).   Just because he printed University of Virginia on his sneakers doesn't mean they've got to graduate him. Uncle Willy!

WILLY (*angrily*).   What're you talking about? With scholarships to three universities they're gonna flunk him?

BERNARD. But I heard Mr. Birnbaum say—

WILLY. Don't be a pest, Bernard! (*To his boys*) What an anemic!

BERNARD. Okay, I'm waiting for you in my house, Biff.

(BERNARD *goes off. The Lomans laugh.*)

WILLY. Bernard is not well liked, is he?

BIFF. He's liked, but he's not well liked.

HAPPY. That's right, Pop.

WILLY. That's just what I mean. Bernard can get the best marks in school, y'understand, but when he gets out in the business world, y'understand, you are going to be five times ahead of him. That's why I thank Almighty God you're both built like Adonises. Because the man who makes an appearance in the business world, the man who creates personal interest, is the man who gets ahead. Be liked and you will never want. You take me, for instance. I never have to wait in line to see a buyer. "Willy Loman is here!" That's all they have to know, and I go right through.

BIFF. Did you knock them dead, Pop?

WILLY. Knocked 'em cold in Providence, slaughtered 'em in Boston.

HAPPY (*on his back, pedaling again*). I'm losing weight, you notice, Pop?

(LINDA *enters, as of old, a ribbon in her hair, carrying a basket of washing.*)

LINDA (*with youthful energy*). Hello, dear!

WILLY. Sweetheart!

LINDA. How'd the Chevvy run?

WILLY. Chevrolet, Linda, is the greatest car ever built. (*To the boys*) Since when do you let your mother carry wash up the stairs?

BIFF. Grab hold there, boy!

HAPPY. Where to, Mom?

LINDA. Hang them up on the line. And you better go down to your friends, Biff. The cellar is full of boys. They don't know what to do with themselves.

BIFF. Ah, when Pop comes home they can wait!

WILLY (*laughs appreciatively*). You better go down and tell them what to do, Biff.

BIFF. I think I'll have them sweep out the furnace room.

WILLY. Good work, Biff.

BIFF (*goes through wall-line of kitchen to doorway at back and calls down*). Fellas! Everybody sweep out the furnace room! I'll be right down!

VOICES. All right! Okay, Biff.

BIFF. George and Sam and Frank, come out back! We're hangin' up the wash! Come on, Hap, on the double! (*He and* HAPPY *carry out the basket.*)

LINDA. The way they obey him!

WILLY. Well, that's training, the training. I'm tellin' you, I was sellin' thousands and thousands, but I had to come home.

LINDA. Oh, the whole block'll be at that game. Did you sell anything?

WILLY. I did five hundred gross in Providence and seven hundred gross in Boston.

LINDA. No! Wait a minute, I've got a pencil. (*She pulls pencil and paper out of her apron pocket.*) That makes your commission . . . Two hundred—my God! Two hundred and twelve dollars!

WILLY. Well, I didn't figure it yet, but . . .

LINDA. How much did you do?

WILLY. Well, I—I did—about a hundred and eighty gross in Providence. Well, no—it came to—roughly two hundred gross on the whole trip.

LINDA (*without hesitation*). Two hundred gross. That's . . . (*She figures.*)

WILLY. The trouble was that three of the stores were half closed for inventory in Boston. Otherwise I woulda broke records.

LINDA. Well, it makes seventy dollars and some pennies. That's very good.

WILLY. What do we owe?

LINDA. Well, on the first there's sixteen dollars on the refrigerator—

WILLY. Why sixteen?

LINDA. Well, the fan belt broke, so it was a dollar eighty.

WILLY. But it's brand new.

LINDA. Well, the man said that's the way it is. Till they work themselves in, y'know.

(*They move through the wall-line into the kitchen.*)

WILLY. I hope we didn't get stuck on that machine.

LINDA. They got the biggest ads of any of them!

WILLY. I know, it's a fine machine. What else?

LINDA. Well, there's nine-sixty for the washing machine. And for the vacuum cleaner there's three and a half due on the fifteenth. Then the roof, you got twenty-one dollars remaining.

WILLY. It don't leak, does it?

LINDA. No, they did a wonderful job. Then you owe Frank for the carburetor.

WILLY. I'm not going to pay that man! That goddam. Chevrolet, they ought to prohibit the manufacture of that car!

LINDA. Well, you owe him three and a half. And odds and ends, comes to around a hundred and twenty dollars by the fifteenth.

WILLY. A hundred and twenty dollars! My God, if business don't pick up I don't know what I'm gonna do!

LINDA. Well, next week you'll do better.

WILLY. Oh, I'll knock 'em dead next week. I'll go to Hartford. I'm very well liked in Hartford. You know, the trouble is, Linda, people don't seem to take to me.

(*They move onto the forestage.*)

LINDA. Oh, don't be foolish.

WILLY. I know it when I walk in. They seem to laugh at me.

LINDA. Why? Why would they laugh at you? Don't talk that way, Willy.

(WILLY *moves to the edge of the stage.* LINDA *goes into the kitchen and starts to darn stockings.*)

WILLY. I don't know the reason for it, but they just pass me by. I'm not noticed.

LINDA. But you're doing wonderful, dear. You're making seventy to a hundred dollars a week.

WILLY. But I gotta be at it ten, twelve hours a day. Other men—I don't know—they do it easier. I don't know why—I can't stop myself—I talk too much. A man oughta come in with a few words. One thing about Charley. He's a man of few words, and they respect him.

LINDA. You don't talk too much, you're just lively.

WILLY (*smiling*). Well, I figure, what the hell, life is short, a couple of jokes. (*To himself*) I joke too much! (*The smile goes.*)

LINDA. Why? You're—

WILLY. I'm fat. I'm very—foolish to look at, Linda. I didn't tell you, but Christmas time I happened to be calling on F. H. Stewarts, and a salesman I know, as I was going in to see the buyer I heard him say something about—walrus. And I—I cracked him right across the face. I won't take that. I simply will not take that. But they do laugh at me. I know that.

LINDA. Darling . . .

WILLY. I gotta overcome it. I know I gotta overcome it. I'm not dressing to advantage, maybe.

LINDA. Willy, darling, you're the handsomest man in the world—

WILLY. Oh, no, Linda.

LINDA. To me you are. (*Slight pause*) The handsomest.

(*From the darkness is heard the laughter of a woman.* WILLY *doesn't turn to it, but it continues through* LINDA's *lines.*)

LINDA. And the boys, Willy. Few men are idolized by their children the way you are.

(*Music is heard as behind a scrim, to the left of the house,* THE WOMAN, *dimly seen, is dressing.*)

WILLY (*with great feeling*). You're the best there is, Linda, you're a pal, you know that? On the road—on the road I want to grab you sometimes and just kiss the life outa you.

(*The laughter is loud now, and he moves into a brightening area at the left, where* THE WOMAN *has come from behind the scrim and is standing, putting on her hat, looking into a "mirror" and laughing.*)

WILLY. 'Cause I get so lonely—especially when business is bad and there's nobody to talk to. I get the feeling that I'll never sell anything again, that I won't make a living for you, or a business, a business for the boys. (*He talks through* THE WOMAN'S *subsiding laughter;* THE WOMAN *primps at the "mirror."*) There's so much I want to make for—

THE WOMAN. Me? You didn't make me, Willy. I picked you.

WILLY (*pleased*). You picked me?

THE WOMAN (*who is quite proper-looking,* WILLY'S *age*). I did. I've been sitting at that desk watching all the salesmen go by, day in, day out. But you've got such a sense of humor, and we do have such a good time together, don't we?

WILLY. Sure, sure. (*He takes her in his arms.*) Why do you have to go now?

THE WOMAN. It's two o'clock . . .

WILLY. No, come on in! (*He pulls her.*)

THE WOMAN. . . . my sisters'll be scandalized. When'll you be back?

WILLY. Oh, two weeks about. Will you come up again?

THE WOMAN. Sure thing. You do make me laugh. It's good for me. (*She squeezes his arm, kisses him.*) And I think you're a wonderful man.

WILLY. You picked me, heh?

THE WOMAN. Sure. Because you're so sweet. And such a kidder.

WILLY. Well, I'll see you next time I'm in Boston.

THE WOMAN. I'll put you right through to the buyers.

WILLY (*slapping her bottom*). Right. Well, bottoms up!

THE WOMAN (*slaps him gently and laughs*). You just kill me, Willy. (*He suddenly grabs her and kisses her roughly.*) You kill me. And thanks for the stockings. I love a lot of stockings. Well, good night.

WILLY. Good night. And keep your pores open!

THE WOMAN. Oh, Willy!

(THE WOMAN *bursts out laughing, and* LINDA'S *laughter blends in.* THE WOMAN *disappears into the dark. Now the area at the kitchen table brightens.* LINDA *is sitting where she was at the kitchen table, but now is mending a pair of her silk stockings.*)

LINDA. You are, Willy. The handsomest man. You've got no reason to feel that—

WILLY (*coming out of* THE WOMAN'S *dimming area and going over to* LINDA). I'll make it all up to you, Linda, I'll—

LINDA. There's nothing to make up, dear. You're doing fine, better than—

WILLY (*noticing her mending*). What's that?

LINDA. Just mending my stockings. They're so expensive—

WILLY (*angrily, taking them from her*). I won't have you mending stockings in this house! Now throw them out!

(LINDA *puts the stockings in her pocket.*)

BERNARD (*entering on the run*). Where is he? If he doesn't study!

WILLY (*moving to the forestage, with great agitation*). You'll give him the answers!

BERNARD. I do, but I can't on a Regents! That's a state exam! They're liable to arrest me!

WILLY. Where is he? I'll whip him, I'll whip him!

LINDA. And he'd better give back that football, Willy, it's not nice.

WILLY. Biff! Where is he? Why is he taking everything?

LINDA. He's too rough with the girls, Willy. All the mothers are afraid of him!

WILLY. I'll whip him!

BERNARD. He's driving the car without a license!

(THE WOMAN's *laugh is heard.*)

WILLY. Shut up!

LINDA. All the mothers—

WILLY. Shut up!

BERNARD (*backing quietly away and out*). Mr. Birnbaum says he's stuck up.

WILLY. Get outa here!

BERNARD. If he doesn't buckle down he'll flunk math! (*He goes off.*)

LINDA. He's right, Willy, you've gotta—

WILLY (*exploding at her*). There's nothing the matter with him! You want him to be a worm like Bernard? He's got spirit, personality . . .

(*As he speaks,* LINDA, *almost in tears, exits into the living-room.* WILLY *is alone in the kitchen, wilting and staring. The leaves are gone. It is night again, and the apartment houses look down from behind.*)

WILLY. Loaded with it. Loaded! What is he stealing? He's giving it back, isn't he? Why is he stealing? What did I tell him? I never in my life told him anything but decent things.

(HAPPY *in pajamas has come down the stairs;* WILLY *suddenly becomes aware of* HAPPY's *presence.*)

HAPPY. Let's go now, come on.

WILLY (*sitting down at the kitchen table*). Huh! Why did she have to wax the floors herself? Everytime she waxes the floors she keels over. She knows that!

HAPPY. Shh! Take it easy. What brought you back tonight?

WILLY. I got an awful scare. Nearly hit a kid in Yonkers. God! Why didn't I go to Alaska with my brother Ben that time! Ben! That man was a genius, that man was success incarnate! What a mistake! He begged me to go.

HAPPY. Well, there's no use in—

WILLY. You guys! There was a man started with the clothes on his back and ended up with diamond mines!

HAPPY. Boy, someday I'd like to know how he did it.

WILLY. What's the mystery? The man knew what he wanted and went out and got it! Walked into a jungle, and comes out, the age of twenty-one, and he's rich! The world is an oyster, but you don't crack it open on a mattress.

HAPPY. Pop, I told you I'm gonna retire you for life.

WILLY. You'll retire me for life on seventy goddam dollars a week? And your women and your car and your apartment, and you'll retire me for life! Christ's sake, I couldn't get past Yonkers today! Where are you guys, where are you? The woods are burning! I can't drive a car!

(CHARLEY *has appeared in the doorway. He is a large man, slow of speech, laconic, immovable. In all he says, despite what he says, there is pity, and, now, trepidation. He has a robe over pajamas, slippers on his feet. He enters the kitchen.*)

CHARLEY. Everything all right?

HAPPY. Yeah, Charley, everything's . . .

WILLY. What's the matter?

CHARLEY. I heard some noise. I thought something happened. Can't we do something about the walls? You sneeze in here, and in my house hats blow off.

HAPPY. Let's go to bed, Dad. Come on.

(CHARLEY *signals to* HAPPY *to go.*)

WILLY. You go ahead, I'm not tired at the moment.

HAPPY (*to* WILLY). Take it easy, huh? (*He exits.*)

WILLY. What're you doin' up?

CHARLEY (*sitting down at the kitchen table opposite* WILLY). Couldn't sleep good. I had a heartburn.

WILLY. Well, you don't know how to eat.

CHARLEY. I eat with my mouth.

WILLY. No, you're ignorant. You gotta know about vitamins and things like that.

CHARLEY. Come on, let's shoot. Tire you out a little.

WILLY (*hesitantly*). All right. You got cards?

CHARLEY (*taking a deck from his pocket*). Yeah, I got them. Some-place. What is it with those vitamins?

WILLY (*dealing*). They build up your bones. Chemistry.

CHARLEY. Yeah, but there's no bones in a heartburn.

WILLY. What are you talkin' about? Do you know the first thing about it?

CHARLEY. Don't get insulted.

WILLY. Don't talk about something you don't know anything about.

(*They are playing. Pause.*)

CHARLEY. What're you doin' home?

WILLY. A little trouble with the car.

CHARLEY. Oh. (*Pause*) I'd like to take a trip to California.

WILLY. Don't say.

CHARLEY. You want a job?

WILLY. I got a job, I told you that. (*After a slight pause*) What the hell are you offering me a job for?

CHARLEY. Don't get insulted.

WILLY. Don't insult me.

CHARLEY. I don't see no sense in it. You don't have to go on this way.

WILLY. I got a good job. (*Slight pause*) What do you keep comin' in here for?

CHARLEY. You want me to go?

WILLY (*after a pause, withering*). I can't understand it. He's going back to Texas again. What the hell is that?

CHARLEY. Let him go.

WILLY. I got nothin' to give him, Charley, I'm clean, I'm clean.

CHARLEY. He won't starve. None a them starve. Forget about him.

WILLY. Then what have I got to remember?

CHARLEY. You take it too hard. To hell with it. When a deposit bottle is broken you don't get your nickel back.

WILLY. That's easy enough for you to say.

CHARLEY. That ain't easy for me to say.

WILLY. Did you see the ceiling I put up in the living-room?

CHARLEY. Yeah, that's a piece of work. To put up a ceiling is a mystery to me. How do you do it?

WILLY. What's the difference?

CHARLEY. Well, talk about it.

WILLY. You gonna put up a ceiling?

CHARLEY. How could I put up a ceiling?

WILLY. Then what the hell are you bothering me for?

CHARLEY. You're insulted again.

WILLY. A man who can't handle tools is not a man. You're disgusting.

CHARLEY. Don't call me disgusting, Willy.

(UNCLE BEN, *carrying a valise and an umbrella, enters the forestage from around the right corner of the house. He is a stolid man, in his sixties, with a mustache and an authoritative air. He is utterly certain of his destiny, and there is an aura of far places about him. He enters exactly as* WILLY *speaks.*)

WILLY.   I'm getting awfully tired, Ben.

(BEN's *music is heard.* BEN *looks around at everything.*)

CHARLEY.   Good, keep playing; you'll sleep better. Did you call me Ben?

(BEN *looks at his watch.*)

WILLY.   That's funny. For a second there you reminded me of my brother Ben.
BEN.   I only have a few minutes.

(*He strolls, inspecting the place.* WILLY *and* CHARLEY *continue playing.*)

CHARLEY.   You never heard from him again, heh? Since that time?
WILLY.   Didn't Linda tell you? Couple of weeks ago we got a letter from his wife in Africa. He died.
CHARLEY.   That so.
BEN (*chuckling*).   So this is Brooklyn, eh?
CHARLEY.   Maybe you're in for some of his money.
WILLY.   Naa, he had seven sons. There's just one opportunity I had with that man . . .
BEN.   I must make a train, William. There are several properties I'm looking at in Alaska.
WILLY.   Sure, sure! If I'd gone with him to Alaska that time, everything would've been totally different.
CHARLEY.   Go on, you'd froze to death up there.
WILLY.   What're you talking about?
BEN.   Opportunity is tremendous in Alaska, William. Surprised you're not up there.
WILLY.   Sure, tremendous.
CHARLEY.   Heh?
WILLY.   There was the only man I ever met who knew the answers.
CHARLEY.   Who?
BEN.   How are you all?
WILLY (*taking a pot, smiling*).   Fine, fine.
CHARLEY.   Pretty sharp tonight.
BEN.   Is Mother living with you?
WILLY.   No, she died a long time ago.
CHARLEY.   Who?
BEN.   That's too bad. Fine specimen of a lady, Mother.

WILLY (to CHARLEY). Heh?

BEN. I'd hoped to see the old girl.

CHARLEY. Who died?

BEN. Heard anything from Father, have you?

WILLY (unnerved). What do you mean, who died?

CHARLEY (taking a pot). What're you talkin' about?

BEN (looking at his watch). William, it's half-past eight!

WILLY (as though to dispel his confusion he angrily stops CHARLEY's hand). That's my build!

CHARLEY. I put the ace—

WILLY. If you don't know how to play the game I'm not gonna throw my money away on you!

CHARLEY (rising). It was my ace, for God's sake!

WILLY. I'm through, I'm through!

BEN. When did Mother die?

WILLY. Long ago. Since the beginning you never knew how to play cards.

CHARLEY (picks up the cards and goes to the door). All right! Next time I'll bring a deck with five aces.

WILLY. I don't play that kind of game!

CHARLEY (turning to him). You ought to be ashamed of yourself!

WILLY. Yeah?

CHARLEY. Yeah! (He goes out.)

WILLY (slamming the door after him). Ignoramus!

BEN (as WILLY comes toward him through the wall-line of the kitchen). So you're William.

WILLY (shaking BEN's hand). Ben! I've been waiting for you so long! What's the answer? How did you do it?

BEN. Oh, there's a story in that.

(LINDA enters the forestage, as of old, carrying the wash basket.)

LINDA. Is this Ben?

BEN (gallantly). How do you do, my dear.

LINDA. Where've you been all these years? Willy's always wondered why you—

WILLY (pulling BEN away from her impatiently). Where is Dad? Didn't you follow him? How did you get started?

BEN. Well, I don't know how much you remember.

WILLY. Well, I was just a baby, of course, only three or four years old—

BEN. Three years and eleven months.

WILLY. What a memory, Ben!

BEN. I have many enterprises, William, and I have never kept books.

WILLY.   I remember I was sitting under the wagon in—was it Nebraska?

BEN.   It was South Dakota, and I gave you a bunch of wild flowers.

WILLY.   I remember you walking away down some open road.

BEN (*laughing*).   I was going to find Father in Alaska.

WILLY.   Where is he?

BEN.   At that age I had a very faulty view of geography, William. I discovered after a few days that I was heading due south, so instead of Alaska, I ended up in Africa.

LINDA.   Africa!

WILLY.   The Gold Coast!

BEN.   Principally diamond mines.

LINDA.   Diamond mines!

BEN.   Yes, my dear. But I've only a few minutes—

WILLY.   No! Boys! Boys! (YOUNG BIFF *and* HAPPY *appear.*) Listen to this. This is your Uncle Ben, a great man! Tell my boys, Ben!

BEN.   Why, boys, when I was seventeen I walked into the jungle, and when I was twenty-one I walked out. (*He laughs.*) And by God I was rich.

WILLY (*to the boys*).   You see what I been talking about? The greatest things can happen!

BEN (*glancing at his watch*).   I have an appointment in Ketchikan Tuesday week.

WILLY.   No, Ben! Please tell about Dad. I want my boys to hear. I want them to know the kind of stock they spring from. All I remember is a man with a big beard, and I was in Mamma's lap, sitting around a fire, and some kind of high music.

BEN.   His flute. He played the flute.

WILLY.   Sure, the flute, that's right!

(*New music is heard, a high, rollicking tune.*)

BEN.   Father was a very great and a very wild-hearted man. We would start in Boston, and he'd toss the whole family into the wagon, and then he'd drive the team right across the country; through Ohio, and Indiana, Michigan, Illinois, and all the Western states. And we'd stop in the towns and sell the flutes that he'd made on the way. Great inventor, Father. With one gadget he made more in a week than a man like you could make in a lifetime.

WILLY.   That's just the way I'm bringing them up, Ben—rugged, well liked, all-around.

BEN.   Yeah? (*To* BIFF) Hit that, boy—hard as you can. (*He pounds his stomach.*)

BIFF.   Oh, no, sir!

BEN (*taking boxing stance*).   Come on, get to me! (*He laughs.*)

WILLY.   Go to it, Biff! Go ahead, show him!

BIFF. Okay! (*He cocks his fists and starts in.*)

LINDA (*to* WILLY). Why must he fight, dear?

BEN (*sparring with* BIFF). Good boy! Good boy!

WILLY. How's that, Ben, heh?

HAPPY. Give him the left, Biff!

LINDA. Why are you fighting?

BEN. Good boy! (*Suddenly comes in, trips* BIFF, *and stands over him, the point of his umbrella poised over* BIFF's *eye.*)

LINDA. Look out, Biff!

BIFF. Gee!

BEN (*patting* BIFF's *knee*). Never fight fair with a stranger, boy. You'll never get out of the jungle that way. (*Taking* LINDA's *hand and bowing*) It was an honor and a pleasure to meet you, Linda.

LINDA (*withdrawing her hand coldly, frightened*). Have a nice—trip.

BEN (*to* WILLY). And good luck with your—what do you do?

WILLY. Selling.

BEN. Yes. Well . . . (*He raises his hand in farewell to all.*)

WILLY. No, Ben, I don't want you to think . . . (*He takes* BEN's *arm to show him.*) It's Brooklyn, I know, but we hunt too.

BEN. Really, now.

WILLY. Oh, sure, there's snakes and rabbits and—that's why I moved out here. Why, Biff can fell any one of these trees in no time! Boys! Go right over to where they're building the apartment house and get some sand. We're gonna rebuild the entire front stoop right now! Watch this, Ben!

BIFF. Yes, sir! On the double, Hap!

HAPPY (*as he and* BIFF *run off*). I lost weight, Pop, you notice?

(CHARLEY *enters in knickers, even before the boys are gone.*)

CHARLEY. Listen, if they steal any more from that building the watchman'll put the cops on them!

LINDA (*to* WILLY). Don't let Biff . . .

(BEN *laughs lustily.*)

WILLY. You shoulda seen the lumber they brought home last week. At least a dozen six-by-tens worth all kinds a money.

CHARLEY. Listen, if that watchman—

WILLY. I gave them hell, understand. But I got a couple of fearless characters there.

CHARLEY. Willy, the jails are full of fearless characters.

BEN (*clapping* WILLY *on the back, with a laugh at* CHARLEY). And the stock exchange, friend!

WILLY (*joining in* BEN's *laughter*). Where are the rest of your pants?

CHARLEY. My wife bought them.

WILLY. Now all you need is a golf club and you can go upstairs and go to sleep. (*To* BEN) Great athlete! Between him and his son Bernard they can't hammer a nail!

BERNARD (*rushing in*). The watchman's chasing Biff!

WILLY (*angrily*). Shut up! He's not stealing anything!

LINDA (*alarmed, hurrying off left*). Where is he? Biff, dear! (*She exits.*)

WILLY (*moving toward the left, away from* BEN). There's nothing wrong. What's the matter with you?

BEN. Nervy boy. Good!

WILLY (*laughing*). Oh, nerves of iron, that Biff!

CHARLEY. Don't know what it is. My New England man comes back and he's bleedin', they murdered him up there.

WILLY. It's contacts, Charley, I got important contacts!

CHARLEY (*sarcastically*). Glad to hear it, Willy. Come in later, we'll shoot a little casino. I'll take some of your Portland money. (*He laughs at* WILLY *and exits.*)

WILLY (*turning to* BEN). Business is bad, it's murderous. But not for me, of course.

BEN. I'll stop by on my way back to Africa.

WILLY (*longingly*). Can't you stay a few days? You're just what I need, Ben, because I—I have a fine position here, but I—well, Dad left when I was such a baby and I never had a chance to talk to him and I still feel—kind of temporary about myself.

BEN. I'll be late for my train.

(*They are at opposite ends of the stage.*)

WILLY. Ben, my boys—can't we talk? They'd go into the jaws of hell for me, but I—

BEN. William, you're being first-rate with your boys. Outstanding, manly chaps!

WILLY (*hanging on to his words*). Oh, Ben, that's good to hear! Because sometimes I'm afraid that I'm not teaching them the right kind of— Ben, how should I teach them?

BEN (*giving great weight to each word, and with a certain vicious audacity*). William, when I walked into the jungle, I was seventeen. When I walked out I was twenty-one. And, by God, I was rich! (*He goes off into darkness around the right corner of the house.*)

WILLY. . . . was rich! That's just the spirit I want to imbue them with! To walk into a jungle! I was right! I was right! I was right!

(BEN *is gone, but* WILLY *is still speaking to him as* LINDA, *in nightgown and robe, enters the kitchen, glances around for* WILLY, *then goes to the door of the house, looks out and sees him. Comes down to his left. He looks at her.*)

LINDA. Willy, dear? Willy?

WILLY. I was right!

LINDA. Did you have some cheese? (*He can't answer.*) It's very late, darling. Come to bed, heh?

WILLY (*looking straight up*). Gotta break your neck to see a star in this yard.

LINDA. You coming in?

WILLY. Whatever happened to that diamond watch fob? Remember? When Ben came from Africa that time? Didn't he give me a watch fob with a diamond in it?

LINDA. You pawned it, dear. Twelve, thirteen years ago. For Biff's radio correspondence course.

WILLY. Gee, that was a beautiful thing. I'll take a walk.

LINDA. But you're in your slippers.

WILLY (*starting to go around the house at the left*). I was right! I was! (*Half to* LINDA, *as he goes, shaking his head*) What a man! There was a man worth talking to. I was right!

LINDA (*calling after* WILLY). But in your slippers, Willy!

(WILLY *is almost gone when* BIFF, *in his pajamas, comes down the stairs and enters the kitchen.*)

BIFF. What is he doing out there?

LINDA. Sh!

BIFF. God Almighty, Mom, how long has he been doing this?

LINDA. Don't, he'll hear you.

BIFF. What the hell is the matter with him?

LINDA. It'll pass by morning.

BIFF. Shouldn't we do anything?

LINDA. Oh, my dear, you should do a lot of things, but there's nothing to do, so go to sleep.

(HAPPY *comes down the stairs and sits on the steps.*)

HAPPY. I never heard him so loud, Mom.

LINDA. Well, come around more often; you'll hear him. (*She sits down at the table and mends the lining of* WILLY's *jacket.*)

BIFF. Why didn't you ever write me about this, Mom?

LINDA. How would I write to you? For over three months you had no address.

BIFF. I was on the move. But you know I thought of you all the time. You know that, don't you, pal?

LINDA. I know, dear, I know. But he likes to have a letter. Just to know that there's still a possibility for better things.

BIFF. He's not like this all the time, is he?

LINDA. It's when you come home he's always the worst.

BIFF. When I come home?

LINDA. When you write you're coming, he's all smiles, and talks about the future, and—he's just wonderful. And then the closer you seem to come, the more shaky he gets, and then, by the time you get here, he's arguing, and he seems angry at you. I think it's just that maybe he can't bring himself to—to open up to you. Why are you so hateful to each other? Why is that?

BIFF (*evasively*). I'm not hateful, Mom.

LINDA. But you no sooner come in the door than you're fighting!

BIFF. I don't know why. I mean to change. I'm tryin', Mom, you understand?

LINDA. Are you home to stay now?

BIFF. I don't know. I want to look around, see what's doin'.

LINDA. Biff, you can't look around all your life, can you?

BIFF. I just can't take hold, Mom. I can't take hold of some kind of a life.

LINDA. Biff, a man is not a bird, to come and go with the springtime.

BIFF. Your hair . . . (*He touches her hair.*) Your hair got so gray.

LINDA. Oh, it's been gray since you were in high school. I just stopped dyeing it, that's all.

BIFF. Dye it again, will ya? I don't want my pal looking old. (*He smiles.*)

LINDA. You're such a boy! You think you can go away for a year and . . . You've got to get it into your head now that one day you'll knock on this door and there'll be strange people here—

BIFF. What are you talking about? You're not even sixty, Mom.

LINDA. But what about your father?

BIFF (*lamely*). Well, I meant him too.

HAPPY. He admires Pop.

LINDA. Biff, dear, if you don't have any feeling for him, then you can't have any feeling for me.

BIFF. Sure I can, Mom.

LINDA. No. You can't just come to see me, because I love him. (*With a threat, but only a threat, of tears*) He's the dearest man in the world to me, and I won't have anyone making him feel unwanted and low and blue. You've got to make up your mind now, darling, there's no leeway any more. Either he's your father and you pay him that respect, or else you're not to come here. I know he's not easy to get along with—nobody knows that better than me—but . . .

WILLY (*from the left, with a laugh*). Hey, hey, Biffo!

BIFF (*starting to go out after* WILLY). What the hell is the matter with him?

(HAPPY *stops him.*)

LINDA. Don't—don't go near him!

BIFF. Stop making excuses for him! He always, always wiped the floor with you. Never had an ounce of respect for you.

HAPPY. He's always had respect for—

BIFF. What the hell do you know about it?

HAPPY (*surlily*). Just don't call him crazy!

BIFF. He's got no character—Charley wouldn't do this. Not in his own house—spewing out that vomit from his mind.

HAPPY. Charley never had to cope with what he's got to.

BIFF. People are worse off than Willy Loman. Believe me, I've seen them.

LINDA. Then make Charley your father, Biff. You can't do that, can you? I don't say he's a great man. Willy Loman never made a lot of money. His name was never in the paper. He's not the finest character that ever lived. But he's a human being, and a terrible thing is happening to him. So attention must be paid. He's not to be allowed to fall into his grave like an old dog. Attention, attention must be finally paid to such a person. You called him crazy—

BIFF. I didn't mean—

LINDA. No, a lot of people think he's lost his—balance. But you don't have to be very smart to know what his trouble is. The man is exhausted.

HAPPY. Sure!

LINDA. A small man can be just as exhausted as a great man. He works for a company thirty-six years this March, opens up unheard of territories to their trademark, and now in his old age they take his salary away.

HAPPY (*indignantly*). I didn't know that, Mom.

LINDA. You never asked, my dear! Now that you get your spending money someplace else you don't trouble your mind with him.

HAPPY. But I gave you money last—

LINDA. Christmas time, fifty dollars! To fix the hot water it cost ninety-seven fifty! For five weeks he's been on straight commission, like a beginner, an unknown!

BIFF. Those ungrateful bastards!

LINDA. Are they any worse than his sons? When he brought them business, when he was young, they were glad to see him. But now his old friends, the old buyers that loved him so and always found some order to hand him in a pinch—they're all dead, retired. He used to be able to make six, seven calls a day in Boston. Now he takes his valises out of the car and puts them back and takes them out again and he's exhausted. Instead of walking he talks now. He drives seven hundred miles, and when he gets there no one knows him any more, no one welcomes him. And what goes through a man's mind, driving seven hundred miles home without having earned a cent? Why shouldn't he talk to himself? Why? When he has to go to Charley and borrow fifty dollars a week and pretend to me that it's his pay? How long can that go on? How long? You see what I'm sitting here and waiting for? And you tell me he has no character? The man who never worked a day but for your benefit? When does he get the medal for that? Is this his reward—to turn around at the age of sixty-three and find his sons, who he loved better than his life, one aphilandering bum—

HAPPY. Mom!

LINDA. That's all you are, my baby! (*To* BIFF) And you! What happened to the love you had for him? You were such pals! How you used to talk to him on the phone every night! How lonely he was till he could come home to you!

BIFF. All right, Mom. I'll live here in my room, and I'll get a job. I'll keep away from him, that's all.

LINDA. No, Biff. You can't stay here and fight all the time.

BIFF. He threw me out of this house, remember that.

LINDA. Why did he do that? I never knew why.

BIFF. Because I know he's a fake and he doesn't like anybody around who knows!

LINDA. Why a fake? In what way? What do you mean?

BIFF. Just don't lay it all at my feet. It's between me and him—that's all I have to say. I'll chip in from now on. He'll settle for half my pay check. He'll be all right. I'm going to bed. (*He starts for the stairs.*)

LINDA. He won't be all right.

BIFF (*turning on the stairs, furiously*). I hate this city and I'll stay here. Now what do you want?

LINDA. He's dying, Biff.

(HAPPY *turns quickly to her, shocked.*)

BIFF (*after a pause*). Why is he dying?

LINDA. He's been trying to kill himself.

BIFF (*with great horror*). How?

LINDA. I live from day to day.

BIFF. What're you talking about?

LINDA. Remember I wrote you that he smashed up the car again? In February?

BIFF. Well?

LINDA. The insurance inspector came. He said that they have evidence. That all these accidents in the last year—weren't—weren't—accidents.

HAPPY. How can they tell that? That's a lie.

{ LINDA. It seems there's a woman . . . (*She takes a breath as*)

{ BIFF (*sharply but contained*). What woman?

LINDA (*simultaneously*). . . . and this woman . . .

LINDA. What?

BIFF. Nothing. Go ahead.

LINDA. What did you say?

BIFF. Nothing. I just said what woman?

HAPPY. What about her?

LINDA. Well, it seems she was walking down the road and saw his car. She says that he wasn't driving fast at all, and that he didn't skid. She says he came to that little bridge, and then deliberately smashed into the railing, and it was only the shallowness of the water that saved him.

BIFF. Oh, no, he probably just fell asleep again.

LINDA. I don't think he fell asleep.

BIFF. Why not?

LINDA. Last month . . . (*With great difficulty*) Oh, boys, it's so hard to say a thing like this! He's just a big stupid man to you, but I tell you there's more good in him than in many other people. (*She chokes, wipes her eyes.*) I was looking for a fuse. The lights blew out, and I went down the cellar. And behind the fuse box—it happened to fall out—was a length of rubber pipe—just short.

HAPPY. No kidding?

LINDA. There's a little attachment on the end of it. I knew right away. And sure enough, on the bottom of the water heater there's a new little nipple on the gas pipe.

HAPPY (*angrily*). That—jerk.

BIFF. Did you have it taken off?

LINDA. I'm—I'm ashamed to. How can I mention it to him? Every day I go down and take away that little rubber pipe. But, when he comes home, I put it back where it was. How can I insult him that way? I don't know what to do. I live from day to day, boys. I tell you, I know every thought in his mind. It sounds so old-fashioned and silly, but I tell you he put his whole life into you and you've turned your backs on him. (*She is bent over in the chair, weeping, her face in her hands.*) Biff, I swear to God! Biff, his life is in your hands!

HAPPY (*to* BIFF). How do you like that damned fool!

BIFF (*kissing her*). All right, pal, all right. It's all settled now. I've been remiss. I know that, Mom. But now I'll stay, and I swear to you, I'll apply myself. (*Kneeling in front of her, in a fever of self-reproach*) It's just—you see, Mom, I don't fit in business. Not that I won't try. I'll try, and I'll make good.

HAPPY. Sure you will. The trouble with you in business was you never tried to please people.

BIFF. I know, I—

HAPPY. Like when you worked for Harrison's. Bob Harrison said you were tops, and then you go and do some damn fool thing like whistling whole songs in the elevator like a comedian.

BIFF (*against* HAPPY). So what? I like to whistle sometimes.

HAPPY. You don't raise a guy to a responsible job who whistles in the elevator!

LINDA. Well, don't argue about it now.

HAPPY. Like when you'd go off and swim in the middle of the day instead of taking the line around.

BIFF (*his resentment rising*). Well, don't you run off? You take off sometimes, don't you? On a nice summer day?

HAPPY. Yeah, but I cover myself!

LINDA. Boys!

HAPPY. If I'm going to take a fade the boss can call any number where I'm supposed to be and they'll swear to him that I just left. I'll tell you something that I hate to say, Biff, but in the business world some of them think you're crazy.

BIFF (*angered*). Screw the business world!

HAPPY. All right, screw it! Great, but cover yourself!

LINDA. Hap, Hap!

BIFF. I don't care what they think! They've laughed at Dad for years, and you know why? Because we don't belong in this nuthouse of a city! We should be mixing cement on some open plain, or—or carpenters. A carpenter is allowed to whistle!

(WILLY *walks in from the entrance of the house, at left.*)

WILLY. Even your grandfather was better than a carpenter. (*Pause. They watch him.*) You never grew up. Bernard does not whistle in the elevator, I assure you.

BIFF (*as though to laugh WILLY out of it*). Yeah, but you do, Pop.

WILLY. I never in my life whistled in an elevator! And who in the business world thinks I'm crazy?

BIFF. I didn't mean it like that, Pop. Now don't make a whole thing out of it, will ya?

WILLY. Go back to the West! Be a carpenter, a cowboy, enjoy yourself!

LINDA. Willy, he was just saying—

WILLY. I heard what he said!

HAPPY (*trying to quiet WILLY*). Hey, Pop, come on now . . .

WILLY (*continuing over HAPPY's line*). They laugh at me, heh? Go to Filene's, go to the Hub, go to Slattery's, Boston. Call out the name Willy Loman and see what happens! Big shot!

BIFF. All right, Pop.

WILLY. Big!

BIFF. All right!

WILLY. Why do you always insult me?

BIFF. I didn't say a word. (*To* LINDA) Did I say a word?

LINDA. He didn't say anything, Willy.

WILLY (*going to the doorway of the living-room*).   All right, good night, good night.

LINDA.   Willy, dear, he just decided . . .

WILLY (*to* BIFF).   If you get tired hanging around tomorrow, paint the ceiling I put up in the living-room.

BIFF.   I'm leaving early tomorrow.

HAPPY.   He's going to see Bill Oliver, Pop.

WILLY (*interestedly*).   Oliver? For what?

BIFF (*with reserve, but trying, trying*).   He always said he'd stake me. I'd like to go into business, so maybe I can take him up on it.

LINDA.   Isn't that wonderful?

WILLY.   Don't interrupt. What's wonderful about it? There's fifty men in the City of New York who'd stake him. (*To* BIFF) Sporting goods?

BIFF.   I guess so. I know something about it and—

WILLY.   He knows something about it! You know sporting goods better than Spalding, for God's sake! How much is he giving you?

BIFF.   I don't know, I didn't even see him yet, but—

WILLY.   Then what're you talkin' about?

BIFF (*getting angry*).   Well, all I said was I'm gonna see him, that's all!

WILLY (*turning away*).   Ah, you're counting your chickens again.

BIFF (*starting left for the stairs*).   Oh, Jesus, I'm going to sleep!

WILLY (*calling after him*).   Don't curse in this house!

BIFF (*turning*).   Since when did you get so clean?

HAPPY (*trying to stop them*).   Wait a . . .

WILLY.   Don't use that language to me! I won't have it!

HAPPY (*grabbing* BIFF, *shouts*).   Wait a minute! I got an idea. I got a feasible idea. Come here, Biff, let's talk this over now, let's talk some sense here. When I was down in Florida last time, I thought of a great idea to sell sporting goods. It just came back to me. You and I, Biff—we have a line, the Loman Line. We train a couple of weeks, and put on a couple of exhibitions, see?

WILLY.   That's an idea!

HAPPY.   Wait! We form two basketball teams, see? Two water-polo teams. We play each other. It's a million dollars' worth of publicity. Two brothers, see? The Loman Brothers. Displays in the Royal Palms—all the hotels. And banners over the ring and the basketball court: "Loman Brothers." Baby, we could sell sporting goods!

WILLY.   That is a one-million-dollar idea!

LINDA.   Marvelous!

BIFF.   I'm in great shape as far as that's concerned.

HAPPY.   And the beauty of it is, Biff, it wouldn't be like a business. We'd be out playin' ball again . . .

BIFF (*enthused*).   Yeah, that's . . .

WILLY.   Million-dollar . . .

HAPPY. And you wouldn't get fed up with it, Biff. It'd be the family again. There'd be the old honor, and comradeship, and if you wanted to go off for a swim or somethin'—well, you'd do it! Without some smart cooky gettin' up ahead of you!

WILLY. Lick the world! You guys together could absolutely lick the civilized world.

BIFF. I'll see Oliver tomorrow. Hap, if we could work that out . . .

LINDA. Maybe things are beginning to—

WILLY (*wildly enthused, to* LINDA). Stop interrupting! (*To* BIFF) But don't wear sport jacket and slacks when you see Oliver.

BIFF. No, I'll—

WILLY. A business suit, and talk as little as possible, and don't crack any jokes.

BIFF. He did like me. Always liked me.

LINDA. He loved you!

WILLY (*to* LINDA). Will you stop! (*To* BIFF) Walk in very serious. You are not applying for a boy's job. Money is to pass. Be quiet, fine, and serious. Everybody likes a kidder, but nobody lends him money.

HAPPY. I'll try to get some myself, Biff. I'm sure I can.

WILLY. I see great things for you kids, I think your troubles are over. But remember, start big and you'll end big. Ask for fifteen. How much you gonna ask for?

BIFF. Gee, I don't know—

WILLY. And don't say "Gee." "Gee" is a boy's word. A man walking in for fifteen thousand dollars does not say "Gee!"

BIFF. Ten, I think, would be top though.

WILLY. Don't be so modest. You always started too low. Walk in with a big laugh. Don't look worried. Start off with a couple of your good stories to lighten things up. It's not what you say, it's how you say it— because personality always wins the day.

LINDA. Oliver always thought the highest of him—

WILLY. Will you let me talk?

BIFF. Don't yell at her, Pop, will ya?

WILLY (*angrily*). I was talking, wasn't I?

BIFF. I don't like you yelling at her all the time, and I'm tellin' you, that's all.

WILLY. What're you, takin' over this house?

LINDA. Willy—

WILLY (*turning on her*). Don't take his side all the time, goddammit!

BIFF (*furiously*). Stop yelling at her!

WILLY (*suddenly pulling on his cheek, beaten down, guilt ridden*). Give my best to Bill Oliver—he may remember me. (*He exits through the living-room doorway.*)

LINDA (*her voice subdued*). What'd you have to start that for? (BIFF *turns away.*) You see how sweet he was as soon as you talked hopefully? (*She goes over to* BIFF.) Come up and say good night to him. Don't let him go to bed that way.

HAPPY. Come on, Biff, let's buck him up.

LINDA. Please, dear. Just say good night. It takes so little to make him happy. Come. (*She goes through the living-room doorway, calling upstairs from within the living-room.*) Your pajamas are hanging in the bathroom, Willy!

HAPPY (*looking toward where* LINDA *went out*). What a woman! They broke the mold when they made her. You know that, Biff?

BIFF. He's off salary. My God, working on commission!

HAPPY. Well, let's face it: he's no hot-shot selling man. Except that sometimes, you have to admit, he's a sweet personality.

BIFF (*deciding*). Lend me ten bucks, will ya? I want to buy some new ties.

HAPPY. I'll take you to a place I know. Beautiful stuff. Wear one of my striped shirts tomorrow.

BIFF. She got gray. Mom got awful old. Gee, I'm gonna go in to Oliver tomorrow and knock him for a—

HAPPY. Come on up. Tell that to Dad. Let's give him a whirl. Come on.

BIFF (*steamed up*). You know, with ten thousand bucks, boy!

HAPPY (*as they go into the living room*). That's the talk, Biff, that's the first time I've heard the old confidence out of you! (*From within the living-room, fading off*) You're gonna live with me, kid, and any babe you want just say the word . . . (*The last lines are hardly heard. They are mounting the stairs to their parents' bedroom.*)

LINDA (*entering her bedroom and addressing* WILLY, *who is in the bathroom. She is straightening the bed for him*). Can you do anything about the shower? It drips.

WILLY (*from the bathroom*). All of a sudden everything falls to pieces! Goddam plumbing, oughta be sued, those people. I hardly finished putting it in and the thing . . . (*His words rumble off.*)

LINDA. I'm just wondering if Oliver will remember him. You think he might?

WILLY (*coming out of the bathroom in his pajamas*). Remember him? What's the matter with you, you crazy? If he'd've stayed with Oliver he'd be on top by now! Wait'll Oliver gets a look at him. You don't know the average caliber any more. The average young man today—(*he is getting into bed*)—is got a caliber of zero. Greatest thing in the world for him was to bum around.

(BIFF *and* HAPPY *enter the bedroom. Slight pause.*)

WILLY (*stops short, looking at* BIFF). Glad to hear it, boy.

HAPPY. He wanted to say good night to you, sport.

WILLY (*to* BIFF). Yeah. Knock him dead, boy. What'd you want to tell me?

BIFF. Just take it easy, Pop. Good night. (*He turns to go.*)

WILLY (*unable to resist*). And if anything falls off the desk while you're talking to him—like a package or something—don't you pick it up. They have office boys for that.

LINDA. I'll make a big breakfast—

WILLY. Will you let me finish? (*To* BIFF) Tell him you were in the business in the West. Not farm work.

BIFF. All right, Dad.

LINDA. I think everything—

WILLY (*going right through her speech*). And don't undersell yourself. No less than fifteen thousand dollars.

BIFF (*unable to bear him*). Okay. Good night, Mom. (*He starts moving.*)

WILLY. Because you got a greatness in you, Biff, remember that. You got all kinds of greatness . . .

(*He lies back, exhausted.* BIFF *walks out.*)

LINDA (*calling after* BIFF). Sleep well, darling!

HAPPY. I'm gonna get married, Mom. I wanted to tell you.

LINDA. Go to sleep, dear.

HAPPY (*going*). I just wanted to tell you.

WILLY. Keep up the good work. (HAPPY *exits.*) God . . . remember that Ebbets Field game? The championship of the city?

LINDA. Just rest. Should I sing to you?

WILLY. Yeah. Sing to me. (LINDA *hums a soft lullaby.*) When that team came out—he was the tallest, remember?

LINDA. Oh, yes. And in gold.

(BIFF *enters the darkened kitchen, takes a cigarette, and leaves the house. He comes downstage into a golden pool of light. He smokes, staring at the night.*)

WILLY. Like a young god. Hercules—something like that. And the sun, the sun all around him. Remember how he waved to me? Right up from the field, with the representatives of three colleges standing by? And the buyers I brought, and the cheers when he came out—Loman, Loman, Loman! God Almighty, he'll be great yet. A star like that, magnificent, can never really fade away!

(*The light on* WILLY *is fading. The gas heater begins to glow through the kitchen wall, near the stairs, a blue flame beneath red coils.*)

LINDA (*timidly*). Willy dear, what has he got against you?

WILLY. I'm so tired. Don't talk any more.

(BIFF *slowly returns to the kitchen. He stops, stares toward the heater.*)

LINDA. Will you ask Howard to let you work in New York?

WILLY. First thing in the morning. Everything'll be all right.

(BIFF *reaches behind the heater and draws out a length of rubber tubing. He is horrified and turns his head toward* WILLY'*s room, still dimly lit, from which the strains of* LINDA'*s desperate but monotonous humming rise.*)

WILLY (*staring through the window into the moonlight*).   Gee, look at the moon moving between the buildings!

(BIFF *wraps the tubing around his hand and quickly goes up the stairs.*)

ACT II

Music is heard, gay and bright. The curtain rises as the music fades away. WILLY, *in shirt sleeves, is sitting at the kitchen table, sipping coffee, his hat in his lap.* LINDA *is filling his cup when she can.*

WILLY. Wonderful coffee. Meal in itself.

LINDA. Can I make you some eggs?

WILLY. No. Take a breath.

LINDA. You look so rested, dear.

WILLY. I slept like a dead one. First time in months. Imagine, sleeping till ten on a Tuesday morning. Boys left nice and early, heh?

LINDA. They were out of here by eight o'clock.

WILLY. Good work!

LINDA. It was so thrilling to see them leaving together. I can't get over the shaving lotion in this house!

WILLY (*smiling*).   Mmm—

LINDA. Biff was very changed this morning. His whole attitude seemed to be hopeful. He couldn't wait to get downtown to see Oliver.

WILLY. He's heading for a change. There's no question, there simply are certain men that take longer to get—solidified. How did he dress?

LINDA. His blue suit. He's so handsome in that suit. He could be a—anything in that suit!

(WILLY *gets up from the table.* LINDA *holds his jacket for him.*)

WILLY. There's no question, no question at all. Gee, on the way home tonight I'd like to buy some seeds.

LINDA (*laughing*).   That'd be wonderful. But not enough sun gets back there. Nothing'll grow any more.

WILLY. You wait, kid, before it's all over we're gonna get a little place out in the country, and I'll raise some vegetables, a couple of chickens . . .

LINDA. You'll do it yet, dear.

(WILLY *walks out of his jacket.* LINDA *follows him.*)

WILLY.   And they'll get married, and come for a weekend. I'd build a little guest house. 'Cause I got so many fine tools, all I'd need would be a little lumber and some peace of mind.

LINDA (*joyfully*).   I sewed the lining . . .

WILLY.   I would build two guest houses, so they'd both come. Did he decide how much he's going to ask Oliver for?

LINDA (*getting him into the jacket*).   He didn't mention it, but I imagine ten or fifteen thousand. You going to talk to Howard today?

WILLY.   Yeah. I'll put it to him straight and simple. He'll just have to take me off the road.

LINDA.   And, Willy, don't forget to ask for a little advance, because we've got the insurance premium. It's the grace period now.

WILLY.   That's a hundred . . .?

LINDA.   A hundred and eight, sixty-eight. Because we're a little short again.

WILLY.   Why are we short?

LINDA.   Well, you had the motor job on the car . . .

WILLY.   That goddam Studebaker!

LINDA.   And you got one more payment on the refrigerator . . .

WILLY.   But it just broke again!

LINDA.   Well, it's old, dear.

WILLY.   I told you we should've bought a well-advertised machine. Charley bought a General Electric and it's twenty years old and it's still good, that son-of-a-bitch.

LINDA.   But, Willy—

WILLY.   Whoever heard of a Hastings refrigerator? Once in my life I would like to own something outright before it's broken! I'm always in a race with the junkyard! I just finished paying for the car and it's on its last legs. The refrigerator consumes belts like a goddam maniac. They time those things. They time them so when you finally paid for them, they're used up.

LINDA (*buttoning up his jacket as he unbuttons it*).   All told, about two hundred dollars would carry us, dear. But that includes the last payment on the mortgage. After this payment, Willy, the house belongs to us.

WILLY.   It's twenty-five years!

LINDA.   Biff was nine years old when we bought it.

WILLY.   Well, that's a great thing. To weather a twenty-five year mortgage is—

LINDA.   It's an accomplishment.

WILLY.   All the cement, the lumber, the reconstruction I put in this house! There ain't a crack to be found in it any more.

LINDA.   Well, it served its purpose.

WILLY. What purpose? Some stranger'll come along, move in, and that's that. If only Biff would take this house, and raise a family . . . (*He starts to go.*) Good-by, I'm late.

LINDA (*suddenly remembering*). Oh, I forgot! You're supposed to meet them for dinner.

WILLY. Me?

LINDA. At Frank's Chop House on Forty-eighth near Sixth Avenue.

WILLY. Is that so! How about you?

LINDA. No, just the three of you. They're gonna blow you to a big meal!

WILLY. Don't say! Who thought of that?

LINDA. Biff came to me this morning, Willy, and he said, "Tell Dad, we want to blow him to a big meal." Be there six o'clock. You and your two boys are going to have dinner.

WILLY. Gee whiz! That's really somethin'. I'm gonna knock Howard for a loop, kid. I'll get an advance, and I'll come home with a New York job. Goddammit, now I'm gonna do it!

LINDA. Oh, that's the spirit, Willy!

WILLY. I will never get behind a wheel the rest of my life!

LINDA. It's changing, Willy, I can feel it changing!

WILLY. Beyond a question. G'by, I'm late. (*He starts to go again.*)

LINDA (*calling after him as she runs to the kitchen table for a handkerchief*). You got your glasses?

WILLY (*feels for them, then comes back in*). Yeah, yeah, got my glasses.

LINDA (*giving him the handkerchief*). And a handkerchief.

WILLY. Yeah, handkerchief.

LINDA. And your saccharine?

WILLY. Yeah, my saccharine.

LINDA. Be careful on the subway stairs.

(*She kisses him, and a silk stocking is seen hanging from her hand.* WILLY *notices it.*)

WILLY. Will you stop mending stockings? At least while I'm in the house. It gets me nervous. I can't tell you. Please.

(LINDA *hides the stocking in her hand as she follows* WILLY *across the forestage in front of the house.*)

LINDA. Remember, Frank's Chop House.

WILLY (*passing the apron*). Maybe beets would grow out there.

LINDA (*laughing*). But you tried so many times.

WILLY. Yeah. Well, don't work hard today. (*He disappears around the right corner of the house.*)

LINDA. Be careful!

(*As* Willy *vanishes,* Linda *waves to him. Suddenly the phone rings. She runs across the stage and into the kitchen and lifts it.*)

Linda.   Hello? Oh, Biff! I'm so glad you called, I just . . . Yes, sure, I just told him. Yes, he'll be there for dinner at six o'clock, I didn't forget. Listen, I was just dying to tell you. You know that little rubber pipe I told you about? That he connected to the gas heater? I finally decided to go down the cellar this morning and take it away and destroy it. But it's gone! Imagine? He took it away himself, it isn't there! (*She listens.*) When? Oh, then you took it. Oh—nothing, it's just that I'd hoped he'd taken it away himself. Oh, I'm not worried, darling, because this morning he left in such high spirits, it was like the old days! I'm not afraid any more. Did Mr. Oliver see you? . . . Well, you wait there then. And make a nice impression on him, darling. Just don't perspire too much before you see him. And have a nice time with Dad. He may have big news too! . . . That's right, a New York job. And be sweet to him tonight, dear. Be loving to him. Because he's only a little boat looking for a harbor. (*She is trembling with sorrow and joy.*) Oh, that's wonderful, Biff, you'll save his life. Thanks, darling. Just put your arm around him when he comes into the restaurant. Give him a smile. That's the boy . . . Good-by, dear . . . You got your comb? . . . That's fine. Good-by, Biff dear.

(*In the middle of her speech,* Howard Wagner, *thirty-six, wheels on a small typewriter table on which is a wire-recording machine and proceeds to plug it in. This is on the left forestage. Light slowly fades on* Linda *as it rises on* Howard. Howard *is intent on threading the machine and only glances over his shoulder as* Willy *appears.*)

Willy.   Pst! Pst!
Howard.   Hello, Willy, come in.
Willy.   Like to have a little talk with you, Howard.
Howard.   Sorry to keep you waiting. I'll be with you in a minute.
Willy.   What's that, Howard?
Howard.   Didn't you ever see one of these? Wire recorder.
Willy.   Oh. Can we talk a minute?
Howard.   Records things. Just got delivery yesterday. Been driving me crazy, the most terrific machine I ever saw in my life. I was up all night with it.
Willy.   What do you do with it?
Howard.   I bought it for dictation, but you can do anything with it. Listen to this. I had it home last night. Listen to what I picked up. The first one is my daughter. Get this. (*He flicks the switch and "Roll Out the Barrel" is heard being whistled.*) Listen to that kid whistle.
Willy.   That is lifelike, isn't it?
Howard.   Seven years old. Get that tone.

WILLY. Ts, ts. Like to ask a little favor if you . . .

(*The whistling breaks off, and the voice of* HOWARD'S *daughter is heard.*)

HIS DAUGHTER. "Now you, Daddy."

HOWARD. She's crazy for me! (*Again the same song is whistled.*) That's me! Ha! (*He winks.*)

WILLY. You're very good!

(*The whistling breaks off again. The machine runs silent for a moment.*)

HOWARD. Sh! Get this now, this is my son.

HIS SON. "The capital of Alabama is Montgomery; the capital of Arizona is Phoenix; the capital of Arkansas is Little Rock; the capital of California is Sacramento . . ." (*and on, and on*).

HOWARD (*holding up five fingers.*) Five years old, Willy!

WILLY. He'll make an announcer some day!

HIS SON (*continuing*). "The capital . . ."

HOWARD. Get that—alphabetical order! (*The machine breaks off suddenly.*) Wait a minute. The maid kicked the plug out.

WILLY. It certainly is a—

HOWARD. Sh, for God's sake!

HIS SON. "It's nine o'clock, Bulova watch time. So I have to go to sleep."

WILLY. That really is—

HOWARD. Wait a minute! The next is my wife.

(*They wait.*)

HOWARD'S VOICE. "Go on, say something." (*Pause*) "Well, you gonna talk?"

HIS WIFE. "I can't think of anything."

HOWARD'S VOICE. "Well, talk—it's turning."

HIS WIFE (*shyly, beaten*). "Hello." (*Silence*) "Oh, Howard, I can't talk into this . . ."

HOWARD (*snapping the machine off*). That was my wife.

WILLY. That is a wonderful machine. Can we—

HOWARD. I tell you, Willy, I'm gonna take my camera, and my bandsaw, and all my hobbies, and out they go. This is the most fascinating relaxation I ever found.

WILLY. I think I'll get one myself.

HOWARD. Sure, they're only a hundred and a half. You can't do without it. Supposing you wanna hear Jack Benny, see? But you can't be at home at that hour. So you tell the maid to turn the radio on when Jack Benny comes on, and this automatically goes on with the radio . . .

WILLY. And when you come home you . . .

HOWARD. You can come home twelve o'clock, one o'clock, any time you like, and you get yourself a Coke and sit yourself down, throw the switch, and there's Jack Benny's program in the middle of the night!

WILLY. I'm definitely going to get one. Because lots of time I'm on the road, and I think to myself, what I must be missing on the radio!

HOWARD. Don't you have a radio in the car?

WILLY. Well, yeah, but who ever thinks of turning it on?

HOWARD. Say, aren't you supposed to be in Boston?

WILLY. That's what I want to talk to you about, Howard. You got a minute? (*He draws a chair in from the wing.*)

HOWARD. What happened? What're you doing here?

WILLY. Well . . .

HOWARD. You didn't crack up again, did you?

WILLY. Oh, no. No . . .

HOWARD. Geez, you had me worried there for a minute. What's the trouble?

WILLY. Well, tell you the truth, Howard. I've come to the decision that I'd rather not travel any more.

HOWARD. Not travel! Well, what'll you do?

WILLY. Remember, Christmas time, when you had the party here? You said you'd try to think of some spot for me here in town.

HOWARD. With us?

WILLY. Well, sure.

HOWARD. Oh, yeah, yeah. I remember. Well, I couldn't think of anything for you, Willy.

WILLY. I tell ya, Howard. The kids are all grown up, y'know. I don't need much any more. If I could take home—well, sixty-five dollars a week, I could swing it.

HOWARD. Yeah, but Willy, see I—

WILLY. I tell ya why, Howard. Speaking frankly and between the two of us, y'know—I'm just a little tired.

HOWARD. Oh, I could understand that, Willy. But you're a road man, Willy, and we do a road business. We've only got a half-dozen salesmen on the floor here.

WILLY. God knows, Howard, I never asked a favor of any man. But I was with the firm when your father used to carry you in here in his arms.

HOWARD. I know that, Willy, but—

WILLY. Your father came to me the day you were born and asked me what I thought of the name of Howard, may he rest in peace.

HOWARD. I appreciate that, Willy, but there just is no spot here for you. If I had a spot I'd slam you right in, but I just don't have a single solitary spot.

(*He looks for his lighter.* WILLY *has picked it up and gives it to him. Pause.*)

WILLY (*with increasing anger*). Howard, all I need to set my table is fifty dollars a week.

HOWARD. But where am I going to put you, kid?

WILLY. Look, it isn't a question of whether I can sell merchandise, is it?

HOWARD. No, but it's a business, kid, and everybody, gotta pull his own weight.

WILLY (*desperately*). Just let me tell you a story, Howard—

HOWARD. 'Cause you gotta admit, business is business.

WILLY (*angrily*). Business is definitely business, but just listen for a minute. You don't understand this. When I was a boy—eighteen, nineteen— I was already on the road. And there was a question in my mind as to whether selling had a future for me. Because in those days I had a yearning to go to Alaska. See, there were three gold strikes in one month in Alaska, and I felt like going out. Just for the ride, you might say.

HOWARD (*barely interested*). Don't say.

WILLY. Oh, yeah, my father lived many years in Alaska. He was an adventurous man. We've got quite a little streak of self-reliance in our family. I thought I'd go out with my older brother and try to locate him, and maybe settle in the North with the old man. And I was almost decided to go, when I met a salesman in the Parker House. His name was Dave Singleman. And he was eighty-four years old, and he'd drummed merchandise in thirty-one states. And old Dave, he'd go up to his room, y'understand, put on his green velvet slippers—I'll never forget—and pick up his phone and call the buyers, and without ever leaving his room, at the age of eighty-four, he made his living. And when I saw that, I realized that selling was the greatest career a man could want. 'Cause what could be more satisfying than to be able to go, at the age of eighty-four, into twenty or thirty different cities, and pick up a phone, and be remembered and loved and helped by so many different people? Do you know? when he died—and by the way he died the death of a salesman, in his green velvet slippers in the smoker of the New York, New Haven and Hartford, going into Boston—when he died, hundreds of salesmen and buyers were at his funeral. Things were sad on a lotta trains for months after that. (*He stands up.* HOWARD *has not looked at him.*) In those days there was personality in it, Howard. There was respect, and comradeship, and gratitude in it. Today, it's all cut and dried, and there's no chance for bringing friendship to bear—or personality. You see what I mean? They don't know me any more.

HOWARD (*moving away, to the right*). That's just the thing, Willy.

WILLY. If I had forty dollars a week—that's all I'd need. Forty dollars, Howard.

HOWARD. Kid, I can't take blood from a stone, I—

WILLY (*desperation is on him now*). Howard, the year Al Smith was nominated, your father came to me and—

HOWARD (*starting to go off*).   I've got to see some people, kid.

WILLY (*stopping him*).   I'm talking about your father! There were promises made across this desk! You mustn't tell me you've got people to see —I put thirty-four years into this firm, Howard, and now I can't pay my insurance! You can't eat the orange and throw the peel away—a man is not a piece of fruit! (*After a pause*) Now pay attention. Your father—in 1928 I had a big year. I averaged a hundred and seventy dollars a week in commissions.

HOWARD (*impatiently*).   Now, Willy, you never averaged—

WILLY (*banging his hand on the desk*).   I averaged a hundred and seventy dollars a week in the year of 1928! And your father came to me— or rather, I was in the office here—it was right over this desk—and he put his hand on my shoulder—

HOWARD (*getting up*).   You'll have to excuse me, Willy, I gotta see some people. Pull yourself together. (*Going out*) I'll be back in a little while.

(*On* HOWARD's *exit, the light on his chair grows very bright and strange.*)

WILLY.   Pull myself together! What the hell did I say to him? My God, I was yelling at him! How could I! (WILLY *breaks off, staring at the light, which occupies the chair, animating it. He approaches this chair, standing across the desk from it.*) Frank, Frank, don't you remember what you told me that time? How you put your hand on my shoulder, and Frank . . . (*He leans on the desk and as he speaks the dead man's name he accidentally switches on the recorder, and instantly*)

HOWARD's SON.   ". . . of New York is Albany. The capital of Ohio is Cincinnati, the capital of Rhode Island is . . ." (*The recitation continues.*)

WILLY (*leaping away with fright, shouting*).   Ha! Howard! Howard! Howard!

HOWARD (*rushing in*).   What happened?

WILLY (*pointing at the machine, which continues nasally, childishly, with the capital cities*).   Shut it off! Shut it off!

HOWARD (*pulling the plug out*).   Look, Willy . . .

WILLY (*pressing his hands to his eyes*).   I gotta get myself some coffee. I'll get some coffee . . .

(WILLY *starts to walk out.* HOWARD *stops him.*)

HOWARD (*rolling up the cord*).   Willy, look . . .

WILLY.   I'll go to Boston.

HOWARD.   Willy, you can't go to Boston for us.

WILLY.   Why can't I go?

HOWARD.   I don't want you to represent us. I've been meaning to tell you for a long time now.

WILLY.   Howard, are you firing me?

HOWARD.   I think you need a good long rest, Willy.

WILLY. Howard—

HOWARD. And when you feel better, come back, and we'll see if we can work something out.

WILLY. But I gotta earn money, Howard. I'm in no position to—

HOWARD. Where are your sons? Why don't your sons give you a hand?

WILLY. They're working on a very big deal.

HOWARD. This is no time for false pride, Willy. You go to your sons and you tell them that you're tired. You've got two great boys, haven't you?

WILLY. Oh, no question, no question, but in the meantime . . .

HOWARD. Then that's that, heh?

WILLY. All right, I'll go to Boston tomorrow.

HOWARD. No, no.

WILLY. I can't throw myself on my sons. I'm not a cripple!

HOWARD. Look, kid, I'm busy this morning.

WILLY (grasping HOWARD's arm). Howard, you've got to let me go to Boston!

HOWARD (hard, keeping himself under control). I've got a line of people to see this morning. Sit down, take five minutes, and pull yourself together, and then go home, will ya? I need the office, Willy. (He starts to go, turns, remembering the recorder, starts to push off the table holding the recorder.) Oh, yeah. Whenever you can this week, stop by and drop off the samples. You'll feel better, Willy, and then come back and we'll talk. Pull yourself together, kid, there's people outside.

(HOWARD exits, pushing the table off left. WILLY stares into space, exhausted. Now the music is heard—BEN's music—first distantly, then closer, closer. As WILLY speaks, BEN enters from the right. He carries valise and umbrella.)

WILLY. Oh, Ben, how did you do it? What is the answer? Did you wind up the Alaska deal already?

BEN. Doesn't take much time if you know what you're doing. Just a short business trip. Boarding ship in an hour. Wanted to say good-by.

WILLY. Ben, I've got to talk to you.

BEN (glancing at his watch). Haven't the time, William.

WILLY (crossing the apron to BEN). Ben, nothing's working out. I don't know what to do.

BEN. Now, look here, William. I've bought timberland in Alaska and I need a man to look after things for me.

WILLY. God, timberland! Me and my boys in those grand outdoors!

BEN. You've a new continent at your doorstep, William. Get out of these cities, they're full of talk and time payments and courts of law. Screw on your fists and you can fight for a fortune up there.

WILLY. Yes, yes! Linda, Linda!

(LINDA enters as of old, with the wash.)

LINDA. Oh, you're back?

BEN. I haven't much time.

WILLY. No, wait! Linda, he's got a proposition for me in Alaska.

LINDA. But you've got—(*To* BEN) He's got a beautiful job here.

WILLY. But in Alaska, kid, I could—

LINDA. You're doing well enough, Willy!

BEN (*to* LINDA). Enough for what, my dear?

LINDA (*frightened of* BEN *and angry at him*). Don't say those things to him! Enough to be happy right here, right now. (*To* WILLY, *while* BEN *laughs*) Why must everybody conquer the world? You're well liked, and the boys love you, and someday—(*to* BEN)—why, old man Wagner told him just the other day that if he keeps it up he'll be a member of the firm, didn't he, Willy?

WILLY. Sure, sure. I am building something with this firm, Ben, and if a man is building something he must be on the right track, mustn't he?

BEN. What are you building? Lay your hand on it. Where is it?

WILLY (*hesitantly*). That's true, Linda, there's nothing.

LINDA. Why? (*To* BEN) There's a man eighty-four years old—

WILLY. That's right, Ben, that's right. When I look at that man I say, what is there to worry about?

BEN. Bah!

WILLY. It's true, Ben. All he has to do is go into any city, pick up the phone, and he's making his living and you know why?

BEN (*picking up his valise*). I've got to go.

WILLY (*holding* BEN *back*). Look at this boy!

(BIFF, *in his high school sweater, enters carrying suitcase.* HAPPY *carries* BIFF's *shoulder guards, gold helmet, and football pants.*)

WILLY. Without a penny to his name, three great universities are begging for him, and from there the sky's the limit, because it's not what you do, Ben. It's who you know and the smile on your face! It's contacts, Ben, contacts! The whole wealth of Alaska passes over the lunch table at the Commodore Hotel, and that's the wonder, the wonder of this country, that a man can end with diamonds here on the basis of being liked! (*He turns to* BIFF) And that's why when you get out on that field today, it's important. Because thousands of people will be rooting for you and loving you. (*To* BEN, *who has again begun to leave*) And Ben! when he walks into a business office his name will sound out like a bell and all the doors will open to him! I've seen it, Ben, I've seen it a thousand times! You can't feel it with your hand like timber, but it's there!

BEN. Good-by, William.

WILLY. Ben, am I right? Don't you think I'm right? I value your advice.

BEN. There's a new continent at your doorstep, William. You could walk out rich. Rich! (*He is gone.*)

WILLY. We'll do it here, Ben! You hear me? We're gonna do it hear!

(YOUNG BERNARD *rushes in. The gay music of the boys is heard.*)

BERNARD. Oh, gee, I was afraid you left already!

WILLY. Why? What time is it?

BERNARD. It's half-past one!

WILLY. Well, come on, everybody! Ebbets Field next stop! Where's the pennants? (*He rushes through the wall-line of the kitchen and out into the living-room.*)

LINDA (*to* BIFF). Did you pack fresh underwear?

BIFF (*who has been limbering up*). I want to go!

BERNARD. Biff, I'm carrying your helmet, ain't I?

HAPPY. No, I'm carrying the helmet.

BERNARD. Oh, Biff, you promised me.

HAPPY. I'm carrying the helmet.

BERNARD. How am I going to get in the locker room?

LINDA. Let him carry the shoulder guards. (*She puts her coat and hat on in the kitchen.*)

BERNARD. Can I, Biff? 'Cause I told everybody I'm going to be in the locker room.

HAPPY. In Ebbets Field it's the clubhouse.

BERNARD. I meant the clubhouse, Biff!

HAPPY. Biff!

BIFF (*grandly, after a slight pause*). Let him carry the shoulder guards.

HAPPY (*as he gives* BERNARD *the shoulder guards*). Stay close to us now.

(WILLY *rushes in with the pennants.*)

WILLY (*handing them out*). Everybody wave when Biff comes out on the field. (HAPPY *and* BERNARD *run off.*) You set now, boy?

(*The music has died away.*)

BIFF. Ready to go, Pop. Every muscle is ready.

WILLY (*at the edge of the apron*). You realize what this means?

BIFF. That's right, Pop.

WILLY (*feeling* BIFF's *muscles*). You're comin' home this afternoon captain of the All-Scholastic Championship Team of the City of New York.

BIFF. I got it, Pop. And remember, pal, when I take off my helmet, that touchdown is for you.

WILLY. Let's go! (*He is starting out, with his arm around* BIFF, *when* CHARLEY *enters, as of old, in knickers.*) I got no room for you, Charley.

CHARLEY. Room? For what?

WILLY. In the car.

CHARLEY. You goin' for a ride? I wanted to shoot some casino.

WILLY (*furiously*).   Casino! (*Incredulously*) Don't you realize what today is?

LINDA.   Oh, he knows, Willy. He's just kidding you.

WILLY.   That's nothing to kid about!

CHARLEY.   No, Linda, what's goin' on?

LINDA.   He's playing in Ebbets Field.

CHARLEY.   Baseball in this weather?

WILLY.   Don't talk to him. Come on, come on! (*He is pushing them out.*)

CHARLEY.   What a minute, didn't you hear the news?

WILLY.   What?

CHARLEY.   Don't you listen to the radio? Ebbets Field just blew up.

WILLY.   You go to hell! (CHARLEY *laughs. Pushing them out*) Come on, come on! We're late.

CHARLEY (*as they go*).   Knock a homer, Biff, knock a homer!

WILLY (*the last to leave, turning to* CHARLEY).   I don't think that was funny, Charley. This is the greatest day of his life.

CHARLEY.   Willy, when are you going to grow up?

WILLY.   Yeah, heh? When this game is over, Charley, you'll be laughing out of the other side of your face. They'll be calling him another Red Grange. Twenty-five thousand a year.

CHARLEY (*kidding*).   Is that so?

WILLY.   Yeah, that's so.

CHARLEY.   Well, then, I'm sorry, Willy. But tell me something.

WILLY.   What?

CHARLEY.   Who is Red Grange?

WILLY.   Put up your hands. Goddam you, put up your hands!

(CHARLEY, *chuckling, shakes his head and walks away, around the left corner of the stage.* WILLY *follows him. The music rises to a mocking frenzy.*)

WILLY.   Who the hell do you think you are, better than everybody else? You don't know everything, you big, ignorant, stupid . . . Put up your hands!

(*Light rises, on the right side of the forestage, on a small table in the reception room of* CHARLEY's *office. Traffic sounds are heard.* BERNARD, *now mature, sits whistling to himself. A pair of tennis rackets and an overnight bag are on the floor beside him.*)

WILLY (*offstage*).   What are you walking away for? Don't walk away! If you're going to say something say it to my face! I know you laugh at me behind my back. You'll laugh out of the other side of your goddam face after this game. Touchdown! Touchdown! Eighty thousand people! Touchdown! Right between the goal posts.

(BERNARD *is a quiet, earnest, but self-assured young man.* WILLY's *voice is coming from right upstage now.* BERNARD *lowers his feet off the table and listens.* JENNY, *his father's secretary, enters.)*

JENNY (*distressed*). Say, Bernard, will you go out in the hall?

BERNARD. What is that noise? Who is it?

JENNY. Mr. Loman. He just got off the elevator.

BERNARD (*getting up*). Who's he arguing with?

JENNY. Nobody. There's nobody with him. I can't deal with him any more, and your father gets all upset everytime he comes. I've got a lot of typing to do, and your father's waiting to sign it. Will you see him?

WILLY (*entering*). Touchdown! Touch—(*He sees* JENNY.) Jenny, Jenny, good to see you. How're ya? Workin'? Or still honest?

JENNY. Fine. How've you been feeling?

WILLY. Not much any more, Jenny. Ha, Ha! (*He is surprised to see the rackets.*)

BERNARD. Hello, Uncle Willy.

WILLY (*almost shocked*). Bernard! Well, look who's here! (*He comes quickly, guiltily, to* BERNARD *and warmly shakes his hand.*)

BERNARD. How are you? Good to see you.

WILLY. What are you doing here?

BERNARD. Oh, just stopped by to see Pop. Get off my feet till my train leaves. I'm going to Washington in a few minutes.

WILLY. Is he in?

BERNARD. Yes, he's in his office with the accountant. Sit down.

WILLY (*sitting down*). What're you going to do in Washington?

BERNARD. Oh, just a case I've got there, Willy.

WILLY. That so? (*Indicating the rackets*) You going to play tennis there?

BERNARD. I'm staying with a friend who's got a court.

WILLY. Don't say. His own tennis court. Must be fine people, I bet.

BERNARD. They are, very nice. Dad tells me Biff's in town.

WILLY (*with a big smile*). Yeah, Biff's in. Working on a very big deal, Bernard.

BERNARD. What's Biff doing?

WILLY. Well, he's been doing very big things in the West. But he decided to establish himself here. Very big. We're having dinner. Did I hear your wife had a boy?

BERNARD. That's right. Our second.

WILLY. Two boys! What do you know!

BERNARD. What kind of a deal has Biff got?

WILLY. Well, Bill Oliver—very big sporting goods man—he wants Biff very badly. Called him in from the West. Long distance, carte blanche, special deliveries. Your friends have their own private tennis court?

BERNARD. You still with the old firm, Willy?

WILLY (*after a pause*). I'm—I'm overjoyed to see how you made the grade, Bernard, overjoyed. It's an encouraging thing to see a young man really—really—Looks very good for Biff—very—(*He breaks off, then*) Bernard—(*He is so full of emotion, he breaks off again.*)

BERNARD. What is it, Willy?

WILLY (*small and alone*). What—what's the secret?

BERNARD. What secret?

WILLY. How—how did you? Why didn't he ever catch on?

BERNARD. I wouldn't know that, Willy.

WILLY (*confidentially, desperately*). You were his friend, his boyhood friend. There's something I don't understand about it. His life ended after that Ebbets Field game. From the age of seventeen nothing good ever happened to him.

BERNARD. He never trained himself for anything.

WILLY. But he did, he did. After high school he took so many correspondence courses. Radio mechanics; television; God knows what, and never made the slightest mark.

BERNARD (*taking off his glasses*). Willy, do you want to talk candidly?

WILLY (*rising, faces* BERNARD). I regard you as a very brilliant man, Bernard. I value your advice.

BERNARD. Oh, the hell with the advice, Willy. I couldn't advise you. There's just one thing I've always wanted to ask you. When he was supposed to graduate, and the math teacher flunked him—

WILLY. Oh, that son-of-a-bitch ruined his life.

BERNARD. Yeah, but, Willy, all he had to do was go to summer school and make up that subject.

WILLY. That's right, that's right.

BERNARD. Did you tell him not to go to summer school?

WILLY. Me? I begged him to go. I ordered him to go!

BERNARD. Then why wouldn't he go?

WILLY. Why? Why! Bernard, that question has been trailing me like a ghost for the last fifteen years. He flunked the subject, and laid down and died like a hammer hit him!

BERNARD. Take it easy, kid.

WILLY. Let me talk to you—I got nobody to talk to. Bernard, Bernard, was it my fault? Y'see? It keeps going around in my mind, maybe I did something to him. I got nothing to give him.

BERNARD. Don't take it so hard.

WILLY. Why did he lay down? What is the story there? You were his friend!

BERNARD. Willy, I remember, it was June, and our grades came out. And he'd flunked math.

WILLY. That son-of-a-bitch!

BERNARD. No, it wasn't right then. Biff just got very angry, I remember, and he was ready to enroll in summer school.

WILLY (*surprised*).   He was?

BERNARD.   He wasn't beaten by it at all. But then, Willy, he disappeared from the block for almost a month. And I got the idea that he'd gone up to New England to see you. Did he have a talk with you then?

(WILLY *stares in silence.*)

BERNARD.   Willy?

WILLY (*with a strong edge of resentment in his voice*).   Yeah, he came to Boston. What about it?

BERNARD.   Well, just that when he came back—I'll never forget this, it always mystifies me. Because I thought so well of Biff, even though he'd always taken advantage of me. I loved him, Willy, y'know? And he came back after that month and took his sneakers—remember those sneakers with "University of Virginia" printed on them? He was so proud of those, wore them every day. And he took them down in the cellar, and burned them up in the furnace. We had a fist fight. It lasted at least half an hour. Just the two of us, punching each other down the cellar, and crying right through it. I've often thought of how strange it was that I knew he'd given up his life. What happened in Boston, Willy?

(WILLY *looks at him as at an intruder.*)

BERNARD.   I just bring it up because you asked me.

WILLY (*angrily*).   Nothing. What do you mean, "What happened?" What's that go to do with anything?

BERNARD.   Well, don't get sore.

WILLY.   What are you trying to do, blame it on me? If a boy lays down is that my fault?

BERNARD.   Now, Willy, don't get—

WILLY.   Well, don't—don't talk to me that way! What does that mean, "What happened?"

(CHARLEY *enters. He is in his vest, and he carries a bottle of bourbon.*)

CHARLEY.   Hey, you're going to miss that train. (*He waves the bottle.*)

BERNARD.   Yeah, I'm going. (*He takes the bottle.*) Thanks, Pop. (*He picks up his rackets and bag.*) Good-by, Willy, and don't worry about it. You know, "If at first you don't succeed . . ."

WILLY.   Yes, I believe in that.

BERNARD.   But sometimes, Willy, it's better for a man just to walk away.

WILLY.   Walk away?

BERNARD.   That's right.

WILLY.   But if you can't walk away?

BERNARD (*after a slight pause*).   I guess that's when it's tough. (*Extending his hand*) Good-by, Willy.

WILLY (*shaking BERNARD's hand*).   Good-by, boy.

CHARLEY (*an arm on* BERNARD'*s shoulder*).   How do you like this kid?
Gonna argue a case in front of the Supreme Court.

BERNARD (*protesting*).   Pop!

WILLY (*genuinely shocked, pained, and happy*).   No! The Supreme
Court!

BERNARD.   I gotta run. 'By, Dad!

CHARLEY.   Knock 'em dead, Bernard!

(BERNARD *goes off.*)

WILLY (*as* CHARLEY *takes out his wallet*).   The Supreme Court! And
he didn't even mention it!

CHARLEY (*counting out money on the desk*).   He don't have to—he's
gonna do it.

WILLY.   And you never told him what to do, did you? You never took
any interest in him.

CHARLEY.   My salvation is that I never took any interest in anything.
There's some money—fifty dollars. I got an accountant inside.

WILLY.   Charley, look . . . (*With difficulty*) I got my insurance to pay.
If you can manage it—I need a hundred and ten dollars.

(CHARLEY *doesn't reply for a moment; merely stops moving.*)

WILLY.   I'd draw it from my bank but Linda would know, and I . . .

CHARLEY.   Sit down, Willy.

WILLY (*moving toward the chair*).   I'm keeping an account of everything, remember. I'll pay every penny back. (*He sits.*)

CHARLEY.   Now listen to me, Willy.

WILLY.   I want you to know I appreciate . . .

CHARLEY (*sitting down on the table*).   Willy, what're you doin'? What
the hell is goin' on in your head?

WILLY.   Why? I'm simply . . .

CHARLEY.   I offered you a job. You can make fifty dollars a week. And
I won't send you on the road.

WILLY.   I've got a job.

CHARLEY.   Without pay? What kind of a job is a job without pay?
(*He rises.*) Now, look, kid, enough is enough. I'm no genius but I know
when I'm being insulted.

WILLY.   Insulted!

CHARLEY.   Why don't you want to work for me?

WILLY.   What's the matter with you? I've got a job.

CHARLEY.   Then what're you walkin' in here every week for?

WILLY (*getting up*).   Well, if you don't want me to walk in here—

CHARLEY.   I am offering you a job.

WILLY.   I don't want your goddam job!

CHARLEY.   When the hell are you going to grow up?

WILLY (*furiously*). You big ignoramus, if you say that to me again I'll rap you one! I don't care how big you are! (*He's ready to fight.*)

(*Pause.*)

CHARLEY (*kindly, going to him*). How much do you need, Willy?

WILLY. Charley, I'm strapped. I'm strapped. I don't know what to do. I was just fired.

CHARLEY. Howard fired you?

WILLY. That snotnose. Imagine that? I named him. I named him Howard.

CHARLEY. Willy, when're you gonna realize that them things don't mean anything? You named him Howard, but you can't sell that. The only thing you got in this world is what you can sell. And the funny thing is that you're a salesman, and you don't know that.

WILLY. I've always tried to think otherwise, I guess. I always felt that if a man was impressive, and well liked, that nothing—

CHARLEY. Why must everybody like you? Who liked J. P. Morgan? Was he impressive? In a Turkish bath he'd look like a butcher. But with his pockets on he was very well liked. Now listen, Willy, I know you don't like me, and nobody can say I'm in love with you, but I'll give you a job be-cause—just for the hell of it, put it that way. Now what do you say?

WILLY. I—I just can't work for you, Charley.

CHARLEY. What're you, jealous of me?

WILLY. I can't work for you, that's all, don't ask me why.

CHARLEY (*angered, takes out more bills*). You been jealous of me all your life, you damned fool! Here, pay your insurance. (*He puts the money in* WILLY's *hand.*)

WILLY. I'm keeping strict accounts.

CHARLEY. I've got some work to do. Take care of yourself. And pay your insurance.

WILLY (*moving to the right*). Funny, y'know? After all the highways, and the trains, and the appointments, and the years, you end up worth more dead than alive.

CHARLEY. Willy, nobody's worth nothin' dead. (*After a slight pause*) Did you hear what I said? (WILLY *stands still, dreaming.*) Willy!

WILLY. Apologize to Bernard for me when you see him. I didn't mean to argue with him. He's a fine boy. They're all fine boys, and they'll end up big—all of them. Someday they'll all play tennis together. Wish me luck, Charley. He saw Bill Oliver today.

CHARLEY. Good luck.

WILLY (*on the verge of tears*). Charley, you're the only friend I got. Isn't that a remarkable thing? (*He goes out.*)

CHARLEY. Jesus!

(CHARLEY *stares after him a moment and follows. All light blacks out. Suddenly raucous music is heard, and a red glow rises behind the screen at right.* STANLEY, *a young waiter, appears, carrying a table, followed by* HAPPY, *who is carrying two chairs.*)

STANLEY (*putting the table down*).   That's all right, Mr. Loman, I can handle it myself. (*He turns and takes the chairs from* HAPPY *and places them at the table.*)

HAPPY (*glancing around*).   Oh, this is better.

STANLEY.   Sure, in the front there you're in the middle of all kinds a noise. Whenever you got a party, Mr. Loman, you just tell me and I'll put you back here. Y'know, there's a lotta people they don't like it private, because when they go out they like to see a lotta action around them because they're sick and tired to stay in the house by theirself. But I know you, you ain't from Hackensack. You know what I mean?

HAPPY (*sitting down*).   So how's it coming, Stanley?

STANLEY.   Ah, it's a dog's life. I only wish during the war they'd a took me in the Army. I coulda been dead by now.

HAPPY.   My brother's back, Stanley.

STANLEY.   Oh, he come back, heh? From the Far West.

HAPPY.   Yeah, big cattle man, my brother, so treat him right. And my father's coming too.

STANLEY.   Oh, your father too!

HAPPY.   You got a couple of nice lobsters?

STANLEY.   Hundred per cent, big.

HAPPY.   I want them with the claws.

STANLEY.   Don't worry, I don't give you no mice. (HAPPY *laughs.*) How about some wine? It'll put a head on the meal.

HAPPY.   No. You remember, Stanley, that recipe I brought you from overseas? With the champagne in it?

STANLEY.   Oh, yeah, sure. I still got it tacked up yet in the kitchen. But that'll have to have to cost a buck apiece anyways.

HAPPY.   That's all right.

STANLEY.   What'd you, hit a number or somethin'?

HAPPY.   No, it's a little celebration. My brother is—I think he pulled off a big deal today. I think we're going into business together.

STANLEY.   Great! That's the best for you. Because a family business, you know what I mean?—that's the best.

HAPPY.   That's what I think.

STANLEY.   'Cause what's the difference? Somebody steals? It's in the family. Know what I mean? (*Sotto voce*) Like this bartender here. The boss is goin' crazy what kinda leak he's got in the cash register. You put it in but it don't come out.

HAPPY (*raising his head*).   Sh!

STANLEY. What?

HAPPY. You notice I wasn't lookin' right or left, was I?

STANLEY. No.

HAPPY. And my eyes are closed.

STANLEY. So what's the—?

HAPPY. Strudel's comin'.

STANLEY (catching on, looks around). Ah, no, there's no—

(He breaks off as a furred, lavishly dressed girl enters and sits at the next table. Both follow her with their eyes.)

STANLEY. Geez, how'd ya know?

HAPPY. I got radar or something. (Staring directly at her profile) Oooooooo . . . Stanley.

STANLEY. I think that's for you, Mr. Loman.

HAPPY. Look at that mouth. Oh, God. And the binoculars.

STANLEY. Geez, you got a life, Mr. Loman.

HAPPY. Wait on her.

STANLEY (going to the GIRL's table). Would you like a menu, ma'am?

GIRL. I'm expecting someone, but I'd like a—

HAPPY. Why don't you bring her—excuse me, miss, do you mind? I sell champagne, and I'd like you to try my brand. Bring her a champagne, Stanley.

GIRL. That's awfully nice of you.

HAPPY. Don't mention it. It's all company money. (He laughs.)

GIRL. That's a charming product to be selling, isn't it?

HAPPY. Oh, gets to be like everything else. Selling is selling, y'know.

GIRL. I suppose.

HAPPY. You don't happen to sell, do you?

GIRL. No, I don't sell.

HAPPY. Would you object to a compliment from a stranger? You ought to be on a magazine cover.

GIRL (looking at him a little archly). I have been.

(STANLEY comes in with a glass of champagne.)

HAPPY. What'd I say before, Stanley? You see? She's a cover girl.

STANLEY. Oh, I could see, I could see.

HAPPY (to the GIRL). What magazine?

GIRL. Oh, a lot of them. (She takes the drink.) Thank you.

HAPPY. You know what they say in France, don't you? "Champagne is the drink of the complexion"—Hya, Biff!

(BIFF has entered and sits with HAPPY.)

BIFF. Hello, kid. Sorry I'm late.

HAPPY. I just got here. Uh, Miss—?

GIRL. Forsythe.

HAPPY. Miss Forsythe, this is my brother.

BIFF. Is Dad here?

HAPPY. His name is Biff. You might've heard of him. Great football player.

GIRL. Really? What team?

HAPPY. Are you familiar with football?

GIRL. No, I'm afraid I'm not.

HAPPY. Biff is quarterback with the New York Giants.

GIRL. Well, that is nice, isn't it? (*She drinks.*)

HAPPY. Good health.

GIRL. I'm happy to meet you.

HAPPY. That's my name. Hap. It's really Harold, but at West Point they called me Happy.

GIRL (*now really impressed*). Oh, I see. How do you do? (*She turns her profile.*)

BIFF. Isn't Dad coming?

HAPPY. You want her?

BIFF. Oh, I could never make that.

HAPPY. I remember the time that idea would never come into your head. Where's the old confidence, Biff?

BIFF. I just saw Oliver—

HAPPY. Wait a minute. I've got to see that old confidence again. Do you want her? She's on call.

BIFF. Oh, no. (*He turns to look at the* GIRL.)

HAPPY. I'm telling you. Watch this. (*Turning to the* GIRL) Honey? (*She turns to him.*) Are you busy?

GIRL. Well, I am . . . but I could make a phone call.

HAPPY. Do that, will you, honey? And see if you can get a friend. We'll be here for a while. Biff is one of the greatest football players in the country.

GIRL (*standing up*). Well, I'm certainly happy to meet you.

HAPPY. Come back soon.

GIRL. I'll try.

HAPPY. Don't try, honey, try hard.

(*The* GIRL *exits.* STANLEY *follows, shaking his head in bewildered admiration.*)

HAPPY. Isn't that a shame now? A beautiful girl like that? That's why I can't get married. There's not a good woman in a thousand. New York is loaded with them, kid!

BIFF. Hap, look—

HAPPY. I told you she was on call!

BIFF (*strangely unnerved*).   Cut it out, will ya? I want to say something to you.

HAPPY.   Did you see Oliver?

BIFF.   I saw him all right. Now look, I want to tell Dad a couple of things and I want you to help me.

HAPPY.   What? Is he going to back you?

BIFF.   Are you crazy? You're out of your goddam head, you know that?

HAPPY.   Why? What happened?

BIFF (*breathlessly*).   I did a terrible thing today, Hap. It's been the strangest day I ever went through. I'm all numb, I swear.

HAPPY.   You mean he wouldn't see you?

BIFF.   Well, I waited six hours for him, see? All day. Kept sending my name in. Even tried to date his secretary so she'd get me to him, but no soap.

HAPPY.   Because you're not showin' the old confidence, Biff. He remembered you, didn't he?

BIFF (*stopping* HAPPY *with a gesture*).   Finally, about five o'clock, he comes out. Didn't remember who I was or anything. I felt like such an idiot, Hap.

HAPPY.   Did you tell him my Florida idea?

BIFF.   He walked away. I saw him for one minute. I got so mad I could've torn the walls down! How the hell did I ever get the idea I was a salesman there? I even believed myself that I'd been a salesman for him! And then he gave me one look and—I realized what a ridiculous lie my whole life has been! We've been talking in a dream for fifteen years. I was a shipping clerk.

HAPPY.   What'd you do?

BIFF (*with great tension and wonder*).   Well, he left, see. And the secretary went out. I was all alone in the waiting-room. I don't know what came over me, Hap. The next thing I know I'm in his office—paneled walls, everything. I can't explain it. I—Hap, I took his fountain pen.

HAPPY.   Geez, did he catch you?

BIFF.   I ran out. I ran down all eleven flights. I ran and ran and ran.

HAPPY.   That was an awful dumb—what'd you do that for?

BIFF (*agonized*).   I don't know, I just—wanted to take something, I don't know. You gotta help me, Hap, I'm gonna tell Pop.

HAPPY.   You crazy? What for?

BIFF.   Hap, he's got to understand that I'm not the man somebody lends that kind of money to. He thinks I've been spiting him all these years and it's eating him up.

HAPPY.   That's just it. You tell him something nice.

BIFF.   I can't.

HAPPY.   Say you got a lunch date with Oliver tomorrow.

BIFF.   So what do I do tomorrow?

HAPPY.   You leave the house tomorrow and come back at night and say Oliver is thinking it over. And he thinks it over for a couple of weeks, and gradually it fades away and nobody's the worse.

BIFF. But it'll go on forever!

HAPPY. Dad is never so happy as when he's looking forward to something!

(WILLY *enters.*)

HAPPY. Hello, scout!

WILLY. Gee, I haven't been here in years!

(STANLEY *has followed* WILLY *in and sets a chair for him.* STANLEY *starts off but* HAPPY *stops him.*)

HAPPY. Stanley!

(STANLEY *stands by, waiting for an order.*)

BIFF (*going to* WILLY *with guilt, as to an invalid*). Sit down, Pop. You want a drink?

WILLY. Sure, I don't mind.

BIFF. Let's get a load on.

WILLY. You look worried.

BIFF. N-no. (*To* STANLEY) Scotch all around. Make it doubles.

STANLEY. Doubles, right. (*He goes.*)

WILLY. You had a couple already, didn't you?

BIFF. Just a couple, yeah.

WILLY. Well, what happened, boy? (*Nodding affirmatively, with a smile*) Everything go all right?

BIFF (*takes a breath, then reaches out and grasps* WILLY's *hand*). Pal . . . (*He is smiling bravely, and* WILLY *is smiling too.*) I had an experience today.

HAPPY. Terrific, Pop.

WILLY. That so? What happened?

BIFF (*high, slightly alcoholic, above the earth*). I'm going to tell you everything from first to last. It's been a strange day. (*Silence. He looks around, composes himself as best he can, but his breath keeps breaking the rhythm of his voice.*) I had to wait quite a while for him, and—

WILLY. Oliver?

BIFF. Yeah, Oliver. All day, as a matter of cold fact. And a lot of— instances—facts, Pop, facts about my life came back to me. Who was it, Pop? Who ever said I was a salesman with Oliver?

WILLY. Well, you were.

BIFF. No, Dad, I was a shipping clerk.

WILLY. But you were practically—

BIFF (*with determination*). Dad, I don't know who said it first, but I was never a salesman for Bill Oliver.

WILLY. What're you talking about?

BIFF. Let's hold on to the facts tonight, Pop. We're not going to get anywhere bullin' around. I was a shipping clerk.

WILLY (*angrily*). All right, now listen to me—

BIFF. Why don't you let me finish?

WILLY. I'm not interested in stories about the past or any crap of that kind because the woods are burning, boys, you understand? There's a big blaze going on all around. I was fired today.

BIFF (*shocked*). How could you be?

WILLY. I was fired, and I'm looking for a little good news to tell your mother, because the woman has waited and the woman has suffered. The gist of it is that I haven't got a story left in my head, Biff. So don't give me a lecture about facts and aspects. I am not interested. Now what've you got to say to me?

(STANLEY *enters with three drinks. They wait until he leaves.*)

WILLY. Did you see Oliver?

BIFF. Jesus, Dad!

WILLY. You mean you didn't go up there?

HAPPY. Sure he went up there.

BIFF. I did. I—saw him. How could they fire you?

WILLY (*on the edge of his chair*). What kind of a welcome did he give you?

BIFF. He won't even let you work on commission?

WILLY. I'm out! (*Driving*) So tell me, he gave you a warm welcome?

HAPPY. Sure, Pop, sure!

BIFF (*driven*). Well, it was kind of—

WILLY. I was wondering if he'd remember you. (*To* HAPPY) Imagine, man doesn't see him for ten, twelve years and gives him that kind of a welcome!

HAPPY. Damn right!

BIFF (*trying to return to the offensive*). Pop look—

WILLY. You know why he remembered you, don't you? Because you impressed him in those days.

BIFF. Let's talk quietly and get this down to the facts, huh?

WILLY (*as though* BIFF *had been interrupting*). Well, what happened? It's great news, Biff. Did he take you into his office or'd you talk in the waiting-room?

BIFF. Well, he came in, see, and—

WILLY (*with a big smile*). What'd he say? Betcha he threw his arm around you.

BIFF. Well, he kinda—

WILLY. He's a fine man. (*To* HAPPY) Very hard man to see, y'know.

HAPPY (*agreeing*). Oh, I know.

WILLY (*to* BIFF). Is that where you had the drinks?

BIFF. Yeah, he gave me a couple of—no, no!

HAPPY (*cutting in*). He told him my Florida idea.

WILLY. Don't interrupt. (*To* BIFF) How'd he react to the Florida idea?

BIFF. Dad, will you give me a minute to explain?

WILLY. I've been waiting for you to explain since I sat down here! What happened? He took you into his office and what?

BIFF. Well—I talked. And—and he listened, see.

WILLY. Famous for the way he listens, y'know. What was his answer?

BIFF. His answer was—(*He breaks off, suddenly angry.*)Dad, you're not letting me tell you what I want to tell you!

WILLY (*accusing, angered*). You didn't see him, did you?

BIFF. I did see him!

WILLY. What'd you insult him or something? You insulted him, didn't you?

BIFF. Listen, will you let me out of it, will you just let me out of it!

HAPPY. What the hell!

WILLY. Tell me what happened!

BIFF (*to* HAPPY). I can't talk to him!

(*A single trumpet note jars the ear. The light of green leaves stains the house, which holds the air of night and a dream.* YOUNG BERNARD *enters and knocks on the door of the house.*)

YOUNG BERNARD (*frantically*). Mrs. Loman, Mrs. Loman!

HAPPY. Tell him what happened!

BIFF (*to* HAPPY). Shut up and leave me alone!

WILLY. No, no! You had to go and flunk math!

BIFF. What math? What're you talking about?

YOUNG BERNARD. Mrs. Loman, Mrs. Loman!

(LINDA *appears in the house, as of old.*)

WILLY (*wildly*). Math, math, math!

BIFF. Take it easy, Pop!

YOUNG BERNARD. Mrs. Loman!

WILLY (*furiously*). If you hadn't flunked you'd've been set by now!

BIFF. Now, look, I'm gonna tell you what happened, and you're going to listen to me.

YOUNG BERNARD. Mrs. Loman!

BIFF. I waited six hours—

HAPPY. What the hell are you saying?

BIFF. I kept sending in my name but he wouldn't see me. So finally he . . . (*He continues unheard as light fades low on the restaurant.*)

YOUNG BERNARD. Biff flunked math!

LINDA. No!

YOUNG BERNARD. Birnbaum flunked him! They won't graduate him!

LINDA. But they have to. He's gotta go to the university. Where is he? Biff! Biff!

YOUNG BERNARD. No, he left. He went to Grand Central.

LINDA. Grand—You mean he went to Boston!

YOUNG BERNARD. Is Uncle Willy in Boston?

LINDA. Oh, maybe Willy can talk to the teacher. Oh, the poor, poor boy!

(*Light on house area snaps out.*)

BIFF (*at the table, now audible, holding up a gold fountain pen*). . . . so I'm washed up with Oliver, you understand? Are you listening to me?

WILLY (*at a loss*). Yeah, sure. If you hadn't flunked—

BIFF. Flunked what? What're you talking about?

WILLY. Don't blame everything on me! I didn't flunk math—you did! What pen?

HAPPY. That was awful dumb, Biff, a pen like that is worth—

WILLY (*seeing the pen for the first time*). You took Oliver's pen?

BIFF (*weakening*). Dad, I just explained it to you.

WILLY. You stole Bill Oliver's fountain pen!

BIFF. I didn't exactly steal it! That's just what I've been explaining to you!

HAPPY. He had it in his hand and just then Oliver walked in, so he got nervous and stuck it in his pocket!

WILLY. My God, Biff!

BIFF. I never intended to do it, Dad!

OPERATOR'S VOICE. Standish Arms, good evening!

WILLY (*shouting*). I'm not in my room!

BIFF (*frightened*). Dad, what's the matter? (*He and* HAPPY *stand up.*)

OPERATOR. Ringing Mr. Loman for you!

WILLY. I'm not there, stop it!

BIFF (*horrified, gets down on one knee before* WILLY). Dad, I'll make good, I'll make good. (WILLY *tries to get to his feet.* BIFF *holds him down.*) Sit down now.

WILLY. No, you're no good, you're no good for anything.

BIFF. I am, Dad, I'll find something else, you understand? Now don't worry about anything. (*He holds up* WILLY's *face.*) Talk to me, Dad.

OPERATOR. Mr. Loman does not answer. Shall I page him?

WILLY (*attempting to stand, as though to rush and silence the* OPERATOR). No, no, no!

HAPPY. He'll strike something, Pop.

WILLY. No, no . . .

BIFF (*desperately, standing over* WILLY). Pop, listen! Listen to me! I'm telling you something good. Oliver talked to his partner about the

Florida idea. You listening? He—he talked to his partner, and he came to me . . . I'm going to be all right, you hear? Dad, listen to me, he said it was just a question of the amount!

WILLY. Then you . . . got it?

HAPPY. He's gonna be terrific, Pop!

WILLY (*trying to stand*). Then you got it, haven't you? You got it! You got it!

BIFF (*agonized, holds* WILLY *down*). No, no. Look, Pop. I'm supposed to have lunch with them tomorrow. I'm just telling you this so you'll know that I can still make an impression, Pop. And I'll make good somewhere, but I can't go tomorrow, see?

WILLY. Why not? You simply—

BIFF. But the pen, Pop!

WILLY. You give it to him and tell him it was an oversight!

HAPPY. Sure, have lunch tomorrow!

BIFF. I can't say that—

WILLY. You were doing a crossword puzzle and accidentally used his pen!

BIFF. Listen, kid, I took those balls years ago, now I walk in with his fountain pen? That clinches it, don't you see? I can't face him like that! I'll try elsewhere.

PAGE's VOICE. Paging Mr. Loman!

WILLY. Don't you want to be anything?

BIFF. Pop, how can I go back?

WILLY. You don't want to be anything, is that what's behind it?

BIFF (*now angry at* WILLY *for not crediting his sympathy*). Don't take it that way! You think it was easy walking into that office after what I'd done to him? A team of horses couldn't have dragged me back to Bill Oliver!

WILLY. Then why'd you go?

BIFF. Why did I go? Why did I go! Look at you! Look at what's become of you!

(*Off left,* THE WOMAN *laughs*.)

WILLY. Biff, you're going to go to that lunch tomorrow, or—

BIFF. I can't go. I've got no appointment!

HAPPY. Biff, for . . . !

WILLY. Are you spiting me?

BIFF. Don't take it that way! Goddammit!

WILLY (*strikes* BIFF *and falters away from the table*). You rotten little louse! Are you spiting me?

THE WOMAN. Someone's at the door, Willy!

BIFF. I'm no good, can't you see what I am?

HAPPY (*separating them*).   Hey, you're in a restaurant! Now cut it out, both of you! (*The* GIRLS *enter.*) Hello, girls, sit down.

(THE WOMAN *laughs, off left.*)

MISS FORSYTHE.   I guess we might as well. This is Letta.
THE WOMAN.   Willy, are you going to wake up?
BIFF (*ignoring* WILLY).   How're ya, miss, sit down. What do you drink?
MISS FORSYTHE.   Letta might not be able to stay long.
LETTA.   I gotta get up very early tomorrow. I got jury duty. I'm so excited! Were you fellows ever on a jury?
BIFF.   No, but I been in front of them! (*The* GIRLS *laugh.*) This is my father.
LETTA.   Isn't he cute? Sit down with us, Pop.
HAPPY.   Sit him down, Biff!
BIFF (*going to him*).   Come on, slugger, drink us under the table. To hell with it! Come on, sit down, pal.

(*On* BIFF's *last insistence,* WILLY *is about to sit.*)

THE WOMAN (*now urgently*).   Willy, are you going to answer the door!

(THE WOMAN's *call pulls* WILLY *back. He starts right, befuddled.*)

BIFF.   Hey, where are you going?
WILLY.   Open the door.
BIFF.   The door?
WILLY.   The washroom . . . the door . . . where's the door?
BIFF (*leading* WILLY *to the left*).   Just go straight down.

(WILLY *moves left.*)

THE WOMAN.   Willy, Willy, are you going to get up, get up, get up, get up?

(WILLY *exits left.,*

LETTA.   I think it's sweet you bring your daddy along.
MISS FORSYTHE.   Oh, he isn't really your father!
BIFF (*at left, turning to her resentfully*).   Miss Forsythe, you've just seen a prince walk by. A fine, troubled prince. A hard-working, unappreciated prince. A pal, you understand? A good companion. Always for his boys.
LETTA.   That's so sweet.
HAPPY.   Well, girls, what's the program? We're wasting time. Come on, Biff. Gather round. Where would you like to go?
BIFF.   Why don't you do something for him?

HAPPY. Me!

BIFF. Don't you give a damn for him, Hap?

HAPPY. What're you talking about? I'm the one who—

BIFF. I sense it, you don't give a good goddam about him. (*He takes the rolled-up hose from his pocket and puts it on the table in front of* HAPPY.) Look what I found in the cellar, for Christ's sake. How can you bear to let it go on?

HAPPY. Me? Who goes away? Who runs off and—

BIFF. Yeah, but he doesn't mean anything to you. You could help him—I can't! Don't you understand what I'm talking about? He's going to kill himself, don't you know that?

HAPPY. Don't I know it! Me!

BIFF. Hap, help him! Jesus . . . help him . . . Help me, help me, I can't bear to look at his face! (*Ready to weep, he hurries out, up right.*)

HAPPY (*starting after him*). Where are you going?

MISS FORSYTHE. What's he so mad about?

HAPPY. Come on, girls, we'll catch up with him.

MISS FORSYTHE (*as* HAPPY *pushes her out*). Say, I don't like that temper of his!

HAPPY. He's just a little overstrung, he'll be all right!

WILLY (*off left, as* THE WOMAN *laughs*). Don't answer! Don't answer!

LETTA. Don't you want to tell your father—

HAPPY. No, that's not my father. He's just a guy. Come on, we'll catch Biff, and, honey, we're going to paint this town! Stanley, where's the check! Hey, Stanley!

(*They exit.* STANLEY *looks toward left.*)

STANLEY (*calling to* HAPPY *indignantly*). Mr. Loman! Mr. Loman!

(STANLEY *picks up a chair and follows them off. Knocking is heard off left.* THE WOMAN *enters, laughing.* WILLY *follows her. She is in a black slip; he is buttoning his shirt. Raw, sensuous music accompanies their speech.*)

WILLY. Will you stop laughing? Will you stop?

THE WOMAN. Aren't you going to answer the door? He'll wake the whole hotel.

WILLY. I'm not expecting anybody.

THE WOMAN. Whyn't you have another drink, honey, and stop being so damn self-centered?

WILLY. I'm so lonely.

THE WOMAN. You know you ruined me, Willy? From now on, whenever you come to the office, I'll see that you go right through to the buyers. No waiting at my desk any more, Willy. You ruined me.

WILLY. That's nice of you to say that.

THE WOMAN. Gee, you are self-centered! Why so sad? You are the saddest, self-centeredest soul I ever did see-saw. (*She laughs. He kisses her.*) Come on inside, drummer boy. It's silly to be dressing in the middle of the night. (*As knocking is heard*) Aren't you going to answer the door?

WILLY. They're knocking on the wrong door.

THE WOMAN. But I felt the knocking. And he heard us talking in here. Maybe the hotel's on fire!

WILLY (*his terror rising*). It's a mistake.

THE WOMAN. Then tell him to go away!

WILLY. There's nobody there.

THE WOMAN. It's getting on my nerves, Willy. There's somebody standing out there and it's getting on my nerves!

WILLY (*pushing her away from him*). All right, stay in the bathroom here, and don't come out. I think there's a law in Massachusetts about it, so don't come out. It may be that new room clerk. He looked very mean. So don't come out. It's a mistake, there's no fire.

(*The knocking is heard again. He takes a few steps away from her, and she vanishes into the wing. The light follows him, and now he is facing* YOUNG BIFF, *who carries a suitcase.* BIFF *steps toward him. The music is gone.*)

BIFF. Why didn't you answer?

WILLY. Biff! What are you doing in Boston?

BIFF. Why didn't you answer? I've been knocking for five minutes, I called you on the phone—

WILLY. I just heard you. I was in the bathroom and had the door shut. Did anything happen home?

BIFF. Dad—I let you down.

WILLY. What do you mean?

BIFF. Dad . . .

WILLY. Biffo, what's this about? (*Putting his arm around* BIFF) Come on, let's go downstairs and get you a malted.

BIFF. Dad, I flunked math.

WILLY. Not for the term?

BIFF. The term. I haven't got enough credits to graduate.

WILLY. You mean to say Bernard wouldn't give you the answers?

BIFF. He did, he tried, but I only got a sixty-one.

WILLY. And they wouldn't give you four points?

BIFF. Birnbaum refused absolutely. I begged him, Pop, but he won't give me those points. You gotta talk to him before they close the school. Because if he saw the kind of man you are, and you just talked to him in your way, I'm sure he'd come through for me. The class came right before practice, see, and I didn't go enough. Would you talk to him? He'd like you, Pop. You know the way you could talk.

WILLY.   You're on. We'll drive right back.

BIFF.   Oh, Dad, good work! I'm sure he'll change it for you!

WILLY.   Go downstairs and tell the clerk I'm checkin' out. Go right down.

BIFF.   Yes, sir! See, the reason he hates me, Pop—one day he was late for class so I got up at the blackboard and imitated him. I crossed my eyes and talked with a lithp.

WILLY (*laughing*).   You did? The kids like it?

BIFF.   They nearly died laughing!

WILLY.   Yeah? What'd you do?

BIFF.   The thquare root of thixthy twee is . . . (WILLY *bursts out laughing;* BIFF *joins him.*) And in the middle of it he walked in!

(WILLY *laughs and* THE WOMAN *joins in offstage.*)

WILLY (*without hesitation*).   Hurry downstairs and—

BIFF.   Somebody in there?

WILLY.   No, that was next door.

(THE WOMAN *laughs offstage.*)

BIFF.   Somebody got in your bathroom!

WILLY.   No, it's the next room, there's a party—

THE WOMAN (*enters, laughing. She lisps this*).   Can I come in? There's something in the bathtub, Willy, and it's moving!

(WILLY *looks at* BIFF, *who is staring open-mouthed and horrified at* THE WOMAN.)

WILLY.   Ah—you better go back to your room. They must be finished painting by now. They're painting her room so I let her take a shower here. Go back, go back . . . (*He pushes her.*)

THE WOMAN (*resisting*).   But I've got to get dressed, Willy, I can't—

WILLY.   Get out of here! Go back, go back . . . (*Suddenly striving for the ordinary*) This is Miss Francis, Biff, she's a buyer. They're painting her room. Go back, Miss Francis, go back . . .

THE WOMAN.   But my clothes, I can't go out naked in the hall!

WILLY (*pushing her offstage*).   Get outa here! Go back, go back!

(BIFF *slowly sits down on his suitcase as the argument continues offstage.*)

THE WOMAN.   Where's my stockings? You promised me stockings, Willy!

WILLY.   I have no stockings here!

THE WOMAN.   You had two boxes of size nine sheers for me, and I want them!

WILLY.   Here, for God's sake, will you get outa here!

THE WOMAN (*enters holding a box of stockings*). I just hope there's nobody in the hall. That's all I hope. (*To* BIFF) Are you football or baseball?

BIFF. Football.

THE WOMAN (*angry, humiliated*). That's me too. G'night. (*She snatches her clothes from* WILLY *and walks out.*)

WILLY (*after a pause*). Well, better get going. I want to get to the school first thing in the morning. Get my suits out of the closet. I'll get my valise. (BIFF *doesn't move.*) What's the matter? (BIFF *remains motionless, tears falling.*) She's a buyer. Buys for J. H. Simmons. She lives down the hall—they're painting. You don't imagine—(*He breaks off. After a pause*) Now listen, pal, she's just a buyer. She sees merchandise in her room and they have to keep it looking just so . . . (*Pause. Assuming command*) All right, get my suits. (BIFF *doesn't move.*) Now stop crying and do as I say. I gave you an order. Biff, I gave you an order! Is that what you do when I give you an order? How dare you cry! (*Putting his arm around* BIFF) Now look, Biff, when you grow up you'll understand about these things. You mustn't—you mustn't overemphasize a thing like this. I'll see Birnbaum first thing in the morning.

BIFF. Never mind.

WILLY (*getting down beside* BIFF). Never mind! He's going to give you those points. I'll see to it.

BIFF. He wouldn't listen to you.

WILLY. He certainly will listen to me. You need those points for the U. of Virginia.

BIFF. I'm not going there.

WILLY. Heh? If I can't get him to change that mark you'll make it up in summer school. You've got all summer to—

BIFF (*his weeping breaking from him*). Dad . . .

WILLY (*infected by it*). Oh, my boy . . .

BIFF. Dad . . .

WILLY. She's nothing to me, Biff. I was lonely, I was terribly lonely.

BIFF. You—you gave her Mama's stockings! (*His tears break through and he rises to go.*)

WILLY (*grabbing for* BIFF). I gave you an order!

BIFF. Don't touch me, you—liar!

WILLY. Apologize for that!

BIFF. You fake! You phony little fake! You fake! (*Overcome, he turns quickly and weeping fully goes out with his suitcase.* WILLY *is left on the floor on his knees.*)

WILLY. I gave you an order! Biff, come back here or I'll beat you! Come back here! I'll whip you!

(STANLEY *comes quickly in from the right and stands in front of* WILLY.)

WILLY (*shouts at* STANLEY). I gave you an order . . .

STANLEY. Hey, let's pick it up, pick it up, Mr. Loman. (*He helps* WILLY *to his feet.*) Your boys left with the chippies. They said they'll see you home.

(*A second waiter watches some distance away.*)

WILLY. But we were supposed to have dinner together.

(*Music is heard,* WILLY's *theme.*)

STANLEY. Can you make it?

WILLY. I'll—sure, I can make it. (*Suddenly concerned about his clothes*) Do I—I look all right?

STANLEY. Sure, you look all right. (*He flicks a speck off* WILLY's *lapel.*)

WILLY. Here—here's a dollar.

STANLEY. Oh, your son paid me. It's all right.

WILLY (*putting it in* STANLEY's *hand*). No, take it. You're a good boy.

STANLEY. Oh, no, you don't have to . . .

WILLY. Here's some more, I don't need it any more. (*After a slight pause*) Tell me—is there a seed store in the neighborhood?

STANLEY. Seeds? You mean like to plant?

(*As* WILLY *turns,* STANLEY *slips the money back into his jacket pocket.*)

WILLY. Yes. Carrots, peas . . .

STANLEY. Well, there's hardware stores on Sixth Avenue, but it may be too late now.

WILLY (*anxiously*). Oh, I'd better hurry. I've got to get some seeds. (*He starts off to the right.*) I've got to get some seeds, right away. Nothing's planted. I don't have a thing in the ground.

(WILLY *hurries out as the light goes down.* STANLEY *moves over to the right after him, watches him off. The other waiter has been staring at* WILLY.)

STANLEY (*to the waiter*). Well, whatta you looking at?

(*The waiter picks up the chairs and moves off right.* STANLEY *takes the table and follows him. The light fades on this area. There is a long pause, the sound of the flute coming over. The light gradually rises on the kitchen, which is empty.* HAPPY *appears at the door of the house, followed by* BIFF. HAPPY *is carrying a large bunch of long-stemmed roses. He enters the kitchen, looks around for* LINDA. *Not seeing her, he turns to* BIFF, *who is just outside the house door, and makes a gesture with his hands, indicating "Not here, I guess." He looks into the living-room and freezes. Inside,* LINDA, *unseen, is seated,* WILLY's *coat on her lap. She rises ominously and quietly and moves toward* HAPPY, *who backs up into the kitchen, afraid.*)

HAPPY. Hey, what're you doing up? (LINDA *says nothing but moves toward him implacably.*) Where's Pop? (*He keeps backing to the right, and now* LINDA *is in full view in the doorway to the living-room.*) Is he sleeping?

LINDA. Where were you?

HAPPY (*trying to laugh it off*). We met two girls, Mom, very fine types. Here, we brought you some flowers. (*Offering them to her*) Put them in your room, Ma.

(*She knocks them to the floor at* BIFF's *feet. He has now come inside and closed the door behind him. She stares at* BIFF, *silent.*)

HAPPY. Now what'd you do that for? Mom, I want you to have some flowers—

LINDA (*cutting* HAPPY *off, violently to* BIFF). Don't you care whether he lives or dies?

HAPPY (*going to the stairs*). Come upstairs, Biff.

BIFF (*with a flare of disgust, to* HAPPY). Go away from me! (*To* LINDA) What do you mean, lives or dies? Nobody's dying around here, pal.

LINDA. Get out of my sight! Get out of here!

BIFF. I wanna see the boss.

LINDA. You're not going near him!

BIFF. Where is he? (*He moves into the living-room and* LINDA *follows.*)

LINDA (*shouting after* BIFF). You invite him for dinner. He looks forward to it all day—(BIFF *appears in his parents' bedroom, looks around, and exits*)—and then you desert him there. There's no stranger you'd do that to!

HAPPY. Why? He had a swell time with us. Listen, when I—(LINDA *comes back into the kitchen*)—desert him I hope I don't outlive the day!

LINDA. Get out of here!

HAPPY. Now look, Mom . . .

LINDA. Did you have to go to women tonight? You and your lousy rotten whores!

(BIFF *re-enters the kitchen.*)

HAPPY. Mom, all we did was follow Biff around trying to cheer him up! (*To* BIFF) Boy, what a night you gave me!

LINDA. Get out of here, both of you, and don't come back! I don't want you tormenting him any more. Go on now, get your things together! (*To* BIFF) You can sleep in his apartment. (*She starts to pick up the flowers and stops herself.*) Pick up this stuff, I'm not your maid any more. Pick it up, you bum, you!

(HAPPY *turns his back to her in refusal.* BIFF *slowly moves over and gets down on his knees, picking up the flowers.*)

LINDA. You're a pair of animals! Not one, not another living soul would have had the cruelty to walk out on that man in a restaurant!

BIFF (*not looking at her*). Is that what he said?

LINDA. He didn't have to say anything. He was so humiliated he nearly limped when he came in.

HAPPY. But, Mom, he had a great time with us—

BIFF (*cutting him off violently*). Shut up!

(*Without another word,* HAPPY *goes upstairs.*)

LINDA. You! You didn't even go in to see if he was all right!

BIFF (*still on the floor in front of* LINDA, *the flowers in his hand; with self-loathing*). No. Didn't. Didn't do a damned thing. How do you like that, heh? Left him babbling in a toilet.

LINDA. You louse. You . . .

BIFF. Now you hit it on the nose! (*He gets up, throws the flowers in the wastebasket.*) The scum of the earth, and you're looking at him!

LINDA. Get out of here!

BIFF. I gotta talk to the boss, Mom. Where is he?

LINDA. You're not going near him. Get out of this house!

BIFF (*with absolute assurance, determination*). No. We're gonna have an abrupt conversation, him and me.

LINDA. You're not talking to him!

(*Hammering is heard from outside the house, off right.* BIFF *turns toward the noise.*)

LINDA (*suddenly pleading*). Will you please leave him alone?

BIFF. What's he doing out there?

LINDA. He's planting the garden!

BIFF (*quietly*). Now? Oh, my God!

(BIFF *moves outside,* LINDA *following. The light dies down on them and comes up on the center of the apron as* WILLY *walks into it. He is carrying a flashlight, a hoe, and a handful of seed packets. He raps the top of the hoe sharply to fix it firmly, and then moves to the left, measuring off the distance with his foot. He holds the flashlight to look at the seed packets, reading off the instructions. He is in the blue of night.*)

WILLY. Carrots . . . quarter-inch apart. Rows . . . one-foot rows. (*He measures it off.*) One foot. (*He puts down a package and measures off.*) Beets. (*He puts down another package and measures again.*) Lettuce. (*He reads the package, puts it down.*) One foot—(*He breaks off as* BEN *appears at the right and moves slowly down to him.*) What a proposition, ts, ts. Terrific, terrific. 'Cause she's suffered, Ben, the woman has suffered. You understand me? A man can't go out the way he came in. Ben, a man has got to add up to something. You can't, you can't—(BEN *moves toward him as though to interrupt.*) You gotta consider, now. Don't answer so quick. Remember, it's a guaranteed twenty-thousand-dollar proposition. Now look,

Ben, I want you to go through the ins and outs of this thing with me. I've got nobody to talk to, Ben, and the woman has suffered, you hear me?

BEN (*standing still, considering*).   What's the proposition?

WILLY.   It's twenty thousand dollars on the barrelhead. Guaranteed, gilt-edged, you understand?

BEN.   You don't want to make a fool of yourself. They might not honor the policy.

WILLY.   How can they dare refuse? Didn't I work like a coolie to meet every premium on the nose? And now they don't pay off? Impossible!

BEN.   It's called a cowardly thing, William.

WILLY.   Why? Does it take more guts to stand here the rest of my life ringing up a zero?

BEN (*yielding*).   That's a point, William. (*He moves, thinking, turns.*) And twenty thousand—that *is* something one can feel with the hand, it is there.

WILLY (*now assured, with rising power*).   Oh, Ben, that's the whole beauty of it! I see it like a diamond, shining in the dark, hard and rough, that I can pick up and touch in my hand. Not like—like an appointment! This would not be another damned-fool appointment, Ben, and it changes all the aspects. Because he thinks I'm nothing, see, and so he spites me. But the funeral—(*Straightening up*) Ben, that funeral will be massive! They'll come from Maine, Massachusetts, Vermont, New Hampshire! All the old-timers with the strange license plates—that boy will be thunder-struck, Ben, because he never realized—I am known! Rhode Island, New York, New Jersey—I am known, Ben, and he'll see it with his eyes once and for all. He'll see what I am, Ben! He's in for a shock, that boy!

BEN (*coming down to the edge of the garden*).   He'll call you a coward.

WILLY (*suddenly fearful*).   No, that would be terrible.

BEN.   Yes. And a damned fool.

WILLY.   No, no, he mustn't, I won't have that! (*He is broken and desperate.*)

BEN.   He'll hate you, William.

(*The gay music of the boys is heard.*)

WILLY.   Oh, Ben, how do we get back to all the great times? Used to be so full of light, and comradeship, the sleigh-riding in winter and the ruddiness on his cheeks. And always some kind of good news coming up, always something nice coming up ahead. And never even let me carry the valises in the house, and simonizing, simonizing that little red car! Why, why can't I give him something and not have him hate me?

BEN.   Let me think about it. (*He glances at his watch.*) I still have a little time. Remarkable proposition, but you've got to be sure you're not making a fool of yourself.

(BEN *drifts off upstage and goes out of sight.* BIFF *comes down from the left.*)

WILLY (*suddenly conscious of* BIFF, *turns and looks up at him, then begins picking up the packages of seeds in confusion*).   Where the hell is that seed? (*Indignantly*) You can't see nothing out here! They boxed in the whole goddam neighborhood!

BIFF.   There are people all around here. Don't you realize that?

WILLY.   I'm busy. Don't bother me.

BIFF (*taking the hoe from* WILLY).   I'm saying good-by to you, Pop. (WILLY *looks at him, silent, unable to move.*) I'm not coming back any more.

WILLY.   You're not going to see Oliver tomorrow?

BIFF.   I've got no appointment, Dad.

WILLY.   He put his arms around you, and you've got no appointment?

BIFF.   Pop, get this now, will you? Every time I've left it's been a fight that sent me out of here. Today I realized something about myself and I tried to explain it to you and I—I think I'm just not smart enough to make any sense out of it for you. To hell with whose fault it is or anything like that. (*He takes* WILLY'S *arm.*) Let's just wrap it up, heh? Come on in, we'll tell Mom. (*He gently tries to pull* WILLY *to left.*)

WILLY (*frozen, immobile, with guilt in his voice*).   No, I don't want to see her.

BIFF.   Come on!

(*He pulls again, and* WILLY *tries to pull away.*)

WILLY (*highly nervous*).   No, no, I don't want to see her.

BIFF (*tries to look into* WILLY'S *face, as if to find the answer there.*) Why don't you want to see her?

WILLY (*more harshly now*).   Don't bother me, will you?

BIFF.   What do you mean, you don't want to see her? You don't want them calling you yellow do you? This isn't your fault; it's me, I'm a bum. Now come inside! (WILLY *strains to get away.*) Did you hear what I said to you?

(WILLY *pulls away and quickly goes by himself into the house.* BIFF *follows.*)

LINDA (*to* WILLY).   Did you plant, dear?

BIFF (*at the door, to* LINDA).   All right, we had it out. I'm going and I'm not writing any more.

LINDA (*going to* WILLY *in the kitchen*).   I think that's the best way, dear. 'Cause there's no use drawing it out, you'll just never get along.

(WILLY *doesn't respond.*)

BIFF.   People ask where I am and what I'm doing, you don't know, and you don't care. That way it'll be off your mind and you can start brightening up again. All right? That clears it, doesn't it? (WILLY *is silent, and* BIFF *goes to him.*) You gonna wish me luck, scout? (*He extends his hand.*) What do you say?

LINDA. Shake his hand, Willy.

WILLY (*turning to her, seething with hurt*). There's no necessity to mention the pen at all, y'know.

BIFF (*gently*). I've got no appointment, Dad.

WILLY (*erupting fiercely*). He put his arm around . . . ?

BIFF. Dad, you're never going to see what I am, so what's the use of arguing? If I strike oil I'll send you a check. Meantime forget I'm alive.

WILLY (*to* LINDA). Spite, see?

BIFF. Shake hands, Dad.

WILLY. Not my hand.

BIFF. I was hoping not to go this way.

WILLY. Well, this is the way you're going. Good-by.

(BIFF *looks at him a moment, then turns sharply and goes to the stairs.*)

WILLY (*stops him with:*) May you rot in hell if you leave this house!

BIFF (*turning*). Exactly what is it that you want from me?

WILLY. I want you to know, on the train, in the mountains, in the valleys, wherever you go, that you cut down your life for spite!

BIFF. No, no.

WILLY. Spite, spite, is the word of your undoing! And when you're down and out, remember what did it. When you're rotting somewhere beside the railroad tracks, remember, and don't you dare blame it on me!

BIFF. I'm not blaming it on you!

WILLY. I won't take the rap for this, you hear?

(HAPPY *comes down the stairs and stands on the bottom step, watching.*)

BIFF. That's just what I'm telling you!

WILLY (*sinking into a chair at the table, with full accusation*). You're trying to put a knife in me—don't think I don't know what you're doing!

BIFF. All right, phony! Then let's lay it on the line. (*He whips the rubber tube out of his pocket and puts it on the table.*)

HAPPY. You crazy—

LINDA. Biff! (*She moves to grab the hose, but* BIFF *holds it down with his hand.*)

BIFF. Leave it there! Don't move it!

WILLY (*not looking at it*). What is that?

BIFF. You know goddam well what that is.

WILLY (*caged, wanting to escape*). I never saw that.

BIFF. You saw it. The mice didn't bring it into the cellar! What is this supposed to do, make a hero out of you? This supposed to make me sorry for you?

WILLY.   Never heard of it.

BIFF.   There'll be no pity for you, you hear it? No pity!

WILLY (*to* LINDA).   You hear the spite!

BIFF.   No, you're going to hear the truth—what you are and what I am!

LINDA.   Stop it!

WILLY.   Spite!

HAPPY (*coming down toward* BIFF).   You cut it now!

BIFF (*to* HAPPY).   The man don't know who we are! The man is gonna know! (*To* WILLY) We never told the truth for ten minutes in this house!

HAPPY.   We always told the truth!

BIFF (*turning on him*).   You big blow, are you the assistant buyer? You're one of the two assistants to the assistant, aren't you?

HAPPY.   Well, I'm practically—

BIFF.   You're practically full of it! We all are! And I'm through with it. (*To* WILLY) Now hear this, Willy, this is me.

WILLY.   I know you!

BIFF.   You know why I had no address for three months? I stole a suit in Kansas City and I was in jail. (*To* LINDA, *who is sobbing*) Stop crying. I'm through with it.

(LINDA *turns away from them, her hands covering her face.*)

WILLY.   I suppose that's my fault!

BIFF.   I stole myself out of every good job since high school!

WILLY.   And whose fault is that?

BIFF.   And I never got anywhere because you blew me so full of hot air I could never stand taking orders from anybody! That's whose fault it is!

WILLY.   I hear that!

LINDA.   Don't, Biff!

BIFF.   It's goddam time you heard that! I had to be boss big shot in two weeks, and I'm through with it!

WILLY.   Then hang yourself! For spite, hang yourself!

BIFF.   No! Nobody's hanging himself, Willy! I ran down eleven flights with a pen in my hand today. And suddenly I stopped, you hear me? And in the middle of that office building, do you hear this? I stopped in the middle of that building and I saw—the sky. I saw the things that I love in this world. The work and the food and time to sit and smoke. And I looked at the pen and said to myself, what the hell am I grabbing this for? Why am I trying to become what I don't want to be? What am I doing in an office, making a contemptuous, begging fool of myself, when all I want is out there, waiting for me the minute I say I know who I am! Why can't I say that, Willy?

(*He tries to make* WILLY *face him, but* WILLY *pulls away and moves to the left.*)

WILLY (*with hatred, threateningly*). The door of your life is wide open!

BIFF. Pop! I'm a dime a dozen, and so are you!

WILLY (*turning on him now in an uncontrolled outburst*). I am not a dime a dozen! I am Willy Loman, and you are Biff Loman!

(BIFF *starts for* WILLY, *but is blocked by* HAPPY. *In his fury*, BIFF *seems on the verge of attacking his father.*)

BIFF. I am not a leader of men, Willy, and neither are you. You were never anything but a hard-working drummer who landed in the ash can like all the rest of them! I'm one dollar an hour, Willy! I tried seven states and couldn't raise it. A buck an hour! Do you gather my meaning? I'm not bringing home any prizes any more, and you're going to stop waiting for me to bring them home!

WILLY (*directly to* BIFF). You vengeful, spiteful mutt!

(BIFF *breaks from* HAPPY. WILLY, *in fright, starts up the stairs.* BIFF *grabs him.*)

BIFF (*at the peak of his fury*). Pop, I'm nothing! I'm nothing, Pop. Can't you understand that? There's no spite in it any more. I'm just what I am, that's all.

(BIFF's *fury has spent itself, and he breaks down, sobbing, holding on to* WILLY, *who dumbly fumbles for* BIFF's *face.*)

WILLY (*astonished*). What're you doing? What're you doing? (*To* LINDA) Why is he crying?

BIFF (*crying, broken*). Will you let me go, for Christ's sake? Will you take that phony dream and burn it before something happens? (*Struggling to contain himself, he pulls away and moves to the stairs.*) I'll go in the morning. Put him—put him to bed. (*Exhausted*, BIFF *moves up the stairs to his room.*)

WILLY (*after a long pause, astonished, elevated*). Isn't that—isn't that remarkable? Biff—he likes me!

LINDA. He loves you, Willy!

HAPPY (*deeply moved*). Always did, Pop.

WILLY. Oh, Biff! (*Staring wildly*) He cried! Cried to me. (*He is choking with his love, and now cries out his promise.*) That boy—that boy is going to be magnificent!

(BEN *appears in the light just outside the kitchen.*)

BEN. Yes, outstanding, with twenty thousand behind him.

LINDA (*sensing the racing of his mind, fearfully, carefully*). Now come to bed, Willy. It's all settled now.

WILLY (*finding it difficult not to rush out of the house*). Yes, we'll sleep. Come on. Go to sleep, Hap.

BEN. And it does take a great kind of a man to crack the jungle.

(*In accents of dread,* BEN's *idyllic music starts up.*)

HAPPY (*his arm around* LINDA). I'm getting married, Pop, don't forget it. I'm changing everything. I'm gonna run that department before the year is up. You'll see, Mom. (*He kisses her.*)

BEN. The jungle is dark but full of diamonds, Willy.

(WILLY *turns, moves, listening to* BEN.)

LINDA. Be good. You're both good boys, just act that way, that's all.

HAPPY. 'Night, Pop. (*He goes upstairs.*)

LINDA (*to* WILLY). Come, dear.

BEN (*with greater force*). One must go in to fetch a diamond out.

WILLY (*to* LINDA, *as he moves slowly along the edge of the kitchen, toward the door*). I just want to get settled down, Linda. Let me sit alone for a little.

LINDA (*almost uttering her fear*). I want you upstairs.

WILLY (*taking her in his arms*). In a few minutes, Linda. I couldn't sleep right now. Go on, you look awful tired. (*He kisses her.*)

BEN. Not like an appointment at all. A diamond is rough and hard to the touch.

WILLY. Go on now. I'll be right up.

LINDA. I think this is the only way, Willy.

WILLY. Sure, it's the best thing.

BEN. Best thing!

WILLY. The only way. Everything is gonna be—go on, kid, get to bed. You look so tired.

LINDA. Come right up.

WILLY. Two minutes.

(LINDA *goes into the living-room, then reappears in her bedroom.* WILLY *moves just outside the kitchen door.*)

WILLY. Loves me. (*Wonderingly*) Always loved me. Isn't that a remarkable thing? Ben, he'll worship me for it!

BEN (*with promise*). It's dark there, but full of diamonds.

WILLY. Can you imagine that magnificence with twenty thousand dollars in his pocket?

LINDA (*calling from her room*). Willy! Come up!

WILLY (*calling into the kitchen*). Yes! Yes. Coming! It's very smart, you realize that, don't you, sweetheart? Even Ben sees it. I gotta go, baby. 'By! 'By! (*Going over to* BEN, *almost dancing*) Imagine? When the mail comes he'll be ahead of Bernard again!

BEN. A perfect proposition all around.

WILLY. Did you see how he cried to me? Oh, if I could kiss him, Ben!

BEN. Time, William, time!

WILLY. Oh, Ben, I always knew one way or another we were gonna make it, Biff and I!

BEN (*looking at his watch*). The boat. We'll be late. (*He moves slowly off into the darkness.*)

WILLY (*elegiacally, turning to the house*). Now when you kick off, boy, I want a seventy-yard boot, and get right down the field under the ball, and when you hit, hit low and hit hard, because it's important, boy. (*He swings around and faces the audience.*) There's all kinds of important people in the stands, and the first thing you know . . . (*Suddenly realizing he is alone*) Ben! Ben, where do I . . . ? (*He makes a sudden movement of search.*) Ben, how do I . . . ?

LINDA (*calling*). Willy, you coming up?

WILLY (*uttering a gasp of fear, whirling about as if to quiet her*). Sh! (*He turns around as if to find his way; sounds, faces, voices, seem to be swarming in upon him and he flicks at them, crying*) Sh! Sh! (*Suddenly music, faint and high, stops him. It rises in intensity, almost to an unbearable scream. He goes up and down on his toes, and rushes off around the house.*) Shhh!

LINDA. Willy?

(*There is no answer. LINDA waits. BIFF gets up off his bed. He is still in his clothes. HAPPY sits up. BIFF stands listening.*)

LINDA (*with real fear*). Willy, answer me! Willy!

(*There is the sound of a car starting and moving away at full speed.*)

LINDA. No!

BIFF (*rushing down the stairs*). Pop!

(*As the car speeds off, the music crashes down in a frenzy of sound, which becomes the soft pulsation of a single cello string. BIFF slowly returns to his bedroom. He and HAPPY gravely don their jackets. LINDA slowly walks out of her room. The music has developed into a dead march. The leaves of day are appearing over everything. CHARLEY and BERNARD, somberly dressed, appear and knock on the kitchen door. BIFF and HAPPY slowly descend the stairs to the kitchen as CHARLEY and BERNARD enter. All stop a moment when LINDA, in clothes of mourning, bearing a little bunch of roses, comes through the draped doorway into the kitchen. She goes to CHARLEY and takes his arm. Now all move toward the audience, through the wall-line of the kitchen. At the limit of the apron, LINDA lays down the flowers, kneels, and sits back on her heels. All stare down at the grave.*)

REQUIEM

CHARLEY. It's getting dark, Linda.

(*LINDA doesn't react. She stares at the grave.*)

BIFF. How about it, Mom? Better get some rest, heh? They'll be closing the gate soon.

(LINDA *makes no move. Pause.*)

HAPPY (*deeply angered*).   He had no right to do that. There was no necessity for it. We would've helped him.

CHARLEY (*grunting*).   Hmmm.

BIFF.   Come along, Mom.

LINDA.   Why didn't anybody come?

CHARLEY.   It was a very nice funeral.

LINDA.   But where are all the people he knew? Maybe they blame him.

CHARLEY.   Naa. It's a rough world, Linda. They wouldn't blame him.

LINDA.   I can't understand it. At this time especially. First time in thirty-five years we were just about free and clear. He only needed a little salary. He was even finished with the dentist.

CHARLEY.   No man only needs a little salary.

LINDA.   I can't understand it.

BIFF.   There were a lot of nice days. When he'd come home from a trip; or on Sundays, making the stoop; finishing the cellar; putting on the new porch; when he built the extra bathroom; and put up the garage. You know something, Charley, there's more of him in that front stoop than in all the sales he ever made.

CHARLEY.   Yeah. He was a happy man with a batch of cement.

LINDA.   He was so wonderful with his hands.

BIFF.   He had the wrong dreams. All, all, wrong.

HAPPY (*almost ready to fight* BIFF).   Don't say that!

BIFF.   He never knew who he was.

CHARLEY (*stopping* HAPPY'S *movement and reply. To* BIFF).   Nobody dast blame this man. You don't understand: Willy was a salesman. And for a salesman, there is no rock bottom to the life. He don't put a bolt to a nut, he don't tell you the law or give you medicine. He's a man way out there in the blue, riding on a smile and a shoestring. And when they start not smiling back—that's an earthquake. And then you get yourself a couple of spots on your hat, and you're finished. Nobody dast blame this man. A salesman is got to dream, boy. It comes with the territory.

BIFF.   Charley, the man didn't know who he was.

HAPPY (*infuriated*).   Don't say that!

BIFF.   Why don't you come with me, Happy?

HAPPY.   I'm not licked that easily. I'm staying right in this city, and I'm gonna beat this racket! (He looks at BIFF, *his chin set.*) The Loman Brothers!

BIFF.   I know who I am, kid.

HAPPY.   All right, boy. I'm gonna show you and everybody else that Willy Loman did not die in vain. He had a good dream. It's the only dream you can have—to come out number-one man. He fought it out here, and this is where I'm gonna win it for him.

BIFF (*with a hopeless glance at* HAPPY, *bends toward his mother*). Let's go, Mom.

LINDA. I'll be with you in a minute. Go on, Charley. (*He hesitates.*) I want to, just for a minute. I never had a chance to say good-by.

(CHARLEY *moves away, followed by* HAPPY. BIFF *remains a slight distance up and left of* LINDA. *She sits there, summoning herself. The flute begins, not far away, playing behind her speech.*)

LINDA. Forgive me, dear. I can't cry. I don't know what it is, but I can't cry. I don't understand it. Why did you ever do that? Help me, Willy, I can't cry. It seems to me that you're just on another trip. I keep expecting you. Willy, dear, I can't cry. Why did you do it? I search and search and I search, and I can't understand it, Willy. I made the last payment on the house today. Today, dear. And there'll be nobody home. (*A sob rises in her throat.*) We're free and clear. (*Sobbing more fully, released*) We're free. (BIFF *comes slowly toward her.*) We're free . . . We're free . . .

(BIFF *lifts her to her feet and moves out up right with her in his arms.* LINDA *sobs quietly.* BERNARD *and* CHARLEY *come together and follow them, followed by* HAPPY. *Only the music of the flute is left on the darkening stage as over the house the hard towers of the apartment buildings rise into sharp focus, and the curtain falls.*)

Appendix

THE SOURCE OF *OTHELLO*

The "Tale of the Moor of Venice" was the seventh novella in the third decade of the Hecatommithi *(Hundred Tales) by Gianbattista Giraldi Cinthio, Venice, 1565. It is possible that Shakespeare read the story in an English version that has not survived.*

There once lived in Venice a Moor, who was very valiant, and of a handsome person; and having given proofs in war of great skill and prudence, he was highly esteemed by the Signoria of the Republic, who in rewarding deeds of valour advanced the interests of the State.

It happened that a virtuous lady, of marvellous beauty, named Disdemona, fell in love with the Moor, moved thereto by his valour; and he, vanquished by the beauty and the noble character of Disdemona, returned her love; and their affection was so mutual, that, although the parents of the lady strove all they could to induce her to take another husband, she consented to marry the Moor; and they lived in such harmony and peace in Venice, that no word ever passed between them that was not affectionate and kind.

Now it happened at this time that the Signoria of Venice made a change in the troops whom they used to maintain in Cyprus, and they appointed the Moor commander of the soldiers whom they despatched thither. Joyful as was the Moor at the honour proffered him—such dignity being only conferred on men of noble rank and well-tried faith, and who had displayed bravery in arms—yet his pleasure was lessened when he reflected on the length and dangers of the voyage, fearing that Disdemona would be pained at his absence. But Disdemona, who had no other happiness in the world than the Moor, and who rejoiced to witness the testimony of his valour her husband had received from so powerful and noble a Republic, was all impatient that he should embark with his troops, and longed to accompany him to so honourable a post. And all the more it vexed her to see the Moor so troubled; and not knowing what could be the reason, one day, when they were at dinner, she said to him, "How is it, O Moor, that when so honourable a post has been conferred on you by the Signoria, you are thus melancholy?"

The Moor answered Disdemona, "My pleasure at the honour I have

THE SOURCE OF OTHELLO From *The Moor of Venice: Cinthio's Tale and Shakespere's Tragedy* by John Edward Taylor (London: Chapman and Hall, 1855).

received is disturbed by the love I bear you; for I see that of necessity one of two things must happen; either that I take you with me, to encounter the perils of the sea, or, to save you from this danger, I must leave you here in Venice. The first could not be otherwise than serious to me, for all the toil you would have to bear, and every danger that might befall you, would cause me extreme anxiety and pain. Yet, were I to leave you behind me, I should be hateful to myself, since in parting from you I should part from my own life."

Disdemona, on hearing this, replied, "My husband, what thoughts are these that wander through your mind? Why let such things disturb you? I will accompany you whithersoe'er you go, were it to pass through fire, as now to cross the water in a safe and well-provided ship: if indeed there are toils and perils to encounter, I will share them with you. And in truth I should think you loved me little, were you to leave me here in Venice, denying me to bear you company, or could believe that I would liefer bide in safety here, than share the dangers that await you. Prepare then for the voyage, with all the readiness which the dignity of the post you hold deserves."

The Moor, in the fulness of his joy, threw his arms around his wife's neck, and with an affectionate and tender kiss exclaimed, "God keep you long in such love, dear wife!" Then speedily donning his armour, and having prepared everything for his expedition, he embarked on board the galley, with his wife and all his troops; and setting sail, they pursued their voyage, and with a perfectly tranquil sea arrived safely at Cyprus.

Now amongst the soldiery there was an Ensign, a man of handsome figure, but of the most depraved nature in the world. This man was in great favour with the Moor, who had not the slightest idea of his wickedness; for despite the malice lurking in his heart, he cloaked with proud and valourous speech, and with a specious presence, the villainy of his soul, with such art, that he was to all outward show another Hector or Achilles. This man had likewise taken with him his wife to Cyprus, a young, and fair, and virtuous lady; and being of Italian birth, she was much loved by Disdemona, who spent the greater part of every day with her.

In the same Company there was a certain Captain of a troop, to whom the Moor was much affectioned. And Disdemona, for this cause, knowing how much her husband valued him, showed him proofs of the greatest kindness, which was all very grateful to the Moor. Now the wicked Ensign, regardless of the faith that he had pledged his wife, no less than of the friendship, fidelity, and obligation which he owed the Moor, fell passionately in love with Disdemona, and bent all his thoughts to achieve his conquest; yet he dared not to declare his passion openly, fearing that, should the Moor perceive it, he would at once kill him. He therefore sought in various ways, and with secret guile, to betray his passion to the lady. But she, whose every wish was centred in the Moor, had no thought for this Ensign more than for any other man; and all the means he tried to gain her love, had no more effect than if he had not tried them. But the Ensign imagined that the cause of his ill success was that Disdemona loved the Captain of the troop; and he pondered how to remove him from her sight. The love which he had borne the lady now changed into the bitterest hate; and, having failed in his purposes, he devoted all his thoughts to plot the death of the Captain of the troop, and to divert the affection of the Moor from Disdemona. After revolving in his mind various schemes, all alike wicked, he at length resolved to accuse her of unfaithfulness to her husband, and to represent the Captain as her paramour. But knowing the singular love the Moor bore to Disdemona, and the friendship which he had for the Captain, he was well aware that, unless he practised an artful fraud upon the Moor, it were impossible to make him give ear to either accusation: wherefore he resolved to wait, until time and circumstance should open a path for him to engage in his foul project.

Not long afterwards, it happened that the Captain, having drawn his sword upon a soldier of the guard, and struck him, the Moor deprived him of his rank; whereat Disdemona was deeply grieved, and endeavoured again and again to reconcile her husband to the man. This the Moor told to the wicked Ensign, and how his wife importuned him so much about the Captain, that he feared he should be forced at last to receive him back to service. Upon this hint the Ensign resolved to act, and began to work his web of intrigue; "Perchance," said he, "the lady Disdemona may have good reason to look kindly on him."

"And wherefore?" said the Moor.

"Nay, I would not step 'twixt man and wife," replied the Ensign; "but let your eyes be witness to themselves."

In vain the Moor went on to question the officer—he would proceed no further; nevertheless his words left a sharp stinging thorn in the Moor's heart, who could think of nothing else, trying to guess their meaning, and lost in melancholy. And one day, when his wife had been endeavouring to pacify his anger toward the Captain, and praying him not to be unmindful of ancient services and friendship, for one small fault, especially since peace had been made between the Captain and the soldier he had struck, the Moor was angered, and exclaimed, "Great cause have you, Disdemona, to care so anxiously about this man! Is he a brother, or your kinsman, that he should be so near your heart?"

The lady, with all gentleness and humility, replied, "Be not angered, my dear lord; I have no other cause to bid me speak, than sorrow that I see you lose so dear a friend as, by your own words, this Captain has been to you: nor has he done so grave a fault, that you should bear him so much enmity. Nay, but you Moors are of so hot a nature, that every little trifle moves you to anger and revenge."

Still more enraged at these words, the Moor replied, "I could bring proofs —by heaven it mocks belief! but for the wrongs I have endured, revenge must satisfy my wrath."

Disdemona, in astonishment and fright, seeing her husband's anger kindled against her, so contrary to his wont, said humbly and with timidness, "None save a good intent has led me thus to speak with you, my lord; but to give cause no longer for offence, I'll never speak a word more on the subject."

The Moor, observing the earnestness with which his wife again pleaded for the Captain, began to guess the meaning of the Ensign's words; and in deep melancholy he went to seek that villain, and induce him to speak more openly of what he knew. Then the Ensign, who was bent upon injuring the unhappy lady, after feigning at first great reluctance to say aught that might displease the Moor, at length pretended to yield to his entreaties, and said, "I can't deny, it pains me to the soul to be thus forced to say what needs must be more hard to hear than any other grief; but since you will it so, and that the regard I owe your honour compels me to confess the truth, I will no longer refuse to satisfy your questions and my duty. Know then, that for no other reason is your lady vext to see the Captain in disfavour, than for the pleasure that she has in his company whenever he comes to your house, and all the more since she has taken an aversion to your blackness."

These words went straight to the Moor's heart; but in order to hear more (now that he believed true all that the Ensign had told him), he replied, with a fierce glance, "By heavens, I scarce can hold this hand from plucking out that tongue of thine, so bold, which dares to speak such slander of my wife!"

"Captain," replied the Ensign, "I looked for such reward, for these my faithful offices—none else; but since my duty, and the jealous care I bear your honour, have carried me thus far, I do repeat, so stands the truth, as you have heard it from these lips: and if the lady Disdemona hath, with a false show of love for you, blinded your eyes to what you should have seen, this is no argument but that I speak the truth. Nay, this same Captain told it me himself, like one whose happiness is incomplete until he can declare it to another: and, but that I feared your anger, I should have given him, when he told it me, his merited reward, and slain him. But since informing you, of what concerns more you than any other man, brings me so undeserved a recompense, would I had held my peace, since silence might have spared me your displeasure."

Then the Moor, burning with indignation and anguish, said, "Make thou these eyes self-witnesses of what thou tell'st, or on thy life I'll make thee wish thou hadst been born without a tongue."

"An easy task it would have been," replied the villain, "when he was used to visit at your house; but now, that you have banished him, not for just cause, but for more frivolous pretext, it will be hard to prove the truth. Still I do not forgo the hope, to make you witness of that which you will not credit from my lips."

Thus they parted. The wretched Moor, struck to the heart as by a barbed dart, returned to his home, and awaited the day when the Ensign should disclose to him the truth which was to make him miserable to the end of his days. But the evil-minded Ensign was, on his part, not less troubled by the chastity which he knew the lady Disdemona observed inviolate; and it seemed to him impossible to discover a means of making the Moor believe what he had falsely told him; and turning the matter over in his thoughts, in various ways, the villain resolved on a new deed of guilt.

Disdemona often used to go, as I have already said, to visit the Ensign's wife, and remained with her a good part of the day. Now the Ensign observed, that she carried about with her a handkerchief, which he knew the Moor had given her, finely embroidered in the Moorish fashion, and which was precious to Disdemona, nor less so to the Moor. Then he conceived the plan, of taking this kerchief from her secretly, and thus laying the snare for her final ruin. The Ensign had a little daughter, a child three years of age who was much loved by Disdemona; and one day, when the unhappy lady had gone to pay a visit at the house of this vile man, he took the little child up in his arms, and carried her to Disdemona, who took her, and pressed her to her bosom; whilst at the same instant this traitor, who had extreme dexterity of hand, drew the kerchief from her sash so cunningly, that she did not notice him, and overjoyed he took his leave of her.

Disdemona, ignorant of what had happened, returned home, and, busied with other thoughts, forgot the handkerchief. But a few days afterwards looking for it, and not finding it, she was in alarm, lest the Moor should ask her for it, as he oft was wont to do. Meanwhile the wicked Ensign, seizing a fit opportunity, went to the Captain of the troop, and with crafty malice left the handkerchief at the head of his bed, without his discovering the trick; until the following morning, when, on his getting out of bed, the handkerchief fell upon the floor, and he set his foot upon it. And not being able to imagine how it had come into his house, knowing that it belonged to Disdemona, he resolved to give it her; and waiting until the Moor had gone from home, he went to the back door, and knocked. It seemed as if fate conspired with the Ensign to work the death of the unhappy Disdemona. Just at that time the Moor returned home, and hearing a knocking at the back door, he went to the window, and in a rage exclaimed, "Who knocks there?" The Captain, hearing the Moor's voice, and fearing lest he should come downstairs and attack him, took to flight without answering a word. The Moor went down, and opening the door, hastened into the street, and looked about, but in vain. Then returning into the house, in great anger, he demanded of his wife who it was that had knocked at the door. Disdemona replied, as was true, that she did not know: but the Moor said, "It seemed to me the Captain."

"I know not," answered Disdemona, "whether it was he, or another person."

The Moor restrained his fury, great as it was, wishing to do nothing before consulting the Ensign, to whom he hastened instantly, and told him all that had passed, praying him to gather from the Captain all he could respecting the affair. The Ensign, overjoyed at the occurrence, promised the Moor to do as he requested; and one day he took occasion to speak with the Captain, when the Moor was so placed that he could see and hear them as they conversed. And whilst talking to him of every other subject than of Disdemona, he kept laughing all the time aloud; and feigning astonishment, he made various movements with his head and hands, as if listening to some tale of marvel. As soon as the Moor saw the Captain depart, he went up to the Ensign, to hear what he had said to him. And the Ensign, after long entreaty, at length said, "He has hidden from me nothing, and has told me that he has been used to visit your wife whenever you went from home, and that on the last occasion she gave him this handkerchief, which you presented to her when you married her."

The Moor thanked the Ensign, and it seemed now clear to him that, should he find Disdemona not to have the handkerchief, it was all true that the Ensign had told to him. One day, therefore, after dinner, in conversation with his wife on various subjects, he asked her for the kerchief. The unhappy lady, who had been in great fear of this, grew red as fire at this demand; and to hide the scarlet of her cheeks, which was closely noted by the Moor, she ran to a chest, and pretended to seek the handkerchief: and after hunting for it a long time, she said, "I know not how it is—I cannot find it—can you perchance have taken it?"

"If I had taken it," said the Moor, "why should I ask it of you? but you will look better another time."

On leaving the room, the Moor fell to meditating how he should put his wife to death, and likewise the Captain of the troop, so that their death should not be laid to his charge. And as he ruminated over this day and night, he could not prevent his wife's observing that he was not the same toward her as he had been wont; and she said to him again and again, "What is the matter? what troubles you? how comes it that you, who were the most light-hearted man in the world, are now so melancholy?"

The Moor feigned various reasons in reply to his wife's questioning, but she was not satisfied; and, although conscious that she had given the Moor no cause, by act or deed, to be so troubled, yet she feared that he might have grown wearied of her; and she would say to the Ensign's wife, "I know not what to say of the Moor; he used to be all love toward me; but within these few days he has become another man; and much I fear, that I shall prove a warning to young girls not to marry against the wishes of their parents, and that the Italian ladies may learn from me not to wed a man whom nature and habitude of life estrange from us. But as I know the Moor is on such terms of friendship with your husband, and communicates to him all his affairs, I pray you, if you have heard from him aught that you may tell me of, fail not to befriend me." And as she said this, she wept bitterly.

The Ensign's wife, who knew the whole truth (her husband wishing to make use of her to compass the death of Disdemona), but could never consent to such a project, dared not, from fear of her husband, disclose a single circumstance: all she said was, "Beware lest you give any cause of suspicion to your husband, and show to him by every means your fidelity and love."

"Indeed I do so," replied Disdemona; "but it is all of no avail."

Meanwhile the Moor sought in every way to convince himself of what he fain would have found untrue; and he prayed the Ensign to contrive that he might see the handkerchief in the possession of the Captain. This was a difficult matter to the wicked Ensign, nevertheless he promised to use every means to satisfy the Moor of the truth of what he said.

Now the Captain had a wife at home, who worked the most marvellous embroidery upon lawn; and seeing the handkerchief which belonged to the Moor's wife, she resolved, before it was returned to her, to work one like it. As she was engaged in this task, the Ensign observed her standing at a window, where she could be seen by all passers-by in the street; and he pointed her out to the Moor, who was now perfectly convinced of his wife's guilt. Then he arranged with the Ensign to slay Disdemona, and the Captain of the troop, treating them as it seemed they both deserved. And the Moor prayed the Ensign that he would kill the Captain, promising eternal gratitude to him. But the Ensign at first refused to undertake so dangerous a task, the Captain being a man of equal skill and courage; until at length, after much entreating, and being richly paid, the Moor prevailed on him to promise to attempt the deed.

Having formed this resolution, the Ensign, going out one dark night, sword in hand, met the Captain, on his way to visit a courtesan, and struck him a blow on his right thigh, which cut off his leg, and felled him to the earth. Then the Ensign was on the point of putting an end to his life, when the Captain, who was a courageous man, and used to the sight of blood and death, drew his sword, and, wounded as he was, kept on his defence, exclaiming with a loud voice, "I'm murdered!" Thereupon the Ensign, hearing the people come running up, with some of the soldiers who were lodged thereabouts, took to his heels, to escape being caught; then turning about again, he joined the crowd, pretending to have been attracted by the noise. And when he saw the Captain's leg cut off, he judged that, if not already dead, the blow must at all events end his life; and whilst in his heart he was rejoiced at this, he yet feigned to compassionate the Captain as he had been his brother.

The next morning the tidings of this affair spread through the whole city, and reached the ears of Disdemona; whereat she, who was kind-hearted and little dreamed that any ill would betide her, evinced the greatest grief at the calamity. This served but to confirm the Moor's suspicions, and he went to seek for the Ensign, and said to him, "Do you know, that ass my wife is in such grief at the Captain's accident, that she is well-nigh gone mad."

"And what could you expect, seeing he is her very soul?" replied the Ensign.

"Ay, soul forsooth!" exclaimed the Moor; "I'll draw the soul from out her body: call me no man, if that I fail to shut the world upon this wretch."

Then they consulted of one means and another—poison and daggers— to kill poor Disdemona, but could resolve on nothing. At length the Ensign said, "A plan comes to my mind, which will give you satisfaction, and raise cause for no suspicion—it is this: the house in which you live is very old, and the ceiling of your chamber has many cracks; I propose we take a stocking, filled with sand, and beat Disdemona with it till she dies; thus will her body bear no signs of violence. When she is dead, we can pull down a portion of the ceiling, and thus make it seem as if a rafter falling on her head had killed the lady. Suspicion can not rest on you, since all men will impute her death to accident."

This cruel counsel pleased the Moor, and he only waited for a fitting time to execute the plot. One night, when he and Disdemona had retired to bed, the Ensign, whom the Moor had concealed in a closet which opened into the chamber, raised a noise in the closet, according to a concerted plan; whereat the Moor said to his wife, "Did you not hear that noise?"

"Indeed I heard it," she replied.

"Rise," said the Moor, "and see what 'tis."

The unhappy Disdemona rose from bed, and the instant she approached the closet, out rushed the Ensign, and being strong and of stout nerve, he beat her cruelly with the bag of sand across her back; upon which Disdemona fell to the ground, scarce able to draw her breath: but with the little voice she had left, she called upon the Moor for aid. But the Moor, leaping from bed, exclaimed, "Thou wickedest of women, thus has thy falseness found its just reward—the recompense to wives, who counterfeiting love, place horns upon their husbands' brows."

The wretched lady, hearing these words, and feeling that she was near her end (for the Ensign had given her another blow), appealed to the justice of Heaven, since justice here had failed her, in proof of her fidelity and truth; and as she was thus calling Heaven to witness, the wicked Ensign inflicted a third blow, under which she sank lifeless on the floor.

Then the Ensign and the Moor, laying Disdemona on the bed, and wounding her head, pulled down part of the ceiling of the chamber, as they had arranged; whereupon the Moor began to call aloud for help, exclaiming that the house was falling. Hearing this uproar, the neighbors all came running up, and there found Disdemona lying dead beneath a rafter—a sight which, from the good life of that poor lady, did fill all hearts with sorrow.

On the following day Disdemona was buried, followed to the grave by the universal grief of the people. But Heaven, the just regarder of all hearts, willed not that so wicked a deed should go unpunished. Ere long the Moor, whom Disdemona had loved more than her own life, began to feel such sorrow at her loss, that he went wandering about, as one bereft of reason, searching in every part of the house. And reflecting in his thoughts that the Ensign had been the cause that he had lost, with Disdemona, all joy in life, he conceived so deep a hatred to that wicked man, he could not bear to set eyes on him; and had it not been for his fear of the inviolable justice of the Signoria of Venice, he would have slain him openly. But being unable to do this with safety, he deprived him of his rank, and would not allow him to remain in his Company; whereat such an enmity arose between the two, that no greater or more deadly can be imagined.

The Ensign, that wickedest of all bad men, now turned his thoughts to injuring the Moor; and seeking out the Captain, whose wound was by this time healed, and who went about with a wooden leg, in place of the one that had been cut off, he said to him, " 'Tis time you should be avenged for your lost limb; and if you will come with me to Venice, I'll tell you who the malefactor is, whom I dare not mention to you here, for many reasons, and I will bring you proofs."

The Captain of the troop, whose anger returned fiercely, but without knowing why, thanked the Ensign, and went with him to Venice. On arriving there, the Ensign told him that it was the Moor who had cut off his leg, on account of the suspicion he had formed of Disdemona's conduct with him; and for that reason he had slain her, and then spread the report that the ceiling had fallen and killed her. Upon hearing which, the Captain accused the Moor to the Signoria, both of having cut off his leg and killed his wife, and called the Ensign to witness the truth of what he said. The Ensign declared both charges to be true, for that the Moor had disclosed to him the whole plot, and had tried to persuade him to perpetrate both crimes; and that having afterwards killed his wife, out of jealousy he had conceived, he had narrated to him the manner in which he had perpetrated her death.

The Signori of Venice, when they heard of the cruelty inflicted by a barbarian upon a lady of their city, commanded that the Moor's arms should be pinioned in Cyprus, and he be brought to Venice, where with many tortures they sought to draw from him the truth. But the Moor, bearing with unyielding courage all the torment, denied the whole charge so resolutely, that no confession could be drawn from him. But although, by his constancy and firmness, he escaped death, he was, after being confined for several days in prison, condemned to perpetual banishment, in which he was eventually slain by the kinsfolk of Disdemona, as he merited. The Ensign returned to his own country, and following up his wonted villainy, he accused one of his companions of having sought to persuade him to kill an enemy of his, who was a man of noble rank; whereupon this person was arrested, and put to the torture; but when he denied the truth of what his accuser had declared, the Ensign himself was likewise tortured, to make him prove the truth of his accusation; and he was tortured so that his body ruptured, upon which he was removed from prison and taken home, where he died a miserable death. Thus did Heaven avenge the innocence of Disdemona; and all these events were narrated by the Ensign's wife, who was privy to the whole, after his death, as I have told them here.